South Asian Perspectives in Mental Health and Psychology

Series Editors

S. M. Yasir Arafat, Department of Psychiatry, Bangladesh Specialized Hospital, Dhaka, Bangladesh

Sujita Kumar Kar, Department of Psychiatry, King George's Medical University, Lucknow, Uttar Pradesh, India

This series of books is an endeavor to gather and present a comprehensive understanding of the various aspects of mental health that are relevant to people living in South Asia. The books aim to provide in-depth guidance and practical solutions to the mental health challenges that are unique to these areas. The content covers a wide range of topics, including but not limited to, climate change and its impact, prison mental health, perinatal mental health, social psychiatry, mental health and disorder among the elderly population, psychiatry education and training, suicide, SDGs and mental health, trauma, addiction, and social isolation. The books also emphasize the importance of early intervention and provide resources for seeking help. The ultimate goal of this series is to empower individuals and communities to take proactive steps toward enhancing their mental wellbeing. The proposed books will fill the existing unmet need in the region with huge populations in low and middle-income country (LMIC) settings.

South Asia, home to about 2 billion people, is a region of diverse cultures, languages, and religions. It caters to about 25% of the global population. This densely populated region faces a myriad of challenges, both natural and man-made. The frequent occurrence of natural disasters, such as earthquakes, floods, and landslides, threaten the lives and livelihoods of millions of people. War, terrorism, and political instability have caused significant disruptions to the region's socio-political fabric. Poverty, migration, and tropical infectious diseases remain major challenges that hinder progress towards sustainable development. Climate change exacerbates these challenges, causing widespread environmental degradation, food insecurity, and water scarcity. Despite these obstacles, South Asian people have shown remarkable resilience and strength in the face of adversity.

Mental health issues in the South Asian region significantly contribute to the global burden of mental illnesses. However, the region faces plenty of challenges such as high stigma, low mental health literacy, poor budgetary allocation, high out-of-pocket expense for mental health services, lack of adequate infrastructure, and limited human resources are significant barriers in mental healthcare. The majority of research on mental health issues is produced by the western countries which may not fit all in the South Asian culture, albeit evidence is needed to test. There is a paucity of research and evidence-based strategies that are region-specific. This series of books is an attempt to compile the important dimensions of mental health that will benefit the regional people.

Salim Al-Huseini · S. M. Yasir Arafat
Editors

Mental Health Care in the Middle East

Springer

Editors
Salim Al-Huseini
Department of Psychiatry
Al Masarra Hospital
Muscat, Oman

S. M. Yasir Arafat
Department of Psychiatry
Bangladesh Specialized Hospital
Dhaka, Bangladesh

ISSN 3059-3646 ISSN 3059-3522 (electronic)
South Asian Perspectives in Mental Health and Psychology
ISBN 978-981-95-0460-2 ISBN 978-981-95-0461-9 (eBook)
https://doi.org/10.1007/978-981-95-0461-9

This Springer imprint is published by the registered company Springer Nature Singapore Pte Ltd.
The registered company address is: 152 Beach Road, #21-01/04 Gateway East, Singapore 189721, Singapore

We dedicate this book to one of the greatest Muslim Physician ***Ibn Sina***

Foreword by Walid Sarhan

It is my pleasure and honor to write about this book, which addresses a critical topic in the region that has been somewhat neglected. Mental health is a cornerstone of human well-being, yet it remains one of the most poorly served areas of healthcare globally. In the Middle East, a region rich in cultural diversity and historical significance, mental health care faces unique challenges shaped by sociopolitical dynamics, cultural norms, and systemic barriers.

This book (Mental Health Care in the Middle East) is a groundbreaking effort to address these challenges and provide a comprehensive overview of mental health services across the region. The editors Dr. Salim Al-Huseini and Dr. S. M. Yasir Arafat, have tried to compile insights into the historical development, current landscape, and future directions of mental health care in the Middle East. By dedicating sixteen chapters, the first chapter provides an overall problem, and the subsequent fourteen chapters focus on specific nations. The last chapter attempts to address the gaps in mental health in the region.

The book offers a good understanding of the region's mental health systems, highlighting both its strengths and persistent gaps. It explores critical issues such as stigma, funding, workforce shortages, and the role of alternative medicine, while also shedding light on innovative solutions like telepsychiatry and country-specific strategies. This book is not just a resource; it is a call to action. It emphasizes the urgent need for research, policy reform, and collaboration to bridge the treatment gap and improve access to evidence-based mental health care. Considering that the Middle East is one of the wealthiest regions globally, the editors and authors have successfully created a valuable tool for researchers, academics, and professionals across various disciplines, thereby fostering a deeper understanding of the challenges and opportunities in mental healthcare in the Middle East.

The book identified the needs, resources, and gaps that can be addressed by national plans and regional cooperation to achieve the goal of good mental health for all. As the first comparative analysis of mental health services in the region, Mental Health Care in the Middle East is a testament to the authors' dedication and expertise.

I want to congratulate the editors and authors on this successful endeavor, and I hope that this book will inspire meaningful change and contribute to the advancement of mental health care in the Middle East and beyond.

Amman-Jordan
2025

Walid Sarhan, MD, FRCPsych, IDFAPA
Senior Consultant Psychiatrist

Preface

The Middle East is a region of Arab countries: Bahrain, Egypt, Iraq, Iran, Israel, Jordan, Kuwait, Lebanon, Oman, Palestine, Qatar, Saudi Arabia, Syria, the United Arab Emirates, and Yemen, rich in diversity, covering various countries and cultures. There are rising socio-geopolitical issues that have resulted in negative attitudes toward mental health. Additionally, culture, religion, and public stigma contribute to adverse outcomes, as there is insufficient mental health care coverage or difficulties accessing services in many of these countries. Most observers have attested to the view that the Middle East countries have a substantial treatment gap for people with mental illness. Only a tiny fraction of the population with mental illness can access evidence-based mental health care. Recently, the region has been significantly affected by war and trauma. Therefore, conducting more research to explore mental health services in the region is crucial. However, limited efforts have been identified to explore access to mental health services, focused on the cultural issues that affect the accessibility of mental health care in Middle Eastern countries. As a result, our objective was to identify and address the persistent cultural barriers and anticipate upcoming challenges to meet the needs of the region's large population. We aim to highlight the problems of accessing mental health services in Middle Eastern countries.

The book begins with an overview of access to mental health care in the Middle East to establish baseline characteristics of the region. Individual chapters will be dedicated to each country, including Bahrain, Egypt, Iran, Iraq, Jordan, Kuwait, Lebanon, Oman, Palestine, Qatar, Saudi Arabia, Syria, the United Arab Emirates, and Yemen. Individual country-wise chapters include an introduction that covers the historical aspects of mental health services development in that country, epidemiology and burden of mental illness, an overview of available mental health services, and a discussion of new avenues such as telepsychiatry. It also includes any potential strengths of mental health services in an individual country, which would be important to know and replicate in another setting. The challenges of mental care, including issues such as poor funding and research, inadequate and inequitable manpower, high out-of-pocket expenses, low mental health literacy, low income and income disparity, high stigma, help-seeking patterns, non-judicious prescribing (polypharmacy), and non-medical management of mental disorders (religious healers, herbalists, Kabiraz, homoeopathy, alternative medicine, and Samans) have been discussed. Each chapter highlights the potential opportunities and country-specific solutions.

It is the first attempt to compare the provision of mental health services in Middle Eastern countries. This book is the first to discuss the historical development of mental health services in the countries of the Middle East. It examines explicitly the practical challenges faced in accessing these services. It sheds light on the issues surrounding mental health service accessibility in the Middle East region. This book will be a valuable resource for researchers, academics, and professionals in various fields such as mental health, public health, public health administration, mass media and communication, behavioral science, and social science.

Muscat, Oman Salim Al-Huseini
Dhaka, Bangladesh S. M. Yasir Arafat

Contents

About the Editors

Dr. Salim Al-Huseini is a Specialist Psychiatrist at Al Masarra Hospital, where he serves in the Department of Psychiatry under the Ministry of Health in Oman. He holds a Doctor of Medicine (MD) Degree from Sultan Qaboos University and is a board-certified Psychiatrist. Dr Al-Huseini completed his psychiatry residency at the Oman Medical Specialty Board.

Dr. Al-Huseini completed his residency training in psychiatry at the Oman Medical Specialty Board (OMSB). He holds a specialty certificate in psychiatry from both OMSB and the Arab Board of Health Specializations. Dr. Al-Huseini is currently undertaking a clinical fellowship in rehabilitation psychiatry with the National Health Service (NHS) in the United Kingdom. He also holds a Postgraduate Certificate in Clinical Psychiatry from the University of Bolton, UK.

Dr. Al-Huseini has co-authored more than 50 peer-reviewed articles and book chapters. He is acting as a reviewer for various journals. His primary research interests include mental health, suicide and suicide prevention, treatment-resistant depression and psychosis, and psychosocial rehabilitation.

Dr. S. M. Yasir Arafat is currently working as an Associate Consultant of Psychiatry at Bangladesh Specialized Hospital, Dhaka, Bangladesh. He is an Associate Professor of Frontier University Garowe, Somalia, an Associated Fellow of the Bangladesh Academy of Sciences, and a Senior Research Fellow of the Biomedical Research Foundation, Bangladesh. He was affiliated with the University of Bristol, UK, as a Visiting Senior Research Associate (August 2021–2023) and an Honorary Research Fellow with Dnet (October 2023–25). He completed an MD in Psychiatry from Bangabandhu Sheikh Mujib Medical University, Dhaka, and an MBBS from the Dhaka Medical College, Dhaka, Bangladesh. He also did an MPH in Health Economics and an MBA in Marketing. Dr. Arafat has (co) co-authored more than 350 peer-reviewed articles and 50 book chapters, and co-edited more than 15 books with Springer. He has been included in the global 2% researcher list in 2021, 2022, 2023, and 2025. He is acting as an editorial member in more than 10 leading journals in mental health published by Elsevier, Wiley, Springer, and Taylor and Francis. His research focused on mental health, suicidal behavior, psychometrics, panic buying, and psycho-sexual disorders.

List of Figures

Chapter 9

Chapter 11

Chapter 12

Chapter 14

Chapter 15

Chapter 16

List of Tables

Chapter 1
Mental Health Care in the Middle East: An Overview

Salim Al-Huseini and S. M. Yasir Arafat

Abstract This chapter comprehensively introduces mental health services in the Middle East, examining the region's geographical features, demographic patterns, and cultural aspects. It explores the prevalence of psychiatric disorders, highlighting how geopolitical issues, economic inequalities, and recent global events, such as the COVID-19 pandemic, which have impacted mental health outcomes. Special emphasis is placed on the evolving trends in mental health conditions, particularly the rising rates of depression, anxiety, and substance abuse disorders. The availability of mental healthcare is discussed as a vital yet frequently underfunded aspect of public health in the Middle East. Key barriers to care are identified, including persistent social stigma, the unequal distribution of healthcare resources, and instability resulting from conflicts. The chapter concludes by proposing strategies to enhance mental health services in the region, underscoring the need for culturally appropriate approaches, comprehensive data collection, and government-initiated efforts to integrate mental health into broader healthcare systems.

Keywords Epidemiology · Psychiatric disorders · Middle East · Mental health care · Mental health services · Challenges of mental health care

1 Introduction

The Middle East is known for its vast geographic, demographic, and cultural diversity (Mohit, 2001). Currently, there are more than 500 million population (2024) in the region (World Population Review, 2025). It comprises 16 countries: Bahrain, Egypt, Iran, Iraq, Israel, Jordan, Kuwait, Lebanon, Oman, Palestine, Qatar, Saudi Arabia, Syria, Turkey, the United Arab Emirates, and Yemen (*The Geography of the*

S. Al-Huseini (✉)
Department of Psychiatry, AL Masarra Hospital, Ministry of Health, Muscat, Sultanate of Oman
e-mail: salimalhuseini@gmail.com

S. M. Y. Arafat
Department of Psychiatry, Bangladesh Specialised Hospital, Dhaka, Bangladesh

S. Al-Huseini and S. M. Y. Arafat (eds.), *Mental Health Care in the Middle East*, South Asian Perspectives in Mental Health and Psychology ,
https://doi.org/10.1007/978-981-95-0461-9_1

Middle East, Geoff Emberling, 2025). The region is extensive, exhibiting considerable wealth and economic stability disparities between and within countries. The dominant economies in the area encompass agriculture (including subsistence and commercial practices), hydrocarbon extraction, and other extractive industries (Waha et al., 2017). Its physical landscape ranges from sprawling deserts with low population density due to limited water and arable land to more temperate areas in the northern regions and along the Mediterranean coast, which support a higher number of inhabitants concentrations. These geographical characteristics directly influence settlement patterns, resource distribution, and, by extension, the differing levels of healthcare infrastructure across the Middle East countries (Alsharhan & Nairn, 1997).

The region is equally diverse culturally and linguistically. While Arabic is the most widely spoken language, countries such as Iran and Israel have distinct linguistic identities. The Middle East is also the birthplace of the three major monotheistic religions, Judaism, Christianity, and Islam, imparting significant spiritual and historical dimensions to social norms and healthcare practices (Lewis, 1998; Mohit, 2001). Although Islam remains the predominant faith, large Jewish populations in Israel, as well as Christian and other religious minorities elsewhere, illustrate the region's multi-religious makeup. Ethnic compositions similarly vary: Arab populations are predominant in many nations, whereas Iran and Israel have their majority groups, and some ethnicities, like the Kurds, lack a formal nation-state yet maintain sizable communities across borders (Zabad, 2020).

In addition to these similarities and dissimilarities, the region has been struggling with enduring political conflicts, war, torture, and violence. Although there are variations in political systems among the countries, there has been a major shift to democracy in recent decades after the Arab Spring (Arafat et al., 2024). The region faces proxy wars, and external political influence while deciding the agenda. The region has also been adapting to the immigrants and overseas workers from South Asian and African countries, which warrants additional aspects of mental health services (Musa, 2024).

Against this backdrop of shared cultural roots and notable differences, Middle Eastern countries have developed distinct approaches to mental health care. Wealthier nations, such as the United Arab Emirates, Saudi Arabia, and Qatar, have invested substantially in mental health infrastructure, integrating awareness campaigns and modern treatment facilities into their healthcare systems (International Trade Administration, 2023; Al-Khathami et al., 2025; Release, 2025). In contrast, conflict-affected countries like Syria and Yemen struggle with severely limited resources and face acute challenges in meeting even basic mental health needs (Truppa et al., 2024). Nevertheless, there is a growing recognition that mental health must be addressed through coordinated policy efforts and community-based interventions. Countries like Lebanon are integrating mental health services into primary care, while Saudi Arabia and others have launched national mental health strategies aimed at improving access and reducing stigma (Al-Subaie et al., 2020; Hijazi et al., 2011). This interplay of geographic, demographic, and cultural forces, coupled with the region's varied socio-economic and political conditions, sets the stage for a complex yet evolving landscape of mental health care. Understanding these dynamics is essential for designing and implementing effective interventions that acknowledge shared values and the diverse realities of the Middle East.

2 Epidemiology of Psychiatric Disorders in the Middle East

The epidemiology of psychiatric disorders in the Middle East reveals a complex landscape characterised by a growing awareness of mental health challenges, rising prevalence rates, and an increasing burden on healthcare systems. Recent research highlights a significant increase in the number of individuals seeking psychiatric help, particularly for depressive and anxiety disorders, influenced by sociocultural shifts and the ramifications of the COVID-19 pandemic. The region revealed high rates of psychiatric disorders with a range from 15.6 to 35.5% (Ibrahim, 2021). It is higher in countries with complex emergencies such as war and famine. The rates of anxiety disorders were also varied and noted up to 54.5% in Egypt (Tanios et al., 2009). Findings from the Global Burden of Disease Study indicate a 13.88% rise in disability-adjusted life years (DALYs) for mental disorders in the Middle East and North Africa (MENA) region from 1990 to 2019, with considerable variations across countries and age groups (Effatpanah et al., 2024). Notably, Palestine displayed the highest DALY rates for depressive disorders, highlighting significant regional disparities (Moradinazar et al., 2022). In Iran, a study conducted at a community mental health centre identified major depressive disorder (MDD) and generalised anxiety disorder (GAD) as significant concerns, particularly among younger, married women (Talebi et al., 2024). Further evidence from a study in Dubai highlighted a rising trend in outpatient clinic visits, with depressive and anxiety disorders representing the most prevalent diagnoses (Salamah et al., 2024). Meanwhile, the Saudi National Mental Health Survey reported that approximately one in three adults in Saudi Arabia has experienced a mental disorder, with higher prevalence rates observed for separation anxiety, obsessive–compulsive disorder, and social phobia (Chatterji, 2020). Alongside these developments, a separate study examining schizophrenia found a relatively stable age-standardised prevalence of 248.2 per 100,000 population and an incidence rate of 14.7 per 100,000 during the same period (Safiri et al., 2024). Factors like intimate partner violence and childhood trauma further increase the burden of MDD, underscoring the impact of social determinants on mental health outcomes (Moradinazar et al., 2022). Despite growing recognition of these issues, stigma and insufficient healthcare resources remain considerable obstacles to effective treatment and prevention in many Middle Eastern countries. Addressing these barriers will improve mental health outcomes, necessitating culturally sensitive interventions, expanded mental health infrastructure, and policies tailored to the region's unique social and political contexts.

3 Changing Trends of Psychiatric Disorders in the Middle East

The Middle East has undergone considerable shifts in mental health patterns over the past few decades, driven by social, cultural, and healthcare transformations. Recent evidence points to a rise in the overall prevalence of psychiatric disorders, coupled with increased public awareness of mental health services. One study noted an increase (25.7%) in visits to the emergency department during the COVID-19 pandemic in Saudi Arabia; females visited more than males and GAD was the most common psychiatric reason for visits (Ramadan et al., 2022). The trend suggests that new psychological stressors and evolving societal attitudes have contributed to an uptick in help-seeking behaviour. In parallel, Salamah et al. (2024) report a growing volume of clinic visits during the pandemic, indicating that acute pressures such as lockdowns, economic uncertainty, and social isolation may have prompted more people to seek professional support (Salamah et al., 2024). Longitudinal analyses further underscore these changes. Effatpanah et al. (2024) indicate that the DALYs related to mental disorders in the MENA region rose by 13.88% from 1990 to 2019, underscoring a significant rise in the regional burden. Schizophrenia, depressive disorders, and substance use disorders showed pronounced increases, a pattern that speaks to the role of urbanisation, shifting family structures, and cultural factors in shaping mental health outcomes (Effatpanah et al., 2024). While these findings point to a growing recognition of mental health concerns, challenges remain. Stigma persists as a formidable barrier, preventing many people from openly discussing or seeking treatment for psychiatric conditions.

Nevertheless, governmental efforts in several Middle Eastern countries to integrate mental health services into primary care, along with public education campaigns, have begun to reduce stigma (Mirzai et al., 2024). The pandemic has also accelerated the adoption of telehealth and e-mental health platforms, providing new avenues for individuals to access care with fewer logistical and cultural obstacles (Alnaqbi et al., 2024). Policymakers and healthcare providers in the Middle East must address long-standing resource constraints, enhance professional training, and expand culturally sensitive outreach initiatives. The region can continue advancing more comprehensive and equitable mental health services by fostering greater community engagement, bolstering research efforts, and incorporating technology-based interventions. Ultimately, these changing trends, while indicative of rising prevalence, also signify promising developments in the public's willingness to acknowledge and seek help for mental health issues.

4 Mental Healthcare in the Middle East

Access to mental healthcare in the Middle East continues to evolve, influenced by cultural beliefs, enduring stigma, historical developments, and emerging technological solutions (Musa, 2024). Historically, mental health services in the region have often been integrated into general healthcare systems, resulting in limited funding and oversight (Mohit, 2001; al-Krenawi & Graham, 2000; Al-Krenawi et al., 2009). This has led to persistent gaps in infrastructure, professional training, and policy focus, hindering the development of comprehensive mental health frameworks. Cultural factors significantly impact access, with stigma surrounding psychiatric conditions posing a significant obstacle in many Middle Eastern societies, as individuals fear social ostracism or bringing shame to their families (al-Krenawi & Graham, 2000). In contrast, Arab immigrants in North America and Europe often experience improved mental health outcomes due to targeted outreach and culturally informed treatment approaches (Mohit, 2001).

Although progress in the Middle East has been gradual, several Gulf Cooperation Council (GCC) countries, including Qatar, have begun prioritising mental health in their national policies (Fakhr El-Islam, 2008; Ghuloum, 2013). These initiatives involve restructuring hospital-based care and implementing comprehensive prevention, early detection, treatment, and rehabilitation strategies. For example, Qatar's national mental health strategy emphasises integrated services across all life stages, supported by public awareness campaigns to reduce stigma (Abou-Saleh & Ibrahim, 2013).

Despite these policy-driven improvements, resource disparities and uneven implementation persist across and within Middle Eastern countries. Community-based engagement and culturally sensitive interventions are crucial to expand mental health services in the region. Many individuals still rely on extended family networks and religious institutions for support, highlighting the importance of incorporating these social structures into public health strategies. Collaborating with religious leaders and community influencers can help dispel misconceptions, reduce stigma, and encourage those seeking professional care (Al-Krenawi et al., 2009).

Additionally, training healthcare providers in culturally informed communication can enhance therapeutic relationships and improve adherence to treatment plans. This combination of community engagement and culturally tailored care provides a foundation for broader, more sustainable developments throughout the Arab Gulf. These developments are increasingly evident in Saudi Arabia, Oman, Bahrain, Qatar, and Kuwait, which exhibit significant variation in mental healthcare accessibility. Saudi Arabia, for instance, has established a comprehensive, hospital-based mental health network, culminating in dedicated mental health legislation enacted in 2014. While the Ministry of Health remains the primary care provider, other governmental agencies also address psychiatric conditions within their workforces (Carlisle, 2018). Building upon these efforts, the Saudi Vision 2030 and its Health Sector Transformation Programme aim to enhance care quality and promote more equitable healthcare access, partly through adopting e-health and other digital technologies (Health Sector

Transformation Program, 2025). Concurrently, although challenges remain, Oman has made consistent progress in mental health services. Before 2014, the Health Ministry reported only 57 psychiatrists and 432 nurses working in mental health facilities (Sultanate of Oman, 2025).

In contrast, Bahrain has adopted a different approach by providing free psychiatric services through its national Psychiatric Hospital, which is available to citizens and foreign residents (Grey et al., 2015; Khaja et al., 2012). Qatar, meanwhile, has made substantial changes through its 2013 National Mental Health Strategy, shifting from specialist-centred care in secondary settings to more community-oriented services (Wadoo et al., 2021). Kuwait also works to improve its mental health counselling and therapy services, emphasising the ongoing need for additional resources (Al-Qimlass, 2015). Across these countries, the implementation of digital mental health services, particularly telepsychiatry—began before the COVID-19 pandemic and has gained momentum in Qatar, Oman, Saudi Arabia, and the United Arab Emirates. This expansion underscores the potential of technology to bridge geographical and social gaps, creating new opportunities to reach underserved populations and improve overall access to care (El Hayek et al., 2020). Each nation encounters challenges related to resource distribution, service coordination, and cultural perceptions. Nevertheless, the increasing focus on policy reform, community engagement, and digital innovation indicates a promising trajectory for mental healthcare throughout the Middle East.

5 Mental Healthcare Challenges in the Middle East

Several interconnected issues hinder the delivery of suitable and culturally sensitive mental health care in the Middle East (Fig. 1). The widespread stigma surrounding mental disorders discourages individuals from seeking professional help and perpetuates misconceptions (Mohit, 2001; Musa, 2024). Furthermore, inadequate training and education among healthcare workers result in gaps in service provision, while limited access to evidence-based treatments further complicates the situation. Cultural barriers also significantly obstruct open dialogue and rapport between patients and mental health professionals. These challenges are particularly evident within Middle Eastern immigrant and refugee communities in host nations, where language barriers, financial difficulties, and the psychological impact of relocation exacerbate existing mental health vulnerabilities.

In Arab societies, physical manifestations frequently serve as the primary indicators of illness, while psychological distress may be overlooked or stigmatised (Okasha et al., 2012, 2024). This tendency may result in exaggerated verbal expressions of distress, reflecting the emotive nature of the Arabic language and complicating diagnosis. Furthermore, the reluctance to seek professional mental health support is often reinforced by cultural beliefs that equate psychological suffering with personal weakness or spiritual deficiency (Sayed, 2015). Even in affluent regions

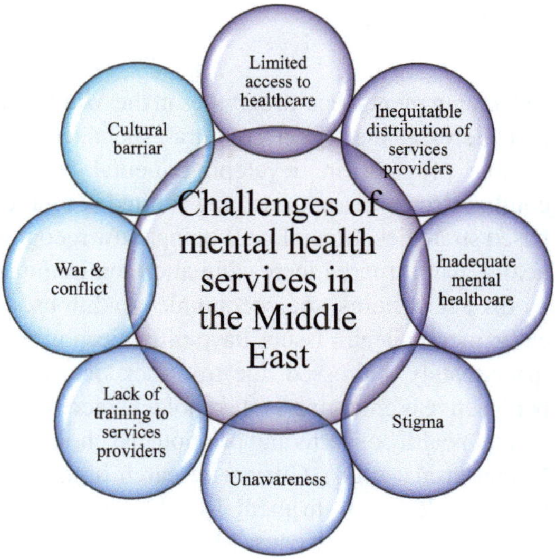

Fig. 1 Major challenges of mental health services in the Middle East

such as the UAE, stigma remains prevalent, leading many individuals to seek assistance from religious figures rather than mental health professionals (Sayed, 2015; Thomas et al., 2015). Mental illnesses are sometimes perceived as indicators of weak faith, prompting individuals to find solace in spiritual practices such as prayer and Qur'anic recitation (Thomas et al., 2015). Similar barriers to accessing mental health services are present across Arab nations, including Egypt, where extended waiting times, inadequate service availability, transportation challenges, and financial constraints further limit access (Khatib et al., 2024). Another barrier to mental healthcare in Middle Eastern countries is the unequal distribution of resources, which highlights the structural limitations of the mental health system and emphasises the need for more equitable funding and decentralised service models. In Egypt, government expenditure on mental health accounts for approximately 2% of total health expenditure, with nearly 59% allocated to large, centralised psychiatric hospitals (Jenkins et al., 2010; Okasha et al., 2024).

Enduring conflict, war, political oppression, and famine significantly hamper mental health care services in the region. It increased the rates of psychiatric disorders and the service burden. At the same time, it destroys the available mental health services and hinders people from accessing those during the conflict time (Younis et al., 2023). Addressing these systemic challenges necessitates a comprehensive approach integrating mental health into primary healthcare, expanding digital mental health solutions, strengthening community support networks, and implementing culturally informed awareness campaigns. By aligning mental health interventions with the social and cultural context of the Middle East, stakeholders can work towards sustainable improvements in mental health care and overall well-being in the region.

6 Ways Ahead

Enhancing mental health services in the Middle East requires a coordinated approach that addresses the region's cultural, social, economic, and political nuances. Despite notable progress in developing mental health infrastructure, persistent stigma, conflict-driven disruptions, and limited resources highlight the need for evidence-based strategies. Mental well-being, now recognised as a vital component of overall health, has garnered increasing attention in the Middle East, a region characterised by diverse cultures, socioeconomic conditions, and political environments. Historically, mental health issues have often been misinterpreted, heavily stigmatised, and inadequately addressed due to a lack of accessible services. However, a shift in perspective is emerging as stakeholders increasingly acknowledge the need to address mental health concerns and promote psychological well-being (Elshamy et al., 2023; Mirzai et al., 2024). Current research highlights the cultural and social obstacles that impede access to mental health services. For instance, (Semrau et al., 2024) emphasise the effectiveness of community-based initiatives in raising awareness and reducing stigma, while (Al Dweik et al., 2024) explore the transformative potential of digital technologies in mental health care, particularly in remote and underserved areas.

These findings align with broader efforts to integrate technological advancements into mental health service delivery to enhance accessibility and effectiveness. This review explores innovative methods for enhancing mental health care in the Middle East, including strategies such as integrating mental health services into primary healthcare, utilising technology, building community support networks, and promoting policy advocacy changes (Alsleem et al., 2024). A comprehensive understanding of the cultural and social factors influencing perceptions of mental health is essential for developing effective interventions. In the Middle East, cultural heritage, religious beliefs, and strong family and community ties significantly shape attitudes towards mental health (Ghuloum et al., 2024; Zolezzi et al., 2018). Tailoring mental health initiatives to align with these cultural frameworks can enhance their acceptance and effectiveness within local communities. Enhancing mental health outcomes in the Middle East necessitates a multifaceted approach that primarily emphasises the importance of increasing awareness and reducing stigma. Educational initiatives directed at the public are essential for disseminating accurate information, promoting help-seeking behaviour, and challenging misconceptions regarding mental health disorders (Javed et al., 2021; Musa, 2024; Sewilam et al., 2015). Moreover, increasingly utilising digital technologies, including smartphone applications, online therapy platforms, and telemedicine, presents promising solutions to bridge service gaps, particularly in underserved rural areas (Long et al., 2018; Maita et al., 2024). Despite these advancements, significant obstacles persist. Long-standing stigma surrounding mental illness, limited access to services, and cultural influences on perceptions of mental health continue to impede progress. Strengthening surveillance systems, particularly in under-resourced and conflict-affected areas, remains crucial; adopting culturally sensitive research methods and fostering cross-border collaborations can significantly improve data reliability (Ben-Zeev et al., 2024; Gearing et al., 2013; Salinas-Pérez et al., 2022). Integrating mental health care into primary healthcare settings is essential, as it allows for early identification of risks while reducing stigma (Coleman & Patrick, 1976; Thielke et al., 2007).

Improving the education and training of healthcare providers to recognise mental health symptoms, psychiatric disorders, and psychosocial responses to abuse and trauma may increase awareness and enable timely referrals to mental health services. To tackle workforce shortages, a multifaceted approach is required, which includes expanding residency training programmes.

Furthermore, collaborating with religious and community leaders to provide culturally sensitive psychoeducation can enhance mental health literacy, improve community outreach, and reduce the stigma surrounding the pursuit of mental health care (Clausen et al., 2019; Sewilam et al., 2015). National awareness campaigns, school-based mental health programs, and ongoing anti-stigma efforts further promote early help-seeking behaviours (Sewilam et al., 2015; Walsh & Foster, 2021). Moreover, telepsychiatry and online self-help platforms offer cost-effective solutions to bridge service gaps in underserved regions (Al Dweik et al., 2024; Al-Worafi, 2023; Chakrabarti, 2024). Addressing conflict-related disorders necessitates trauma-informed care and psychosocial interventions, particularly for refugees and internally displaced persons (Grasser, 2022; Nocon et al., 2017). Ultimately, sustained government commitment, intersectoral collaboration, and comprehensive policy frameworks, including adequate funding, are vital for enduring improvements in mental health outcomes across the Middle East (Mirzai et al., 2024).

7 Conclusion

Mental health in the Middle East is shaped by a unique interplay of historical developments, cultural traditions, and religious beliefs that profoundly influence perceptions of illness, treatment approaches, and societal attitudes. This chapter has provided an overview of how these factors have enriched mental health practices in the region and posed significant challenges to delivering comprehensive, equitable care. Although many Middle Eastern countries have made strides in increasing awareness and strengthening mental health services, pervasive stigma, uneven resource distribution, and limited community support remain considerable barriers. Moving forward, adopting a multifaceted approach that integrates culturally sensitive care, incorporates mental health services into primary healthcare frameworks, employs technological innovations, and fosters robust community support networks will be key. By acknowledging the region's diverse social and religious contexts and building on its rich healing and communal care heritage, Middle Eastern nations can continue evolving towards more accessible, equitable, and effective mental health services. This holistic effort will enhance individual well-being and contribute to healthier, more resilient communities across the region.

References

Abou-Saleh, M. T., & Ibrahim, M. A. (2013). Mental health law in Qatar. *International Psychiatry, 10*(4), 88–90. https://doi.org/10.1192/S1749367600004045

Al Dweik, R., Ajaj, R., Kotb, R., Halabi, D. E., Sadier, N. S., Sarsour, H., & Elhadi, Y. A. M. (2024). Opportunities and challenges in leveraging digital technology for mental health system strengthening: A systematic review to inform interventions in the United Arab Emirates. *BMC Public Health, 24*(1), 2592. https://doi.org/10.1186/s12889-024-19980-y

Al-Khathami, A. D., Alharbi, L. S., Alomari, S. A., Alqahtani, A. A., & Alfadhli, D. S. (2025). Integrating mental healthcare into primary healthcare services: Saudi Arabia progress and achievements (1995–2022). *Current Research in Psychiatry, 5*(1), 42–49. https://doi.org/10.46439/Psychiatry.5.035

al-Krenawi, A., & Graham, J. R. (2000). Culturally sensitive social work practice with Arab clients in mental health settings. *Health & Social Work, 25*(1), 9–22. https://doi.org/10.1093/hsw/25.1.9

Al-Krenawi, A., Graham, J. R., Al-Bedah, E. A., Kadri, H. M., & Sehwail, M. A. (2009). Cross-national comparison of Middle Eastern university students: Help-seeking behaviors, attitudes toward helping professionals, and cultural beliefs about mental health problems. *Community Mental Health Journal, 45*(1), 26–36. https://doi.org/10.1007/s10597-008-9175-2

Alnaqbi, A. A. S. R., Alhelali, M. O. A. M., Kong, A.S.-Y., Cheng, W.-H., Olayanju, L., Awad, H., Lai, K. S., & Nare, T. (2024). Navigating telemedicine in the Middle Eastern countries: A scoping review. *Dubai Medical Journal, 7*(4), 244–265. https://doi.org/10.18502/dmj.v7i4.17802

Al-Qimlass, A. (2015). The counseling profession in Kuwait: Its journey and future. *International Journal for the Advancement of Counselling, 37*(4), 355–366. https://doi.org/10.1007/s10447-015-9249-0

Alsharhan, A., & Nairn, A. (1997). *Chapter 1—An Introductory Overview*. 1–13. https://doi.org/10.1016/B978-044482465-3/50002-4

Alsleem, H. S. S., Jufaysh, J. S. G. A., Yami, A. S. S. A., Alqufayli, M. H. M., Alyami, M. M., Alyami, S. M. M., Alyami, W. M. M., Althaiban, S. H. A., & Althaiban, A. H. A. (2024). Comprehensive review of mental health integration, community health services, and technological innovations for vulnerable populations. *Journal of Ecohumanism, 3*(8), 6797–6805. https://doi.org/10.62754/joe.v3i8.5335

Al-Subaie, A. S., Al-Habeeb, A., & Altwaijri, Y. A. (2020). Overview of the Saudi National Mental Health Survey. *International Journal of Methods in Psychiatric Research, 29*(3), Article e1835. https://doi.org/10.1002/mpr.1835

Al-Worafi, Y. M. (2023). Telehealth and telemedicine in developing countries. In Y. M. Al-Worafi (Ed.), *Handbook of Medical and Health Sciences in developing countries: Education, practice, and research* (pp. 1–26). Springer. https://doi.org/10.1007/978-3-030-74786-2_309-1

Arafat, S. M. Y., Rezaeian, M., & Khan, M. M. (2024). Suicidal behavior in Islamic countries: An overview. In S. M. Y. Arafat, M. Rezaeian, & M. M. Khan (Eds.), *Suicidal behavior in Muslim majority countries*. Springer. https://doi.org/10.1007/978-981-97-2519-9_1

Ben-Zeev, D., Larsen, A., Beaulieu, A., Guler, J., & Bawaneh, A. (2024). Mental health priorities in the Arab world: Insights from Jordan. *Psychiatric Services*. https://doi.org/10.1176/appi.ps.20230365

Carlisle, J. (2018). Mental health law in Saudi Arabia. *Bjpsych International, 15*(1), 17–19. https://doi.org/10.1192/bji.2017.10

Chakrabarti, S. (2024). Digital psychiatry in low-and-middle-income countries: New developments and the way forward. *World Journal of Psychiatry, 14*(3), 350–361. https://doi.org/10.5498/wjp.v14.i3.350

Chatterji, S. (2020). The Saudi National Mental Health Survey: Filling critical gaps in methodology and data in mental health epidemiology. *International Journal of Methods in Psychiatric Research, 29*(3), Article e1852. https://doi.org/10.1002/mpr.1852

Clausen, C. E., Bazaid, K., Azeem, M., Abdelrahim, F., Elgawad, A., Alamiri, B., AlAnsari, A. M. S., Alhamzawi, A., Mai, A. M. A., Bakhiet, A., Bashtawi, M., Çuhadaroğlu, F., Hedar, M., Holdar, M., Jabr, S., Jafri, A. S., Jumaian, A., Moussa, S., Osman, A. H., & Skokauskas, N. (2019). Child and adolescent psychiatry training and services in the Middle East region: A current status assessment. *European Child & Adolescent Psychiatry, 29*, 51–61. https://doi.org/10.1007/s00787-019-01360-2

Coleman, J., & Patrick, D. (1976). Integrating mental health services into primary medical care. *Medical Care, 14*, 654–661. https://doi.org/10.1097/00005650-197608000-00002

Effatpanah, M., Nakhostin-Ansari, A., Gorgani, F., Khotbehsara, S. T., Seifi, S., Nasoori, H., Memari, A. H., & Darijani, S. R. (2024). Burden and Epidemiology of Mental Disorders in the Middle East and North Africa from 1990 to 2019: Findings from the Global Burden of Disease Study. *Balkan Medical Journal, 41*(2), 121–129. https://doi.org/10.4274/balkanmedj.galenos.2024.2023-11-55

El Hayek, S., Nofal, M., Abdelrahman, D., Adra, A., Al Harthi, M., Al Shamli, S., AlNuaimi, N., Bensid, L., Cheaito, M. A., Emberish, A. M., Larnaout, A., Radwan, A., Slaih, M., Kobeissy, F., & Bizri, M. (2020). Telepsychiatry in the Arab world: A viewpoint before and during COVID-19. *Neuropsychiatric Disease and Treatment, 16*, 2805–2815. https://doi.org/10.2147/NDT.S277224

Elshamy, F., Hamadeh, A., Billings, J., & Alyafei, A. (2023). Mental illness and help-seeking behaviours among Middle Eastern cultures: A systematic review and meta-synthesis of qualitative data. *PLoS ONE, 18*(10), Article e0293525. https://doi.org/10.1371/journal.pone.0293525

Fakhr El-Islam, M. (2008). Arab culture and mental health care. *Transcultural Psychiatry, 45*(4), 671–682. https://doi.org/10.1177/1363461508100788

Gearing, R., Schwalbe, C., Mackenzie, M., Brewer, K., Ibrahim, R. W., Olimat, H., Al-Makhamreh, S., Mian, I. A., & Al-Krenawi, A. (2013). Adaptation and translation of mental health interventions in Middle Eastern Arab countries: A systematic review of barriers to and strategies for effective treatment implementation. *International Journal of Social Psychiatry, 59*, 671–681. https://doi.org/10.1177/0020764012452349

Ghuloum, S. (2013). Gender differences in mental health in the Middle East. *International Psychiatry, 10*(4), 79–80. https://doi.org/10.1192/S1749367600003982

Ghuloum, S., Al-Thani, H. A. Q. F., & Al-Amin, H. (2024). Religion and mental health: An Eastern Mediterranean region perspective. *Frontiers in Psychology, 15*, Article 1441560. https://doi.org/10.3389/fpsyg.2024.1441560

Grasser, L. R. (2022). Addressing mental health concerns in refugees and displaced populations: Is enough being done? *Risk Management and Healthcare Policy, 15*, 909–922. https://doi.org/10.2147/RMHP.S270233

Grey, I., Al-Saihati, B. A., Al-Haddad, M., & McClean, B. (2015). Reasons for referral, intervention approaches and demographic characteristics of clients with intellectual disability attending adult psychiatric outpatient services in the Kingdom of Bahrain. *Journal of Intellectual Disability Research: JIDR, 59*(2), 186–192. https://doi.org/10.1111/jir.12077

Health Sector Transformation Program. (2025). Retrieved 9 March 2025, from https://www.vision2030.gov.sa/en/explore/programs/health-sector-transformation-program

Hijazi, Z., Weissbecker, I., & Chammay, R. (2011). The integration of mental health into primary health care in Lebanon. *Intervention: International Journal of Mental Health, Psychosocial Work & Counselling in Areas of Armed Conflict, 9*(3), 265–278.

Ibrahim, N. K. (2021). Epidemiology of Mental Health Problems in the Middle East. In I. Laher (Ed.), *Handbook of healthcare in the Arab world*.Springer. https://doi.org/10.1007/978-3-030-36811-1_1

International Trade Administration. (2023). *Qatar Healthcare Mental Health Services*. https://www.trade.gov/market-intelligence/qatar-healthcare-mental-health-services

Javed, A., Lee, C., Zakaria, H., Buenaventura, R., Cetkovich-Bakmas, M., Duailibi, K., Ng, B., Ramy, H., Saha, G., Arifeen, S., Elorza, P. M., Ratnasingham, P., & Azeem, M. (2021). Reducing the stigma of mental health disorders with a focus on low- and middle-income countries. *Asian Journal of Psychiatry, 58*, 102601. https://doi.org/10.1016/j.ajp.2021.102601

Jenkins, R., Heshmat, A., Loza, N., Siekkonen, I., & Sorour, E. (2010). Mental health policy and development in Egypt—Integrating mental health into health sector reforms 2001–9. *International Journal of Mental Health Systems, 4*, 17. https://doi.org/10.1186/1752-4458-4-17

Khaja, K. A. J. A., Al-Haddad, M. K., Sequeira, R. P., & Al-Offi, A. R. (2012). Antipsychotic and anticholinergic drug prescribing pattern in psychiatry: Extent of evidence-based practice in Bahrain. *Pharmacology & Pharmacy, 03*(04), 409–416. https://doi.org/10.4236/pp.2012.34055

Khatib, A., Abo-Rass, F., & Khatib, A. (2024). Barriers to mental health service utilization among Arab society in Israel: Perspectives from service providers. *Archives of Psychiatric Nursing, 51*, 127–132. https://doi.org/10.1016/j.apnu.2024.06.001

Lewis, B. (1998). The multiple identities of the Middle East. *Journal of Balkan and Near Eastern Studies*. https://doi.org/10.2307/20049591

Long, L., Pariyo, G., & Kallander, K. (2018). Digital technologies for health workforce development in low- and middle-income countries: A scoping review. *Global Health: Science and Practice, 6*, 41–48. https://doi.org/10.9745/GHSP-D-18-00167

Maita, K. C., Maniaci, M., Haider, C. R., Avila, F. R., Torres-Guzman, R. A., Borna, S., Lunde, J. J., Coffey, J. D., Demaerschalk, B. M., & Forte, A. J. (2024). The impact of digital health solutions on bridging the health care gap in rural areas: A scoping review. *The Permanente Journal, 28*, 130–143. https://doi.org/10.7812/TPP/23.134

Mirzai, F., Nasiri, Z., Naeim, M., Imannezhad, S., & Javedani, M. (2024). Advancing mental health in the Middle East: A paradigm shift. *Asian Journal of Psychiatry, 101*, Article 104220. https://doi.org/10.1016/j.ajp.2024.104220

Mohit, A. (2001). Mental health and psychiatry in the Middle East: Historical development. *Eastern Mediterranean Health Journal, 7*(3), 336–347.

Moradinazar, M., Mirzaei, P., Moradivafa, S., Saeedi, M., Basiri, M., & Shakiba, M. (2022). Epidemiological status of depressive disorders in the Middle East and North Africa from 1990 to 2019. *Health Promotion Perspectives, 12*(3), 301–309. https://doi.org/10.34172/hpp.2022.39

Musa, M. (2024). Mental health in the Middle East: Historical perspectives, current challenges, and future implications. *Saudi Journal of Humanities and Social Sciences*. https://doi.org/10.36348/sjhss.2024.v09i05.001

Nocon, A., Eberle-Sejari, R., Unterhitzenberger, J., & Rosner, R. (2017). The effectiveness of psychosocial interventions in war-traumatized refugee and internally displaced minors: Systematic review and meta-analysis. *European Journal of Psychotraumatology, 8*(sup2), 1388709. https://doi.org/10.1080/20008198.2017.1388709

Okasha, A., Karam, E., & Okasha, T. (2012). Mental health services in the Arab world. *World Psychiatry, 11*(1), 52–54. https://doi.org/10.1016/j.wpsyc.2012.01.008

Okasha, T., Shaker, N. M., & El-Gabry, D. A. (2024). Mental health services in Egypt, the Middle East, and North Africa. *International Review of Psychiatry*. https://doi.org/10.1080/09540261.2024.2400143

Ramadan, M., Fallatah, A. M., Batwa, Y. F., et al. (2022). Trends in emergency department visits for mental health disorder diagnoses before and during the COVID-19 pandemic: A retrospective cohort study 2018–2021. *BMC Psychiatry, 22*, 378. https://doi.org/10.1186/s12888-022-03988-y

Release, P. (2025). *Emirates Health Services launches 15 specialized mental health clinics across 6 emirates*. Zawya. (2025, February 27). https://www.zawya.com/en/press-release/government-news/emirates-health-services-launches-15-specialized-mental-health-clinics-across-6-emirates-atn6d8vi

Safiri, S., Mousavi, S. E., Nejadghaderi, S. A., Noori, M., Sullman, M. J. M., Kolahi, A.-A., & Shekarriz-Foumani, R. (2024). The burden of major depressive disorder in the Middle East and North Africa region, 1990–2019. *Acta Neuropsychiatrica, 36*(3), 139–152. https://doi.org/10.1017/neu.2023.42

Salamah, F., Khan, Z., Alaa Ibrahim Hassan, L., Mahmoud Marashi, S., Ahmed Ali Ahmed Shukry, A., Ahmed Abdelmuti Murad, L., Ahmed Alshehhi, M., Nasir Mohamed Sabir Alameeri, S., & Abdulla Alghaithi, S. (2024). Sociodemographic and diagnostic trends of users accessing psychiatry outpatient clinic in Dubai from 2019 to 2023: A cross-sectional retrospective study. *International Review of Psychiatry*, 1–13. https://doi.org/10.1080/09540261.2024.2434568

Salinas-Pérez, J., Ghuloum, S., Gutiérrez-Colosía, M., Bagheri, N., & Salvador-Carulla, L. (2022). Analysis of the mental health service provision in Qatar: Progressing in community mental health in a Middle East country. *Frontiers in Psychiatry, 13*, 1095788. https://doi.org/10.3389/fpsyt.2022.1095788

Sayed, M. A. (2015). Mental health services in the United Arab Emirates: Challenges and opportunities. *International Journal of Emergency Mental Health and Human Resilience, 17*(3), 661–663. https://doi.org/10.4172/1522-4821.1000263

Semrau, M., Gronholm, P. C., Eaton, J., Maulik, P. K., Ayele, B., Bakolis, I., Mendon, G. B., Bhattarai, K., Brohan, E., Cherian, A. V., Daniel, M., Girma, E., Gurung, D., Hailemariam, A., Hanlon, C., Healey, A., Kallakuri, S., Li, J., Loganathan, S., & Votruba, N. (2024). Reducing stigma and improving access to care for people with mental health conditions in the community: Protocol for a multi-site feasibility intervention study (Indigo-Local). *International Journal of Mental Health Systems, 18*(1), 35. https://doi.org/10.1186/s13033-024-00649-3

Sewilam, A., Watson, A. M., Kassem, A. M., Clifton, S., Mcdonald, M., Lipski, R., Deshpande, S., Mansour, H. A., & Nimgaonkar, V. (2015). Suggested avenues to reduce the stigma of mental illness in the Middle East. *International Journal of Social Psychiatry, 61*, 111–120. https://doi.org/10.1177/0020764014537234

Sultanate of Oman | Electronic Health Portal. (2025). Retrieved 9 March 2025, from https://moh.gov.om/en/

Talebi, M., Niroumand, S., Gholami, M., Samarghandi, A., Shaygani, F., Radfar, M., & Nemati, A. (2024). Epidemiological aspects of individuals with mental disorders in the referral system: The experience of a Community Mental Health Center in the northeast of Iran. *Discover Mental Health, 4*(1), 22. https://doi.org/10.1007/s44192-024-00078-1

Tanios, C. Y., Abou-Saleh, M. T., Karam, A. N., Salamoun, M. M., Mneimneh, Z. N., & Karam, E. G. (2009). The epidemiology of anxiety disorders in the Arab world: A review. *Journal of Anxiety Disorders, 23*(4), 409–419. https://doi.org/10.1016/j.janxdis.2008.10.009

The Geography of the Middle East, Geoff Emberling. (2025). Retrieved 9 March 2025, from http://teachmiddleeast.lib.uchicago.edu/foundations/geography/essay/essay-01.html

Thielke, S., Vannoy, S., & Unützer, J. (2007). Integrating mental health and primary care. *Primary Care, 34*(3), 571–592. https://doi.org/10.1016/J.POP.2007.05.007

Thomas, J., Al-Qarni, N., & Furber, S. W. (2015). Conceptualising mental health in the United Arab Emirates: The perspective of traditional healers. *Mental Health, Religion & Culture, 18*(2), 134–145. https://doi.org/10.1080/13674676.2015.1010196

Truppa, C., Yaacoub, S., Valente, M., Celentano, G., Ragazzoni, L., & Saulnier, D. (2024). Health systems resilience in fragile and conflict-affected settings: A systematic scoping review. *Conflict and Health, 18*(1), 2. https://doi.org/10.1186/s13031-023-00560-7

Wadoo, O., Ahmed, M. A. S., Reagu, S., Al Abdulla, S. A., & Al Abdulla, M. A. Y. A. (2021). Primary care mental health services in Qatar. *Bjpsych International, 18*(1), 15–18. https://doi.org/10.1192/bji.2020.45

Waha, K., Krummenauer, L., Adams, S., Aich, V., Baarsch, F., Coumou, D., Fader, M., Hoff, H., Jobbins, G., Marcus, R., Mengel, M., Otto, I. M., Perrette, M., Rocha, M., Robinson, A., & Schleussner, C.-F. (2017). Climate change impacts in the Middle East and Northern Africa (MENA) region and their implications for vulnerable population groups. *Regional Environmental Change, 17*(6), 1623–1638. https://doi.org/10.1007/s10113-017-1144-2

Walsh, D., & Foster, J. L. (2021). A call to action. A critical review of mental health related anti-stigma campaigns. *Frontiers in Public Health, 8*, 569539. https://doi.org/10.3389/fpubh.2020.569539

World Population Review. (2025). *The Middle East Population 2024.* (n.d.). Retrieved 9 March 2025, from https://worldpopulationreview.com/continents/the-middle-east

Younis, M. S., Abdullah, A. S., & Arafat, S. Y. (2023). Posttraumatic stress disorder among university students of Mosul, Iraq: An after effect of war atrocities. *Intervention Journal of Mental Health and Psychosocial Support in Conflict Affected Areas, 21*(1), 9–13. https://doi.org/10.4103/intv.intv_16_21

Zabad, I. M. (2020). Minorities in the Middle East. *International Relations.* https://doi.org/10.1093/obo/9780199743292-0275

Zolezzi, M., Alamri, M., Shaar, S., & Rainkie, D. (2018). Stigma associated with mental illness and its treatment in the Arab culture: A systematic review. *International Journal of Social Psychiatry, 64*(6), 597–609. https://doi.org/10.1177/0020764018789200

Chapter 2
Bahrain's Mental Health Sector: Pillars of Excellence and Strategic Directions

Ahmed H. Ebrahim, Haitham Jahrami, and Randah R. Hamadeh

Abstract Mental disorders and psychosocial disabilities represent a globally acknowledged healthcare challenge, demanding a well-modeled and functioning mental health system. In Bahrain, strategically mobilizing national efforts toward fostering population mental health is one of the utmost priorities. Hence, to reinforce these vital efforts, this chapter will first provide a review of Bahrain's mental health sector, its progression, factors that potentially influence its success, highlight areas of attention to support advancements in national mental health strategic work, and propose strategies to overcome the sector's challenges that Bahrain and other regional countries encounter. Five excellence pillars were focused on and inspired by international evidence, specifically: (1) developing a mental health surveillance system, (2) mental health workforce planning, (3) architecting mental health facilities, (4) national mental health strategic planning, and (5) comprehensive mental health legislation and governance. These pillars are crucial for supporting health policy development and determining areas for action.

Keywords Psychiatry · Mental health · Strategic excellence · Health development · Bahrain

A. H. Ebrahim · H. Jahrami (✉)
Government Hospitals, Manama, Bahrain
e-mail: haitham.jahrami@outlook.com

A. H. Ebrahim
Department of Research & Studies, Ahlia University, Manama, Bahrain

H. Jahrami · R. R. Hamadeh
College of Medicine and Health Sciences, Arabian Gulf University, Manama, Bahrain

S. Al-Huseini and S. M. Y. Arafat (eds.), *Mental Health Care in the Middle East*, South Asian Perspectives in Mental Health and Psychology ,
https://doi.org/10.1007/978-981-95-0461-9_2

1 Introduction

1.1 Mental Health: Global Overview

Mental disorders rank third among the top common diseases, with a prevalence rate of 36.6% in patients with chronic physical diseases (Daré et al., 2019). It is estimated that one in four persons globally will suffer a psychological problem in their lifetime (World Health Organization, 2001), and approximately one in five persons experience a common mental disorder within 12 months (Steel et al., 2014). Mental disorders continue to be among the top ten leading causes of death, accounting for 14.3% of deaths worldwide and approximately 8 million deaths each year (Walker et al., 2015). The global burden of mental illness accounts for 32.4% of years lived with disability (YLD) and 13.0% of disability-adjusted life-years (DALYs) (Vigo et al., 2016). Mental disorders were the seventh leading cause of DALYs in 2019 and the second leading cause of YLDs worldwide in both 1990 and 2019. Between 1990 and 2019, the number of DALYs due to mental disorders increased from 80.8 to 125.3 million (GBD 2019 Mental Disorders Collaborators, 2022). Suicide is responsible for almost one million deaths every year and remains the second leading cause of death among young people aged 15–29 (Bilsen, 2018). Dementia is the seventh leading cause of mortality and is a significant cause of disability among older adults (World Health Organization, 2022a). Globally, depression is the leading cause of disability worldwide, affecting more than 300 million people, ranking third in the global burden of disease, and is projected to become the first in 2030 (United Nations, 2017). At the disorder level, depressive disorders were ranked 13th among the top 25 leading causes of DALYs and second among the top 25 leading causes of YLDs in 2019 (GBD 2019 Mental Disorders Collaborators, 2022). Hence, national health systems are urged to include excellent planning, management, and development practices to lead the mental health sector according to the best applicable strategies and standards.

1.2 Brief Overview of Bahrain and its Healthcare Sector

The Kingdom of Bahrain is an Arab Middle Eastern country located in the heart of the Arabian Gulf with a land area of 786.5 km^2. The population of Bahrain is 1.6 million (47% Bahraini nationals), with 5.7% aged 60 and above, a life expectancy at birth of 77.3 years (Information & eGovernment Authority, 2020). Bahrain has a gross domestic product (GDP) of 38.9 billion US dollars (The World Bank, 2022), and it is placed in the very high human development category, with a Human Development Index (HDI) of 0.888 in 2022 (United Nations Development Programme, 2025). Bahrain's HDI value increased by 18.6% compared to 0.749 in 1990, reflecting progress in living standards, education, and health.

In the health sector, Bahrain is known for its rich history. It was the first country in the Arabian Gulf region to open a clinic in 1888 and establish a specialist health facility called the Mason Memorial Hospital in 1902 (Abuzeyad et al., 2018). Bahrain embraces the Health for All policy through the provision of free and accessible public primary and secondary healthcare services to all citizens. Expatriates can benefit from publicly subsidized health services or health insurance mandated by their employers.

Bahrain's healthcare system comprises three major segments: public primary healthcare, public secondary and tertiary healthcare, and private healthcare. Notably, secondary and tertiary care have been incorporated under the umbrella of "Government Hospitals Subject to Health Insurance." Considering the National Health Plan (2016–2025), Bahrain's healthcare system has been transformed over the past few years by adopting more sustainable financing schemes, autonomizing public health providers, and activating the Social Health Insurance Program (SEHATI) in consecutive phases (Ebrahim, 2020; Supreme Council for Health, 2017). In general, the healthcare sector has experienced exponential growth over the past decade, and the total number of hospital beds exceeded 2661, with a total of 29 hospitals in 2020 (Alpen Capital, 2023).

Bahrain's current healthcare expenditure (CHE) reached 4.2% of its GDP in 2020, below the average rate of the overall average of the Gulf Cooperation Council (GCC) countries (6.1%) (Alpen Capital, 2023). However, the health system encountered several challenges, such as fiscal deficits, the aging of the population, and the high prevalence of non-communicable diseases (NCDS), associated with an 86% NCD-related mortality rate, the highest among its GCC peers as of 2019. The COVID-19 pandemic has been detrimental to the healthcare system; however, Bahrain's model of combating the pandemic and its adaptability were well-recognized internationally (United Nations, 2020). The rise of health-related challenges coupled with urban living styles is seen as a push and demand-creating factor for comprehensive long-term care and advanced mental health services.

1.3 *Bahrain's Mental Health Sector*

Bahrain did not have hospitals or institutions designated for psychiatric patient care before 1930. Mentally ill patients were mostly cared for by their families, but some were abandoned and wandered in the streets and were subjected to abuse or ridicule. During that decade, Sir Charles Belgrave, a British advisor to the rulers of Bahrain from 1926 to 1957, requested the municipality to provide a place for the mentally disabled, and a small house called the "Mad House" was rented in the capital of Manama for that purpose (Al-Haddad & Al-Offi, 2009). This was the first initiative that later developed into a hospital. In 1937, the service was moved to another building on the same site as the current psychiatric hospital, and was called the "Insane Asylum." In 1974, Dr. Imad Farid was appointed director of the hospital. He changed its name to the Hospital for Psychiatry and Neurological Disorders. Since then and until now, the hospital has been in continuous development and expansion, to become the only public hospital for psychiatric diseases. In the context of mental health sector development, geographically distributed psychiatric services based on the liaison approach are provided in a spectrum of primary care centers. The private mental health sector is still relatively new. Two private psychiatric hospitals have recently been established, and two medical centers provide psychiatric services out of the 46 private medical centers in the country.

1.4 The Prevalence of Mental Disorders

The prevalence of depression and anxiety disorders in Bahrain is 4.8% and 4.3%, respectively (World Health Organization, 2017). According to the 2020 census, 7468 individuals suffered from intellectual disability, of whom 93% were Bahraini and 64% were males. This showed a 140% increase compared to what was reported in 2012 (3099) (Information & eGovernment Authority, 2020). A study that aimed at assessing the pattern of mental disorders in the outpatient department of the Psychiatric Hospital in 2013 reported that most of the patients suffered from depression (33.4%), anxiety disorders (19.9%), and psychotic disorders (14.8%) (Ali et al., 2015). Furthermore, the odds of having high depression or anxiety scores are significantly greater in patients aged < 45 years, with low income, low education, a personal history of mental illness, and a personal history of NCDs (AlSharbati et al., 2018). However, there is a lack of information published about the prevalence of several psychiatric diseases, such as bipolar disorder, schizophrenia, addiction, and eating disorders. This aspect is evident in the conclusion reached in a recent study conducted in Bahrain that stated that "long-term follow-up studies, cohort studies, a national prevalence rate of disorders, and clinical trials were lacking" (AlAnsari & Jahrami, 2021).

1.5 Socioeconomic, Cultural, and Legal Context

An examination of the literature suggests that psychological health is linked to resource availability, equality, political stability, social justice, employment, and economic security (Jenkins et al., 2011; Sharma et al., 2021). Moreover, crises, whether natural, man-made, health-related, financial, or humanitarian, are major factors and catalysts that affect the overall mental well-being of people and communities. A healthy politico–legal environment, modern infrastructure, and sustainable socioeconomic development are conducive elements for populations to mentally flourish and enjoy the implications of a higher standard of living. In Bahrain, the discovery of oil in the 1930s and its generated income reinforced the transformation of the country's economy and the building of its infrastructure for education, transportation, health, commercial, financial, and industrial sectors. Additionally, the government's pioneering programs of economic liberalization and diversification have been influential in increasing human development standards and achieving the

Sustainable Development Goals (SDGs) set by the United Nations General Assembly (United Nations, 2018; United Nations Development Programme, 2025).

Bahrain witnessed a new phase of political transformation following the 2001 National Action Charter (Al-Serhan et al., 2017). Article 8 states that "Every citizen is entitled to health care. The State cares for public health, and the State ensures the means of prevention and treatment by establishing various hospitals and health care institutions." Alongside the constitutional health-promoting/guaranteeing decrees, in 2018, the Health Insurance Law was issued to achieve an integrated health system, establish an efficient and sustainable health financing system, empower citizens' freedom in selecting their health providers, and heighten the competitiveness of the healthcare sector. Notably, novel mental health laws have been drawn up by the Parliament and the Government, which still require ratification and issuance, to cover all mental health services provided in the country and address rights and obligations in the provision of such services through legislative frameworks. However, in consideration of the above political and economic aspirations, the need for investments in Bahrain's mental health sector becomes imperative to bridge the demand–supply gap and take the sector forward to a higher level, particularly with the increase of NCDs and transformations occurring in different facets of people's lives.

Sociocultural values are imperative in general health care practice, and they become more sensitive and significant in mental health care due to multidimensional factors, including but not limited to the stigmatization of mental illness, etiological beliefs, religious orientations, traditions, discrimination, societal support, and communal values (Huang & Zane, 2016; Lee et al., 2021). In the Arab community, mental illness stigma is one of the major concerns affecting people's behavior toward psychiatric care and the subsequent necessity for inaugurating mechanisms to encourage the activation of sociocultural models of mental health care and destigmatize mental illness. Mental illness stigma has been linked with fear or reluctance to seek mental health, adherence to treatment, life satisfaction, life- or marriage-related decisions, and other negative consequences (Dardas & Simmons, 2015; Merhej, 2019; Verhaeghe et al., 2010). Like many Middle Eastern societies, the stigma of mental illness in Bahrain has a long history and is an area of public and health debate. Despite the importance of investigating and addressing stigma through evidence-based models, studies relevant to this subject are scarce in the country. One of these studies pointed toward prevalent patterns of observed behaviors among patients and their families when seeking psychiatric care, such as the tendency to avoid being physically recognized by others (Alani & Alhusaini, 2019). Interestingly, another study indicated that providers in mental health services exhibit less stigma compared to those in primary care (Al Saif et al., 2019). However, research on the prevalence, tendencies, and nature of stigma experiences is desirable in Bahrain and other regional countries.

2 Mental Health Sector Excellence Pillar

2.1 Mental Health Surveillance System

Nationwide epidemiological studies and screening tactics must be considered as health priorities to track mental health and determine the main psychiatric illnesses, their prevalence rates, risk factors, associations, and vulnerable populations. This requires an active Mental Health Surveillance System (MHSS) and the administration of periodical screening. While the MHSS can establish important baseline data and identify gaps in mental health, repeated observations help track trends in psychological well-being, evaluate the effectiveness of mental health interventions and programs, and control mental health risks. In the Middle East in general and Bahrain in particular, studies assessing the efficacy of health systems for the detection and monitoring of mental health disorders, which may present changes in prevalence over time, particularly during times of crisis or major socioeconomic contextual alterations, are lacking. Additionally, mental health data specific to psychiatric care remains limited and varies widely among Arab countries, especially regarding the prevalence of mental disorders among patients attending health facilities such as primary health care centers, chronic disease clinics, and community-based palliative care. During the COVID-19 pandemic, public health surveillance has become essential for decision-makers to lead and manage public health crises with early and effective recognition of issues and interventions (BinDhim et al., 2020). However, despite the robustness of the MHSS role in developed countries, the spectrum of population segments and the number of mental health indicators represent a great challenge for capturing an inclusive view of public health concerns. Therefore, planning, developing, and operating a comprehensive MHSS necessitates the experience and understanding of community-specific needs, particularly for vulnerable groups like children, youth, and the elderly (Bitsko et al., 2022).

2.2 Mental Health Workforce Planning

Mental health human resources dedicated to the healthcare sector are essential for the success of health strategies and the community's well-being. Hence, planning, recruiting, and developing the quantity and quality of competencies dedicated to mental health should be strategically and institutionally prioritized (Jarmain, 2016). The World Health Organization (WHO) defines health human resource planning as "the process of estimating the number of persons and the kinds of knowledge, skills, and attitudes they need to achieve predetermined health targets and ultimately health status objectives" (Hall & Mejía, 1978, p. 18). It has been attributed as an essential component and an integral part of national health planning. In the mental health context, this process could be complex and requires careful and skilled modeling to meet the new expectations of services; factors related to such complexity include, but

Table 1 Rates (per 100,000 inhabitants) of health workers in mental health sectors in Bahrain, GCC, Europe, and globally

Specialty/location	Bahrain	Average GCC region[a]	Europe ($N = 40$)	Global ($N = 156$)
Psychiatrists	5.5	1.9	9.7	1.7
Mental health nurses	28.0	7.0	25.2	3.8
Psychologists	1.2	1.3	5.4	1.4
Social workers	1.5	1.5	2.0	0.7

[a]The average is based on including the following countries as per data availability: Saudi Arabia, Qatar, Oman, and the United Arab Emirates. Oman data were unavailable for the Social Worker speciality, and none were available for Kuwait (World Health Organization, 2021, 2022b)

are not limited to the woven relationship between mental health and all other forms of health, ongoing health transformations and increasing rates of mental disorders among many different community segments. In general, Bahrain's rate of psychiatrists and nurses per 100,000 inhabitants is approximately 3–4 times greater than the average of GCC countries (Table 1). However, identifying the optimal rates of the specialized mental health workforce in Bahrain constitutes an area of development that needs scrutiny of the supply–demand gap. Another vital aspect that should be taken into consideration in mental health workforce planning is the integration of psychiatric services into primary care, secondary care, and community care. There is now growing evidence of improved accessibility and effectiveness of care upon establishing innovative and context-specific integrative frameworks in the provision of mental healthcare. This includes mental health training of health workers in all the health care facilities, consultation-liaison, collaborative care, and referral tactics (Bower & Gilbody, 2005; van Ginneken et al., 2017).

2.3 *Architecting Mental Health Facilities*

While Bahrain had more than 30 psychiatric beds per 100,000 people in 2007, it decreased to 19.3 in 2017 (Okasha et al., 2012; World Health Organization, 2022c). Despite the population increase within that period, this drastic change should not necessarily be negatively viewed. One of the main reasons could be deinstitutionalization, such as reducing hospital beds and increasing community mental health services. An evident model that can be inspired by this is Trieste's strategy, which is based on mitigating hospitalizations and involuntary treatments while increasing family involvement and promoting viable recreation and living environments (Frances, 2021). Based on the Delphi method, a recent study indicated that 60 psychiatric beds per 100,000 people is optimal, with a minimum of 30 beds (Mundt et al., 2022). However, classic bed rate calculations may mismanage mental health demands and incur costs over the long term. Hence, bed resource planning and utilization require expert consensus techniques and epidemiological estimations, which should serve as guiding tools to determine the optimal psychiatric inpatient bed capacity for the country. Conclusively, defining acceptable psychiatric bed numbers seems complex and requires careful situational and trend evaluation due to many factors, including but not limited to coverage and quality of community care and outreach programs, length of stays, relapse rates, mental illness trends, and institutionalization patterns (Mundt et al., 2021, 2022).

Other essential aspects when planning psychiatric facilities are their characteristics, specializations, and geographical coverage for areas in demand. There has been evidence suggesting an association between certain clinical characteristics and engagement in mental health services; for example, outreach was linked with greater engagement (Stein et al., 2014). Additionally, prophylaxis in mental health facilities is a means for high standards of quality. These characteristics can include offering suicide prevention services and outcome follow-up after discharge (Kuramoto-Crawford et al., 2016). In the late twentieth century, psychiatry as a medical specialty has evolved within a wide range of diagnostic, therapeutic, and rehabilitative specializations to overcome clinical, neuroscientific, and pharmacological challenges (Bilikiewicz, 1998; Gaebel et al., 2010). Therefore, analyzing the supply–demand of psychiatric subspecialties is an essential task when developing national mental health sectors. First, the following questions should be answered: What are the subspecialties? How can the supply–demand gaps be closed? What socioeconomic or public health crises have the potential to emerge in the future? Inspiring international experiences, as part of the answer to such questions, relies on tactics for building an architecture for mental health research, developing prediction capabilities, supporting subspecialty training, and sponsoring college programs and fellowships (Aoun et al., 2004; Armstrong et al., 2022).

2.4 National Mental Health Strategic Planning

Many high-income countries have initiated mental health reforms based on the design and implementation of a National Action Plan on Mental Health alongside the development and implementation of inclusive mental health policies (Zhou et al., 2018). Strategic planning is crucial for developing a clear-cut direction toward a conducive mental health landscape and defining major priorities for financing, providing, regulating, and developing mental health services. This includes specialized acute, subacute, and residential care, in which the public sector usually takes a major lead. Such strategies aim to improve access to mental health, promote preventive programs against mental health disorders, and minimize stigma and discrimination. The key aspects to be considered in strategic frameworks include but are not limited to (1) the integration of the public and private sectors for delivering mental health services through hospitals and community settings; (2) mainstreaming mental health services within and outside the general health system; (3) developing effective surveillance and monitoring mental health systems; and (4) community programs for reducing stigma and discrimination. (5) governance and regulation of the mental health sector;

(6) mental health competence building; (7) mental health quality and accreditation; and (8) fostering partnerships and coordinating stakeholders (Jenkins et al., 2002; Ramsay, 1996; Waddell et al., 2005). However, in strategy development, there is no "one size fits all," and the success of strategic frameworks requires holistic context evaluation, understanding of the culture, proper modeling of improvement programs alongside the existence of implementation capacities, and periodical strategic revisions. India's National Mental Health Programme and Uganda's implementation of a Western mental health model are evident experiences that generated learned lessons over their course, explicitly that constraints to success could be multidimensional and complex, such as struggles in budgetary allocation, deficient community participation, limited non-governmental organizations and private sector partnerships, a shortage of training, weak cyclical monitoring, and poor risk assessment (Kopinak, 2015; Gupta & Sagar, 2018).

Like some other GCC countries, Bahrain has made progress in mental health policies and strategic directions. However, more work is still needed concerning comprehensive mental health-wide strategies, policies, and laws that strengthen the mental health sector's sustainability, autonomy, financing, integration, and spectrum throughout the life stages and whole-of-community. This mission requires focusing on the feasibility of investment in inclusive infrastructure projects for specialized mental health facilities, a national research and knowledge economy, innovative community outreach programs, and digital and artificial intelligence technologies. Undoubtedly, mental health leadership is fundamental to leading the desired paradigm shift in mental health care. This has been demonstrated through the creation of mental health advisory councils or boards in some countries.

2.5 *Legislation and Governance*

In general, the concept of governance is multidimensional and may pertain to the culture and institutional environment in which the processes and norms of accountability, transparency, stakeholders' interaction, the rule of law, and values of equity and inclusiveness are demonstrated and intertwined (Addink, 2019). In mental health, governance encompasses "standards of quality and attention centered on the patient and incorporates the consumers of mental healthcare in the decision-making process" (Díaz-Castro et al., 2017). Hence, we understand that the good governance approach involves the assurance of effective policy and legislative frameworks to enhance and protect the mental well-being of a population and the ability to exercise empowerment for optimal policy implementation and the assurance of the integrative influence of sociopolitical and health systems in the promotion and protection of public mental health. While some countries may fare well to formulating governance strategies, whether at clinical, sectoral, or integrative levels, the implementation element emerges as the greatest challenge for good governance, especially with the existence of barriers such as inadequate technical and financing resources, low public health priority of mental health, poor management models, insufficient participation, and collaboration between relevant stakeholders (Petersen et al., 2017). In Bahrain, national health authorities are exercising influential governance levels in all healthcare disciplines, including mental health; however, there is promising potential to develop and implement higher levels of specialized mental health governance practices soon because of the robust national orientation toward developing new/progressive mental health legislation and policies.

3 Conclusion

Based on the combined holistic review of relevant mental health literature and experts' points of view, national efforts need to be determined and strategically architected for the different areas of attention. Therefore, it is important to warrant a concrete core for the highlighted excellence pillars. First, the development of an advanced and functional mental health surveillance system should remain a priority for targeted prevention and intervention. Second, in mental health workforce planning, competence, adequacy, and motivation should be considered with equal importance. Third, planning mental health facilities that encourage community engagement is a key factor in improving the quality of life. Fourth, in national mental health strategic planning, intersectoral collaboration and coordination are crucial for attaining outcomes; however, setting indicators and reasonable time scales are determinant elements for such strategic work. Fifth, in comprehensive mental health legislation and governance, the inauguration of an independent national mental health body is a feasible model that can help propose mental health policies, promote interaction among stakeholders, and provide large-scale consultations in financial, regulatory, and ethical matters concerning the mental health sector in the country.

References

Abuzeyad, F., Alqasem, L., Al Farras, M. I., Alsenany, S., Al Ansari, A., & Sadeq, H. (2018). Emergency medicine in the Kingdom of Bahrain. *International Journal of Emergency Medicine, 11*(1), 4. https://doi.org/10.1186/s12245-018-0163-1

Addink, H. (2019). *Good governance: Concept and context*. Oxford University Press. https://doi.org/10.1093/oso/9780198841159.001.0001

Al Saif, F., Al Shakhoori, H., Nooh, S., & Jahrami, H. (2019). Association between attitudes of stigma toward mental illness and attitudes toward adoption of evidence-based practice within health care providers in Bahrain. *PLoS ONE, 14*(12), Article e0225738. https://doi.org/10.1371/journal.pone.0225738

Alani, W., & Alhusaini, T. (2019). The stigma of mental illness at the Bahrain Defense Force (BDF) Hospital. *World Cultural Psychiatry Research Review, 14*(1/2), 3–8.

AlAnsari, A. M., & Jahrami, H. (2021). Mapping the research activity on psychiatric disorders in Bahrain: A 40-year analysis. *Bahrain Medical Bulletin, 43*(1), 376–378.

Al-Haddad, M. K., & Al-Offi, A. (2009). Psychiatric services in Bahrain: Past, present and future. *International Psychiatry, 6*(1), 14–16. https://doi.org/10.1192/S1749367600000242
Ali, M. K., Jahrami, H. A., & Ghareeb, A. (2015). Pattern of mental disorders at psychiatric hospital: A retrospective study of the outpatient. *Bahrain Medical Bulletin, 37*(4), 1–4.
Alpen Capital. (2023). *GCC Healthcare Sector*. Alpen Capital.
Al-Serhan, S. F., Mashagbeh, A. A., & Salameh, M. T. B. (2017). Challenges facing national security in the Arab Gulf states: A case study of Bahrain. *International Journal of Humanities and Social Science, 7*(9), 131–142.
AlSharbati, W., Bucheeri, S., Alkawari, M., Alromaihi, N., Algarf, R., & Alfara, W. (2018). Prevalence of depression and anxiety among patients with noncommunicable diseases in the Kingdom of Bahrain. *Journal of the Bahrain Medical Society, 30*(3), 10–19.
Aoun, S., Pennebaker, D., & Wood, C. (2004). Assessing population need for mental health care: A review of approaches and predictors. *Mental Health Services Research, 6*(1), 33–46. https://doi.org/10.1023/B:MHSR.0000011255.10887.59
Armstrong, A. G., Mayorga, A. K., & Brown, R. M. (2022). Kansas needs psychiatric subspecialists. *Kansas Journal of Medicine, 15*, 222–225. https://doi.org/10.17161/kjm.vol15.16506
Bilikiewicz, A. (1998). Psychiatria na przełomie XX i XXI stulecia [Psychiatry at the turn of the 20th and 21st centuries]. *Psychiatria Polska, 32*(5), 547–555.
Bilsen, J. (2018). Suicide and youth: Risk factors. *Frontiers in Psychiatry, 9*, 540. https://doi.org/10.3389/fpsyt.2018.00540
BinDhim, N. F., Althumiri, N. A., Basyouni, M. H., Alageel, A. A., Alghnam, S., Al-Qunaibet, A. M., & Ad-Dab'bagh, Y. (2020). A mental health surveillance system for the general population during the COVID-19 pandemic: Protocol for a multiwave cross-sectional survey study. *JMIR Research Protocols, 9*(11), Article e23748. https://doi.org/10.2196/23748
Bitsko, R. H., Claussen, A. H., Lichstein, J., Black, L. I., Jones, S. E., Danielson, M. L., & Ghandour, R. M. (2022). Mental health surveillance among children—United States, 2013–2019. *MMWR Supplements, 71*(2), 1–42. https://doi.org/10.15585/mmwr.su7102a1
Bower, P., & Gilbody, S. (2005). Managing common mental health disorders in primary care: Conceptual models and evidence base. *BMJ, 330*(7495), 839–842. https://doi.org/10.1136/bmj.330.7495.839
Dardas, L. A., & Simmons, L. A. (2015). The stigma of mental illness in Arab families: A concept analysis. *Journal of Psychiatric and Mental Health Nursing, 22*(9), 668–679. https://doi.org/10.1111/jpm.12237
Daré, L. O., Bruand, P. E., Gérard, D., Marin, B., Lameyre, V., Boumédiène, F., & Preux, P. M. (2019). Comorbidities of mental disorders and chronic physical diseases in developing and emerging countries: A meta-analysis. *BMC Public Health, 19*(1), 304. https://doi.org/10.1186/s12889-019-6623-6
Díaz-Castro, L., Arredondo, A., Pelcastre-Villafuerte, B. E., & Hufty, M. (2017). Governance and mental health: Contributions for public policy approach. *Revista de Saúde Pública, 51*, 4. https://doi.org/10.1590/S1518-8787.2017051006991
Ebrahim, A. (2020). *Determinants of public trust in private medical sector of Bahrain: An empirical study*. Swiss Business School.
Frances, A. (2021). Save Trieste's mental health system. *The Lancet Psychiatry, 8*(9), 744–746.
Gaebel, W., Zielasek, J., & Cleveland, H. R. (2010). Psychiatry as a medical specialty: Challenges and opportunities. *World Psychiatry, 9*(1), 36–38. https://doi.org/10.1002/j.2051-5545.2010.tb00265.x
GBD 2019 Mental Disorders Collaborators. (2022). Global, regional, and national burden of 12 mental disorders in 204 countries and territories, 1990–2019: A systematic analysis for the Global Burden of Disease Study 2019. *The Lancet Psychiatry, 9*(2), 137–150. https://doi.org/10.1016/S2215-0366(21)00395-3
Gupta, S., & Sagar, R. (2018). National mental health programme—optimism and caution: A narrative review. *Indian Journal of Psychological Medicine, 40*(6), 509–516. https://doi.org/10.4103/IJPSYM.IJPSYM_191_18

Hall, T. L., & Mejía, A. (1978). *Health manpower planning: Principles, methods, issues.* World Health Organization. https://apps.who.int/iris/handle/10665/40341

Huang, C. Y., & Zane, N. (2016). Cultural influences in mental health treatment. *Current Opinion in Psychology, 8*, 131–136. https://doi.org/10.1016/j.copsyc.2015.10.013

Information & eGovernment Authority. (2020). *Bahrain Open Data Portal.* https://data.gov.bh/

Jarmain, S. (2016). Psychiatrist health human resource planning: An essential component of a hospital-based mental healthcare system transformation. *Healthcare Quarterly, 18*, 22–26. https://doi.org/10.12927/hcq.2016.24478

Jenkins, R., Baingana, F., Ahmad, R., McDaid, D., & Atun, R. (2011). Social, economic, human rights and political challenges to global mental health. *Mental Health in Family Medicine, 8*(2), 87–96.

Jenkins, R., McCulloch, A., Friedli, L., & Parker, C. (2002). *Developing a national mental health policy.* Psychology Press.

Kopinak, J. K. (2015). Mental health in developing countries: Challenges and opportunities in introducing Western mental health systems in Uganda. *International Journal of MCH and AIDS, 3*(1), 22. https://doi.org/10.21106/ijma.35

Kuramoto-Crawford, S. J., Smith, K. E., & McKeon, R. (2016). Characteristics of US mental health facilities that offer suicide prevention services. *Psychiatric Services, 67*(1), 119–123. https://doi.org/10.1176/appi.ps.201500024

Lee, S., Park, S. J., Yon, K. J., Choi, B. K., Kim, P. Y., & Kim, C. M. (2021). Etiology beliefs, religious coping, perceived church climates, and beliefs about psychological services. *The Counseling Psychologist, 49*(6), 818–846. https://doi.org/10.1177/00110000211019483

Merhej, R. (2019). Stigma on mental illness in the Arab world: Beyond the sociocultural barriers. *International Journal of Human Rights in Healthcare, 12*(5), 285–298.

Mundt, A. P., Delhey Langerfeldt, S., Rozas Serri, E., Siebenförcher, M., & Priebe, S. (2021). Expert arguments for trends of psychiatric bed numbers: A systematic review of qualitative data. *Frontiers in Psychiatry, 12*, Article 745247. https://doi.org/10.3389/fpsyt.2021.745247

Mundt, A. P., Rozas Serri, E., Irarrázaval, M., O'Reilly, R., Allison, S., Bastiampillai, T., & Priebe, S. (2022). Minimum and optimal numbers of psychiatric beds: Expert consensus using a Delphi process. *Molecular Psychiatry, 27*(4), 1873–1879. https://doi.org/10.1038/s41380-021-01272-1

Okasha, A., Karam, E., & Okasha, T. (2012). Mental health services in the Arab world. *World Psychiatry, 11*(1), 52–54. https://doi.org/10.1016/j.wpsyc.2012.01.008

Petersen, I., Marais, D., Abdulmalik, J., Ahuja, S., Alem, A., Chisholm, D., Egbe, C., Gureje, O., Hanlon, C., Lund, C., Shidhaye, R., Jordans, M., Kigozi, F., Mugisha, J., Upadhaya, N., & Thornicroft, G. (2017). Strengthening mental health system governance in six low- and middle-income countries in Africa and South Asia: Challenges, needs and potential strategies. *Health Policy and Planning, 32*(5), 699–709. https://doi.org/10.1093/heapol/czx014

Ramsay, J. (1996). The national mental health strategy. *Australian Journal of Rural Health, 4*(1), 53–56. https://doi.org/10.1111/j.1440-1584.1996.tb00187.x

Sharma, S., Singhal, S., & Tarp, F. (2021). Corruption and mental health: Evidence from Vietnam. *Journal of Economic Behavior & Organization, 185*, 125–137. https://doi.org/10.1016/j.jebo.2021.02.009

Steel, Z., Marnane, C., Iranpour, C., Chey, T., Jackson, J. W., Patel, V., & Silove, D. (2014). The global prevalence of common mental disorders: A systematic review and meta-analysis 1980–2013. *International Journal of Epidemiology, 43*(2), 476–493. https://doi.org/10.1093/ije/dyu038

Stein, G. L., Lee, C. S., Shi, P., Cook, B. L., Papajorgji-Taylor, D., Carson, N. J., & Alegría, M. (2014). Characteristics of community mental health clinics associated with treatment engagement. *Psychiatric Services, 65*(8), 1020–1025. https://doi.org/10.1176/appi.ps.201300250

Supreme Council for Health. (2017). *Road to SEHATI: National Social Health Insurance Program.* SCH.

The World Bank. (2022). *Bahrain.* https://data.worldbank.org/country/BH

United Nations. (2017, February 23). *UN health agency reports depression now "leading cause of disability worldwide."* https://news.un.org/en/story/2017/02/552062

United Nations. (2018). *Bahrain's first voluntary national review on the implementation of the 2030 Agenda for Sustainable Development*. https://sustainabledevelopment.un.org/content/documents/21329Bahrain_VNR_English_translation.pdf

United Nations. (2020). *Joint United Nations COVID-19 socioeconomic response & recovery framework*. https://unsdg.un.org/sites/default/files/2020-11/BHR_Socioeconomic-Response-Plan_2020.pdf

United Nations Development Programme. (2025). *Human Development Index (HDI)*. https://hdr.undp.org/data-center/human-development-index

van Ginneken, N., Maheedhariah, M. S., Ghani, S., Ramakrishna, J., Raja, A., & Patel, V. (2017). Human resources and models of mental healthcare integration into primary and community care in India: Case studies of 72 programmes. *PLoS ONE, 12*(6), Article e0178954. https://doi.org/10.1371/journal.pone.0178954

Verhaeghe, M., Bracke, P., & Christiaens, W. (2010). Stigma and client satisfaction in mental health services. *Journal of Applied Social Psychology, 40*(9), 2295–2318. https://doi.org/10.1111/j.1559-1816.2010.00663.x

Vigo, D., Thornicroft, G., & Atun, R. (2016). Estimating the true global burden of mental illness. *The Lancet Psychiatry, 3*(2), 171–178. https://doi.org/10.1016/S2215-0366(15)00505-2

Waddell, C., McEwan, K., Shepherd, C. A., Offord, D. R., & Hua, J. M. (2005). A public health strategy to improve the mental health of Canadian children. *The Canadian Journal of Psychiatry, 50*(4), 226–233. https://doi.org/10.1177/070674370505000406

Walker, E. R., McGee, R. E., & Druss, B. G. (2015). Mortality in mental disorders and global disease burden implications: A systematic review and meta-analysis. *JAMA Psychiatry, 72*(4), 334–341. https://doi.org/10.1001/jamapsychiatry.2014.2502

World Health Organization. (2001). *The World Health Report 2001: Mental health: New understanding, new hope*. https://www.who.int/whr/2001/en/

World Health Organization. (2017). *Depression and other common mental disorders: Global health estimates*. https://apps.who.int/iris/handle/10665/254610

World Health Organization. (2021). *Mental health atlas 2020*. https://www.who.int/publications/i/item/9789240036703

World Health Organization. (2022a). *Dementia*. https://www.who.int/news-room/fact-sheets/detail/dementia

World Health Organization. (2022b). *Global Health Observatory data repository: Mental health workers data by country*. Retrieved January 26, 2022, from https://apps.who.int/gho/data/view.main.HWF11v

World Health Organization. (2022c). *Global Health Observatory data repository*. https://apps.who.int/gho/data/node.main.MHBEDS

Zhou, W., Yu, Y., Yang, M., Chen, L., & Xiao, S. (2018). Policy development and challenges of global mental health: A systematic review of published studies of national-level mental health policies. *BMC Psychiatry, 18*(1), 1–9. https://doi.org/10.1186/s12888-018-1711-1

Chapter 3
Mental Health Care in Egypt

Walid Hassan and Sally Elnoby

Abstract Egypt, a lower middle-income country in North Africa, is witnessing increasing attention toward mental health amidst a shifting burden of non-communicable diseases. Psychiatric disorders are among the most pressing public health concerns, yet the country faces a significant treatment gap, particularly in underserved regions. This chapter explores the historical evolution, current structure, and challenges of mental health care access in Egypt. It begins by outlining the development of psychiatric institutions and the integration of mental health into the primary care system. Key barriers discussed include inadequate funding and research, workforce shortages, geographic disparities in service distribution, limited child and adolescent services, high out-of-pocket costs, poor mental health literacy, persistent stigma, and non-standardized referral and prescribing practices. Special emphasis is placed on the roles of the *General Secretariat of Mental Health and Addiction Treatment (GSMHAT)*, private sector clinics, telepsychiatry platforms, and day care centers for addiction treatment. The chapter concludes with a set of evidence-based policy recommendations focused on expanding community-based care, enhancing training and regulation, reducing stigma, strengthening legislation, and promoting national and international collaboration to improve mental health service delivery in Egypt.

Keywords Mental health care · Egypt · Pathway of mental health care · Mental health services · Challenges of mental health care

W. Hassan (✉)
Institute of Psychiatry, Ain Shams University, Cairo, Egypt
e-mail: ebrahimw@alumni.vcu.edu

S. Elnoby
General Secretariat of Mental Health and Addiction Treatment-MOH, Cairo, Egypt

S. Al-Huseini and S. M. Y. Arafat (eds.), *Mental Health Care in the Middle East*, South Asian Perspectives in Mental Health and Psychology ,
https://doi.org/10.1007/978-981-95-0461-9_3

1 Introduction

1.1 Country Profile

Egypt is situated in northeastern Africa, bordered by the Mediterranean Sea to the north, the Red Sea to the east, Libya to the west, Sudan to the south, and Palestine to the northeast (Fig. 1). The Nile River, a lifeline for its agriculture and settlements, flows through the country. Egypt, historically part of the Arab world, was under British occupation from 1882 until its revolution in 1952, after which it abolished its monarchy in 1953 and became a republic. It briefly unified with Syria as the United Arab Republic (1958–1961) and later experienced military leadership until the 2011 Arab Spring uprising. Post-revolution, Egypt transitioned to a short-lived democratic government (2012–2013) before returning to military-influenced governance.

The World Bank (2025) classifies Egypt as a lower middle-income economy. Egypt has seen growth driven by sectors like tourism, Suez Canal revenues, natural gas exports, and agriculture. However, challenges such as inflation, high public debt,

Fig. 1 Map of Egypt

and wealth inequality persist, with significant disparities between urban and rural areas.

Egypt is the Arab world's most populous nation, with over 110 million people, and benefits from a large youth population, though youth unemployment remains a critical issue. Approximately 90% of Egyptians identify as Muslim, predominantly Sunni, with a Coptic Christian minority (World Population Review, 2023).

The country has faced severe inflationary pressures on essential goods in recent years, exacerbated by the dual shocks of the COVID-19 pandemic and the Russia–Ukraine war, which disrupted global supply chains and raised energy and food prices. Compounded by systemic financial corruption, tax evasion, and allegations of money laundering, these factors have strained household incomes and widened poverty gaps, particularly among low-income communities. The devaluation of the Egyptian pound and reliance on imports for staples like wheat, much of which came from Russia and Ukraine, intensified the crisis, pushing inflation to over 30% in 2023 (World Bank, 2025).

Culturally, Egypt's identity has been shaped by its Arab heritage, Mediterranean influences, and African roots, with historical ties to neighboring regions like the Levant and Sudan. Notably, Egypt has emerged as a regional hub for medical tourism in the Middle East and Africa, attracting patients from Libya, Sudan, and Gulf countries seeking affordable, high-quality healthcare.

1.2 Evolution of Psychiatric Services in Egypt

1.2.1 Mental Health Awareness in Egypt: A Historical Overview

The historical understanding of mental health in ancient Egypt traces back over five millennia, with early records such as the Ebers and Kahun papyri describing psychological conditions as physical afflictions linked to organs like the heart or uterus. The papers also described one of the psychotherapeutic methods used, "temple sleep," which involved the use of herbs, quite possibly opium (Okasha & Okasha, 2000). Unlike modern distinctions between mind and body, these disorders were not stigmatized, as ancient Egyptian medicine viewed mental and physical health as interconnected. By the fourteenth century, a mental healthcare unit was established as one of four departments at Cairo's Kalaoon Hospital—a groundbreaking development that predated comparable European facilities by nearly six centuries (Okasha, 2004).

1.2.2 Asylum Period

Throughout Egyptian history, care of people with a mental illness appears to have been community-based, while institutional care for those suffering from mental health problems was within general hospitals.

During the French colonization of Egypt in the early 1800s, Claude, a French physician who served as the director of medical services in the Egyptian Armed Forces, contacted the Egyptian monarch about the terrible conditions of mental patients in Cairo. Since all medical facilities were then under military control, mental health patients in Cairo were moved to Al Azbakia, a military hospital in the center of the city. They were moved to a nearby independent building in Boloaque after a few years (Okasha, 1993).

Separating patients with mental illness in separate buildings away from inhabited areas began only in the late nineteenth century, following a visit from the Royal Medico-Psychological Association in 1879. British colonization has influenced the modern practice of asylum care in Egypt (Loza & Nawawi, 2012).

One of the royal palaces was destroyed by fire in 1880, with the exception of a two-story structure. In 1883, this was painted yellow and opened as Cairo's first psychiatric hospital. The Yellow Palace was its name. It was located in Abbassia, a secluded desert district of Cairo, at the time. It is currently in the center of a congested, enlarged metropolis, and preparations are in place to demolish it. Khanka saw the construction of a second state psychiatric hospital in 1912. It was located a few kilometers north of Cairo and covered roughly 300 acres, including a sizable plantation. A third psychiatric hospital was founded in Alexandria in 1967, another in Helwan in 1979, and a third close to the airport in 1990 (Okasha, 1993).

In 1920, Egypt had 12 psychiatric beds for every 100,000 population, compared to England (250/100,000) and India (3/100,000). In 1992, Egypt had a ratio of 14 psychiatric beds for every 100,000 population, considering that Egypt's population in 1920 was 15 million, and in 1992, 57 million. Starting from 1949, outpatient facilities were extended to central hospitals in almost all governorates of Egypt (Okasha, 1993).

1.2.3 Modern Era

The institutional mental health care progressed steadily. This included the development of major facilities such as El Khanka Hospital, El Abbassia Hospital in Cairo, and Maamoura Hospital in Alexandria, which became the backbone of inpatient psychiatric care in the country (Saeed, 2018). In parallel, psychiatric departments were gradually integrated into university-affiliated medical schools and teaching hospitals. Notably, the Okasha Institute of Psychiatry at Ain Shams University has played a leading role in advancing clinical care, postgraduate training, and research in psychiatry. Psychiatric units were also introduced into major public hospitals, such as Kasr Al Ainy and Helwan General Hospital, though many general and district-level hospitals still lack dedicated inpatient psychiatric beds (Okasha et al., 2024). The integration of psychiatric care into medical universities—like Cairo University, Zagazig University, and Alexandria University—has contributed to a decentralized model of service, although coverage remains variable.

Currently, Egypt has approximately 21 specialized mental health hospitals under the *General Secretariat of Mental Health and Addiction Treatment (GSMHAT)* and over 70 psychiatric departments within general or university hospitals across the country (GSMHAT, 2023a, 2023b). However, inpatient capacity remains limited relative to demand, and forensic psychiatric services are centralized in only a few secure institutions. While urban areas are relatively well served, rural governorates such as Damietta and Beni Suef report significantly lower patient intake and specialist availability, reflecting persistent regional disparities in psychiatric infrastructure (GSMHAT, 2023a, 2023b; Okasha et al., 2024).

1.2.4 Private Clinics and Psychiatric Services in Egypt

The private sector plays a growing and crucial role in psychiatric services in Egypt, especially given the limitations of public mental health facilities. Many psychiatrists operate private clinics alongside public sector work, offering faster access, more privacy, and individualized care. Fees vary depending on the clinician's experience, and most services are paid out-of-pocket due to limited insurance coverage for mental health (Okasha et al., 2024; World Health Organization, 2006). In addition to face-to-face consultations, telepsychiatry has expanded rapidly in private practice through platforms like Shezlong, O7 Therapy, WhatsApp consultations, and video conferencing, particularly following the COVID-19 pandemic (MobiHealthNews, 2022).

Alongside private clinics, Egypt has seen the emergence of specialized private psychiatric hospitals. These facilities typically offer inpatient care, outpatient psychotherapy, addiction rehabilitation, and multidisciplinary services, but mainly cater to middle- and upper-income populations (Saeed, 2018). While the quality of care in private settings is often higher compared to overstretched public hospitals, concerns about variable treatment standards, absence of national accreditation, and occasional unethical practices like unnecessary hospitalization persist (Okasha et al., 2024). There is also a shortage of mental health professionals in private practice in rural areas, leading to significant geographical disparities in access.

1.2.5 Major Advocacy Group: Egyptian Psychiatric Association (EPA)

In Egypt, advocacy for mental health has historically been limited but has expanded significantly in the last two decades. One of the leading players is the GSMHAT under the Ministry of Health, which not only oversees service provision but also actively advocates for mental health rights, awareness campaigns, and policy reforms (Okasha et al., 2024). GSMHAT has played a crucial role in pushing forward the 2009 Mental Health Act and launching initiatives to reduce stigma and integrate mental health services into primary care (GSMHAT, 2023a, 2023b).

The Egyptian Psychiatric Association (EPA) is the principal professional body representing psychiatrists in Egypt. Established to advance mental health care, the EPA promotes Mental Health Care and plays a vital role in shaping Egypt's mental health landscape through its commitment to professional excellence and public advocacy.

1.2.6 Mental Health Legislation in Egypt

Efforts to formalize mental health law in Egypt can be traced back to the early twentieth century. In 1921, a draft proposal for a lunacy law was first mentioned in the annual report of the Lunacy Division of the Ministry of the Interior (Loza & El Nawawi, 2012).

Egypt's parliament passed its first **Mental Health Act** in 1944. This law introduced structured procedures for the involuntary detention of individuals diagnosed with psychosis, required second medical opinions, outlined patients' rights concerning consent to treatment, and established avenues for appeal (Zaki, 2009). While the 1944 Act provided the foundation for psychiatric practice in Egypt for approximately three decades, it gradually became outdated.

The **Mental Health Act of 2009** (Law 71) introduced significant reforms in the treatment and rights of people with mental illnesses in Egypt. It emphasized patients' rights to consent, independent second opinions, and protections within mental health institutions. Alongside legislative change, awareness campaigns using media, billboards, and school education were launched to advocate for community integration. Initially funded by the Ministry of Health, advocacy efforts were later driven by NGOs and human rights organizations. (Loza & El Nawawi, 2012).

The National Mental Health Council (NMHC) is the governmental body responsible for supervising the Mental Health Act 71 for the year 2009. Its main role is to develop the general policies for admission and treatment of mentally ill patients, policies for protection of rights of the mentally ill, policies for licensing facilities working in the field of mental health service provision, and policies regulating the work of forensic psychiatry units.

2 Epidemiology and Burden of Mental Illness in Egypt

The GSMHAT, Ministry of Health (MOH), has carried out a number of researches on the incidence of substance use and mental illnesses in recent years as part of health care policy and planning.

Psychiatric illnesses were found to be 17% prevalent in Egypt's northern governorates, which are primarily rural, according to Ghanem et al. (2009). Mood disorders accounted for 6.43%, anxiety disorders for 4.75%, and multiple disorders for 4.72% of all disorders. A report from the Mental Health Secretariat: Report to WHO-EMRO on 2009 revealed a number of important findings about mental illness in Upper Egypt. Mood (depressive) disorders and anxiety disorders were the most common (10.7% and 9.1%, respectively) (Saeed, 2018).

In collaboration with the WHO, GSMHAT in 2017 found that psychiatric disorders are proven to be 7%. The most prevalent disorders are mood disorders and substance disorders (3.1% and 2.17%, respectively). The prevalence is more in rural than in urban areas.

The National Survey on Psychiatric and Substance Use Disorders was conducted in 2017 and 2023. The prevalence Egyptian population exhibiting minor psychiatric morbidity was reported to be 25% and 20% in 2017 and 2023, respectively. The difference in prevalence rate in both studies may be due to methodological differences as including old age, children, and adolescents in the targeted population of the current study.

The first survey research on addiction was done in 1996, and reported substance use prevalence of around 6%. In 2014, 6–9% prevalence rate of substance use was reported. The last study survey on substance use was done in 2021 in collaboration with the Narcotic Control Fund and the National Center for Social and Criminal Research, and a 2.4% prevalence rate of substance use was reported.

The National Survey on Psychiatric and Substance Use Disorders (2023) Prevalence of any psychiatric disorder in adults and the elderly was 13.1%. Major depressive disorder was the most common diagnosis (6.78%), followed by anxiety disorders (4.96%), then obsessive–compulsive disorder (2.32%). In the last 12 months, substance use was found to be 7.1%, substance use disorder was 5.4%, while alcohol use disorder was 1.25%.

The prevalence of psychiatric disorders among children and adolescents was 14.9%. Attention-Deficit/Hyperactivity Disorder was the most prevalent disorder (6.83%), followed by Oppositional Defiant Disorder (3.05%), in the national survey 2023. Drug use among school students was carried out in The Egyptian Mediterranean School Survey Project on alcohol and other drugs (Medspad) in 2016 and 2020. Tobacco was the most used substance among teenagers, reaching 14.2%. Last year, the prevalence of alcohol detected in the current study was 4.6%, and the prevalence of illicit drugs reached 16.4%. The most prevalent substances were non-prescribed tranquilizers, alcohol, and inhalants.

Mental health screening of the elderly revealed that 20.5% of the old age group (1.4% of the whole sample) suffered from major neurocognitive impairment, and 27.6% of the old age group (1.9% of the whole sample) suffered from mild cognitive impairment.

According to WHO statistics, 7881 people committed suicide in Egypt alone in 2022, while in 2019, 3022 people died by suicide in Egypt. Egypt has a suicide rate of < 5.0 per 100,000 people, compared to an average of 9.0 worldwide. This low rate of suicide may be due to either defects in surveillance or religious traditions of the country, leading to underreporting consequences.

3 Mental Health Services in Egypt

3.1 Conventional Services

Many systems in Egypt provide mental health services. GSMHAT is considered the main provider of service in the field of mental health in Egypt. It was established after the Ministerial Decree (No. 32) for the year 1998, as a central administrative entity, directly affiliated to the Minister of Health, for the management of mental health hospitals and centers. At the beginning, the General Secretariat included only five hospitals; at present, 21 hospitals and centers are affiliated to the General Secretariat, which provides mental health services around the country (While the General Administration in MOHP supervises the private mental hospitals, NGOs, and outpatient clinics all over the country. (Elnemais Fawzy, 2017).

University psychiatric hospitals are under the supervision of the Ministry of Higher Education, while the psychiatric departments in hospitals under the supervision of the Ministry of Interior and the Ministry of Defense are directly under the supervision of those ministries. Finally, there are facilities managed by the Addiction Treatment and Abuse Fund.

Mental health services in Egypt include outpatient clinics, residential inpatient facilities, and specialized addiction treatment units. National Mental Health Platform Final Report—Phase III (2023) issued by GSMHAT, 83% of patients utilized outpatient services, while 17% received both outpatient and inpatient care. The delivery model typically begins with an outpatient consultation and inpatient admission if necessary. There is significant geographic variation in service utilization. The Abbasia Hospital in Cairo reported the highest number of cases (13.38%), followed by Heliopolis, Mamoura, and Khanka Hospitals. In contrast, hospitals in more remote governorates such as Damietta and Beni Suef had minimal patient intake, reflecting disparities in regional health infrastructure.

There is a disproportionate distribution of mental health facilities and services between urban and rural areas, as they are more prevalent in urban areas (especially in large cities) than in rural areas. They are deficient in areas such as Sinai, Matrouh, Hurghada, and New Waadi. In addition, there is a deficiency of community and preventive mental health services all over the country. (Saeed, 2018).

According to the World Health Organization—Country Cooperation Strategies—Egypt (2013), most primary healthcare physicians and nurses have not undergone formal mental health training in the past five years. While standardized manuals on diagnosing and managing mental health conditions are available in many primary care settings, structured referral pathways from primary to secondary or tertiary care remain absent.

Efforts to incorporate psychiatry into the primary healthcare system have encountered resistance. Despite, GSMHAT conducted mhGAP training projects for different PHC staff (Saeed, 2018). Mental health is commonly perceived by the public as a specialized field that falls outside the scope of general practice, which discourages patients from seeking psychiatric care through primary care channels. (Okasha et al., 2012).

Egypt's primary healthcare system is organized into two levels: the basic Family Health Units (FHUs) and the more specialized Family Health Centers (FHCs). Both structures include a core team of healthcare providers such as physicians, nurses, health educators, and social workers. FHCs, however, also host additional specialists (e.g., pediatricians) and serve a referral and coordination role for affiliated FHUs. In terms of mental health services, FHUS is responsible for initial assessments, after which patients may be referred to FHCS, where a visiting psychiatrist, typically from a local mental hospital, conducts outpatient clinics twice weekly and collaborates with general practitioners on complex cases (GSMHAT, 2017; Okasha et al., 2024).

While FHCs are envisioned to manage catchment area oversight, this function is not yet formally defined in their scope. Mental health integration into primary care is overseen by the GSMHAT, the governmental authority responsible for supervising 18 public mental health hospitals, managing outpatient and inpatient services, and delivering nationwide training programs for professionals across various sectors. As of 2017, Egypt had 5391 primary care units staffed by nearly 9000 physicians, although the target workforce was over 16,000—highlighting a significant human resource gap in primary care delivery (GSMHAT, 2017).

GSMHAT has expanded addiction day care centers in four hospitals—Abbassia, El-Matar, El-Maamoura, and El Khanka—to support individuals in recovery post-rehabilitation or those achieving clinical stability without inpatient care. Currently, 15 of the 18 GSMHAT hospitals offer addiction treatment through outpatient, inpatient, and day care services, with 563 dedicated addiction treatment beds, a large share of which are centralized in Abbassia Hospital (GSMHAT, 2017).

Forensic psychiatry services are primarily concentrated in El Khanka and El Abbassia hospitals. By 2016, these two institutions hosted around 600 forensic beds, with occupancy rates between 90 and 100%, demonstrating high demand and limited capacity.

With nearly 40% of Egypt's population under 18, the need for child and adolescent mental health services is significant. Yet, only 5% of children who require care actually receive it. Mental health services for youth are delivered through both public and private sectors. Providers include pediatricians (50%), general psychiatrists (20%), non-professionals (20%), and a limited number of child psychiatrists (7%). Primary care physicians account for only 3% of service providers in this population (Hussien et al., 2012).

3.2 New Developments-Tele-Psychiatry

In Egypt, telepsychiatry has emerged as a pivotal component of mental health care, particularly accentuated during the COVID-19 pandemic (Okasha et al., 2024). Many practitioners now provide online follow-ups and therapy sessions through mobile applications, particularly in private practice, offering patients increased privacy and flexibility.

The Ministry of Health's GSMHAT led projects like the creation of two round-the-clock psychological support hotlines and a nationwide **Mental Health Platform** that would enable remote services nationwide. Statistics from the national mental health platform since its launch in 2022 indicate that there are 17,153 registered users and 44,105 site visitors (Noby, 2023).

Academic institutions also contributed to this digital transformation. The Okasha Institute of Psychiatry at Ain Shams University implemented a comprehensive telepsychiatry program, offering services through video consultations, WhatsApp triage systems, and online group therapy sessions (Sayed et al., 2023).

The **Fund for Combating and Treating Addiction and Abuse (FDCTA)** operates a national addiction hotline—**16023**—providing free, confidential, and round-the-clock support for individuals struggling with substance use disorders. This hotline serves as a critical entry point for those seeking assistance, offering services such as counseling, referrals to treatment centers, and follow-up support.

Private sector platforms, such as Shezlong and O7 Therapy, have further expanded access to mental health care by offering online therapy sessions, corporate wellness programs, and psychoeducational resources. These platforms have been instrumental in reaching populations hesitant to seek in-person consultations due to stigma or logistical barriers (MobiHealthNews, 2022).

Despite these advancements, challenges persist, including the need for standardized regulations, data privacy concerns, and ensuring equitable access across different regions.

4 Challenges of Mental Health Care

4.1 High Treatment Gap in Egypt

Historically, mental health care in Egypt has been under-prioritized, leading to a substantial treatment gap across various population groups. Many individuals seek psychiatric support only at advanced stages of distress, when symptoms severely interfere with social or occupational functioning. Cultural beliefs attributing mental illness to supernatural causes, such as possession or the evil eye, further delay formal psychiatric intervention. This often results in individuals turning first to religious or traditional healers, bypassing clinical services entirely (Saeed, 2018).

According to Egypt's National Survey for Psychiatric and Substance Use Disorders (2023), while 16.93% of adults were found to experience psychiatric disorders, only a small fraction receive timely and appropriate care (GSMHAT, 2023a, 2023b). For example, a study among university students found that although over two-thirds (68.1%) reported significant psychological distress, only 11.2% sought professional mental health support (Baklola et al., 2024). Similar trends were observed among medical students, where nearly 78% reported needing mental health care but only 23% pursued it (El-gabry et al., 2022).

The treatment gap is especially pronounced among children and adolescents. Data from the MedSPAD Egypt 2020 study showed minimal formal mental health service utilization in this group, with many turning instead to peers, families, or spiritual authorities. Estimates from GSMHAT suggest that less than 20% of individuals with mental health conditions access specialized care, indicating that upward of 80% may remain untreated (Saeed, 2018). This gap reflects systemic service availability, cultural acceptance, and workforce distribution issues.

Compounding the issue, Egypt's psychiatric infrastructure also remains inadequate. The 2018 data show 5508 licensed psychiatric beds are distributed across 18 governmental mental health hospitals. Notably, nearly one-third (1755 beds) of this capacity is located et al. Khanka Hospital, a forensic and male inpatient facility, while Abbassia Hospital, the largest mental health facility in the Middle East, holds 1,381 beds. This distribution highlights the highly centralized and hospital-based nature of Egypt's mental health system, leaving many governorates with limited or no inpatient capacity.

4.2 Unregulated Help-Seeking Patterns in Egypt

Egypt's mental health care system exhibits a fragmented and pluralistic help-seeking landscape, shaped by a combination of limited access to formal psychiatric care, cultural stigma, and reliance on traditional healing practices.

According to the National Survey for Psychiatric and Substance Use Disorders (2023), many individuals initiate their care journey with non-specialist providers. These include general practitioners, pharmacists, religious leaders, or traditional healers, often well before accessing specialized psychiatric care. In rural areas and underserved governorates, first-line consultations are more likely to occur in the form of religious rituals or traditional practices than through clinical channels. This trend is consistent with findings from the National Addiction Mapping Report (2018), which reported a high rate of traditional and spiritual consultations prior to formal treatment engagement.

MedSPAD Egypt (2020) also showed that adolescents frequently rely on peers, online sources, and informal guidance for managing psychological distress or experimenting with substances, without any engagement with mental health professionals. Among adults, religious and spiritual explanations for mental illness remain prevalent, delaying diagnosis and treatment.

Recent academic reviews (Okasha et al., 2024) reinforce these findings, reporting that more than half of mental health patients consult non-specialist sources, such as traditional healers or non-psychiatric physicians, before reaching psychiatric services. Additionally, family members often act as gatekeepers to care, determining when and where individuals seek help, which can either support or obstruct timely treatment.

4.3 Poor Funding and Research in Egypt

Despite increasing recognition of mental health as a public health priority, Egypt continues to allocate a limited proportion of its overall health budget to mental health services. According to estimates referenced in WHO reports and national assessments, only around 2% of Egypt's total health expenditure is dedicated to mental health. Of this, approximately 59% is spent on mental hospitals, leaving community-based care and research initiatives underfunded (Saeed, 2018).

This financial constraint severely limits the scale and quality of services, particularly in underresourced regions. The cost of psychotropic medications is borne entirely by the government in public facilities, but logistical delays and inadequate distribution channels often hinder continuous access, especially in rural areas. Additionally, the absence of mental health insurance coverage in most health plans further exacerbates the financial burden on families seeking long-term care.

Research output in the field of mental health remains insufficient. Although institutions like Ain Shams University and Cairo University contribute to psychiatric research, Egypt lags behind international and regional benchmarks in terms of peer-reviewed publications, especially in areas like implementation science, health economics, and community mental health. For instance, between 2015 and 2020, Egypt produced fewer than 50 indexed articles annually related to mental health in PubMed-listed journals (Elnemais Fawzy, 2017).

4.4 Inadequate and Inequitable Manpower in Egypt

Mental health care in Egypt suffers from a critical shortage and inequitable distribution of professionals, significantly hindering access to care. According to the most recent data, Egypt has approximately 1100 registered psychiatrists, with 889 employed within the GSMHAT system (Okasha et al., 2022). This number falls well below the WHO-recommended minimum of 70 psychiatrists per 100,000 population, especially in the context of Egypt's population exceeding 114 million. Moreover, Doctors' immigration has been encouraged by policymakers in wealthy Arab Gulf countries to contribute to the foreign currency to the local economy (Loza & Sorour, 2016).

Despite steady efforts to train new professionals, the output of psychiatrists and clinical psychologists remains limited, and many prefer to work in the private sector or abroad. As a result, public sector institutions—especially in rural and underserved regions—remain severely understaffed. A pronounced urban–rural disparity in workforce distribution exacerbates the issue. Most mental health professionals are concentrated in Cairo, Giza, and Alexandria, while regions such as Upper Egypt and frontier governorates often lack even a single full-time psychiatrist. Many districts are served only by general practitioners with limited psychiatric training, resulting in delayed diagnosis and inadequate treatment (GSMHAT National Survey, 2023a, 2023b).

Mental health services in Egypt are predominantly hospital-centered, with a relatively underdeveloped network of community-based services. While initiatives like the National Mental Health Platform and WHO-supported mhGAP training aim to expand access, especially through telepsychiatry and primary care integration, their reach is still limited in terms of personnel and geographical coverage (Noby, 2022).

4.5 Out-of-Pocket Expense in Egypt

Mental health care in Egypt imposes a significant financial burden on individuals, primarily due to limited insurance coverage and high out-of-pocket (OOP) expenses. As of the Egypt National Health Accounts (2019/2020), OOP payments accounted for approximately 77% of the expenditure on mental health. This level of OOP spending is significantly higher than the global average and exceeds the averages for both the Middle East and North Africa (MENA) region and lower middle-income countries.

While public hospitals under GSMHAT provide free psychiatric medications and inpatient care, many essential services, such as outpatient psychotherapy, private consultations, and long-term rehabilitation, are not covered by public insurance schemes. Consequently, patients often bear the full cost of these services, which can be prohibitively expensive, especially for those in lower income.

The Egyptian government's expenditure on mental health constitutes approximately 2% of the total health budget, with a significant portion allocated to inpatient services. This limited investment in mental health infrastructure and services further exacerbates the financial strain on individuals seeking care (Okasha et al., 2024).

4.6 Malfunctioning Referral System in Egypt

Egypt's mental health referral system remains fragmented and underdeveloped. Although mental health is included in Egypt's Basic Benefit Package for family health practice, there is no standardized referral protocol linking primary care with specialized psychiatric services. Many general practitioners in Primary Health Care Units (PHUs) lack mental health training (Saeed, 2018). Patients often bypass primary care and present directly at GSMHAT hospitals, university clinics, or private providers. This open-access model leads to overburdening of tertiary services, inefficient triaging, and a lack of continuity in treatment. Public perceptions of mental health as an issue requiring specialist care also reduce early engagement with primary-level services (Okasha et al., 2024; Saeed, 2018).

4.7 Poor Mental Health Literacy in Egypt

Mental health literacy across Egypt remains low, particularly in rural and marginalized communities (Okasha et al., 2024). Formal mental health education is absent from primary and secondary school curricula, and no national literacy campaign or strategy is embedded in the educational system. While some public awareness initiatives have been launched by GSMHAT and civil society organizations, these remain limited in reach and sustainability (GSMHAT, 2023a, 2023b).

University-level training in psychiatry is integrated into medical curricula, but this does not translate to widespread community awareness. Misinformation, fear of labeling, and lack of public discourse continue as barriers. Developing mental health awareness curricula, engaging media and religious institutions, and supporting community health outreach are essential to raising mental health literacy nationwide (Okasha et al., 2024; GSMHAT, 2023a, 2023b).

4.8 High Stigma in Egypt

Stigma surrounding mental illness remains one of the most critical barriers to mental health care in Egypt. A nationwide study by Rabea et al. (2023) found that 74.8% of patients attending a mental health outpatient clinic in Fayoum experienced significant levels of stigma, with 36.6% demonstrating low self-concept. In her comprehensive review, Raafat (2015) explains that stigma in Egypt stems from cultural myths, religious interpretations, and false media narratives. Mental illness is often seen as a reflection of weakness or moral failure, leading individuals to avoid psychiatric services and conceal symptoms from family and community. Her work also emphasizes that mass media often reinforces damaging stereotypes, portraying those with mental illness as violent, unpredictable, or socially undesirable. This environment fosters an internalized stigma that patients themselves begin to accept. As Ghanem et al. (2009) note, self-stigma compounds the social stigma, reducing patients' likelihood of adhering to treatment, pursuing employment, or maintaining social relationships.

Education level, employment status, and age also correlate strongly with stigma levels. Rabea et al. (2023) found that illiterate patients and those unemployed were more likely to report internalized stigma, indicating the intersectional impact of socioeconomic status on mental health experiences. Despite efforts by Egypt's GSMHAT to lead national awareness campaigns and adopt more compassionate language (e.g., replacing "electroshock" with "brain synchronization"), these initiatives remain limited in scope and evaluation.

4.9 Non-judicious Prescribing (Polypharmacy) in Egypt

In Egypt, polypharmacy—particularly the concurrent use of multiple antipsychotics—is common, especially in inpatient psychiatric settings. Antipsychotics are often used at higher doses than recommended, and off-label prescribing (e.g., clozapine for sedation) has been observed (Abolmagd et al., 2020). A study on child psychiatry prescribing practices found that 76% of medications used did not align with established international guidelines, such as the Maudsley Prescribing Manual (Ghaly et al., 2020). Contributing to this issue is the lack of standardized training, with only 37% of psychiatrists having received refresher courses on the rational use of psychotropic medication (WHO-AIMS, 2006). These patterns not only reflect clinical inconsistencies but also reinforce public stigma, as psychiatric medication is commonly perceived as overly sedative.

4.10 Scarcity of Medications in Egypt

Egypt faces a significant shortage of psychiatric medications, posing a critical challenge to mental health care delivery. Despite the inclusion of essential psychotropic drugs—such as haloperidol, risperidone, fluoxetine, and lithium carbonate—in the national essential medicines list, their availability across healthcare facilities is inconsistent and often inadequate (Okasha et al., 2024; Saeed, 2018).

A 2024 investigative report described a worsening psychiatric medication crisis, noting that patients with chronic conditions like bipolar disorder were forced to interrupt treatment due to the unavailability of medicines such as Lamictal (Ammar, 2024). This reflects a broader problem across Egypt's health system, where economic instability, bureaucratic delays, and foreign currency shortages have severely disrupted pharmaceutical imports and production (Diab, 2025; Saad, 2019).

According to the Ministry of Health's own assessments, while major GSMHAT hospitals may have access to a basic psychotropic inventory, general hospitals, outpatient units, and rural pharmacies often experience long-term stock-outs (Saeed, 2018). Additionally, many medications are acquired informally or at inflated prices due to supply disruptions, posing risks related to quality and affordability (Ammar, 2024).

This scarcity is further aggravated by the limited budget allocated to mental health: in 2017, while EGP 20.8 million was proposed for mental health services, only EGP 2 million was disbursed (Saeed, 2018). Without sustainable supply chains, regulatory reform, and local manufacturing support, medication shortages will continue to jeopardize patient outcomes.

5 Non-medical Management of Mental Disorders in Egypt

In Egypt, non-medical approaches to mental health remain deeply embedded in societal care-seeking patterns, particularly in rural areas and among socioeconomically disadvantaged groups. Many individuals first consult traditional or religious healers, rather than medical professionals, due to long-standing cultural beliefs that attribute mental illness to supernatural causes such as jinn possession, black magic (sihr), or the evil eye (al-ayn) (Okasha et al., 2024).

Traditional healers in Egypt—often referred to as sheikhs, fakirs, or spiritual guides—are commonly seen as more accessible and trustworthy than formal psychiatric services, especially in communities with limited mental health literacy. Rituals such as Qur'anic recitation, talismanic treatments, and spiritual cleansing are widely practiced and sometimes even preferred over pharmacological or psychotherapeutic interventions (Assad et al., 2015). Okasha et al. (2024) further note that the high religiosity of Egyptian society shapes symptom interpretation and treatment choices. A qualitative study on care pathways for patients with bipolar disorder in Egypt found that over 60% of patients engaged with traditional healers before accessing psychiatric care, often leading to treatment delays and reduced medication adherence (Assad et al., 2015).

Despite the scale of traditional healing, there is no formal integration between traditional and psychiatric care in Egypt. Unlike some other countries in the region, Egypt has not implemented collaborative models that involve traditional healers in referral or awareness systems (Green & Colucci, 2020). As such, traditional healers operate in parallel to, rather than in partnership with, formal services.

Family remains a primary support system for individuals with mental health conditions. However, due to a lack of awareness, families often fail to provide the necessary psychological support, and in some cases, contribute to the stigma and isolation of affected individuals. There is a growing interest in alternative therapies such as meditation, herbal medicine, and physical fitness as adjuncts to conventional treatment. While these approaches can be beneficial, they should be integrated with professional medical care rather than used as substitutes.

6 Way Forward for Mental Health Reform in Egypt

6.1 Augmented Research and Funding in Egypt: A Path Forward

One of the key barriers to advancing mental health services in Egypt has been the historically low funding allocated for research and service development. According to the World Health Organization (2006), only 2% of the total governmental health budget was allocated to mental health, with 59% directed toward psychiatric hospitals. Recent steps, such as the Egyptian government's decision to raise mental health hospital budgets by LE 50 million for 2024–2025 (Egypt Independent, 2024), are promising but mainly focus on service infrastructure rather than scientific innovation. To overcome this, Egypt must strengthen research capacity through scholarships and fellowships like the Fulbright Commission Egypt, foster international collaboration Science for Africa Foundation, and encourage public–private partnerships to fund community interventions, as exemplified by the success of O7 Therapy in securing $2.1 million for mental health service expansion (MobiHealthNews, 2022).

6.2 Building an Equitable Mental Health Workforce in Egypt: A Strategic Priority

Egypt faces a critical shortage of mental health professionals, with approximately 1.44 psychiatrists per 100,000 population (Okasha et al., 2024). This shortage is particularly acute in rural and underserved areas (Saeed, 2018). Addressing this gap requires expanding psychiatric residency positions (World Health Organization, 2006), incentivizing rural placements, integrating mental health into primary care via WHO's mhGAP (Okasha et al., 2024), and promoting task-shifting by training community health workers (Green & Colucci, 2020).

6.3 Expanding Community-Based Mental Health Services in Egypt

Egypt's system remains highly centralized around large psychiatric hospitals, with limited access to community-based services (Okasha et al., 2024). Pilot programs in Helwan and El Khanka (Saeed, 2018) showed the potential for decentralization. Building on these pilots, Egypt must integrate mental health services into primary health care following mhGAP (World Health Organization, 2006), develop mobile teams, partner with NGOs to provide community mental health (MobiHealthNews, 2022), and legislate community mental health protection.

6.4 Improving Mental Health Literacy and Public Awareness in Egypt

Mental health literacy remains low, with widespread misconceptions about mental illness (Okasha et al., 2024; Rabea et al., 2023). School-based programs (Raafat, 2015), mass media campaigns, healthcare worker training, religious leader engagement, and digital platforms (MobiHealthNews, 2022) are essential strategies to enhance awareness and encourage earlier help-seeking.

6.5 Strengthening Medication Supply Chains for Psychiatric Care in Egypt

Frequent medication shortages—particularly for lithium, risperidone, and fluoxetine—disrupt patient care (Ammar, 2024; Saeed, 2018). Egypt must improve centralized procurement (World Health Organization, 2021), stimulate local production (Saad, 2019), streamline regulatory pathways, and ensure inclusion of psychotropic drugs in Universal Health Insurance plans (Dinana et al., 2024).

6.6 Expanding Telepsychiatry and Digital Mental Health Services in Egypt

The pandemic accelerated telepsychiatry growth via informal channels like WhatsApp and Skype (Okasha et al., 2024). However, formal regulation, digital training, platform expansion, subsidization of teleconsultations, and strengthened hotline services like 16,023 (GSMHAT, 2023a, 2023b) are needed to sustain momentum and ensure equitable digital access.

6.7 Reducing Stigma Through National Programs in Egypt

Stigma remains a pervasive barrier to accessing care (Okasha et al., 2024; Rabea et al., 2023). Egypt should launch a national anti-stigma campaign, engage religious leaders, use popular media narratives, educate youth through schools (Raafat, 2015), and systematically evaluate program impact (World Health Organization, 2021).

6.8 Strengthening Mental Health Legislation and Human Rights Protections in Egypt

While the 2009 Mental Health Act was a milestone, gaps in enforcement remain (Okasha et al., 2024). Strengthening judicial oversight, establishing independent monitoring bodies (World Health Organization, 2021), promoting community-based alternatives, and creating patient advocacy services are necessary steps to protect rights and dignity.

6.9 Fostering Collaboration and International Partnerships in Egypt

International partnerships are crucial for system strengthening. Egypt should engage with the WHO and the World Psychiatric Association (WPA) (World Health Organization, 2021), join global research initiatives (Science for Africa Foundation, sign bilateral mental health agreements, promote NGO involvement, and align with the Sustainable Development Goals, especially SDG 3.4 (United Nations, 2015).

7 Conclusion

Egypt has made significant strides in addressing the mental health needs of its population. The establishment of GSMHAT, the implementation of national surveys, and the creation of the National Drug Observatory reflect a growing commitment to mental health care. However, substantial challenges remain, including stigma, lack of resources, and geographic disparities in service availability. Egypt must invest in infrastructure, human resources, and public education to build a resilient and inclusive mental health system. Multisectoral collaboration, legislative reform, and community engagement are critical to advancing the mental health agenda. By adopting a holistic and rights-based approach, Egypt can pave the way for accessible, equitable, and effective mental health care for all its citizens.

References

Abolmagd, S., El-Gabry, D., Elkholy, H., et al. (2020). Tackling myths of common prescribing patterns in schizophrenia amongst Egyptian psychiatrists. *Middle East Current Psychiatry, 27*(1), 52. https://doi.org/10.1186/s43045-020-00059-4

Ammar, R. (2024). *Shortage of psychiatric medications in Egypt: A daily struggle for survival*. Zawia3. https://zawia3.com/en/psychiatric-medications/

Assad, T., Okasha, T., Ramy, H., et al. (2015). Role of traditional healers in the pathway to care of patients with bipolar disorder in Egypt. *International Journal of Social Psychiatry, 61*(6), 583–590. https://doi.org/10.1177/0020764014565799

Baklola, M., Terra, M., Taha, A., et al. (2024). Mental health literacy and help-seeking behaviour among Egyptian undergraduates: A cross-sectional national study. *BMC Psychiatry, 24*(1), 202. https://doi.org/10.1186/s12888-024-05620-7

Diab, A. (2025). Egypt's drug shortage. *The Borgen Project*. https://borgenproject.org/egypts-drug-shortage/

Dinana, H., Saleh, B., Aly, E., Ismail, H., et al. (2024). *Sustainability and Resilience in the Egyptian Health System EGYPT*. Partnership for Health System Sustainability and Resilience (PHSSR) https://www3.weforum.org/docs/WEF_PHSSR_Egypt_2024.pdf

Economist Impact. (2023). Tackling mental health in Egypt. https://impact.economist.com/perspectives/health/tackling-mental-health-egypt

Egypt National Health Accounts. (2019/2020). https://applications.emro.who.int/docs/9789292741549-eng.pdf

Egypt National Health Accounts 2019/2020. (2020). World Health Organization. https://applications.emro.who.int/docs/9789292741549-eng.pdf

El-Gabry, D., Okasha, T., Shaker, N., et al. (2022). Mental health and wellbeing among Egyptian medical students: A cross-sectional study. *Middle East Current Psychiatry, 29*(1), 25. https://doi.org/10.1186/s43045-022-00193-1

Elnemais Fawzy, M. (2017). Mental health care in Egypt: Review of current state, policy, and needs. *International Journal of Mental Health, 46*(4), 339–345. https://doi.org/10.1080/00207411.2017.1367447

Fund for Combating and Treating Addiction and Abuse (FDCTA). http://www.drugcontrol.org.eg/

General Secretariat of Mental Health and Addiction Treatment (GSMHAT). (2017). *Annual statistical report on mental health services in Egypt*. Ministry of Health and Population. https://mentalhealth.mohp.gov.eg/mental/web/sites/default/files/files/National%20survey%20report.pdf

General Secretariat of Mental Health and Addiction Treatment (GSMHAT). (2020). *MedSPAD Egypt survey report*. https://rm.coe.int/p-pg-mednet-2021-8-medspad-guidelines-2020-2021-en/1680a2c80f

General Secretariat of Mental Health and Addiction Treatment (GSMHAT). (2023a). *National mental health platform final report—Phase III*. Ministry of Health and Population. https://mentalhealth.mohp.gov.eg

General Secretariat of Mental Health and Addiction Treatment (GSMHAT). (2023b). *National psychiatric and substance use disorders survey*. https://mentalhealth.mohp.gov.eg

Ghaly, A. S., Tobar, S. M. S., El-Hadidy, M. A., et al. (2020). Prescribed psychiatric interventions for children presented to a university psychiatric clinic in Egypt: A descriptive cross-sectional study. *Middle East Current Psychiatry, 27*(1), 53. https://doi.org/10.1186/s43045-020-00056-7

Ghanem, M., Gadallah, M., Meky, F. A., et al. (2009). National survey of prevalence of mental disorders in Egypt: Preliminary survey. *Eastern Mediterranean Health Journal, 15*(1), 65–75.

Green, B., & Colucci, E. (2020). Traditional healers' and biomedical practitioners' perceptions of collaborative mental healthcare in low- and middle-income countries: A systematic review. *Transcultural Psychiatry, 57*(1), 94–107. https://doi.org/10.1177/1363461519894396

Hussein, H., Shaker, N., El-Sheikh, M., et al. (2012). Pathways to child mental health services among patients in an urban clinical setting in Egypt. *Psychiatric Services, 63*(12), 1225–1230. https://doi.org/10.1176/appi.ps.201200039

Loza, N., & El Nawawi, M. (2012). Mental health legislation in Egypt. *International Psychiatry, 9*(3), 64–66. https://doi.org/10.1192/S1749367600003246

Loza, N., & Sorour, E. (2016). Brain drain: The issues raised for Egypt by the emigration of psychiatrists. *Bjpsych International, 13*(3), 59–61. https://doi.org/10.1192/s2056474000001239

MobiHealthNews. (2022). *Egypt's O7 Therapy lands game-changing $2.1M in funding*. https://www.mobihealthnews.com/news/emea/egypt-s-o7-therapy-lands-game-changing-21m-funding

Noby, S. (2022). National Mental Health Platform in Egypt, revolution of mental health services. *European Psychiatry, 65*(S1), S574–S574. https://doi.org/10.1192/j.eurpsy.2022.1471.PMCID: PMC9567546

Noby, S. I. (2023). Reform of mental health care in Egypt: Telepsychiatry perspective. *European Psychiatry, 66*(S1), S861. https://doi.org/10.1192/j.eurpsy.2023.1823

Okasha, A. (1993). Psychiatry in Egypt. *Psychiatric Bulletin, 17*(9), 548–551. https://doi.org/10.1192/pb.17.9.548

Okasha, A. (2004). Focus on psychiatry in Egypt. *The British Journal of Psychiatry, 185*(3), 266–272. https://doi.org/10.1192/bjp.185.3.266

Okasha, A., & Okasha, T. (2000). Notes on mental disorders in pharaonic Egypt. *History of Psychiatry, 11*(44), 413–424. https://doi.org/10.1177/0957154X0001104406

Okasha, A., Karam, E., & Okasha, T. (2012). Mental health services in the Arab world. *World Psychiatry, 11*(1), 52–54. https://doi.org/10.1016/j.wpsyc.2012.01.008

Okasha, T., Shaker, N., El-Gabry D. (2022). Community mental health services in Egypt. *Consortium Psychiatricum, 3*(2), 123–128. https://doi.org/10.17816/CP165

Okasha, T., Shaker, N. M., & El-Gabry, D. A. (2024). Mental health services in Egypt, the Middle East, and North Africa. *International Review of Psychiatry*. https://doi.org/10.1080/09540261.2024.2400143

Raafat, M. (2015). Mental illness stigma in Egypt. *Misr International University*. https://doi.org/10.13140/RG.2.2.20832.99841

Rabea, A., Mourad, M., & Mohamed, S. (2023). Stigma and its relation to self-concept among patients with mental disorders. *Egyptian Journal of Health Care, 14*(1), 279–298. https://doi.org/10.21608/ejhc.2023.282510

Saad, A. A. (2019). *Drug shortage in Egypt: Causes and mitigation measures* [Master's thesis, The American University in Cairo]. AUC Knowledge Fountain. https://fount.aucegypt.edu/etds/1711

Saeed, S. (2018). *Assessment of governmental mental health system in Egypt (2016–2017)* [Master's thesis, Universidade NOVA de Lisboa]. RUN Repository. http://hdl.handle.net/10362/40174

Sayed, M., Gafary, M. E., Mohsen, N., et al. (2023). Assessment of telepsychiatry services provided by Okasha Institute of Psychiatry during COVID-19 pandemic. *Middle East Current Psychiatry, 30*(1), 84. https://doi.org/10.1186/s43045-023-00356-8

United Nations. (2015). Department of Economic and Social Affairs Sustainable Development. https://sdgs.un.org/goals/goal3.

World Bank. (2025). *Egypt Overview*. https://www.worldbank.org/en/country/egypt/overview

World Health Organization. (2006). *WHO-AIMS report on mental health system in Egypt*. https://cdn.who.int/media/docs/default-source/mental-health/who-aims-country-reports/who_aims_report_egypt.pdf

World Health Organization. (2013). *Country cooperation strategy: Egypt*. https://apps.who.int/iris/handle/10665/113237

World Health Organization. (2021). *Mental Health Atlas 2020*. https://www.who.int/publications/i/item/9789240036703

World Population Review. (2023). *Egypt Population 2023*. https://worldpopulationreview.com/countries/egypt

Zaki, M. M. (2009). Egyptian legislation on the compulsory treatment of persons with psychiatric disorders: The old and the new. *International Psychiatry, 6*(3), 57–58. https://doi.org/10.1192/S1749367600000576

Chapter 4
Mental Health Care in Iran

Marjan Fathi

Abstract Mental health in Iran has evolved through years of sustained efforts, overcoming cultural, economic, and social barriers to expand access to care. The nation's mental health programs have progressively developed and integrated into the primary health care system, ensuring comprehensive services from primary prevention to harm reduction initiatives. This integration is a key strength, providing accessible, structured, and continuity-based support across different levels of intervention. Despite challenges such as stigma, workforce shortages, and resource constraints, efforts continue to enhance mental health awareness and accessibility. The emphasis on community participation, structured training for health professionals, and inter-sectoral collaboration has strengthened the program's impact. As mental health disorders remain a growing concern, Iran's integrated approach offers a scalable and sustainable model for developing countries aiming to improve mental health care within existing healthcare systems.

Keywords Community participation · Cultural adaptation · Harm reduction · Healthcare accessibility · Inter-sectoral collaboration · Public awareness · Sustainable model

1 Introduction

Iran is a beautiful, expansive country with a rich mix of cultures and histories that go back around 7,000 years. It is in the Eastern Mediterranean region, and its people come from many ethnic backgrounds. By 2025, over 92 million Iranians will call this land home, and most will live in cities where life is rapidly changing. People there can expect to live around 78 years on average, with women generally living longer than men (Iran Demographics, 2025).

M. Fathi (✉)
Suicidology, Postdoctoral, Iran University of Medical Sciences (IUMS), Tehran, Iran
e-mail: fathi.ma@iums.ac.ir

S. Al-Huseini and S. M. Y. Arafat (eds.), *Mental Health Care in the Middle East*, South Asian Perspectives in Mental Health and Psychology ,
https://doi.org/10.1007/978-981-95-0461-9_4

Iran is a nation characterized by its cultural diversity, with Persians, Kurds, Azerbaijanis, Turkmens, Lurs, Arabs, and Baloch. This ethnic diversity contributes to the country's rich cultural heritage. Persian culture exerts significant influence on literature, art, and architecture, while each ethnic group preserves its unique traditions. Islam is the predominant religion in Iran. Zoroastrians, Christians, and Jews also form part of the country's diverse religious composition. Regionality and urbanization are influential factors that shape interethnic relations.

Iran's socioeconomic landscape is shaped by its hydrocarbon-based economy, agricultural sector, and service industries, with a significant state presence in manufacturing and financial services. The country holds the second-largest natural gas reserves and the fourth-largest proven crude oil reserves, making energy exports a key driver of economic activity. The main Industries included Petroleum, petrochemicals, automotive, pharmaceuticals, textiles, construction, food processing. Traditional occupations are prevalent in accordance with the geographical situation of each region.

According to the World Bank report in 2025, Iran's socioeconomic outlook remains complex, with economic resilience driven by policy adjustments, trade diversification, and domestic production strategies. However, inflation (29.5%, 2025), unemployment (8.9%, 2021), and climate-related challenges continue to pose significant hurdles to sustainable growth.

Public health as well as mental health are the most concerning indicators in Iran. In recent years, research in the field of mental health has been increasing. The integration of mental health into the primary care system has facilitated access to mental health indicators more precisely.

The latest research showed that the number of people affected by mental disorders in Iran is growing much faster than the global rate. Mental health issues now account for approximately 10% of all health problems, up from 4.6% in 1990 (Badrfam & Zandifar, 2025). Different methods of studying the population show that around a third of Iranians may face some mental health challenges during their lives. These numbers are higher than in nearby countries like Iraq, India, and Turkey, but lower than in Pakistan and Afghanistan.

Many social and economic troubles contribute to this situation. Economic instability, unemployment, and poverty increase stress and make mental health issues worse. These issues can lead to serious problems like depression, suicide, and addiction (Mirghaed et al., 2020). Political unrest, financial crises, and social upheaval can influence mental health trends. In Iran, ongoing economic and political crises seem to weigh heavily, making it even more urgent to find solutions (Hosseinzadeh-Shanjani et al., 2024).

The rising tide of mental health struggles calls for immediate action. Leaders and policymakers have focused on improving mental health services, making them more accessible, transparent, and compassionate. Only by working together can we be hopeful to support the well-being of Iran's people and ensure they get the care they deserve.

2 The History of Mental Health Policy in Iran

Over the years, Iran has made progress in caring for mental health. Starting in the 1920s, efforts began to treat mental health issues, and today, the country has developed dedicated services, laws, and community programs aimed at helping those in need (Rastegar et al., 2025).

Mental health care in Iran has evolved significantly over the past century, shaped by government policies and institutional reforms. In the early twentieth century, psychiatric care was rudimentary, with municipal authorities managing psychiatric hospitals and assuming financial responsibility for patient care. In 1924, Tehran Municipality officially took over the administration of psychiatric hospitals, marking a pivotal moment in mental health governance.

Early Institutional Development (1920s–1940s)

During the 1930s and 1940s, psychiatric hospital management continued under municipal oversight, with financial support provided for patients unable to afford treatment. In 1946, Iran established its first dedicated psychiatric hospital, which catalyzed the expansion of mental health services in provincial centers.

Legal and Financial Framework (1950s–1970s)

By the 1950s, Iran introduced legal procedures for appointing guardians for mentally ill individuals and solidified municipal financial responsibility for psychiatric care. National laws formalized these obligations in the 1960s, further clarifying cost-sharing mechanisms. However, budget deficits and financial mismanagement led to irregular funding, prompting a transfer of psychiatric hospital oversight to the Ministry of Labor and Social Affairs in 1974.

Revolutionary Changes and Welfare Expansion (1980s–1990s)

Following the 1979 Revolution, Iran's constitution emphasized universal healthcare and social security as fundamental rights. The newly established State Welfare Organization took responsibility for mental health rehabilitation, ensuring financial aid for individuals with chronic conditions. The expansion of social insurance in the 1990s further improved coverage for vulnerable populations, culminating in the Universal Health Insurance Law of 1994 (Rastegar et al., 2025).

Systematic Reform and Inclusion (2000s–Present)

The integration of mental health services into primary care in Iran was mentioned for the first time in the mid-1980s by a team of mental health professionals with experience in public health issues and approved of by senior authorities in the Ministry of Health (MOH). It started to be launched in the late 1980s (Hajebi et al., 2021). The 2000s saw the integration of mental health into Iran's broader social and economic development policies, including comprehensive rehabilitation programs for chronic mental illness. The 2018 *Comprehensive Law on the Protection of the Disabled* enhanced subsidies for non-governmental psychiatric institutions, strengthening financial assistance for families caring for individuals with severe mental disorders (Rastegar et al., 2025).

Gradual migration from rural to urban areas throughout the past four decades, the shift of disease pattern from communicable diseases to non-communicable diseases, including mental disorders, showed the need for reform in mental health policy. On the other hand, the National Mental Health Survey revealed that a significant proportion of people with a reported mental disorder had not received any health services during the last 12 months of the study, revealing significant unmet needs (Hajebi et al., 2021).

In 2022, Iran introduced a specialized fund to support individuals with severe psychiatric conditions, providing financial protection through health insurance and exempting them from hospitalization costs. National hospital accreditation standards now incorporate financial assistance measures, further advancing equity in mental health care.

From municipal governance to nationwide welfare policies, Iran's mental health system has undergone continuous transformation, reflecting a growing recognition of psychiatric care as a critical public health concern. While financing and accessibility remain challenges, recent policy advancements suggest a broader commitment to reducing the burden of mental illness through structured legal and financial support (Rastegar et al., 2025).

3 Prevalence of Mental Disorders in Iran

3.1 Mental Disorders

Access to high-quality data on epidemiological measures of mental disorders is a major issue in Iran, as with many other countries in the region. Although there were several mental health surveys in Iran during the past decades, some of them used non-standard methods or non-representative samples that made them unsuitable for GBD models. However, the Global Burden of Disease (GBD) 2019 study highlights significant epidemiological shifts in mental health disorders across Iran over three decades. Total disability-adjusted life years (DALYs) due to mental disorders increased by 77.1%, rising from 1.16 million (4.6% of total disease burden) in 1990 to 2.05 million (10.3%) in 2019. This growth rate surpassed the global average (55%) but remained below the Eastern Mediterranean regional trend (114%). The modest increase in age-standardized DALY rates (1.8%) suggests that demographic shifts—particularly population growth among young and middle-aged adults—are the primary drivers rather than increased age-specific prevalence. Depressive disorders saw the highest absolute burden increase (104%), affecting 4.8 million cases by 2019, followed by anxiety disorders with a 67% increase (totaling 7.3 million cases). Schizophrenia demonstrated the most rapid relative growth (129%), though its prevalence remained lower (~254,000 cases). Eating disorders exhibited the highest rise in age-standardized rates (+26%), possibly due to lifestyle and media influences, while developmental intellectual disability (−23%) and conduct disorders (−19%) showed declining trends, likely due to improved diagnostic measures and childhood prevention programs. Gender disparities were evident, with women experiencing a 34% higher burden than men (DALY ratio: 1.34 vs. global 1.19), largely driven by socioeconomic constraints, domestic violence, and healthcare access barriers. Provincial variations showed Zanjan and Gilan as the highest burden growth areas, while Sistan-Baluchestan had elevated untreated disorder rates due to service shortages. Key contributing factors include economic sanctions, high social inequality (elevated Gini coefficient), critical gaps in mental health services (with only 33% of affected individuals accessing care), and urban–rural disparities (only 1.2 psychiatrists per 100,000 population). Emerging mental health trends include post-pandemic effects, with Iran reporting a 58% increase in anxiety symptoms following COVID-19, and a growing youth mental health crisis, as suicide rates among Iranian medical residents rose 300% from 2010 to 2020. Given the rapid rise in mental disorders, urgent policy action is required, including national mental health programs targeting social determinants, integration of mental health services into primary care, interventions for high-risk populations (women, youth), equitable resource distribution, and public education campaigns to reduce stigma. Mental disorders now represent Iran's fastest-growing non-communicable disease category, necessitating immediate policy response and systemic improvements to ensure accessible and effective care (Devi, 2024; Ghalichi et al., 2024; Khademi et al., 2020; Mohammadi et al., 2005; Tajik et al., 2023).

3.2 Suicide Risk and Mental Health Disparities

While mental health challenges, particularly depression, are more prevalent among individuals over 25, younger populations are also at risk, including those struggling with suicidal ideation. Factors such as urban living and lower education levels are linked to an increased likelihood of mental health disorders and suicide. Regional differences also play a role, with significant variations in gender, age distribution, and suicide methods between Western and non-Western regions.

A systematic review of 68 studies (54 included in meta-analysis) identified several contributing factors to suicide risk, with pooled prevalence rates as follows: male gender (64.3%, 95% CI: 62.6–66.0%), age over 25 (57.9%, 95% CI: 51.0–64.5%), education below a diploma level (73.4%, 95% CI: 62.1–82.3%), employment issues (66.4%, 95% CI: 59.7–72.5%), urban living (61.7%, 95% CI: 53.8–69.1%), past medical history (8.5%, 95% CI: 4.9–14.2%), past psychiatric history (20.7%, 95% CI: 15.5–27.1%), previous suicide attempt (12.2%, 95% CI: 8.5–17.0%), substance abuse history (28.4%, 95% CI: 20.1–38.3%), suicide incidents occurring in the spring season (29.8%, 95% CI: 26.7–33%), and hanging as the most common method (46.1%, 95% CI: 41.6–50.6%). These findings highlight regional disparities and the need for targeted suicide prevention strategies.

A review started with 1,646 articles, narrowing to 68 for detailed review and 54 for meta-analysis. Key contributing factors to the studied condition showed pooled prevalence rates, including male gender (64.3%), age over 25 (57.9%), lower education levels (73.4%), employment issues (66.4%), urban living (61.7%), past medical and psychiatric histories, previous suicide attempts, substance abuse, spring season (29.8%), and hanging as a method (46.1%). Notably, regional differences were found in gender, age, and suicide methods between Western and non-Western areas (Rahmani et al., 2025). The pattern of suicides shows regional differences in the country. The suicide rate in the west of the country is significantly higher than in other regions. A significant increase in suicide rates after the COVID-19 pandemic, particularly among young adults and women, highlights the urgent need for targeted mental health interventions, especially for vulnerable groups such as housewives and single individuals. Additionally, the correlation between education levels and suicide rates underscores the importance of addressing educational disparities as part of comprehensive mental health strategies (Movahed et al., 2025).

3.3 Alcohol and Substance Use Disorders

Iran faces significant challenges related to substance use, with opium being the most frequently used drug. A study conducted in Tehran found that 5.6% of the adult population reported substance use, with 95.8% of users consuming opium (Masoudkabir et al., 2024). The prevalence of substance use is notably higher among men, with factors such as alcohol intake and smoking being independently associated with opium use.

A national survey estimated that 11.9% of Iranian adults have experienced drug use, with socioeconomic status playing a major role in substance use patterns (Moradinazar et al., 2020). Drug use is more concentrated among individuals with lower socioeconomic status, highlighting the need for targeted prevention programs. Additionally, Iran's proximity to Afghanistan, the world's largest producer of opium, contributes to the availability and trafficking of illicit substances (UNODC, 2025).

Efforts to estimate the population size of individuals using illicit drugs and alcohol have revealed that opium remains the most prevalent illicit drug, followed by hashish, stimulants, and heroin (Rastegari et al., 2022). Alcohol use is also widespread, with an estimated prevalence of 2,797 per 100,000 population (WHO, 2024). These findings underscore the importance of substance use disorders as a public health issue in Iran.

4 Overview of Mental Health Initiatives and Programs in Iran

Over the years, Iran has made progress in caring for mental health. Starting in the 1920s, efforts began to treat mental health issues, and today, the country has developed dedicated services, laws, and community programs aimed at helping those in need (Rastegar et al., 2025).

Iran has been working to make mental health care more accessible and integrated into everyday life, especially in its rural communities. A key part of this effort involves embedding mental health services into the primary health care system. It means that general practitioners and local health workers are trained to recognize and manage mental health issues, making help reachable even in the most remote areas (Rastegar et al., 2025).

The story of the rural mental health care system goes back to a period of experimentation before the 1979 Revolution and then leaped forward after establishing the country's primary health care (PHC) system. Starting in the 1980s, Iran began to weave mental health care into this broader framework—treating mental illnesses similarly to infectious diseases, which helped address them more systematically. The country developed treatment approaches compatible with existing services, offered specialized training to healthcare providers, and brought mental health specialists to support these efforts. This integration led to notable improvements in health outcomes, reaching many previously underserved populations.

However, alongside these successes, some unintended challenges emerged. The focus on pharmaceutical treatments grew, sometimes at the expense of holistic approaches—especially for conditions like somatization, where mental health symptoms are expressed through physical complaints (Smith, 2020).

Today, the core principles of integrating mental health into primary care remain vital. However, real-world challenges like administrative hurdles and resource limitations have tested the system's resilience. Continuous monitoring, evaluation, and strategic efforts to secure stable funding are essential to succeed. Only then can Iran's mental health services become more sustainable, effective, and accessible for everyone (Hajebi et al., 2021).

4.1 Mental Health Infrastructure

Iran has a limited number of psychiatrists, psychologists, and social workers relative to its population. The country has approximately 1 psychiatrist per 100,000 people, which is significantly lower than global standards (Rastegar et al., 2025). Iran has several psychiatric hospitals that provide specialized mental health care. One of the most well-known facilities is Roozbeh Hospital, affiliated with Tehran University of Medical Sciences. It is the oldest teaching psychiatry hospital in Iran and has trained hundreds of psychiatrists over the years.

Iran's healthcare system operates on a three-tiered structure to ensure effective service delivery across rural and urban areas. The first level consists of comprehensive health service centers, which serve as the primary access points for healthcare. These include health homes and rural health bases under rural comprehensive centers, while urban health bases function within urban comprehensive centers. For cases requiring specific programs, comprehensive health service centers act as the initial service providers in the referral system. The second level encompasses county health centers and county hospitals, offering more advanced medical services and facilitating specialized referrals. At the third level, provincial health centers and specialized hospitals provide high-level medical care, handling complex cases and specialized treatments. This hierarchical system ensures efficient patient management, referral coordination, and access to appropriate care at different levels of need.

Iran's healthcare system is structured around key principles that ensure equitable access and efficiency in service delivery. Geographical accessibility is a priority, ensuring that health services reach even the most remote communities. Cultural accessibility is also emphasized, requiring that healthcare services align with societal traditions while avoiding ethnic, cultural, and religious conflicts. To minimize waiting times and optimize service delivery, resource efficiency is achieved through appropriate workforce distribution, clearly defined service-level tasks, and standardized efficiency measures. Effective training is tailored to practical needs, ensuring that healthcare workers possess clearly defined knowledge and skills, trainers understand community priorities, and personnel are locally deployed to maximize impact. Decentralized management empowers healthcare units with autonomy in planning, budgeting, and organizing, fostering efficiency and responsiveness. Community participation plays a critical role, encouraging public engagement in health initiatives to promote self-care and preventative health measures. Comprehensive healthcare delivery depends on intra-sectoral coordination, where collaboration within the health sector prevents fragmentation and enhances service integration. Cross-sector cooperation with private and cooperative entities strengthens infrastructure, funding, and service outreach. A tiered healthcare network supports equitable access through integrated services for target populations, strategic population-based planning, standardized primary care guidelines, structured health worker training, optimized human resource deployment, and a reliable data system tailored to rural healthcare challenges. These principles collectively reinforce Iran's commitment to an accessible, efficient, and well-coordinated healthcare system.

4.2 Key Activities in Mental Health Service Improvement

The mental health program focuses on connecting people to the care they need through targeted activities designed to strengthen mental health support across Iran.

4.2.1 Training General Practitioners

The foundation for successful health initiatives often lies in the strength of existing systems. Iran's primary health care (PHC) network, especially in rural areas, has proven vital. General Practitioners (GPs) also play a key role, offering mental health and substance use prevention services in urban and rural settings. While they have brief training, mhGAP instruction, in mental health care, it's crucial for them to be well-equipped to serve their communities effectively (Hajebi et al., 2021). By training general practitioners (GPs), they are empowered to recognize and manage mental health issues early on. This approach helps bring mental health care closer to communities that need it most (Takian et al., 2013).

4.2.2 Equipping Healthcare Workers to Screen and Identify Risks

Community Health Workers (CHWs) are essential members of the healthcare system, especially in urban and underserved areas. They typically have a bachelor's degree in fields like nursing, family health, or midwifery and receive specialized training that equips them to address mental health and substance use issues. With a focus on early detection, CHWs conduct initial screenings for mental health and social challenges, ensuring that one health protector is available for every 2,500 urban residents (Hajebi et al., 2021). The Ministry of Health provides specialized training for health workers and community health volunteers—known as Community Health Workers (CHWs) to help identify individuals at risk for mental health problems, substance abuse, domestic violence, and child abuse. These dedicated professionals are essential in reaching vulnerable populations, and their training takes place in centers managed by district health networks that offer comprehensive education, boosting their skills, motivation, and capacity to serve local families. As programs grow and evolve, adapting training to meet local needs becomes increasingly important (Javanparast et al., 2012).

4.2.3 Recruiting Psychologists to Support Mental Well-Being

Mental Health Workers are another vital resource, bringing expertise in clinical psychology and completing extensive training to help manage the growing rates of mental health disorders. These professionals work in health centers, providing support and care where needed most (Hajebi et al., 2021). To expand mental health services, the Ministry of Health has recruited psychologists to work directly within community health centers, offering brief interventions for depression, anxiety, suicide, and substance use. This initiative began with workshops for health workers, physicians, and psychologists, creating a collaborative effort to bring mental health support into the primary care setting. Since then, many individuals have benefited from immediate, accessible psychological care (Dorosti et al., 2024). In addition to providing brief interventions, psychologists are responsible for educating the general population.

4.2.4 Providing Specialized Support for Severe Mental Disorders

Community Mental Health Centers (CMHCs), part of Iran's Seraj program, serve as local hubs for mental health care, offering ongoing support for patients with common and severe mental illnesses. These centers deliver various services, including collaborative care with primary physicians, follow-up after hospital discharge—via phone or home visits—and day programs focused on psychoeducation and skill-building. Over four years in the two pilot regions, more than 6,200 patients have received care through these centers, demonstrating their vital role in patient recovery and stability (Sharifi et al., 2021). Supporting families and caregivers through responsive and accessible networks remains a cornerstone of this work (Akbari et al., 2019).

4.2.5 Harm Reduction for Substance and Alcohol Use

Iran's approach to substance use and alcohol abuse emphasizes harm reduction—an evidence-based strategy aimed at minimizing health, social, and economic harms associated with drug use, without insisting on total abstinence. The services include needle exchange programs, supervised consumption sites, medication-assisted treatments, naloxone distribution, and policies that decriminalize certain drug-related behaviors. Supported by firm commitments from high-level health officials, these strategies prioritize human rights, public health, and social justice, helping reduce overdose deaths, disease transmission, and stigma (Hajebi et al., 2022; Omiyefa, 2022).

4.2.6 Drop-In Centers for Vulnerable Populations

Drop-in centers (DICs) serve as safe spaces where drug users, especially women vulnerable to HIV transmission through sharing needles, can access harm reduction services. Iran's shift from a purely supply-reduction policy to one that encourages treatment and support led to the establishment of these centers, which are critical in expanding harm-reduction efforts and reaching those most at risk (Ravaghi et al., 2016).

4.2.7 Community Education on Parenting and Life Skills

Prevention and early intervention are key. The mental health education packages focus on educating parents and communities about healthy parenting techniques and important life skills. Empowering families with knowledge helps build resilient communities and promote mental well-being from a young age.

4.2.8 National Suicide Prevention Program and Registry

Recognizing the urgent need to address suicide, Iran has launched a national suicide prevention program and established a registry system to better understand and respond to these tragedies. Forensic medicine organization records Suicide death cases, while attempted suicides are documented in the Ministry of Health's suicide registration system. This system helps track patterns and identify risk factors, enabling more effective prevention efforts.

Based on the national suicide prevention program, medical universities in the country must refer cases to healthcare networks for follow-up and intervention. Brief interventions are provided by psychologists for people with suicidal thoughts in healthcare centers.

4.2.9 Post-discharge Support for Suicide Attempts

Supporting individuals after a suicide attempt is crucial. Integrating mental health services into primary care and expanding psychosocial support centers remain fundamental public health strategies, not only in Iran but worldwide, to reduce suicide risks and promote healing (WHO, 2013). The health system offers follow-up services by phone and in person to ensure continued care during recovery. To prevent the reattempt, the ASSIP method is used by psychologists in the healthcare centers.

The master chart for providing mental health services in the PHC system is shown in Figure 1.

4.3 Expanding Mental Health Care: Role of Private Clinics, Hospitals, and NGOs

Private clinics and hospitals offer specialized mental health services such as therapy sessions and psychiatric consultations.

There are notable institutions and Psychiatric Hospitals, even hold an ISO 9001 certification and are recognized as one of the top private psychiatric hospitals in the country. They offer various treatments, including electroconvulsive therapy (ECT), transcranial magnetic stimulation (rTMS), and ketamine therapy for depression.

While these services often come with a higher price tag, they are valued for providing quicker access and a broader range of treatment options. For many, especially those seeking immediate help or more personalized care, these places can be a vital part of their journey toward well-being.

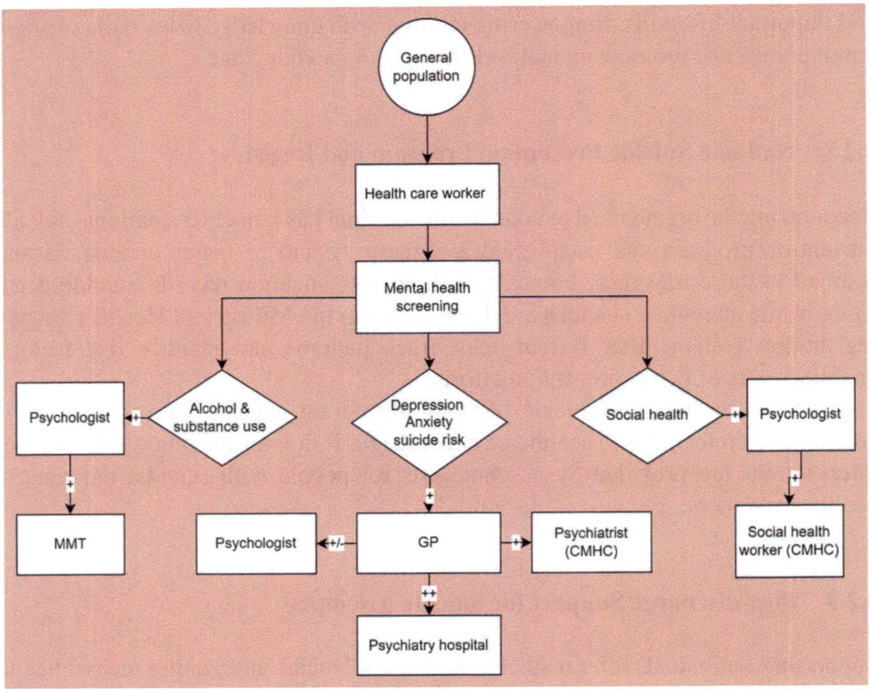

Fig. 1 The feature of providing mental health services in the PHC system

The non-governmental organizations (NGOs) play an essential role beyond the walls of clinics and hospitals. They work tirelessly to raise awareness about mental health, offer support to those in need, and advocate for the rights of individuals struggling with mental health issues. Some NGOs and private institutions also promote mental wellness among employees and students, running programs that foster early intervention and prevent problems before they escalate. Most NGOs operate under the oversight of welfare organizations, ensuring their efforts align with national policies and standards.

4.4 Crisis Support and Emergency Mental Health HOT Lines

Many hotlines are available for emergency situations. Well-known 24-h hotlines are associated with the Welfare Organization (123) and the Ministry of Health (115). Some psychiatric hospitals, such as Roozbeh Hospital, also have hotlines accessible.

Together, these various sectors create a diverse and supportive mental health landscape that strives to reach many people, wherever they are, in their journey toward mental well-being.

5 Current Challenges in Mental Health Care

5.1 Breaking Down Barriers: Tackling Mental Health Stigma in Iran

Stigma around mental health is a challenge faced by countries all over the world, and Iran is no exception. Deep-rooted cultural beliefs and misconceptions create significant barriers that prevent many from seeking help or receiving proper care. Addressing this stigma requires more than just awareness—it calls for targeted, sustained interventions (Taghva et al., 2024).

Stigma deeply affects every aspect of psychiatric care, touching not only the individuals struggling with mental health issues but also their families. It discourages those living with depression or other conditions from reaching out for help and can even impact the quality of treatment they receive. Cultural perfectionism, which emphasizes an idealized image of strength and resilience, often makes these issues harder to see and talk about, leading many mental health problems to stay hidden.

Media representations frequently reinforce harmful stereotypes and unscientific views about mental health, further fueling misunderstanding and prejudice. For meaningful change, the government must provide strong support and resources to mental health programs, along with comprehensive plans that challenge existing stigma. Unfortunately, limited budgets often constrain these efforts, and discrimination can even exist within the healthcare system itself—highlighting the urgent need for awareness, education, and structural reforms. Only through collective effort—policy change, community engagement, and increased investment—stigma will be reduced and a more accepting environment where everyone feels safe to seek the help they deserve will be created (Taghva et al., 2017).

5.2 Infrastructure Decay: Slow Growth Rate of Infrastructure Compared to Increasing Demands

Despite all advances, many Iranians still struggle with mental health problems, and the efforts have not yet made a big dent. Challenges like lack of transparency about services, unclear roles among healthcare workers, crumbling infrastructure, and a shortage of trained specialists—like psychiatrists, psychologists, and social workers—stand in the way (Sharifi et al., 2021).

5.3 Addressing Mental Health Inequities

Despite efforts to expand healthcare access, rural areas in Iran continue to face a shortage of mental health professionals, as many prefer urban settings with better amenities. The scarcity of specialized providers in rural regions, especially for children, poses a significant challenge. Policymakers must prioritize equitable resource distribution and funding to improve accessibility (Hajebi et al., 2021). Many professionals prefer urban settings due to better infrastructure and career opportunities, leaving rural areas with limited specialized services.

The increasing burden of mental disorders in Iran, particularly the rise in DALYs, underscores the need for comprehensive prevention and intervention strategies. Addressing socioeconomic and regional disparities will be key to ensuring effective mental health care for all population segments. Telehealth technique also offers a promising solution to bridge service gaps and provide essential mental health care to underserved communities. Expanding remote consultation capabilities and training sufficient professionals will be critical in ensuring equitable care across regions (Mirmoeini et al., 2019).

5.4 Non-medical Management of Mental Disorders (Help-Seeking Behavior and Traditional Healing Practice in Iran)

Despite the increasing availability of clinical psychiatric services, mental health stigma continues to drive many Iranians toward alternative healing methods rather than formal medical treatment. Traditional practices, including herbal medicine, faith healing, and spiritual rituals, remain prevalent, particularly in rural areas where access to psychiatric services is limited. Religious and spiritual healing methods play a significant role in mental health management (Soltani et al., 2024). Additionally, traditional Persian medicine, which incorporates dietary and lifestyle modifications alongside herbal remedies, is widely used to alleviate symptoms of anxiety and depression (Hajebi et al., 2021).

In Iran, help-seeking behaviors for mental health issues are strongly influenced by cultural and religious beliefs. Many individuals rely on spiritual and community-based support, including religious leaders, family elders, and social networks, as their primary source of emotional and psychological relief (Mirmoeini et al., 2019). However, significant barriers to seeking formal treatment persist, including low perceived need for psychiatric care, financial constraints, and misconceptions about mental disorders (Soltani et al., 2024). Among those diagnosed with psychiatric conditions, fear of social stigma, concerns about burdening family members, and a reliance on self-coping mechanisms further discourage engagement with professional mental health services (Khademi et al., 2020).

Research indicates that social capital—defined by trust, community cohesion, and interpersonal support—has a protective effect against mental illnesses such as major depressive disorder (Ghalichi et al., 2024). Strong community ties reduce vulnerability to psychiatric conditions, reinforcing the importance of social support networks in non-medical mental health management. Gender disparities also play a role, as women in Iran experience higher rates of mental illness due to socioeconomic challenges, cultural expectations, and domestic pressures (Mohammadi et al., 2005).

To address these gaps, community-based interventions such as peer support groups and culturally adapted psychotherapy are being promoted to bridge traditional and modern approaches to mental health care. Such initiatives aim to improve mental health literacy, enhance access to professional services, and reduce stigma associated with psychiatric disorders. Strengthening collaboration between traditional healing practitioners and mental health professionals may further support effective mental health care delivery in Iran.

5.5 *Government Policies on Mental Health Awareness and Suicide Prevention*

Iran has developed national policies to address mental health awareness and suicide prevention. The National Suicide Prevention Program integrates evidence-based strategies into policy and practice, focusing on improving suicide attempt registration, reducing stigma, and increasing service availability through primary healthcare. The government has also engaged media outlets to improve the quality of suicide reporting, aiming to reduce harmful portrayals that may contribute to suicide contagion.

Historically, Iran's mental health policies have evolved from institutional care to community-based interventions. While significant progress has been made, challenges remain in ensuring sustainable financing and inter-agency coordination for mental health initiatives.

There is a clear need for reform, particularly around infrastructure, including adequate human resources and financial support. Ensuring these services' ongoing success and growth depended heavily on strong backing from the upper levels of the Ministry of Health. Without committed leadership and sustained funding, these programs risk losing momentum.

These findings highlight the need for continued investment in mental health infrastructure, public awareness campaigns, and culturally sensitive interventions to address the growing burden of psychiatric disorders in Iran.

6 Future Directions: Strengthening Iran's Mental Health System

Since 1986, dedicated teams within the Iranian Ministry of Health and Medical Education (MOHME) have carefully designed and implemented a national program to integrate mental health services into primary health care. This approach is essentially top-down, with policies communicated from the highest levels of the system down to local communities. Building on the success of pilot projects, senior health officials remain committed to expanding this integrated model nationwide, training General Practitioners and psychologists alike to provide better mental health support (Dorosti et al., 2024).

However, strengthening mental health in Iran is about policy and addressing broader social and economic challenges. The efforts must extend beyond healthcare: reducing international tensions, lifting restrictive sanctions, fostering stronger global connections, and improving education, medical services, and rehabilitation infrastructure are all vital steps. Community mental health centers, particularly those under the national SERAJ program, must be expanded and adequately equipped with the necessary resources and trained staff. Policymakers must actively seek ways to secure sufficient funding, including engaging community voices and offering incentives—like financial benefits—to encourage qualified professionals to serve in these centers. Partnering with private sector investors can also help fill gaps and boost capacity.

Equally important are educational initiatives aimed at reducing the stigma surrounding mental health. Changing perceptions and fostering acceptance require tailored programs that fit the unique capacity of local health systems. A comprehensive reform of mental health services that combines policy, community engagement, resource allocation, and education will be essential in creating a healthier, more resilient Iran where everyone's mental well-being matters.

Everyone has a part to play in shaping a kinder, more understanding Iran—one where mental health is openly spoken about and truly supported. No matter what people's role, everyone can make a difference. Speaking up, sharing stories, challenging stigma, and supporting initiatives that promote mental well-being. Small steps, taken together, can lead to a society where no one feels alone in their struggles, and everyone can find the help they need.

7 Conclusion

Iran is making significant progress in developing a mental health system that supports everyone. By continuing to raise awareness, investing in community care, and uniting with compassion, we can create a future where mental health is seen as essential. This will foster a healthier and more resilient Iran.

References

Akbari, M., Alavi, M., Maghsoudi, J., Irajpour, A., Lopez, V., & Cleary, M. (2019). Mastering the art of collaboration: Supporting family caregivers of mental health patients by service providers in Iran. *Administration and Policy in Mental Health and Mental Health Services Research, 46*, 54–61. https://doi.org/10.1007/s10488-018-0893-7

Badrfam, R., & Zandifar, A. (2025). Improving mental health care in Iran. *The Lancet Psychiatry*, 12(6), e8. https://doi.org/10.1016/S2215-0366(25)00104-X

Devi, S. (2024). Iranian medic suicides spark criticism of working conditions. *The Lancet, 403*(10431), 1010. https://doi.org/10.1016/S0140-6736(24)00530-0

Dorosti, A., Karamouz, M., Rahimi, V. A., Azimzadeh, S., Gharaee, H., Azami-Aghdash, S., & Farahbakhsh, M. (2024). Mental health services integration in primary health care in Iran: A policy analysis. *Iranian Journal of Psychiatry, 19*(1), 57. https://doi.org/10.18502/ijps.v19i1.14339

Ghalichi, L., Shariat, S. V., Naserbakht, M., Taban, M., Abbasi-Kangevari, M., Afrashteh, F., Ajami, M., Akbarialiabad, H., Amiri, S., Arabloo, J., Azizi, H., Baghcheghi, N., Bagherieh, S., Bitaraf, S., Eskandarieh, S., Ghadirian, F., Gholami, A., Goleij, P., Habibi Asgarabad, M., … Naghavi, M. (2024). National and subnational burden of mental disorders in Iran (1990–2019): Findings of the Global Burden of Disease 2019 study. *The Lancet Global Health, 12*(12), e1984–e1992. https://doi.org/10.1016/S2214-109X(24)00342-5

Hajebi, A., Asadi, A., Ghoddousi, S. E., Ziadlou, T., Mehrabi, M., Vaezi, Z., Hajebi, A., & Abbasinejad, M. (2022). Mental health and prevention of substance use programs in iran: component of the national action plan for prevention and control of non-communicable diseases. *Medical Journal of The Islamic Republic of Iran, 36*, 171. https://doi.org/10.47176/mjiri.36.171

Hajebi, A., Sharifi, V., Abbasinejad, M., Asadi, A., Jafari, N., Ziadlou, T., Khadem, S., Asgardoon, M. H., & Damari, B. (2021). Integrating mental health services into the primary health care system: The need for reform in Iran. *Iranian Journal of Psychiatry, 16*(3), 320. https://doi.org/10.18502/ijps.v16i3.6258

Hosseinzadeh-Shanjani, Z., Khodayari-Zarnaq, R., Khosravi, M. F., Arab-Zozani, M., & Alizadeh, G. (2024, 2024/05/27). Factors affecting major depression in Iran: a mixed-method study. *Journal of Health, Population and Nutrition, 43*(1), 73. https://doi.org/10.1186/s41043-024-00571-x

Iran Demographics. (2025). https://www.worldometers.info/demographics/iran-demographics/

Javanparast, S., Baum, F., Labonte, R., Sanders, D., Rajabi, Z., & Heidari, G. (2012). The experience of community health workers training in Iran: A qualitative study. *BMC Health Services Research, 12*, 1–8. https://doi.org/10.1186/1472-6963-12-291

Khademi, M., Zohrabi, S., Mohtashamalsharieh, A., & Zahiroddin, A. (2020). Investigation of the results of collaborative care in the diagnosis and treatment of anxiety and depressive disorders in Community Mental Health Center (CMHC), Shahid Beheshti University of Medical Sciences. *Iranian Journal of Psychiatry and Behavioral Sciences, 14*(2). https://doi.org/10.5812/ijpbs.66117

Masoudkabir, F., Shafiee, A., Heidari, A., Mohammadi, N. S. H., Tavakoli, K., Jalali, A., Nayebirad, S., Alaeddini, F., Saadat, S., & Vasheghani-Farahani, A. (2024). Epidemiology of substance and opium use among adult residents of Tehran; a comprehensive report from Tehran cohort study (TeCS). *BMC Psychiatry, 24*(1), 132. https://doi.org/10.1186/s12888-024-05561-1

Mirghaed, M. T., Gorji, H. A., & Panahi, S. (2020). Prevalence of psychiatric disorders in Iran: A systematic review and meta-analysis. *International Journal of Preventive Medicine, 11*(1), 21. https://doi.org/10.4103/ijpvm.IJPVM_510_18

Mirmoeini, S. M., Marashi Shooshtari, S. S., Battineni, G., Amenta, F., & Tayebati, S. K. (2019). Policies and challenges on the distribution of specialists and subspecialists in rural areas of Iran. *Medicina, 55*(12), 783. https://doi.org/10.3390/medicina55120783

Mohammadi, M.-R., Davidian, H., Noorbala, A. A., Malekafzali, H., Naghavi, H. R., Pouretemad, H. R., Yazdi, S. A. B., Rahgozar, M., Alaghebandrad, J., & Amini, H. (2005). An epidemiological survey of psychiatric disorders in Iran. *Clinical Practice and Epidemiology in Mental Health, 1*, 1–8. https://doi.org/10.1186/1745-0179-1-16

Moradinazar, M., Najafi, F., Jalilian, F., Pasdar, Y., Hamzeh, B., Shakiba, E., Hajizadeh, M., Haghdoost, A. A., Malekzadeh, R., & Poustchi, H. (2020). Prevalence of drug use, alcohol consumption, cigarette smoking and measure of socioeconomic-related inequalities of drug use among Iranian people: Findings from a national survey. *Substance Abuse Treatment, Prevention, and Policy, 15*, 1–11. https://doi.org/10.1186/s13011-020-00279-1

Movahed, E., Afsharmanesh, A., Aqarabi, H., Raesi, R., Hushmandi, K., & Daneshi, S. (2025). Comparison of the trend of suicide before and after the COVID-19 pandemic in Southeast Iran from 2016 to 2023. *BMC Public Health, 25*(1), 66. https://doi.org/10.1186/s12889-024-21265-3

Omiyefa, S. (2022). *Comprehensive harm reduction strategies in substance use disorders: Evaluating policy, treatment, and public health outcomes.* https://ijetrm.com/issues/files/Mar-2022-02-1740918345-SEP06.pdf

Rahmani, A., Vazirinejad, R., Ahmadinia, H., Hamzeh, S., Nabardi, M., Nicholas, A., Souresrafil, A., & Rezaeian, M. (2025). Key messages for suicide prevention media campaigns in Iran: Findings from a Delphi study. *BMC Public Health, 25*(1), 697. https://doi.org/10.1186/s12889-025-21810-8

Rastegar, H., Morasae, E. K., & Doshmangir, L. (2025). The dynamics of mental health policy in Iran over the last century. *BMC Psychology, 13*(1), 51. https://doi.org/10.1186/s40359-025-023 84-x

Rastegari, A., Baneshi, M. R., Hajebi, A., Noroozi, A., Karamouzian, M., Shokoohi, M., Mirzazadeh, A., Bojnourdi, T. K., Nasiri, N., & Maghsoudi, S. H. (2022). Population size estimation of people who use illicit drugs and alcohol in Iran (2015–2016). *International Journal of Health Policy and Management, 12*, 6578. https://doi.org/10.34172/ijhpm.2022.6578

Ravaghi, H., Zandian, H., Kazerooni, P. A., Sabet, M., Mostafavi, H., & Sakha, M. A. (2016). Challenges and successes of harm reduction services in drop-in centers: Perspectives of service providers. *International Journal of High Risk Behaviors and Addiction, 6*(2). https://doi.org/10.5812/ijhrba.29391

Sharifi, V., Hajebi, A., Damari, B., & Mohammadjafari, A. (2021). Specialized outpatient services: Community Mental Health Centers (CMHCs). *Iranian Journal of Psychiatry, 16*(1), 87. https://doi.org/10.18502/ijps.v16i1.5383

Smith, A. K. (2020). The integration of mental health care in rural Iran. *Iranian Studies, 53*(1–2), 93–111. https://doi.org/10.1080/00210862.2019.1670625

Soltani, E., Bazrafshanb, A., Bahreini, F., & Zaremohazabiyeh, S. (2024). Identifying barriers to help-seeking from mental health professionals in the general population and mental disorders. https://doi.org/10.21203/rs.3.rs-4583884/v1

Taghva, A., Farsi, Z., Javanmard, Y., Atashi, A., Hajebi, A., & Khademi, M. (2017). Stigma barriers of mental health in Iran: A qualitative study by stakeholders of mental health. *Iranian Journal of Psychiatry, 12*(3), 163. https://pmc.ncbi.nlm.nih.gov/articles/PMC5640577/

Taghva, A., Hajebi, A., Noorbala, A. A., Khademi, M., Asadi, A., Rahnejat, A. M., Alizadeh, K., Shalbafan, M., Bolhari, J., & Hashemian, S. S. (2024). Mental health stigma in Iran: A systematic review. *Stigma and Health.* https://psycnet.apa.org/doi/10.1037/sah0000559

Tajik, F., Shalbafan, M., & Shariat, S. V. (2023). A disastrous year that ends with corona outbreak: Effects on mental health of university students. *Journal of American College HealtH, 71*(9), 2726–2729. https://doi.org/10.1080/07448481.2021.1988958

Takian, A., Doshmangir, L., & Rashidian, A. (2013). Implementing family physician programme in rural Iran: Exploring the role of an existing primary health care network. *Family Practice, 30*(5), 551–559. https://doi.org/10.1093/fampra/cmt025

UNODC. (2025). *Drug trafficking and border control situation analysis.* https://www.unodc.org/islamicrepublicofiran/drug-trafficking-and-border-control.html
WHO. (2024, 2024). *Global status report on alcohol and health and treatment of substance use disorders.* https://www.who.int/publications/i/item/9789240096745
WHO. (2013, January 6). https://iris.who.int/bitstream/handle/10665/89966/9789241506021_eng.pdf?sequence=1

Chapter 5
Mental Health Services in Iraq

Maha Sulaiman Younis

Abstract This chapter aims to discuss the historical background, current status, challenges, and areas of insufficiency in mental health care access in Iraq, focusing on the impact of wars, political unrest, economic sanctions, and other barriers such as social stigma and stagnation of development plans and scientific growth. It was considered a regional leader in psychiatric care during the 1970s and 1980s with widespread access to free services, specialized hospitals, and highly qualified psychiatrists. Mental disorders are common, with recent rising rates of depression, anxiety, post-traumatic stress disorder, suicide, and substance abuse, with no prevention strategies. Despite post-war international support and efforts at reconstruction, the psychiatric system in Iraq remains underdeveloped. Inadequate and inequitable manpower through the exodus of experienced psychiatrists caused by the war-related anarchy and acts of violence in the country created challenges for mental health care. The psychiatrist-to-population ratio falls considerably below international standards, with a similar lag in other mental health workers. Services are overly centralized in major cities, with minimal access in rural and conflict-affected areas, manifested by the inadequacy of infrastructure, medication supply, and psychosocial support systems.

Keywords Iraq · Mental health services · War and mental health · History · Epidemiology

---

M. S. Younis (✉)
College of Medicine, Baghdad University, Baghdad, Iraq
e-mail: maha.younis@gmail.com

S. Al-Huseini and S. M. Y. Arafat (eds.), *Mental Health Care in the Middle East*, South Asian Perspectives in Mental Health and Psychology ,
https://doi.org/10.1007/978-981-95-0461-9_5

1 Introduction

1.1 Country Profile

The Republic of Iraq is in the central region of the Middle East, bordered by four Arab nations: Kuwait and the Kingdom of Saudi Arabia to the south, Syria and Jordan to the west, and two Muslim non-Arab countries, Turkey to the north and Iran to the east, encompassing a total area of 438,317 km^2. The population of Iraq is 46,652,321, with a density of 108 people per square kilometer. (World Meter, 2025). Iraq had substantial oil reserves, ranking sixth globally with 143,069,000,000 barrels, and exported oil valued at 25,868.10 million USD in the third quarter of 2024. The gross domestic product (GDP) is $264.15 billion, with a GDP per capita of $136.20, ranking 34th out of 142 countries in the annual GDP review of upper middle-income nations and 134th out of 204 countries in the Human Development Index for 2021–22 (World Bank, 2025). Iraq has a growth rate of 2.9% and a life expectancy of 71.35 years, characterized by one of the youngest demographics worldwide, with those under 19 years old constituting half of the population (World Meter, 2025). The population predominantly comprises Arab Muslims, with Arabs representing 75–80% and Muslims around 97–99%. Baghdad serves as the capital, boasting a population of 7,921,000 and a growth rate of 2.72%. The country comprises eighteen governorates, three of which are in the semi-autonomous Kurdistan Region of Iraq (KRI), with a Kurdish population of 6,370,000, predominantly Muslims (80%) (Wikipedia, 2025) (Fig. 1).

1.2 Historical and Geopolitical Background

Iraq, known as Mesopotamia, was the cradle of one of the world's earliest civilizations. Their inventions, such as the wheel, plough, mathematics, time calculation, and building techniques, revolutionized technology. The Sumerians also developed "cuneiform," the first known writing system. Successive empires like the Akkadian, Neo-Sumerian, Babylonian, Neo-Assyrian, and Neo-Babylonian dominated Mesopotamia and the Near East; they contributed further innovations, including law codes like the Code of Hammurabi (1754 BC) and foundational knowledge in medicine and pharmacology. By the seventh century, Baghdad had become a renowned center for intellectual activities and scientific achievements. The city was devastated in 1258 by Mongol invaders. In the sixteenth century, the Ottomans took control of Iraq, leading to conflicts with the Safavids and a decline in development (Wikipedia, 2025). Nearly 400 years later, the British took over from March 11, 1917, until October 3, 1932, when Iraq was admitted to the League of Nations as an independent Arab country, with the Iraqis winning their independence from colonial rule. On July 14, 1958, a military coup successfully overthrew the ruling Hashemite monarchy, leading to the establishment of Iraq as a sovereign republic. The Iran–Iraq

Fig. 1 Map of Iraq (google image)

War, 1980–1988, resulted in the deaths of one million Iraqi military personnel and significantly strained the country's budget; however, the government succeeded in constructing advanced infrastructure and a high-quality, free education system. In May 1978, the National Comprehensive Campaign for Compulsory Literacy Law was issued; the obligatory applications led to the eradication of adult illiteracy, earning Iraq the United Nations Educational, Scientific, and Cultural Organization (UNESCO) prize in 1979 (Al-Shaikhly & Cui, 2017).

2 Evolution of Psychiatric Services in Iraq

2.1 *Ancient Period*

In ancient Iraq, also known as Mesopotamia, many cuneiform clay texts documented symptoms of mental disorders, attributing them to punishment by gods and goddesses for misdeeds or possession by evil spirits. Priests treated these patients within temples using exorcism to extract the possessing spirit, or often employing herbal remedies to alter consciousness, and reciting prayers. Healing the mentally ill was primarily the responsibility of shamans and priests during paganism and after the introduction of heavenly religions in Iraq. Some of the discovered clay texts in the Sumerian capital, Uruk, 2600 years B.C., and Babylon, 1800 B.C., described psychiatric symptoms such as paranoid delusions, passivity phenomena, and depression. Later, around 800 clay texts, like medical literature, were found in Mosel, 1200 B.C. Ancient Iraqis believed that epilepsy, or "miqtu," was the result of the punishment of an evil spirit called "alu limnu." Anxiety symptoms were described as a short temper (ikkašu Kurri) and symptoms of depression (tādirta irašši); the verb (samû) means troubled or discontented, while the term (Leibschmerzen) describes somatic symptoms with mental causes. Treatment of mental and non-mental illnesses used to be conducted by two therapists: the Assipu, who read a prayer, and the Assue, who provided herbal remedies. The treatment setting should be within a temple near the river, and both therapists wear fish skin based on the belief in the healing power of the river god (Parys, 2014; Younis, 2005) (Fig. 2).

2.2 *Psychiatry in Arab Islamic Civilization*

Like other Arab cultures, mental disorders were attributed to the possession of supernatural spirits known as "jinn," by Islamic beliefs, and the Arabic term of "Al-Jinon" symbolized the concept of "insanity" (Khalifa & Hardie, 2005). Arab Muslim scientists significantly contributed to the world's knowledge about mental disorders; they authored many articles and book chapters about symptoms, classifications, and treatment methods during their heyday in the seventh to the twelfth centuries. Abu Bakr Mohammed Ibn Zakariya Al-Razi, an influential Muslim scholar, authored 237 books, including the renowned "Bible of Medicine," Al-Hawi. He integrated psychological methods with physiological explanations for dissociative disorders, rectifying mistakes made by Galen. The emergence of professional pharmacy as an independent entity from medicine during his era was another recognized scientific achievement. Al-Razi's contributions to medicine and pharmacy inspired the European physicians during the Dark Ages. Another eminent scientist, Abo Ali Al-Hasan Ibn Sina (Avicenna) (980–1037 AD), highlighted the connection between physical and psychological illnesses. He pioneered the concept of hypnosis for treating

Fig. 2 The "Assipu" and the "Assue" are the priests responsible for treatment (Library of the Iraq Museum, Baghdad, Circa 2001)

mental disorders and elucidated the causes of somatic illnesses such as hallucinations, insomnia, mania, and melancholia. He contributed to the establishment of free hospitals and employed various psychological techniques to aid his patients (Sarhan, 2017). A remarkable pioneer psychologist, Abu Zayd al-Balkhi (850–934), introduced the concepts of mental health and mental hygiene in Islamic psychology, with a strong emphasis on spiritual and mental well-being, offering a critique of medical professionals who often prioritize physical ailments over psychological conditions (Saeed et al., 2024). He proposed a comprehensive theory to elucidate the underlying causes of psychological disorders, which encompassed psychological, developmental factors, internal states, and social and environmental influences on the somatic presentations of physical or mental disorders (Saeed et al., 2024).

2.3 *Modern Psychiatric Services*

Modern mental health services in Iraq began with the British authorities opening Dar Al Shafaa Hospital in 1922. Initially, a horse stable, it functioned as a custodial hospital with poor facilities and inadequate care. Patients, mostly vagrants with severe psychotic disorders, were admitted by local police. The hospital lacked outpatient services and death records, treating 795,628 male and 167 female patients with limited resources. Treatment methods included restraints, insulin shock therapy, and sedatives. Until the late 1950s, it was known as a "lunatic asylum," and a World Health Organization (WHO) representative deemed it unfit for proper medical care during a visit in 1950 (Younis, 2009a, 2009b). Dar Al-Shafaa Hospital was shut down in 1960, and all its remaining patients were transferred to the newly established mental hospital with 400 beds, mostly for chronic care facilities, known as Shammaiyia, which was founded in 1953 in Baghdad's suburb, known now as Al-Rashad Mental Hospital. Additional wards increased the capacity to 1300 beds (Bazzoui & Al-Issa, 1966; Younis, 2009a). Dr. Jack Abboudy Shaby, the first qualified psychiatrist to join the Iraqi health services, was born into a Jewish family in Basra in 1908. He graduated from the Iraqi Royal College of Medicine in 1932 as one of its earliest graduates. After training in the United Kingdom in 1934, he returned to Iraq and was appointed to Dar Al-Shafaa Mental Hospital, eventually becoming its director. Dr. Abboudy also established the only private psychiatric clinic in Baghdad. In 1936, Dr. Abboudy began teaching in the neurosciences department and was promoted to assistant professor in 1942. He opened the first private mental hospital, Al-Rasheed Mental Hospital, in 1944. He introduced electroconvulsive therapy (ECT) at the government-run Dar-Al Shafaa Hospital, replacing insulin shock therapy (Younis & Arafat, 2022). Dr. Abboudy retired from medical college in 1954 and continued his private practice until 1972, after which he emigrated to the UK and worked at the Brixton prison clinic in London until he passed away in 1981 (Younis, 2009b). The Ministry of Health (Moh) established the Ibn Rushd Mental Hospital with 70 beds in 1968 in Baghdad to treat acute mental disorders (Younis, 2009a). Al-Rashad and Ibn-Rushd mental hospitals in Baghdad played central roles in treating patients and training medical students and psychiatric trainees. During 1970–1990, psychiatric services were extended to major cities outside Baghdad, primarily providing outpatient care with limited inpatient beds for urgent acute cases (Younis, 2008) (Fig. 3).

Fig. 3 Dar-Al-Shaffa mental hospital, guide of the kingdom of Iraq, 1936 (personal archive)

3 Epidemiology of Mental Disorders

Due to missing electronic documentation and damage to academic archives after 2003, little is known about the prevalence of mental disorders during the 1980s–1990s. The World Health Organization reported that over 20% of Iraqis suffer from mental illnesses, driven by wars, conflicts, and political instability (World Health Oorganization [WHO], 2023). Accurate, updated data on psychiatric services in Iraq is scarce, with only one national study, the Iraq Mental Health Survey (IMHS), supervised by the WHO and funded by the European Commission and the Government of Japan as part of the project of developing a mental health system in Iraq (WHO, 2006b). The research team used the Self-Reporting Questionnaire (SRQ-20) and Diagnostic and Statistical Manual of Mental Disorders (DSM-IV) on 4,332 respondents from 18 governorates during 2006–2007. The findings indicated that the lifetime prevalence of mental disorders in Iraq is 18.8%, with bipolar disorder and substance-related disorders being the most serious. Twelve-month prevalence of any disorder was 13.6%, with 42.1% of cases classified as mild, 36.0% as moderate, and 21.9% as serious. The disorders most often classified as serious were bipolar disorder (76.9%) and substance-related disorders (54.9%). Only 2.2% of IMHS respondents reported receiving treatment (Al-Hasnawi et al., 2009; WHO, 2006). In 2019, the prevalence of mental disorders among Iraqis was 29%, which is higher than in some neighboring Arab countries. According to the WHO, there are 104,838 patients diagnosed with mental disorders, with a prevalence rate of 29 per 100,000. Males account for 60% and females, 40% (WHO Mental Health Atlas, 2020).

3.1 *Common Mental Disorders*

3.1.1 Anxiety Disorders

It is agreed upon through many studies that anxiety disorders are commonly encountered in mental health settings, for example, among 10,101 patients who attended the neuropsychiatric outpatient clinic in Baghdad in 1993, 18.9% suffered from anxiety disorders (Younis & Lafta, 2014). A decade later, anxiety disorders comprised 33.4% of the attendees to the same clinic (Younis & Al-Naaimi, 2006). Again, anxiety disorders comprised 18% of 2,979 attendees to the same clinic during 2010 (Younis et al., 2013). Recently, it was found that anxiety disorders comprise 14% and 9.7% of the attendees to two psychiatric outpatient clinics in Baghdad (Younis & Saeed, 2023). Similarly, the IMHS found that anxiety disorders affected 13.8% of the studied general population sample with a male-to-female ratio of 1:1.8 for any the disorders, particularly among the youngest cohorts, panic disorder and Post-traumatic stress disorder (PTSD) being the most prevalent: while Obsessive–Compulsive Disorder (OCD), was less common but more impairing (Al Hasnawi et al., 2009). Like other countries, anxiety symptoms were found to be increased during the COVID-19 pandemic by a recent study where 28.4%, 39.3%, and 22.9% of the studied 370 physicians suffered mild, moderate, and severe degrees, respectively (Saeed et al., 2021). Similarly, another study indicated a high prevalence of OCD symptoms; 43% of 1644 medical students during the COVID-19 pandemic (Taher et al., 2021).

3.1.2 Depression

Many local and international studies have found that depression is more common than other mental disorders and is associated with war-related traumas and persistent PTSD. For example, depression affected 16%, 33.4%, and stood at 30% of the total attendees to the psychiatric outpatient clinic in Medical City Teaching Hospital during the years of 1993, 2003, and 2010, respectively (Younis & Al-Naaimi, 2006; Younis & Lafta, 2014; Younis et al., 2013). A recent study reported a ratio of 30% in the same clinic, which is higher than 15.7% of attendees at the Ibn-Rushd Hospital clinic. This may indicate that patients prefer general hospitals over mental hospitals due to the social stigma associated with mental hospitals when experiencing depression (Younis & Saeed, 2023). Various other small-scale studies targeting clinical and general population samples have demonstrated significant prevalence and morbidity rates among specific groups such as medical students, physicians, and war-traumatized individuals (Ahmed et al., 2024a). Regarding depression in the non-clinical population, the IMHS found that the lifetime prevalence of affective disorders was 6.13% for males and 9.3% for females (Al-Hasnawi et al., 2009). Further analysis of IMHS data revealed that major depressive disorder had a lifetime prevalence of 7.4% and a twelve-month prevalence of 4.0%, with 46% of the twelve-month cases being severe; notably, many affected individuals did not seek formal treatment (Al-Hamzawi et al., 2015).

3.1.3 Psychotic Disorders

Among the few publications in 1990s, one study explored the outcomes of schizophrenia by following up with 298 patients revealed that 47% of the subjects had good or partial symptomatic and psychosocial outcomes at the final assessment, while approximately 53% exhibited poor outcomes with male-to-female ratio of 20:31.3%, and concluding that the outcomes of schizophrenia in Iraq are comparable to those in developing countries and could be attribute to large, supportive families and a committed regimen for active follow-up treatment (Younis & Moselhy, 2009a). Psychotic disorders affected 7.3%, 13.3%, and 24% of the total attendees at the psychiatric outpatient clinic at Medical City Teaching Hospital during the years 1993, 2003, and 2010, respectively (Younis & Al-Naaimi, 2006; Younis & Lafta, 2014; Younis et al., 2013), while the ratio was 47.7% of the total attendees of Ibn-Rushd clinic indicating the tendency of patients with psychotic disorders mainly schizophrenia to attend specialized psychiatric hospital as a first station and for follow-up (Younis & Saeed, 2023). A study revealed that 29% of 200 patients diagnosed with schizophrenia attributed their symptoms to sorcery, witchcraft, and the evil eye, while 44% blamed life stresses such as war-related trauma, imprisonment, and social or family problems (Al-Abbudi, 2016). In the same context, a sample of 328 patients with first-episode schizophrenia expressed prodromal signs of sleep disturbances, aggression, restlessness, disorganized speech, suspiciousness, social withdrawal, odd behavior, and somatic complaints. The author emphasized the importance of early intervention through psycho-educational management to prevent complicated and advanced presentations of schizophrenia (Al-Abbudi, 2018). Due to beliefs in supernatural powers and the social stigma, a significant number of patients with psychotic disorders do not rely on medical treatment, instead, they seek help from faith healers(FHs), such behavior may lead to delayed diagnosis and advanced or complicated presentations, consequently, the actual prevalence rates are believed to be higher than those reported in existing studies and medical sources (Fekih-Romdhan et al., 2013).

3.1.4 Alcohol and Substance Abuse

The prevalence of alcohol and substance abuse disorders is lower in Arab Muslim countries, including Iraq, compared to Western nations. However, there has been an increase in the abuse of more hazardous illicit drugs over the past two decades (Muzil et al., 2023). A retrospective analysis of the inpatient records from 1991 to 2000 found that 354 patients were treated for Benzhexol tablet abuse and co-morbid depression and anxiety (Younis & Moselhy, 2009b). A study on a non-consulting sample of 3200 adults found that past-month alcohol use was 3.2%, and 1.4% abuse of non-prescribed medications, mostly sedatives and strong analgesics; only 0.2% of men reported using any illicit drugs in the past month (Al-Hemiery et al., 2017). While a retrospective cross-sectional study found that the number of hospital admissions for alcohol and substance abuse increased from 2,979 in 2017 to 6,101 in 2021with more than doubled related offences: 6,393 to 14,391 for the same time (Al Ansari et al., 2022). The Ministry of Interior reported increased rates of drug trafficking and secret factories of Methamphetamines in particular, leading to around a 40% increase in the prevalence of abuse after 2017 and an increase in the number of drug dealers to 14,000, with 120 kg of drugs captured in 2022 (Ministry of Interior, 2025). It is believed that the black market for illicit drugs became easily accessible after 2003 due to post-conflict chaotic situations and poor security measures on Iraq's extensive borders.

3.1.5 Suicide and Suicidality

The WHO reported that there were over 590 suicide deaths and 1112 attempted suicides in Iraq during 2019 (World Health Organization Eastern Mediterranean Regional Office [WHO EMRO], 2020). However, the actual prevalence is believed to be higher due to underreported cases. A study conducted in 1998 revealed that

8.8% of patients admitted to the emergency room were involved in self-poisoning by drug overdose or chemical substances like pesticides. Among those attempting suicide, 70.7% were under 30 years old, with a male-to-female ratio of 1:2.2 (Al-Samarrai & Hussein, 2000). The Iraq National Study of Suicide (INSS) found the crude suicide rate in 2015 was 1.09/100,000 population; 1.2, males, and 0.97 females, and this increased to 1.31/100000 1.54 males,1.07 females during the year 2016, comprising a lower suicide rate compared to international figures, with 68% of cases aged under 30. The most frequent methods of suicide are firearms, self-burning, and self-poisoning by overdose or chemicals (Abbas et al., 2018). A large-scale study found that 15.5% of 1000 non-consulting adults confirmed having suicidal thoughts, with a male to female ratio of 10.36: 19.31%, and a higher prevalence of 23.33% among housewives (Stewart et al., 2015). Another comparable study found that of 113 self-harm patients predominantly females; 79.6% admitted to the emergency room, suicide intentions were strongly held by 7.1% of the total sample, ed with an average age of 26 years, 8% had psychiatric disorders, and 31.3% had the intent to die shortly before the act and described their attempts as an "escape," or "relief" from their emotional problems (Al-Haidary& Al-Badri, 2015). One of the rarest methods of self-harm was the dermal injection of Kerosene (which is used for cooking and heating), five out of ten females admitted having suicidal intent before their act as a reaction to emotional problems, the rest had confused emotions, such condition if not treated can be fatal by causing irreversible necrosis and suppuration leading to septicemia. However, self-injection by Kerosene was unreported in Western countries; it is an increasing practice in Iraq (Sharquie et al., 2014). A recent study about suicidal ideations found that among 388 patients with psychiatric disorders recruited from two psychiatric outpatient clinics in Baghdad found that 37.1% of the patients expressed suicidal ideas during the last year, the majority of suicidal ideations fell into a low severity range on the *Colombia -Suicide Severity Rating Scale* (C-SSRS) and suicidal ideations were significantly associated with female gender, recent psychological trauma, family history of suicidal behavior and family history of mental illness (Younis et al., 2025). Suicidal ideations may progress to attempts by different means and are usually encountered in emergency departments. Such attempts could be an impulsive act without real suicidal intent and could be easily overlooked as accidental injury. It is believed that the rising rates of suicide, suicidal thoughts, and suicide attempts are associated with war-related traumas, with a changing trend toward more violent methods, such as hanging and shooting by small firearms, in association with a higher prevalence of affective disorders (Younis, 2024). Despite increasing suicide rates, reaching 4.47% for the age-standardized suicide mortality rate per 100,000 population, and the fact that the Moh sought suicide prevention strategies based on the INSS data, such strategies were not activated or implemented (Abbas et al., 2018; WHO Mental Health Atlas, 2020).

4 Mental Health Services in Iraq: Structure and Challenges

4.1 Mental Health Services (1960–1990)

There are no official documents about the structure and function of psychiatric services in Iraq before 2003 due to the incidents of vandalism affecting the Ministry of Health building, leading to the loss of the archives and files during the post-conflict chaotic situation and loss of law and order on April, 9th, 2003. Mental health services in Iraq could be considered one of the earliest systems in the Arab countries regarding the time of commencement and stability, mostly limited to Baghdad and major cities. The neuro-psychiatric unit in the Iraqi Royal Teaching Hospital, renamed to (Al-Jamhori Teaching Hospital after 1958, used to receive 150 outpatients daily (Bazzoui & Al-Issa, 1966; Younis, 2008). Al-Rasheed Military Hospital, created in 1938 by the Ministry of Defense, served as the sole main and tertiary institution for assessing and treating military and police forces. The hospital included a psychiatric unit during the 1950s. It expanded over time to contain two outpatient clinics, an ECT department, approximately 30 beds for acute admission, a department for psychology, and social workers. It served as a venue for the central military psychiatric committee for any determination concerning mental illnesses under the military regulations. Al-Rasheed Hospital was a recognized training center for military interns in medical and surgical specialties, including psychiatry. The number of military psychiatrists was below the growing demands, particularly following the conflicts of the 1980s and 1991, which resulted in war-related casualties across all medical specialties, including psychiatric emergencies (Younis, 2008). Psychotherapy and occupational therapy were initiated with a limited scope due to a shortage of budget and a lack of trained supervisors. The Moh established the first mental health advocacy department in 1960. During the 1960s–1970s, the health care system flourished and was a model for the region, including mental health services, due to an increased number of qualified psychiatrists returning mainly from the UK to provide psychiatric carefree of charge in government hospitals. The health care services provided access to 97% of the urban and 79% of the rural population (Sharma & Piachaud, 2011; Younis, 2009a). During the 1970s, large sums of oil revenue allowed the government to start advanced comprehensive projects all over Iraq, including education and health institutions. In the early 1980s, Iraq was a rapidly developing middle-income country with a well-developed health system and was known to be industrialized, had a high rate of literacy, and had a skilled workforce (Al-Hilfi et al., 2013; Hamada & Everett, 2007). Opening the psychiatric unit attached to Al-Yarmouk Teaching Hospital in Baghdad was a step forward in strengthening the psychiatric services. It contained a spacious forty-bed ward, an outpatient clinic, ECT compartments for general anesthesia, a social worker unit, an electroencephalogram (EEG), and a pharmacy. This integrated psychiatric unit was operated by four MRCPsych-qualified psychiatrists and one psychiatric practitioner who provided education and training to medical students and psychiatric residents. Unfortunately, this ideal unit was converted to an obstetrics and gynecology department by a decision made by the MOH in 1989

(Younis, 2008). In 1978, the first child and adolescent psychiatry clinic was opened in Ibn-Rushd Mental Hospital, staffed by a UK-trained psychiatrist, social worker, psychologist, and psychiatric registrar (Younis, 2008; Younis & Khunda, 2020). In the late 1970s, another psychiatric outpatient clinic was established in Baghdad City Centre to provide treatment and follow-up for patients discharged from Al-Rashad Mental Hospital and other walk-in patients. This clinic saw an average of 60–70 attendees per day and was managed by Dr. Ali Kamal and Abdul-Mohsen Al-Khiatt, along with one psychiatric practitioner, EEG department and social worker Additionally, the building housed the Central Psychiatric Civil Committee, which was operated by a panel of three specialist psychiatrists convened biweekly to evaluate the mental status of individuals referred for non-forensic medico-legal decisions till 2000 when the building closed. The committee moved to another location, maintaining its role. (personal experience) Younger mental health professionals and workers were required to join military forces as service members or reserve soldiers during Iran–Iraq war 1980–1988, which resulted in a shortage of personnel and increased the workload for remaining workforce, additionally, the military expenditure rose from 19.4% to 38.4% of the state budget, leading to the cutoff of training opportunities abroad and hurdle building new psychiatric hospitals and units (Sharma & Piachaud, 2011; Okasha et al., 2012). Despite these challenges, the World Bank and the WHO described Iraq's infrastructure as sophisticated and comparable to that of advanced countries. Health services were effective, widely expanded, and provided free of charge. Medicines and equipment were imported from reputable sources, and numerous fully equipped general hospitals were opened in Baghdad and various other governorates (Al-Nasrawi, 2001; Sharma & Piachaud, 2011). In 1970, the Medical City Teaching Hospital was established, and it was the primary teaching and training center for medical students of Baghdad College of Medicine. It's 11 floors include a 23-bed neuro-psychiatric ward, an outpatient department staffed by psychiatric residents, specialist psychiatrists, and a social worker. It continued to serve as a major training center for psychiatric residents (Younis & Khunda, 2020). In 1988, a new well-equipped medical college and teaching hospital were established in Al-Kadhimiya, Baghdad. The hospital featured a psychiatric outpatient clinic and a few beds of a psychiatric ward run by a UK-trained consultant psychiatrist (Al-Samarrai, 2002). Another psychiatric unit opened in the mid-1980s et al.-Karama General Hospital in Baghdad-Al-Karkh, closed in 1994 after the immigration of its two psychiatrists, reopened as an outpatient clinic in the last decade (Younis, 2008). Regarding other governorates, the teaching hospital of the Mosul College of Medicine in Mosul city, north of Iraq, has included a well-equipped psychiatric ward administered by Dr. Fakhry Al Dabbagh, a UK-trained professor of psychiatry during the 1960s, who authored numerous literature publications about mental health and facilitated government scholarships for postgraduate training opportunities, especially for the UK Diploma in Psychiatry He also advocated mental health literacy through television programs during the 1970s (ArabPsyNet, 2025; Younis, 2008). With the establishment of the University of Basra in southern Iraq in 1964, the Basra teaching hospital included a psychiatric outpatient clinic and a few beds supervised by Dr. Fadhel Zaiya, joined by Dr. Salih Al-Shekh Gomer, an MRCPsych consultant psychiatrist and tutor from 1978 to 1983, assisted by a psychiatric registrar. Other southern provinces, such as Al-Diwaniya and Al-Nasiriyah, had psychiatric outpatient clinics managed by psychiatric practitioners, who were responsible for serving the nearby provinces that lacked psychiatric services. Psychiatric outpatient clinics served governorates of central Iraq, and some had few beds for acute admissions run by UK-trained psychiatrists, including Al-Hilla city, Al-Najaf, Karbala, Al-Anbar, Al-Kut, and Diyala. In 2000, Sulaymaniyah and Erbil had acute psychiatric beds available to serve their million-plus populations, but Duhok, with a slightly smaller population, had none. In 1984, the Ministry of Health established new 400-bed general hospitals in 14 governorates, including the KRI, built by the Marubeni Japanese Corporation, which in turn improved the quality of the existing psychiatric units and may offer space for opening new ones (Ministry of Health, 2025; Relief Web, 2000).

4.2 Mental Health Services (1990–2003)

4.2.1 The Impact of Economic Sanctions on Mental Health Services

When the United Nations Security Council (UNSC) adopted resolution 986, which imposed a comprehensive trade embargo against Iraq as a political punishment four days after the invasion, the first sanction of its kind since the UN's founding in October 1945, the Iraqi army invaded Kuwait on August 2, 1990. It annexed the entire country on August 28, 1990, beginning an era of chaos that affected every aspect of life (United Nations Security Council [UNSC], 1995). The economic sanction significantly affected the world economy regarding health, as Moh's financing for healthcare fell by 90%. The country's health spending fell from 3.72% of GDP in 1990, the pre-sanction era, to 81% in 1997. The country experienced food insecurity, unemployment, and a sharp decline in the value of the Iraqi dinar (Hamid & Everett, 2007). The number of Iraqis living below the national poverty line has increased to 22.9%, and health indicators have gotten worse (Al-Nasrawi, 2001; Rawaf et al., 2004). According to the WHO, the number of patients attending psychiatric outpatient clinics has increased despite profound shortages in medicines and manpower, reflecting the increase in people's needs for treatment. For example, psychiatric attendees at outpatient clinics increased from 197,000 in 1990 to 220,000 in 1994. It rose to 507,000 in 1998, with the prevalence of 10% of the population affected by different psychiatric disorders, especially PTSD (WHO, 2006a). Many patients with schizophrenia suffer frequent relapses with catatonia, requiring ECT as a first-line treatment because of the deprivation of antipsychotic medications, especially the atypical antipsychotics (Younis & Moselhy, 2009a). Psychological distress affected the life qualities of healthy people also as reflected by a representative sample of 579 college students who expressed their dissatisfaction with overall poor life quality. The students were residents of Baghdad, the capital, Diyala province in central Iraq, and Nasiriyah in the south during the year 2001 (Younis, 2003). One local study revealed that 24–57% of 130 school-age children in the Al-Ameriyah district of Baghdad showed PTSD symptoms following the bombing of a nearby shelter that killed 40 civilians in February 1991 (Younis & Aswad, 2018). Like other government employees, mental health professionals and workers experienced low wages and financial hardships. Additionally, they lacked access to global medical advancements and educational resources and were affected by strict limitations on travel and communication with the outside world. Consequently, the number and caliber of working psychiatrists were hampered, and psychiatric units in hospitals experienced a decline in both medical and therapeutic outcomes (Younis & Aswad, 2018). In 1995, the UNSC established the Oil-for-Food Program under Resolution 986. This program permitted Iraq to sell oil on the global market in exchange for food, medicine, and other humanitarian necessities (UNSC, 1995). During the 1990s, the Iraq Ministry of Health (Moh) and the state-owned pharmaceutical company, Samara Drug Industry (SDI), were the main providers of basic psychiatric drugs, including anxiolytics, antidepressants, and antipsychotics, which were imported or locally made. Some international organizations, such as the *International Committee of the Red Cross (ICRC)* and the *Iraqi Red Crescent Society (IRCS)*, provided basic psychiatric medications through donations. However, the overall drug supply was inconsistent and did not meet the increasing demands (Hamada & Everett, 2007; Younis & Aswad, 2018). In 1997, the Moh initiated a new policy to cover the cost of streaming health services by charging the patients as affordably as possible, called a "self-financing system," replacing the government funding scheme. For example, there were fees for plain or modified ECT treatment and a minimal fee for psychiatric consultation, investigations, and admission in a psychiatric ward, keeping in mind that all state hospitals are affiliated with the Moh (Al-Alwan, 2004; Sharma & Piachaud, 2011). Many psychiatric units were hardly functioning to provide basic services, leading to the closure of some units, like the psychiatric unit in Al-Karama General Hospital in Baghdad, after the immigration of its two specialist psychiatrists in 1994 and the paralysis of a few other outpatient clinics (Younis & Aswad, 2018). The financial strain of the sanctions and the stringent restrictions on traveling and communications with the outside world led to a lack of access to educational materials and global medical advances, this, in turn, hindered the quantity and caliber of the working psychiatrists. The shattered economy, coupled with political unrest and the impending Gulf War, resulted in a decrease in the number of psychiatrists due to brain drain, particularly those qualified in the UK who fled to Arab or Western countries for financial security, better life quality, and safer environments. The dramatic devaluation of the local currency, the Iraqi Dinar (ID), valued at 0.3108 to 1 US dollar in 1985, dropped to 3000 ID for 1 dollar in 1995; the estimated inflation rate was 800 times more than in the pre-sanction era (Central Bank of Iraq, 2025). From August 1990, the monthly wages of specialist psychiatrists ranged from 3,000 to 10,000 Iraqi Dinar (ID), equivalent to 1–5 USD (IPA, 2001; Younis & Aswad, 2018).

4.2.2 The Impact of the Gulf War (1991) on Mental Health Services

In November 1990, the UNSC adopted Resolution 678 and officially issued Iraq an ultimatum to withdraw from Kuwait unconditionally and authorized the assembly of an American-led military coalition. The coalition pursued the directive to forcefully expel Iraqi troops from Kuwait by initiating the Gulf War aerial bombardment campaign on January 17, 1991 (Al-Nasrawi, 2001). Over 120,000 air raids occurred in Iraq, taking the lives of more than 82,000 Iraqi soldier during their retreat. Inadequate. The extensive bombing and ground battles destroyed many military and civilian structures, including bridges, roads, power stations, and water sanitation plants (Al-Nasrawi, 2001; Harvard Study Team, 1991). This invasion led to anti-government revolts in the northern Kurdish provinces and southern cities, causing increased hospital casualties and chaotic conditions, which in turn added more numbers of war-traumatized patients and exacerbated other acute or chronic mental disorders. As a result, a few psychiatric centers, like Ibn Rushd Hospital in Baghdad, continued to function, with self-motivated psychiatrists and nurses willing to endure continuous bombing, minimal medication and food donations, as well as severe shortages of fuel and total disruption of telecommunications (Younis & Khunda, 2020). Psychiatric medications were offered in a few central hospitals, mainly for urgent cases like acute psychosis with agitation, suicidal attempts, and severe grief reactions presented with dissociative symptoms.

The working psychiatrists had to use plain ECT treatment more than before for serious presentations of psychotic disorders because of a shortage or absence of antipsychotic and antidepressant medications during or shortly after the time of bombardment. The rehabilitation of psychiatric units was at a minimum, and plans for establishing new ones were suspended. Because of the war and chaotic situation, many hospitals were vandalized, especially in southern provinces. In Baghdad, the Al Rashad Mental Hospital was affected by looting and vandalism, and many patients escaped or died due to the collapse of effective administration and a lack of proper medical care. The ICRC delegate in Baghdad sponsored and supervised a rehabilitation process in cooperation with the MOH. After the cease-fire on February 28, 1991, the government launched a national campaign to rebuild infrastructure, including health institutes, investing in the local experts and national workforce despite the strict embargo conditions (Younis & Aswad, 2018). The resilience and preservations of the mental health professionals and workers r were the prime motivations for streaming the basic psychiatric care; also, the sincere efforts of health authorities play a significant role in inspecting and supervising g psychiatric units and hospitals, despite dropping the fund of to 90% and prioritizing urgent public health problems over mental health services, such as controlling endemic diseases, infant and maternal mortality rates, malnutrition, maintaining the national vaccination campaigns, and water sanitation (Ministry of Health, 2025; Lafta & Al-Nuaimi, 2019). The international community took notice of such an impact on Iraq's health system during the reconstruction phase, however, out of the approximately $4 billion allocated initially for reconstruction funding, only 4.8% went to the health sector, and 97% of that funding was spent on construction and equipment with little or no space for improvement or training (WHO, 2006a; Hamid & Everett, 2007).

4.2.3 Mental Health Services After 2003

The Immediate Impact of the 2003 War

The Bush administration was authorized to deploy military forces against Iraq by a resolution passed by the US Congress in October 2002. During that extensive bombardment, the invading coalition's forces occupied all Iraqi territories, tanks roared on the streets of Baghdad and other main cities in Iraq, and their heavily armed personnel patrolled all over cities and towns. The US, second de facto head of state of Iraq and the leader of the Coalition Provisional Authority (CPA), Paul Bremer, signed two subversive pieces of legislation, the first one, the "De-Ba'athification," outlined in CPA Order 1 on May 16, 2003, declaring that all public sector employees affiliated with the Ba'ath Party were to be removed from their positions and to be banned from any future employment in the public sector without receiving any pension for their civil service, this decision involved four military specialists and psychiatrists (personal experience). Authority Order Number 2, issued on May 23, 2003, dissolved the Iraqi military, security, police, and intelligence infrastructure (Kameel, 2007). As a result, military psychiatric services ceased to exist, where Al-Rasheed military hospital became a deserted, ruined building, and military mental health professionals were reassigned to civilian health institutes, with some fleeing the country. Dissolution of the Iraqi military and security forces led to disastrous effects on civil life by creating a security vacuum that set the stage for subsequent generalized disruption, where looting, arson, vandalism, theft, and sabotage affected almost all state buildings, including hospitals and health centers (Sharma & Piachaud, 2011; Younis, 2008). The Iraq Family Health Survey Study group visited 89.4% of 1086 household clusters from January 2002 through June 2006; the overall rate of death per 1000 person-years was 5.31, and the estimated rate of violence-related death was 1.09, while the rate of violence-related death was estimated to be 1.67. This rate translates into an estimated number of violent deaths of 151,000 from March 2003 through June 2006 (Iraq Family Health Survey Study, 2008). Additionally, 654,965 persons had died during the 40 months since the US-led invasion, as compared with prewar numbers, keeping in mind the strong possibility of underreporting because of people's fear of disclosing such sensitive data to strangers. Another national cross-sectional cohort study on 12,801 individuals from 16 governorates concluded that pre-invasion mortality rates were 5.5 per 1,000 people per year, compared with 13.3 per 1,000 per year (Burnham et al., 2006; Roberts et al., 2004). Estimates indicate that the US troops assassinated over 140 doctors, or that street bombs claimed their lives. Between 2003 and 2007, four psychiatrists were assassinated, three others were victims of threats, and two specialists were kidnapped for ransom. The situation of sectarian conflicts and civil war continued for the following years, driving hundreds of doctors to flee Iraq; among them, seven academic tutors of psychiatry, six specialists, and 10 psychiatric residents and practitioners (Iraqi Psychiatric Association, 2025, personal communications). The loss of psychiatrists by immigration, quitting, and death comprises 40% of the total number of psychiatrists, and 2% of the total number of doctors (Laborte, 2005). The Moh estimated that 628 physicians have been murdered since 2003, while the Iraqi Medical Syndicate has put the number closer to 2000. (Webster, 2011). The atmosphere of violence caused some other psychiatrists to leave their jobs in Baghdad or other cities in central Iraq for other secure provinces, mainly KRI. Additionally, the intimidating presence of heavily armed US troops and their unexpected raids on some hospitals within their "Anti-Insurgency" campaigns worsened the sense of humiliation. It suppressed scientific activities regarding basic training or educational forums, for example, the conference hall attached to the Medical City Teaching Campus, where I worked, was known before as "Saddam Conference Hall," changing its name and turning it into a military base (personal experience). Many psychiatric units were damaged by looting and vandalism, including Ibn-Rushd mental hospital and psychiatric outpatient clinics in general hospitals. At the same time, they were closed for at least six weeks of bombardment and its aftermath (Younis & Al-Naaimi, 2006). The only private psychiatric hospital (Al-Mokhtar Psychiatric Hospital, which opened in 1998 in Baghdad) was closed for months and then transferred to a surgical private hospital (Younis, 2009b). Looters invaded Al-Rashad, wrecking its facilities such as the kitchen, laundry, patient areas, and rehabilitation rooms. Around 600 patients escaped from the hospital, including 100 from the highly secure psychiatric ward at Ibn-Al-Haytham. The remaining 300 patients experienced hazardous relapses, with some dying from diseases, poor nutrition, and neglect (Humaidi, 2006; Kammel, 2007). A western author attributed this act to the previous government, suggesting a politically biased attitude by quoting: "Saddam Hussein forcibly evacuated all the patients in Al-Rashad as part of a military strategy to inject chaos into Baghdad during the initial invasion" (Levin, 2008), again the ICRC significantly contributed to rebuilding Al-Rashad Mental Hospital (Fig. 4). Such chaotic situations led to a decreasing ratio of psychiatric beds per 100,000 from 7 in 1998 to 6.3 in 2007 (Okasha et al., 2012). Many other international organizations tried to help the collapsing psychiatric services; the Japanese and the US-Aid funds were handed over to the newly founded mental health office in the MoH to be used for developing the infrastructure of psychiatric services together with improving the professional and scientific levels of the mental health professionals and workers through providing training opportunities inside Iraq or in other Arab and western countries (WHO, 2006a; WHO, EMRO, 2006b).

4.2.4 Mental Health Services Long After 2003

As in other war-related situations, the incidence of mental disorders increased, with more complex presentations such as PTSD, anxiety, and depression persisting after the 2003 war, which exceeded the capacity of existing mental health facilities (Freh,

Fig. 4 Al-Rashad mental hospital, following the US-led invasion in 2003 (Copyrights ICRC, Reference: V-P-IQ-D-00035)

2016). According to the WHO, there were 25 outpatient mental health facilities available in the country, of which four were for children and adolescents with no appointment or follow-up protocols and no community facilities or mobile teams; also, there are no records about the average number of contacts per user of the clinics, leading to inaccurate registration data. Additionally, less than 20% of the outpatient facilities offer psychosocial treatment and depend on the personal interest of the attending psychiatrists (WHO, 2006a, 2023). The mental health system remains two-tiered, with 92% of psychiatrists working both in public and private services, 2% in government only, and 5% solely in private practice. Moreover, the rate of 1.6 mental health professionals per 100,000, when Iraq's population was 27 million, and the absence of multi-disciplinary practice could be pinpointed as the principal shortfall (Sharma & Piachaud, 2011). Despite the passage of 22 years since 2003, infrastructure, such as intermittent electricity and associated sanitation problems, is still poor and defective, which negatively affected the quality of psychiatric services in the context of the slow overhauling of public health, where the physician-to-population ratio is about 60% lower than the average for the other 23 nations in WHO's Eastern Mediterranean Region (Al-Hilfi et al., 2013). According to Al-Uzri et al., the following data were addressed as positive indicators for the development of the mental health system after 2003: Psychiatric units: 12–23; Psychiatrists and other doctors working in psychiatric settings: 98–206; Psychiatric nurses: 145–335; Psychologists: 16–47; Social workers: 25–33. The study concluded that while the quality of mental healthcare in Iraq is improving, there remains a significant disparity between the need for services and the capacity of healthcare providers (Al-Uzri et al., 2012). Opposite to such indicators, some authors described Iraq's mental health system as unable to meet people's needs due to the previously mentioned shortfalls, despite the international support and increasing the number of psychiatrists, ancillaries, and psychiatric units, if an increase in Iraq's population is undertaken. Since 2017, standalone mental health policies have not been adequately implemented, and many specialized psychiatric services remain limited and underdeveloped due to multiple factors, such as a lack of a mental health perspective within the national educational system. Substandard medications and equipment, like ECT apparatuses with inconsistent branded medications, hence switching medications may be mandated by stock rather than clinical considerations, making national clinical guidelines more challenging to design and adhere (Saied et al., 2023).

4.2.5 The Impact of the 2014–2017 Conflict on Mental Health Services

The ensuing violence following the 2003 war persisted and multiplied when the Islamic State of Iraq and Syria (ISIS) took control of the northern and western parts of Iraq in June 2014, Mosul city was exclusively seized and ruled by ISIS imposing brutal and tyrannical governance for 29 months until the battle to retake Mosul S started October 16, 2016 and ended in July 21, 2017, taking the lives of approximately 40,000 civilians with the highest mortality rate during the military operations inside the densely populated neighborhoods, and an estimated 1.2 million internally displaced people (IDP), increasing the total number of IDP to approximately four million comprising 10% of Iraq's overall population, leading to serious humanitarian situations with inadequate health care facilities (Lafta & Al Nuaimi, 2019; Lafta et al., 2018). As a result of nefarious air strikes and intense artillery, the psychiatric department ward and outpatient clinic were obliterated as part of the Mosul Teaching Hospital together with the psychiatric department and lecture halls of Mosul College of Medicine located on the "west side." On the one hand, the psychiatric unit in Ibn-Sennas Hospital was damaged and closed, and on the other hand, psychiatric private clinics located on the west side were also destroyed depriving patients from any form of psychiatric care. Such atrocities caused the development of severe anxiety, depression, PTSD, and induced relapses in patients with psychotic or bipolar disorders (Younis et al., 2023). There is a dearth of national data regarding the devastating effects of recent conflicts on people, women and children in IDP settlements experience many health-hazardous conditions, while some external assistance was received, much more is needed to meet their needs, additionally they feel insecure and feared the possibility of not returning home soon (Lafta et al., 2016). A recent cross-sectional study conducted on 1321 women living in in KRI's refugees camps, found that around two-thirds of women attended the camp's healthcare facilities, and 16.4% could afford to pay for private facilities, more than half of the IDP women reported symptoms of depression, anxiety, emotional traumas, and PTSD Iraqi government, local NGOs s, and international aid agencies need to strengthen their efforts (Ahmed et al., 2024a).

5 Other Challenges Facing Psychiatric Services

5.1 The Impact of Social Stigma

Although societal stigma toward mental illnesses is a global concern, it seems explicit in Arab countries, adversely affecting the psychiatric services in almost all aspects, where public perceptions mimic mental health issues with "insanity," personal failure, social flaws, or weak Islamic faith. Such negative attitudes are usually mixed with the non-medical causes for any mental illnesses and were addressed in many studies either as direct objectives of the studies or in the context of studies about psychiatric disorders or services (Khatib et al., 2023). The following summaries implied the strength of such stigmatizing attitudes; the first one is a multinational study on a general population sample across 16 Arab countries that concluded that more than one in four individuals exhibited stigmatizing attitudes toward mental illness (26.5%), had poor knowledge (31.7%), and held negative attitudes toward help-seeking (28.0%). In the overall sample, being female, older, having higher knowledge, having more positive attitudes toward mental illness, and endorsing biomedical and psychosocial causes were associated with fewer stigmatizing attitudes (Fekih-Romdhane et al., 2013). The second study looked at 33 articles that examined social stigma among people of Arab heritage, showing how stigmatizing behaviors are shown and how they relate to negative beliefs, actions, and attitudes toward mental health treatments, with a wide range of differences found within the Arab population. The third one is a cross-sectional study aimed at exploring self and public stigma toward mental illness and associated factors among 4241 university students from 11 Arabic-speaking countries. The study found that the average agreement on stigma toward mental illnesses among university students was 19.7 (SD = 6.0). This level of agreement was linked to the participants' backgrounds in terms of demographics and education (Al-Omari et al., 2023). Like other Arab nations, societal stigma surrounding mental diseases is a significant issue encountered daily in the mental health sector, affecting a considerable portion of the general populace, hindering the efficiency of the provided psychiatric care. Such negative attitudes impact the mental health system at its core in many ways, including choosing non-medical therapy over psychiatric consultation, poor or non-drug adherence, not showing up for the follow-up, pre-conception, and distrustful beliefs about psychiatrists as persons, psychiatric medications, and psychiatric hospitals (Younis et al., 2021). It seems that the current psychiatrist's impressions are not novel and resistant to change, first referred to six decades ago (Bazzoui & Al-Issa, 1966), continued to be addressed by numerous studies afterward till the most recent ones, for example, one study found that over half of 418 non-consulting adults expressed feeling ashamed if a family member had a mental illness, and over half would avoid working with the mentally ill person, or communicating with them, while three-quarters of respondents chose to hide their mental health issues, on the other hand, the respondents showed their sympathy and support if they would have a sick family member (Sadik et al., 2010). In consistency with the two most recent studies conducted in the KRI, a sample of 294 university students in the KRI found that most of the participants held negative attitudes toward individuals with mental health disorders and that they are often singled out and subjected to stereotypes, limitations, stigmatization, pessimistic forecasts, and a lack of benevolence, resulting in a negative perception (Omar et al., 2024). The second similar study on 407 young adults indicated that stigma-related barriers were significant, with participants fearing being considered weak (mean score = 2.14, SD = 0.96) and concerns about being labeled "crazy" (mean score = 1.80, SD = 1.19). There was a notable preference for dealing with mental health issues independently without professional help, which was described as rare and lacking culturally diverse mental health professionals (Ahmed et al., 2024b). In Baghdad city, a study conducted on 300 adults randomly sampled from the general population revealed that 80% of the participants showed a moderate degree of stigmatizing attitude toward mental illness and negative attitudes toward mental health care and professionals, and around 20% of respondents showed a low degree of stigmatizing attitude toward mental illness; there were no clear roles of sociodemographic factors in the stigmatic attitude toward mental illnesses (Younis et al., 2021). Unlike the general population, 158 senior medical students who completed their training course in psychiatry at Baghdad College of Medicine, 86.6% of them advocated the psychiatrist's role in the medical field by providing the proper treatment for mental illness, and that mental illness is a medical disease; 23% of the students expressed their wish to pursue psychiatry. It is thought that education and training in psychiatry had influenced their reflections (Younis & Al-Rubayee, 2018). The social stigma was addressed by the national studies conducted on thousands of adult population samples at different times, such as IMHS, INSS, and IFHS, confirming its impact and consistency (WHO, 2006/7; Abbas et al., 2018; Iraq Family Health Survey Study, 2008). Moreover, social stigma was deemed a solid barrier to developing psychiatric services by its effect on patients and their families, recruiting a greater number of mental health professionals and workers, expanding services to remote areas, and deterring medical students and interns from pursuing psychiatry. Additionally, many psychiatric trainees and specialists experience frustrating feelings and depolarization caused by such stigmatizing attitudes during their career journeys (Ahmed et al., 2024b; Jaff et al., 2024).

5.1.1 Non-medical Management of Mental Disorders

Traditional and religious beliefs significantly influence the conception of mental disorders and help-seeking behavior, challenging the biomedical model of mental illnesses. Despite the little research to substantiate the cultural impact, it is agreed upon by many studies that Arab patients may or may not seek formal psychiatric services, influenced by the dominating family traditions and decision-making (Al Shelali et al., 2024). The use of informal Indigenous resources is a common phenomenon in Arab Muslim countries, and Iraq is no exception where the role of "loyalty" is highest to the parents, brothers, and sisters and less toward tribal members in determining behavior toward others and creating a close-knit system of interdependence and mutual support, thus the need to seek formal psychiatric care could be weakened and non-medical help is preferred (Al-Issa & Al-Issa, 1970). The changes of speech and behavior among individuals with psychotic or dissociative disorders are commonly attributed to supernatural power; thus, seeking therapy from FHs would be more rational and less stigmatized than relying on mental health settings, this was reflected by a cross-sectional study conducted on 482 attendees of the psychiatric outpatient clinic in Baghdad revealing that 57% of the participants visited FHs before, during, or after their psychiatric consultation, 84.6% reported visiting FHs less than 10 times, while 15.4% went 10 times or more; 36.9% believed that the treatment of FHs is accepted or even good, while 30.9% realized that it is useless. Patients with schizophrenia/psychosis or bipolar disorders visited FHs significantly more often than those with other diagnoses (Younis et al., 2019). Large scale studies and local community research focusing on mental health help-seeking issues are needed to understand the people's preferences and how to bring them into more medical models together with examining the alternative resources such as family therapy, Quranic treatment (Al-Ruqiyah) instead of some other harmful methods. Additionally, integrating mental health into the primary health care system is thought to mitigate the social stigma about mental health care settings (Fekih-Romdhane et al., 2013). Action plans should be taken concerning the following: promoting mental health literacy, substantiating medical education with mental health training, implementing an anti-stigma strategy, and improving the work environment and standards of care in mental clinics and hospitals (Khatib et al., 2023).

6 Mental Health Services Availability and Uptake

6.1 Integrating Mental Health into the Primary Health Care System

The Moh sought to integrate mental health into primary health care by arranging short training courses for the general practitioners working in primary care health centers in collaboration with the regional advisor on mental health, Dr. Taha Baʿashar, during his visit to Baghdad in 1988. The plan was designed to expand the integrating strategy to some major cities other than Baghdad by implementing the policy of "training the trainers" (ToT) to increase the number of trainers recruited from mental health fields and primary health care centers; however, the Gulf War and economic sanctions hindered further development due to a shortage of human and financial resources and kept those plans within limitations (personal experience). According to a study supervised by the Moh, it was found that 42.3–59% of trained primary health care workers achieved improvement regarding their psychiatric skills after two weeks of interactive training. An evaluation questionnaire measured the program in comparison with its untrained counterparts. The study concluded that systematic training programs can succeed even in complex conflict situations and achieve measurable improvements in physician behaviors (Sadik et al., 2011). This study was not reproduced with no available official data regarding the current situations of primary health care practice, it seems that monitoring such comprehensive strategy face the challenges of not having enough number of psychiatrists to deal with extended primary health care centers along Iraq, moreover, the bureaucratic and disorganized (Moh) structures resulted by frequent changes in the top officials, which in turn led to changes in their visions and policies toward mental health services (Bolton, 2013). A recent study evaluated the psychiatric morbidities and the psychosocial support services in primary health care centers found that symptoms of anxiety were the most prevalent 57%, followed by depression (17%), psychosomatic disorders 9%, behavioral and developmental disorders 6%, PTSD 5%, and substance use disorder 3%. Specific tools designed by the WHO were used for psychiatric assessments, and the authors concluded the following:

1. Primary health centers lack the presence of psychiatrists, psychologists, or social workers.
2. The staff receiving mental health training is too small compared to the heavy workload.
3. The trained staff showed flaws and incompetencies regarding service skills, diagnosis of priority disorders, and managing mental health issues.
4. There are shortages of essential psychotropic medications hindering treatment effectiveness.
5. Absence of a strict referral protocol to mental health facilities with a low referral rate, with no liaison services for the patients referred to the mental health facilities (Al-Rudaini et al., 2024). The WHO's recent report provides an updated summary of psychiatric services available in Iraq 0, as follows:

   - Outpatient clinics: 30 units, 283.04 visits per 100,000 population
   - Child and adolescent facilities: 9 units, 42.58 visits per 100,000 population
   - Mental hospitals (inpatient care): 2 units, 3.21–2.29 visits per 100,000 population
   - Psychiatric units in general hospitals: 21 units, 0.53 visits per 100,000 population.

The WHO report indicated that there were 4,408 admissions in mental hospitals, of which 250 were involuntary. Long-stay admissions, defined as stays exceeding five years, included 1,389 patients. The follow-up services accounted for 25–50% of the total number of discharged patients from hospitals (WHO Mental Health Atlas, 2020).

While the above data was published by international source, the Research Office in the Iraqi Parliament released an updated report about mental health services based on official data from MoH summarized by the following data: There are four mental hospitals in Baghdad including Al-Qanat Center with bed capacity of 125, and Al-Attah center with bed capacity of 150 for treatment and rehabilitation of persons with

Table 1 The newly established psychiatric units in Iraq in 2024

Governorate	General psychiatry bed capacity	Bed capacity, alcohol, and substance abuse
Dyialah	12	10
Najaf	10	
Thi-Qar		18
Mosul	16	16
Basra	36	44
Diwaniyah	8	
Wasit	12	
Babil	10	18
Muthanna	10	10

alcohol and substance abuse which were opened during 2021–2023 (Baghdad Al-Russafa Health Directory, 2022). According to updated official data, Table 1 shows the newly opened psychiatric units in nine governorates.

The total number of bed capacity for Baghdad and governorates other than KRI is 1617, representing 4.4 beds for a 100,000 population, which is lower than the ratio of 6.1/100,000 in Middle Eastern countries and the international ratio of 7.04/100,000 (The Iraqi Parliament, Office of Parliamentary Research, 2024).

6.2 *Forensic Mental Health Services*

Following the WHO's constitution for mental health legislation, the National Council for Mental Health arranged its first meeting in Baghdad in 2004, and the allocated working committee issued the final draft of the Iraq Mental Health Act (IMHA), abiding by the human rights covenants. And was approved by the Cabinet in 2005 (WHO, 2006a). However, active implementation of the act did not take place either in the judiciary or in forensic psychiatric settings, for which some literature attributed such failure to the issue of security, insufficiency of allocated human resources, and absence of dedicated authority to assess compliance with mental health legislation with international human rights, keeping in mind that the mental health plan contains specified cultural and religious precautions against complete surveillance (Kameel, 2007; WHO, Mental Health Atlas, 2020). Forensic psychiatric services in Iraq abide by the standard of "significantly impaired decision-making ability" (SIDMA) caused by mental disorders, which is the basis for the insanity verdict released by the court to reduce criminal responsibility to the minimum, that is, the McNaughton rule (Hummadi et al., 2020). The Iraqi judiciary system confirmed the diminished responsibility due to mental illness as the Iraqi Penal Code with amendment 1969, Chapter 4, Sect. 1, Paragraph 60, titled Loss of Volition Stated: "Any person who, at the time of the commission of the offense, suffers from a loss of reason or volition due to insanity or infirmity of mind or in a state of intoxication or under the influence of narcotic substances given to them against their will or without their knowledge or due to any other reason, which leads one to believe that they have lost their reason or that volition is not criminally liable, it is considered a mitigating circumstance" (Ministry of Justice Iraq, 1969). There is no available data on the actual commencement of forensic psychiatric services in Iraq due to the loss of the hospital's archives by the acts of vandalism during the Gulf War on January 17, 1991, and the US-led invasion on March 21, 2003 (Humaidi, 2006; Hummadi et al., 2020). However, it is believed that the nucleus of forensic psychiatry was established in the Ibn-Al Haitham unit in Al Rashad Hospital in the late 1950s. It is a highly secured unit with 250 detainee beds and a forensic psychiatric committee compartment. The panelists include three consultant psychiatrists, a psychiatric resident, a clinical psychologist, a social worker, and a psychiatric nurse. Their meetings take place twice weekly to determine the defendant's criminal responsibility in the context of their mental capacity. Those who are mentally incompetent stay in custody in the same unit for treatment and future assessment within 3–6 months; others who are mentally sound are returned by the police force, the so-called "Al Tasferaat," to continue their statutory procedures. Al Rashad Mental Hospital is the sole center for forensic psychiatry in Iraq, serving a population of 37,400,468 in Baghdad and other governorates, apart from the KRI, which is a daunting workload conducted in risky settings (Muslim & Chaleby, 2007). Apart from scattered small-scale studies, national data about forensic psychiatric services is lacking; hence, knowledge about mental disorders within the context of the criminal justice system is insufficient and has not been updated.

6.3 Mental Health Advocacy: Non-government Organizations

In 1970, the Iraqi Association for Neurologists, Neurosurgeons, and Psychiatrists (IANP) was founded by Dr. Tariq Ibrahim Hamdi, a pioneer psychiatrist and professor of neurology-psychiatry at Baghdad's College of Medicine. He was the president of the Iraqi Medical Syndicate in 1968 and was elected president of the IANP with an executive committee comprised of distinguished psychiatrists, neurologists, and neurosurgeons in 1971. Later on was appointed as the college's dean in 1976. The pioneer members published a peer-reviewed psychiatric journal, Al-Razi, from 1978 until 1993, when economic sanctions halted production due to financial constraints (Younis, 2009b; Younis & Aswad, 2018). The executive committee members of the IANP decided to designate the association for psychiatrists only in 1993. They renamed it the Iraqi Society for Psychiatrists (ISP), affiliated to the Supreme Council of Scientific Societies in concordance with the bylaw of Scientific Societies code 55, issued by the Ministry of Higher Education and Scientific Research in 1981 (Ministry of Justice, 2025). The ISP joined the Arab Federation of Psychiatrists and continued to function with limited communication with the outside world because of the economic sanctions and the government's strict regulations for traveling. A new batch of 8 specialist psychiatrists was elected for the ISP's executive committee in a voting session supervised by the president of the Iraqi Medical Syndicate, Professor Mohamad Al Rawi, assassinated in his clinic in April 2003, and a representative of the Ministry of Justice, among the elected members; the author was the first woman psychiatrist in the 2000–2007 (Younis & Khunda, 2020). Despite the financial constraints and lack of international support, the ISP organized the first and second psychiatric conferences in Baghdad in 2000 and 2002 (The Iraqi Psychiatric Association [IPA], 2025). The ISP organizes many scientific events and voting sessions every 4 years. After the election of 2020, the association was renamed the Iraqi Psychiatric Association (IPA) and later organized two successful psychiatric conferences in Baghdad city center, the fourth and the fifth international conferences on November 23–24, 2023 and February 20–21, 2025. Notably, the number of women members of the executive committee rose from one in 2020 to four in 2023, especially reflecting the growing number of young women doctors pursuing psychiatry in general (IPA, 2025). In addition to the WHO delegate and the EMRO office in Baghdad and KRI, some other international NGOs, such as ICRC, UNICEF, and humanitarian organizations like Médecins Sans Frontières (MSF), in collaboration with the local Iraqi Red Crescent Society (IRCS), donated some basic psychiatric medicines within their charity campaigns during the wars of 1991 and 2003 (Younis & Aswad, 2018). Many other international bodies, like the US-Aid, International Medical Corps (IMC), Substance Abuse and Mental Health Services Administration (SAMHSA), UK Department of Health, Heartland Alliance, Johns Hopkins University delegate, Royal College of Psychiatrists (RCP), and collaboration with Dr. Sabah Sadik, an Iraqi consultant psychiatrist based in the UK who joined the Iraq (MoH) as the National Advisor for Mental Health System leading the projects for development in 2004 by investing the Japanese and US funds of $6 M and $5 M, respectively (WHO, 2006a: WHO, 2006). These international (Kammel, 2007; Younis, 2008). The partnership with that international foreign expertise introduced an international action planning group that supported mental health service development in Iraq, which was described by some authors as a unique and successful model of inviting multidisciplinary teams from Iraq to propose service developments through training courses for the Iraqi psychiatrists in the US and the UK, hoping to implement those initiatives on their return (Al-Uzri et al., 2012). Those initiatives covered various mental health aspects, such as providing these community mental health workers with training and supervision in several evidence-based psychotherapies (Bolton, 2013), while a US-based IMC delegate claimed to improve medical education and community mental health planning by involving US military physicians, staffers from the SAMHSA, and many others. (Levin, 2008). Their professional activities included three-month specialty training in the UK and system-planning assistance and medical education in neighboring countries, in addition to attending the American Psychiatric Association (APA) annual meetings in the US. Many other meetings and forums were designed to improve medical education by implementing the UK medical models, however, the factual advances were minimal due to multiple factors.

6.4 Mental Health Education and Training

6.4.1 Undergraduate Education

Mental health education began with the Iraqi Royal College of Medicine in Baghdad in 1927, renamed the College of Medicine affiliated with the University of Baghdad after its establishment in 1956. Theoretical lectures on mental diseases were included for fourth-year students starting in 1929 (Fig. 5). Clinical training occurred et al.-Shaffa Mental Hospital and the Neuro-Psychiatry outpatient clinic, with tutoring by British lecturer Dr. Jack Abboudy and faculty members Dr. Moamer Al Shabender (1941), Dr. Saffa Al-Deen Hamid (1944), and Dr. Ali Kamal (1951). In 1953, a hospital ward was dedicated to mental health training, enhancing the learning experience (Younis, 2009a, 2009b). Presently, psychiatry is taught to fifth-year students through 38 one-hour lectures covering psychiatry over two semesters, plus three weeks of training in psychiatric wards and clinics. Fourth-year students receive approximately 28 one-hour lectures on Behavioral Science over the calendar year. Although a four-week psychiatry internship was planned, it was not fully implemented due to wartime needs. It is observed that training for other mental health professionals remains underdeveloped despite some international courses (Younis & Al Rubayee, 2018).

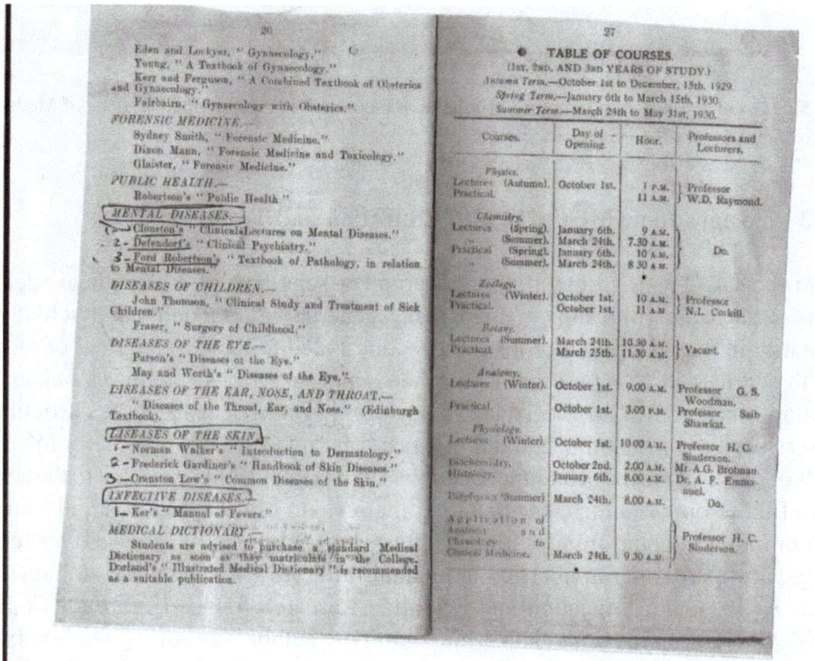

26

Eden and Lockyer, "Gynaecology."
Young, "A Textbook of Gynaecology."
Kerr and Ferguson, "A Combined Textbook of Obsterics and Gynaecology."
Fairbairn, "Gynaecology with Obsterics."

FORENSIC MEDICINE.—
Sydney Smith, "Forensic Medicine."
Dixon Mann, "Forensic Medicine and Toxicology."
Glaister, "Forensic Medicine."

PUBLIC HEALTH.—
Robertson's "Public Health."

MENTAL DISEASES.—
1- Clouston's "Clinical Lectures on Mental Diseases."
2- Defendorf's "Clinical Psychiatry."
3- Ford Robertson's "Textbook of Pathology, in relation to Mental Diseases."

DISEASES OF CHILDREN.—
John Thomson, "Clinical Study and Treatment of Sick Children."
Fraser, "Surgery of Childhood."

DISEASES OF THE EYE.—
Parson's "Diseases of the Eye."
May and Worth's "Diseases of the Eye."

DISEASES OF THE EAR, NOSE, AND THROAT.—
"Diseases of the Throat, Ear, and Nose." (Edinburgh Textbook).

DISEASES OF THE SKIN.—
1- Norman Walker's "Introduction to Dermatology."
2- Frederick Gardiner's "Handbook of Skin Diseases."
3- Cranston Low's "Common Diseases of the Skin."

INFECTIVE DISEASES.—
1- Ker's "Manual of Fevers."

MEDICAL DICTIONARY.—
Students are advised to purchase a standard Medical Dictionary as soon as they matriculate in the College. Dorland's "Illustrated Medical Dictionary" is recommended as a suitable publication.

27

TABLE OF COURSES.
(1st, 2nd, AND 3rd YEARS OF STUDY.)
Autumn Term.—October 1st to December, 15th, 1929.
Spring Term.—January 6th to March 15th, 1930.
Summer Term.—March 24th to May 31st, 1930.

Courses.	Day of Opening.	Hour.	Professors and Lecturers.
Physics.			
Lectures (Autumn).	October 1st.	1 P.M.	Professor W.D. Raymond.
Practical.		11 A.M.	
Chemistry.			
Lectures (Spring).	January 6th.	9 A.M.	Do.
" (Summer).	March 24th.	7.30 A.M.	
Practical (Spring).	January 6th.	10 A.M.	
" (Summer).	March 24th.	8 30 A.M.	
Zoology.			
Lectures (Winter).	October 1st.	10 A.M.	Professor N.L. Corkill.
Practical.	October 1st.	11 A.M.	
Botany.			
Lectures (Summer).	March 24th.	10.30 A.M.	Vacant.
Practical.	March 25th.	11.30 A.M.	
Anatomy.			
Lectures (Winter).	October 1st.	9.00 A.M.	Professor G. S. Woodman.
Practical.	October 1st.	3.00 P.M.	Professor Saib Shawkat.
Physiology.			
Lectures (Winter).	October 1st.	10 00 A.M.	Professor H. C. Sinderson.
Biochemistry.	October 2nd.	2.00 A.M.	Mr. A.G. Brotman.
Histology.	January 6th.	8.00 A.M.	Dr. A. F. Emmanuel.
[illegible] (Summer)	March 24th.	8.00 A.M.	Do.
Application of Anatomy and Physiology to Clinical Medicine.	March 24th.	9.30 A.M.	Professor H. C. Sinderson.

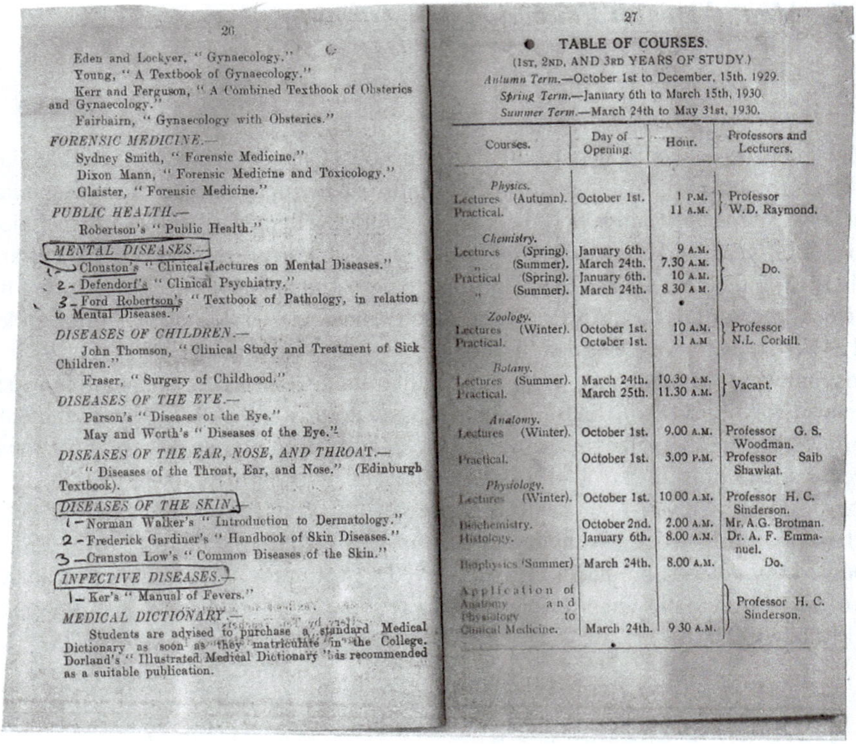

26

Eden and Lockyer, " Gynaecology."
Young, " A Textbook of Gynaecology."
Kerr and Ferguson, " A Combined Textbook of Obsterics and Gynaecology."
Fairbairn, " Gynaecology with Obsterics."

FORENSIC MEDICINE.—
Sydney Smith, " Forensic Medicine."
Dixon Mann, " Forensic Medicine and Toxicology."
Glaister, " Forensic Medicine."

PUBLIC HEALTH.—
Robertson's " Public Health."

MENTAL DISEASES.—
Clouston's " Clinical Lectures on Mental Diseases."
Defendorf's " Clinical Psychiatry."
Ford Robertson's " Textbook of Pathology, in relation to Mental Diseases."

DISEASES OF CHILDREN.—
John Thomson, " Clinical Study and Treatment of Sick Children."
Fraser, " Surgery of Childhood."

DISEASES OF THE EYE.—
Parson's " Diseases of the Eye."
May and Worth's " Diseases of the Eye."

DISEASES OF THE EAR, NOSE, AND THROAT.—
" Diseases of the Throat, Ear, and Nose." (Edinburgh Textbook).

DISEASES OF THE SKIN.—
Norman Walker's " Introduction to Dermatology."
Frederick Gardiner's " Handbook of Skin Diseases."
Cranston Low's " Common Diseases of the Skin."

INFECTIVE DISEASES.—
Ker's " Manual of Fevers."

MEDICAL DICTIONARY.—
Students are advised to purchase a standard Medical Dictionary as soon as they matriculate in the College. Dorland's " Illustrated Medical Dictionary " has recommended as a suitable publication.

27

TABLE OF COURSES.
(1st, 2nd, AND 3rd YEARS OF STUDY.)
Autumn Term.—October 1st to December, 15th. 1929.
Spring Term.—January 6th to March 15th, 1930.
Summer Term.—March 24th to May 31st, 1930.

Courses.	Day of Opening.	Hour.	Professors and Lecturers.
Physics.			
Lectures (Autumn).	October 1st.	1 P.M.	Professor W.D. Raymond.
Practical.		11 A.M.	
Chemistry.			
Lectures (Spring).	January 6th.	9 A.M.	Do.
" (Summer).	March 24th.	7.30 A.M.	
Practical (Spring).	January 6th.	10 A.M.	
" (Summer).	March 24th.	8 30 A.M.	
Zoology.			
Lectures (Winter).	October 1st.	10 A.M.	Professor N.L. Corkill.
Practical.	October 1st.	11 A.M	
Botany.			
Lectures (Summer).	March 24th.	10.30 A.M.	Vacant.
Practical.	March 25th.	11.30 A.M.	
Anatomy.			
Lectures (Winter).	October 1st.	9.00 A.M.	Professor G. S. Woodman.
Practical.	October 1st.	3.00 P.M.	Professor Saib Shawkat.
Physiology.			
Lectures (Winter).	October 1st.	10 00 A.M.	Professor H. C. Sinderson.
Biochemistry.	October 2nd.	2.00 A.M.	Mr. A.G. Brotman.
Histology.	January 6th.	8.00 A.M.	Dr. A. F. Emmanuel.
Biophysics (Summer)	March 24th.	8.00 A.M.	Do.
Application of Anatomy and Physiology to Clinical Medicine.	March 24th.	9 30 A.M.	Professor H. C. Sinderson.

Fig. 5 The curriculum of the Iraqi royal college of medicine, 1929 (Baghdad College of Medicine, Department of Archives, Baghdad, 2015)

6.4.2 Postgraduate Mental Health Education and Training

From the late 1930s to the 1980s, government scholarships for medical specializations abroad significantly trained many generations of qualified psychiatrists, primarily in the UK. These professionals contributed to the development of mental health services in Iraq by establishing new units in various provinces, enhancing existing standards of medical care, enriching psychiatric education curricula at universities, and promoting training for residents interested in psychiatry (Younis, 2009a). The war and the economic sanctions 1980–1988, 1990–2003, led to the cessation of these opportunities, necessitating the revamp of the education and training system into a national framework to address gaps in mental health services, especially with increasing numbers of individuals affected by war-related trauma. The Ministry of Higher Education and Scientific Research founded the Iraqi Council for Medical Specializations (ICMS) in 1986. The author was among the first batch to join the postgraduate training program of the Scientific Council of Psychiatry and obtained the degree from the Iraqi Board of Psychiatry in October 1988. Of 11 trainees, 10 graduated in October 1992, with only four currently working and living

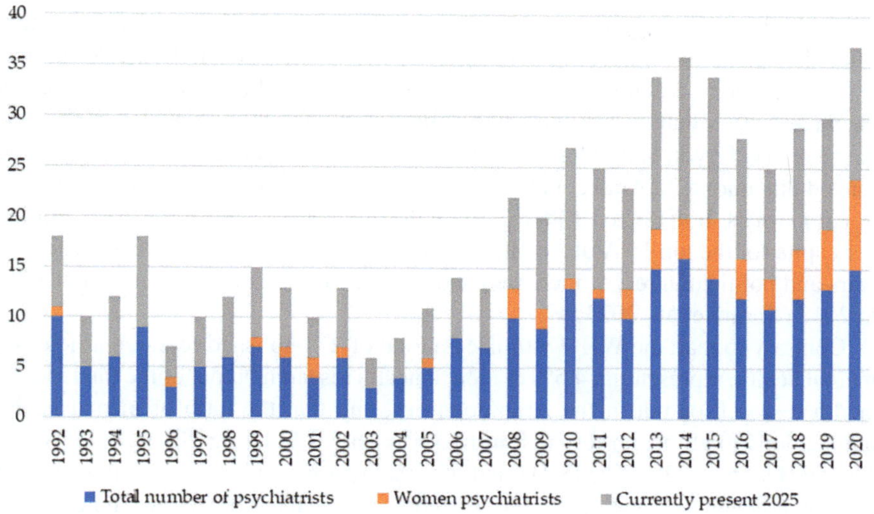

Fig. 6 Number of psychiatrists who graduated from the Iraqi and Arab board of psychiatry (1992–2020) currently working and living in Iraq (Hussein et al., 2025)

in Iraq (Iraqi Council for Medical Specializations [ICMS], 2025). Another opportunity was provided by the Council of Psychiatry and the Iraq Office of The Arab Board for Health Specializations (ABHS); both institutions have a comprehensive four-year training program in psychiatric centers, mainly in Baghdad, with two qualifying exams: primary and final. The author was the first Iraqi woman to qualify with the Arab Board of Psychiatry in 2000 (Iraq Office of The Arab Board for Health Specializations, 2025; Younis & Khunda, 2020). As of 2025, the total number of psychiatrists who graduated from the Iraqi and Arab Board of Psychiatry and who are currently working and living in Iraq is documented by ICMS and ABHS. After 2003, travelling abroad became unrestricted, allowing some Iraqi interns to continue their medical education in psychiatry in the US, the UK, Europe, or Arab countries independently. However, their numbers are not reported (Iraq Office of The Arab Board for Health Specializations, 2015; ICMS, 2025) (Fig. 6).

6.5 *Mental Health Research Activities*

Few published studies focused on mental health research in Arab countries, none in Iraq. Despite more psychiatrists, new universities and research centers, and internet services that aid international collaboration, quantitative and qualitative reviews remain lacking. Studies show that Arab countries have a low contribution to global mental health publications. However, the Gulf Cooperation Council countries are highly productive, with 408 indexed biomedical mental health research publications. Iraq contributed only 0.5% of the total mental health publications between 1987 and

2002 (Afifi, 2005). According to Karam et al., reviews of 3373 related articles identified the cumulative number of publications per $10 billion GDP during 2018; also, it was not among the top five producers in the Arab world and was not included in the three Arab countries with the highest number of mental health publications in the past century: Egypt, Kingdom of Saudi Arabia (KSA), and Lebanon. However, Iraq ranked 8th among 20 Arab countries with 77 articles; 62 were published in international journals. Iraq ranked 13th regarding the number of publications per 1 million per capita for the top 15 Arab countries yearly. Despite the adverse consequences of wars and political unrest, it increased and had the most significant jump from 1998 to 2018 (Karam et al., 2023).

Contrary to that, the WHO estimated a total of 27 published research articles on mental health, representing 4.5% of mental health research output of the total mental health research output in the Arab countries, and that the ratio of mental health publications to all health research in Iraq was only 2% during 2016–2020 (WHO, Mental Healths, 2020). The IMHS and other sources have identified the low number of mental health publications in Index Medicus journals as a negative indicator for mental health development in Iraq, calling for more epidemiological and national studies (Bolton, 2013; Sadik et al., 2010; WHO, 2006). The rise in research activities is due to more psychiatrists working in academia, access to Internet services, and board candidates needing to complete research for their psychiatry specialization degree.

7 Human Resources in Mental Health Services

7.1 Number of Psychiatrists

There is confusion about how many psychiatrists there are and the number per 100,000 people in different time zones. The reported total of 108 psychiatrists in 2008 (Younis, 2008; IPA, 2015) has often changed in international reports about mental health services in Iraq. Many of these reports relied on personal interviews, limited official documents, WHO representatives, and foreign NGOs visiting Iraq, which resulted in inconsistent and rarely updated information. For example, the WHO reported a total of 91 psychiatrists, with a ratio of is 0.3 psychiatrists for every 100,000 people in 2004 when Iraq's population was 25.85 million while the total number of psychiatrists was 108 during 1998–2000 (IPA, 2001; WHO, 2006b), a similar number of 90–100 was repeated in many other international studies over the years despite the rising number of interns and psychiatric specialists; also, the ratio of 0.1–0.3/100,000 population was not updated despite the growing Iraq population from 28.62 million in 2006 to 44.496 million in 2021 (Al-Uzri et al., 2012; Bolton, 2013; IMHS, 2006/7; Sharma & Piachaud, 2011). A recent article revealed the same total number of 100 psychiatrists with a ratio of 0.34/100,000 population during 2020 (Sadik, 2021). The WHO released an updated total number of 226 psychiatrists, equating to 0.57/100,000 population, when Iraq had a 42.12 million population (WHO, Mental Health Atlas, 2020). Furthermore, Okasha et al., noted a ratio of psychiatrists ranging from 0.2 to 0.5 per 100,000 population during the 1980s, dropping to 0.1 per 100,000 in 1998 due to the psychiatrist exodus caused by the Gulf War economic sanctions. In the 1990s, the Iraqi population was 23.05 million (Okasha et al., 2012). In contradiction to such figures, a total number of 178 psychiatrists with 0.4–0.12/100000 population was revealed by the Iraqi Parliament reports, which is a much lower ratio than the neighboring Gulf countries and lower than middle- and low-income Arab countries like Egypt (0.8/100000) and Jordan (1.04/100000) (The Iraqi Parliament, 2024). To elucidate such data, we searched the related websites, reviewed the available literature, and examined the graduation lists of the ICMS and the ABHS offices to count their total numbers; names were verified and matched with the records of the IPA. Currently, the total number of psychiatrists is 422, 245 consultants and specialists who graduated from ICMS, 1992–2024, or the ABHS, 2000–2024; on the other hand, there are 143 trainees in either of these programs. This total includes ten psychiatrists qualified by MRCPSYC, D.P.M. from the UK, and MS from Egypt, as well as five psychiatric practitioners. Additionally, nine specialists graduated from the Kurdish Board of Psychiatry between 2011 and 2024, and ten residents are currently in training stages, distributed across four governorates of the KRI. (Hussein et al., 2025, in press) According to the most recent census, the ratio of psychiatrists is 1.1 per 100,000, based on Iraq's population of 46,042,015 (World Meter, Iraq, 2025). Psychiatrists in Iraq have worked hard since the commencement of mental health services to provide psychiatric care in adverse work and life environments in state hospitals and private clinics.

7.2 *Other Mental Health Workers*

As well as psychiatrists, other mental health workers who are adequately trained are also beyond the international standard of care even in comparison with Arab countries; for example, the ratios of psychiatric nurses, psychologists, and social workers remained constant during 1998–2007: 0.1, 0.05, and 0.2/100,000 population, respectively (Okasha et al., 2012). The ratio of 2.09 psychiatric nurses/100,000 population in Iraq is lower than 5.1 psychiatric nurses/100,000 population reported by other middle-income countries and lower than 3.9/100,000 reported in low-income countries like Egypt, for example; psychologists and social workers have similar roles in mental health settings, representing 0.2, which is also lower than 1.6 reported in middle-income countries and 0.3 reported in the low-income countries, with a much lower rate than 10.7 reported in the high-income countries per 100,000 population (The Iraqi Parliament, 2024).

8 Mental Health Delays in Iraq

Despite the international support for developing mental health services after 2003, there many areas of shortcomings that were expected to be dealt through external fund and foreign expertise, summarized in the followings: there are lack of community residential facilities, community nursing, mental health insurance policy, mobile teams, and day treatment facilities, with no organizational integration unites mental hospitals and outpatient facilities (WHO, 2006). Specialized mental health services for women, war-traumatized, and IDPS have not been established yet despite the large number of such needy populations. Only four out of the twenty-five outpatient facilities dedicated to child and adolescent psychiatry have no available data on service utilization. The strategies of integrating mental health into primary health care are still at the minimal levels (WHO-Atlas, 2020; Younis, 2015). The suicide prevention strategies set by the MoH in 2017 have not been implemented yet, keeping in mind the rising rates of death by suicide and suicidal behavior (Younis, 2024). The Iraqi government ought to establish a new mental hospital with chronic cases and forensic services facilities since Al-Rashad Mental Hospital is the only large long-stay mental hospital since 1953 and could not meet the growing numbers of needy patients, and remote pastoral areas. Many literatures about mental health services were published by foreign authors or Iraqis living abroad for decades based on their short visits to Iraq, with poor access to internal documents and the inside mental health professionals making it challenging to provide a clear picture of the country's turmoil that influenced the quality and quantity of psychiatric care ever. Some of the decided strategies came out with negative consequences, for instance, foreign experts, in collaboration with mental health authorities from the Moh, decided to prohibit the practice of plain ECT in Iraq to be replaced by the modified practice throughout the country. Consequently, an effort to enhance mental health care led to the closure of the ECT unit et al.-Rashad Mental Hospital. This decision limited ECT access to just two hospitals in Baghdad with general anesthesia, burdening patients and families who must endure long transfers and frequent delays (Saied et al., 2023; Younis & Arafat, 2022).

9 Conclusions

Iraq is recovering from years of conflict, but its mental health challenges persist due to harsh living conditions and political unrest. Addressing these issues requires a comprehensive mental health policy, including community-based initiatives, trauma-informed care, telehealth services, culturally sensitive therapies, education, workplace mental health programs, resilience-building, peer support networks, and stakeholder collaboration. Regular evaluation and monitoring are crucial for effectiveness. Iraq's historical contributions to psychiatry demonstrate its intellectual and cultural foundation for a world-class mental health system. A multifaceted strategy, considering international and internal conflicts, cultural factors, and substance abuse, is needed to improve Iraq's health system. There is a need to establish additional mental hospitals specifically for long-term admissions, mental health units in general hospitals, mental health facilities within primary care units, and community services. MHA, mental health research, and postgraduate training programs should also be activated and developed.

References

Abbas, M. J., Alhemiary, N., Razaq, E. A., Naosh, S., & Appleby, L. (2018). The Iraqi national study of suicide: Report on suicide data in Iraq in 2015 and 2016. *Journal of Affective Disorders, 229*, 56–62. https://doi.org/10.1016/j.jad.2017.12.037

Afifi, M. M. (2005). Mental health publications from the Arab world cited in PubMed, 1987–2002. *Eastern Mediterranean Health Journal, 11*(3), 319–328. https://iris.who.int/handle/10665/116948

Ahmed, H. M., Abdulla, S. A., Al-Tawil, N., Mishkin, K., & Al-Tawil, N., Sr. (2024a). Maternal health experiences, depression, and anxiety among refugees and displaced persons in Iraq: A cross-sectional study. *Cureus, 16*(8), Article e67645. https://doi.org/10.7759/cureus.67645

Ahmed, S. M., Sabre, F., Naif, A. A. A., Hamad, A. H., Ahmed, S. K., Abdullah, A. Y., Qurbani, K., & Hussein, S. (2024b). Exploring young adults' reluctance to engage with psychiatric hospitals in Erbil, Iraq: Identifying barriers to psychiatric care. *Cereus, 16*(6), Article e62164. https://doi.org/10.7759/cureus.62164

Al-Abbudi, S. J. (2016). Causal beliefs of schizophrenia among sample of Iraqi schizophrenic inpatients' families in Iraq. *Iraqi Journal of Medical Sciences, 14*(3), 237. https://doi.org/10.32474/LOJMS.2020.04.00019

Al-Abbudi, S. J. R. (2018). Prodromal symptoms and signs of first episode schizophrenia in Iraq. *Journal of Psychiatry and Mental Illness, 1*(1), 102.

Al-Alwan, A. (2004). Health in Iraq: The current situation, our vision for the future, and areas of work. Baghdad, Iraqi Ministry of Health. https://moh.gov.iq

Al Ansari, M., Dawson, A., & Conigrave, K. (2022). Alcohol among young people in Iraq: A systematic scoping review. *Discover Psychology, 2*, 16. https://doi.org/10.1007/s44202-022-00024-8

Al-Haidary, A. & Al-Badri, S. (2015). Deliberate self-harm cases presented to the emergency unit of al-Hussein general teaching hospital in Karbala/Iraq. *AlQadisiyah Medical Journal, 11*(20), 92–97. https://doi.org/10.28922/qmj.2015.11.20.92-97

Al-Hamzawi, A. O., Bruffaerts, R., Bromet, E. J., AlKhafaji, A. M., & Kessler, R. C. (2015). The epidemiology of major depressive episodes in the Iraqi general population. *PLoS ONE, 10*(7), Article e0131937. https://doi.org/10.1371/journal.pone.0131937

Al-Hasnawi, S., Sadik, S., Rasheed, M., Baban, A., Al-Alak, M. M., Othman, A. Y., et al. (2009). The prevalence and correlates of DSM-IV disorders in the Iraq Mental Health Survey (IMHS). World Psychiatry. 2009; 8:97–109.

Al-Hemiery, N., Dabbagh, R., Hashim, M. T., Al-Hasnawi, S., Abutiheen, A., Abdulghani, E. A., & Rawson, R. A. (2017). Self-reported substance use in Iraq: Findings from the Iraqi National Household Survey of Alcohol and Drug Use. *Addiction, 112*(8), 1470–1479. https://doi.org/10.1111/add.13300

Al-Hilfi, T. K., Lafta, R., & Burnham, G. (2013). Health services in Iraq. *The Lancet, 381*(9870), 939–948. https://doi.org/10.1016/S0140-6736(13)60320-7

Al-Issa, I., & Al-Issa, B. (1970). Psychiatric problems in a developing country: Iraq. *International Journal of Social Psychiatry, 16*(1), 15–22. https://doi.org/10.1177/002076407001600102

Al-Nasrawi, A. (2001). Iraq: Economic sanctions and consequences, 1990–2000. *Journal of Third World Quarterly, 22*, 205–218. https://www.jstor.org/stable/3993407

Al-Omari, O., Valsaraj, B. P., Khatatbeh, M., Al-Jubouri, M. B., Emam, M., Al Hashmi, I., & Mohamed, N. (2023). Self and public stigma towards mental illnesses and its predictors among university students in 11 Arabic-speaking countries: A multi-site study. *International Journal of Mental Health Nursing, 32*(6), 1745–1755. https://doi.org/10.1111/inm.13206

Al-Rudaini, R. S., Awad, Z. W., Attalla, M., Faris Al-lami. (2024). Integration of mental health services into Primary healthcare, Iraq: Key findings and recommendations. *International Journal of Advanced Community Medicine, 7*(2), 01–06. https://doi.org/10.33545/comed.2024.v7.i2a.303

Al-Samarrai, M., & Hussein, M. (2000). Parasuicide with self-poisoning in an emergency department in Baghdad. *The Arab Journal of Psychiatry, 11*(2), 113–121.

Al-Samarrai, M., & Hussein, M. (2002). A study of the pattern of psychiatric consultation: A general hospital psychiatric outpatient clinic in Baghdad. *The Arab Journal of Psychiatry, 13*(1), 55–63.

Al-Shaikhly, S., & Cui, J. (2017). Education in Iraq, education system profiles. Retrieved March 13, 2025, from https://www.scholaro.com/pro/countries/iraq/education-system

Al Shelali, M., AL Ibrahim, H., Alomar, N., Pandi-Perumal, S. R., Seeman, M. V., & Jahrami, H. (2024). The good, the bad, and the ugly of faith healers and psychiatric illnesses: A systematic review of the literature in the Arab world. *Journal of Religion and Health, 63*(2), 857–876.https://doi.org/10.1007/s10943-023-01898

Al-Uzri, M., Abed, R., & Abbas, M. J. (2012). Rebuilding mental health services in Iraq. *International Psychiatry, 9*(3), 58–60. https://doi.org/10.1192/S1749367600003209

ArabPsyNet. Fakhry Al Dabbagh retrieved 13 March 2025 from haattp://arabpsynet.com›Documents›

Baghdad Al-Russafa Health Directory. The opening of Al Attah Centre for Drug Dependence 2022. Retrieved April 1, 2022, from https://www.brhd.gov.iq

Bazzoui, W., & Al-Issa, I. (1966). Psychiatry in Iraq. *British Journal of Psychiatry, 112*(489), 827. https://doi.org/10.1192/bjp.112.489.827

Bolton, P. (2013). Mental health in Iraq: Issues and challenges. *The Lancet, 381*(9870), 879–881.

Burnham, G., Lafta, R., Doocy, S. H., & Roberts, L. (2006). Mortality after the 2003 invasion of Iraq: A cross-sectional cluster sample survey. *The Lancet, 368*(9545), 1421–1428.

Central Bank of Iraq. (CBI). *History of the Central Bank of Iraq*. Retrieved March 13, 2025, from http://ww.cbi.iq/?pid=home&lang=en

Fekih-Romdhane, F., Jahrami, H., Stambouli, M., et al. (2013). Cross-cultural comparison of mental illness stigma and help-seeking attitudes: A multinational population-based study from 16 Arab countries and 10,036 individuals. *Social Psychiatry Psychiatric Epidemiology, 58*, 641–656. https://doi.org/10.1007/s00127-022-02403-x

Freh, F. M. (2016). PTSD, depression, and anxiety among young people in Iraq, one decade after the American invasion. *Traumatology, 22*(1), 56.

Hamid, H. I., & Everett, A. (2007). Developing Iraq's mental health policy. *Psychiatric Services, 58*(10), 1355–1357. https://doi.org/10.1176/ps.2007.58.10.1355

Harvard Study Team. (1991). The effect of the Gulf crises on the children of Iraq: Special report. *New England Journal of Medicine, 325*(13), 977–980. https://doi.org/10.1056/NEJM199109263251330

Humaidi, N. S. (2006). Resettlement prospects for inpatients at Al Rashad mental hospital. *Journal of Muslim Mental Health, 1*(2), 177–183. https://doi.org/10.1080/15564900600980798

Hummadi, B. F., Firas, Al-Kadhimi, F. A., & Al-Mashhadani, G. A. (2020). Criminal responsibility among murderers presented to the forensic committee in Al-Rashad training hospital/forensic department, 20162017. *Indian Journal of Forensic Medicine & Toxicology, 14*(1). https://doi.org/10.37506/v14/i1/2020/ijfmt/192942

Hussein, N. A., Younis, M. S., & Saied, A. A. (2025). *Women psychiatrists in Iraq: An updated briefing*. In press.

Iraq Family Health Survey Study Group (IFHS). (2008). Violence-related mortality in Iraq from 2002 to 2006. *New England Journal of Medicine, 358*(5), 484–493. https://doi.org/10.1056/NEJMsa0707782

Iraq Office of The Arab Board for Health Specializations (ABHS). Retrieved January 13, 2025, from https://www.abhs.edu.iq

Jaff, D., Abas, N., Leatherman, S., Seidi, P., & Ankamah, D. (2024). Barriers to mental healthcare in the Kurdistan region of Iraq: Practitioner perspectives. *Medicine, Conflict and Survival*, 1–12. https://doi.org/10.1080/13623699.2024.2437565

Kammel, K. P. (2007). Rebuilding the mental health system in Iraq in the context of transitional justice. *DePaul Journal of Health Care Law, 11*, 369. http://hdl.handle.net/10822/957049

Karam, E. G., Okasha, A., Trojanovic, N., et al. (2023). Research in mental health in the Arab-speaking world, 1920 to 2018. *Middle East Current Psychiatry, 30*, 109. https://doi.org/10.1186/s43045-023-00382-6

Khalifa, N., & Hardie, T. (2005). Possession and jinn. *Journal of the Royal Society of Medicine, 89*(8), 351–353. https://doi.org/10.1177/014107680509800805

Khatib, H. E., Al yafei, A., & Shaikh, M. (2023). Understanding experiences of mental health help-seeking in Arab populations around the world: a systematic review and narrative synthesis. *BMC Psychiatry, 23*, 324. https://doi.org/10.1186/s12888-023-04827-4

Laborte, R. (2005). Iraqi doctors tell of health crimes. *British Medical Journal, 331*(30), 252–255. https://doi.org/10.1136/bmj.331.7511.252-b

Lafta, R., Aflouk, N., Dhiaa, S., Lyles, E., & Burnham, G. (2016). Needs of internally displaced women and children in Baghdad, Karbala, and Kirkuk, Iraq. *Plos Currents, 8*, 1–8. https://doi.org/10.1371/currents.dis.fefc1fc62c02ecaedec2c

Lafta, R. K., & Al-Nuaimi, M. A. (2019). War or health: A four-decade armed conflict in Iraq. *Medicine, Conflict and Survival, 35*(3), 209–226. https://doi.org/10.1080/13623699.2019.1670431

Lafta, R., Al-Nuaimi, M. A., & Burnham, G. (2018). Injury and death during the ISIS occupation of Mosul and its liberation: Results from a 40-cluster household survey. *PLoS Medicine, 15*(5), Article e1002567. https://doi.org/10.1371/journal.pmed.1002567

Levin, A. (2006). Iraq tackles daunting task of rebuilding MH system. *Psychiatric News, 41*(5), 5–5. https://doi.org/10.1176/pn.41.5.0005

Levin, A. (2008). Psychiatry in Iraq on long, slow road to recovery. *Psychiatric News, 43*(12), 15–26. https://doi.org/10.1176/pn.43.12.0015

Ministry of Health (MoH). *The national adviser for mental health*. Retrieved February 25, 2025, from https://moh.gov.iq

Ministry of Interior. The Directory of Drug Control. Retrieved March 3, 2025, from https://moi.gov.iq

Ministry of Justice, Iraq. (1969). Statutory Notice, The Penal Code with amendment No. (111. https://uoajournal.com › user.

Muslim, J. K., & Chaleby, K. (2007). The insanity defense in Iraq. *Journal of Muslim Mental Health, 2*(1), 57–64. https://doi.org/10.1080/15564900701238575

Muzil, J. A., Abdulwahid, D. A., Abed, A. H., & Kammad, Z. A. (2023). Substance abuse in Iraq, quantifying the picture. *Journal of Population Therapeutics and Clinical Pharmacology, 30*(12), 302–313.

Okasha, A., Karam, E., & Okasha, T. (2012). Mental health services in the Arab world. *World Psychiatry, 11*(1), 52–54. https://doi.org/10.1016/j.wpsyc.2012.01.008

Omar, R. M., Ahmed, S. K., & Haji, R. M. (2024). Attitudes of university students towards people with mental health disorders: a survey-based study. *Discover Psychology, 4*, 97. https://doi.org/10.1007/s44202-024-00220-8

Parys, M. (2014). "Introduction to mental illness in Ancient Mesopotamia." Conference Paper. 10. No. 2.1. 4830-1443. https://doi.org/10.13140/2.1.4830.1443

Rawaf, S., Bahri, S., Alsheikh, G., & Mahgoub, A. (2004). Public health in Iraq. *Public Health Medicine, 5*(2), 76–83.

Relief Web. (2000). Briefing on Northern Governorates: Hospitals, Retrieved March 13, 2025, from Iraq -b report, https://reliefweb.int

Roberts, L., et al. (2004). Mortality before and after the 2003 invasion of Iraq: Cluster sample survey. *The Lancet, 364*(9448), 1857–1864.

Sadik. S., Abdulrahman, S., Bradley, M., & Jenkins, R. (2011). Integrating mental health into primary health care in Iraq. *Mental Health in Family Medicine, 8*(1), 39–49. PMCID: PMC3134212

Sadik, A. (2021). A snapshot of Iraqi psychiatry. *BJPsych International, 18*(1), 9–11. https://doi.org/10.1192/bji.2020.19

Sadik, S., Bradley, M., Al-Hasoon, S., & Jenkins, R. (2010). Public perception of mental health in Iraq. *International Journal of Mental Health Systems, 4*, 26, https://doi.org/10.1186/1752-4458-4-26

Sarhan, W (2017). The contribution of Arab Islamic civilization to mental health. *The Editorial Assistants–Jordan, 28*(1), 57–66. https://doi.org/10.12816/0046445

Saeed, B. A., Shabila, N. P., & Aziz, A. J. (2021). Stress and anxiety among physicians during the COVID-19 outbreak in the Iraqi Kurdistan Region: An online survey. *PLoS ONE, 16*(6), Article e0253903.

Saeed, S. I., Ahmed Sr, J. O., Kakamad, K., & Najmadden, Z. (2024). Abu Zayd Ahmed ibn Sahl Al-Balkhi (850–934): A pioneer in the field of psychotherapy and mental health. *Cureus, 16*(8). https://doi.org/10.7759/cureus.67998

Saied, A. A., Ahmed, S. K., Metwally, A. A., & Aiash, H. (2023). Iraq's mental health crises: A way forward? *Lancet, 402*(10409), 1235–1236. https://doi.org/10.1016/S0140-6736(23)01283-7

Sharma, S., & Piachaud, J. (2011). Iraq and mental health policy: A post-invasion analysis. *Intervention, 9*(3), 32–344.

Sharquie, K., Al Noaimi, A., Younis, M., & Sultani, B. (2014). Kerosene-induced panniculitis in Iraqi patients. *Journal of Cosmetics, Dermatological Sciences and Applications, 4*, 323–328. https://doi.org/10.4236/jcdsa.2014.45042

Stewart, B., Lafta, R., Al Shatari, S., Cherewick, M., Burnham, G., Hagopian, A., et al. (2015). Burns in Baghdad from 2003–2014: Results of a randomized household cluster survey. *Burns, 42*(1), 48–55. https://doi.org/10.1016/j.burns.2015.10.002

Taher, T. M. J., Al-Fadhil, S. A. L., Abutiheen, A. A., Ghazi, H. F., & Abood, N. S. (2021). Prevalence of obsessive-compulsive disorder (OCD) among Iraqi undergraduate medical students in time of COVID-19 pandemic. *Middle East Current Psychiatry, 28*, 8. https://doi.org/10.1186/s43045-021-00086-9

The Iraqi Parliament, Office of Parliamentary Research, A Study Report (2024). *The gaps in mental health services in Iraq*. Retrieved February 25, 2025, from haattps://iq.parliament.iq›uploads›2024/05

The Iraqi Psychiatric Association (IPA). Retrieved April 1, 2025, from www.iq-pa.com

The Scientific Council of Psychiatry, Iraqi Council for Medical Specializations (ICMS). Retrieved January 13, 2025, from https://www.iraqiboard.edu.iq

United Nations Security Council (UNSC). (1995). *Resolution 986*. Retrieved April 1, 2025, from http://www.securitycouncilreport.org/undocuments/Iraq%20SRES986.php

Webster, P. C. (2011). Iraq's health system is yet to heal from the ravages of war. *The Lancet, 78*(9794), 863–866. Available at: The Lancet.

Wikipedia, Iraq. Retrieved February 12, 2025, from https://en.wikipedia.org

World Bank. (2025). *Country classification, Iraq*. Retrieved January 1, from https://data.worldbank.org

World Health Organization. (2006a). WHO–AIMS Report on Mental Health System in Iraq, Geneva: WHO. http://www.who.int/mental_health/evidence/iraq_who_aims_report.pdf

World Health Organization. (2006b). Country Office in Iraq, Eastern Mediterranean Regional Office (EMRO), Bi-weekly Bulletin. Retrieved April 13, 2025, from http://www.emro.who.int

World Health Organization (WHO). *Iraq mental health survey (IMHS)*. 2006/7 Report. https://applications.emro.who.int

World Health Organization. (WHO). *Mental health atlas 2020 country profile: Iraq*. Retrieved April 1, 2025, from https://www.who.int/publications/m/item/mental-health-atlas-irq-2020-country-profile

World Health Organization Eastern Mediterranean Regional Office (WHO EMRO). (2020). *An increasing number of suicide cases in Iraq worries public health experts amid COVID-19 pandemic*. Retrieved April 13, 2025, from http://www.emro.who.int.irq, Iraq news.

World Health Organization. (2023). Mental disorders. Geneva: World Health Organization. https://www.who.int/newsroom/factsheets/detail/mental-disorders

World meter. Iraq population. (2025). Retrieved January 28, 2025, from https://www.worldometers.info

Younis, M. S. (2003). Application of QOL–Brief in Iraq. *Journal of the Arab Board of Medical Specializations, 5*(4), 103–107.

Younis, M. S. (2005). *History of psychiatry in Iraq*. Data presented in the 13th world congress of psychiatry. Cairo 2005, articles. https://pmc.ncbi.nlm.nih.gov

Younis, M. S. (2008). A view of mental health in system Iraq, Route and challenges. *The Arab Journal of Psychiatry, 19*(1), 80–66, em Ar | IMEMR | ID: emr-85770.

Younis, M. S. (2009a). Historical highlights on mental health education in Iraq. *Journal of the Faculty of Medicine Baghdad, 51*(3), 272–275. https://doi.org/10.32007/jfacmedbagdad.5131124

Younis, M. S. (2009b). The foundation of modern psychiatry in Iraq: exploring personal archives. *AJP, 20*(1), 78–83. http://arabjournalpsychiatry.com

Younis, M. S. (2015). Tears of Ishtar: Women's mental health in Iraq. *The Lancet Psychiatry, 2*(2), 119–121. https://doi.org/10.1016/S2215-0366(14)00061-3

Younis, M. S. (2024). Suicidal behavior in Iraq. In *Suicidal Behavior in Muslim Majority Countries: Epidemiology, Risk Factors, and Prevention* (pp. 115–131). Springer Nature Singapore. https://doi.org/10.1007/978-981-97-2519-9_9

Younis, M. S., Abdullah, A. S., & Arafat, S. Y. (2023). Posttraumatic stress disorder among university students of Mosul, Iraq: An after effect of war atrocities. *Intervention Journal of Mental Health and Psychosocial Support in Conflict-Affected Areas, 21*(1), 9–13. https://doi.org/10.4103/intv.intv_16_21

Younis, M. S., Al-Naaimi, A. S. (2006). Cross-sectional study of psychiatric outpatients clinic in Baghdad university hospital over the year 2003. *Journal of the Arab Board Medical Specializations, 8*(1), 85–87. https://www.researchgate.net/publication/362112666

Younis, M. S., Al-Rubayee, A. F. (2018). Attitude of medical students university of Baghdad towards psychiatry: Clinical significance and as a future career. *Journal of the Faculty of Medicine Baghdad, 60*(4). https://doi.org/10.32007/med.1936/jfacmedbagdad.v60i4.8

Younis, M. S., Anwer, A. H., & Hussain, H. Y. (2021). Stigmatizing attitude and reflections towards mental illness a community setting, population-based approach, Baghdad City 2020. *International Journal of Social Psychiatry, 67*(5), 461–466. https://doi.org/10.1177/0020764020961797

Younis, M. S., & Arafat, S. M. Y. (2022). Historical highlights on electroconvulsive therapy practice in Iraq: A brief narrative. *The Journal of ECT, 38*(3), 151–155. https://doi.org/10.1097/YCT.0000000000000824

Younis, M. S., & Aswad, A. M. (2018). The impact of war and economic sanctions on the mental health system in Iraq from 1990 to 2003: A preliminary report. *Intervention, 16*(1), 54–58. https://doi.org/10.1097/WTF.0000000000000144

Younis, M. S., Kamal, M. M., & Arafat, S. M. Y. (2025). Suicidal ideation among persons with psychiatric disorders: A cross-sectional study at outpatient clinics in Iraq. *Journal of Health Science Reports, 5*(8), Article e70517. https://doi.org/10.1002/hsr2.70517

Younis, M. S., & Khunda, D. (2020). Maha Sulaiman Younis: A personal history of psychiatry in Iraq through war and conflict. *Journal of Global Psychiatry, 3*(2), 1–6. https://doi.org/10.2478/gp-2020-0017

Younis, M. S., & Lafta, R. K. (2014). Working in a conflict region: A total year work load of a psychiatry-neurology outpatient clinic in Baghdad. *American Journal of Bioterrorism, Biosecurity and Biodefense, 1*(1), 1–4.

Younis, M. S., Lafta, R. K., Dhiaa, S. (2019). Faith healers are taking over the role of psychiatrists in Iraq. *Qatar Medical Journal, 13.* https://doi.org/10.5339/qmj.2019.13

Younis, A. A., & Moselhy, H. F. (2009a). A nation under siege: The 15-year outcome of Iraqi patients with schizophrenia in Babylon, Iraq. *Journal of Mental Health, 18*(5), 398–404. https://doi.org/10.3109/09638230902968266

Younis, A. A. R., & Moselhy, H. M. (2009b). Benzhexol dependence resulting from self-medication for intermittent explosive disorders. *International Journal of Psychiatry in Clinical Practice, 13*(1), 11–15. https://doi.org/10.1080/13651500802192421

Younis, M. S., Al-Noaimi, A. S., Zaidan, Z. A., Al-Rubayie, A. F., Al-Farsi, Y., Al-Zakwani, I., & Al-Adawi, S. (2013). Clinical and demographic profile of attendees at Baghdad's walk-in psychiatric clinic. *Oman Medical Journal, 28*(5), 365–370. https://doi.org/10.5001/omj.2013.104

Chapter 6
Mental Health Services in Jordan

Mohammed Qutishat and Majdi Al-Hadidi

Abstract This comprehensive overview examines the state of mental health services in Jordan, a nation grappling with significant mental health challenges exacerbated by demographic factors, including a high refugee population and complex sociopolitical dynamics. The mental health landscape has evolved from traditional healing practices to a more structured system influenced by historical developments and governmental policies. Key statistics indicate a substantial rise in mental disorders, with anxiety and depression being the most common. While Jordan's healthcare system boasts advanced infrastructure and a commitment to integrating mental health into primary care, severe gaps remain, including underfunding, a shortage of qualified professionals, and pervasive stigma surrounding mental illness. Innovative approaches, community initiatives, and international collaborations show promise in enhancing mental health services. Addressing barriers such as financial constraints and societal stigma is crucial for improving accessibility and quality of care, ultimately promoting better mental health outcomes for both refugees and local populations.

Keywords Mental health · Jordan · Middle East · Services · History

1 Country Profile

Jordan, officially known as the Hashemite Kingdom of Jordan, is a landlocked country in the Middle East, bordered by Israel and Palestine to the west, Syria to the north, Iraq to the east, and Saudi Arabia to the south (Bank, 2019). The country features a diverse landscape, including deserts, mountains, and the iconic Jordan Rift Valley.

M. Qutishat (✉)
Community and Mental Health Department, College of Nursing, Sultan Qaboos University, Muscat, Sultanate of Oman
e-mail: mohqut@squ.edu.om

M. Al-Hadidi
Health Nursing, Faculty of Nursing, Al-Zaytoonah University of Jordan, Amman, Jordan
e-mail: m.alhadidi@zuj.edu.jo

S. Al-Huseini and S. M. Y. Arafat (eds.), *Mental Health Care in the Middle East*, South Asian Perspectives in Mental Health and Psychology ,
https://doi.org/10.1007/978-981-95-0461-9_6

The capital, Amman, is in the north-central region and is the nation's political, economic, and cultural epicenter (Bank, 2019; Erkekoğlu & Madi, 2018).

As of recent estimates, Jordan is home to approximately 11.3 million people, with a significant demographic proportion being young individuals under 30 (Csicsmann, 2024; Marwene, 2024). The population is ethnically diverse, comprising Arabs, Circassians, and Chechens (Sharnoff, 2024). A notable characteristic of Jordan's demographic landscape is the substantial influx of refugees, particularly from neighboring countries like Syria and Palestine, significantly influencing the nation's multicultural dynamics (Hoffman, 2024).

2 Health Care System in Jordan

Jordan's healthcare system is divided between public/semi-public and private sectors, offering hospitals, clinics, pharmacies, and other support services. With more than 106 hospitals and 12,081 beds serving the country, the public sector provides most healthcare services in Jordan (67%) (Council, 2015). While Jordan's hospital bed rate of 18 per 10,000 people is higher than some neighboring Arab countries, it falls below the global average. It is considered insufficient to meet the current needs of a growing population and the influx of refugees, straining existing resources (Council, 2015; Nazer & Tuffaha, 2017).

In urban and rural areas, Jordan's healthcare system offers readily available primary care services, including vaccinations, maternal and child health care, and chronic disease management. However, a significant weakness is the limited and largely unaffordable private home healthcare options (Alduraidi et al., 2021; Nazer & Tuffaha, 2017). This lack of alternative care forces patients to remain in acute care facilities for prolonged periods, putting considerable strain on resources, especially as the country's aging population increases (Alduraidi et al., 2021). This situation highlights the critical need for long-term care facilities. The system is further complicated by relying heavily on international aid and non-governmental organizations (NGOs) for essential support. For instance, the United Nations Relief and Works Agency (UNRWA) has provided crucial Healthcare to Palestinian refugees since 1950, serving over 1 million people. UNRWA assists these refugees in accessing hospital care by contracting beds or offering partial cost reimbursement at public and private facilities. This dependence underscores the need for more sustainable domestic healthcare solutions to address the growing needs of the nation's overall population (Alduraidi et al., 2021; Nazer & Tuffaha, 2017).

3 Historical Background of Mental Health Services Development

Mental health in Jordan is a significant concern, with prevalence rates of mental illness estimated to be high, potentially as high as 20% of the population (roughly 1.75 million people). Studies show a high prevalence of mental disorders, particularly anxiety and depression, across the region (Al-Qerem et al., 2024). This is further complicated by the fact that Jordan, like other countries in the Eastern Mediterranean, experiences a higher burden of mental health disorders than the global average. A notable trend is that, the highest incidence is among adults aged 25–49 (Al-Qerem et al., 2024). The situation is exacerbated by the presence of complex emergencies like food shortages and war, which are linked to increased mental health issues. These findings underscore a pressing need for increased research and resources to address mental health in Jordan (Charara et al., 2017).

Mental health care in Jordan has deep historical roots influenced by cultural, religious, and social factors. In ancient times, mental health issues were frequently attributed to supernatural causes or spiritual possessions (Musa, 2024). Traditional healing practices involving religious rituals and herbal remedies were predominant. The roles of faith healers, community leaders, and family networks were crucial in addressing mental health concerns (Rayan, 2024).

3.1 Ottoman Era

During the Ottoman Empire, which lasted until the early twentieth century, some organization of care for individuals with mental health issues was initiated. However, this care was largely informal and primarily reliant on family and community support. The understanding of mental illnesses at the time was limited, leading to significant social stigma and marginalization of individuals with mental health disorders.

3.2 British Mandate Period

The British Mandate (1921–1946) marked a significant turning point in Jordan's mental health approach. British authorities initiated a gradual transition from informal community care to more structured forms of medical treatment, establishing the first psychiatric hospitals. Despite these efforts, resources remained scarce, and most care was confined to institutionalized patients.

3.3 Post-independence Developments

After gaining independence in 1946, the Jordanian government began to formalize mental health services, recognizing the need for better treatment and support for individuals suffering from mental illnesses. The establishment of the *Jordanian Ministry of Health* (JMH) and later the *Department of Mental Health* aimed to organize and deliver mental health services nationwide.

3.4 The 1980s and 1990s: Expanding Services

The 1980s and 1990s reflected a shift toward community-based mental health care, emphasizing integrating mental health services into primary health care. In 1993, the JMH implemented its first national mental health strategy to address the population's mental health needs by enhancing community awareness, prevention programs, and establishing outpatient clinics. Additionally, the government emphasized mental health education and reduced stigma.

3.5 Mental Health Policy in Jordan

Jordan's mental health is guided by the 2011 National Mental Health Policy, which was updated and deemed relevant in 2016. This policy was the basis for the 2018–2021 National Mental Health and Substance Use Action Plan. A progress report is anticipated for 2020 to evaluate the plan's implementation, identify areas needing improvement, and help create a new action plan (WHO, 2020).

The policy and plan prioritize integrating mental health services into primary Healthcare (PHC). This includes early detection, basic interventions, medication, referrals, and follow-up, delivered by trained PHC staff like family doctors, general practitioners, and nurses, aligned with the WHO guidelines. The plan explicitly targets the implementation of mhGAP in 80 primary care centers and integrates mhGAP training into pre-service medical and nursing education (WHO, 2020). The policy aims to bolster mental health services at secondary and tertiary levels. Secondary care should be available in all governorates, including acute inpatient units, outpatient clinics, and community mental health centers. The plan outlines the creation of three additional inpatient units, nine community mental health centers, and nationwide outpatient clinics. Tertiary care is to be reorganized (WHO, 2020). New admissions to tertiary facilities will be phased out in favor of discharge plans recommending alternative care, including family care. Resource redistribution, particularly for beds and specialists, is planned for tertiary to secondary care hospitals (WHO, 2020). Currently, mental health is not addressed by dedicated legislation but by provisions within the Public Health Law (2008) and the Persons with Disabilities

Act (2017). These laws cover involuntary treatment and free care for citizens with mental health conditions, respectively (WHO, 2020).

4 Epidemiology of Mental Disorders

The Global Burden of Disease (GBD) 2021 study reveals a significant and alarming increase in the prevalence of mental disorders in Jordan between 1990 and 2021. The total number of mental disorder cases increased by a substantial 279.8%, rising from 514,234 to 1,953,087. This rise was particularly pronounced across various categories, including other mental disorders (376.3%), other drug use disorders (374.5%), schizophrenia (358.6%), depressive disorders (327.0%), and anxiety disorders (326.2%) (Altobaishat et al., 2025). By 2021, anxiety disorders, depressive disorders, and other mental disorders were the most prevalent conditions, highlighting a pressing need for increased access to mental health resources and interventions. The study also reveals substantial gender disparities, with women consistently demonstrating higher prevalence rates for many mental health conditions (Altobaishat et al., 2025). Further investigation into risk factors like behavioral issues, bullying, childhood trauma, and substance use is crucial for developing effective prevention and treatment strategies.

This increased prevalence underscores the urgent need for targeted mental health interventions in Jordan. The substantial rise across various diagnostic categories indicates a complex and multifaceted problem requiring a comprehensive approach. Key findings include significant gender disparities in prevalence, with women experiencing higher rates for many mental disorders. Identifying and addressing risk factors like behavioral issues, bullying, childhood trauma, and substance use is vital for designing effective prevention and treatment programs, particularly considering the substantial impact on healthy life years lost (Altobaishat et al., 2025).

4.1 Suicide in Jordan

In Jordan, a Middle Eastern nation with about 11.5 million residents, the suicide mortality rate is estimated at 3.7 per 100,000. This rate is significantly lower than the global average but is similar to that of the eastern Mediterranean region, which is 3.9 per 100,000 (Li, 2020). Over the last decade, Jordan has witnessed a slight uptick in reported suicides (Li, 2020), and there are concerns regarding the underreporting of such incidents, primarily due to the stigma surrounding mental health. This intricate situation highlights the urgent need for enhanced mental health services and increased public consciousness.

5 Mental Health Conditions and Services in Jordan

Jordan's mental health services are delivered through a complex system involving the public, private, and charitable sectors. The public sector, including government hospitals and the Ministry of Health, plays a crucial role. Still, its mental health responsibilities are specifically housed within a specialized directorate dedicated to disability and mental health. Private hospitals, clinics, non-governmental organizations (NGOs), and international humanitarian agencies like UNHCR and UNRWA also provide services. These various components operate independently, with separate funding and service delivery structures. This complex organizational arrangement can present opportunities and challenges for coordinating care and ensuring comprehensive access to mental health services for the population.

Jordan's mental health services are fragmented across public, private, and charitable sectors. Primary care is delivered through 93 primary health care clinics (PHCs) with integrated mental health services (though with limited pharmacy stock), and UNRWA clinics face challenges of accessibility due to fears of community stigma. Secondary care includes partially operational inpatient units, such as the 15-bed Ma'an Governmental Hospital unit (with a male-only ward), the 12-bed Jordan University Hospital unit, and the 12-bed King Abdullah University Hospital unit (with a female-only ward), as well as four community mental health centers (CMHCs) (WHO, 2020). Some CMHCs, like Al-Hashmi and Princess Basma, offer biopsychosocial care, while others (Al-Istisharia and Karak) are primarily outpatient clinics focusing on biomedical care. The International Medical Corps runs additional CMHCs. Psychiatric outpatient clinics (48 run by the MOH, and five more at major hospitals) and 16 from the RMS also form part of secondary care. Private sector clinics, mainly in Amman, further supplement this level. Tertiary care comprises three mental hospitals—the NCMH (205 beds), Al-Karama Hospital (150 beds), and the National Center for the Rehabilitation of Addicts (47 beds). A forensic facility (140 beds) awaits staffing, and the private sector includes Al Rasheed Hospital (120 beds), along with a specialized acute inpatient unit from RMS. Significant gaps remain in staffing, particularly for psychologists and other providers, impacting comprehensive care (WHO, 2020).

Jordan has a relatively high density of doctors, nurses, and pharmacists, exceeding 200 per 100,000 population. However, the country has a shortage of psychiatrists and psychiatric nurses, with approximately one psychiatrist and 0.13 psychiatric nurses per 100,000 people. While 42 psychiatrists are in the public sector and 49 in the private sector, the overall supply of psychiatrists, psychologists, and social workers providing mental health services isn't readily available. Additional mental health professionals include psychiatric residents and a significant number of NGO workers. Training for psychiatric residents and basic mental health knowledge for other healthcare professionals occurs through rotations and pre-service training (WHO, 2020).

5.1 *Impact of War on Mental Health Services*

The ongoing Syrian conflict, which began in 2011, has led to a significant mental health crisis in Jordan, which hosts over 660,000 registered Syrian refugees as of May 2021, with estimates of total displaced individuals (both registered and unregistered) reaching upward of 1.3 million (Al-Soleiti et al., 2021). Many refugees have faced extreme trauma, with studies indicating that more than 50% experience symptoms of post-traumatic stress disorder (PTSD), and over 30% suffer from depression or anxiety disorders. This psychological burden is compounded by various barriers to accessing mental health care, including financial constraints, limited availability of trained professionals, and societal stigma surrounding mental health issues. Approximately, 58–79% of urban Syrian refugees report difficulties accessing mental health services, exacerbated by challenges in transportation and the high cost of care, despite some services being offered at subsidized rates due to UNHCR registration (Gougazeh et al., 2024).

The impact of the Syrian conflict, for example, extends beyond the refugee population, affecting local Jordanian communities as well. Research reveals that stigma surrounding mental health treatment persists in Jordan, often deterring individuals from seeking the help they need (Gougazeh et al., 2024). Furthermore, as the influx of refugees strains healthcare resources, approximately 70% of local healthcare providers report feeling overwhelmed by the increased demand, which can lead to reduced quality of care for both refugees and Jordanian citizens (Al-Soleiti et al., 2021). In response, NGOs and community organizations are making concerted efforts to address these mental health challenges through community-based interventions and training for local practitioners in trauma-informed care. Still, more sustained efforts are necessary to effectively mitigate the long-term mental health consequences of this humanitarian crisis (Atrooz et al., 2023; Bawadi et al., 2022). The strain on Jordan's existing mental health infrastructure has been exacerbated by the sharp increase in demand for services resulting from the Syrian refugee crisis. Resource limitations are a critical concern; despite Jordan's relatively advanced healthcare system compared to neighboring countries, mental health services were already underfunded and understaffed before the influx of refugees (AlHamawi et al., 2023; Bawadi et al., 2022). The added burden of treating individuals suffering from trauma, PTSD, and other mental health disorders complicates efforts to provide adequate care. Moreover, the integration of mental health services into primary Healthcare remains incomplete, leaving many refugees facing logistical barriers, pervasive stigma, and a significant shortage of trained professionals (Atrooz et al., 2023; Khader, 2021).

The impact of this crisis also reverberates through local Jordanian communities, where the presence of a large refugee population has created tensions that exacerbate stress and mental health issues for both groups (Khader, 2021). Research indicates that local Jordanians experience increased anxiety, particularly in areas heavily populated by refugees. The cultural stigma surrounding mental health further discourages individuals from seeking help, complicating the prospect of addressing the mental health needs of both the refugee and Jordanian populations. As many avoid discussing their symptoms due to fear of judgment, this collective struggle underscores the need for enhanced mental health support systems that can accommodate and unify the diverse needs of both communities effectively (Khader, 2021).

6 Strengths of Mental Health Services in Jordan

6.1 Innovative Approaches

Jordan has made significant strides in adopting innovative solutions to address mental health needs. The integration of telepsychiatry and digital platforms has revolutionized access to mental health care, particularly during the challenges posed by the COVID-19 pandemic (El Hayek et al., 2020). By enabling mental health professionals to provide remote consultations, these innovations are especially beneficial for individuals living in remote areas or those hesitant to seek traditional face-to-face help (Abu-Farha et al., 2023). This ensures timely access to care and support and enhances the overall convenience and affordability of mental health services, making it easier for individuals to prioritize their mental well-being.

6.2 Community Initiatives

Non-governmental organizations (NGOs) and local community groups have developed programs to promote mental health awareness and support. These initiatives often target specific demographics, providing tailored education on mental health issues and de-stigmatizing the subject through workshops, seminars, and support groups (Bader et al., 2009). By fostering open dialogues within communities, these programs encourage people to seek help and share their experiences without fear of judgment. Additionally, community-based psychosocial support initiatives foster understanding and compassion, helping build a support network for individuals facing mental health challenges (Abdalla, 2023).

6.3 Decentralization of Healthcare Services

The Jordanian government has undertaken efforts to decentralize mental health services to enhance accessibility, particularly in rural and underserved areas. This decentralization allows local organizations and healthcare providers to tailor mental health support to address community-specific needs, resulting in more relevant and effective interventions (Abdalla, 2023). This approach ensures a more responsive and efficient mental health system by facilitating easier access to mental health resources.

It empowers local communities to take ownership of their mental health initiatives, leading to better health outcomes and increased community engagement in mental health issues.

6.4 *Government Commitment*

The National Mental Health Policy reflects Jordan's commitment to improving mental health services in response to growing societal needs. Recognizing the rising mental health challenges stemming from regional instability, economic pressures, and societal changes, the government has emphasized the integration of mental health care into primary healthcare systems. This holistic approach ensures that mental health is treated as a core component of overall health, enabling individuals to receive comprehensive care that addresses physical and psychological needs. Ongoing government initiatives also focus on increasing funding and resources dedicated to mental health, reinforcing its importance in national health agendas.

6.5 *The Role of Family Support*

The family unit plays a crucial role in the mental health support system in Jordan, often serving as the first line of defense for individuals facing mental health challenges. Families provide essential emotional support, encouragement, and understanding, which can significantly impact an individual's recovery journey (Khader et al., 2023). Engaging family members in treatment processes can be particularly effective, as it helps address familial dynamics that may contribute to mental health issues and fosters open communication about mental wellness. This collaborative approach ensures that individuals in care benefit from a supportive and understanding environment, which is vital for fostering resilience and facilitating recovery.

6.6 *Increasing Awareness of Mental Health Issues in Jordan*

In recent years, there has been a significant increase in awareness regarding mental health issues in Jordan. This shift can be attributed to several key factors, including educational campaigns that have helped destigmatize mental health issues and raise awareness about available resources (Abojaradeh et al., 2019). These initiatives aim to inform the public about common mental health disorders, their symptoms, and the importance of seeking help. Additionally, social media platforms have emerged as valuable tools for disseminating information about mental health, with influencers and mental health advocates sharing their personal stories and promoting resources that effectively bridge the gap between professional help and public understanding

(Al-Dmour et al., 2020). Furthermore, schools and universities are increasingly incorporating mental health education into their curricula, which empowers students with coping strategies and resources that encourage them to seek help, thus normalizing conversations about mental health among the youth (AlAzzam & Abuhammad, 2021; Alshammari et al., 2021).

6.7 *The Reputation of Healthcare in Jordan and Its Impact on Mental Health*

The reputation of Jordan's healthcare system, recognized as one of the leading healthcare providers in the Middle East, positively impacts mental health services in several ways. High-quality medical services result from significant medical infrastructure and training investments, leading to skilled healthcare professionals and well-equipped facilities (Tamimi et al., 2024). Consequently, patients often feel more confident seeking mental health services, understanding they will receive high-quality care. This strong healthcare reputation contributes to stigma reduction, as it encourages individuals to seek help and promotes broader acceptance of mental health issues (Sewilam et al., 2015). While mental health services have historically faced underfunding compared to physical health services, growing awareness and advocacy efforts are prompting a shift toward providing equal attention and resources for mental health. Additionally, the government's increasing focus on mental health, exemplified by the National Mental Health Policy, is crucial for addressing the disparities between physical and mental health services (Ben-Zeev et al., 2024). The commitment to improving mental health facilities and integrating them into general Healthcare is significant in transforming the landscape of mental health care in Jordan.

6.8 *International Collaboration*

International collaboration significantly enhances Jordan's mental health services through partnerships with organizations such as the World Health Organization (WHO) and various NGOs. These collaborations promote capacity building and training for mental health professionals, ensuring they remain equipped with the latest evidence-based practices. Jordan can develop community programs and improve infrastructure by sharing resources like funding and research. Joint efforts also facilitate awareness campaigns that reduce stigma and emphasize the importance of mental health care. Furthermore, these collaborations support the development of national mental health strategies aligned with international best practices and help establish monitoring frameworks to assess program effectiveness. This comprehensive approach enables Jordan to address its mental health challenges better while fostering global best practices.

6.9 *Skilled Workforce*

Jordan's mental health sector is supported by a diverse and skilled workforce, including psychiatrists, psychologists, social workers, and counsellors, essential for delivering comprehensive care (Ghuloum et al., 2022). Ongoing professional development and training initiatives enable these professionals to remain abreast of the latest research, therapeutic techniques, and best practices in mental health. This commitment to continuous education enhances the quality of care for individuals seeking mental health services. It fosters a culture of excellence and innovation within the mental health community in Jordan.

7 Challenges of Mental Health Care in Jordan

Jordan's mental health care system encounters numerous challenges that impede the delivery of effective and equitable care. These challenges are multifaceted and can be categorized into several crucial areas:

7.1 *Funding and Research*

Mental health services in Jordan are significantly underfunded, leading to significant gaps in care. About 3% of the health budget is allocated to mental health, far below the WHO's recommendations. This situation hinders the establishment and sustaining of effective programs that could address refugees' and local populations' diverse mental health needs (Halasa-Rappel et al., 2022). Insufficient funding also restricts research efforts; evidence-based practices tailored to local needs are lacking without studies focused on Jordan's unique cultural and socioeconomic factors (Ben-Zeev et al., 2024). Investing in research could help identify specific mental health challenges communities face and cultivate culturally relevant interventions.

7.2 *Inadequate and Inequitable Manpower*

A severe shortage of mental health professionals in Jordan poses a significant barrier to effective care. There are insufficient psychiatrists, psychologists, and counselors, often disproportionately concentrated in urban areas, leaving rural regions with a lack of mental health support (Dardas et al., 2025; Dator et al., 2018; Hamdan-Mansour et al., 2011). Consequently, individuals in these areas face long travel distances to secure necessary care or may not access it. Furthermore, continuous professional development opportunities for existing mental health staff are inadequate, hindering updates in practices and treatments (Rosal & Al-Delaimy, 2022). Strengthening the mental health workforce through more training programs and incentivizing recruitment in underserved areas is critical for improving access and care quality (Dardas et al., 2025).

7.3 Huge Out-Of-Pocket Expenses

Out-of-pocket costs for mental health care in Jordan can be substantial, further dissuading individuals from seeking necessary treatment. Many Jordanians, especially refugees, face economic hardships, and these expenses create barriers to accessing care (Bawadi et al., 2022; Dator et al., 2018). Individuals typically prioritize urgent needs such as food and shelter over mental health services, and the unpredictability of mental health-related expenses can make it difficult for families to budget (Bawadi et al., 2022). Policy reforms that provide subsidized mental health services, affordable insurance options, and integrated mental health care into primary healthcare settings could alleviate these financial burdens (Al-Krenawi, 2024).

7.4 High Stigma and Help-Seeking Patterns

The stigma surrounding mental health remains deeply ingrained in Jordanian society, where mental illness is often associated with shame and social isolation (Rayan & Jaradat, 2016). Negative perceptions discourage individuals from seeking help due to fear of judgment and ostracism. This stigma is exacerbated by a lack of awareness and understanding, leading people to avoid discussing symptoms or reaching out for support (Hasan & Musleh, 2017). Traditional attitudes may prioritize spiritual or familial assistance over professional help, causing delays in care that worsen mental health conditions. Community education campaigns emphasizing normalized discussions about mental health and sharing recovery stories are crucial to combat stigma and create a supportive atmosphere where seeking help is embraced rather than frowned upon (Dalky et al., 2017; Rayan et al., 2018).

7.5 *Non-judicious Prescribing (Polypharmacy)*

Polypharmacy, defined as the use of multiple medications simultaneously, raises concerns about the prescribing practices of mental health professionals in Jordan. Non-judicious prescribing may arise from insufficient training, limited time for comprehensive patient evaluations, and the urgency to address complex symptoms quickly (Barakat et al., 2024). This practice can result in unfavorable side effects that detract from treatment outcomes and compromise the overall quality of care (Akour et al., 2021). Ensuring that mental health professionals receive appropriate training in medication management and remain updated on best practices for prescribing is essential. Promoting collaboration between psychiatrists and general practitioners can foster a holistic understanding of patient health, ultimately improving care quality.

7.6 *Poor Mental Health Literacy*

The deficiency of mental health literacy is a significant impediment to accessing care in Jordan. Many individuals lack an understanding of mental health issues or available treatments, leading to misconceptions that can result in viewing mental disorders as moral failings instead of legitimate medical conditions. Educational initiatives designed to increase awareness and understanding of mental health can help reduce stigma and encourage individuals to seek help. Such education should not only target the general population but also healthcare providers, ensuring they can adequately recognize and manage mental health issues. Integrating mental health education within schools, communities, and primary healthcare centers can contribute to promoting an understanding of mental health as an integral part of overall well-being.

7.7 *Workplace Violence*

Workplace violence has become a critical issue in various sectors, particularly affecting healthcare professionals such as nurses and physicians. In psychiatric hospitals, approximately 27.5% of nurses report physical attacks, while an alarming 71.9% experience verbal abuse within a year (Al-Omari et al., 2019). A study in Jordan found that 63.1% of physicians faced some form of violence, with governmental healthcare settings exhibiting the highest prevalence due to factors like overcrowding and inadequate security. Male physicians are more affected, with 67.2% reporting incidents compared to 55.3% of female doctors (Alhamad et al., 2021). The implications of such violence extend beyond physical harm, significantly impacting mental health and job performance; around 71.8% of affected physicians acknowledged a decline in their work effectiveness. This atmosphere of fear and anxiety can undermine staff morale and the quality of patient care (Al-Omari et al., 2019). Urgent action is needed by healthcare authorities to implement robust preventive measures, including comprehensive anti-violence policies and effective training programs. Fostering a supportive workplace and encouraging open communication are essential for safeguarding healthcare professionals (Alhamad et al., 2021). Addressing this issue is crucial not only for the safety of employees but also for enhancing the overall quality of care provided to patients.

8 Non-medical Management of Mental Disorders in Jordan

Many individuals seek help from various non-conventional approaches, including religious healers, herbalists, kabiraz (traditional healers), homoeopathy, and alternative medicine practitioners like shamans. This shift reflects societal trends where non-medical methods are perceived as accessible, cost-effective, and culturally relevant alternatives to formal mental health care.

8.1 Religious Healers and Spiritual Practices

In Jordan, religious beliefs profoundly influence the understanding and treatment of mental health issues (Ghuloum et al., 2024). Religious healers command a respected place in communities, as individuals often consult them for spiritual guidance, prayer, and rituals believed to possess healing properties. Standard practices—such as prayer, recitation of holy texts, and collective rituals—address mental health concerns (Al Shelali et al., 2024). Although these spiritual practices can provide comfort and community support, they may have potential drawbacks. In clinical cases of severe psychological distress, reliance on spiritual healing exclusively may delay access to necessary medical treatments and exacerbate mental health conditions (Valaitė & Berniūnas, 2024). Striking a balance between spiritual and conventional care is essential, ensuring individuals receive comprehensive support that encompasses medical interventions when warranted (Ghuloum et al., 2024).

8.2 Herbalists and Traditional Remedies

Herbalists have long been a part of Jordanian culture, prescribing natural remedies derived from plants believed to possess therapeutic properties (Abu-Irmaileh & Afifi, 2003; Wazaify et al., 2011). Commonly used herbs for mental health issues include chamomile, St. John's Wort, and valerian root, which are associated with calming effects. The appeal of herbal remedies stems from their perceived safety and "natural" origins compared to pharmaceuticals (Wazaify et al., 2011). However, concerns arise regarding the lack of scientific evidence, standardization, and quality control surrounding these treatments. Self-medication with herbal remedies can also increase the risk of interactions with prescribed medications. Awareness and education regarding herbal treatments' safety, efficacy, and potential side effects are necessary. Engaging in research to verify the clinical benefits of these remedies can bridge the gap between traditional practices and modern medical standards.

9 Future Directions

Future directions for enhancing mental health services in Jordan should concentrate on several critical areas. First and foremost, increasing funding dedicated to mental health care is essential to tackle resource shortages and broaden service availability; this financial support will facilitate the establishment of additional facilities and comprehensive programs. Secondly, improving the training of healthcare professionals, especially in rural regions, is vital to closing the manpower gap and enhancing the quality of care delivered, ensuring that mental health practitioners are equipped with the latest evidence-based methodologies. Thirdly, integrating mental health education into school curricula can boost mental health literacy among young people, thereby reducing stigma and fostering early intervention, while equipping students with effective coping strategies and resources. Lastly, harnessing technology, such as telehealth services, can significantly enhance accessibility for underserved populations by enabling remote consultations and follow-ups, ensuring that individuals receive timely support, regardless of their geographical circumstances.

10 Conclusion

Mental health services in Jordan face significant challenges, exacerbated by the refugee crisis and socio-cultural stigma surrounding mental illness. While the government has made strides towards integrating mental health care into primary health services, issues like underfunding, workforce shortages, and high out-of-pocket expenses continue to hinder access. Innovative approaches, such as telepsychiatry and community initiatives, promise to address these gaps. However, more comprehensive strategies are needed to improve mental health literacy and reduce stigma. Overall, a commitment to enhancing resources and support systems will be vital for achieving better mental health outcomes for both Jordanians and refugees.

References

Abdalla, D. (2023). A multi-factorial analysis of the sustainability of non-governmental organizations' psychosocial support programs in Jordan. https://digitalcollections.sit.edu/cgi/viewcontent.cgi?article=4771&context=isp_collection

Abojaradeh, A. M., Shehadeh, J., Abojaradeh, A., & Bsisu, I. K. (2019). Effectiveness of community-based mental health education programs on mental health issues awareness level among students in Jordan. *Malaysian Journal of Medicine & Health Sciences, 15*. https://www.researchgate.net/publication/332991772_Effectiveness_of_communitybased_mental_health_education_programs_on_mental_health_issues_awareness_level_among_students_in_Jordan

Abu-Farha, R., Alzoubi, K. H., Abu Assab, M., Awwad, O., Gharaibeh, L., Mukattash, T. L., & Halboup, A. M. (2023). Perception and willingness to use telepharmacy among the general population in Jordan. *Patient Preference and Adherence*, 2131–2140. https://doi.org/10.2147/PPA.S428470

Abu-Irmaileh, B. E., & Afifi, F. U. (2003). Herbal medicine in Jordan with special emphasis on commonly used herbs. *Journal of Ethnopharmacology, 89*(2–3), 193–197. https://doi.org/10.1016/s0378-8741(03)00283-6

Akour, A., Halloush, S., Nusair, M., Barakat, M., Abdulla, F., & Al Momani, M. (2021). Pharmacists' and mental health, between perceptions and practice: A cross-sectional study. https://doi.org/10.21203/rs.3.rs-805582/v1

Al-Dmour, H., Masa'deh, R. E., Salman, A., Abuhashesh, M., & Al-Dmour, R. (2020). Influence of social media platforms on public health protection against the COVID-19 pandemic via the mediating effects of public health awareness and behavioral changes: Integrated model. *Journal of Medical Internet Research, 22*(8), e19996. https://doi.org/10.2196/19996

Al-Krenawi, A. (2024). *Syrian refugees in Jordan and mental health: Challenges and culturally sensitive practice*: Brill. https://brill.com/display/title/70576#:~:text=This%20innovative%20book%20provides%20a%20thorough%20and%20compassionate,effectively%20intervene%20when%20working%20with%20this%20vulnerable%20population

Al-Omari, H., Khait, A. A., Al-Modallal, H., Al-Awabdeh, E., & Hamaideh, S. (2019). Workplace violence against nurses working in psychiatric hospitals in Jordan. *Archives of Psychiatric Nursing, 33*(5), 58–62. https://doi.org/10.1016/j.apnu.2019.08.002

Al-Qerem, W., Jarab, A., Khdour, M., Eberhardt, J., Alasmari, F., Hammad, A., Zumot, R., & Khalil, S. (2024). Assessing mental health literacy in Jordan: A factor analysis and Rasch analysis study. *Frontiers in Public Health, 12*, 1396255. https://doi.org/10.3389/fpubh.2024.1396255

Al-Soleiti, M., Adi, M. A., Nashwan, A., & Rafla-Yuan, E. (2021). Barriers and opportunities for refugee mental health services: Clinician recommendations from Jordan. *Global Mental Health, 8*, Article e38. https://doi.org/10.1017/gmh.2021.36

Al Shelali, M., Alibrahim, H., Alomar, N., Pandi-Perumal, S. R., Seeman, M. V., & Jahrami, H. (2024). The good, the bad, and the ugly of faith healers and psychiatric illnesses: A systematic review of the literature in the Arab world. *Journal of Religion and Health, 63*(2), 857–876. https://doi.org/10.1007/s10943-023-01898-1

AlAzzam, M., & Abuhammad, S. (2021). Knowledge and attitude toward mental health and mental health problems among secondary school students in Jordan. *Journal of Child and Adolescent Psychiatric Nursing, 34*(1), 57–67. https://doi.org/10.1111/jcap.12301

Alduraidi, H., Abdulla Aqel, A., Saleh, Z., Almansour, I., & Darawad, M. (2021). UNRWA's role in promoting health outcomes of Palestinian refugees in Jordan: A systematic literature review. *Public Health Nursing, 38*(4), 692–700. https://doi.org/10.1111/phn.12889

Alhamad, R., Suleiman, A., Bsisu, I., Santarisi, A., Al Owaidat, A., Sabri, A., Farraj, M., Al Omar, M., Almazaydeh, R., Odeh, G., & Al Mousa, M. (2021). Violence against physicians in Jordan: An analytical cross-sectional study. *PloS one, 16*(1), e0245192. https://doi.org/10.1371/journal.pone.0245192

AlHamawi, R., Khader, Y., Abu Khudair, S., Tanaka, E., & Al Nsour, M. (2023). Mental health and psychosocial problems among children and adolescents in Jordan: A scoping review. *Children, 10*(7), 1165. https://doi.org/10.3390/children10071165

Alshammari, A. S., Piko, B. F., & Fitzpatrick, K. M. (2021). Social support and adolescent mental health and well-being among Jordanian students. *International Journal of Adolescence and Youth, 26*(1), 211–223. https://www.tandfonline.com/doi/pdf/10.1080/02673843.2021.1908375#:~:text=Social%20support%20from%20family%2C%20friends%2C%20and%20others%20enhances,related%20to%20mental%20health%20outcomes%20among%20Jordanian%20adolescents

Altobaishat, O., Abouzid, M., Omari, D., Sange, W., Al-Zoubi, A. K., Bani-Salameh, A., & Al-Ajlouni, Y. A. (2025). Examining the burden of mental disorders in Jordan: An ecological study over three decades. *BMC Psychiatry, 25*(1), 218. https://doi.org/10.1186/s12888-025-06658-x

Atrooz, F., Aljararwah, S. M., Chen, T. A., Khabour, O. F., & Salim, S. (2023). Understanding mental health status of Syrian refugee and Jordanian women: Novel insights from a comparative study. *International Journal of Environmental Research and Public Health, 20*(4), 2976. https://doi.org/10.3390/ijerph20042976

Bader, F., Sinha, R., Leigh, J., Goyal, N., Andrews, A., Valeeva, N., Sirois, A., Doocy, S., & Team, I. S. (2009). Psychosocial health in displaced Iraqi care-seekers in non-governmental organization clinics in Amman, Jordan: An unmet need. *Prehospital and Disaster Medicine, 24*(4), 312–320. https://doi.org/10.1017/s1049023x00007032

Bank, A. (2019). *Hashemite kingdom of Jordan government and politics of the Middle East and North Africa* (pp. 377–408). Routledge. https://www.taylorfrancis.com/chapters/edit/10.4324/9780429494482-4/hashemite-kingdom-jordan-curtis-ryan

Barakat, M., Nassar, R., Gharaibeh, L., Thiab, S., & Nashwan, A. J. (2024). Current landscape and future directions of deprescribing and polypharmacy practices in Jordan. *Medical Principles and Practice, 33*(6), 505–518. https://doi.org/10.1159/000541009

Bawadi, H., Al-Hamdan, Z., Khader, Y., & Aldalaykeh, M. (2022). Barriers to the use of mental health services by Syrian refugees in Jordan: A qualitative study. *Eastern Mediterranean Health Journal, 28*(3), 197–203. https://doi.org/10.26719/emhj.22.030

Ben-Zeev, D., Larsen, A., Beaulieu, A., Guler, J., & Bawaneh, A. (2024). Mental health priorities in the Arab world: Insights from Jordan. *Psychiatric Services, 75*(6), 604–607. https://doi.org/10.1176/appi.ps.20230365

Charara, R., Forouzanfar, M., Naghavi, M., Moradi-Lakeh, M., Afshin, A., Vos, T., Daoud, F., Wang, H., El Bcheraoui, C., Khalil, I., & Hamadeh, R. R. (2017). The burden of mental disorders in the eastern Mediterranean region, 1990–2013. *PloS One, 12*(1), e0169575. https://doi.org/10.1371/journal.pone.0169575

Council, H. H. (2015). The National Strategy for Health Sector in Jordan 2015–2019. *National Strategy for Health Sector in Jordan 2015–2019. pdf*. https://p4h.world/en/news/the-national-strategy-for-health-sector-in-jordan/#:~:text=This%20document%20presents%20the%20key%20features%20of%20the,Higher%20Health%20Council%20Law%20No.%209%20of%201999

Csicsmann, L. (2024). Political reform as regime survival strategy in the Hashemite kingdom of Jordan after the Arab uprisings. *Alternatives*. https://doi.org/10.1177/03043754241304518

Dalky, H. F., Qandil, A. M., Natour, A. S., & Janet, M. C. (2017). Quality of life, stigma and burden perception among family caregivers and patients with psychiatric illnesses in Jordan. *Community Mental Health Journal, 53*, 266–274. https://doi.org/10.1007/s10597-016-0028-0

Dardas, L. A., Habashneh, R., Keyan, D., Ali, A., Saleh, R., Aqel, I. S., Abualhaija, A., & Bryant, R. (2025). Successes and challenges in implementing stepped care for mental health in Jordan: A qualitative process evaluation. *Nursing & Health Sciences, 27*(1), e70054. https://doi.org/10.1111/nhs.70054

Dator, W., Abunab, H., & Dao-Ayen, N. (2018). Health challenges and access to health care among Syrian refugees in Jordan: A review. *Eastern Mediterranean Health Journal, 24*(7), 680–686. https://doi.org/10.26719/2018.24.7.680

El Hayek, S., Nofal, M., Abdelrahman, D., Adra, A., Al Harthi, M., Al Shamli, S., AlNuaimi, N., Bensid, L., Cheaito, M. A., Emberish, A. M., & Larnaout, A. (2020). Telepsychiatry in the Arab world: A viewpoint before and during COVID-19. *Neuropsychiatric Disease and Treatment*, 2805–2815. https://doi.org/10.2147/NDT.S277224

Erkekoğlu, L. C., & Madi, İ. (2018). *The Hashemite kingdom of Jordan Handbook of research on sociopolitical factors impacting economic growth in Islamic nations* (pp. 95–121). IGI Global. https://books.google.com.om/books/about/Handbook_of_Research_on_Sociopolitical_F.html?id=bYwtDwAAQBAJ&redir_esc=y#:~:text=Featuring%20extensive%20coverage%20on%20sociopolitical%20structures%2C%20economic%20sector,techniques%20in%20the%20economic%20infrastructures%20of%20Islamic%20nations

Ghuloum, S., Al-Thani, H. A., & Al-Amin, H. (2024). Religion and mental health: An Eastern Mediterranean region perspective. *Frontiers in Psychology, 15*, 1441560. https://doi.org/10.3389/fpsyg.2024.1441560

Ghuloum, S., Mahfoud, Z. R., Al-Amin, H., Marji, T., & Kehyayan, V. (2022). Healthcare professionals' attitudes toward patients with mental illness: A cross-sectional study in Qatar. *Frontiers in Psychiatry, 13*, Article 884947. https://doi.org/10.3389/fpsyt.2022.884947

Gougazeh, Y. M., AlHussami, M. O., Tsaras, K., Almegewly, W. H., Karavasileiadou, S., & Kleisiaris, C. (2024). Assessing barriers and difficulties to healthcare access among syrian refugees in Jordan: An observational study. *Paper Presented at the Healthcare*. https://doi.org/10.3390/healthcare12222276

Halasa-Rappel, Y., Jarawan, E., Diab, J. L., Hashoush, M., & Fouad, F. M. (2022). Jordan country report.

Hamdan-Mansour, A. M., Al-Gamal, E., Puskar, K., Yacoub, M., & Marini, A. (2011). Mental health nursing in Jordan: An investigation into experience, work stress and organizational support. *International Journal of Mental Health Nursing, 20*(2), 86–94. https://doi.org/10.1111/j.1447-0349.2010.00716.x

Hasan, A.A.-H., & Musleh, M. (2017). Public stigma toward mental illness in Jordan: A cross-sectional survey of family members of individuals with schizophrenia, depression, and anxiety. *Journal of Psychosocial Nursing and Mental Health Services, 55*(6), 36–43. https://doi.org/10.3928/02793695-20170519-05

Hoffman, R. U. (2024). *Jordan and the refugee crisis: Impact on the host nation.* University of Exeter (United Kingdom). https://ore.exeter.ac.uk/repository/bitstream/handle/10871/135262/HoffmanR.pdf?sequence=1

Khader, Y., Al Nsour, M., Abu Khudair, S., Saad, R., Tarawneh, M. R., & Lami, F. (2023). *Strengthening primary healthcare in Jordan for achieving universal health coverage: a need for family health team approach.* Paper presented at the Healthcare. https://emphnet.net/media/4e2p0nyw/strengthening-primary-healthcare-a-summary-of-emphnet-roadmap.pdf#:~:text=The%20Eastern%20Mediterranean%20Public%20Health%20Network%20%28EMPHNET%29%20has,EMR%20through%20the%20Family%20Health%20Team%20%28FHT%29%20approach

Khader, Y. S. (2021). Mental health and psychosocial concerns and provision of services for adolescent Syrian refugees in Jordan. In *Handbook of Healthcare in the Arab World*, 2967–2989. https://link.springer.com/referenceworkentry/10.1007/978-3-030-36811-1_170

Li, J. (2020). *A study on suicide*: Springer. https://doi.org/10.30773/pi.2019.0171

Marwene, B. J. (2024). Mapping the role of the Hashemite kingdom of Jordan in the Palestinian refugee crisis. *UPA Strategic Affairs, 5*(1), 155–174. https://dergipark.org.tr/en/pub/upa/issue/83406/1446386

Musa, M. (2024). Mental Health in the Middle East: Historical perspectives, current challenges, and future implications. *Saudi Journal of Humanities and Social Sciences, 9*(5), 138–148. https://doi.org/10.36348/sjhss.2024.v09i05.001

Nazer, L. H., & Tuffaha, H. (2017). Health care and pharmacy practice in Jordan. *The Canadian Journal of Hospital Pharmacy, 70*(2), 150. https://doi.org/10.4212/cjhp.v70i2.1649

Rayan, A. (2024). Stigma of mental illness: A comparative study of demographic and cultural correlates among nursing students and registered nurses in Jordan. *BMC Nursing, 23*(1), 924. https://doi.org/10.1186/s12912-024-02616-2

Rayan, A., & Jaradat, A. (2016). Stigma of mental illness and attitudes toward psychological help-seeking in Jordanian university students. *Research in Psychology and Behavioral Sciences, 4*(1), 7–14. https://doi.org/10.12691/rpbs-4-1-2

Rayan, A., Mahroum, M. H., & Khasawneh, A. (2018). The correlates of stigma toward mental illness among Jordanian patients with major depressive disorder. *Perspectives in Psychiatric Care, 54*(2), 192–197. https://doi.org/10.1111/ppc.12222

Rosal, J. L., & Al-Delaimy, W. K. (2022). Opportunities and limitations in global mental health training: A qualitative study of Jordanian primary care physicians. *International Journal of Systemic Therapy, 33*(3), 150–174. https://doi.org/10.1080/2692398X.2022.2055430

Sewilam, A. M., Watson, A. M., Kassem, A. M., Clifton, S., McDonald, M. C., Lipski, R., Deshpande, S., Mansour, H., & Nimgaonkar, V. L. (2015). Suggested avenues to reduce the stigma of mental illness in the Middle East. *International Journal of Social Psychiatry, 61*(2), 111–120. https://doi.org/10.1177/0020764014537234

Sharnoff, M. (2024). The Hashemite regime on Jordanian postage stamps: A visual history of nation-building. *Alternatives.* https://doi.org/10.1177/03043754241292574

Tamimi, A., Al-Abbadi, M., Tamimi, I., Juweid, M., Ahmad, M., & Tamimi, F. (2024). The transformation of Jordan's healthcare system in an area of conflict. *BMC Health Services Research, 24*(1), 1033. https://doi.org/10.1186/s12913-024-11467-1

Valaitė, D., & Berniūnas, R. (2024). Majnūn or mental disorders: Between cultural traditions and Western psychology in Jordan. *Culture, Medicine, and Psychiatry, 48*(1), 136–157. https://doi.org/10.1007/s11013-022-09787-0

Wazaify, M., Afifi, F. U., El-Khateeb, M., & Ajlouni, K. (2011). Complementary and alternative medicine use among Jordanian patients with diabetes. *Complementary Therapies in Clinical Practice, 17*(2), 71–75. https://doi.org/10.1016/j.ctcp.2011.02.002

WHO. (2020). Jordan-WHO special initiative for mental health-situational assessment. https://www.who.int/publications/m/item/jordan---who-special-initiative-for-mental-health

Chapter 7
Mental Health Care in Kuwait

Noura AlNouri, Ammar AlSayegh, and Aseel AlIbrahim

Abstract Mental health care in Kuwait has undergone significant evolution over the past century, transitioning from traditional healing methods rooted in religious and cultural practices to a more structured, institutionalized healthcare system. This chapter outlines the historical development of psychiatric services in Kuwait, emphasizing key milestones such as establishing the first mental hospital in the 1950s, the post-Gulf War recovery, and implementing the Mental Health Act of 2019. It explores the current landscape of mental health services across primary, secondary, and tertiary levels, highlights epidemiological data on the burden of mental disorders, and identifies challenges, including workforce limitations, infrastructure gaps, and persistent stigma. The chapter also discusses emerging strengths such as improved policy frameworks, increased public awareness, and international collaborations, concluding with strategic recommendations for future service expansion, integration, and reform. Kuwait's experience underscores the complex interplay between cultural, legal, and systemic factors in shaping mental health care delivery in the Gulf region.

Keywords Mental health services · Kuwait · Psychiatric care · Cultural beliefs and stigma · Traditional healing · Mental health policy · Community mental health · Primary care integration · Substance use disorders · Mental health epidemiology · Mental health workforce · Mental health legislation · Public vs Private sector healthcare · Migrant worker mental health · Post-Gulf War healthcare

---

N. AlNouri (✉)
Psychiatry Unit, Internal Medicine Department, Mubarak AlKabeer Hospital, Hawalli, Kuwait
e-mail: contact@eicarekw.org

A. AlSayegh
Kuwait Center for Mental Health, Sabah Health Region, Kuwait City, Kuwait
e-mail: ammar.alsayegh@moh.gov.kw

A. AlIbrahim
General Psychiatry Unit, Kuwait Center for Mental Health, Sabah Health Region, Kuwait City, Kuwait
e-mail: Aseel.alibrahim@moh.gov.kw

S. Al-Huseini and S. M. Y. Arafat (eds.), *Mental Health Care in the Middle East*, South Asian Perspectives in Mental Health and Psychology ,
https://doi.org/10.1007/978-981-95-0461-9_7

1 Introduction

Kuwait is a high-income country in the Middle East, bordered by Iraq to the north and west, Saudi Arabia to the south, and the Persian Gulf to the east. As of mid-2025, Kuwait's estimated population is approximately 5,026,078, with a significant majority (over 91%) residing in urban areas (Worldometer, 2025). The nation's demographic profile is characterized by a youthful median age of 34.8 years and a total fertility rate of 1.5 children per woman, which is currently below the replacement level.

The population structure is notably influenced by a substantial expatriate community, which comprises around 60% of the total population. The largest expatriate groups include individuals from India and Egypt. This diverse demographic composition has implications for the country's social services and policy planning.

Kuwait has made significant strides in terms of health, with life expectancy at birth reaching 80.8 years in 2025 (82.1 years for females and 79.6 years for males). However, the nation faces challenges related to non-communicable diseases (NCDs), which are the leading causes of mortality. The World Health Organization (WHO) estimates that nearly one in five adults in Kuwait dies from NCDs before the age of 70, imposing a substantial economic burden estimated at KD 1.6 billion (approximately USD 5.2 billion) annually (UNDP & WHO, 2023).

Mental health is an emerging public health priority in Kuwait. While comprehensive national data on mental health prevalence is limited, there is growing recognition of the need to address mental health issues. Efforts are underway to integrate mental health care into primary health services and to expand community-based support systems.

2 Historical Aspects of Mental Health Care in Kuwait

The history of mental health care can be generally viewed through the lens of the Pre-Modern Era and Post-Oil Discovery Era. This Pre-Modern Era can be loosely defined as anything prior to the discovery of oil in Kuwait in the 1940s/1950s. After Kuwait's oil boom, the modernization of all healthcare services started, including the introduction of formal psychiatric care. The evolution of mental health services underwent many stages. There were notable leaps in growth in services after the Gulf War (1990–1991) and after the COVID-19 pandemic (2020), before arriving at where we are today.

2.1 Pre-modern Era; Early Understanding of Mental Health

As with most Arab countries at the time, in the Pre-Modern Era, individuals with mental health needs were cared for in the community by their family, clan, and/or traditional faith healers. As the Middle East was and remains a family-oriented community, many times psychiatric illness would be tolerated and absorbed by the family system until highly unusual behaviors would become disruptive or even dangerous.

As with most pre-modern world views on mental distress, it was not unusual for it to be interpreted as a paranormal or supernatural experience. However, there were some specific religiously influenced cultural interpretations unique to the region, such as beliefs concerning spiritual possession by jinn, the "evil eye," and the impact of sorcery or black magic (El-Islam, 1982). Such explanations are widespread across different social classes and persist even among educated segments of the population.

For example, individuals suffering from obsessional thoughts or ruminations—symptoms that would typically be classified under obsessive-compulsive disorder (OCD) in psychiatric terms—are frequently believed to be under the influence of the devil (Shayṭān). Similarly, depressive or psychotic symptoms are often interpreted not as medical illnesses, but as signs of jinn possession or the result of a malevolent spell (El-Islam, 1982; Gearing et al., 2013).

Initially, families may try healing through reciting Quranic verses at home or practicing "Ruqya" (see below). If this is unsuccessful, the first point of contact would be a traditional faith healer, locally known as "sheikhs" or sometimes "raqi" (Al-Krenawi & Graham, 2000; El-Islam, 1982).

The role of traditional faith healers was especially critical in historical Kuwait. They employ a variety of conventional practices that blend religious, spiritual, and symbolic healing methods:

- **Recitation of Quranic Verses**: Healing sessions often involve the intensive recitation of specific verses from the Quran believed to have protective and curative powers (known as Ruqyah).
- **Amulets and Talismans**: Healers may write Quranic verses on small pieces of paper, tie them to the patient's body, or place them under pillows to ward off evil spirits.
- **"Washings" of the Verses**: Some faith healers write Quranic text on a plate, wash it off with water, and instruct patients to drink it, believing that the holy words will cleanse them spiritually and physically (El-Islam, 1982).
- **Anti-Sorcery Practices**: In cases attributed to black magic, healers often seek "traces"—personal items like hair, clothing, or possessions of the afflicted individual—to negotiate disengagement with the adverse spirit thought to be responsible.
- **Cauterization (Kai)**: Another traditional intervention involves burning the skin at specific points on the body. Cautery is believed to treat physical illnesses and expel the possessing jinni that may have overwhelmed a person's mind (El-Islam, 1982).

Table 1 Timeline of mental health service development in Kuwait

Period	Development highlight
Pre-1950	Traditional healing practices dominate (spiritual healers, sorcery beliefs)
1950s	Establishment of the first psychiatric hospital (Sulaibikhat)
1970s–1990s	Expansion of institutional psychiatry; imported medical models
Late 1990s	Initiation of community-based outpatient services
2013–Present	Policy alignment with the WHO Mental Health Action Plan; slow transition

Source World Health Organization (2020) and Mills (2014)

This historical context of how mental health was addressed provides valuable insights into understanding how regional traditions, cultural values, and stigmas can shape past and present help-seeking patterns (Table 1). While seeking professional support is more widely accepted nowadays, many Kuwaiti patients, especially those with severe psychiatric illnesses, such as schizophrenia, bipolar disorder, and major depression, may never reach psychiatric services. In pockets of Kuwait where families are still deeply attached to traditional values, societal stigma surrounding mental illness can lead families to pursue discreet consultations with healers rather than public psychiatric care. Consequently, this poses another complication, in which a faction of the population with mental health needs remains epidemiologically unaccounted for, given that they are exclusively managed within the traditional healing system.

2.2 *Formalization of Psychiatric Care (Post-oil Discovery Era)*

According to a paper by Zahid and Al-Zayed (2009) the first asylum was opened by the Ministry of Health in 1950 in the Sharq area. The asylum was staffed mostly by physicians and nurses from the Arab region, and the management was mostly custodial at the time. Eventually, the influences of more modern and humane treatments reached Kuwait through the employment of regional doctors who also escorted patients to Lebanon and Egypt for more advanced treatment. This led to opening a bigger, newer, barracks-style hospital in the Sulaibaikhat Area in the mid-1950s. Notably, this area was more isolated and further from the Sharq area, which was close to Kuwait City, which probably perpetuated many of the current societal stigmas of separating and secluding individuals with mental health needs.

The facility was launched at the time as the Hospital for Mental and Neurological Diseases. Over the next few decades, until around the 1970s, bed capacity increased to about 400 beds. However, staffing remained an issue as only 8–9 psychiatrists were manning the facility.

In the mid-1980s, the first evolution to services started due to an Amir Decree (Law no. 74) being passed, which dictated the opening of a new and separate facility for addiction treatment services with a 60-bed capacity. The Ministry of Health also launched outpatient mental health clinics in all 5 general hospitals across Kuwait. By the end of the decade in 1989, mental health services were fairly comprehensive, including a 400-bed inpatient facility, outpatient services, 24-h emergency psychiatric care, and addiction treatment services.

Unfortunately, the whole country, including all medical services, suffered major setbacks during the Gulf War in 1990 when Iraq invaded Kuwait. The addiction treatment facility was destroyed, all but severely unwell patients were sent home during the war, and staffing was down to about 10%. The main mental health hospital's infrastructure also suffered; the water supply and air conditioning systems were severely damaged (Zahid & Al-Zayed, 2009). Fortunately, within 2 months of Kuwait's liberation in February 1991, the Ministry of Health managed to restore basic medical and psychiatric services. A specialist center, the Al-Riggai Centre for Post Traumatic Stress Disorder (PTSD), was established, and a Danish group was recruited to identify, evaluate, and specifically support patients suffering from PTSD after the war.

In the 1990s, a gradual shift to community-based care started with integrating into primary care centers, though Kuwait still relied on a mostly institutional model of care (WHO Mental Health Atlas, 2020). Further development followed in 1993, the addiction treatment center was reopened, and the main psychiatric hospital was fully renovated. Inpatient services were divided into five units, each serving one of Kuwait's five governorates. Inpatient care remained centralized only at the main psychiatric hospital, as it does to the present day. A forensic unit and an electroencephalogram (EEG)-equipped sleep lab were also added to the facility. In 1996, the Ministry of Health contracted the UK-based Priory Group for 4 years to further develop and upgrade services; at this time, rehabilitation services, psychological and social service departments were added in addition to the establishment of a department of auditing and quality assurance.

In 2006, opening a new state-of-the-art facility marked a major turn in mental healthcare in Kuwait. The main psychiatric center's bed capacity was upgraded to accommodate upward of 600 patients. A newer Addiction Treatment Centre was built, which had a bed capacity of 250+ beds. The Ministry of Health consulted specialist mental health architects from Europe to design the facilities, including multiple recreational spaces. The facilities continued to undergo further development, including adding a geriatric and child/family unit. The center was renamed to the Kuwait Centre for Mental Health in 2012. In 2013, the Al-Manara Centre, specifically for child mental health, was launched.

From 2013 onward, Kuwait has aligned it's polices with the World Health Organization's Mental Health Action Plan 2013–2020, which emphasizes expanding to community-based care, reducing mental health stigma, and promoting human rights for people with mental illness. Despite, multiple developments and commitment to mental health funding for mental health remains comparatively low (less than 2% of health budget), and implementation of reforms is inconsistent (WHO, 2013, 2020).

Table 2 Prevalence of mental illnesses in Kuwait

Mental health condition	Estimated prevalence (%)
Depression (general population) (Arab Times, 2023)	20
Depression (primary care attendees) (Alkhadhari et al., 2016)	22.9
Anxiety (primary care attendees) (Alkhadhari et al., 2016)	17.7
Somatization disorder (primary care attendees) (Alkhadhari et al., 2016)	33.4
Bipolar disorder (Arab Times, 2023)	<1
Schizophrenia (Arab Times, 2023)	<1
Youth depression (under 30) (Times Kuwait, 2024)	25

Table 3 Burden of mental illness in Kuwait

Indicator	Value (Kuwait)	Global average
YLDs due to depression (%)	5.6%	4.7%
Suicide rate (per 100,000)	2.7	9.0
Mental health expenditure (% of total health budget)	<2%	~5%
Psychiatrists per 100,000 people	6.4	9.0

Sources WHO Mental Health Atlas (2020) and GBD 2019 Mental Disorders Collaborators (2022)

3 Epidemiology and Mental Health Burden in Kuwait

3.1 Overview of Mental Health Epidemiology

Mental health disorders represent a growing public health challenge in Kuwait, consistent with global trends but amplified by specific local factors such as rapid effects of globalization and digitalization, lifestyle changes, and cultural stigma surrounding mental illness. Mental health disorders contribute to 12–14% of the total disease burden in Kuwait (Tables 2 and 3), which is in keeping with global rates. Unfortunately, many challenges exist in getting fulsome data on mental illness, such as underreporting, poor infrastructure in place to encourage research, and in general paucity of data in the region.

3.2 Prevalence of Common Mental Disorders

3.2.1 Depression

In Kuwait, prevalence estimates for major depressive disorder (MDD) range from 4% to 7% in community surveys (GBD 2019 Mental Disorders Collaborators, 2022),

Table 4 Prevalence of depression among different age groups in Kuwait (Times Kuwait, 2024)

Age group	Prevalence of depression (%)
Under 16	33.3
16–29	25.0
18–39 (females)	33.3
General population	20.0

in comparison to global estimates around 4%. Depression is particularly prevalent among vulnerable populations such as young adults, women, and especially migrant workers (Table 4). Research focusing on Indian expatriates in the Middle East, including Kuwait, during the COVID-19 pandemic found that 33.2% suffered from clinically significant depression, with 8.8% reporting suicidal thoughts (Alsharji, 2020; Uvais, 2021). A 2019 study reported that 24.4% of patients attending primary healthcare centers in Kuwait exhibited moderate to severe depression (AlGhareeb et al., 2019). Additionally, according to the Institute of Health Metrics and Evaluation (IHME), the latest reports rank depression as number 5 out of the top 10 causes of death and disability combined.

3.2.2 Anxiety Disorders

The prevalence of anxiety disorders in Kuwait has been the subject of several studies, particularly in the context of the COVID-19 pandemic (Alali et al., 2025). Thus, it is hard to delineate an accurate general prevalence. The closest reported number from one study has been 17% in primary care attendees (AlQaysi et al., 2024). These studies have examined various populations, including the general public, children and adolescents, and individuals with chronic health conditions. Anxiety disorders in one study have been found to have increased to 53.7% during the COVID-19 pandemic (AlKandari et al., 2022). Another study found anxiety disorders among children and adolescents to be at around 20%, especially among females (AlAmiri Bibi et al., 2024). In general, local factors that can also contribute to anxiety include regional tensions, pressure for social conformity, and the global financial post-COVID situation.

3.2.3 Psychotic Disorders

Schizophrenia has a stable prevalence of around 0.5–1% of the population globally, and the prevalence in Kuwait is around the same. A study in 2019 found that Kuwait had an age-standardized point prevalence of schizophrenia at 273.8 cases per 100,000 population (Safiri et al., 2024). The same study found that the age-standardized incidence rate of schizophrenia in Kuwait was 15.5 per 100,000 population in 2019. A significant number of individuals with psychosis first consult faith healers rather than psychiatric services, delaying early intervention. Schizophrenia poses a huge burden on individuals and society, with the reported rate of Years Lived with Disability (YLD) in Kuwait in 2019 rated at 175.6 per 100,000 (Safiri et al., 2024). Recently, a study done in 2010 has found that Schizophrenia presents as it does globally, with 72% of outpatients presenting with delusions, 58.5% with hallucinations, and 25% with negative symptoms (Zahid et al., 2010).

3.2.4 Bipolar Disorder

While specific prevalence data for bipolar disorder in Kuwait are limited, a review of bipolar disorders in the Arab world indicates a general prevalence ranging from 1% to 5% globally. The review highlights a shortage of data from the Arab world on bipolar disorders and emphasizes the need for more country-specific research (Kronfol et al., 2015).

3.2.5 Substance Use Disorders (SUD)

Substance use disorders are an increasing concern in Kuwait, particularly among young males. The lifetime prevalence for any SUD is 14% (Bajwa et al., 2013). Alcohol use disorder is relatively low due to strict legal prohibitions. Still, illicit drug use, particularly cannabis, amphetamines (particularly methamphetamines), and prescription drug abuse, is rising (UNODC, 2021) in addition to rampant use of benzodiazepines and heroin. Another study conducted over 3 years from 2015 to 2018 found that the most commonly used substance is marijuana/hashish (Al-Matrouk et al., 2021). The same study found that the most common single drugs identified in postmortem specimens from suspected drug-related deaths were heroin, benzodiazepines, and methamphetamine. Combinations such as heroin-benzodiazepines and cannabis-amphetamines were also frequently detected. Additionally, Kuwait is a transit country for illicit drug trafficking, which impacts local availability (UNODC, 2021).

3.2.6 Suicide and Self-Harm

The official suicide rate in Kuwait is 2.7 per 100,000 population (WHO, 2025). Underreporting is common, as suicide is highly stigmatized and considered a religious taboo under Islam. Higher rates of suicide attempts are reported among migrant workers, particularly from South Asia, often linked to financial stress, abuse, and social isolation (Al-Sharifi et al., 2015). According to a study done by Al-Waheeb et al. (2015), suicide demographics were in keeping with global trends, with it being more prevalent in males and the most common method being hanging.

3.3 *Special Populations at Risk*

3.3.1 Migrant Workers

Out of a population of 4.7 million, approximately 70% of Kuwait's population is expatriates. Like immigrants/migrants anywhere in the world, this population is especially vulnerable to mental health issues. In Kuwait, migrant workers experience higher rates of depression, anxiety, and suicide attempts, exacerbated by limited access to mental health services (International Labour Organization, 2020). Additionally, those from South Asia were more likely to die by suicide (Al-Waheeb et al., 2015).

3.3.2 Youth and Adolescents

Youth and adolescents are an especially vulnerable population globally, and mental health problems are increasingly recognized among adolescents in Kuwait, too. Studies in the region indicate that depression in the GCC, including Kuwait, ranges from 6.12% to 45.09% (Chan et al., 2021). The same study found that rates of ADHD in Kuwaiti youth are comparable to those in the region, ranging between 12.83% and 26.14%. Additionally, a 2023 UNICEF report indicates that disordered eating is quite prevalent among youth in Kuwait, with 47.3% of male adolescents and 42.8% of female adolescents affected. Factors found to increase the risk of mental health problems in youth in Kuwait include bullying, cyberbullying, tobacco use, exposure to physical violence, feelings of loneliness, and child abuse, or even a lack of empathetic parental relationships.

3.3.3 Women

Few studies have explored women's mental health in Kuwait. However, within previous studies done on depression and anxiety in Kuwait, female gender was found to be a significant risk factor. Furthermore, studies done during the COVID-19 pandemic showed that women over 50 years old, those with higher educational qualifications, and private business owners reported higher incidences of depression, anxiety, and stress. Notably, Kuwaiti women exhibited significantly elevated rates of these mental health conditions compared to non-Kuwaiti women (Al-Ma'Seb & Al-Sejari, 2023). Additionally, during the pandemic, 19.6% of participants in a study (AlEnezi et al., 2024) experienced postnatal depression, 14.6% were highly likely to have it, and 32.9% were probable cases, highlighting the unique circumstances that can make women more vulnerable to mental health struggles. Finally, women in Kuwait were no different from their counterparts in other countries, and a study done in 2023 on domestic violence found that 56.1% of married or previously married women attending primary healthcare centers had experienced some form of domestic violence. Breakdown of the types of violence included psychological

(42.4%), physical (35.1%), sexual (28.8%), and economic (41.4%), and were closely linked to adverse mental health outcomes (AlShammari et al., 2023). Beyond this, some regional factors could be related to cultural expectations, family roles, and restricted autonomy in some spheres.

4 Current Mental Health Services

4.1 Overview

Mental health services in Kuwait have drastically evolved over the past few decades, reflecting the broader shifts in society's acceptance of mental health struggles, expanding healthcare services, government policy, and a push toward fulfilling and maintaining accreditation standards in training programs and hospitals. Over the past decade or so, the Ministry of Health has invested in collaborations with the Royal College to have accreditation standards met and maintained for all healthcare services in Kuwait.

While this has pushed Kuwait to make great strides in expanding psychiatric services at the secondary and tertiary levels, integration of mental health care into the primary healthcare system remains limited (Table 5). Additionally, due to multiple governmental constraints and regulations, mental healthcare lies predominantly under the umbrella of the public sector, with a growing but relatively minimal contribution from private providers. Specialized services such as those for children, adolescents, the elderly, and individuals with substance use disorders are available but face significant gaps due to challenges with human resources and funding. While a report from the WHO in 2020 indicates Kuwait has a higher number of psychiatrists in comparison to regional averages, servicing the area remains a challenge due to the expanding population.

Table 5 Overview of provision of health services

Service aspect	Status
Primary care integration	Limited
Secondary outpatient services	Available but overloaded
Tertiary inpatient services	Centralized at the Kuwait Center for Mental Health
Specialized child psychiatry	Limited access
Geriatric psychiatry	No specialized units
Substance abuse services	Limited outpatient aftercare
Private sector involvement	Minimal
NGO/International role	Advocacy-focused

Table 6 Distribution of primary mental health clinics across Kuwait's governorates

Governorate	Number of clinics
Capital	15
Hawalli	12
Farwaniya	14
Ahmadi	13
Jahra	10
Mubarak Al-Kabeer	8
Total	72

Source ArabTimes (2025)

4.2 *Structure of Mental Health Services: Primary, Secondary, and Tertiary Levels*

4.2.1 Primary Level: Primary Care Clinics

At the primary care level, services remain limited in comparison to other high-income countries (Kaladchibachi & Al-Dhafiri, 2016; Scull et al., 2020). However, over the past two decades, many efforts have been made to support intervention at the primary care centers, including starting with informal training programs in the early 2010s to having formal training programs for GPs (general practitioners) from the Kuwait Institute for Medical Sciences over the past few years. Currently, 72 primary care clinics are able to provide basic mental health assessments, but treatments are limited to managing simple cases of depression or anxiety with restricted access to psychotropics (Table 6). However, since 2020, each governate has 1–2 specialized mental health clinics at the major primary care centers where family physicians trained in mental health can provide more care with more expansive management options, including medications and psychosocial support.

4.2.2 Secondary Level: General Hospitals

At the secondary level, currently, all six major general hospitals in Kuwait have psychiatric units attached to them. Services provided range from consultation and liaison services, outpatient clinics, to specialized clinics such as child psychiatry clinics. Services include assessment and management of all psychiatric disorders, access to most psychotropic drugs (with exceptions for medications such as clozapine, lithium, and some long-acting injectables which are constrained to use at the Kuwait Center for Mental Health due to monitoring regulations), access to psychotherapeutic support, emergency psychiatric assessments at the general emergency department (no formal inpatient or psychiatric emergency department exists within the general hospitals framework yet).

4.2.3 Tertiary Level: Kuwait Center for Mental Health (KCMH)

Psychiatric services are mostly provided at the Kuwait Centre for Mental Health. The center is the country's only mental health facility; it contains a comprehensive departmental structure that strives to ensure integrated and holistic care for patients. It currently houses the following departments:

Clinical Departments

- Medical Department: includes six inpatient units, one unit per governorate, and specialty inpatient units, including geriatrics, pediatrics, and forensics.
- Specialized Treatment Units:
  - ECT (Electroconvulsive Therapy) Unit
  - EEG and Sleep Lab Unit: For neurological diagnostics and sleep disorders
  - Day Care Unit: Providing structured daytime treatment programs
  - Emergency Unit: For urgent psychiatric care needs
- Psychology Unit: Psychological assessment and therapeutic interventions
- Pharmacy Department
- Nursing Department
- Lab Department
- Radiology Department
- Social Worker Department
- Dental Clinic

Support Departments

- Biomedical Department
- Dietary Department
- Engineering Office
- Medical Record Department
- Quality and Accreditation Office
- Infection Control Office
- Administrative Affairs Department
- Hotel Service Department
- Public Relations Department

Since the launch of the newer building in 2006, the Kuwait Center for Mental Health has continued to develop. Its commitment to quality healthcare has been recognized through multiple accreditations and awards. KCMH achieved accreditation in both 2014 and 2017, demonstrating its adherence to international standards of mental healthcare delivery. Additionally, the center has been honored with the prestigious Safety Star Award three times (2016, 2018, 2021).

4.3 *Public vs. Private Sector Contributions*

In keeping with the rest of the healthcare landscape in Kuwait, mental health care is provided both in the public and private sectors. However, due to government regulations restricting inpatient care only to the public sector, the private sector's role remains limited. Initially, clinics offered limited outpatient services provided by a psychiatrist only; more recently, looser governmental regulations have allowed the development of centers where multidisciplinary teams can provide outpatient care, including psychiatrists, psychologists, nurses, etc. However, due to the higher cost of maintaining services in the private sector, access remains confined mostly to middle and high-income populations. Further challenges in the private sector include further limitations by the government on medications allowed to be sold commercially. Contrarily, governmental oversight of prescriptions is not as judicious as in the public sector. Finally, psychological and therapeutic services are not regulated by the Ministry of Health and are governed under the Ministry of Commerce, which creates unique challenges for regulations.

Ultimately, the majority of care is provided through the Ministry of Health public sector, while care is free for citizens and subsidized for non-citizens, it is more accessible, less costly, but can have long wait times and at times may be complicated to navigate.

4.4 *Mental Health Workforce*

As with the current state of healthcare nationwide, human resources is a major challenge. According to the WHO in 2020, there was a total of 789 mental health professionals servicing a population of 4 million. However, newer data may reflect an increase in staffing, as there was a decrease in healthcare professionals in general during the COVID-19 pandemic when this census was collected. Nonetheless, most mental health professionals are generally concentrated in the public sector. While actively working on recruitment and improving training by providing pathways to scholarships and training opportunities within the country and abroad, psychiatrist attrition out of the public sector remains a drain on human resources (Table 7).

Table 7 Mental health workforce in Kuwait

Professional category	Number per 100,000 population
Psychiatrists	2.35
Psychologists	1.35
Mental health nurses	14.5
Social workers	0.43
Occupational therapists	0.12

Source WHO Mental Health Atlas (2020)

4.5 Mental Health Act

A milestone achievement in Kuwait's mental health policy landscape was the enactment of the **Mental Health Act No. 14 of 2019**, representing the country's first comprehensive legislative framework dedicated to the rights and treatment of individuals with mental disorders. Before this legislation, mental health care in Kuwait operated without a specific legal structure, often relying on general medical laws and informal practices. The act introduced critical reforms, including the formal definition of mental illness, **voluntary and involuntary admissions procedures**, and the establishment of **patient rights protections**, such as the right to informed consent, privacy, and the ability to appeal involuntary detention. It mandates the creation of **Mental Health Review Committees** to oversee cases of compulsory hospitalization, ensuring that admissions are reviewed independently and regularly (STA Law Firm, 2020). The Act also stipulates the rights of psychiatric patients to privacy, dignity, and the least restrictive form of care possible (Table 8).

Table 8 Key provisions of Kuwait's Mental Health Act

Provision	Description
Voluntary admission	Individuals can seek psychiatric treatment voluntarily, with the right to consent to or refuse treatment
Involuntary admission	Permitted under strict conditions if the individual poses a danger to self or others
Consent to treatment	Patients must give informed consent for treatments; emergency treatment exceptions
Mental health committees	Independent committees to review contested involuntary admissions, appeals, consent and capacity for treatment decisions, forensic admissions, and reviews
Patient rights	Affirms patient rights to dignity, privacy, least restrictive care, access to legal counsel, and communication with families
Judicial review	Judicial authorities must be notified of all cases of involuntary admission within set timeframes to prevent abuse
Oversight and accountability	Regular reporting to the Ministry of Health; grievances mechanisms available for patients and families
Alignment with international standards	The act references principles similar to those found in the UN Convention on the Rights of Persons with Disabilities (CRPD)

5 Potential Strengths of Mental Health Services

5.1 *Cultural Strengths: Strong Family Systems, Community Solidarity*

Similar to other Middle Eastern and Arab cultures, Kuwaiti society is characterized by strong family bonds, intergenerational households, and collective decision-making, which can be strategically leveraged for mental health interventions. Families often provide primary emotional, financial, and caregiving support for individuals with mental illness, reducing the risk of homelessness and severe social isolation compared to Western contexts (El-Islam, 2008). Community solidarity and religious coping mechanisms—such as communal prayers, family mediation, and charity—also offer culturally congruent pathways to resilience-building and rehabilitation.

5.2 *Emerging Policy Frameworks Recognizing Mental Health*

Kuwait's government has increasingly acknowledged mental health as a national priority in health policy planning. The passing of the Mental Health Act formalized rights-based psychiatric care and provided the legal infrastructure for regulating services. Furthermore, Kuwait's Vision 2035 National Development Plan explicitly mentions improving mental health services as part of its broader healthcare modernization strategy (Kuwait Vision 2035, 2018). Kuwait has also engaged with international frameworks such as the WHO Mental Health Action Plan 2013–2030, signaling political will to expand services, reduce stigma, and integrate mental health into universal health coverage. These emerging policy initiatives create an enabling environment for future reforms and investments.

5.3 *High Government Spending on Healthcare*

Kuwait has one of the highest per capita healthcare expenditures in the Gulf region (World Bank, 2022), meaning there's potential for sustained funding of mental health reforms. In 2023, Kuwait spent 5.1% of its GDP on healthcare, positioning Kuwait as the second-highest in the Gulf Cooperation Council (GCC) after Saudi Arabia. Per capita spending reached $2292, significantly above the global median of $440. More importantly, most of the healthcare in Kuwait is state-funded and free for Kuwaiti citizens and subsidized at minimal cost for non-citizens, thus removing financial barriers to accessing care. While specific mental health budgets are not publicly itemized from the Ministry of Health, general increased spending on healthcare usually impacts increased spending on subsets of healthcare, such as mental health.

5.4 Young Workforce and Expanding Training Programs

One of the notable strengths of Kuwait's mental health sector is its young and growing psychiatric workforce. Several national initiatives have prioritized training new psychiatrists, psychiatric nurses, and psychologists through local postgraduate programs and international fellowships. Kuwait's Ministry of Health supports scholarships for specialization in psychiatry abroad (particularly in Canada, the USA, Europe, and other Gulf countries), fostering a new generation of highly trained mental health professionals (World Health Organization, 2020). Locally, the Kuwait Institute for Medical Specialization (KIMS) offers a structured psychiatry residency program working to get accredited by international bodies, with a growing intake of young doctors. This influx of younger professionals brings up-to-date clinical knowledge, greater openness to innovation, and reduced stigma among providers, representing a promising foundation for service expansion and modernization in the coming years (AlKandari et al., 2022).

5.5 Growing Public Awareness and Media Campaigns

Over the past decade or so, there's been an increase in public and private initiatives for mental health awareness. Multiple grassroots campaigns by NGOs and civil societies, as well as the Ministries of Health and Education, have all invested in community efforts to spread awareness through hosting events, TV programs, and using social media influencers. Normalizing conversations around mental health has helped reduce stigma and encourage early help-seeking behavior.

5.6 Early Mental Health Promotion in Schools

Additionally, pilot programs have been introduced to increase mental health literacy among children and adolescents, such as anti-bullying campaigns, school counseling programs, and mental wellness education (Ministry of Education, Kuwait, 2020).

5.7 *International Collaborations*

Kuwait values international expertise in health and invests heavily in training and consulting opportunities, which can enhance the current mental health landscape. In addition to Western expertise, Kuwait collaborates with regional and GCC partners to improve mental health services through shared strategies, training, and policy development. Partnerships with organizations like **WHO-EMRO** (Eastern Mediterranean Regional Office), UNICEF, and various UN bodies ensure bringing **global best practices** into the local system (WHO-EMRO, 2023). In collaboration with WHO, Kuwait developed the Country Cooperation Strategy (CCS) for 2023–2027, which outlines priorities including integrating mental health into primary care and promoting community-based mental health services. This partnership also facilitated the launch of initiatives like the "Ghad" national campaign aimed at preventing self-harm and the establishment of a mental health hotline during the COVID-19 pandemic to provide remote consultations and psychosocial support.

6 Challenges in Mental Health Care

While Kuwait has been making strides to advance care in mental health over the past two decades, many challenges ranging from systemic, cultural, to logistical persist. Key issues will be discussed in the following section.

6.1 *Limited Mental Health Workforce*

The most pressing issue across health care and mental health care specifically is understaffing, across all disciplines in mental health, including psychiatrists, nursing staff, clinically trained psychologists, social workers, occupational therapists, and administrative staff. Kuwait faces a shortage of qualified mental health professionals. The country has approximately 18.75 mental health professionals per 100,000 people, significantly lower than the global average in high-income countries. Additionally, service distribution may not be equitable, with rural areas being underserved and staffing not having adequate training. These challenges affect the quality of care that patients receive. They can translate into inadequate assessments due to increased patient volume, long waiting times, medical errors, staff burnout, and staff and patient safety hazards.

6.2 *Inadequate Infrastructure and Overreliance on Tertiary Care*

Mental health services are largely centralized in hospitals like the Kuwait Center for Mental Health (KCMH), with insufficient integration into primary care. Although mental health clinics are expanding across primary health centers (e.g., 72 centers reported by 2025), capacity remains insufficient, especially in rural or underserved areas. According to the WHO, mental health services at Kuwait's primary healthcare (PHC) level should be strengthened. It is estimated that 287,732 people did not receive the mental health services they needed at the primary care level in the public sector in 2019.

6.3 *Stigma and Cultural Beliefs*

While progress has been made to battle stigma, especially since the COVID-19 pandemic, after which people have been more accepting of mental health struggles, mental illness is still heavily stigmatized in Kuwaiti society. Aside from cultural beliefs in **jinn possession, the evil eye, or sorcery**, which often lead people to seek help from **faith healers** rather than mental health professionals, people also avoid care at centralized institutions like the KCMH. Having mental health clinics at primary care facilities and general hospitals has mitigated a lot of the stigma. However, stigma remains against mental health conditions even among healthcare professionals. Unfortunately, this can result in delays in diagnosis and treatment, which is especially impactful for serious conditions like psychosis and mood disorders (El-Islam, 1982; Al-Krenawi & Graham, 2020).

6.4 *Limited Mental Health Legislation Enforcement*

Although the Mental Health Act was a landmark legislative achievement, full implementation remains a challenge. Challenges in coordination between the Ministry of Health and the Ministry of Interior lead to gaps in ensuring that patient rights and safety are protected. Additionally, poor awareness of the Mental Health Act among non-mental health professionals also leads to a lack of application of the law. Finally, lack of awareness among the public also poses a challenge, as individuals with mental health problems or loved ones may not be aware of patient rights, which can lead to avoidance of care.

6.5 Out-Of-Pocket Expenditures & Inequitable Access

Despite public healthcare being largely free for citizens, non-citizens (a substantial portion of Kuwait's population) may face high out-of-pocket costs for mental health care, particularly in the private sector. Additionally, most insurance plans do not cover mental health care in the private sector. A distinctive challenge to accessing psychological therapy persists; as clinically trained psychologists in the public sector are in short supply and care is mostly centralized at the KCMH, not everyone can access psychotherapy due to sheer volume, long wait times, and stigma around attending the KCMH. Certified psychotherapists in the private sector are numerous; however, care is quite expensive and not affordable to most.

6.6 Lack of Mental Health Research and Data

There is a paucity of local epidemiological research, which limits evidence-based policymaking. Most data are extrapolated from small-scale or global studies, leaving gaps in understanding the local mental health burden. Despite rising mental health concerns, there has been minimal investment in longitudinal studies or nationwide mental health surveys. The existing research is often limited to academic case studies or clinic-based findings, which do not provide a comprehensive picture of the prevalence, incidence, or socioeconomic burden of mental illnesses across different population groups, such as adolescents, women, or migrant workers. Furthermore, the absence of a centralized mental health registry or surveillance system restricts the ability to track trends, monitor outcomes, and evaluate interventions systematically. This limitation also affects the development of culturally adapted screening tools and evaluating mental health services' effectiveness.

6.7 Limited NGO and Community Involvement

The role of **non-governmental organizations (NGOs)** in mental health is underdeveloped, and community-based support systems are still emerging compared to other countries. Additionally, most mental health awareness efforts are fragmented and are not embedded within a larger national mental health framework, reducing their long-term impact. There is a strong need for structured partnerships between government entities, NGOs, and academic institutions to build community resilience and support continuity of care beyond hospital settings. Without these, the burden continues to fall disproportionately on overstrained tertiary facilities like the KCMH.

7 Future Directions

Kuwait continues to work on overcoming healthcare challenges to improve users' services. Ultimately, aspiring to provide a comprehensive and holistic service involves bridging systemic and sociocultural gaps. A multifaceted approach, including collaborations between multiple government facets, international collaborations, and proactive awareness and prevention strategies, is integral to moving forward. Some proposed solutions are outlined in the section below.

7.1 National Mental Health Strategy

An effective mental health care system has to have a strong foundation, starting with developing a national mental health strategy with a harmonized national strategy across all institutes involved in mental health care provision. The policy should ensure that clear goals, such as funding allocations and monitoring indicators, are addressed. It can be done in alignment with the WHO's *Mental Health Action Plan 2013–2030* and drawing on other pertinent international bodies for expertise, support, or collaboration.

7.2 Expansion and Decentralization of Mental Health Services

In continuation with global standards and Kuwait's vision to integrate mental health into community care, expansion and decentralization of mental health services should continue to ensure accessibility to care. Kuwait has initiated the process of integrating mental health services into primary care centers and should continue to ensure access to services is available at all centers, including appropriately training staff and ensuring the availability of pharmacological and psychotherapeutic management options.

Beyond this, developing the nascent stage of mental health departments at general hospitals is essential; ensuring the population can have access to inpatient, outpatient, and emergency mental health care in each governorate reduces the burden on tertiary centers such as the KCMH and ensures timely delivery of care as well as decreasing sociocultural barriers to accessing care such as stigma.

Finally, expansion into the community should be an integral consideration with the provision of mobile mental health teams. Mobile mental health teams can provide crisis care and bridge a huge gap for individuals/loved ones who have difficulty delivering care to their loved ones. Additionally, mobile teams can also be used to support those with severe persistent mental illness who are unable to travel to medical centers for care and provide care at home, thus decreasing the burden on secondary and tertiary centers and reducing the costs of care in the long term. Furthermore, mobile teams can be used for follow-up care for geriatric or bedridden patients and as part of assertive community treatment for those with necessary community treatment plans.

7.3 Investing in the Mental Health Workforce

As Kuwait currently has fewer mental health professionals needed to service its population, increasing the number of trained healthcare professionals is integral to providing an equitable service. Increasing the number of psychiatrists, clinical psychologists, and psychiatric nurses, particularly Arabic-speaking professionals, is invaluable to ensuring adequate and timely care. Solutions can include bolstering existing in-country postgraduate training programs for psychiatrists, psychologists, and mental health nurses by including train-the-trainer components to ensure sustainability of these programs. Additionally, expanding training opportunities for general practitioners in the community and increasing shared care with primary care providers decreases a huge burden on tertiary centers.

7.4 Enhance Data Collection and Research

Quality care cannot exist without metrics to track, measure, and improve services. Monitoring the system's success will be unfeasible without adequate data collection and research. Establishing a national registry for mental health prevalence, service utilization, and outcomes should be a natural first step. Beyond this, encouraging academic-clinical partnerships to drive research is integral to understanding existing challenges and driving evidence-based policy changes. Encouraging longitudinal and population-based research starts with teaching and fostering a research culture from the undergraduate training level to encouraging it at an institutional level.

7.5 Leverage Digital and Tele-mental Health Solutions

During the COVID-19 pandemic, many global services adopted telemedicine services to continue service provision. In the public sector in Kuwait, hotlines were provided during working hours. Still, formal tele-psychiatry services were not adopted, mostly due to the system being technologically unprepared to launch secure tele-psychiatry systems. Telepsychiatry has been effectively and safely used globally for many years and is currently being utilized in the private sector. The Ministry of Health can consider expanding services by partnering with tech startups and institutions to develop secure mental health service delivery platforms. Having the option of doing virtual consultations and follow-ups will not only decrease barriers to access for remote and underserved populations, but can reduce stigma and reduce costs on institutions. Additionally, using Arabic-speaking mobile mental health apps, online therapy platforms, and AI-supported screening tools can also decrease the burden on the existing mental health establishment.

7.6 Address Stigma and Promote Awareness

Actively addressing mental health stigma and local sociocultural beliefs around mental health is an integral part of decreasing barriers to care. Launching nationwide mental health literacy campaigns across schools, universities, private and public employment establishments, and healthcare establishments helps battle stigma. Leveraging the use of local influencers, leaders, religious figures, and social media is a critical part of reaching the community effectively. Furthermore, working with the Ministry of Education to embed mental health literacy in school and university curricula can support early recognition of mental health struggles. Finally, promoting open dialogue on mental health through media, especially targeting vulnerable and conservative populations such as youth, men, and migrant workers.

7.7 Regulate and Collaborate with Traditional Healers and Civil Societies in the Community

Recognizing that many reach out to faith healers initially for support with mental health struggles, it would be prudent to involve them in the pathway to appropriate medical care. Offering training workshops on mental illness recognition and developing effective referral pathways to the mental health system could uncover a large portion of the population who may have been otherwise lost to care. Collaboration with the Ministry of Awqaf and Islamic Affairs can ensure the regulation of services.

7.8 Enhance Mental Health Legislation and Human Rights

As with any newly passed law, full enforcement and implementation will take some time. Since passing the **Mental Health Law**, ensuring protection of patient rights, consent, and ethical treatment, slowly but steadily, establishments have become more proficient at implementing it. However, promoting awareness of the actual law to involved parties (healthcare, law enforcement, and the public) would ensure smoother operation of the law. Additionally, expanding independent oversight bodies to monitor involuntary admissions, institutional conditions, and service quality supports upholding the law. Finally, actively training non-psychiatric healthcare providers and law enforcement in the logistics of implementing the law may enhance service delivery.

8 Conclusion

Kuwait has made remarkable strides in the development of its mental health system since the beginning of its journey about a century ago. While legislative reforms, expanding service availability, and increasing public awareness have formed substantial changes, challenges remain. Kuwait's mental health agenda must prioritize integration into primary care, invest in training and research, and embrace culturally informed and community-driven solutions to ensure a holistic approach to mental health.

References

Alali, S. M., Abdalla, D. K. H., Alsaqabi, A., et al. (2025). Generalised anxiety disorder and its determinants amongst patients with diabetes in primary healthcare clinics: A cross-sectional study in Kuwait City, 2024. *BMC Public Health, 25*, 188. https://doi.org/10.1186/s12889-024-21150-z

Alamiri Bibi, A., Alkhamis, M. A., Naguy, A., Alenezi, H. F., & Al Shekaili, M. (2024). Anxiety disorders among children and adolescents during COVID-19 lockdowns and school closures: A cross-sectional study in Kuwait. *Frontiers in Psychiatry, 15*. https://doi.org/10.3389/fpsyt.2024.1322745

Alenezi, R., Alduosari, M., Alotaibi, A., Alrasheedi, D., Alenezi, L., Naser, D., Alshammari, A., Alrasman, S., Aldein, L., Almarabheh, A., & Ahmed, J. (2024). An evaluation of postnatal depression among women in Kuwait: Findings from a web-based survey. *Khyber Medical University Journal, 16*(3), 187–194. https://doi.org/10.35845/kmuj.2024.23371

Al-Ghareeb, H. Y., Al-Wotayan, R., Al-Busairi, H. F., Al-Merza, A. A., & Boresli, I. M. (2019). Prevalence of depression among patients attending the primary health care clinics in Kuwait. *Middle East Journal of Family Medicine, 17*(11), 36–41. https://doi.org/10.5742/MEWFM.2019.93689

AlKandari, S., Salman, A., Al-Ghadban, F., & Ahmad, R. (2022). A cross-sectional study to examine the psychological impact of the COVID-19 pandemic on healthcare workers in Kuwait. *International Journal of Environmental Research and Public Health, 19*(17), 10464. https://doi.org/10.3390/ijerph191710464

Alkhadhari, S., Alsabbrri, A. O., Mohammad, I. H., Atwan, A. A., Alqudaihi, F., & Zahid, M. A. (2016). Prevalence of psychiatric morbidity in the primary health clinic attendees in Kuwait. *Journal of Affective Disorders, 195*, 15–20. https://doi.org/10.1016/j.jad.2016.01.037

Al-Krenawi, A., & Graham, J. R. (2000). Culturally sensitive social work practice with Arab clients in mental health settings. *Health & social work, 25*(1), 9–22. https://doi.org/10.1093/hsw/25.1.9

Al-Ma'Seb, H. B., & Al-Sejari, M. M. (2023). Depression, anxiety, and stress during COVID-19 pandemic among females who live in Kuwait. *Social Work in Public Health, 38*(3), 182–192. https://doi.org/10.1080/19371918.2022.2117254

Al-Matrouk, A., Al-Hasan, M., Naqi, H., Al-Abkal, N., Mohammed, H., Haider, M., Al-Shammeri, D., & Bojbarah, H. (2021). Snapshot of narcotic drugs and psychoactive substances in Kuwait: Analysis of illicit drugs use in Kuwait from 2015 to 2018. *BMC Public Health, 21*(1), 671. https://doi.org/10.1186/s12889-021-10705-z

Alqaysi, L., Alenezi, A. F., Malallah, K., Alsabea, E., Khalfan, M., Alnouri, A., & Jahrami, H. (2024). Analyzing the prevalence of depression and anxiety symptoms among relatives of cancer patients in Kuwait. *Cureus, 16*(3), Article e56989. https://doi.org/10.7759/cureus.56989

Alshammari, F. J., Labib, N. A., Radwan, G. N., El-Shazly, M., Hassan, H. A., & El Aguizy, F. H. (2023). Prevalence and associated factors of domestic violence among women attending primary healthcare centres in Kuwait: A cross-sectional study. *African Journal of Reproductive Health, 27*(11), 33–43. https://www.ajrh.info/index.php/ajrh/article/view/4187

Al-Sharifi, A., Krynicki, C. R., & Upthegrove, R. (2015). Self-harm and ethnicity: A systematic review. *The International Journal of Social Psychiatry, 61*(6), 600–612. https://doi.org/10.1177/0020764015573085

Alsharji, K. E. (2020). Anxiety and depression during the COVID-19 pandemic in Kuwait: The importance of physical activity. *Middle East Current Psychiatry, 27*(1), 1–8. https://doi.org/10.1186/s43045-020-00065-6

Al-Waheeb, S., & Al-Kandary, N. (2015). Patterns of suicide in Kuwait: A retrospective descriptive study from 2003–2009. *BMC Public Health, 15*, 527. https://doi.org/10.1186/s12889-015-1862-7

Arab Times. (2023). *20% people in Kuwait depressed*. https://www.arabtimesonline.com/news/20-people-in-kuwait-depressed/. Accessed May 26, 2025.

Arab Times. (2025). *Kuwait launches 72 primary mental health clinics in all governorates*. https://www.arabtimesonline.com/news/kuwait-launches-72-primary-mental-health-clinics-in-all-governorates/?utm_source=chatgpt.com. Accessed May 26, 2025.

Bajwa, H. Z., Al-Turki, A. S., Dawas, A. M., Behbehani, M. Q., Al-Mutairi, A. M., Al-Mahmoud, S., Shukkur, M., & Thalib, L. (2013). Prevalence and factors associated with the use of illicit substances among male university students in Kuwait. *Medical Principles and Practice, 22*(5), 458–463. https://doi.org/10.1159/000350609

Chan, M. F., Al Balushi, R., Al Falahi, M., Mahadevan, S., Al Saadoon, M., & Al-Adawi, S. (2021). Child and adolescent mental health disorders in the GCC: A systematic review and meta-analysis. *International Journal of Pediatrics and Adolescent Medicine, 8*(3), 134–145. https://doi.org/10.1016/j.ijpam.2021.04.002

El-Islam, M. F. (1982). Arabic cultural psychiatry. *Transcultural Psychiatric Research Review, 19*(1), 5–24. https://doi.org/10.1177/136346158201900101

El-Islam, M. F. (2008). Arab culture and mental health care. *Transcultural Psychiatry, 45*(4), 671–682. https://doi.org/10.1177/1363461508100788

GBD 2019 Mental Disorders Collaborators. (2022). Global, regional, and national burden of 12 mental disorders in 204 countries and territories, 1990-2019: A systematic analysis for the Global Burden of Disease Study 2019. *The Lancet Psychiatry, 9*(2), 137–150. https://doi.org/10.1016/S2215-0366(21)00395-3

Gearing, R. E., Schwalbe, C. S., MacKenzie, M. J., Brewer, K. B., Ibrahim, R. W., Olimat, H. S., & Al-Krenawi, A. (2013). Adaptation and translation of mental health interventions in Middle Eastern Arab countries. *International Journal of Social Psychiatry, 59*(7), 671–681. https://doi.org/10.1177/0020764012452349

International Labour Organization. (2020). *Protection legislation and legal frameworks for migrant workers in the Arab States*. https://www.ilo.org/sites/default/files/wcmsp5/groups/public/@arabstates/@ro-beirut/documents/publication/wcms_886063.pdf

Kaladchibachi, S., & Al-Dhafiri, A. M. (2016). Mental health care in Kuwait: Toward a community-based decentralized approach. *International Social Work, 61*(3), 329–334. https://doi.org/10.1177/0020872816661403

Kronfol, Z., Zakaria Khalil, M., Kumar, P., Suhre, K., Karam, E., & McInnis, M. (2015). Bipolar disorders in the Arab world: A critical review. *Annals of the New York Academy of Sciences, 1345*(1), 59–66. https://doi.org/10.1111/nyas.12652

Mills, A. (2014). Health care systems in low- and middle-income countries. *New England Journal of Medicine. 370*(6), 552–557. https://doi.org/10.1056/NEJMra1110897

Oxford Business Group. (2024). *Kuwait is improving quality of education and health care, and local talent.* https://oxfordbusinessgroup.com/reports/kuwait/2024-report/education-health/markers-of-excellence-the-government-is-seeking-a-balance-between-improved-quality-and-the-fostering-of-local-talent-as-the-private-sector-expands-its-role-in-both-health-care-and-education-overview/

Safiri, S., Noori, M., Nejadghaderi, S. A., Shamekh, A., Sullman, M. J. M., Collins, G. S., & Kolahi, A. A. (2024). The burden of schizophrenia in the Middle East and North Africa region, 1990–2019. *Scientific Reports, 14*(1), 9720. https://doi.org/10.1038/s41598-024-59905-8

Scull, N. C., Khullar, N., Al-Awadhi, N., & Erheim, R. (2020). A qualitative study of the perceptions of mental health care in Kuwait. *International Perspectives in Psychology: Research, Practice, Consultation, 3*(4), 284–299. https://doi.org/10.1037/ipp0000023

STA Law Firm. (2020). *Kuwait's first mental health law: A step forward.* https://www.mondaq.com/healthcare/887534/kuwaits-first-mental-health-law-a-step-forward#:~:text=14%20of%202019%20is%20the,term%20mental%20illness%20as%20%E2%80%9Cpsychological. Accessed May 26, 2025.

The New Arab. (2022, March 1). *Kuwait shaken by suicide surge.* https://www.newarab.com/features/kuwait-shaken-suicide-surge

Times Kuwait. (2024). "*16% of young people in Kuwait suffer from depression: Mental Health Survey.*" https://timeskuwait.com/news/16-of-young-people-in-kuwait-suffer-from-depression-mental-health-survey/. Accessed May 26, 2025.

UNDP and WHO. (2023). The cost of health services delivered at primary care facilities in Kuwait. https://uniatf.who.int/docs/librariesprovider22/default-document-library/kuwait-phc-costing-report.pdf?sfvrsn=f7939cdc_3. Accessed June 1, 2025.

UNICEF Gulf Area Office. (2023). *Integration of mental health and psychosocial support in primary health care for children, adolescents, pregnant women and new mothers in the Middle East and North Africa region: Kuwait country report.* https://www.unicef.org/mena/media/26291/file/240314%20UNICEF%20MENARO%20MHPSS%20Report%20Kuwait%20Web%20Final.pdf

United Nations. (2006). *Convention on the rights of persons with disabilities (CRPD).* https://www.un.org/development/desa/disabilities/convention-on-the-rights-of-persons-with-disabilities.html

United Nations Development Programme (UNDP) & Supreme Council for Planning and Development (Kuwait). (2020). *Effects of COVID-19 on mental health, food consumption, and relationship dynamics in Kuwait.* UNDP. https://www.undp.org/arab-states/publications/effects-covid-19-mental-health-food-consumption-and-relationship-dynamics-kuwait

United Nations Office on Drugs and Crime. (2021). *World drug report 2021.* https://www.unodc.org/unodc/en/data-and-analysis/wdr2021.html

Uvais, N. A. (2021). Suicidal ideation among Indian expats in the Middle East during the COVID-19 pandemic. *Primary Care Companion for CNS Disorders, 23*(6), 21br02974. https://doi.org/10.4088/PCC.21br02974

World Bank. (2022). *Current health expenditure per capita (current US$)—Kuwait.* https://data.worldbank.org/indicator/SH.XPD.CHEX.PC.CD?locations=KW

World Health Organization. (2013). *Mental health action plan 2013–2020.* https://www.who.int/publications/i/item/9789241506021

World Health Organization. (2020). *Mental health atlas: Kuwait country profile.* https://cdn.who.int/media/docs/default-source/mental-health/mental-health-atlas-2020-country-profiles/kwt.pdf

World Health Organization. (2025). *Suicide worldwide in 2021: Global health estimates.* https://iris.who.int/bitstream/handle/10665/381495/9789240110069-eng.pdf

World Health Organization Regional Office for the Eastern Mediterranean. (2023). *Kuwait: The impact of the COVID-19 pandemic on mental health.* https://www.emro.who.int/mnh/news/kuwait-the-impact-of-the-covid-19-pandemic-on-mental-health.html

Worldometer. (2025). *Kuwait population (LIVE).* https://www.worldometers.info/world-population/kuwait-population/

Zahid, M. A., & Al-Zayed, A. (2009). Psychiatry in Kuwait. *International Psychiatry, 6*(2), 34–36.

Zahid, M. A., Ohaeri, J. U., & Al-Zayed, A. A. (2010). Factors associated with hospital service satisfaction in a sample of Arab subjects with schizophrenia. *BMC Health Services Research, 10*, 294. https://doi.org/10.1186/1472-6963-10-294

Chapter 8
Mental Health Care in Lebanon: History, Challenges, and Current Status

Ahmad Nsouli, Celine Zeineldine, and Fadi Maalouf

Abstract Lebanon is a small developing country, which is facing the added burden of political unrest, economic instability, and the unresolved effects of compounded intergenerational trauma. This chapter provides an overview of the historical development of mental health care, current status, and possible future directions. It begins by giving an overview of the evolution of psychiatric services, followed by the epidemiology of the most burdensome mental illnesses and substance use, and an outline of the current services and the role each service plays in the community. Moreover, it provides insight into key challenges like workforce shortages, geographic inequities, stigma, and underdeveloped referral systems. Finally, the chapter highlights relevant and innovative initiatives, especially the National Mental Health Program, and proposes strategies to strengthen the infrastructure and framework of Lebanon's mental health care system, such as insurance reform, better governance, improved training, and enhanced research capacity.

Keywords Lebanon · Mental health challenges · Psychiatric services · Health policy · Primary health care

1 Introduction

1.1 Country Profile

Lebanon's cultural and commercial crossroads history is still evident in its rich heritage. From ancient Phoenicia to successive periods of Greek, Roman, Byzantine, Islamic, Ottoman, and French rule, the country's historical depth adds further complexity to its modern identity. Lebanon is a small, low-income country in the Middle East that covers an area of 10,452 km^2. It has a population of approximately

A. Nsouli · C. Zeineldine · F. Maalouf (✉)
Department of Psychiatry, American University of Beirut, Beirut, Lebanon
e-mail: fm38@aub.edu.lb

S. Al-Huseini and S. M. Y. Arafat (eds.), *Mental Health Care in the Middle East*, South Asian Perspectives in Mental Health and Psychology ,
https://doi.org/10.1007/978-981-95-0461-9_8

5.77 million Lebanese citizens alongside 1.5 million Syrian refugees and several hundred thousand Palestinian refugees (UNHCR, 2024; World Health Organization, 2023). Despite its small size, Lebanon is home to a very diverse group. The country officially recognizes 18 religious sects, including Maronite Christians, Sunni and Shia Muslims, Druze, Greek Orthodox, Armenian Christians, and other minorities (U.S. Department of State, 2023). The political system, a parliamentary democratic republic where political power is distributed among religious communities, further exemplifies the sectarian diversity; In contrast, this system serves to preserve balance, it has also fuelled sectarian divisions, contributed to political deadlocks, economic crises, and a 15-year civil war from 1975 to 1990 (Makdisi & El-Khalil, 2013). Moreover, Lebanon has been the focal point of regional and global interest due to its strategic geographic position; where it borders Syria, Palestine, and the Mediterranean Sea; as a result, the country has been exposed to repeated external interventions and conflicts, most notably the Israeli invasions, a prolonged Syrian military presence, and more recently, the renewed conflict with Israel in 2024 (Deeb et al., 2025).

Despite a reputation in the mid-twentieth century as a regional hub for finance, culture, and tourism, Lebanon's golden days are behind it, as it's been bombarded with crisis after the other for the past 50 years. In addition to the civil war, recent shocks such as the COVID-19 pandemic, the 2020 Beirut Port explosion, and a severe economic collapse marked by hyperinflation have severely weakened Lebanon's healthcare system, especially mental health services (Mjaess et al., 2021).

1.2 Evolution of Psychiatric Services in Lebanon

1.2.1 Early Period: Echoes from the Past

Before the dawn of the twentieth century, Lebanon, like much of the broader region, lacked a formal framework for understanding and treating mental illness. Mental disorders were interpreted primarily through deeply rooted cultural, social, and religious lenses and often viewed as the result of supernatural forces such as possession by spirits or jinn, or as divine tests of faith. Treatments reflected these beliefs and commonly included folk remedies, religious rituals, and spiritual exorcisms (El-Khoury et al., 2020). While such interpretations occasionally provided individuals with a sense of closure, they also led to significant issues, including widespread misdiagnosis, social marginalization, and a lack of effective medical treatment.

Accounts from nineteenth-century missionaries and Western travellers described conditions of extreme neglect of people suffering from mental illnesses, who were often hidden from society, confined to poorhouses or prisons, or left to wander the streets without care or compassion. Toward the end of Ottoman rule, and influenced by European ideas, a number of Lebanese physicians and intellectuals began advocating for scientific explanations of mental illness rather than spiritual or moral ones. This shift marked the beginning of a more humane and medical approach to mental health, thus laying the groundwork for institutional reform and the establishment of the region's first psychiatric facility.

1.2.2 Institutional Beginnings: The Turning Point

The evolution of psychiatric services in Lebanon can be dated back to the early twentieth century, 1900 to be exact, with the founding of the "Lebanon Hospital for the Insane" at Asfūrīyah by Dr. Theophilus Waldmeier. Later, commonly known as Asfūrīyah, the first modern psychiatric hospital in the Middle East became the hub for countries all over the region. Initially, it was the leading hospital in mental health, where patients benefited from relatively advanced and humane institutionalization. Influenced by European models of "moral treatment," it emphasized structured care, occupational therapy, and basic human dignity, although stigmatization remained deeply rooted in society (Moghnieh, 2019). In 1923, the Franciscan Sisters of the Cross established a convent in Jal El Dib, which later became the Hospital of the Cross in 1951, is still operational and one of the largest psychiatric facilities in the country (Syndicate of Hospitals, n.d.). Other notable institutions followed, including the Armenian Sanatorium of Azounieh in 1938, which integrated psychiatric services alongside general care, and Dar Al-Ajaza Al-Islamiya in Beirut, which began offering mental health services in 1959. During this period, there was a gradual, yet promising move away from mere custodial care toward more therapeutic models. All institutions delivered asylum-based care that was in line with the standards of the time and appropriate for the perceived needs of society. Yet, the stigmatization surrounding psychiatric hospitalization meant that Asfourieh and Deir El Saleeb became associated with horror and desolation in the popular imagination (El-Khoury et al., 2020).

1.2.3 Civil War and Post-war Developments

The momentum toward improving mental health services in Lebanon came to an abrupt halt during the Lebanese Civil War (1975–1990), which severely disrupted the sector due to widespread infrastructure damage and mass displacement. Prior to the conflict, Lebanon had a relatively well-developed health care system, primarily driven by private institutions and supplemented by international non-governmental organizations. However, the onset of civil unrest caused significant dysfunction across the sector, leading to a sharp decline in the accessibility and quality of services, particularly mental health services; among the most notable casualties was the historic ʿAṣfūriyyeh Hospital, which, after operating under extreme conditions amid ongoing shelling, damaged infrastructure, and a traumatized workforce, was forced to close its doors in 1982. Its closure symbolized a broader national mental health crisis whose consequences are still visible today. The war left deep psychological scars on the Lebanese population, contributing to a legacy of intergenerational trauma (MIT Press Reader, 2023). Despite the evident need, mental health remained largely neglected in national policy in the decades following the war. Between the end of the conflict and 2013, the absence of centralized coordination further fragmented mental health services. Most psychiatric facilities were either privately operated or established through joint efforts by local and international NGOs, often in isolated regions with limited oversight.

Post-war reconstruction efforts prioritized physical health infrastructure, sidelining psychiatric care. In this vacuum, NGOs played a critical role in addressing mental health needs, particularly in delivering trauma-informed care, rehabilitation, and community-based mental health support.

1.2.4 Recent Developments and Integration with Primary Care

In the aftermath of decades of neglect, Lebanon's mental health infrastructure entered a pivotal period of development in the mid-2010s. The most crucial initiative at the time was the establishment of the *National Mental Health Programme* (NMHP) within the Ministry of Public Health (MoPH) in May of 2014. This initiative was created in response to the country's fragmented mental health system and lack of coordinated national strategy, this initiative was done in partnership with international bodies like the World Health Organization (WHO), UNICEF, and the International Medical Corps (IMC), with the aim of establishing a comprehensive, inclusive, and rights-based mental health system for all individuals residing in Lebanon, regardless of nationality or socioeconomic status (Ministry of Public Health, n.d.; World Health Organization (WHO), 2023).

The NMHP's main publication, the *Mental Health and Substance Use Strategy 2015–2020,* later followed by an updated version 2024–2030 strategy, marked the first attempt in Lebanon's history to structure national mental health services under a common policy framework. One of the cornerstone objectives of the strategy was the integration of mental health into the country's existing network of primary healthcare centers, which will help tackle the lack of available services. In addition, it aimed to reduce stigma and promote community-based, humane mental health services. This integration emphasizes building the capacity of non-specialist health workers—including general practitioners, nurses, and social workers—to identify, manage, and refer individuals with common mental, neurological, and substance use disorders. Over the next several years, this integration effort led to the implementation of mental health services across primary health care centers distributed throughout the country. This approach was particularly critical in a context marked by a shortage of mental health specialists and a health system strained by overlapping crises.

The NMHP also played a coordinating role in Lebanon's mental health response during major crises. Following the Beirut Port explosion in 2020, the NMHP mobilized emergency psychosocial support, psychological first aid, and trauma care. Beyond crisis response, the NMHP has pushed for systemic integration of mental health into schools and prisons. In education, it partnered with the Ministry of Education and UNICEF to train teachers and counsellors and introduce mental health programming into public schools. The justice sector began piloting efforts to offer mental health screenings and consultations in detention settings (Rabih El Chammay, 2023; Obeid, 2024).

Community-based mental health services in Lebanon have seen notable progress in recent years, especially amid mounting social and economic pressures. Atoui et al. (2024) highlight the effectiveness of assertive follow-up and continuous psychoeducation in enhancing mental health service use and compliance, particularly among women, who made up 67% of the service users. Similarly, El-Khoury et al. (2020) describe a gradual shift toward community mental healthcare, with efforts to standardize early detection and treatment despite significant gaps, especially for severe psychiatric disorders and for populations outside Beirut. The system remains fragmented, relying heavily on private clinics and lacking adequate integration into primary healthcare, which hinders access for vulnerable groups such as the elderly. Karam et al. (2025) note a growing public willingness to seek help, indicating increased awareness of mental health as a priority. Building on these developments, the Ministry of Public Health (2024) launched the National Mental Health Strategy (2024–2030) to establish a sustainable, inclusive, and rights-based mental health system. The strategy emphasizes equitable access, quality community-based services, legal reform, stakeholder engagement, and evidence-based practices to address Lebanon's long-standing and emerging mental health challenges (El-Khoury et al., 2020).

Despite these achievements, challenges persist. Many primary care providers continue to feel underprepared to address severe or complex psychiatric conditions, and referrals to secondary or tertiary care remain inconsistent due to logistical, financial, and infrastructural barriers. Nevertheless, the integration of mental health into primary care in Lebanon represents a foundational shift in both policy and practice, one that lays the groundwork for a more decentralized, accessible, and preventive system of care.

1.2.5 Role of Private Sector, NGOs, and Academic Medical Institutions

Although efforts to publicize mental services are underway to provide Mental health care, Lebanon remains heavily dominated by the private sector, where services are often concentrated in urban centers, particularly in and around Beirut. The cost of private psychiatric consultations and psychotherapy sessions is prohibitively high for many individuals, especially in the absence of insurance coverage for mental health conditions. As a result, there exists a two-tiered system in which high-quality care is available to a minority who can afford it, while the majority rely on under-resourced public facilities or NGO-led initiatives.

Non-governmental organizations (NGOs) have emerged as key actors in addressing these disparities, providing vital mental health and psychosocial support (MHPSS) to both Lebanese nationals and refugee populations. Organizations such as Embrace and Médecins Sans Frontières (MSF) have played instrumental roles in bridging the treatment gap. Embrace, under the influence of, for instance, operates Lebanon's national suicide prevention hotline (1564) and offers community-based mental health services, including psychiatric consultations, psychotherapy, and awareness-raising campaigns, similarly while MSF and other local NGOs deliver little to no-cost mental health care to displaced and underserved populations, particularly in the Bekaa Valley and northern regions.

2 Epidemiology and Burden of Mental Illness

2.1 Common Mental Health Disorders

About 25% of the Lebanese population suffers from at least one mental health disorder (Atoui et al., 2024; El-Khoury et al., 2020; Karam, 2024). From this percentage, Karam (2024) found that 18% of the population suffers from anxiety, while 13% suffers from depression. It seems that the most common mental health disorders are Major Depressive Disorder (MDD) (Atoui et al., 2024; Ministry of Public Health, 2024), Generalized Anxiety Disorder (GAD) (Atoui et al., 2024; Ministry of Public Health, 2024), and Post-Traumatic Stress Disorder (PTSD) (Atoui et al., 2024).

In Lebanon, the most vulnerable populations concerning mental health include older adults, particularly those suffering from dementia (Ministry of Public Health, 2024), as well as displaced individuals and elderly refugees. Notably, one study indicated that 80% of elderly refugees experience depression (Karam, 2024). Additionally, younger individuals aged 18–24 years (Atoui et al., 2024) and incarcerated populations, who exhibit a higher prevalence of bipolar and psychotic disorders (Ministry of Public Health, 2024), are also at increased risk.

Moreover, two notable trends emerge from these observations. Firstly, the prevalence of mental health disorders tends to be inversely related to age; for instance, 32.7% of children and adolescents have at least one mental disorder (Maalouf et al., 2022; Ministry of Public Health, 2024). The 2016 BEI-PSY by Maalouf et al., showed that 26.1% of adolescents in Beirut struggle with at least one mental health disorder, with specific rates for anxiety disorders (13.1%), ADHD (10.2%), mood disorders (6.7%), and disruptive behavior disorders (4.7%) (Maalouf et al., 2016). On a national level, the PALS study by Maalouf et al. reported 32.7% prevalence of positive psychiatric screening tests in children and adolescents, with the most prevalent disorders being depression and anxiety (Maalouf et al., 2022). Secondly, populations exposed to higher levels of trauma generally exhibit a greater prevalence of mental health disorders among the Lebanese population, driven by war-related trauma, which does not correlate with socioeconomic background. This finding suggests that historical trauma affects individuals across various backgrounds. Furthermore, the studies reveal that women have higher prevalence rates of anxiety and depression compared to men (Atoui et al., 2024; Karam et al., 2006).

This is particularly concerning, considering that earlier studies reported vastly smaller prevalences. For example, in a 2002–2003 survey, Chahine and Chemali (2009) found a 12-month prevalence of 11.2% for anxiety disorders and 6.6% for mood disorders. Furthermore, among children aged 3–16, the 12-month prevalence rate was 10.3% for PTSD symptoms and 33.3% for Major Depressive Disorder (MDD) within a year following the civil war. Additionally, Karam (2024) reported a prevalence rate of 18% for anxiety and 13% for depression in his 2024 study.

Consequently, the increase in prevalence rates could be due to the instability the Lebanese population has endured amidst the numerous crises affecting the country (Ministry of Public Health, 2024). Notably, Karam and Baaklini (2024) found a strong link between the severity of individuals' exposure to recent crises and their mental health, underscoring the urgent need for effective mental health interventions.

Intersecting with these predictors, certain risk factors further exacerbate mental health issues. Individuals who are female, children, adolescents, and refugees are notably more vulnerable (Chahine & Chemali, 2009; Karam, 2024). Trauma, in particular, has had a profound impact on mental health. Karam et al. (2006) reported that research indicates that factors such as socioeconomic status, governorate, marital status, and employment status do not significantly correlate with mental health disorders when exposure to trauma is a significant factor. This finding suggests that trauma transcends individuals' backgrounds and affects all individuals regardless of their circumstances. Furthermore, the high prevalence rates of PTSD in Lebanon, especially when compared to global statistics, underscore the enduring impact of trauma on the Lebanese population (Karam et al., 2025).

A notable and concerning phenomenon in Lebanon is the overwhelmingly low percentage of individuals with mental health disorders who seek treatment. Current statistics reveal a staggering treatment gap of over 90%, with only about 10.9% of those suffering from mental health issues actively pursuing care. Maalouf et al. (2022) found that only 5% of children and adolescents who screened positive for a psychiatric illness sought help. One study indicated that merely 3.7% of individuals with mental disorders and 14.6% of those with severe mental disorders received any form of treatment (Chahine & Chemali, 2009). Interestingly, another study found that 45% of individuals receiving treatment were aged between 18 and 24 years, which supports the notion that mental health disorders have a higher prevalence among younger populations and suggests that they may be more inclined to seek help (Atoui et al., 2024).

2.2 *Suicide and Substance Abuse*

Historically, literature on suicide has been limited, but the past decade has seen a rise in national studies addressing the prevalence, characteristics, and risk factors of suicide. In Lebanon, suicide rates have increased in recent years, which is largely driven by the cascade of crises, the country is going through alongside better reporting and awareness (Bou Khalil, 2019). The suicide rate is estimated at 1 person every

2.1 days (Embrace, 2024) or 2.8 per 100,000 population, with under-reporting suggesting even higher rates due to stigma and inadequate surveillance (International Society of Substance Use Professionals, 2025; Ministry of Public Health, 2024). According to Karam et al., the lifetime prevalence of suicide attempts in adults is 2%. In addition, evidence from Lebanon shows that the first onset of suicidal ideation, planning, and attempts is significantly associated with war exposure, younger age, female gender, and mental disorders such as depression, impulse-control disorders, and social phobia (Karam et al., 2012). Among children and adolescents in Lebanon, Baroud et al., (2019) reported that 11.5% endorsed suicidal ideation while another study by Chahine et al., (2020) showed that suicidal ideations among adolescents reached a staggering 28.9%. Between 2008 and 2018, 1366 documented suicide cases were noted, with rates fluctuating during that period (Bizri et al., 2021).

A review of suicide attempts from a tertiary hospital in Lebanon between 2009 and 2015 identified 108 cases, with females accounting for 71.4% of attempts, with ages ranging from 22 to 49. Most individuals were unmarried (61.1%) and unemployed (43%). The majority of attempts occurring at home using prescription medication (61.3%) or over-the-counter medications (27.9) (Wazir et al., 2024). Men are statistically more likely to die by suicide than women at a ratio of 2:1, with the majority of methods being violent, notably using firearms (41.4%), followed by hanging (26.5%). Completed suicides were most common in the Mount Lebanon region (Bizri et al., 2021). The rise in suicide rates correlates with the ongoing economic crisis, highlighting a link between socioeconomic decline, mental health deterioration, and substance abuse (Ayoubi, 2024). While Lebanon lacks a national suicide prevention strategy, multiple initiatives like Embrace's National Lifeline (1564) represent progress and show promise for the future (Wazir et al., 2024).

Additionally, commonly used substances in Lebanon include marijuana, hashish, heroin, and synthetic drugs, alongside tobacco and alcohol use among the population (International Society of Substance Use Professionals, 2025; Kerbage & Haddad, 2014). Recent studies on opioid use have discovered concerning levels of risk for Opioid Use Disorder, correlating with factors such as personal and family history of substance abuse (Chamoun et al., 2023).

Lebanon's socioeconomic turmoil has significantly influenced substance abuse patterns (Kerbage & Haddad, 2014). The onset of Lebanon's economic crisis in 2019 precipitated increased relapse rates among recovering drug addicts, primarily due to limited resources and financial instability. This financial distress contributed to various stressors, such as employment changes and reduced work hours, all of which are known risk factors for substance abuse (Gibon, 2025). Moreover, as the crisis prolonged, individuals began to shift from recreational drug use to utilizing substances as coping mechanisms for mental health issues, such as stress, depression, and insomnia. Consequently, there was an observable shift in drug consumption toward cheaper alternatives such as cannabis, salvia, alcohol, and crystal meth, in place of more expensive options such as MDMA and cocaine (Gibon, 2025). The collapse of Lebanon's healthcare system exacerbated addiction treatment challenges, leading to increased reliance on NGOs, such as Skoun, which often operate with limited funding and accessibility (Gibon, 2025).

A cross-sectional study by Khoshnood et al. (2021) further highlighted the alarming prevalence of drug overdose among people who inject drugs (PWID) in Lebanon, reporting that 44.8% had experienced a non-fatal overdose. The study also linked overdose incidents to factors such as a history of incarceration and prior substance treatment. Heroin remained the most commonly injected drug among PWID, with a marked increase in relapse risks attributed to a shortage of affordable opioid agonist therapy medications due to the rising black market prices (Gibon, 2025). It is critical to establish overdose prevention strategies, particularly for individuals recently incarcerated or in drug treatment, to mitigate overdose risks (Khoshnood et al., 2021). Additionally, the lack of reliable death documentation in Lebanon complicates the ability to discern the causes of death, including drug-related and suicide cases (Ministry of Public Health, 2017). The correlation between substance use disorders and incarceration is evident, with Khoshnood et al. (2021) reporting that 80.1% of people who inject drugs (PWID) have a history of arrest, highlighting the urgent need for a cohesive drug policy that differentiates between drug use/possession and trafficking (Kerbage & Haddad, 2014). Treating drug users similarly to traffickers impedes rehabilitation efforts and deters treatment-seeking behaviors, which can increase the risk of suicide.

In conclusion, tackling the intertwined issues of economic instability, mental health services, and substance abuse treatment within a more comprehensive public health framework can significantly reduce substance abuse and suicide rates in Lebanon (Ayoubi, 2024).

3 Mental Health Services in Lebanon

3.1 Conventional Services

Lebanon's health system is a pluralistic one that includes public health services governed by the Ministry of Public Health (MoPH), a dominant private sector, local non-governmental organizations (NGOs), and international donors and humanitarian agencies like UNRWA, UN. Knowing that the model for health care in Lebanon was largely designed outside the public sector's framework, it is no one's surprise that most of health services are delivered through the private sector, especially mental health care (MoPH, 2022). This has led to a system in which access to mental health services is significantly influenced by factors such as geographic location, socioeconomic status, and insurance coverage.

Within the public sector, mental health services are delivered through primary health care centers (PHCCs), district hospitals, and a few tertiary public hospitals. Since 2014, the MoPH's National Mental Health Programme (NMHP) has worked to integrate mental health into primary care, training general practitioners, nurses, and social workers to detect and manage common mental disorders. As of 2023, approximately 75 PHCCs out of more than 240 have implemented some form of integrated mental health service delivery. Despite these advancements, the public sector continues to suffer from a shortage of trained personnel, the absence of psychiatrists in primary and district health facilities, a limited range of medications, and insufficient inpatient psychiatric beds. Most public hospitals lack specialized psychiatric units, and there is little infrastructure for the management of complex or severe mental illness outside the capital region (MoPH, 2023).

The private sector, which dominates the provision of specialized psychiatric care, includes private psychiatric hospitals, outpatient clinics, and private practitioners. Facilities such as Fanar Hospital, Deir el Salib Hospital, and psychiatric wards in general hospitals like Hôtel-Dieu de France and the American University of Beirut Medical Centre (AUBMC) offer a wide range of services. Private practitioners, including psychiatrists, clinical psychologists, and psychotherapists, also operate individual clinics, particularly in urban centers. While private services are generally more advanced and provide higher quality care, they are often unaffordable for the average Lebanese citizen. Consultation fees typically range from 30 to 100 US dollars per session, with few insurance plans, including the National Social Security Fund, offering meaningful reimbursement for mental health treatment (Chahine & Chemali, 2009). Compounding the problem is the lack of oversight and regulation of private mental health services, leading to inconsistencies in care quality and ethical practices.

Informal care pathways are also prevalent in Lebanon and often serve as the first point of contact for individuals experiencing mental distress, particularly in rural and underserved communities. Many people turn to religious figures such as sheikhs and priests, or traditional healers known for spiritual or herbal interventions. These providers are often sought when symptoms are interpreted through a cultural or spiritual lens, with beliefs in jinn possession, the evil eye, or divine punishment frequently informing people's understanding of mental illness. While such practices may offer emotional support and community integration, they can delay access to professional help, reinforce stigma, and result in the use of unproven or even harmful treatment methods; The Ministry of Public Health (2023) notes that traditional and religious beliefs, stigma, and low perceived need are among the key barriers to timely professional help-seeking in Lebanon (MOPH, 2023).

Non-governmental organizations and international humanitarian agencies have stepped in to fill some of the service gaps, especially among vulnerable populations such as refugees, survivors of trauma, and those in low-income or rural areas. Organizations like Médecins Sans Frontières (MSF) offer free psychiatric services and medications in underserved regions, while the International Medical Corps (IMC) runs mobile mental health teams and community-based psychosocial programs. The Restart Center provides trauma-focused services for survivors of torture and detention. At the same time, Embrace, a locally founded NGO, has become a national leader in suicide prevention, crisis helpline support, and public mental health education. These initiatives have become increasingly vital, particularly in light of the growing demand for services and the limited capacity of the state to provide them (UNHCR, 2022).

A critical issue that cuts across all sectors of mental health care in Lebanon is the absence of a coordinated referral system. Individuals can access services through any channel—public, private, NGO, or informal, without a structured pathway or gatekeeping mechanism. While this theoretically offers flexibility, it often results in misdiagnosis, fragmentation of care, duplication of services, and preventable costs to patients. Geographic and financial disparities persist as major barriers to access. Rural areas continue to be underserved, and many people forego treatment altogether due to the high costs, social stigma, or limited awareness of mental health conditions. According to recent figures from the NMHP, Lebanon has only about 1.26 psychiatrists per 100,000 people, well below the World Health Organization's recommended minimum of 10 (Kheir et al, 2024).

3.2 New Developments—Telepsychiatry

The COVID-19 pandemic served as a catalyst for the development and adoption of telepsychiatry in Lebanon (Mohtar et al., 2025). As in many parts of the world, the pandemic created a surge in demand for mental health services; in response, several public and private initiatives began offering remote psychiatric consultations and therapy sessions through digital platforms. In contrast, telepsychiatry has improved access in certain contexts, especially for individuals in remote areas or those facing mobility limitations. The downside is that no formal guidelines or national standards governing licensure, confidentiality, or data protection for tele-mental health services in Lebanon. Additionally, disparities in digital access and literacy pose significant challenges as many individuals, particularly older adults, refugees, and residents of rural areas, face difficulties related to internet connectivity, lack of private space at home, and limited familiarity with digital tools. The potential of telepsychiatry lies in bridging the gap and providing access to care. These barriers have restricted the equitable adoption of telepsychiatry, even as its potential to extend access remains promising. Looking ahead, telepsychiatry could play an important role in scaling up mental health services and reducing stigma by offering a more discrete and convenient mode of care. However, its success will depend on the development of a comprehensive digital health strategy, investments in infrastructure, and the establishment of regulatory frameworks that ensure both quality and accessibility.

4 Challenges in Mental Health Care

4.1 Financial Constraints

A significant barrier to effective mental health care in Lebanon is insufficient funding (Atoui et al., 2024; Chahine & Chemali, 2009; El-Khoury et al., 2020; Karam, 2024; Kerbage & Haddad, 2014; Ministry of Public Health, 2017). This is partly due to the misallocation of health expenditures, with 70% of mental health funding directed toward inpatient care, leaving outpatient services reliant on out-of-pocket payments, NGOs, or external donors. The lack of comprehensive mental health policies and dedicated financial strategies further limits the system's effectiveness (Karam, 2024). Since 2019, services and medications have become increasingly expensive and sometimes unavailable. With most services in the private sector and no private insurance coverage for mental health, treatment remains financially burdensome and inaccessible for many. While NGOs provide low-fee services, sustained financial support is challenging (Atoui et al., 2024).

4.2 Workforce Shortages

Lebanon faces a critical shortage of mental health professionals, with approximately 1.26 psychiatrists, 3.42 psychologists, and 1.38 social workers per 100,000 people, far below the 70 mental health workers per 100,000 seen in high-income countries (Atoui et al., 2024). This shortage makes it difficult to meet the population's mental health needs and contributes to overburdened professionals, burnout, and "brain drain" (El-Khoury et al., 2020; Ministry of Public Health, 2024). The economic crisis has accelerated the migration of professionals, worsening the gap (Ayoubi, 2024). There is also a lack of training among primary care physicians to identify and manage mental health conditions effectively. While efforts exist through organizations such as the Lebanese Order of Psychologists and national psychiatric societies, they have not been sufficient to close workforce gaps (Ministry of Public Health, 2024). Moreover, professionals are concentrated in Beirut and coastal cities, leaving rural areas underrepresented (International Society of Substance Use Professionals, 2025). NGOs offer support but cannot substitute for a fully staffed mental health workforce. To improve access and quality of care, Lebanon urgently needs more trained, geographically distributed mental health providers (El-Khoury et al., 2020; Karam et al., 2006; Ministry of Public Health, 2017).

4.3 Access Barriers

Access to mental health care in Lebanon is hindered by geographic, economic, and systemic barriers (Bizri et al., 2021; Chahine & Chemali, 2009; Karam & Baaklini, 2024; Ministry of Public Health, 2017). Services are often concentrated in Beirut, leading to shortages in rural areas and creating significant disparities in access (Atoui et al., 2024; Ayoubi, 2024; El-Khoury et al., 2020; Karam et al., 2006; Kerbage & Haddad, 2014). For instance, 80% of the country's 15 substance-use or dual-diagnosis treatment facilities are located in Beirut and Mount Lebanon (International Society of Substance Use Professionals, 2025). Poor public transportation and rising travel costs further limit access to care (El-Khoury et al., 2020; Ministry of Public Health, 2024). Telehealth services have been suggested as a potential solution (Ministry of Public Health, 2024). Economic hardship is another major barrier, both as a contributing factor to mental health conditions and as a deterrent to seeking help due to the high cost of private care and limited affordability of services (Atoui et al., 2024; Karam, 2024; Kerbage & Haddad, 2014). Additional issues include deteriorating supply chains, reprioritization of health services, lack of professional regulation, and widespread normalization of mental distress, all of which reduce help-seeking behavior (Atoui et al., 2024; Karam & Baaklini, 2024; Trieu, 2024).

4.4 Stigma

Cultural perceptions have historically played a role in shaping attitudes toward mental health and help-seeking behaviors, with stigma showing to be a contributor to low help-seeking behaviors (Atoui et al., 2024; Ayoubi, 2024; Chahine & Chemali, 2009; Karam, 2024; Karam & Baaklini, 2024; Kerbage & Haddad, 2014; Ministry of Public Health, 2017, 2024). In a large portion of the Lebanese population, attitudes toward mental health issues and toward seeing a professional about them are mostly negative (Ministry of Public Health, 2024). Negative societal attitudes, fears of being discriminated against or labeled, as well as a lack of awareness, have previously been discouraging factors in seeking help (Atoui et al., 2024; El-Khoury et al., 2020; International Society of Substance Use Professionals, 2025; Karam, 2024; Karam et al., 2006; Kerbage & Haddad, 2014; Ministry of Public Health, 2017; Trieu, 2024). 90% of people who deal with mental health problems do not seek treatment (Karam, 2024), which is in line with the fact that even physicians tend to have negative attitudes toward mental health patients (Chahine & Chemali, 2009). Although mental health issues, suicide, and drug-use problems are prevalent, they tend to be underreported due to social and religious taboos (Bizri et al., 2021; International Society of Substance Use Professionals, 2025). This shows how prominent this type of stigma is. This creates a cycle of avoidance of mental health services due to the silence that is expected when mental health is in question, since it is deemed a taboo subject in Lebanon (El-Khoury et al., 2020; Karam et al., 2006). Limited knowledge about mental health also contributes to the treatment gap (Karam et al., 2025).

However, there has been recent progress: in a Lebanese sample, 65% recognized that mental health disorders are a primary concern (Karam et al., 2025). More recent data from the nationally representative PALS study showed that, among parents of children with a psychiatric disorder, stigma, discomfort discussing mental health, and distrust in care were not deemed barriers to seeking help. These findings show progress in mental health awareness in Lebanon.

4.5 Non-medical Management

Another potential barrier to seeking medical treatment is the influence of religious healers and alternative medicine in Lebanon (El-Khoury et al., 2020). Due to the stigma surrounding mental health and its medical treatment, people often rely on non-conventional treatment approaches (Bizri et al., 2021; Chahine & Chemali, 2009). Thus, societal and cultural beliefs, along with the distrust in health institutions due to past experiences, may encourage individuals who struggle with mental health to seek help from religious or informal healers (Atoui et al., 2024). Another reason why treatment is often sought from spiritual healers is the lack of awareness about mental health or the unavailability of scientific treatments, especially in rural areas (El-Khoury et al., 2020; Karam & Baaklini, 2024; Ministry of Public Health, 2024). Moreover, in the cultural context of Lebanon, people tend to turn to religious and traditional healers, such as Cheikhs, during crises which could further explain the overreliance on alternative treatments for mental health which is deemed more culturally acceptable (Ayoubi, 2024; Karam et al., 2025; Ministry of Public Health, 2017, 2024; Trieu, 2024). Such non-medical approaches can be problematic since they push people away from seeking professional help, further complicating the treatment of mental health disorders (El-Khoury et al., 2020; Karam et al., 2006; Kerbage & Haddad, 2014; Ministry of Public Health, 2017). However, recent findings suggest a shift in attitudes, especially in the context of childhood and adolescent mental health, where data from the PALS study showed that among parents of children with psychiatric disorders, stigma, discomfort discussing mental health, and distrust in care were not considered major barriers. This indicates increasing awareness and changing perceptions around professional mental health care in Lebanon.

4.6 Research Gaps

There is a lack of data to inform evidence-based practices in Lebanon (Chahine & Chemali, 2009). There is a deficiency in data collection when it comes to the prevalence of mental health disorders (Chahine & Chemali, 2009). There is a lack of research into mental health conditions, especially when it comes to psychotic disorders (El-Khoury et al., 2020). The effectiveness of existing mental health services has not been well studied (Chahine & Chemali, 2009). Moreover, there is a significant gap in intervention research, including evaluating treatment outcomes and culturally adapted therapeutic approaches. These research gaps indicate that there are gaps in evidence-based practices that influence the creation of informed policies in Lebanon (Ayoubi, 2024; Chahine & Chemali, 2009; El-Khoury et al., 2020; Kerbage & Haddad, 2014; Ministry of Public Health, 2024). Developing a robust database, such as a national health information system for mental health-related indicators, could help solve this issue (Ministry of Public Health, 2017, 2024). Additionally, reliable data involving suicide has been shown to be difficult to attain due to unorganized reporting and a lack of detailed demographic information (Bizri et al., 2021).

5 Strengths

Despite the innumerable challenges facing the mental health system, there is a silver lining in the form of strengths that have yielded great progress in the past decade. These strengths highlight the country's resilience and drive toward innovation and improvement, and serve as a beacon of hope for the potential of the Lebanese mental health system.

5.1 A Robust Mental Health Policy Framework

As previously mentioned, the National Mental Health Programme (NMHP) developed in 2014 which developed the Mental health and Substance Use Strategy (2015–2020) alongside the update 2021–2030 laid the groundwork toward high quality, reasonably priced, and more accessible mental health services for everyone and have worked on the integration of mental health services into primary health care center which is decentralizing services and further improving access.

5.2 Strong NGO and Civil Society Engagement

NGOs have played a pivotal role in the progression of mental health in Lebanon. They are filling service gaps and providing aid to vulnerable populations all over Lebanon. Moreover, they've played a huge role in raising public awareness and crisis response.

5.3 Growing Public Awareness

Growing media coverage, social campaigns, and youth engagement in schools, as well as NGOs, the public sector, and the private sector leading anti-stigma campaigns all over Lebanon, have improved public awareness regarding mental illnesses and treatment.

5.4 Academic Institutions: The Backbone of Lebanon's Mental Health System

A key strength of Lebanon's mental health system is its strong academic institutions, which prioritize teaching and research in psychiatry and psychology. Furthermore, universities across the country offer top-tier educational programs in mental health that train future professionals to uphold the highest standards of care. In addition, these institutions play a pivotal role in shaping and disseminating evidence-based practices while addressing critical research points like stigma, culturally appropriate interventions, and the epidemiological landscape of mental illness in Lebanon.

6 Ways Out

6.1 Enhancing Research and Funding

Although multiple university hospitals and NGOs produce mental health research, there is sparse national data about service utilization and treatment outcomes. Thus, bridging this gap requires investment in epidemiological research, assessment of treatments, and culturally relevant interventions. In addition, collaboration between academic centers and ministries to secure national and international grants to fund huge research projects aimed at improving mental health services all over Lebanon.

6.2 Equitable Distribution of Mental Health Professionals

As previously mentioned, most mental health professionals are concentrated in urban areas, especially the capital, Beirut, whereas remote areas like Akkar, Bekaa, and parts of the South are underserved and face shortages. A plan to decentralize training and offer incentives for rural deployment will help expand coverage and compensate for the current shortage.

6.3 Health Insurance Coverage for Mental Health

Mental health is generally not covered by most insurance plans in Lebanon. Therefore, reforms to mandate mental health coverage in national health insurance and private insurance companies will increase equity in access for all patients, regardless of socioeconomic status or background.

6.4 Improving Referral Pathways

Lebanon's referral system is highly fragmented and confusing, requiring patients to navigate a system filled with disconnected providers. Therefore, a user-friendly digital interface with interface linking primary health centers, NGOs, and private practitioners is needed to streamline access and continuity of care.

6.5 Collaboration

Collaboration across education, justice, social affairs, and health sectors is crucial. Lebanon's NMHP has laid the groundwork with interministerial coordination platforms, but more structured intersectoral mechanisms are needed, particularly in schools and juvenile justice settings.

7 Conclusion

Lebanon has made significant progress in strengthening its healthcare system, and in recent years, there has been a growing recognition of the importance of mental health. While the country continues to face challenges that inevitably impact the mental health system, there is clear and encouraging momentum toward nationwide improvement. Dedicated efforts are being made to address gaps, such as limited and inequitable access to mental health services and stigma, by integrating mental health into primary care, the development of national strategies, and increased involvement from NGOs and the private sector.

Although the shortage of mental health professionals and underfunding remain pressing concerns that render a significant portion of the population without access to essential mental health care, promising initiatives aimed at expanding training and building community-based services are paving the way to a more inclusive and equitable system. By securing investments in mental health research, promoting a more balanced geographical distribution of services, building a reliable referral system, and improving clinical regulation, Lebanon is laying the ground for a more robust and accessible mental health system.

Finally, the progress made so far is gradual yet steady. It provides a solid foundation for a future where mental health care is a right delivered with equity and quality to the people of Lebanon.

References

Atoui, M., Zeinoun, L., Akiki, Z., & Zeinoun, P. (2024). What does it take to offer high-quality, community-based, accessible mental health care in Lebanon? *Eastern Mediterranean Health Journal, 30*(8), 584–592. https://doi.org/10.26719/2024.30.8.584

Ayoubi, B. R. (2024). Suicide in Lebanon amidst economic collapse, political stalemate, and societal disintegration. *Silent Pain and Public Policy*, 134–157. https://doi.org/10.4337/9781035338801.00014

Baroud, E., Al Rojolah, L., Ghandour, L. A., Akoury Dirani, L., Barakat, M., Elbejjani, M., Shamseddeen, W., Brent, D., & Maalouf, F. T. (2020). Risk and protective factors for depressive symptoms and suicidality among children and adolescents in Lebanon: Results from a national survey. *Journal of Affective Disorders Reports, 2*, Article 100036. https://doi.org/10.1016/j.jadr.2020.100036

Baroud, E., Ghandour, L. A., Alrojolah, L., Zeinoun, P., & Maalouf, F. T. (2019). Suicidality among Lebanese adolescents: Prevalence, predictors and service utilization. *Psychiatry Research, 275*, 338–344. https://doi.org/10.1016/j.psychres.2019.03.033

Bizri, M., Zeinoun, L., Mihailescu, A. M., Daher, M., Atoui, M., Chammay, R., & Nahas, Z. (2021). A closer look at patterns and characteristics of suicide in Lebanon: A first nationwide report of cases from 2008 to 2018. *Asian Journal of Psychiatry, 59*, Article 102635. https://doi.org/10.1016/j.ajp.2021.102635

Bou Khalil, R. (2019). The psychological wellbeing of the Lebanese society lies between incremental suicide rates and financial stress. *Asian Journal of Psychiatry, 42*, 85–86. https://doi.org/10.1016/j.ajp.2019.04.002

Chahine, L. M., & Chemali, Z. (2009). Report: Mental health care in Lebanon: Policy, plans and programmes. *World Health Organization*. https://www.emro.who.int/emhj-volume-15-2009/volume-15-issue-6/report-mental-health-care-in-lebanon-policy-plans-and-programmes.html

Chahine, M., Salameh, P., Haddad, C., Sacre, H., Soufia, M., Akel, M., Obeid, S., Hallit, R., & Hallit, S. (2020). Suicidal ideation among Lebanese adolescents: Scale validation, prevalence and correlates. *BMC Psychiatry, 20*(1), 304. https://doi.org/10.1186/s12888-020-02726-6

Chamoun, K., Mouawad, J., Salameh, P., Sacre, H., Haddad, R., Khabbaz, L. R., Megarbane, B., & Hajj, A. (2023). Opioid use disorder in two samples of the Lebanese population: Scale validation and correlation with sleep and mood disorders. *BMC Psychiatry, 23*(1). https://doi.org/10.1186/s12888-023-05304-8

Dar Al-Ajaza Al-Islamia. (n.d.). *About us*. Retrieved April 28, 2025, from https://daih.org/aboutus

Deeb, L., Mikdashi, M., Nalbantian, T., & Sbaiti, N. (2025, January). A primer on Lebanon—History, Palestine and resistance to Israeli violence. *Middle East Research and Information Project*. https://merip.org/2025/01/a-primer-on-lebanon-history-palestine-and-resistance-to-israeli-violence-2/

El-Khoury, J., Haidar, R., & Charara, R. (2020). Community mental healthcare in Lebanon. *Consortium Psychiatricum, 1*(1), 71–77. https://doi.org/10.17650/2712-7672-2020-1-1-71-77

Embrace. (n.d.). *Embrace Mental Health Center (EMHC)*. https://embracelebanon.org/en/whatwedo/EMHC

Embrace. (2024, February). *Lebanon's 2023 suicide rates: What do this year's numbers tell us about mental health in the country*. https://www.embracelebanon.org/Media/publications/pdfs/dc722868-a519-4afb-89fc-31b2165c442d.pdf

Gibon, C. (2025). Lebanon's recovering drug addicts risk relapse as economic crisis destroys hope. *Middle East Eye*. https://www.middleeasteye.net/news/lebanon-drug-addicts-recovering-risk-falling-back-economic-crisis

IDRAAC. (n.d.). *About us*. https://www.idraac.org/page/about-us

International Medical Corps. (n.d.). *Lebanon*. https://internationalmedicalcorps.org/country/lebanon/

International Society of Substance Use Professionals. (2025). *Lebanon Country Profile*. https://www.issup.net/national-chapters/issup-lebanon/country-profile

Karam, E., & Baaklini, S. (2024, September 12). Two-thirds of Lebanese people suffer from at least one mental health disorder. *L'Orient Today*. https://today.lorientlejour.com/article/1426938/two-thirds-of-lebanese-people-suffer-from-at-least-one-mental-health-disorder.html

Karam, E. G., El-Jamal, M., Osman, R., Toukan, S., Mouawad, G. I., & Al Barathie, J. (2025). The aftermath of multiple trauma on a nation: Unraveling Lebanon's unique mental health struggle. *Frontiers in Psychiatry, 15*. https://doi.org/10.3389/fpsyt.2024.1444245

Karam, E. G., Mneimneh, Z. N., Karam, A. N., Fayyad, J. A., Nasser, S. C., Chatterji, S., & Kessler, R. C. (2006). Prevalence and treatment of mental disorders in Lebanon: A national epidemiological survey. *The Lancet, 367*(9515), 1000–1006. https://doi.org/10.1016/s0140-6736(06)68427-4

Karam, E. G., Salamoun, M. M., Mneimneh, Z. N., Fayyad, J. A., Karam, A. N., Hajjar, R., Dimassi, H., Nock, M. K., & Kessler, R. C. (2012). War and first onset of suicidality: The role of mental disorders. *Psychological Medicine, 42*(10), 2109–2118. https://doi.org/10.1017/s0033291712000268

Karam, G. E. (2024). The prevalence of mental health disorders in Lebanon: 25% of the population is at risk. *Human & Health* (53, pp. 16–17). Syndicate of Hospitals in Lebanon. https://syndicateofhospitals.org.lb/Content/uploads/SyndicateMagazinePdfs/1535_16-17.pdf

Kerbage, H., & Haddad, R. (2014). Lebanon drug situation and policy. Accessed September 18, 2017, from https://www.coe.int/T/DG3/Pompidou/Source/Images/country%20pro-files%20flags/profiles/CP%20Lebanon%20English%20V2.pdf

Kheir, W., Zoghbi, E., Bteich, R., Rady, A., & El Chammay, R. (2024). Modelling target workforce estimates for community-based mental health services in Lebanon [Preprint]. *Research Square*. https://doi.org/10.21203/rs.3.rs-1192774/v1

Khoshnood, K., Sheb, F., Khouri, D., Aaraj, E., Barbour, R., Crawford, F., Mokhbat, J., Parpia, A., & Heimer, R. (2021). Reported history and correlates of drug overdose among people who inject drugs in Lebanon. *Eastern Mediterranean Health Journal, 27*(6), 571–579. https://doi.org/10.26719/2021.27.6.571

Maalouf, F. T., Alrojolah, L., Akoury-Dirani, L., Barakat, M., Brent, D., Elbejjani, M., Shamseddeen, W., & Ghandour, L. A. (2022, April). Psychopathology in children and adolescents in Lebanon study (PALS): A national household survey. *Social Psychiatry and Psychiatric Epidemiology, 57*(4), 761–774. https://doi.org/10.1007/s00127-021-02208-4

Maalouf, F. T., Ghandour, L. A., Halabi, F., Zeinoun, P., Shehab, A. A., & Tavitian, L. (2016, August). Psychiatric disorders among adolescents from Lebanon: Prevalence, correlates, and treatment gap. *Social Psychiatry and Psychiatric Epidemiology, 51*(8), 1105–1116. https://doi.org/10.1007/s00127-016-1241-4

Makdisi, S., & El-Khalil, Y. (2013, March). *Lebanon: The legacy of sectarian consociationalism and the transition to a fully-fledged democracy* (Working Paper No. 14). Issam Fares Institute for Public Policy and International Affairs, American University of Beirut. https://www.aub.edu.lb/ifi/Documents/20130301samir_makdesi_youssef_khalil_rapp_wp.pdf

Médecins Sans Frontières. (n.d.). *Lebanon*. Médecins Sans Frontières. https://www.msf.org/lebanon

Ministry of Public Health. (n.d.). *About the national mental health program.* Retrieved April 28, 2025, from https://www.moph.gov.lb/en/Pages/0/8872/about-the-national-mental-health-program
Ministry of Public Health. (2017). *National report on drug situation in Lebanon 2017.* Available at: https://www.moph.gov.lb/userfiles/files/HealthCareSystem/Narcotics/NODDA_2017_english.pdf
Ministry of Public Health. (2022, January 24). Lebanon national health strategy: Vision 2030: Out of the crisis and towards better health for all. *Beirut.* https://www.moph.gov.lb/userfiles/files/About%20MOPH/StrategicPlans/National-Health-Strategy–Vision2030/LHS_220124.pdf
Ministry of Public Health. (2023). National mental health strategy for Lebanon (2023–2030) [Draft version for stakeholder review]. *Beirut.* https://www.moph.gov.lb/userfiles/files/ENG%20Mental%20health%20strategy-Lebanon-2023-2030-DRAFT%20FOR%20REVIEW.pdf
Ministry of Public Health. (2024). *National mental health strategy for Lebanon (2024–2030): Reforming the mental health system.* Available at: https://moph.gov.lb
MIT Press Reader. (2023, January 19). The tragic downfall of ʿAṣfūriyyeh (The Lebanon Hospital for the Insane). *The MIT Press Reader.* https://thereader.mitpress.mit.edu/the-tragic-downfall-of-aşfuriyyeh-the-lebanon-hospital-for-the-insane/
Mjaess, G., Karam, A., Chebel, R., Tayeh, G. A., & Aoun, F. (2021). COVID-19, the economic crisis, and the Beirut blast: What 2020 meant to the Lebanese health-care system. *Eastern Mediterranean Health Journal, 27*(6), 535–537. https://doi.org/10.26719/2021.27.6.535
Moghnieh, L. (2019, May 22). Asfourieh: A history of institutional psychiatry, madness and society in Lebanon. *Forum Transregionale Studien.* https://www.forum-transregionale-studien.de/en/events/calendar/details/asfourieh-a-history-of-institutional-psychiatry-madness-and-society-in-lebanon
Mohtar, L., Badr, N., Asmar, M. K., Bou-Orm, I., Maalouf, F. T., & Haddad, P. E. (2025). March 20) Adoption of tele health technology in mental and psychiatric services in Lebanon: A quantitative study. *Discover Mental Health, 5*(1), 40. https://doi.org/10.1007/s44192-025-00169-7.PMID:40111657;PMCID:PMC11925833
Obeid, B. (2024, October 18). The national mental health program: What you need to know. *Beirut.com.* Retrieved April 28, 2025, from https://www.beirut.com/en/733899/the-national-mental-health-program-what-you-need-to-know/
Rabih El Chammay: addressing mental health in crises. *Bulletin of the World Health Organization, 101*(12), 756–757 (2023, December 1). https://doi.org/10.2471/BLT.23.031223
Syndicate of Hospitals. (n.d.). *Armenian Sanatorium of Azounieh.* Retrieved April 28, 2025, from https://www.syndicateofhospitals.org.lb/Hospitals/Details/137
Syndicate of Hospitals. (n.d.). *Psychiatric Hospital of the Cross (Jal El Dib).* Retrieved April 28, 2025, from https://www.syndicateofhospitals.org.lb/Hospitals/Details/137
Trieu. (2024, October 10). Break the stigma: Let's talk about mental health in Lebanon. *Première Urgence Internationale.* https://www.premiere-urgence.org/en/break-the-stigma-lets-talk-about-mental-health-in-lebanon/
UNHCR. (2022, October). Lebanon fact sheet: October 2022. *UNHCR.* https://www.unhcr.org/lb/sites/lb/files/legacy-pdf/UNHCR-Lebanon-FactSheet-October-2022.pdf
UNHCR. (2024, May 30). *Lebanon annual results report 2023.* United Nations High Commissioner for Refugees. Retrieved April 28, 2025, from https://reporting.unhcr.org/sites/default/files/2024-06/MENA%20-%20Lebanon%20ARR%202023_0.pdf
U.S. Department of State. (2023, May 15). *2022 report on international religious freedom: Lebanon.* https://www.state.gov/reports/2022-report-on-international-religious-freedom/lebanon/
Wazir, A., El Hayek, S., Zeinoun, P. (2024). Suicidal behavior in Lebanon. In S. M. Y. Arafat, M. Rezaeian, & M. M. Khan (Eds.), *Suicidal behavior in Muslim majority countries.* Springer. https://doi.org/10.1007/978-981-97-2519-9_10
World Health Organization. (2023). Lebanon: Health data overview. *WHO Data.* https://data.who.int/countries/422

Chapter 9
Mental Health Care in Oman: Current Landscape, Challenges, and Future Directions

Salim Al-Huseini and Mandhar Al Maqbali

Abstract This chapter presents a comprehensive overview of mental health care in Oman, commencing with a historical analysis of service development and an evaluation of the current epidemiological burden of mental health disease across various demographic groups. It subsequently identifies the strengths of mental health care in Oman, followed by the barriers to effective care delivery, including limitations in treatment options and polypharmacy, the lack of dedicated mental health legislation, high out-of-pocket expenses, stigma, as well as sociocultural constraints. The chapter then proposes six strategic pillars designed to facilitate reform: Research and Evidence-Informed Policy; Workforce Development and Retention; Expansion of Community-Based Mental Health Services; Digital Mental Health and Telepsychiatry; Policy and Implementation of Mental Health Legislation in Oman; and Promotion of Mental Health Literacy and Stigma Reduction. This chapter outlines culturally sensitive, integrated strategies, offering a framework for policymakers and practitioners to enhance access, quality, and sustainability of mental health care across Oman.

Keywords Mental health care · Oman · Pathway of mental health care · Mental health services · Challenges of mental health care · Middle East

S. Al-Huseini (✉)
Department of Psychiatry, AL Masarra Hospital, Ministry of Health, Muscat, Sultanate of Oman
e-mail: salimalhuseini@gmial.com

M. Al Maqbali
Department of Psychiatry, Sohar Hospital, Ministry of Health, Sohar, Sultanate of Oman
e-mail: Mandhar.almaqbali@mail.mcdill.ca

S. Al-Huseini and S. M. Y. Arafat (eds.), *Mental Health Care in the Middle East*, South Asian Perspectives in Mental Health and Psychology ,
https://doi.org/10.1007/978-981-95-0461-9_9

1 Introduction

1.1 Country Profile: Geography and Strategic Importance

The Sultanate of Oman is in the far southeastern corner of the Arabian Peninsula, occupying a strategic position that has significantly influenced its political stability and economic growth. Its coastline stretches over 3,165 km, connecting the Arabian Sea, the Sea of Oman, and the Arabian Gulf. In the far north, the Musandam Governorate overlooks the Strait of Hormuz, a narrow waterway through which nearly one-third of the world's oil trade flows, granting Oman a vital geopolitical advantage without the instability often seen in nearby regions (Team, 2025). Oman shares land borders with the United Arab Emirates, Saudi Arabia, and Yemen. This unique location places it at the heart of Gulf Cooperation Council (GCC) markets and makes it a potential logistics hub for trade routes linking South and Southeast Asia to Africa and Europe. Over the years, Oman has pursued a foreign policy focussed on regional cooperation, neutrality, and balanced international relations. This diplomatic approach has helped the country attract foreign direct investment (FDI), preserve its rich cultural heritage, and steadily improve the living standards of its citizens (Ramady, 2014). Geographically, Oman is diverse. About 82% of its land are deserts and wadis, 15% is mountain ranges, and only a small portion is fertile coastal plains. The climate varies greatly, from hot and dry inland to more temperate conditions in the southern Dhofar region and higher mountain areas. The country is divided into eleven governorates and sixty-three districts (wilayats) (Wihaibi, 2019).

With a population of approximately five million, and nearly two-thirds of its residents under 29, Oman is considered a high-income country within the World Health Organisation's Eastern Mediterranean Region. While economic and social development has been rapid, mental health services have not always kept pace, highlighting a key area for further progress.

1.2 The Healthcare System

Since the 1970s, Oman's healthcare system has experienced a significant transformation. Initially characterised by minimal services, it has evolved into a structured, multitiered network that provides universal healthcare coverage. The Ministry of Health (MOH) is the primary provider, offering complimentary healthcare services to all Omani citizens and public-sector expatriates.

The healthcare system is organised into three principal levels:

Primary care, administered through local and extended health centres, emphasises preventive services, health promotion, and the management of common illnesses. These centres function as patients' initial point of contact.

Wilayat and Regional Hospitals offer **secondary care** and specialised outpatient services, inpatient care, and surgical procedures.

Tertiary care, accessible at Governorate Hospitals and select larger Regional Hospitals, delivers highly specialised services, advanced treatments, and the management of complex medical conditions.

As of 2023, the MOH operated 50 hospitals, 21 polyclinics, and 1,944 health centres nationwide, ensuring equitable healthcare services for individuals across all regions. This growth has resulted in significant improvements in health outcomes. Life expectancy at birth reached 78.3 years in 2023, while the infant and under-five mortality rates declined to 8.8 and 10.8 deaths per 1,000 live births, respectively. Oman has made substantial investments in its workforce to support the expanding healthcare system. In 2023, the MOH employed over 39,500 healthcare professionals, including approximately 6,117 physicians and 16,000 nurses (Ministry of Health, 2023). Looking ahead, Oman's Health Vision 2050 provides a strategic framework for modernising the healthcare system. This plan focusses on enhancing quality and efficiency, integrating services across all levels of care, advancing digital health and research capabilities, and strengthening public–private partnerships (Al Hinai et al., 2020; Al Mawali et al., 2017; Al-Riyami, 2012; Ministry of Health, 2012).

2 Epidemiology and Burden of Mental Illness in Oman

2.1 *Overview*

Oman has a relatively young population, but the country is going through important changes, such as longer life expectancy, increased urbanisation, and shifting social structures. These changes have led to greater awareness of mental health issues. Early clinical observations suggest that mental health conditions common in other countries, such as depression, anxiety, psychosis, and substance use disorders, also occur frequently in Oman. However, they may appear in ways shaped by local cultural and social factors (Al-Adawi et al., 1997). Despite this, there is still a lack of extensive, nationwide studies on mental health in the country. Most available information comes from hospital-based research or studies focussing on specific groups. In this section, we discussed the prevalence and epidemiology of common mental health disorders across diverse age groups in Oman, with particular emphasis on specific populations, including women, students, trainee doctors, youth, adolescents, and the geriatric population. Additionally, we address the prevalence of suicide and substance use disorders within the country.

2.2 *Prevalence of Common Mental Disorders*

Mental health disorders are increasingly recognised as a crucial aspect of public health in Oman. This section examines the prevalence of common conditions such as depression, anxiety, and psychotic disorders within the general population, as well as the rates of anxiety and depression among individuals with chronic physical health issues. The significant burden of psychological distress, especially when it coexists with physical illnesses, emphasises the importance of a comprehensive biopsychosocial approach to healthcare. Mental health symptoms not only undermine individual well-being but also worsen physical health problems and impede recovery. These insights underscore the need for integrating mental and physical health services to enhance overall health outcomes (Al-Adawi et al., 2014).

2.2.1 Depression

Depression remains one of the most diagnosed mental disorders in Oman and is frequently observed in individuals with co-occurring physical health conditions. According to the Ministry of Health, Sultanate of Oman (2023); mood disorders, including depression and bipolar affective disorder, and psychotic disorders, constitute approximately 37% of psychiatric visits, Fig. 1 highlighting sustained demand for specialist mental health services and access (Ministry of Health, 2023). The burden of depressive symptoms appears particularly high among patients with chronic illnesses. For instance, 23.4% of individuals with inflammatory bowel disease (IBD) were found to have depressive symptoms (Al-Aamri et al., 2022). Similarly, 26.0% of patients attending pain clinics screened positive for depression (Al Shukaili et al., 2022), suggesting a strong link between chronic pain and mental health comorbidities. Among patients with type 2 diabetes mellitus (T2DM) attending urban primary healthcare centres, the prevalence of depression was reported at 26% (Alsumry et al., 2022), which further reinforces the intersection between physical and mental health in clinical populations.

2.2.2 Anxiety Disorders

Anxiety disorders are also highly prevalent among adults in Oman and constitute a significant portion of mental health service utilisation. According to the Ministry of Health's, 2023 report, anxiety and other somatoform disorders accounted for 31.5% of total psychiatric consultations (Fig. 1) (Ministry of Health, 2023) (*Ministry of Health, Sultanate of Oman.*, n.d.). The COVID-19 pandemic further amplified this trend. A study conducted among healthcare workers during the early stages of the pandemic found that 34.1% reported anxiety symptoms (Alshekaili et al., 2020). Notably, among female healthcare professionals, 27.9% experienced moderate-to-severe symptoms of generalised anxiety disorder (Khamis et al., 2020), suggesting possible gender-based vulnerabilities within clinical environments. Beyond healthcare settings, anxiety remains a widespread concern in the general population. A national survey on social anxiety disorder (SAD) revealed that 45.9% met the diagnostic criteria for SAD (Ambusaidi et al., 2022), illustrating the extensive, and perhaps under-recognised, burden of anxiety disorders on the broader community.

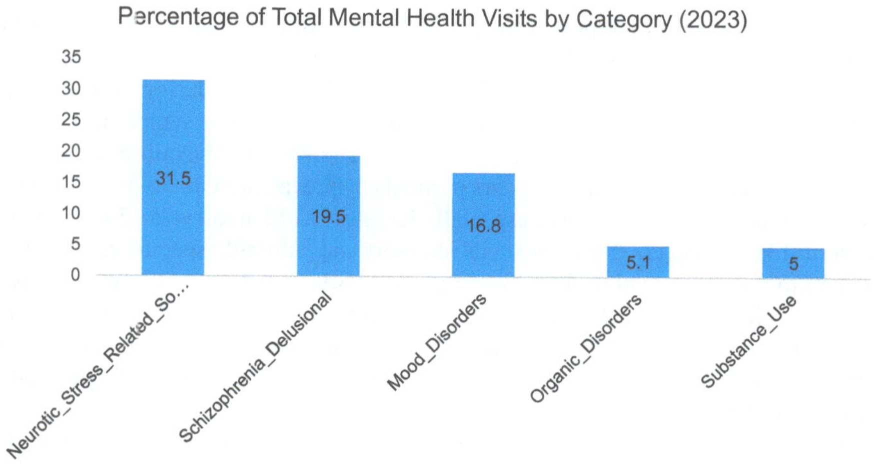

Fig. 1 Distribution of mental health visits by diagnostic category, Oman, 2023 (Ministry of Health, 2023)

2.2.3 Psychotic Disorders

Although no nationwide epidemiological studies have been conducted to estimate the prevalence of schizophrenia or related psychotic disorders in Oman, available service data offer valuable insights. According to the Ministry of Health's, 2023 Annual Health Report, schizophrenia and other psychotic disorders account for approximately 19.5% of all community-based psychiatric cases (Ministry of Health, 2023).

2.3 *Mental Disorders Among Specific Populations*

2.3.1 Youth and Adolescents

Adolescence and youth are crucial developmental stages marked by increased vulnerability to mental health disorders due to a combination of biological, psychological, and social changes. In Oman, emerging evidence underscores a rising prevalence of psychiatric conditions in this demographic, making youth mental health an urgent public health priority. Epidemiological data suggest a substantial burden of depressive disorders among Omani adolescents. School-based surveys estimate that around 17% report depressive symptoms, with lifetime prevalence rates for major depressive disorder (MDD) and bipolar disorder at 3% and 1%, respectively (Abraham & Scaria, 2018; Afifi et al., 2006; Al Riyami et al., 2009). A nationally representative study using the Composite International Diagnostic Interview (CIDI) similarly found that 13.9% of adolescents met criteria for at least one DSM-IV mental disorder, including MDD (3.0%), bipolar disorder (1.0%), specific phobia (5.8%), and social phobia (1.6%) (Jaju et al., 2009). The COVID-19 pandemic further exacerbated mental health challenges among youth. A cross-sectional study during the pandemic found that 13.9% of children and adolescents reported depressive symptoms (Zadjali et al., 2022), while 33.3% screened positive for anxiety (Al-Shekaili et al., 2024). Social anxiety disorder (SAD) appears particularly prevalent, with 36.6% of adolescents meeting diagnostic criteria, especially females (Al-Sharbati et al., 2012). These patterns likely reflect both psychosocial stressors and culturally specific sensitivities related to social evaluation. Psychiatric comorbidities are particularly pronounced among adolescents with chronic medical conditions. In a prospective study of youth with cancer, high rates of anxiety (43.5%), depression (56.5%), and post-traumatic stress disorder (32.6%) were reported three months post-diagnosis, with symptoms often persisting (Al-Saadi et al., 2024).

Eating disorders, once considered rare in non-Western settings, are increasingly recognised in Oman. A school-based study found that 33% of adolescents demonstrated disordered eating attitudes, with 12.3% exhibiting bulimic or binge-eating patterns, particularly among girls (Al-Adawi et al., 2002a, 2002b). Although data on night eating syndrome are more limited, sub-threshold symptoms affect up to 20% of adults, suggesting a broader spectrum of disordered eating behaviours (Mirza et al., 2013; Zadjali et al., 2015).

With regards to the prevalence of the neurodevelopmental disorders, particularly ADHD and autism spectrum disorder (ASD), they are increasingly recognised as significant challenges. A school-based study reported that 8.8% of children aged 9–10 met ADHD criteria (Al-Ghannami et al., 2018). In adulthood, ADHD remains underdiagnosed but significant, with outpatient data showing 1.77% of visits were related to adult ADHD, often with the inattentive subtype being the most prevalent and with comorbidities, including substance use and depression (Bedawi et al., 2024; Mirza et al., 2022). ASD prevalence is estimated at 20.35 per 10,000 children, with higher rates among boys (Al-Mamri et al., 2019), emphasising the need for early diagnosis and tailored support services. Despite the growing recognition of the mental health needs of youth, systemic barriers continue to impede access to care. Qualitative research underscores stigma, limited mental health literacy, and insufficient specialised services as significant obstacles to effective treatment (Al Omari et al., 2022a, 2022b). Addressing these challenges is crucial for developing Oman's responsive and youth-friendly mental health system.

2.3.2 Mental Health Among Older Adults in Oman

Despite the predominance of a youthful demographic within Oman, the proportion of older adults is steadily increasing, thereby necessitating greater attention to their mental health requirements. A study involving 1,682 older adults who attended primary care clinics in the Al-Dakhiliyah governorate revealed that 16.9% exhibited signs of depression, with a higher prevalence among women (19.3%) compared to men (14.3%) (Al-Sabahi et al., 2014). Furthermore, another investigation indicated that 67.3% of older adults experienced moderate to severe loneliness (Yazeedi & Shin, 2025). These findings underscore the critical need for mental health support tailored to older adults. A study evaluating a life-story review programme demonstrated its efficacy in reducing depressive symptoms while enhancing life satisfaction and overall quality of life after an eight-week intervention (Al-Ghafri et al., 2024). This evidence suggests that culturally sensitive psychological programmes can significantly benefit the mental health of this demographic. Additionally, further research is warranted to address issues such as dementia, which are anticipated to become increasingly prevalent as the population continues to age.

2.3.3 Mental Health: Women's Mental Health

A combination of biological, psychological, and sociocultural factors influences mental health among women. One of the most critical periods of vulnerability is the perinatal phase, during which women may experience significant emotional and psychological challenges. Perinatal depression has been identified in many studies in Oman and affects a considerable proportion of pregnant and postpartum women. A cross-sectional survey by Al-Azri et al. (2016) reported that 24.3% of women screened positive for antenatal depression (Al-Azri et al., 2016). Similarly, a prospective cohort study conducted by Al Rawahi et al. (2020) found that 24.4% of pregnant women scored 13 or higher on the Edinburgh Postnatal Depression Scale (EPDS). In this study, depressive symptoms were reported by 27.1% of participants during late pregnancy and by 29.3% in the postnatal period (Al Rawahi et al., 2020). Further research by Al-Abri et al. (2024) showed that women experiencing perinatal depression were more likely to have babies with low birth weight (Al-abri et al., 2024). These women also reported higher levels of antenatal stress and lower levels of perceived social support, indicating the broader psychosocial impact of perinatal mental health conditions.

2.3.4 Mental Health Among Students and Trainees

Mental health concerns among students and medical trainees in Oman are increasingly recognised, with depression, anxiety, and sleep disturbances being the most reported conditions. These issues can significantly affect academic performance, clinical competence, and long-term well-being.

Depression is among the most prevalent mental health conditions documented in this population. Depression is particularly prevalent. Among OMSB residents, 28.8% screened positive for depressive symptoms, including 8.7% with severe depression (Al-Houqani et al., 2020). Similar trends are seen in university students, with 27.7% at Sultan Qaboos University reporting depressive symptoms (Al-Busaidi et al., 2011), and higher rates reported in more recent studies: 41.3% among medical students (Al-Maashani et al., 2020), and 33.7% in a broader university sample (Al Salmani et al., 2025). Anxiety, though reported less frequently than depression, also appears to be a significant concern. A study of OMSB residents reported that 14.7% experienced anxiety symptoms (AlJahwari et al., 2022), highlighting the emotional toll of high-pressure training environments. Sleep disturbances are another widespread issue. A survey of 637 university students found high rates of insomnia, narcolepsy, restless leg syndrome, and sleep apnoea, particularly among females, with negative effects on academic performance (Salmani et al., 2020). In another study, nearly two-thirds of students reported insomnia, with exam stress, smartphone use, and age identified as key factors (Al Omari et al., 2022a, 2022b). The COVID-19 pandemic further worsened these issues. Among quarantined Omani students returning from abroad, 49.5% reported insomnia symptoms (Al Mukhaini et al., 2022), demonstrating how acute stressors can intensify existing vulnerabilities. These findings underscore the urgent need for targeted mental health strategies within academic and training institutions, including early screening, support services, and structural reforms to reduce stress.

2.4 Suicide in Oman

Although suicide rates in Oman are relatively low compared to global figures, it remains a significant and complex public health issue. In 2019, the crude suicide rate was 4.9 deaths per 100,000 people—an increase of 4.26% from the previous year (WHO, 2021b). By 2020, suicide accounted for around 1.62% of all deaths, with an age-standardised mortality rate of 4.47 per 100,000, according to the WHO Mental Health Atlas (2020) (*Mental Health ATLAS*, 2020). The most recent clinical data on suicide attempts comes from studies conducted between 2015 and 2018. Al Khatri et al. (2023) examined individuals seeking emergency care after suicide attempts and found that drug overdose was the most common method, used in 48.1% of cases (Al Khatri et al., 2023). Another study showed that 35.7% of patients who had previously attempted suicide went on to reattempt, and psychiatric comorbidity emerged as a significant risk factor, elevating the likelihood of reattempting by more than fourfold (Odds Ratio = 4.534, $p = 0.002$) (Al-Huseini et al., 2024). Earlier research also provides important insights. Koussous and AlAdawi (2006) analysed 436 autopsies from a medico-legal centre and found that 22.4% were due to suicide and 9.2% were homicides (Koussous & AlAdawi, 2006). Another study by Al Hashmi et al. (2011) analysed suicide data from the Royal Oman Police Forensic Department between 2000 and 2010. There were 599 recorded suicide cases, of which 83.8% (502 cases) were male (Al Hashmi et al., 2012). Patterns of deliberate self-harm (DSH) are also concerning. Zaidan et al. (2002) reported an increase in DSH among adolescent females, rising from 1.9 per 100,000 in 1993 to 12.8 per 100,000 by 1998 (Zaidan et al., 2002). A later study by Muna et al. (2016) examined 117 cases of deliberate self-harm (DSH) admitted to a tertiary hospital over three years. The average age of the patients was 23.5 years, with 65.8% aged 15–24 (Muna et al., 2016).

The COVID-19 pandemic further exacerbated mental health challenges. A multinational study, including data from Oman, reported a significant rise in psychiatric emergency visits by young people with self-harm behaviour during the pandemic (Wong et al., 2023). Expatriates in Oman show a higher incidence of suicidal behaviour and self-harm during the pandemic. This trend is likely linked to socio-economic challenges and social isolation (Al Maqbali et al., 2023). Despite growing awareness of the problem, Oman still lacks a national suicide registry and large-scale community-based studies, leading to gaps in data collection and understanding of suicide trends. Evidence indicates higher vulnerability among youth, women, and migrant workers, while cultural stigma and limited awareness hinder prevention efforts (Al-Adawi et al., 2024).

2.5 *Substance Misuse Disorder in Oman*

Substance misuse in Oman presents a growing public health concern, with evidence indicating a steady increase in prevalence and service utilisation over the past two decades. According to the WHO ATLAS (2012), alcohol use disorder in Oman was estimated at 0.37%, and psychoactive substance use disorders at 0.02%. Among university and college students, 2.2% reported alcohol use, 2.7% had experimented with psychoactive substances, and 2.0% with inhalants (World Health Organisation, 2012). More recently, the Ministry of Health (2023) reported that addiction-related consultations accounted for approximately 5% of all mental health visits nationwide (Ministry of Health, 2023).

While substance misuse has long existed in Oman, early analyses noted a rise in rehabilitation admissions and overdose emergencies, with cannabis being the most commonly abused illicit substance (Al-Harthi & Al-Adawi, 2002). More recent school- and university-based surveys suggest higher rates among youth. Al-Hinaai et al. (2021) found a 41.3% lifetime prevalence of substance use among university students, with tobacco (23.5%) and alcohol (10.7%) most common (Al-Hinaai et al., 2021). Among secondary school students, the prevalence of current use ranged from 9.7% in Muscat and Al-Mudhaibi (Jaffer et al., 2006) to 20.7% in Al-Dhahirah (Hamed Al-Alawi & Shaikh, 2018), with tobacco, sedatives, and stimulants frequently reported. Hospital-based surveillance confirms a shifting pattern. Between 2004 and 2018, 6,453 substance misuse cases were reported nationally, 97.9% involving Omani nationals (Al Abri et al., 2020). Opiates were the most frequently misused (66.6%), over half engaged in polydrug use, and 53.4% reported intravenous drug use. Cannabis and alcohol were often the initiating substances, while cannabis and benzodiazepine users showed greater treatment response (Wahaibi et al., 2019). Rising emergency presentations for overdose further highlight the clinical burden (Jayakrishnan et al., 2012). In response, Oman revised its drug laws in 2015 to include stricter penalties, including capital punishment for major trafficking offences (Al-Balushi, 2004). Despite comparatively lower prevalence than global averages, Oman's substance use patterns indicate escalating trends across settings. Robust population-based and longitudinal research is needed to track emerging patterns, refine prevalence estimates, and evaluate policy impact.

3 Mental Health Services in Oman

3.1 Historical Development of Mental Health

Mental health services in Oman have developed predominantly according to the Anglo-American model. Initial outpatient services were established in the 1970s Al-Rahma Hospital in Muscat. In 1983, the Ibn Sina Hospital, the nation's first specialised mental health facility, was inaugurated, which provided inpatient and outpatient services. Subsequently, in the early 1990s, Sultan Qaboos University Hospital (SQUH) integrated psychiatric education into its curriculum (Al-Sinawi & Al-Adawi, 2006). The World Health Organisation (2008) later ranked Oman's healthcare system as the most efficient globally, though mental health services were acknowledged as still underdeveloped relative to physical healthcare sectors (World Health Organisation, 2008).

3.2 Structure of Mental Health Services in Oman

3.2.1 Inpatient Facilities

Most psychiatric inpatient services in Oman are provided Al Masarra Hospital and SQUH in Muscat. Al Masarra Hospital, inaugurated in 2013, is the Sultanate's largest and only dedicated psychiatric hospital. It serves as the national psychiatric referral centre, offering 245 inpatient beds and delivering a comprehensive range of specialised services, including general adult psychiatry, geriatric psychiatry, child and adolescent psychiatry, forensic psychiatry, and addiction services, Rehabilitation services, clinical psychology, social work, physiotherapy, occupational therapy, and speech therapy are integral components of the multidisciplinary care provided. Emergency psychiatric services are available 24/7 for individuals presenting with acute mental health crises or risk.

In addition to its clinical role, Al Masarra Hospital functions as a significant national training centre, providing structured psychiatric education and clinical placements for resident doctors enrolled in the Oman Medical Speciality Board (OMSB), medical students from Sultan Qaboos University (SQU), and nursing students from various institutions across the country (*Al Masarra Hospital*, 2025). In 2023, Al Masarra Hospital recorded approximately 2,550 outpatient visits, reflecting its highly specialised role within the mental health system (Ministry of Health, 2023).

The SQUH, located within University Medical City, provides 28 psychiatric beds and subspecialties including general adult psychiatry, child and adolescent psychiatry, geriatric psychiatry, and consultation-liaison psychiatry (Al-Sinawi et al., 2020). In southern Oman, Sultan Qaboos Hospital in Salalah operates a smaller psychiatric unit offering limited inpatient mental health services to the Dhofar Governorate.

3.2.2 Outpatient Facilities

According to the Ministry of Health's Annual Report 2023, the MOH operates 23 outpatient mental health facilities. These facilities are primarily embedded within extended polyclinics and wilayat hospitals, ensuring broad geographic coverage across the Sultanate (Table 1). Mental health services are also increasingly integrated into primary health care (PHC) settings, where they address common psychiatric conditions such as depression and anxiety (Ministry of Health, 2023). Data from the 2023 Ministry of Health annual report demonstrates high utilisation of outpatient services, with 104,475 mental health outpatient contacts recorded across MOH institutions. Utilisation rates were highest in North Al Batinah Governorate, 29,540 visits, and Muscat Governorate, 24,233 visits, although all governorates reported substantial mental health caseloads. The predominant clinical presentations were mood disorders, anxiety- and stress-related conditions, and schizophrenia-spectrum psychoses (Ministry of Health, 2023) (Fig. 1). Additional psychiatric services are provided through sector-specific institutions. The Medical City Hospital for Military and Security Services hosts an outpatient psychiatric unit and SQUH (University Medical City).

3.3 Mental Health Workforce

According to the *WHO Mental Health Atlas*(2020) for Oman, the country has 82 psychiatrists across all sectors, including those employed by the Ministry of Health (MOH), resulting in a national density of 1.65 psychiatrists per 100,000 population. The psychiatric nursing workforce consists of 493 nurses, 9.91 per 100,000 individuals. However, the distribution of psychiatrists is markedly uneven, with psychiatrist density outside the capital, Muscat, falling below 0.7 per 100,000 population (WHO, 2021a). According to the Ministry of Health workforce, as of 2023, the MOH employed 71 psychiatrists, of whom 45 were Omani nationals, and 330 psychiatric nurses, including 231 Omani nationals. Despite advancements in workforce development, significant gaps persist in the availability of allied mental health professionals within the medical and nursing workforce (Ministry of Health, 2023).

3.4 Specialised Services

3.4.1 Rehabilitation and Community Services in Oman

Rehabilitation services for individuals with severe mental illness in Oman remain in the early stages of development. At Al-Masarra Hospital, the country's sole tertiary psychiatric facility, the Rehabilitation Department offers a range of therapeutic activities, including physiotherapy, music therapy, and various occupational

Table 1 Location of Ministry of Health (MOH) mental health facilities across the Sultanate of Oman

Governorate	Wilayats	Name of the hospital/Extended Health Centre (EHC)
Muscat	Al Amerat	Al Masarra Hospital
	A Seeb	Seeb (EHC)
	Bowsher	Bowsher (EHC)
North Al Batinah	Al Suwaiq	Suwaiq (EHC)
	Shinas	Shinas (EHC)
	Saham	Saham (EHC)
	Sohar	Sohar (EHC)
	Al Khaburah	Al Khaburah (EHC)
	Sohar	Sohar Hospital
South Al Batinah	Rustaq	Rustaq (EHC)
	Barka	Barka (EHC)
	Al Musannah	Al Musanaa (EHC)
Ad Dakhiliyah	Nizwa	Nizwa Hospital
	Nizwa	Nizwa (EHC)
	Samail	Sama'il Hospital
Ash Sharqiyah North	Sinaw	Sinaw Hospital
	Ibra	Ibra (EHC)
Ash Sharqiyah South	Jalan Bani Buali	Ja'alan (EHC)
	Sur	Sur (EHC)
Al Dhahirah	Ibri	Ibri Hospital
Al Buraimi	Al Buraimi	Al Buraimi (EHC)
Musandam	Khasab	Khasab Hospital
Dhofar	Salalah	Sultan Qaboos Hospital

Distribution of mental health clinics in the Ministry of Health in 2023 (Ministry of Health, 2023)

therapy modalities. However, these interventions are generally provided as stand-alone activities, rather than delivered through structured, goal-oriented rehabilitation pathways tailored to each patient's needs. Beyond the hospital setting, Oman's first organised Community Mental Health Service (CMHS) was established in Muscat in 2013. Early evaluations suggest that providing community mental health services has contributed to a reduction in psychiatric readmission rates by providing proactive monitoring and continuity of care for individuals with psychotic and mood disorders (Al-Jadidi et al., 2021). Nevertheless, the expansion of community services remains limited by persistent challenges, including shortages of trained professionals and funding.

At present, there are no dedicated residential rehabilitation units specifically for individuals with psychiatric disorders in Oman. The only available non-hospital residential options are those managed by the Ministry of Social Affairs, primarily serving individuals with multiple physical and intellectual disabilities, with one facility designated for children under 14 (World Health Organisation, 2008, n.d.). As part of future service development Al Masarra hospital, there are plans to establish inpatient psychiatric rehabilitation wards staffed by full multidisciplinary teams and create assertive outreach community (AOT) teams to deliver intensive, community-based interventions. Post-discharge, community rehabilitation teams will provide comprehensive biopsychosocial interventions, including medication management, skills development, family psychoeducation, and vocational support, thereby maximising service users' opportunities for independent living and improving their overall quality of life. Furthermore, given the absence of dedicated residential facilities for individuals with severe and enduring mental illnesses within the community, future strategic plans aim to establish supported and semi-supported accommodation options as a crucial part of the rehabilitation pathway. These facilities are intended to facilitate long-term community reintegration and recovery. Successful implementation of these initiatives will require sustained intersectoral collaboration, particularly between the Ministry of Health and the Ministry of Social Affairs, ensuring an integrated approach to holistic mental health rehabilitation.

3.4.2 Child and Adolescent Mental Health Services

The demand for multidisciplinary child and adolescent mental health services (CAMHS) in Oman has markedly escalated in recent decades, driven by factors such as rapid urbanisation, demographic transitions, and changes in family structures. The inaugural child psychiatry service was established at Sultan Qaboos University Hospital (SQUH) in the late 1990s (Al-Adawi, 2014). Currently, two main hospitals provide inpatient psychiatric services for young people. Al Masarra Hospital in Muscat operates two dedicated child and adolescent wards, one for males and one for females. It offers a comprehensive range of outpatient services, including speech therapy, clinical psychology, and occupational therapy. Similarly, SQUH, situated within the University Medical City, delivers inpatient and outpatient services for children and adolescents. It has expanded its offerings to include a specialised service for adults with attention-deficit/hyperactivity disorder (ADHD) (Mirza et al., 2022). Child and adolescent psychiatric services are gradually expanding outside the capital, Muscat, aided by the return of Omani psychiatrists who have completed subspecialty fellowships abroad. These developments have led to the establishment of outpatient CAMHS clinics within regional polyclinics. As of 2024, Oman has 13 Omani child and adolescent psychiatrists practising nationwide, with four additional fellows currently pursuing subspecialty training internationally. This growing specialist workforce reflects a broader national commitment to enhancing child and adolescent mental health services across the Sultanate.

3.4.3 Mental Health Services for Older Adults.

Oman's elderly population has remained stable at about 3% from 1950 to 2015 and is expected to maintain this level until 2025. A significant increase is projected thereafter, with the proportion rising from 4.4% in 2030 to nearly 22% by 2065, reflecting broader demographic shifts in the region (Islam, 2020). In Oman, two leading hospitals currently provide mental health services for older adults (Geriatric). Al Masarra Hospital in Muscat offers outpatient and inpatient geriatric psychiatric services, supported by multidisciplinary teams. At the same time, SQUH at the University Medical City also delivers specialised inpatient and outpatient care for elderly patients (Al-Sinawi & Mirza, 2023). The availability of geriatric psychiatry specialists, however, remains limited. Currently, two consultants are based Al Masarra Hospital and three consultants at SQUH. In addition, geriatric outpatient psychiatric services have expanded outside Muscat, with one consultant psychiatrist providing outpatient care for older adults at Sohar Hospital in the Al Batinah region. Despite these developments, the distribution of geriatric psychiatry services remains uneven across the country, necessitating further strategic expansion to meet the growing mental health needs of Oman's ageing population.

3.4.4 Forensic Services in Oman

Forensic psychiatric provision in Oman remains highly centralised and limited in scope. The country's sole specialised forensic psychiatry unit is located Al Masarra Hospital in Muscat; it comprises separate male and female wards that undertake medico-legal assessments, prepare court reports, and provide inpatient and outpatient treatment for individuals judged unfit to plead or requiring psychiatric observation (World Health Organisation, 2008). Professional staffing is likewise constrained: only one consultant psychiatrist in Oman holds formal subspecialty training in forensic psychiatry. However, a second clinician is scheduled to commence overseas fellowship training during the coming year. This marked shortage of forensic expertise and infrastructure highlights an urgent need for strategic investment in secure clinical facilities, multidisciplinary staffing, and legislative frameworks to ensure that individuals with mental disorders who come into conflict with the law receive timely, rights-based assessment and care.

3.4.5 Neuropsychiatry Services

Al Masarra Hospital has a specialised Neuropsychiatry Department that offers comprehensive services for a variety of neuropsychiatric conditions, including post-traumatic brain injury, sleep disorders, and other complex neurobehavioural syndromes. The department operates a sleep laboratory that conducts diagnostic sleep studies, thereby facilitating the assessment and management of various sleep-related disorders (*Al Masarra Hospital*, n.d.-a). The hospital also provides advanced neurostimulation treatments, such as repetitive transcranial magnetic stimulation (rTMS), specifically targeting treatment-resistant mental health disorders. Currently, the facility is equipped with two rTMS machines: one situated within Al Masarra Hospital and the other located at a community polyclinic (Al-Ruhaili et al., 2023; Qutishat et al., 2025). Moreover, electroconvulsive therapy (ECT) is administered three times weekly as part of the hospital's extensive treatment (Al Saadi et al., 2022; Al-Balushi et al., 2025). In addition to therapeutic interventions, the department offers neurodiagnostic evaluations, which include electroencephalogram (EEG) monitoring and polysomnography (Al-Kaabi et al., 2020). Notably, Al Masarra Hospital is recognised as the only mental health facility in Oman providing these comprehensive neuropsychiatric services. The country has only one neuropsychiatry consultant, with two additional physicians anticipated to begin fellowship training in neuropsychiatry later this year.

3.4.6 Addiction Services

Addiction services in Oman are predominantly administered by the MOH, with Al Masarra Hospital serving a pivotal function through its specialised Substance Misuse Unit (SMU). The SMU encompasses outpatient clinics and male inpatient wards, which include a detoxification unit, a rehabilitation unit, and a halfway house (*Al Masarra Hospital*, n.d.-b). Presently, there are no inpatient services available for women; however, women who use substances can avail themselves of outpatient care. Patients can access treatment through the Emergency Department (ED) or outpatient clinics, where they undergo an initial assessment to ascertain the appropriate level of care and the necessity for admission. Depending on the evaluation, they may receive supportive care, be scheduled for future admission, or be placed on a waiting list. Efforts are underway to expand and diversify addiction treatment services in Oman. The Ministry of Health is leading the establishment of the Muscat Centre for Recovery, a dedicated facility offering detoxification and rehabilitation services with emergency access. The Al Taafi Suhar Centre for Drug Treatment and Rehabilitation operates through a public–private partnership (PPP) model (Prabhu, 2025). Despite these advancements, significant gaps remain within the national addiction treatment framework. These gaps include a deficiency of trained addiction psychiatrists, an underdeveloped multidisciplinary team (MDT), and the absence of evidence-based harm reduction strategies, such as opioid substitution therapy (OST), needle exchange programme (NEP), and naloxone distribution. Addressing these challenges is crucial for the establishment of a comprehensive, equitable, and effective system of care for individuals who use drugs in Oman.

4 Potential Strengths of Mental Health Services in Oman

4.1 Government Commitment to Health Sector Development

Oman has established a comprehensive, publicly funded healthcare system that provides free medical services to all citizens throughout their lifespan, ensuring universal access to essential healthcare (Alshishtawy, 2010). In its inaugural comparative analysis of health systems conducted in 2000, the World Health Organisation (WHO) ranked Oman first among 191 member states regarding overall health system performance (*The World Health Report*, 2000), a distinction indicative of the country's sustained investment in health over preceding decades. Additional recognition was bestowed upon Oman in 2001, when the WHO lauded the nation for its "spectacular performance" in reducing infant mortality rates, identifying it as one of the most significant improvements in child health outcomes globally (Al Dhawi et al., 2007). Building on these achievements, Oman Vision 2040 places healthcare at the forefront of national priorities, recognising it as a key pillar for sustainable development. As part of this strategy, the National Health Policy emphasises innovation, evidence-based practice, and inclusive service delivery under the "Health for All, by All". By tailoring policy to evolving demographic, epidemiological, and technological trends, Oman aims to maintain high-quality coverage, involve communities effectively, and continually strengthen its healthcare infrastructure (Ministry of Health, 2025b). The MOH is continuing efforts to integrate mental health services within primary care settings (Ministry of Health, 2023). This strategy is designed to enhance timely access to care, improve the early detection of mood and anxiety disorders, and develop the competencies of frontline providers in managing mental health presentations.

4.2 Growing Awareness and Acceptance of Mental Health Issues

In the past five years, Oman has witnessed a marked shift towards greater awareness and acceptance of mental health issues, driven by coordinated initiatives across governmental, non-governmental (NGO), and private sectors. The Ministry of Health (MOH), in collaboration with NGOs and professional associations, has mounted nationwide public-education campaigns, most notably the Al-Masarra Hospital "Awareness Convoy", to dispel misconceptions, improve knowledge of services, and engage school, college, and university communities on mental-health and substance-use topics (*Al Masarra Hospital*, n.d.-a). Concurrently, digital platforms managed by the MOH and Al-Masarra amplify these messages, extending their reach and normalising help-seeking behaviours. Private clinics have also contributed: the Whispers of Serenity Clinic's "Not Alone" campaign provides targeted support for depression, anxiety, and bullying (Whispers Of Serenity Clinic, n.d.). Together, these efforts have reduced stigma, fostered a more supportive environment, and empowered the public and healthcare providers to address mental health concerns proactively.

4.3 Opportunities for Public–Private Partnerships

Oman has a long-standing record of leveraging public–private partnerships (PPPS) to bolster its infrastructure, successfully applying these models in sectors such as electricity and water (*The Report*, 2018). Building on this track record, the country has turned its attention to healthcare, recognising PPPS as a critical engine for socio-economic growth. Guided by the Directorate General of Private Health Establishments, the Ministry of Health (MOH) oversees and regulates private-sector facilities, integrating them into national emergency preparedness and broader health initiatives. In line with Oman Vision 2040, a key priority area centres on healthcare enhancements and explicitly supports greater private sector involvement (*Oman-Vision2040*). Such commitments are reflected in forthcoming initiatives, including the Sohar Recovery Centre Project, which provides excellence for the treatment and rehabilitation of drug and psychoactive substance addicts (Ministry of Health, 2025a). Ultimately, these collaborations are positioned to foster sustainable, high-quality mental healthcare through shared governance, clear regulations, and ongoing infrastructural support.

4.4 Training and Education

The OMSB offers a five-year psychiatry residency programme accredited by the Accreditation Council for Graduate Medical Education International (ACGME-I). Trainees are required to complete Part I of the Board examination at the end of their second year, followed by Part II, which includes both Objective Structured Clinical Examination (OSCE) and theoretical components, at the end of their fifth year. Graduates who successfully complete the programme are appointed as specialist psychiatrists within the mental health institute. To address deficiencies in subspecialty care, the Ministry of Health sponsors a select group of psychiatrists to pursue fellowships abroad, ranging from one to three years, in areas identified as national priorities. Concurrently, higher education institutions in Oman have expanded their postgraduate offerings in allied health fields, particularly mental health nursing. Ongoing professional development is facilitated through local workshops, international conferences, and online learning platforms. This ensures that mental health workers, allied health professionals, and primary care providers remain informed about evidence-based treatments, emerging therapeutic modalities, and best practices in patient-centred care.

5 Challenges in Mental Health Care in Oman

5.1 Stigma, Cultural, and Societal Barriers

Various cultural factors significantly impede the timely utilisation of formal mental health services in Oman. Limited public understanding of mental illness, often marked by confusion about symptoms and treatment options, reinforces stigma and delays help-seeking. Persistent beliefs attributing mental illness to supernatural causes, such as jinn possession or the evil eye, remain widespread (Dein & Illaiee, 2013; Ran et al., 2021). Consequently, individuals frequently turn to traditional or faith healers before accessing psychiatric care, often presenting to clinics only after alternative approaches have failed (Al-Adawi et al., 2002a, 2002b). Stigma remains a central barrier, influencing service use, medication adherence, and recovery. Paradoxically, attributing symptoms to external agents like jinn may reduce blame and foster communal tolerance in some contexts (Al-Adawi et al., 2001). A recent study indicates a decline in public attitudes towards mental illness, particularly among younger populations. Low mental health literacy contributes to both public and self-stigma. Additionally, internalised stigma, characterised by feelings of shame, secrecy, and social withdrawal, is common among patients (Alawi, 2016).

Sociocultural beliefs also shape treatment preferences. For instance, a recent study found that while most parents were open to using psychotropic medication for children, 25.4% would first consult a faith healer (Al-Harthi et al., 2023). Similarly, Al-Maamari et al. (2025) highlight a disconnect between biomedical models used by clinicians and the traditional frameworks preferred by families (Al-Maamari et al., 2025). This divergence contributes to delays in psychiatric care and longer durations of untreated illness, which are associated with poorer outcomes (Mirza et al., 2020). Stigma is also evident within healthcare settings. Al-Huseini et al. (2016) found that psychiatric patients in emergency departments were often referred to psychiatry without complete medical evaluations, reflecting systemic biases (Al-Huseini et al., 2016). Overall, perceptions of mental illness in Oman are shaped by a complex interplay of cultural beliefs, religious interpretations, and institutional practices. Addressing these challenges will require culturally sensitive, community-informed interventions and greater collaboration between biomedical and traditional care systems.

5.2 Out-of-Pocket Expenses

In Oman, total health expenditure allocation to mental health services remains ambiguous. The financing system implemented by the MOH does not separate mental health expenditures from other health sector costs, primarily due to the absence of a programme-based budgeting framework. The mental health programme is estimated to constitute less than 1% of total health expenditures, attributable mainly to low service coverage rates (Okasha et al., 2012). More recent data, however, indicate that government spending on mental health comprised 6.9% of total health outlays in 2016 and declined to 5.7% by 2020 (WHO, 2021a). In 2023, the MOH's overall health budget represented approximately 6.0% of total government expenditure (Ministry of Health, 2023).

Regarding affordability, all medical services, including access to mental health care and essential psychotropic medications, are provided at no cost to Omani citizens. Nevertheless, the availability of psychotropic medications through MOH clinics is inconsistent, often requiring patients to purchase these medications from private pharmacies at substantial personal expense, and due to waiting lists for psychotherapy, many patients choose to go to private clinics to get the services. For many individuals, such out-of-pocket costs pose significant financial challenges. Despite the critical significance of financial accessibility in mental health care, there exists a pronounced deficiency of empirical studies examining out-of-pocket expenditures related to mental health care in Oman. Specifically, no research has evaluated the costs of specific psychiatric disorders.

5.3 Treatment Challenges: *Polypharmacy*

Even when individuals access formal psychiatric services in Oman, significant challenges persist in pharmacological management. One major concern is polypharmacy, often resulting from training deficits, high patient volumes, and fragmented care pathways. Despite the clinical relevance, there is a paucity of research assessing psychotropic prescribing patterns in Oman. A recent national study reported that 38.9% of psychiatric prescriptions involved polypharmacy, with 9.3% deemed potentially inappropriate (Al-Shehhi et al., 2023).

Particularly concerning are prescribing practices in vulnerable populations. A study focussing on patients with dementia found that 56% were prescribed antipsychotics for behavioural and psychological symptoms of dementia (BPSD), a rate considerably higher than global averages. Alarmingly, antipsychotics were more frequently prescribed for non-Alzheimer's dementias, despite limited evidence supporting their effectiveness and growing concerns about adverse outcomes in this population (Al-Rashdi et al., 2023). In addition to prescribing practices, drug availability also shapes clinical decision-making. In Oman, the availability of specific antidepressants is often limited to psychiatric facilities, constraining psychiatrists' options. A national survey of psychiatric professionals found that over half believed one class of antidepressants to be superior in efficacy, most favouring SSRIS, with paroxetine most commonly linked to sexual dysfunction (Albalushi et al., 2021). Side effects, such as antidepressant-induced weight gain, further complicate treatment. A study of Omani patients identified significant weight gain associated particularly with mirtazapine and paroxetine, underscoring the need for routine monitoring and the development of personalised treatment strategies that account for both psychiatric and metabolic concerns (AL-Jahwari et al., 2025). Finally, public misperceptions about psychiatric medication continue to deter early engagement with services. A common belief among laypersons is that psychiatrists prescribe hypnotics merely to sedate patients. This stigma contributes to the tendency for individuals with mild psychiatric symptoms to seek help first from traditional or faith healers rather than mental health professionals (Al-Harthi et al., 2023).

5.4 *System Governance and Legislation*

Oman's national mental health policy was last revised in 1992. It included key components such as the development of community mental health services, integration of mental health into primary healthcare, human resources development, user and family involvement, advocacy and promotion, protection of users' human rights, equity of access, financing, quality improvement, and monitoring systems. A subsequent revision in 2005 produced a more detailed mental health plan, which identified specific goals, budgets, and timelines. This plan focussed on reforming mental hospitals to provide more comprehensive care, further developing community-based services, strengthening human resources, promoting human rights, and establishing quality improvement mechanisms (World Health Organization, 2008).

Currently, Oman does not have a standalone Mental Health Act. Psychiatric services operate under general healthcare laws and criminal codes, which address some aspects of psychiatric care, such as involuntary admission and forensic assessments. However, the absence of dedicated, rights-based mental health legislation has created significant gaps in safeguarding service users' rights, informed consent procedures, and independent oversight (Al-Maamari et al., 2021). Efforts to address these deficiencies are underway. A comprehensive Mental Health Act has been drafted and submitted for approval. Public health legislation has recently been approved (*Royal Decree Promulgates Public Health Law*, 2025). In 2000, Oman established the National Committee for Narcotics and Psychoactive Substances (NCNP) through a Royal Decree issued in 1999, outlining the national policy for substance misuse and regulation (Abri et al., 2020). However, despite the Ministry of Health's Centre for Emergency Management coordinating responses to public health emergencies (MOH, 2024), a National Disaster Preparedness Plan for Mental Health has not been developed.

6 Recommendations and Way Forward

Since the early 1980s, mental health services in Oman have witnessed gradual expansion; however, they remain relatively underdeveloped when measured against international standards. While current services address some immediate and acute needs, serious concerns persist regarding their long-term capacity and scalability,

Fig. 2 Strategic pillars for advancing mental health in Oman. Adapted from national policy priorities and aligned with the WHO mental health system strengthening frameworks (World Health Orgnisation, 2004)

particularly considering the rising mental health burden and evolving societal expectations.

A comprehensive, multi-tiered, and culturally appropriate approach is essential to ensure the sustainable and effective development of the mental health sector. This must include the National Mental Health Policy, service reconfiguration, workforce development, and community engagement. In this section, we propose **six strategic pillars** to guide the advancement of mental health care in Oman. These pillars align closely with the World Health Organisation's mental health system strengthening framework (World Health Organisation, 2005) (Fig. 2).

6.1 Research, Data, and Evidence-Informed Policy

Although mental health is gaining recognition as a national priority in Oman, research in this field remains limited, fragmented, and underfunded. Most available studies are small-scale, cross-sectional, and survey-based, offering only a partial view of mental health trends and service needs (AlAdawi, 2017; Quigley, 2015). The lack of robust, locally generated evidence hinders the development of effective, data-driven policies and limits the capacity of the health system to respond to emerging challenges. To build a responsive and sustainable mental health system, Oman must invest in research infrastructure and develop reliable data collection, analysis, and application systems. Current gaps in knowledge include the prevalence and distribution of mental disorders, service utilisation patterns, treatment outcomes, and the influence of social, cultural, and environmental factors on mental health. In particular, there is a pressing need for studies on suicide prevention, stigma, and the development of culturally appropriate psychological interventions, areas that remain underexplored at the national level (AlAdawi, 2017). Building national research capacity is essential. This includes supporting epidemiological research, promoting academic policy collaborations, and fostering a culture of inquiry within clinical services.

6.2 Workforce Development and Retention

There are several barriers to workforce distribution in Oman, including the maldistribution of services due to geographical and logistical challenges, pervasive social issues, and stigma (AlAdawi, 2017). Expanding mental health services in Oman necessitates a comprehensive approach to workforce development across multiple disciplines. First, it is essential to strengthen the psychiatry residency programme at the Oman Medical Speciality Board. This enhancement should focus on improving the quality of training, increasing the programme's intake to meet the growing demand, and expanding scholarship opportunities for subspecialty fellowships in areas such as emergency psychiatry, eating disorders, learning disabilities, personality disorders, and rehabilitation psychiatry. Second, the development of structured undergraduate programmes in psychology, which include clinical placements within mental health facilities, would facilitate the cultivation of a pipeline of trained clinical psychologists. Increasing the number of clinical psychologists is vital for delivering a broad spectrum of evidence-based psychological therapies throughout the country. Third, addressing the shortage of clinical pharmacists with a specialisation in mental health is critical. Expanding training opportunities in psychiatric pharmacy would bolster the multidisciplinary team (MDT) by providing expert consultation on psychopharmacology and optimising medication management. Finally, offering competitive career incentives, structured professional development pathways, and supportive working environments is crucial for enhancing workforce retention.

6.3 Expansion of Community-Based Mental Health Services

The development of community and rehabilitation psychiatry in Oman remains limited, contributing to the long-term institutionalisation of inpatients. This, in turn, exacerbates the shortage of beds in acute psychiatric wards and leads to higher readmission rates. A study conducted in Oman reported a 1-year psychiatric readmission rate of 39%, highlighting the inefficiencies of the current model (Al-Shehhi et al., 2023). Prolonged institutionalisation reinforces stigma and restricts patients' opportunities for reintegration into family and community life (Thornicroft & Tansella, 2004). To address these challenges, community rehabilitation outreach teams are urgently needed to support individuals in maintaining their recovery within community settings and to prevent unnecessary hospital admissions (*Rehabilitation for Adults with Complex Psychosis*, 2020). Furthermore, developing local community mental health teams and expanding outpatient clinic services would enhance accessibility and promote recovery-oriented, patient-centred care, particularly for populations residing outside major urban centres (Breslau et al., 2018). Given the centrality of the family unit in Omani society, integrating families into the therapeutic and rehabilitation processes is critical. Family involvement can foster more supportive environments, strengthen treatment adherence, and improve long-term outcomes for individuals with mental illness (Norheim et al., 2024).

6.4 Digital Mental Health and Telepsychiatry

Expanding telepsychiatry and other digital health innovations constitutes a crucial strategy for addressing logistical and systemic barriers to mental healthcare, particularly in remote and underserved regions. Video consultations, online support groups, and digital therapy applications provide significant opportunities for consistent follow-up, continuity of care, and early intervention when traditional face-to-face services are challenging (Achtyes et al., 2023).

In the Arab world, the COVID-19 pandemic markedly accelerated the adoption of telepsychiatry, transforming numerous clinics and hospitals into digital mental health systems. Before the pandemic, digital services primarily encompassed hotlines and messaging platforms; however, the pandemic highlighted the critical importance of telepsychiatry, despite challenges such as limited resources, knowledge gaps, and confidentiality concerns (Hayek et al., 2020). Before the pandemic, telehealth initiatives in Oman were limited due to apprehensions regarding litigation risks stemming from the absence of a regulatory framework (Altaei & Abdul-Mehdi, 2013). Nevertheless, during the pandemic, considerable efforts were undertaken. For instance, the urology department implemented telephone consultations and WhatsApp-based prescription renewals, significantly decreasing outpatient clinic traffic (Al-Marhoon, 2020). These experiences illustrate the feasibility and advantages of digital healthcare transformation in Oman. A recent study investigated the perspectives of both clients and healthcare providers, revealing a generally positive perception of telepsychiatry due to its convenience, enhanced access to specialised care, reduced healthcare costs, and diminished stigma. However, concerns persisted regarding the lack of public telepsychiatry services, standardised national guidelines, a shortage of trained professionals, and insufficient technological infrastructure (Al-Mahrouqi et al., 2022, 2024). Further research involving family physicians utilising mobile phone consultations identified additional barriers, including challenges in maintaining patient privacy and securing adequate technical support. Despite these obstacles, telehealth proved particularly beneficial for patients with chronic conditions (Hasani et al., 2020).

Addressing these challenges necessitates critical policy interventions. The establishment of governmental telepsychiatry services and the development of comprehensive national tele-mental health guidelines are imperative. The Ministry of Health in Oman must urgently expand digital mental health services to ensure widespread availability and accessibility. Telepsychiatry presents transformative opportunities to enhance the quality of mental healthcare in Oman. Systematic efforts to address infrastructural, regulatory, and educational barriers can facilitate the establishment of sustainable, effective, and equitable mental health services for the future.

6.5 *Policy and Implementation of Mental Health Legislation in Oman*

To ensure robust and equitable mental healthcare, the government should prioritise enacting and implementing a comprehensive national Mental Health Act that explicitly codifies patient rights, provider responsibilities, and standards of care. According to the WHO (2023), such legislation significantly reduces stigma, protects patient autonomy, and improves service quality through clear legal frameworks and human rights-based approaches (Mental Health, Human Rights and Legislation, 2023). This legislation must embed explicit legal protections such as anti-discrimination clauses, informed-consent protocols, and accessible appeals mechanisms to safeguard individual autonomy and well-being (WHO-OHCHR, n.d.). It should also establish strong accountability structures, including independent oversight bodies and mandatory reporting requirements, which have proven essential for monitoring compliance and driving continuous quality improvement (Millar et al., 2013). Finally, formally recognising and regulating partnerships between traditional healers and modern mental health professionals has improved treatment adherence and outcomes, creating integrated care models that respect local culture while meeting international standards (Berhe et al., 2024).

6.6 Building Mental Health Literacy and Reducing Stigma

Promoting mental health awareness and addressing stigma are essential to improving help-seeking behaviours and enhancing early intervention in Oman. Despite the increasing prevalence of mental disorders, stigma remains a major barrier to accessing care, often leading to delays in treatment or avoidance of services altogether (Fekih-Romdhane et al., 2023). Public misconceptions, cultural taboos, and fear of social exclusion continue to shape attitudes towards mental illness. Culturally grounded mental health promotion initiatives are needed across multiple sectors, including education, media, and religious institutions. These approaches align with the broader preventive goals outlined in *Oman Vision 2040* and *Health Vision 2050*, which advocate for intersectoral collaboration and community engagement in mental health.

7 Conclusion

Oman's mental health landscape is characterised by evolving awareness. Yet, it continues to face significant challenges, including underdeveloped community-based services, workforce shortages, logistical barriers, and stigma rooted in cultural and religious traditions. These hurdles are further compounded by inadequate funding and a dearth of local research, both of which hamper efforts to expand and refine mental health care. Nevertheless, amid the country's rapid development and demographic shifts over the past four decades, there is a growing emphasis on policy reforms, gradual development of multidisciplinary care teams, and increased integration of digital health solutions, which collectively suggest a constructive path forward.

Looking ahead, a well-rounded approach that merges increased government support, research capacity, and culturally tailored interventions can accelerate progress in Oman's mental health sector. Fostering greater collaboration with traditional healers, religious leaders, and private entities can bolster access to care in underserved areas while helping to break down persistent stigmas. Should Oman continue to advance these strategies while scaling up training, community outreach programmes, and telepsychiatry solutions, it will create a more equitable, evidence-based mental health system that effectively serves its diverse and rapidly changing population.

References

Abraham, J., & Scaria, J. (2018). Empirical directives in defeating adolescent depression in Oman: A systematic review. *Journal of Psychology & Clinical Psychiatry, 9*(6). https://doi.org/10.15406/jpcpy.2018.09.00613

Achtyes, E. D., Glenn, T., Monteith, S., Geddes, J. R., Whybrow, P. C., Martini, J., & Bauer, M. (2023). Telepsychiatry in an era of digital mental health startups. *Current Psychiatry Reports, 25*(6), 263–272. https://doi.org/10.1007/s11920-023-01425-9

Afifi, M., Al Riyami, A., Morsi, M., & Al Kharusil, H. (2006). Depressive symptoms among high school adolescents in Oman. *Eastern Mediterranean Health Journal, 12*(Suppl 2), S126–S137.

Al Abri, M. Z., Farag, M. A. H., Al Mosawi, A. S., & Al Awaidy, S. T. (2020). Socio-demographic characteristics and patterns of substance use disorder in Oman. *Sultan Qaboos University Medical Journal, 20*(4), e296–e303. https://doi.org/10.18295/squmj.2020.20.04.004

Al-Adawi, S., Burjorjee, R., & al-Issa, I. (1997). Mu-Ghayeb: A culture-specific response to bereavement in Oman. *The International Journal of Social Psychiatry, 43*(2), 144–151. https://doi.org/10.1177/002076409704300207

Al-Adawi S. (2014). Tomorrow's people matters: Evidence for action in Oman. *Oman medical journal, 29*(2), 83–85. https://doi.org/10.5001/omj.2014.21

Al Dhawi, A. A., West, D. J. J., Spinelli, R. J., & Gompf, T. A. (2007). The challenge of sustaining health care in Oman. *The Health Care Manager, 26*(1), 19.

Al Hinai, H., Al Mufarji, K., Al Siyabi, H., Al Anqoudi, Z., Al Saadi, R., & Al Awaidy, S. (2020). Health promotion strategy as part of Vision 2050 in Oman: The way forward. *Global Health Promotion, 27*(4), 145–149. https://doi.org/10.1177/1757975920909115

Al Khatri, M., Al Huseini, S., Almaqbali, M., Cucchi, A., Al Saadi, A., Al Farsi, A., Jose, S., Al-Sibani, N., & Al-Adawi, S. (2023). Sociodemographic characteristics and clinical profile of suicide attempters attending the emergency department at a tertiary care hospital in Oman: A retrospective study. *Journal of Psychiatric Practice®, 29*(5), 390. https://doi.org/10.1097/PRA.0000000000000726

Al Maqbali, M., Mohamed Eltanahy, A., Elawdy, M., & Al-Huseini, S. (2023). The psychological impact and suicidal behaviour in the context of the COVID-19 pandemic: Four case reports from Oman. *Cureus, 15*(12), Article e50867. https://doi.org/10.7759/cureus.50867

Al Masarra Hospital. (n.d.-a). Retrieved April 15, 2025, from https://moh.gov.om/en/hospitals-directorates/hospitals/al-masarra-hospital/

Al Masarra Hospital. (n.d.-b). Retrieved April 27, 2025, from https://moh.gov.om/en/hospitals-directorates/hospitals/al-masarra-hospital/

Al Mawali, A. H. N., Al Qasmi, A. M., Al Sabahi, S. M. S., Idikula, J., Elaty, M. A. A., Morsi, M., & Al Hinai, A. T. (2017). Oman vision 2050 for health research: A strategic plan for the future based on the past and present experience. *Oman Medical Journal, 32*(2), 86–96. https://doi.org/10.5001/omj.2017.18

Al Mukhaini, A., Al-Huseini, S., Al Kaabi,S., Chan, M. F., Al Balushi, R., Ganguly, S. S., Al-Adawi, S., & Anwar, H. (2022). Psychological and sleep-related factors among quarantined Omani students returning from abroad. *Biological Rhythm Research, 53*(8), 1273–1284. https://doi.org/10.1080/09291016.2021.1922826

Al Omari, O., Khalaf, A., Al Sabei, S., Al Hashmi, I., Al Qadire, M., Joseph, M., & Damra, J. (2022a). Facilitators and barriers of mental health help-seeking behaviours among adolescents in Oman: A cross-sectional study. *Nordic Journal of Psychiatry, 76*(8), 591–601. https://doi.org/10.1080/08039488.2022.2038666

Al Omari, O., Khalaf, A., Al Sabei, S., Ann Ballad, C., Abdel Ghani, R. M., Al-Hashmi, I., Aldirawi, A., AlBashtawy, M., & Al Qadire, M. (2022b). Insomnia thresholds and associated factors among Omani university students. *International Journal of Africa Nursing Sciences, 17*, Article 100500. https://doi.org/10.1016/j.ijans.2022.100500

Al Rawahi, A., Al Kiyumi, M. H., Al Kimyani, R., Al-Lawati, I., Murthi, S., Davidson, R., Al Maniri, A., & Al Azri, M. (2020). The effect of antepartum depression on the outcomes of pregnancy and development of postpartum depression: A prospective cohort study of Omani women. *Sultan Qaboos University Medical Journal, 20*(2), e179–e186. https://doi.org/10.18295/squmj.2020.20.02.008

Al Riyami, A. A., Al Adawi, S. H., Al Kharusi, H. A., Morsi, M. M., & Jaju, S. S. (2009). Health services utilization by school going Omani adolescents and youths with DSM IV mental disorders and barriers to service use. *International Journal of Mental Health Systems, 3*, 22. https://doi.org/10.1186/1752-4458-3-22

Al Saadi, A., Chan, M. F., Al-Kaabi, S., Al Shukaili, M., Al-Mamari, F., Al Abdali, M., Al Fazari, Z., & Al-Huseini, S. (2022). Demographic and clinical profile of patients receiving electroconvulsive therapy at a tertiary care hospital in Oman: A cluster analysis. *Oman Medical Journal, 37*(4), Article e401. https://doi.org/10.5001/omj.2022.82

Al Salmani, A., Al-Kindi, R., Alawi, N., Maskari, B., Bahri, R., Khamisi, S., & Al-Hadhrami, R. (2025). Prevalence and characterization of symptoms of depression among college students attending Sultan Qaboos University, Muscat, Oman. *Oman Medical Journal*. https://doi.org/10.5001/omj.2025.61

Al Shukaili, M., Al Alawi, M., Al Huseini, S., Al Shukaili, A., Al Muharrami, M., Al Abdali, M., Al Harthi, H., Al Saadi, A., Al Balushi, R., Al Kasbi, F., Al-Fahdi, A., Panchatcharam, S. M., Cucchi, A., & Al-Adawi, S. (2022). Exploring factors associated with depressive symptoms among patients with chronic pain: A cross-sectional multicenter study. *The Journal of Nervous and Mental Disease, 210*(1), 45–53. https://doi.org/10.1097/NMD.0000000000001409

Al-Aamri, H., Al-Huseini, S., Chan, M. F., Al Saadi, A., Al-Sibani, N., Al-Dughaishi, Z., & Al-Alawi, M. (2022). Clinical predictors of depression among patients with inflammatory bowel diseases: A cross-sectional analytical study from Oman. *Oman Medical Journal, 37*(2), Article e352. https://doi.org/10.5001/omj.2022.48

Al-abri, K., Edge, D., & Armitage, C. J. (2024). Prospective analysis of factors associated with perinatal depression. *Midwifery, 128*, Article 103871. https://doi.org/10.1016/j.midw.2023.103871

Al-Adawi, S. (2014). Tomorrow's people matters: Evidence for action in Oman. *Oman Medical Journal, 29*(2), 83–85. https://doi.org/10.5001/omj.2014.21

AlAdawi, S. (2017). Mental health services in Oman: The need for more cultural relevance. *Oman Medical Journal, 32*, 83–85. https://doi.org/10.5001/omj.2017.17

Al-Adawi, S., Al-Huseini, S., Shetty, M., Al-Abdali, H., Ganesh, A., & Al-Sibani, N. (2024). Suicidal behaviour in Oman: emerging trends and challenges. In S. M. Y. Arafat, M. Rezaeian, & M. M. Khan (Eds.), *Suicidal behavior in Muslim majority countries: Epidemiology, risk factors, and prevention* (pp. 207–222). Springer Nature. https://doi.org/10.1007/978-981-97-2519-9_14

Al-Adawi, S., Al-Ismaily, S., Martin, R., Al-Naamani, A., Al-Riyamy, K., Al-Maskari, M., & Al-Hussaini, A. (2001). Psychosocial aspects of epilepsy in Oman: Attitude of health personnel. *Epilepsia, 42*(11), 1476–1481. https://doi.org/10.1046/j.1528-1157.2001.05599.x

Al-Adawi, S., Dorvlo, A. S. S., Al-Ismaily, S. S., Al-Ghafry, D. A., Al-Noobi, B. Z., Al-Salmi, A., Burke, D. T., Shah, M. K., Ghassany, H., & Chand, S. P. (2002a). Perception of and attitude towards mental illness in Oman. *The International Journal of Social Psychiatry, 48*(4), 305–317. https://doi.org/10.1177/002076402128783334

Al-Adawi, S., Dorvlo, A. S. S., Burke, D. T., Al-Bahlani, S., Martin, R. G., & Al-Ismaily, S. (2002b). Presence and severity of anorexia and bulimia among male and female Omani and Non-Omani adolescents. *Journal of the American Academy of Child & Adolescent Psychiatry, 41*(9), 1124–1130. https://doi.org/10.1097/00004583-200209000-00013

Alawi, M. A. (2016). Perception of stigma among attendees of tertiary care psychiatric clinic in Oman. *International Journal of Public Health and Safety, 1*(1).

Al-Azri, M., Al-Lawati, I., Al-Kamyani, R., Al-Kiyumi, M., Al-Rawahi, A., Davidson, R., & Al-Maniri, A. (2016). Prevalence and risk factors of antenatal depression among Omani women in a primary care setting. *Sultan Qaboos University Medical Journal, 16*(1), e35–e41. https://doi.org/10.18295/squmj.2016.16.01.007

Albalushi, M. A., Almaqbali, Mandhar. H., Al-Huseini, S. K., & Alsinawi, H. N. (2021). Prescribing practices in the treatment of depression among psychiatrists in Oman. *Neurosciences, 26*(2), 152–157. https://doi.org/10.17712/nsj.2021.2.20200110

Al-Balushi, M., Al-Huseini, S., Chan, M. F., Al-Kaabi, S., Al-Balushi, N., Qashta, A., & Al-Adawi, S. (2025). Awareness and attitudes toward transcranial magnetic stimulation among psychiatrists in Oman. *New Emirates Medical Journal, 5*(1), 1–9. https://doi.org/10.2174/010250688236177 4250217044041

Al-Balushi, R. B. H. (2004). *Drugs and drug policies in Oman with special reference to the death penalty*. https://hull-repository.worktribe.com/output/4212442/drugs-and-drug-policies-in-oman-with-special-reference-to-the-death-penalty

Al-Busaidi, Z., Bhargava, K., Al-Ismaily, A., Al-Lawati, H., Al-Kindi, R., Al-Shafaee, M., & Al-Maniri, A. (2011). Prevalence of depressive symptoms among university students in Oman. *Oman Medical Journal, 26*(4), 235–239. https://doi.org/10.5001/omj.2011.58

AL-Fahdi, A., Al-Mahrouqi, T., AlZain, I., AL-Aamri, H., & AL-Huseini, S. (n.d.). Self-inflicted total amputation of the external genitalia as a psychological repercussion of the COVID-19 pandemic: A case report. *Cureus, 14*(12), e32725. https://doi.org/10.7759/cureus.32725

Al-Ghafri, B. R., Al-Sinawi, H., Al-Harrasi, A. M., Al-Saidi, Y., Al-Mahrezi, A., Al-Ghusaini, Z. B., Al-Zeedy, K. B. R., & Chan, M. F. (2024). Effects of life-story review on quality of life, depression, and life satisfaction in older adults in Oman: A randomized controlled study. *BMC Geriatrics, 24*(1), 530. https://doi.org/10.1186/s12877-024-05133-8

Al-Ghannami, S. S., Al-Adawi, S., Ghebremeskel, K., Cramer, M. T., Hussein, I. S., Min, Y., Jeyaseelan, L., Al-Sibani, N., Al-Shammakhi, S. M., Al-Mamari, F., & Dorvlo, A. S. S. (2018). Attention deficit hyperactivity disorder and parental factors in school children aged nine to ten years in Muscat, Oman. *Oman Medical Journal, 33*(3), 193–199. https://doi.org/10.5001/omj.2018.37

Al-Harthi, A., & Al-Adawi, S. (2002). Enemy within?: The silent epidemic of substance dependency in GCC countries. *Journal for Scientific Research. Medical Sciences, 4*(1–2), 1–7.

Al-Harthi, H., Al-Huseini, S., Al-Shukaili, M., Chan, M. F., Al-Mahrouqi, T., Al-Breiki, M., Al-Hosni, A., & Mirza, H. (2023). Parental attitude towards the prescription of psychotropic medications for mental disorders in children in a tertiary care university hospital in Oman. *Sultan Qaboos University Medical Journal, 23*(2), 190–197. https://doi.org/10.18295/squmj.8.2022.049

Al Hashmi, S., Al Sabri, A., & Al Felati, N. (2012). Suicide rate in Oman in the period from January 2000 to December 2010. *Journal of US-China Medical Science, 9*(4). https://doi.org/10.17265/1548-6648/2012.04.009

Al-Hinaai, H., Al-Busaidi, I., Al Farsi, B., & Al Saidi, Y. (2021). The prevalence of substance misuse and its effects among omani college students: A cross-sectional study. *Oman Medical Journal, 36*(1), Article e224. https://doi.org/10.5001/omj.2021.04

Al-Houqani, F., Al-Mukhaini, A., & Al-Kindi, R. (2020). Prevalence of depression among oman medical specialty board (OMSB) residents. *Oman Medical Journal, 35*(2), Article e116. https://doi.org/10.5001/omj.2020.34

Al-Huseini, S., Al maqbali, M., Mirza, H., Al Khatri, M., Al Saadi, A., Chan, M.-F., & Al-Adawi, S. (2024). Prevalence and associated factors of a repeat of suicide attempt among individuals attending an emergency department in Oman. *Discover Psychology, 4*(1), 181. https://doi.org/10.1007/s44202-024-00294-4

Al-Huseini, S., Al-Madhani, A., Al-Shehhi, A., & Al-Sinawi, H. (2016). Physical examinations of psychiatric patients who presented at the emergency department of a tertiary-care hospital in Oman. *Saudi Journal of Medicine & Medical Sciences, 4*(3), 206–211. https://doi.org/10.4103/1658-631X.188248

Al-Jadidi, S., Aboalatta, A., Al-Rahbi, I., Al-Harrasi, M., AlRauzaiqi, H., Sabeih, M. A., AlGammari, T., & Al-Shammakhi, A. (2021). Effectiveness of community mental health service in Oman: A pilot study. *World Family Medicine Journal /middle East Journal of Family Medicine*. https://doi.org/10.5742/mewfm.2021.94180

AlJahwari, B., AlKamli, A., Al-Huseini, S., Chan, M. F., AlMahroqi, B., Al Saadoon, M., Ambusaidi, A., Ganesh, A., & Al-Adawi, S. (2022). The prevalence and factors associated with anxiety symptoms among resident physicians in Oman: A cross-sectional study. *Middle East Current Psychiatry, 29*(1), 47. https://doi.org/10.1186/s43045-022-00214-z

AL-Jahwari, L., Qutishat, M., Almaqbali, M., Al Risi, K., AlBreiki, M., Albalushi, M., & Al-Huseini, S. (2025). Effects of antidepressants on body weight in patients treated in a naturalistic setting in Oman. *Middle East Current Psychiatry, 32*(1), 3. https://doi.org/10.1186/s43045-025-00496-z

Al-Kaabi, S., Al-Huseini, S., AL-Habsi, B., Balushi, N. A., Al-Ruzaiqi, M., Al-Wahibi, A., Al-Ghammari, S., Al-Sibani, N., & Al-Adawi, S. (2020). Appropriateness of electroencephalographic referrals in a tertiary care psychiatric hospital: Retrospective study from Oman. *International Journal of Nutrition, Pharmacology, Neurological Diseases, 10*(4), 188. https://doi.org/10.4103/ijnpnd.ijnpnd_85_20

Al-Maamari, A., Al-Kindi, Q., & Mirza, H. (2021). Ethical dilemmas in child and adolescent mental health services in Oman. *Ethics and Social Welfare, 15*(2), 219–223. https://doi.org/10.1080/17496535.2021.1897641

Al-Maamari, A.-M., Al-Huseini, S., AL Sawafi, A., Al-kiyumi, H., Jose, S., Cucchi, A., Aria, F., & Mirza, H. (2025). Culturally shaped explanatory models of psychological and psychiatric distress in family caregivers and their impact on help-seeking behavior: A cross-sectional study from Oman. *Journal of Psychosocial Rehabilitation and Mental Health*. https://doi.org/10.1007/s40737-025-00466-y

Al-Maashani, M., Al-Balushi, N., Al-Alawi, M., Mirza, H., Al-Huseini, S., Al-Balushi, M., Obeid, Y., Jose, S., Al-Sibani, N., & Al-Adawi, S. (2020). Prevalence and correlates of depressive symptoms among medical students: A cross-sectional single-centre study. *East Asian Archives of Psychiatry: Official Journal of the Hong Kong College of Psychiatrists = Dong Ya Jing Shen Ke Xue Zhi: Xianggang Jing Shen Ke Yi Xue Yuan Qi Kan,30*(1), 28–31. https://doi.org/10.12809/eaap1882

Al-Mahrouqi, T., Al-Alawi, K., Al-Alawi, M., Al Balushi, N., Al Ghailani, A., Al Sabti, H., & Al Sinawi, H. (2022). A promising future for tele-mental health in Oman: A qualitative exploration of clients and therapists' experiences. *SAGE Open Medicine, 10*, 20503121221086372. https://doi.org/10.1177/20503121221086372

Al-Mahrouqi, T., Al-Alawi, K., Al-Sabahi, F., Al-Harrasi, A., Al-Sinawi, H., Al-Balushi, N., Al-Shekaili, M., & Al-Alawi, M. (2024). Telephone-based telepsychiatry consultations: A qualitative exploration of psychiatrists' experiences in Oman. *British Medical Journal Open, 14*(3), Article e079033. https://doi.org/10.1136/bmjopen-2023-079033

Al-Mamri, W., Idris, A. B., Dakak, S., Al-Shekaili, M., Al-Harthi, Z., Alnaamani, A. M., Alhinai, F. I., Jalees, S., Al Hatmi, M., El-Naggari, M. A., & Islam, M. M. (2019). Revisiting the prevalence of autism spectrum disorder among omani children. *Sultan Qaboos University Medical Journal, 19*(4), e305–e309. https://doi.org/10.18295/squmj.2019.19.04.005

Al-Marhoon, M. S. (2020). The impact of COVID-19 on urology practice in Oman. *Sultan Qaboos University Medical Journal, 20*(4), e404–e405. https://doi.org/10.18295/squmj.2020.20.04.023

Al-Rashdi, Z., Al-Mahrouqi, T., Al-Shamli, S., Panchatcharam, S., Al-Busaidi, F., Al-Afani, R., Al-Balushi, N., & Al-Sinawi, H. (2023). Prescribing pattern of anti-psychotic medications in patients with dementia in Oman: A retrospective observational study. *Middle East Current Psychiatry, Ain Shams University, 30*(1), 2. https://doi.org/10.1186/s43045-022-00275-0

Al-Riyami, A. (2012). Health vision 2050 Oman: A committed step towards reforms. *Oman Medical Journal, 27*(3), 190–191. https://doi.org/10.5001/omj.2012.43

Al-Ruhaili, I., Al-Huseini, S., Al-Kaabi, S., Mahadevan, S., Al-Sibani, N., Al Balushi, N., Islam, M. M., Jose, S., Mehr, G. K., & Al-Adawi, S. (2023). An evaluation of the effectiveness of repetitive transcranial magnetic stimulation (rTMS) for the management of treatment-resistant depression with somatic attributes: A hospital-based study in Oman. *Brain Sciences, 13*(9), Article 9. https://doi.org/10.3390/brainsci13091289

Al-Saadi, L. S., Chan, M. F., Al Sabahi, A., Alkendi, J., Al-Mashaikhi, N., Sumri, H. A., Al-Fahdi, A., & Al-Azri, M. (2024). Prevalence of anxiety, depression, and post-traumatic stress disorder among Omani children and adolescents diagnosed with cancer: A prospective cross-sectional study. *BMC Cancer, 24*(1), 518. https://doi.org/10.1186/s12885-024-12272-z

Al-Sabahi, S. M., Al Sinawi, H. N., Al-Hinai, S. S., & Youssef, R. M. (2014). Rate and correlates of depression among elderly people attending primary health care centres in Al-Dakhiliyah governorate, Oman. *Eastern Mediterranean Health Journal,20*(3), 181–189.

Al-Sharbati, M., Al-Adawi, S., Petrini, K., Bait Amer, A. S., Al-Suleimani, A., Al-Lawatiya, S., Zaidan, Z., Al-Adawi, S. S., & Al Hussaini, A. (2012). Two-phase survey to determine social anxiety and gender differences in Omani adolescents. *Asia-Pacific Psychiatry, 4*(2), 131–139. https://doi.org/10.1111/j.1758-5872.2012.00181.x

Al-Shehhi, A., Al-Qamshooei, M., Al-Kaabi, L., Al-Suqri, M., Al-Kalbani, Y., Al-Kasbi, S., Al-Saadi, S., Al-Farsi, A., Al-Busaidi, S., Al-Jahwari, L., Al-Hinai, A., Al-Balushi, M., Al-Shekaili, W., & Al-Sinawi, H. (2023). National prescribing patterns of psychotropic medications in older adults in Oman. *Bjpsych Open, 9*(Suppl 1), S43. https://doi.org/10.1192/bjo.2023.174

Al-Shekaili, M., Al-Huseini, S., Al-Kalbani, Y., Mirza, H., Chan, M. F., Hassan, W., Al-Sulimani, F., Al-Ghafri, G. S., Al-Sumri, H. S., Amer, A. B., Ganesh, A., Al-Saadoon, M., & Al-Adawi, S. (2024). Factors associated with anxiety-related symptoms in children and adolescents during COVID-19 in Oman: A cross-sectional study. *Scientific Reports, 14*(1), 9812. https://doi.org/10.1038/s41598-024-59769-y

Alshekaili, M., Hassan, W., Al Said, N., Al Sulaimani, F., Jayapal, S. K., Al-Mawali, A., Chan, M. F., Mahadevan, S., & Al-Adawi, S. (2020). Factors associated with mental health outcomes across healthcare settings in Oman during COVID-19: Frontline versus non-frontline healthcare workers. *British Medical Journal Open, 10*(10), Article e042030. https://doi.org/10.1136/bmjopen-2020-042030

Alshishtawy, M. M. (2010). Four decades of progress: Evolution of the health system in Oman. *Sultan Qaboos University Medical Journal, 10*(1), 12–22.

Al-Sinawi, H., & Al-Adawi, S. (2006). Psychiatry in the Sultanate of Oman. *International Psychiatry, 3*(4), 14–16.

Al-Sinawi, H., & Mirza, H. (2023). Psychiatry in the Sultanate of Oman. *Bjpsych International, 20*(4), 81–84. https://doi.org/10.1192/bji.2023.24

Al-Sinawi, H., Mirza, H., & Al Alawi, M. (2020). Mental health services in the Sultanate of Oman. In I. Laher (Ed.), *Handbook of healthcare in the Arab World* (pp. 1–12). Springer International Publishing. https://doi.org/10.1007/978-3-319-74365-3_131-1

Alsumry, S. H., Al Ghelani, T., & Jaju, S. (2022). Depression in urban omani adults with type 2 diabetes. *Sultan Qaboos University Medical Journal, 22*(1), 45–50. https://doi.org/10.18295/squmj.4.2021.065

Altaei, M. H., & Abdul-Mehdi, Z. T. (2013). Telemedicine requirements for treatment network in Oman. *Journal of Advances in Computer Networks*, 246–249. https://doi.org/10.7763/JACN.2013.V1.49

Ambusaidi, A., Al-Huseini, S., Alshaqsi, H., AlGhafri, M., Chan, M.-F., Al-Sibani, N., Al-Adawi, S., & Qoronfleh, M. W. (2022). The prevalence and sociodemographic correlates of social anxiety disorder: A focused national survey. *Chronic Stress, 6*, 24705470221081216. https://doi.org/10.1177/24705470221081215

Bedawi, R. M., Al-Farsi, Y., Mirza, H., Al-Huseini, S., Al-Mahrouqi, T., Al-Kiyumi, O., Al-Azri, M., & Al-Adawi, S. (2024). Prevalence and clinical profile of adults with ADHD attending a tertiary care hospital for five years. *International Journal of Environmental Research and Public Health, 21*(5), Article 5. https://doi.org/10.3390/ijerph21050566

Berhe, K. T., Gesesew, H. A., & Ward, P. R. (2024). Traditional healing practices, factors influencing to access the practices and its complementary effect on mental health in sub-Saharan Africa: A systematic review. *British Medical Journal Open, 14*(9), Article e083004. https://doi.org/10.1136/bmjopen-2023-083004

Breslau, J., Leckman-Westin, E., Yu, H., Han, B., Pritam, R., Guarasi, D., Horvitz-Lennon, M., Scharf, D. M., Pincus, H. A., & Finnerty, M. T. (2018). Impact of a mental health based primary care program on quality of physical health care. *Administration and Policy in Mental Health and Mental Health Services Research, 45*(2), 276–285. https://doi.org/10.1007/s10488-017-0822-1

Dein, S., & Illaiee, A. S. (2013). Jinn and mental health: Looking at jinn possession in modern psychiatric practice. *The Psychiatrist, 37*(9), 290–293. https://doi.org/10.1192/pb.bp.113.042721

Fekih-Romdhane, F., Jahrami, H., Stambouli, M., Alhuwailah, A., Helmy, M., Shuwiekh, H. A. M., Lemine, C. M. F. M., Radwan, E., Saquib, J., Saquib, N., Fawaz, M., Zarrouq, B., Naser, A. Y., Obeid, S., Hallit, S., Saleh, M., Haider, S., Daher-Nashif, S., Miloud, L., … Cheour, M. (2023). Cross-cultural comparison of mental illness stigma and help-seeking attitudes: A multinational population-based study from 16 Arab countries and 10,036 individuals. *Social Psychiatry and Psychiatric Epidemiology, 58*(4), 641–656. https://doi.org/10.1007/s00127-022-02403-x

Green, B., & Colucci, E. (2020). Traditional healers' and biomedical practitioners' perceptions of collaborative mental healthcare in low- and middle-income countries: A systematic review. *Transcultural Psychiatry, 57*(1), 94–107. https://doi.org/10.1177/1363461519894396

Hamed Al-Alawi, A. S., & Shaikh, J. (2018).Prevalence of substance abuse among the school students in Al-Dhahirah Governorate, Sultanate of Oman. *Madridge Journal of Nursing, 3*(1), 118–123. https://doi.org/10.18689/mjn-1000121

Hasani, S. A., Ghafri, T. A., Al Lawati, H., Mohammed, J., Al Mukhainai, A., Al Ajmi, F., & Anwar, H. (2020). The use of telephone consultation in primary health care during COVID-19 pandemic, Oman: Perceptions from physicians. *Journal of Primary Care & Community Health, 11*, 2150132720976480. https://doi.org/10.1177/2150132720976480

Hayek, S. E., Nofal, M., Abdelrahman, D., Adra, A., Harthi, M. A., Shamli, S. A., AlNuaimi, N., Bensid, L., Cheaito, M. A., Emberish, A. M., Larnaout, A., Radwan, A., Slaih, M., Kobeissy, F., & Bizri, M. (2020). Telepsychiatry in the Arab World: A viewpoint before and during COVID-19. *Neuropsychiatric Disease and Treatment, 16*, 2805–2815. https://doi.org/10.2147/NDT.S277224

Islam, M. M. (2020). Demographic transition in Sultanate of Oman: Emerging demographic dividend and challenges. *Middle East Fertility Society Journal, 25*(1), 7. https://doi.org/10.1186/s43043-020-00022-7

Jaffer, Y. A., Afifi, M., Al Ajmi, F., & Alouhaishi, K. (2006). Knowledge, attitudes and practices of secondary-school pupils in Oman: I. health-compromising behaviours. *Eastern Mediterranean Health Journal = La Revue De Sante De La Mediterranee Orientale = Al-Majallah Al-Sihhiyah Li-Sharq Al-Mutawassit, 12*(1–2), 35–49.

Jaju, S., Al-Adawi, S., Al-Kharusi, H., Morsi, M., & Al-Riyami, A. (2009). Prevalence and age-of-onset distributions of DSM IV mental disorders and their severity among school going Omani adolescents and youths: WMH-CIDI findings. *Child and Adolescent Psychiatry and Mental Health, 3*, 29. https://doi.org/10.1186/1753-2000-3-29

Jayakrishnan, B., Al Asmi, A., Al Qassabi, A., Nandhagopal, R., & Mohammed, I. (2012). Acute drug overdose: Clinical profile, etiologic spectrum and determinants of duration of intensive medical treatment. *Oman Medical Journal, 27*(6), 501–504. https://doi.org/10.5001/omj.2012.120

Khamis, F., Al Mahyijari, N., Al Lawati, F., & Badahdah, A. M. (2020). The mental health of female physicians and nurses in Oman during the COVID-19 pandemic. *Oman Medical Journal, 35*(6), Article e203. https://doi.org/10.5001/omj.2020.103

Koussous, J., & AlAdawi, S. (2006). Sucide in Sultanate of Oman descriptive study among Omanis and expartiates. *Sultan Qaboos University Medical Journal, 6*, 7–13.

Mental Health ATLAS 2020. (n.d.). Retrieved April 27, 2025, from https://www.who.int/publications/i/item/9789240036703

Mental health, human rights and legislation: Guidance and practice. (n.d.). Retrieved April 26, 2025, from https://www.who.int/publications/i/item/9789240080737

Millar, R., Mannion, R., Freeman, T., & Davies, H. T. O. (2013). Hospital board oversight of quality and patient safety: A narrative review and synthesis of recent empirical research. *The Milbank Quarterly, 91*(4), 738–770. https://doi.org/10.1111/1468-0009.12032

Ministry of Health. (2012). *Oman health Vision 2050*. http://www.moh.gov.o/healthvision2050/eng

Ministry of Health. (2023). *Annual Health Report 2023*. https://moh.gov.om/en/statistics/annual-health-reports/annual-health-report-2023/?utm_source=chatgpt.com

Ministry of Health. (2025a). *Agreement signed to operate, manage, & Expand new recovery center in Sohar*. https://moh.gov.om/en/media-center/news/agreement-signed-to-operate-manage-expand-new-recovery-center-in-sohar/

Ministry of Health. (2025b, April 10). *Omans-national-health-policy*. https://moh.gov.om/media/t3ykfej3/english_omans-national-health-policy.pdf

Ministry of Health, Sultanate of Oman. (n.d.). Retrieved April 22, 2025, from https://moh.gov.om/media/v3xfdvmd/annual-health-report-2023.pdf

Mirza, H., Al sinawi, H., & Ruqaishi, N. (2013). Eating disorders among Omani adolescents attendees at a tertiary care center. *International Journal of Nutrition, Pharmacology, Neurological Diseases, 3*, 313–317.

Mirza, H., Al-Huseini, S., Al-Jamoodi, S., Al-Balushi, N., Al-Hosni, A., Chan, M.-F., & Zadjali, F. (2022). Socio-demographic and clinical profiles of adult attention deficit hyperactivity disorder patients in a university hospital in Oman. *Sultan Qaboos University Medical Journal, 22*(2), 206–211. https://doi.org/10.18295/squmj.5.2021.104

Mirza, H., Al-Huseini, S., Al-Shamli, S., Al-Dhahri, M., Al-Rashdi, Z., Al-Hosni, A., Al-Hasani, H., Jaju, S., Al-Sibani, N., & Al-Adawi, S. (2020). The relationship of sociodemographic and clinical profiles to the duration of untreated psychosis among adolescents with first-episode psychosis in an Oman tertiary hospital. *Psychosis, 12*(2), 172–181. https://doi.org/10.1080/17522439.2020.1720272

MOH. (2024). *Center for Emergency Management*. https://moh.gov.om/en/hospitals-directorates/directorates-and-centers-at-hq/center-for-emergency-management/

Muna, D., Salmi, A., Al-Difai, Z., Al-Senawi, H., & Fahdi, A. (2016). Predictors of duration of admission following an act of deliberate self-harm: A cross section study from oman. *Middle East Journal of Psychiatry and AlzheimERS, 8*. https://doi.org/10.5742/MEPA.2016.92886

Norheim, I., Pedersen, R., Selle, M. L., Røssberg, J., Hestmark, L., Heiervang, K., Ruud, T., Åsholt, V. M., Hansson, K., Møller, P., Fosse, R., & Romøren, M. (2024). Implementation of guidelines on family involvement for persons with psychotic disorders: A pragmatic cluster randomized trial. Effect on relatives' outcomes and family interventions received. *Frontiers in Psychiatry, 15*. https://doi.org/10.3389/fpsyt.2024.1381007

Okasha, A., Karam, E., & Okasha, T. (2012). Mental health services in the Arab world. *World Psychiatry: Official Journal of the World Psychiatric Association (WPA), 11*(1), 52–54. https://doi.org/10.1016/j.wpsyc.2012.01.008

Oman Medical Specialty Board-Leading the advancement of medical professions. (n.d.). Retrieved May 1, 2025, from https://omsb.gov.om/

OmanVision2040Report.pdf. (n.d.). Retrieved April 22, 2025, from https://www.oman2040.om/OmanVision2040Report?lang=en

Prabhu, C. (2025, March 8). *Omani-Malaysian JV wins Suhar drug rehab PPP project*. Oman Observer. https://www.omanobserver.om/article/1167351/business/omani-malaysian-jv-wins-suhar-drug-rehab-ppp-project

Quigley, A. (2015). Book review. *Journal of Mental Health, 24*(3), 174–174. https://doi.org/10.3109/09638237.2015.1036979

Qutishat, M., Al-Huseini, S., & Al-Balushi, M. (2025). Transforming mental health care in the Arab World: A scoping review of Arab TMS studies for psychiatric disorders. *General Hospital Psychiatry, 94*, 159–166. https://doi.org/10.1016/j.genhosppsych.2025.03.008

Ramady, M. A. (2014). Sultanate of Oman: Risk analysis. In M. A. Ramady (Ed.), *Political, economic and financial country risk: Analysis of the gulf cooperation council* (pp. 161–178). Springer International Publishing. https://doi.org/10.1007/978-3-319-02177-5_10

Ran, M.-S., Hall, B. J., Su, T. T., Prawira, B., Breth-Petersen, M., Li, X.-H., & Zhang, T.-M. (2021). Stigma of mental illness and cultural factors in Pacific Rim region: A systematic review. *BMC Psychiatry, 21*(1), 8. https://doi.org/10.1186/s12888-020-02991-5

Rehabilitation for adults with complex psychosis. (2020). National Institute for Health and Care Excellence (NICE). http://www.ncbi.nlm.nih.gov/books/NBK562555/

Royal Decree promulgates Public Health Law. (2025, April 24). Oman Observer. https://www.omanobserver.om/article/1169565/oman/his-majesty/royal-decree-promulgates-public-health-law

Salmani, A. A. A., Shidhani, A. A., Qassabi, S. S. A., Yaaribi, S. A. A., & Musharfi, A. M. A. (2020). Prevalence of sleep disorders among university students and its impact on academic performance. *International Journal of Adolescence and Youth.* https://www.tandfonline.com/doi/full/https://doi.org/10.1080/02673843.2020.1815550

Team, F. (n.d.). *History and Geography.* Ministry of Information | Sultanate of Oman - EN. Retrieved April 29, 2025, from https://omaninfo.om/

The Report: Oman 2018 - Oxford Business Group. (2018, February 25). https://oxfordbusinessgroup.com/product/the-report-oman-2018/

The world health report 2000. (n.d.). Retrieved April 15, 2025, from https://www.who.int/publications/i/item/924156198X

Thornicroft, G., & Tansella, M. (2004). Components of a modern mental health service: A pragmatic balance of community and hospital care: Overview of systematic evidence. *The British Journal of Psychiatry: THe Journal of Mental Science, 185*, 283–290. https://doi.org/10.1192/bjp.185.4.283

Wahaibi, N. A., Lawati, A. A., Ruqeishy, F. A., Khatri, A. A., Al-Farsi, Y., Juma, T. M. A., Hinai, F. A., Al-Sibani, N., Mahadevan, S., & Al-Adawi, S. (2019). The characteristics and patterns of utilization of healthcare services among Omanis with substance use disorders attending therapy for cessation. *PLoS ONE, 14.* https://doi.org/10.1371/journal.pone.0210532

Whispers Of Serenity clinic. (n.d.). *Whispers of serenity – whispers of serenity.* Retrieved May 4, 2025, from https://www.whispers-of-serenity.com/

WHO. (2021a). *Mental health atlas 2020* (1st ed). World Health Organization.

WHO. (2021b). *Suicide worldwide in 2019: Global health estimates* (1st ed). World Health Organization.

WHO. (2023). Mental health, human rights and legislation: Guidance and practice. (n.d.). Retrieved 26 April 2025, from https://www.who.int/publications/i/item/9789240080737

Who_aims_oman_report.pdf. (n.d.). Retrieved April 27, 2025, from https://cdn.who.int/media/docs/default-source/mental-health/who-aims-country-reports/who_aims_oman_report.pdf?sfvrsn=6830b334_3&utm_source=chatgpt.com

WHO-OHCHR launch new guidance to improve laws addressing human rights abuses in mental health care. (n.d.). Retrieved April 26, 2025, from https://www.who.int/news/item/09-10-2023-who-ohchr-launch-new-guidance-to-improve-laws-addressing-human-rights-abuses-in-mental-health-care

Wihaibi, K. K. A. (2019). Geographical and administrative divisions of Oman peninsula in Islamic Middle Ages from 1 H/ 7 Ad to the end of 9 H/ 15 AD. *Journal of Arts and Social Sciences [JASS], 10*(1), Article 1. https://doi.org/10.53542/jass.v10i1.3217

Wong, B. H.-C., Cross, S., Zavaleta-Ramírez, P., Bauda, I., Hoffman, P., Ibeziako, P., Nussbaum, L., Berger, G. E., Hassanian-Moghaddam, H., Kapornai, K., Mehdi, T., Tolmac, J., Barrett, E., Romaniuk, L., Davico, C., Moghraby, O. S., Ostrauskaite, G., Chakrabarti, S., Carucci, S., … Ougrin, D. (2023). Self-harm in children and adolescents who presented at emergency units during the COVID-19 Pandemic: An international retrospective cohort study. *Journal of the American Academy of Child & Adolescent Psychiatry, 62*(9), 998–1009. https://doi.org/10.1016/j.jaac.2022.11.016

World bank Data. (n.d.). *Oman economy.* World Bank Data360. Retrieved April 29, 2025, from https://data360.worldbank.org/en/economy/OMN

World Health Organization. (2008). (n.d.). Retrieved May 2, 2025, from https://cdn.who.int/media/docs/default-source/mental-health/who-aims-country-reports/who_aims_oman_report.pdf?sfvrsn=6830b334_3

World Health Orgnization. (2004). *The WHO mental health policy and service guidance package.* https://www.who.int/publications/i/item/9241546468

World Health Organization. (2005). Department of Mental Health and Substance, & World Health Organization Mental Health Evidence and Research. *Mental Health Atlas 2005*. World Health Organization.

World Health Organisation. (2012). Country Profile: OMAN ATLAS of Substance use disorders resources for the prevention and treatment of substance use disorders (SUD) 2012. Accessed on May 8, 2025, from https://www.emro.who.int/mnh/publications/substance-use-atlas.html

Yazeedi, S. A., & Shin, C. (2025). Loneliness and health status among omani older adults. *Journal of Gerontological Nursing, 51*(2), 33–42. https://doi.org/10.3928/00989134-20241122-01

Zadjali, F., Al-Bulushi, A., AlHassani, F., & Al Hinai, M. (2015). Proportion of night eating syndrome in Arab population of Oman. *Journal of Eating Disorders, 3*(1), 43. https://doi.org/10.1186/s40337-015-0079-6

Zadjali, F., Al-Futaisi, A., Al-Hosni, A., Al-Huseini, S., Crommelin, M., & Mirza, H. (2022). The parental and children report of the prevalence of depressive symptoms in children and adolescents amid the COVID-19 pandemic: A cross-sectional study from Oman. *International Journal of Public Health, 67*. https://doi.org/10.3389/ijph.2022.1604474

Zaidan, Z. A. J., Burke, D. T., Dorvlo, A. S. S., Al-Naamani, A., Al-Suleimani, A., Al-Hussaini, A., Al-Sharbati, M. M., & Al-Adawi, S. (2002). Deliberate self-poisoning in Oman. *Tropical Medicine & International Health: TM & IH, 7*(6), 549–556. https://doi.org/10.1046/j.1365-3156.2002.00887.x

Chapter 10
Mental Health Care in Palestine

Salam Khatib, Abdallah Alwawi, and Kawther Elissa

Abstract Mental health disorders in Palestine represent a growing public health concern, compounded by the protracted political conflict, socioeconomic instability, and systemic barriers to care. The epidemiological landscape of mental illness is shaped by multiple intersecting factors, including exposure to violence, displacement, chronic unemployment, and constrained access to health services. Mental health services in Palestine are severely affected by military attacks on Gaza and the military operations in the West Bank, especially the northern districts, such as Jenin and Tulkarem. Mental health services in Palestine face significant challenges as a result of the healthcare infrastructure being destroyed and a shortage of skilled, trained professionals. This situation exacerbates conditions like depression, anxiety, and post-traumatic stress disorder. Due to widespread anxiety and disruption in the community, access to psychological care is restricted, making rehabilitation more difficult. The destructions of mental health services such as hospitals and community mental health centers, entail the need to offer short-term and long-term interventions. This includes the continuous supply of psychiatric medications to ensure consistent access for patients; training of mental health professionals to handle mental health issues, working with the community to reduce stigma, offering psychoeducation, and focusing on the establishment of networking with patients and their families.

Keywords Challenges · Epidemiology · Mental health · Palestine · Telepsychiatry

S. Khatib (✉) · A. Alwawi · K. Elissa
Faculty of Health Profession, Abu Dis Campus, Al Quds University, Jerusalem, Palestine, Israel
e-mail: Salam.khatib@staff.alquds.edu

A. Alwawi
e-mail: aalwawi@staff.alquds.edu

K. Elissa
e-mail: kelissa@staff.alquds.edu

S. Al-Huseini and S. M. Y. Arafat (eds.), *Mental Health Care in the Middle East*, South Asian Perspectives in Mental Health and Psychology ,
https://doi.org/10.1007/978-981-95-0461-9_10

1 Historical Development of Mental Health Services in Palestine

The evolution of mental health services in Palestine is inextricably linked to the region's complex sociopolitical landscape, characterized by occupation, conflict, and systemic structural challenges. Since 1967, the Israeli military occupation has had a profound impact on health infrastructures, social services, and the psychological well-being of Palestinians. This section explores the historical trajectory of mental health care systems in Palestine, with attention to institutional developments, international aid efforts, and the role of local and non-governmental actors in response to chronic stressors under occupation.

1.1 Colonial and Political Backdrop

The Israeli occupation of the West Bank and Gaza Strip following the Six-Day War in 1967 restructured Palestinian civil services, including health care. The imposed administrative control disrupted the organic development of public health systems, including mental health. The fragmentation of Palestinian land, imposition of checkpoints, closure policies, and military incursions created barriers not only to physical health care but also to mental health service delivery (Giacaman et al., 2009). Over the decades, mental health concerns were subordinated to immediate medical emergencies, and psychiatric services were largely reactive rather than preventive. As Marie et al. (2016) emphasize, the psychological consequences of political oppression were largely under-researched and under-addressed, given the lack of systemic investment and long-term planning.

1.2 The Establishment of Mental Health Initiatives

Despite structural barriers, Palestine witnessed the emergence of mental health institutions through civil society actors. The Gaza Community Mental Health Program (GCMHP), founded in 1990, became a flagship initiative, integrating psychological care with community-based rehabilitation and human rights advocacy. Counselling services began taking root through Palestinian universities and NGOS, such as the Palestinian Counselling Centre and the Palestine Red Crescent Society, which provided trauma-informed care and psychosocial support in schools and refugee camps (Ziadni et al., 2011).

Giacaman et al. (2011) note that while traditional psychiatry was historically marginalized, especially among the rural and refugee populations, local cultural idioms of distress began to influence how services were conceptualized. Mental distress was often interpreted through spiritual or social lenses, requiring practitioners to adopt culturally competent approaches grounded in collective identity, familial systems, and resistance narratives.

1.3 Oslo Accords and Health System Fragmentation

The Oslo Accords in the 1990s introduced new administrative divisions (Areas A, B, and C), which not only impacted sovereignty but also fragmented health planning and delivery. The Palestinian Ministry of Health (PMoH), established under the Palestinian Authority in 1994, began modest reforms in integrating mental health into public service provision. However, challenges persisted, including a lack of trained psychiatrists, stigma around psychiatric care, and insufficient funding (Marie et al., 2016).

Keelan (2016) emphasizes that by 2005, mental health services remained critically under-resourced: out of 380 public health clinics, only a handful offered psychiatric care, and psychotropic medications were inconsistently available. Community-based mental health continued to rely heavily on donor-funded NGOS with limited integration into the national system.

1.4 Shifting Narratives and Western Discourse

A notable critique raised by Giacaman et al. (2009) concerns the framing of Palestinian mental health solely through the lens of Western biomedical psychiatry. The authors argue that this framework often pathologizes natural reactions to political trauma, such as fear, grief, and resistance. Instead, they advocate for a contextualized model that recognizes the chronic nature of occupation-related stressors and the resilience mechanisms employed by Palestinian communities.

Mental health narratives have gradually shifted from individualized diagnoses to broader psychosocial frameworks, which include concepts such as collective trauma, intergenerational transmission of distress, and the psychological effects of displacement. The reframing of mental health from merely a clinical condition to a social and political outcome has gained traction in Palestinian research and practice.

2 Epidemiology and Burden of Mental Illness in Palestine

Mental health disorders in Palestine represent a growing public health concern, compounded by the protracted political conflict, socioeconomic instability, and systemic barriers to care. The epidemiological landscape of mental illness is shaped by multiple intersecting factors, including exposure to violence, displacement, chronic unemployment, and constrained access to health services. This section examines the prevalence and burden of common mental health disorders, particularly depression, anxiety, substance abuse, and suicidal behavior, based on recent evidence from both the West Bank and the Gaza Strip. It also highlights demographic vulnerabilities and systemic gaps in early detection and intervention.

2.1 Prevalence of Mental Disorders

Palestinian communities face one of the highest burdens of mental illness in the Eastern Mediterranean Region (EMR), according to the World Health Organization (WHO). A study by Charlson et al. (2016) on the global burden of mental disorders revealed that conditions such as depressive and anxiety disorders account for a substantial proportion of years lived with disability (YLDS) in the occupied Palestinian territory (oPt). In particular, major depressive disorder and post-traumatic stress disorder (PTSD) are highly prevalent, especially among youth, women, and individuals exposed to repeated violence. The WHO (2020) further reports that nearly 30% of adults and adolescents in Gaza and the West Bank exhibit symptoms consistent with depression or anxiety. In a nationally representative survey, up to 54% of adolescents in Gaza reported at least one mental health symptom following armed conflict. These rates are exacerbated by repeated military escalations, chronic uncertainty, and restricted freedom of movement.

2.2 Substance Abuse and Stigma

Substance abuse is an emerging public health concern, particularly among marginalized youth and displaced populations. While data remain limited due to stigma and underreporting, local studies have identified a growing pattern of drug misuse, especially of painkillers, sedatives, and illicit substances such as Tramadol in Gaza. According to Diab et al. (2021), substance use in Palestinian territories often reflects self-medicating behaviors in response to trauma, psychological distress, and lack of coping resources.

Despite the burden, addiction services remain sparse and culturally stigmatized. Many individuals with substance use disorders do not seek help, fearing legal consequences or social rejection. Treatment infrastructure for substance abuse is almost entirely reliant on NGOs or foreign assistance, with little integration into the national health system.

2.3 *Suicidal Ideation and Self-harm*

Suicide, historically considered a cultural taboo in Palestinian society, has gained attention in recent epidemiological literature due to a rising trend in ideation and attempts, particularly among adolescents and young adults. A notable study by El-Khodary and Samara (2020) found that 25% of middle school students in Gaza reported suicidal thoughts, and 14% had formulated suicide plans. Risk factors include exposure to violence, bullying, poor family relations, and untreated psychiatric symptoms. While suicide completion rates remain lower than global averages, the psychosocial burden is significant. The Palestinian Ministry of Health (2022) has acknowledged suicide as a growing concern, calling for targeted prevention and mental health literacy campaigns. However, the lack of comprehensive suicide surveillance systems hinders timely intervention.

2.4 *Vulnerable Populations*

Certain demographic groups bear a disproportionate burden of mental illness in Palestine. Children and adolescents living in refugee camps or areas of high military activity experience higher rates of PTSD, emotional dysregulation, and academic difficulties. Women, particularly widows and female-headed households, exhibit higher prevalence of depressive symptoms and anxiety (Marie et al., 2016). Internally displaced persons (IDPs), particularly in Gaza following major military offensives, are also at heightened risk for trauma-related disorders.

Moreover, persons with disabilities and individuals with chronic illnesses face a dual vulnerability, as they often encounter barriers to accessing both general health care and psychosocial support. Mental health stigma, limited mobility, and the absence of inclusive services contribute to their marginalization.

2.5 *Systemic Challenges and Data Gaps*

Reliable data on mental health disorders in Palestine are limited due to fragmented health information systems and an under-resourced research infrastructure. Most epidemiological studies are conducted in partnership with international organizations or academic institutions, leading to inconsistent methodologies and population coverage. This hinders the formulation of evidence-based policy and the scaling up of effective interventions. Additionally, the mental health workforce is insufficient to meet the growing demand. There are fewer than 1.5 psychiatrists per 100,000 people in the West Bank, and the majority of mental health professionals are concentrated in urban areas. Rural and marginalized communities remain underserved, reinforcing cycles of unmet need and delayed care (WHO, 2020).

3 Current Mental Health Services in Palestine

3.1 Introduction

Palestine's mental health system exists within a landscape of chronic political instability, occupation, and underfunding. Despite these constraints, recent decades have seen the gradual development of a fragmented but evolving network of mental health services delivered through public, private, and nongovernmental sectors. This section offers a critical appraisal of the existing infrastructure, service delivery models, accessibility challenges, and workforce limitations. It also examines the role of local and international stakeholders in shaping mental health policy and expanding service coverage.

3.2 Structure and Key Service Providers

The mental health system in Palestine is primarily composed of four service providers: the Palestinian Ministry of Health (PMoH), the United Nations Relief and Works Agency for Palestine Refugees (UNRWA), local and international NGOs, and the Gaza Community Mental Health Programme (GCMHP). These entities operate decentralized, with varying levels of coordination and coverage between the West Bank and the Gaza Strip.

The PMoH is the principal governmental body responsible for planning and overseeing public mental health services. However, resources are limited. As of 2020, there were only two public psychiatric hospitals—one in Bethlehem and another in Gaza—serving over five million people (Marie et al., 2016). In addition, general hospitals with psychiatric departments are few, and community mental health centers (CMHCS) are distributed unevenly across governorates. Many lack multidisciplinary teams or offer only basic outpatient consultations.

UNRWA provides mental health and psychosocial support (MHPSS) services to Palestinian refugees, primarily in schools and primary care settings. Their work includes deploying school counsellors, psychosocial case managers, and referrals for children exhibiting signs of emotional distress (WHO, 2020). While these programs are essential, they are often constrained by political funding cycles and shifting donor priorities. NGOs have been instrumental in filling service gaps, especially in marginalized and conflict-affected communities. Organizations such as the Palestinian Counseling Center and Médecins Sans Frontières provide free counseling, trauma therapy, and capacity-building programs. Yet, their services are often project-based and lack integration into national health systems, raising concerns about sustainability and continuity of care (Marie et al., 2016).

3.3 Accessibility and Equity Challenges

Access to mental health care in Palestine remains severely constrained by a combination of structural, political, and cultural barriers. Geopolitical fragmentation—the separation of Gaza from the West Bank, the division of the West Bank into Areas A, B, and C, and the presence of checkpoints and the separation wall—impedes the movement of both patients and health professionals. For instance, patients in Area C face severe challenges in reaching care facilities due to a lack of transportation, permit restrictions, and security threats (WHO, 2020).

Cultural stigma surrounding mental illness also discourages many Palestinians from seeking help. In traditional Palestinian society, mental health issues are often perceived as signs of personal weakness or family dishonor. Consequently, individuals may delay seeking treatment or turn to religious or traditional healers as a first step. A lack of mental health literacy exacerbates this situation, particularly in rural areas and among older populations.

Furthermore, gender-based barriers affect women's access to care. Women suffering from depression, trauma, or domestic violence may face additional layers of stigma, restrictions on mobility, and fear of social reprisal, all of which limit their willingness and ability to engage with formal mental health services (Ziadni et al., 2011).

3.4 Human Resources and Workforce Shortages

One of the most pressing challenges to mental health service provision in Palestine is the shortage of trained personnel. According to WHO estimates, there are fewer than 50 psychiatrists across the entire oPt, and most are located in urban areas such as Ramallah, Gaza City, and Bethlehem (WHO, 2020). The mental health workforce also includes clinical psychologists, social workers, nurses, and counsellors, but their training is often variable, and continuing education opportunities are rare.

The GCMHP and other institutions have played a critical role in workforce development through specialized diploma programs, internships, and international collaborations. Still, the number of professionals remains insufficient to meet growing demands, particularly in areas affected by conflict, poverty, and displacement. The absence of professional licensing standards, formal accreditation pathways, and mental health integration into primary care further hinders service expansion.

3.5 Policy Developments and International Support

In recent years, the PMoH has taken steps toward the institutionalization of mental health within the broader health policy framework. The adoption of the WHO Mental

Health Gap Action Programme (mhGAP) in Palestine has facilitated the training of non-specialist health workers in the identification and management of common mental disorders in primary care settings. This task-sharing model is especially valuable in resource-constrained contexts where psychiatric specialists are scarce (World Health Organization Regional Office for the Eastern Mediterranean, 2022). Donor agencies and UN bodies continue to play a pivotal role in supporting mental health programming, research, and service delivery. However, funding inconsistencies and political interference pose ongoing risks. Mental health is often deprioritized in humanitarian response plans, receiving only a fraction of total health sector funding.

3.6 Integration and Future Prospects

There is a growing consensus among mental health stakeholders that future efforts must prioritize the integration of mental health services into primary care and community health systems. The WHO recommends a model of decentralized, community-based mental health services tailored to local cultural norms and supported by multi-sectoral partnerships. Such integration can improve early detection, reduce stigma, and improve care coordination for patients with complex needs (Marie et al., 2016). Yet, systemic change will require investment in infrastructure, training, and evidence-based policy development. Effective scale-up also hinges on strengthening inter-agency coordination, establishing national mental health registries, and enhancing public awareness through culturally appropriate outreach campaigns.

4 Innovations in Mental Health Care: Telepsychiatry in Palestine

Innovations in mental health care are crucial to overcoming access barriers in regions affected by conflict, occupation, and infrastructural limitations—such as Palestine. One of the most promising developments in this context is telepsychiatry: using digital and remote communication technologies to provide psychiatric assessment, therapy, and follow-up services. In Palestine, where geopolitical fragmentation, security constraints, and mental health stigma limit in-person access to care, telepsychiatry offers a transformative model for delivering mental health services. This section explores telepsychiatry's emergence, implementation, effectiveness, and challenges in Palestine, situating it within the broader push toward digital health equity.

4.1 The Rationale for Telepsychiatry in Palestine

The unique context of Palestine—marked by occupation-related travel restrictions, chronic humanitarian crises, and fragmented governance—has made traditional, facility-based mental health services difficult to access for large portions of the population. Residents of rural areas, refugee camps, and Area C of the West Bank often face military checkpoints, roadblocks, and curfews that delay or prevent travel to clinics (Keelan, 2016). In Gaza, frequent electricity outages and movement restrictions further isolate patients from care. Additionally, the shortage of mental health professionals, especially psychiatrists and clinical psychologists, makes it nearly impossible to meet the rising demand.

Telepsychiatry addresses these structural barriers by enabling remote consultations and follow-ups, often through mobile devices or secure video conferencing platforms. It also provides an added layer of privacy for patients concerned with stigma, allowing them to receive care from the comfort of their homes. As such, telepsychiatry holds unique potential to democratize access to mental health care in the oPt.

4.2 Early Models and Implementation

Initial attempts to integrate telemedicine into Palestinian health services date back to the early 2000s. A study by Zatari et al. (1999) described the feasibility of telemedicine in Palestine, identifying mental health as one of its most promising applications due to the shortage of trained professionals. By 2010, more structured pilot programs emerged, primarily supported by international NGOs and academic partnerships. These included basic video-based psychiatric assessments between patients in Gaza and clinicians in the West Bank or abroad. One of the notable early models was developed through collaborations between Palestinian IT specialists, mental health practitioners, and the international NGO sector. It aimed to provide low-cost, real-time consultation. According to Zatari and Tahboub (2000), these programs demonstrated high patient satisfaction, improved attendance rates, and reduced unnecessary referrals.

4.3 Expansion and Institutional Support

In recent years, the use of telepsychiatry has gained more institutional support. The Gaza Community Mental Health Programme (GCMHP), one of the region's leading mental health NGOs, integrated teletherapy into its post-crisis response during the COVID-19 pandemic and in the aftermath of armed escalations. Telepsychiatry proved especially critical when traditional clinic-based services were suspended due to security or public health restrictions. Additionally, several Palestinian startups and digital health platforms have emerged to meet this growing demand. One pioneering initiative, "Shezlong Palestine," adapted the Egyptian online therapy platform to serve the Palestinian population with Arabic-speaking psychologists offering online sessions at reduced costs (Mercy Corps, 2022). The platform saw a rapid increase in users during the COVID-19 lockdowns and escalations in Gaza.

The Palestinian Ministry of Health has also expressed interest in scaling up digital health solutions. While regulatory frameworks remain underdeveloped, recent policy discussions have included telemedicine as a strategic objective within the broader national eHealth agenda.

4.4 Effectiveness, Challenges, and Ethical Considerations

Studies have shown that telepsychiatry in Palestine is generally well-received by patients and providers alike. It has proven particularly effective for patients with anxiety, depression, and trauma-related disorders who may have difficulty travelling or prefer privacy (Helbich & Jabr, 2022). However, its use for more severe psychiatric conditions such as psychosis remains limited, given the need for close clinical supervision and medication management.

Despite its promise, telepsychiatry in Palestine faces several logistical and ethical hurdles:

Infrastructure: Poor internet connectivity disrupts session continuity, especially in Gaza and rural areas.
Digital Literacy: Older adults and patients with limited education may struggle with platforms or lack access to appropriate devices.
Confidentiality: Ensuring secure and private communication is challenging in overcrowded living environments.
Provider Training: Many mental health professionals have not received formal training in delivering teletherapy, raising concerns about quality and consistency.

Furthermore, there is a need for standardized protocols, licensing for online mental health services, and culturally adapted digital platforms that maintain ethical standards.

4.5 Future Directions and Sustainability

The long-term success of telepsychiatry in Palestine depends on its integration into the formal health system, adequate investment in digital infrastructure, and the development of evidence-based guidelines for remote care. Given Palestine's relatively young and tech-savvy population, the expansion of mobile mental health applications, chatbots for psychoeducation, and SMS-based interventions is a promising future pathway (Zatari & Tahboub, 2000).

To ensure equity, telepsychiatry programs must be designed with inclusion in mind, reaching refugees, women in conservative settings, and persons with disabilities. Collaboration between local universities, the PMoH, and international academic partners can further support research, training, and scaling initiatives. Telepsychiatry represents a transformative innovation in Palestinian mental health care. Amid mobility restrictions, stigma, and workforce shortages, it offers a viable path toward more equitable, accessible, and resilient mental health services. While infrastructure, policy, and ethical challenges remain, the groundwork laid by NGOs, startups, and public initiatives offers a promising foundation for scaling up digital mental health solutions across the occupied Palestinian territory.

5 Impact of War on Mental Health Services in Palestine

Palestine is a conflict-affected region. The Palestinian dispute, which began in the late nineteenth century, is a long-running conflict between Israelis, a militarily rich and nuclear state, and Palestinians, landowners (Bhowmick & Khan, 2024). In the Gaza Strip, two million people have faced four wars (in 2008, 2012, 2014, 2021, 2023). The Israel–Palestinian conflict, triggered on October 7, 2023, has resulted in high fatality rates, mass casualties, significant damage to homes and infrastructure, and a huge humanitarian crisis in the region. In the Gaza Strip, civilians have suffered the most direct conflict deaths. Most of the population has been internally displaced, with little access to food, water, housing, sanitation, and essential health services, including mental health services (Ugarte et al., 2024). Additionally, Israeli military operations in the West Bank have caused substantial deaths, infrastructural damage, and economic losses (ESCWA & UNDP, 2023). Also, the current war in Gaza, unstable political situations, and settler violence in the West Bank, including closures, checkpoints, and the separation wall, continue to separate families and compromise the organization of the Palestinian health care system and the quality of healthcare services provided in Palestine (Bromley, 2021).

Aldabbour et al. (2024a, 2024b) reported that 97.05% of medical students experienced mild depression symptoms or worse, whereas 84.37% and 90.56%, respectively, reported mild anxiety and mild stress symptoms or worse. PTSD affected 63.40% of the population, all participants with PTSD had at least one psychiatric comorbidity, and high levels of life dissatisfaction were also reported. In the Gaza Strip, people of all ages express a desire to die rather than endure more hardship, violence, and displacement (ACAPS, 2024). This report also mentioned that nearly all of the people living in Gaza have been a part of or observed violent and traumatic events, such as direct aggression and threats to their lives. All of these situations exacerbate people's underlying psychosocial and mental health issues and raise their risk of getting new ones. Furthermore, ongoing displacement, relentless physical struggles, and the ever-present threat to safety have inflicted profound mental health damage on all Gazans, particularly devastating for children. Children in the Gaza Strip have signs of extreme mental strain and trauma, including worry, fear, eating disorders, bedwetting, hypervigilance, and trouble sleeping (Save the Children, 2024).

Thabet and Vostanis (2017) found that high rates of PTSD and anxiety were found among both parents (PTSD: 60%; anxiety: 26.5%) and children (PTSD: 70.1%; anxiety: 33.9%). Children exhibited additional mental health challenges, including conduct disorders (36.8%), hyperactivity (22.8%), and peer problems (60.1%). The severity of these issues often correlates with exposure to violence, loss, and displacement (Thabet & Thabet, 2017). Similarly, Aldabbour et al. (2024a, 2024b) revealed that 40% of adults screened positive for PTSD, with anxiety affecting 37% and depression affecting 45% of the population. Additionally, a study among internally displaced persons in the Gaza Strip found extremely high rates of mental health issues, including depression at 99.5%, anxiety at 99.7%, and stress at 93.7%. Individuals over 40 and those displaced more than four times had significantly higher risks of psychological distress (Albelbeisi et al., 2025).

According to UNICEF (2024), almost every child in Gaza is thought to require mental health support. Even prior to the onset of the ongoing war, UNICEF reported that more than half a million children in Gaza were in need of psychological and psychosocial assistance.

According to WHO (2024), in Gaza, more than 1.7 million displaced individuals are enduring severe psychological distress and require urgent mental health and psychosocial support (MHPSS). Among them, approximately 485,000 individuals with pre-existing mental health conditions face interrupted treatment and lack access to specialized care, including essential medications. In response, WHO has secured psychotropic drugs sufficient for more than 30,000 patients and distributed emergency MHPSS kits. To improve mental health services, WHO is collaborating with the Gaza Community Mental Health Program (GCMHP) to deliver specialized care, including sending teams to UNRWA shelters to provide on-site psychosocial support. Additionally, WHO has evaluated and mapped MHPSS resources within the Ministry of Health, concentrating on two primary healthcare facilities. Plans are underway to conduct refresher training for health workers using the Mental Health Gap Action Programme (mhgap) guidelines. Furthermore, WHO strives to incorporate MHPSS into the emergency medical teams (EMT) response to ensure comprehensive crisis intervention.

Altawil et al. (2023) conducted a longitudinal study that examined the impact of chronic war trauma on PTSD among 607 Palestinian adolescents and adults in the Gaza Strip from 2006 to 2021. According to this study, four categories of responses to chronic war trauma were identified: the acute group (52.9%) displayed severe PTSD symptoms in both 2006 and 2021, while the remitters group (8.9%) showed symptoms in 2006 but not in 2021. In contrast, the delayed group (33.6%) developed significant PTSD symptoms by 2021 despite having none in 2006. Finally, the resilient group (4.6%) remained symptom-free throughout the study.

Abed Alah (2024) reported that the ongoing war and deprivation of basic needs severely compromise the mental health of the healthcare workers in Gaza. This creates a vicious cycle where their ability to deliver adequate care is impacted not just by external challenges such as the shortage of medical supplies and overcrowding, but also by their declining health and well-being. Between October 2023 and March 14, 2025, 670 Israeli military attacks against healthcare facilities and 170 ambulances occurred in the Gaza Strip, according to the WHO (2025a, 2025b). In addition, this report mentioned that 122 Health facilities were affected, 33 of 36 hospitals were destroyed, and fewer than half of the primary care centers were functional due to the ongoing war in Gaza. This leads to overwhelmed facilities and limited access to care (Aqtam, 2025). Forty-three ambulances and seven health facilities have been damaged by ongoing Israeli operations in the West Bank, resulting in 23 of them not functioning. Health facilities operated by UNRWA in Jenin, Tulkarm, and Nur Shams refugee camps are currently non-operational. Ongoing restrictions on movement continue to disrupt ambulance services and the ability of medical staff to travel, severely limiting access to critical health care (WHO, 2025a, 2025b).

Mental health services in Palestine are severely affected by military attacks on Gaza and the military operations in the West Bank, especially the northern districts, such as Jenin and Tulkarem. Mental health services in Palestine face significant challenges because of the healthcare infrastructure being destroyed and a shortage of skilled, trained professionals (Aqtam, 2025). This situation exacerbates conditions like depression, anxiety, and PTSD. Due to widespread anxiety and disruption in the community, access to psychological care is restricted, making rehabilitation more difficult (Qutishat, 2025). Gaza's mental health infrastructure is severely inadequate; just six community mental health facilities, thirty-six clinical psychologists, and ten psychiatrists serve the two million people living there (Altawil et al., 2023). Prior to the current war in Gaza, there was less than one psychiatrist for every 100,000 people, a situation that was made worse by displacement and war fatalities (Thabet & Vostanis, 2017). Five regional support centers have been established, one for each governorate, to help those affected by trauma increase access. The Gaza Community Mental Health Program is still the area's most well-known mental health provider, with three facilities and about 70 employees (Altawil et al., 2023).

6 Challenges of Mental Health Care in Palestine

The challenges of mental health care have three main factors that influence mental health needs and the provided services: the Israeli occupation, the stereotypical ideas of society about mental illness, and the scarcity of resources. The long-standing war and occupation of Palestine have consequences for the mental health situation and the infrastructure of the health system.

Studies emphasized that the type of trauma plays a tremendous role in people's mental health. Therefore, repeated ongoing trauma is undeniable to the Palestinians, making attempts to protect the health system insufficient. Insecure environments and emergency settings force mental health institutions to focus exclusively on trauma-focused care at the expense of other psychological interventions. Furthermore, life-saving protection services and treating severely injured individuals are prioritized over mental health needs (Palestine Red Crescent Society, 2025).

WHO (2001) stressed that adopting specialized trauma-focused services without integrating them into the broader mental health system is a significant challenge in providing holistic, comprehensive mental health treatments in Palestine. Therefore, they advised linking a short-term trauma approach with a long-term service-building approach, which will help conflict-zone countries to avoid the fragmentation of services and low-quality mental health services (WHO, 2001). However, as a result of unpredictable intensification of violence in the West Bank and the ongoing large-scale military operations in Gaza, most health institutions and NGOs in Palestine immediately provide frontline and short-term crisis relief and healthcare to all affected by the war in Gaza and the West Bank (Palestine Red Crescent Society, 2025). The catastrophic humanitarian conditions negatively impact any previous initiatives to establish long-term stable MH services for people with mental illnesses and worsen even more the pre-existing shortfalls of MH services. Prior to the war in Gaza and despite the widespread mental health problems in Palestine, the mental health system in Palestine suffers from many shortfalls. It is described as weak, with insufficient services, weak training possibilities, limited adequate, formally qualified MH professionals, a lack of funding for multidimensional interventions, and a lack of human resources. During the war in the Gaza Strip, Albelbeisi et al. (2025) study found alarming results concerning depression, anxiety and stress among displaced individuals as the prevalence of those disorders was (99.5%, 99.7%, and 93.7%, respectively). In the same study, it was found that participants aged >40 years had a significantly higher likelihood of experiencing a mental health disorder ($P < 0.05$), and those who were forcefully displaced more than 4 times had a significantly higher likelihood of experiencing a mental health disorder ($P < 0.05$). Those results are shocking if compared to the World Bank Group (2022) survey, which found that the symptom levels of depression are particularly high in Gaza (71%) compared to 50% in the West Bank. They concluded that people in Palestine have a higher risk of mental health problems compared to other countries using the same WHO instruments. In light of the complex mental health problems and the collective nature of trauma among individuals in Palestine, mental health services have to respond appropriately to those needs. This could not be separated from the economic hardships, limited resources, and cultural barriers that undermine mental health status among the Palestinians. Issues related to stigma toward mental illness create additional barriers to seeking mental health services and make many people with mental health problems undiagnosed (WHO, 2025a, 2025b). WHO (2025a, 2025b) provided training to 300 health workers on the Mental Health Gap Action Program (mhGAP) Intervention Guide (2.0) in the West Bank and Gaza Strip. The training was operated to overcome many challenges to seeking mental health services, including limitations in staff and facilities, inadequate and insufficient services, and cultural barriers such as stigma and discrimination.

Therefore, any intervention should take into consideration social stigma to accommodate low health and mental health literacy (MHL), as individuals with low health literacy have more difficulty in the utilization of mental health services. A study by Abo-Ras and Abu-Kaf (2023) examined MHL among 214 Palestinian-Arabs from Israel who reported moderate or high levels on all MHL dimensions (ability to recognize disorders, knowledge of risk factors and causes, knowledge of self-treatment, knowledge of professional help available, knowledge of where to seek information, and attitudes that promote recognition or appropriate help-seeking behavior). Participants who reported using mental health services had significantly ($p < 0.001$) higher MHL levels on three dimensions than those who did not use mental health services: knowledge of professional help available, knowledge of where to seek information, and attitudes that promote recognition or appropriate help-seeking behavior. The study by Abo-Ras and Abu-Kaf (2023) found that the main determinants of mental health service use were psychological distress, knowledge of where to seek information, and attitudes that promote recognition or appropriate help-seeking behavior. Those findings are significant and may provide an understanding of factors underlying the lower utilization of MH services in Palestine. Sarhan et al. (2020) assessed health literacy on 472 students at Birzeit University using the Arabic version of the Health Literacy Questionnaire and a locally developed distress scale to measure students' distress levels. University students' average total health literacy score was 135.3, and interestingly, the study found that distress can moderate university female students' health literacy and health-related behavior, as the study found that females' high distress levels were associated with lower levels of health literacy. Therefore, it can be stipulated that women with mental health issues and with low literacy may refrain from seeking mental health services. This entails the necessity of providing mental health education to Palestinian women to raise their literacy regarding the identification of emotional distress.

Additionally, Abo-Ras and Abu-Kaf (2023) highlighted another critical determinant of mental health services and the link between attitudes and stigma and mental health help-seeking behaviors. Their study found that Palestinian-Arabs from Israel with positive attitudes toward mental disorders and their treatment had a higher rate of mental health service utilization. Consistently, Sarhan et al. (2020) explained their result regarding high psychological distress among female university students in the context of Palestinian society. From their point of view, females in patriarchal societies, as in Palestine, were more likely to report mental health problems than men. Masculine stereotypes in Palestine shape gender differences in expressing emotions as well as seeking mental health-related services (Swan, 2018). This is mainly because men find themselves confined within the narrative of self-governing decision-makers, guardians, and breadwinners to their families; they are not motivated to become anything other than these roles. This provides minimal space for men to manage the emotions that arise when they cannot meet these responsibilities (Swan, 2018). As a consequence, Palestinian men refrain from seeking mental health services, and NGOs and MHPs should adopt new strategies such as "men-streaming," which means engaging men and boys in any psychological interventions where men have safe spaces to speak out about their feelings, as well as offering emotional support if needed (Swan, 2018).

6.1 *Imparity of Manpower, Hospital Beds, and Community Mental Health Centers*

Mentally ill patients faced many challenges, and one of the disturbing conditions that leads to inadequate mental health care is the limited-resource hospitals in the West Bank and the Gaza Strip. There is one Ministry of Health (MoH) mental health hospital in the West Bank and one in the Gaza Strip. The Bethlehem Psychiatric Hospital has only 140 beds. The average duration of patient stay is 64.6 days, and the bed occupancy rate stands at 84.3% (Moh, 2023). The Moh community mental health services are provided through 22 community mental health clinics (15 in the West Bank, 1 for children and adolescents, and 6 in the Gaza Strip). Although there are significant levels of mental health issues and decades of violence and occupation, there are only 23 physicians in the Bethlehem Psychiatric Hospital (8 specialists and 15 general) and 86 nurses. One physician is assigned to each community mental health clinic. Mental health forces play a major role in improving Mental health status in every country, and the severe shortage of medical infrastructures in general and psychiatrists and MHPS in particular indicates that current clinical services are not meeting the demand for mental health services.

6.2 *Economic Hardship and Affordability of Mental Health Treatment*

Poverty rate is high in Palestine compared to other countries in the Middle East (53% in the Gaza Strip; 13.9% in the West Bank) (Palestinian Center for Human Rights, 2022). The unemployment rate in Palestine has increased from 25.7% in 2022 to 49.9% in 2024 (ESCWA & UNDP, 2023). This is caused mainly by the outbreak of the war in the Gaza Strip and the large-scale military operation on the West Bank. Therefore, it is expected that the prevalence of poverty will increase in the year 2025, which will impact all sectors in Palestine, including the economic situation of the mentally ill (ESCWA & UNDP, 2023). The struggle of the mentally ill to secure a full-time job as a result of the deterioration of the economic situation and the stigma surrounding them will affect their psychological conditions (Jabir, 2023). The World Bank report in 2023 stressed that poor mental health among the Palestinians is correlated with economic hardships. Palestinian Moh provides free-of-charge treatments to mentally ill patients, which particularly focus on medication rather than psychotherapy. However, not all psychotropic medications are available through Moh clinics, and buying them from the private pharmacies is not affordable to many patients (Jabir, 2023; World Bank, 2023).

In Palestine, the financial budget for mental health programs comes from governmental and non-governmental sources (Moh, 2023). Although this funding can facilitate various beneficial programs, the quality, coordination, and overall effectiveness of these programs can differ widely (Moh, 2023).

6.3 *Treatment Challenges for the Mentally Ill*

6.3.1 Poly Pharmacy

In Palestine, the practice of polypharmacy persists, even though research indicates that monotherapy frequently proves effective and that non-pharmacological treatments may be more desirable alternatives. A study by Hattab et al. (2023) examined the medical prescriptions of 1045 mentally ill patients in the West Bank. The study found alarming results, as it shows that polypharmacy is widespread in Palestine. 84% (N = 877) of the analyzed prescriptions were prescribed with Polypharmacy, and only one-third of the prescriptions were with two medications. The patients with higher use of polypharmacy were diagnosed with schizophrenia, schizoaffective disorder, and bipolar disorder (Hattab et al., 2023).

6.3.2 Medication, Psychotherapy, and Religious Healers

The treatment for the mentally ill in Palestine focuses on psycho-pharmacological interventions more than psychological treatment (Marie et al., 2020). Due to the large number of patients seen by PMoH professionals in the community mental health centers and the insufficient number of highly skilled mental health professionals, providing counseling and psychotherapy (i.e., cognitive behavioral therapy, family therapy, psychodynamic therapy, etc.) is difficult and therefore those centers offer mainly and only psychotropic medications to mentally ill patients. The inability of patients with mental illness to receive psychotherapy may lead to relapses and exacerbate their condition.

Many NGOs and individuals in the Gaza Strip and the West Bank provide psychosocial and mental health services. Numerous organizations offer a vertical service to specific targeted patients. Mental health professionals who can potentially support a general mental health care system, particularly in the area of training, are usually employed by NGOs. Because they can also take referrals from the general mental health care system, competent NGOs can be considered a valuable resource (UNICEF, 2019). However, the psychosocial projects assessment framework is derived mostly from Western countries, and many MHPS questioned their applicability to the Palestinian context. Therefore, many studies highlight the critical need for expanded funding for mental health services, capacity-building programs, and legislative changes (Abo-Rass et al., 2024; Hillel, 2023; Shalhoub-Kevorkian, 2005). Collaboration between stakeholders, such as NGOS, local communities, and policymakers, can lead to a more effective, equitable, and inclusive mental health-care system that can co-design and implement culturally sensitive interventions that address the various needs of the Palestinian population.

People of all ages and backgrounds are impacted by the significant issue of mental health. Understanding the significance of a comprehensive approach to mental health treatment that incorporates both homeopathy and clinical psychology is crucial. Nevertheless, in Palestine, people frequently turn to religious leaders like Sheikhs or Imams for assistance instead of seeking help from mental health professionals. This may be caused by the widespread belief that mental illness could be caused by supernatural causes such as possession by evil spirits, like Jinn (Elshamy et al., 2023). Additionally, some of the Palestinians blamed their symptoms on "weak faith and disobeying [God's] commandments," or a lack of religious belief. Consequently, they believed overcoming adversity and deepening their relationship with God were more suitable than obtaining expert help (Elshamy et al., 2023).

6.4 Poor Funding and Research

The Lancet series on global mental health significantly elevated the importance of mental health systems in low- and middle-income countries (LMICs) (Patel et al., 2008), aiming to address the challenge of expanding mental health services. Global action was urged, with recommendations for research focused on evaluating mental health systems, particularly in LMICs, to enhance the provision of mental health care to meet the needs of various populations. However, there has been a lack of systematic research conducted in Palestine to date. Establishing comprehensive baseline data regarding the mental health system in Palestine is crucial for informing the development of policies and plans aimed at strengthening and expanding services. However, financial support is a challenge for many researchers, and resource shortages hinder study implementation (Abo-Rass et al., 2024; Rabaia et al, 2014).

7 Potential Strengths of Mental Health Services in the Gaza Strip and the West Bank

Despite the challenges that face mental health services in Gaza and the West Bank, the Palestinian mental health system demonstrates resilience. This system is supported by community-based organizations, regional non-governmental organizations (NGOs), and collaborations with international organizations to carry out a variety of MHPSS interventions.

Collaborations between local Palestinian organizations and international Non-Governmental Organizations (NGOs) and community groups have improved mental health service delivery to Palestinian people in Gaza and the West Bank. This collaboration is vital for a comprehensive, long-term approach, addressing immediate and ongoing needs. For example, MHPSS activities in Gaza are coordinated through the Gaza MHPSS Technical Working Group (TWG). Since the TWG's formation in February 2023, United Nations Relief and Works Agency for Palestine Refugees (UNRWA) has served as co-chair, with assistance from an MHPSS Coordinator (UNRWA, 2024). In light of the ongoing crisis, UNRWA has modified its approach to mental health to give priority to emergency interventions. This includes raising awareness about the psychological effects of war, encouraging adaptive coping mechanisms, strengthening community bonds, providing group and individual psychosocial support (PSS) for at-risk individuals, and offering counselling, psychiatric care, and psychotropic medications when available (UNRWA, 2024).

Numerous NGOS offer specialized mental health treatments or create programs centered on trauma and psychosocial assistance (Arslan, 2024). The World Health Organization (WHO) offers substantial funding and technical assistance to the Ministry of Health. This support primarily focuses on incorporating mental health services into primary healthcare systems, training local medical staff in psychological first aid, and setting up dedicated mental health units within healthcare facilities (Aqtam, 2025; Arslan, 2024). UNICEF delivers essential mental health and psychosocial support services in refugee camps and temporary shelters, creating safe environments where children can play, interact with peers, and reclaim aspects of their childhood. These interventions are being expanded to help children cope with their traumatic experiences (UNICEF, 2025). Humanitarian organizations, including Save the Children, the Palestine Red Crescent Society (PRCS), and Médecins Sans Frontières (MSF), provide mental health services to vulnerable groups in Gaza. These organizations provide counselling, psychotherapy, and psychosocial support to displaced individuals and others facing barriers to accessing traditional healthcare facilities through mobile clinics and outreach teams (Arslan, 2024; Médecins Sans Frontières, 2024).

Gaza Community Mental Health Program (GCMHP) is a non-profit organization established in 1990 to improve the Palestinian community's mental health. GCMHP provides many mental health services such as psychological first aid to affected people and displaced families, which include women, men, children, the elderly, and people with disabilities, telephone counselling services, and expanding the professional foundation of mental health workers in the Gaza Strip to provide the population with a better level of services and occupational therapy and rehabilitation services (GCMHP, 2025).

CARE International has implemented a six-month after-school program to support the emotional and social development of children and young adolescents (ages 10–14) in Gaza. This program provides safe spaces for over 5,000 children to interact with peers and mentors. The program seeks to enhance mental health outcomes and foster resilience in both home and school environments (Arslan, 2024).

8 Ways Out

The development of mental health services in Palestine is a reflection of resilience amid systemic adversity. Despite decades of occupation, institutional neglect, and political instability, local professionals and civil society organizations have sustained and expanded services through culturally grounded, community-based interventions. The historical trajectory underscores the need for an integrated, rights-based, and context-sensitive approach to mental health in Palestine. The burden of mental illness in Palestine is significant and multifaceted, driven by political conflict, economic hardship, and cultural stigma. Despite the high prevalence of disorders such as depression, anxiety, and PTSD—as well as the emerging concerns of substance abuse and suicide—services remain limited and underutilized. A robust, evidence-informed public mental health strategy is urgently needed, incorporating early screening, stigma reduction, and targeted services for high-risk groups. Epidemiological surveillance and research must also be strengthened to provide an accurate picture of mental health needs across the population. Mental health service delivery in Palestine reflects a system under strain but not without resilience. Despite political fragmentation, resource limitations, and pervasive stigma, service providers have made notable strides in expanding access to care. However, significant gaps remain in workforce capacity, geographic equity, and service integration. Advancing mental health care in Palestine requires a holistic, rights-based strategy rooted in sustainability, community engagement, and cultural responsiveness.

9 Conclusion

The destructions of mental health services, such as hospitals and community mental health centers entail the need to offer short-term and long-term interventions. This includes the continuous supply of psychiatric medications to ensure consistent access for patients and the training of mental health professionals to handle mental health issues. Working with the community to reduce stigma, offering psychoeducation, and focusing on the establishment of networking with patients and their families are additional measures that should be implemented. There is a need to research and gather data on the mental health impact of the war to inform targeted, evidence-based interventions. Any emergency plan should consider the use of mobile units to deal with urgent psychiatric care, such as psychological first aid and counselling for those unable to access other health centers.

References

Abed Alah, M. (2024). Echoes of conflict: The enduring mental health struggle of Gaza's healthcare workers. *Conflict and Health, 18*(1), 21. https://doi.org/10.1186/s13031-024-00577-6

Abo-Ras, F., & Abu-Kaf, S. (2023). Mental health literacy among the Palestinian-Arab minority in Israel and its correlates with mental health service use. *Perspectives in Psychiatric Care*, 3001191. https://doi.org/10.1155/2023/3001191

Abo-Rass F, Khatib A, Abu-Kaf S, & Nakash, O. (2024). Association between mental health literacy and formal help-seeking behaviors among students from the Palestinian-Arab minority in Israel. Archives of Psychiatric Nursing 53: 158–164. https://doi.org/10.1016/j.apnu.2024.10.018

ACAPS. (2024). Thematic report – Palestine: Impact of the conflict on mental health and psychosocial support needs in Gaza. Available at: https://www.acaps.org. Accessed (2024, September 3).

Albelbeisi, A. H., Hajizadeh, A., Al-Zeer, A. M., Saeidpour, J., & Kakemam, E. (2025). Prevalence and associated factors of mental health disorders among internally displaced persons in Gaza. *East Mediterr Health Journal, 31*(2), 81–88. https://doi.org/10.26719/2025.31.2.81

Aldabbour, B., Abuabada, A., Lahlouh, A., Halimy, M., Elamassie, S., Sammour, A. A. K., Skaik, A., & Nadarajah, S. (2024a). Psychological impacts of the Gaza war on Palestinian young adults: A cross-sectional study of depression, anxiety, stress, and PTSD symptoms. *BMC Psychology, 12*(1), 696. https://doi.org/10.1186/s40359-024-02188-5

Aldabbour, B., Abuabada, A., Lahlouh, A., et al. (2024b). Psychological impacts of the Gaza war on Palestinian young adults: A cross-sectional study of depression, anxiety, stress, and PTSD symptoms. *BMC Psychology, 12*, 696. https://doi.org/10.1186/s40359-024-02188-5

Altawil, M. A. S., El-Asam, A., & Khadaroo, A. (2023). Impact of chronic war trauma exposure on PTSD diagnosis from 2006–2021: A longitudinal study in Palestine. *Middle East Current Psychiatry*, 30(14). https://doi.org/10.1186/s43045-023-00286-5

Aqtam, I. (2025) A narrative review of mental health and psychosocial impact of the war in Gaza. *Eastern Mediterranean Health Journal, 31*(2), 89–96. https://doi.org/10.26719/2025.31.2.89.

Arslan, B. (2024). Mental health services in Gaza. *Anatolian Clinic the Journal of Medical Sciences, 29*(Special Issue on Gaza), 105–111. https://doi.org/10.21673/anadoluklin.1568415

Bhowmick, R., & Khan, H. (2024). Impact of Israel–Palestine conflict on the economy and businesses of the region. SSRN: https://ssrn.com/abstract=4759320 or https://doi.org/10.2139/ssrn.4759320

Bromley, R. (2021). Fragmented spaces/broken time: Restoring the absence of story in the West Bank of Palestine. In *Narratives of forced mobility and displacement in contemporary literature and culture*(pp. 181–231). Springer Nature Switzerland. https://doi.org/10.1007/978-3-030-73596-8_6

Charlson, F. J., Baxter, A. J., Cheng, H. G., Shidhaye, R., & Whiteford, H. A. (2016). The burden of mental, neurological, and substance use disorders in China and India: A systematic analysis of community representative epidemiological studies. *Lancet, 388*(10042), 376–389. https://doi.org/10.1016/S0140-6736(16)30590-6.

Diab, M., Veronese, G., Jamei, Y. A., et al. (2021). Risk and protective factors of tramadol abuse in the Gaza Strip: The perspective of tramadol abusers and psychiatrists. *International Journal of Mental Health and Addiction, 19*, 2074–2090. https://doi.org/10.1007/s11469-020-00301-4

El-Khodary, B., & Samara, M. (2020). The relationship between multiple exposures to violence and mental health symptoms among Palestinian adolescents. *European Child & Adolescent Psychiatry, 29*, 719–731. https://doi.org/10.1007/s00787-019-01376-8

Elshamy, F., Hamadeh, A., Billings, J., & Alyafei, A. (2023). Mental illness and help-seeking behaviours among Middle Eastern cultures: A systematic review and meta-synthesis of qualitative data. *PLoS ONE, 18*(10), Article e0293525. https://doi.org/10.1371/journal.pone.0293525

ESCWA & UNDP. (2023). Gaza war: Expected socioeconomic impacts on the State of Palestine: Preliminary estimations until 5 November 2023. United Nations. Available at: https://www.unescwa.org/sites/default/files/pubs/pdf/war-gaza-expected-socioeconomic-impact-palestine-english_4.pdf

Gaza Community Mental Health Programme. (2025). Available at: https://www.gcmhp.org/

Giacaman, R., Rabaia, Y., Nguyen-Gillham, V., Batniji, R., Punamäki, R. L., & Summerfield, D. (2011). Mental health, social distress and political oppression: The case of the occupied Palestinian territory. *Glob Public Health, 6*(5), 547–559. https://doi.org/10.1080/17441692.2010.528443.

Giacaman, R., Khatib, R., Shabaneh, L., Ramlawi, A., Sabri, B., Sabatinelli, G., Khawaja, M., Laurance, T., & Nguyen-Gillham, V. (2009). Health status and health services in the occupied Palestinian territory. *The Lancet, 373*(9666), 837–849. https://doi.org/10.1016/S0140-6736(09)60107-0

Hattab, S., Kittana, N., Qasarweh, L., & Tayem, Y. (2023). Prevalence and factors associated with polypharmacy among patients treated for psychiatric disorders in Palestine. *Palestinian Medical and Pharmaceutical Journal, 8*(1), Article 1. https://doi.org/10.59049/2790-0231.1137

Helbich, M. & Jabr, S. (2022). A call for social justice and for a human rights approach with regard to mental health in the occupied Palestinian Territories.

Hillel, R. S. (2023). Decolonising mental health and psychosocial support (MHPSS) interventions in the humanitarian system. *Intervention Journal of Mental Health and Psychosocial Support in Conflict Affected Areas, 21*(1), 20–29. https://doi.org/10.4103/intv.intv_20_22

International Bank for Reconstruction and Development/The World Bank. (2022). Mental health in West Bank and Gaza. Available at: https://documents1.worldbank.org/curated/en/099153502102330181/pdf/P17925303fca130e30936d016a378b6a1e9.pdf

Jabir, S. (2023). Pathogenic poverty and impoverished disease. Jerusalem newspaper. Available at: https://www.alquds.com/en/posts/66807

Keelan, E. (2016). Medical care in Palestine: Working in a conflict zone. *Ulster Med Journal, 85*(1), 3–7.

Marie, M., Hannigan, B., & Jones, A. (2016). Mental health needs and services in the West Bank, Palestine. *International Journal of Mental Health Systems, 10*(1), 23. https://doi.org/10.1186/s13033-016-0056-8

Marie, M., Shaabna, Z., & Saleh, M. (2020). Schizophrenia in the context of mental health services in Palestine: A literature review. *International Journal of Mental Health Systems*, 14, Article 44. https://doi.org/10.1186/s13033-020-00375-6

Médecins Sans Frontières. (2024). Gaza's healthcare workers grapple with the mental health impact of unyielding war. Available at: https://www.msf.org/gazas-healthcare-workers-grapple-mental-health-impact-unyielding-war

Mercy Crop. (2022). The first startup in Palestine devoted to mental health and wellbeing. Available at: https://www.mercycorps.org/blog/startup-palestine-mental-health-wellbeing

Ministry of Health. (2023). Child and Adolescent mental health national strategy 2023–2028: 'Every child deserves a childhood, every child deserves a future'. Available at: https://site.moh.ps/Content/Books/7nV6BevAx3csVSIXvu8A4NaEzUDUxmGIPsowVjwZNidXaUJyomJe7c_7dHoHom7Mc8LrmKz6RGy9R6yCRNpfdWQFtygtYZk5oVdTEiO1xo1L6.pdf

Palestinian Ministry of Health. (2022). Health annual Report Palestine 2021. Accessed June 2022. Available at: https://site.moh.ps/Content/Books/Hqgu4D5vfT6bDhDUtl36GHhx9oYlCS9JplXYDfOMKrnDt6YoDPkPdl_I6mhnD3xb5MaPpX1mx6k6J4WowTnGUc1135KRHMmuMwEi1Zh1QUmFY.pdf

Palestinian Centre for Human Right. (2022). Poverty in Palestine: "Nonstop Upward Indicator" a report on repercussions of non-payment of social affairs dues on humanitarian conditions of the poor in Palestine. Available at: https://pchrgaza.org/poverty-in-palestine-nonstop-upward-indicator-a-report-on-repercussions-of-non-payment-of-social-affairs-dues-on-humanitarian-conditions-of-the-poor-in-palestine/

Palestine Red Crescent Society. (2025). Palestine red crescent society emergency master plan 2025–2027 [EN/AR]. Available at: https://www.palestinercs.org/public/files/image/2025/news/PRCS%20Emergency%20Master%20Plan%202025-2027.pdf

Patel, V., Garrison, P., Mari, J. D. J., Minas, H., Prince, M., & Saxena, Sh. (2008). The Lancet's series on global mental health: 1 year on. *The Lancet, 372*(9646), 1354–1357. https://doi.org/10.1016/S0140-6736(08)61556-1

Qutishat, M. (2025). Mental health in Gaza: Addressing sustainability challenges of ongoing war conflict. *Middle East Current Psychiatry, 32*(1), 27. https://doi.org/10.1186/s43045-025-00520-2

Rabaia, Y., Saleh, M. F., & Giacaman, R. (2014). Sick or sad? Supporting Palestinian children living in conditions of chronic political violence. *Children & Society,* 28, 172–181. https://doi.org/10.1111/chso.12061

Sarhan, M. B. A., Fujii, Y., Kiriya, J., Fujiya, R., Giacaman, R., Kitamura, A., & Jimba, M. (2020). Exploring health literacy and its associated factors among Palestinian university students: A cross-sectional study. *Health Promotion International, 2020,* 1–12. https://doi.org/10.1093/heapro/daaa089

Save the Children. (2024). Trapped and scarred: The compounding mental harm inflicted on Palestinian children in Gaza. Available at: https://resourcecentre.savethechildren.net/document/trapped-and-scarred-the-compounding-mental-harm-inflicted-on-palestinian-children-in-gaza/

Shalhoub-Kevorkian, N. (2005). Voice therapy for women aligned with political prisoners: A case study of trauma among Palestinian women in the second Intifada. *Social Service Review, 79*(2), 322–343. https://doi.org/10.1086/429141

Swan, E. (2018). Study on masculine identities and men's role in the Gaza strip, Palestine. Action Against Hunger. Available at: https://accioncontraelhambre.org/sites/default/files/documents/aah_gaza_masculinities_study.pdf

Thabet, A., & Vostanis, P. (2017). Effect of trauma on mental health of parents and children in the middle area of the Gaza strip. *JOJ Nursing & Health Care, 3*(4), 269–278. https://doi.org/10.19080/JOJNHC.2017.03.555621.

Thabet, A. M., & Thabet, S. S. (2017). Stress, trauma and post-traumatic stress disorder among adolescents in the Gaza strip. *Journal of Trauma and Critical Care, 1*(2), 25–33. https://doi.org/10.4236/oalib.1104929

Ugarte, A. C. G., Acosta, E., Basellini, U., & Alburez-Gutierrez, D. (2024). The effect of war on Palestinian life expectancy in 2023. SocArXiv 8smy2, center for open science. https://doi.org/10.31219/osf.io/8smy2

UNICEF. (2019). A review of the humanitarian mental health and psychosocial needs and gaps in West Bank and Gaza. Available at: https://www.unicef.org/sop/media/1031/file/MHPSS%20Rapid%20Review%20Palestine%202019.pdf

UNICEF. (2024). Humanitarian action for children - State of Palestine. Available at: https://reliefweb.int/report/occupied-palestinian-territory/humanitarian-action-children-2024-state-palestine-revision-3-june-2024

UNICEF. (2025). Children in Gaza need life-saving support. Available at: https://www.unicef.org/emergencies/children-gaza-need-lifesaving-support

United Nations Relief and Works Agency for Palestine Refugees. (2024). Mental health and psychosocial support (MHPSS) in Gaza: Analysis after 300 days of war. Available at: https://www.unrwa.org/sites/default/files/content/resources/22.8.24__mhpss_300_day_report_final.pdf

World Bank. (2023). Mental health in the West Bank and Gaza (English). World Bank Group. Available at: http://documents.worldbank.org/curated/en/099153502102330181

World Health Organization. (2001). The World Health Organizations involvement in Community Mental Health Development in the occupied Palestinian territory a work in progress with WHO. Available at: https://www.mhinnovation.net/sites/default/files/content/document/Report-Community-Mental-Health-Development-in-Palestine.pdf

World Health Organization. (2020). Mental health and psychosocial well-being among Palestinians in the West Bank and Gaza. Regional office for the Eastern Mediterranean. https://www.emro.who.int/images/stories/palestine/documents/Mental_health_report_Palestine.pdf

World Health Organization Regional Office for the Eastern Mediterranean. (2022). Scaling up mental health services in Palestine. https://www.emro.who.int/opt/news/scaling-up-mental-health-services-in-palestine.html

World Health Organization. (2024). WHO's response in the occupied Palestinian territory: Annual report 2024. https://www.emro.who.int/images/stories/palestine/WHO_oPT_Response_Report_March_2024.pdf

World Health Organization. (2025a). oPt emergency situation update (Issue 57): 7 October 2023–14 March 2025. https://www.emro.who.int/images/stories/Sitrep_57.pdf

World Health Organization. (2025b). Scaling-up mental health services in Palestine. https://www.emro.who.int/opt/news/scaling-up-mental-health-services-in-palestine.html

Zatari, D., & Tahboub, R. (2000). Realtime implementation of a simple telemedicine model in Palestine. *Journal of Telemedicine and Telecare, 6*(1), 202–202. https://doi.org/10.1258/1357633001934771

Zatari, D. I., Tahboub, R., Nawahda, M., & Aljabari, T. (1999). Design and implementation of a telemedicine system in Palestine. *Journal of Telemedicine and Telecare, 5*(1), S39–S41. https://doi.org/10.1258/1357633991932487

Ziadni, M., Hammoudeh, W., Abu Rmeileh, N. M., Hogan, D., Shannon, H., & Giacaman, R. (2011). Sources of human insecurity in post-war situations: The case of Gaza. *Journal of Human Security, 7*(3), 23–36. https://doi.org/10.3316/JHS0703023

Chapter 11
Mental Healthcare in Qatar: Services, Developments, and Challenges

Mohammed Mohammed, Samreen Mohammed, and Suhaila Ghuloum

Abstract The health sector in the State of Qatar witnessed progressive development over the years, with a focus on health, education, and research. It secured international accreditations for its services and training programs, such as the Joint Commission International and the Accreditation Council of Graduate Medical Education. Mental health services were pivotal in these initiatives. In a country where the majority of the population is formed of expatriates, with different languages, cultural backgrounds, and mental health needs, this can be very challenging. Local resources are never sufficient to meet the manpower demands in health; the gap is very evident in mental health services. In this chapter, we will describe the evolution of mental health in Qatar and its progress to the current provisions. We will allude to the influence of culture and religion throughout, from stigma to treatment-seeking. The multiple achievements will be discussed while also addressing the many challenges. We followed with a discussion of suggested opportunities for improvement.

Keywords Mental health · Qatar · Psychiatry · Services · Developments · Challenges

1 Introduction

1.1 Country Profile

The State of Qatar is a country in West Asia, at the north eastern coast of the Arabian Peninsula, projecting into the Arabian Gulf, and shares a land border only to the south with Saudi Arabia.

M. Mohammed · S. Mohammed · S. Ghuloum (✉)
Mental Health Services, Hamad Medical Corporation, Doha, Qatar
e-mail: sghuloum@hamad.qa

S. Ghuloum
College of Medicine, QU Health, Qatar University, Doha, Qatar

S. Al-Huseini and S. M. Y. Arafat (eds.), *Mental Health Care in the Middle East*, South Asian Perspectives in Mental Health and Psychology ,
https://doi.org/10.1007/978-981-95-0461-9_11

The land covers an area of approximately 11,571 square kilometers, with a population of around 3 million, mostly living in the capital, Doha. The majority of the population is formed by expatriates. The population is considered "young," where 84.61% are 15–64 years of age. Arabic is the official language of Qatar, but English is widely spoken as a second language. The country gained its independence from the United Kingdom in 1971 and has been ruled by the Al-Thani family since the 1800s as a constitutional monarchy. Islam is the official religion and plays a major role in daily life and culture.

Qatar is one of the largest natural gas and oil reserves in the world, and has one of the highest incomes per capita, with a diversified economy and worldwide investments. Over the past couple of decades, the country has seen rapid growth and a high development index driven by large-scale projects, the most notable being hosting the 2022 FIFA World Cup. These initiatives have brought in waves of both highly skilled professionals and lower-skilled workers and laborers as needed. As a result, the population has multiplied to contribute to the expanding infrastructure and fast-paced progress. Furthermore, the country has focused heavily on promoting education, health, culture, and sports, and made significant investments in cultural institutions to promote and preserve its heritage. Politically, the country plays a major role in mediations and conflict resolutions in the region.

1.2 Evolution of Psychiatric Services in Qatar

1.2.1 Asylum Period

The Middle East has a rich history of establishing institutions for mental health care, with great achievements by Islamic scholars such as Al Razi and Ibn Sina. The mental institutions established in the Arab and Middle East region historically were not asylums in the way Western asylums developed in the nineteenth and eighteenth centuries. Care has adopted more integration into medical practices. Mental illness was seen as a medical condition, and treatment focused on interventions with dignity and respect as opposed to isolation.

This "golden age," roughly from the eighth to fourteenth centuries, began to decline gradually due to multiple factors, including invasion by the Mongols, political fragmentation, intellectual suppression, military conflicts, economic decline, and the rise of the European scientific revolution leading to colonialism and external domination. This is thought to contribute to the rise of folk practices, in the absence of structured medical practice (Mitha, 2020; Mohit, 2001).

1.2.2 Evolution from Folk Medicine to Current

Traditional healing and folk medicine practices are part of the cultural fabric of Qatar and the region. Traditional healing remains a choice for many, provided by the healer called "mutawa." The term often refers to religious and cultural practices interchangeably, despite the distinctions.

Religious healing relies on reciting verses from the Holy Quran and reading prayers, and to a lesser extent, cupping. Other cultural approaches that are not religiously driven include tying down or locking the individual at home, depriving them from specific food items, or even beating to get rid of evil spirits "jinn." Historically, these were the primary interventions for treatment, while the more affluent people would opt for treatment abroad.

The post-oil economy of the region introduced a move toward the adoption of modern medicine in health care practices. A new general hospital, Rumailah Hospital, was opened, and a few psychiatrists were recruited. In 1979, Hamad Medical Corporation (HMC) was established as the country's main provider of secondary and tertiary healthcare, governed by the Ministry of Public Health. HMC has grown steadily and currently oversees 15 specialist hospitals, 13 of which hold Academic Medical Center accreditation by the Joint Commission International (JCI), including mental health. Alongside the hospitals, HMC also runs national ambulance services, home care, and residential care. In 2023, HMC had four hospitals ranked among the world's top 250 academic medical centers, with two achieving a top 100 ranking, highlighting the commitment to combine the best patient care with medical research and education to achieve the best outcome (Bolorunduru, 2025). In addition, Primary Health Care Corporation operates 31 health centers geographically distributed across various areas in the country, providing a wide range of healthcare services around 16 in total, including family medicine, mental health, child and adolescent care, oral and dental health, women's wellness, and other specialized services.

Treatment in the public sector is provided free of charge for all citizens and is heavily subsidized for other residents. During the rule of Shaikh Hamad Bin Khalifa Al-Thani and his wife, Shaikha Moza Bint Nasser, billions of dollars were invested in education and health (Goodman, 2015). The first medical school, Weill Cornell Medicine, was opened as part of Qatar Foundation in 2001, followed by another medical college under Qatar University, founded in 2015.

1.2.3 Private Clinics and Psychiatric Services in Qatar

The private sector plays a relatively small part in the provision of mental health care in Qatar. The services are predominantly provided by public institutions, and there are no more than 10 private clinics. These private clinics provide only outpatient clinical care and usually liaise with public hospitals for inpatient admission, community mental health care, or emergency situations. Health Insurance was recently introduced as mandatory, and it remains to be seen what impact it will have on the growth of private psychiatric care.

The first private psychiatric clinic was opened in 2003 by an expatriate psychiatrist. Others followed, though at a slow rate, until the past few years, with more private clinics opening either as standalone facilities or parts of a general hospital.

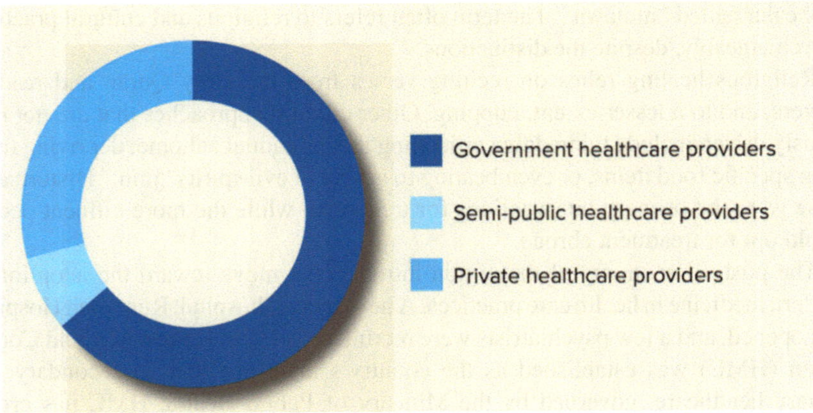

Fig. 1 Health workforce distribution by sector and speciality (World Health Organization & United Nations Development Programme, 2021)

Psychological therapies have also witnessed a major expansion with increased public appreciation of the role of therapy.

Figure 1 shows the availability within the private sector.

1.2.4 Mental Health Act

Mental Health Law was enacted under Law No. 16 in 2016 (Al Meezan, n.d). The legislation was passed by a Royal decree guided by the World Health Organization (WHO) assessment instrument for mental health systems (Sharkey, 2017). The law is influenced by the mental health legislation of the UK and Australia, and the Arab Charter of Human Rights.

The mental health legislation is a relatively short document consisting of seven chapters divided into 35 articles and accompanied by a more comprehensive code of practice. The law has Articles that address aspects of voluntary and involuntary admissions, the appeal process, legal admissions, and penalties. It emphasizes the rights of patients with mental illness, safeguarding their rights, with a view to protecting them and others while providing psychiatrists a legal framework within which they can safely practice. Training of mental health practitioners was conducted, and necessary forms were created (Abou-Saleh & Ibrahim, 2013). However, implementation requires the creation of a supervisory body, referred to as "the competent authority," that oversees the lawful applications of involuntary admissions and ensures codes of practice are upheld. Independent psychiatrists should provide second opinions. These procedural aspects of implementation have faced challenges, resulting in delays in implementing the law (Wadoo et al., 2023).

2 Epidemiology and Burden of Mental Illness in Qatar

Very few studies have explored the prevalence of mental illness, while little is known about its burden. A cross-sectional study conducted in 2010–2011 at the primary healthcare centers among the Qatari population showed that about 1:5 of all Qatari adults who attended PHC had at least one type of mental disorder. Generalized anxiety disorder was the most prevalent at 20.4%, followed closely by depression at 19.1%. Females and those of a younger age had the highest prevalence. The study explored 30-day functioning, which was also worse in women, and 20.6% of the sample had a chronic physical illness (Ghuloum et al., 2014). A more recent study reported lifetime prevalence rates of 13.5% for depression and 10.3% for generalized anxiety disorder among Qatari nationals attending primary healthcare settings (Khaled et al., 2024a, 2024b).

According to the WHO and the United Nations Development Programme 2021, the three leading causes of non-communicable disease burden in Qatar (in Disability Adjusted Life Years-DALYS) are mental health disorders, accounting for 13.7 percent of total DALYS, musculoskeletal disorders, accounting for 11.3 percent, and cardiovascular diseases, at 8.6 percent.

In 2019, the cost of clinical services modeled at the primary healthcare level in Qatar was almost half a billion USD, most aimed toward non-communicable diseases (Table 1). General practice with mental health costs around 450,000 USD, making the total cost of the mental health program around 0.1%. It is estimated that 430,720 people who needed mental health services did not receive them (World Health Organization & United Nations Development Programme, 2021). This figure is considerable if the total population of the country, of less than 3 million, is taken into account. It emphasizes the need to increase funding for mental health at the primary care level and increase coverage. The Qatar National Mental Health Strategy 2013–2018 indicated that 25% of the mental health needs of the Qatari population were met, and only 5% of the needs of the expatriate population.

Table 1 Cost of clinical services at primary care level in Qatar, 2019

Program	Cost (US$)
Immunization	14,852,268
Non-communicable diseases	256,519,723
Child health	51,350,124
Nutrition	2,166,068
Mental health	456,384
Reproductive, maternal, and child health	7,700,850
Oral and dental care	4,966,086
General practice	109,146,069
Cost of clinical services	447,157,572

Source World Health Organization & United Nations Development Programme, 2021

Contrary to established findings of a shorter life expectancy associated with mental illness, the mortality rate among Qatari nationals with mental illness is in fact, lower. Individuals with mental illness had a higher median age at death (76.5 years) compared to those without mental illness (62.7 years). This unexpected result may be attributed to sociocultural factors, accessible healthcare services, and the proactive roles of mental health professionals in managing comorbidities (Ouanes et al., 2024). Generally, WHO figures reflect an improvement in life expectancy at birth in Qatar by 6.33 years from 70.4 [70–71.1] years in 2000 to 76.7 [76.2–77.4] years in 2021. Suicide mortality rate per 100.000 population has also dropped steadily from 13.2 in the year 2000 to 4.7 in 2021 (World Health Organization, 2024).

3 Mental Health Services in Qatar

3.1 *Conventional Services*

Mental healthcare in Qatar is primarily provided by the public health sector through the Mental Health Services of Hamad Medical Corporation. The private sector plays a minor role, limited to outpatient settings. The services witnessed expansion and development as a result of major investment over the past three decades in the healthcare system to align with health indicators in the developed country (World Health Organization, 2018).

The National Mental Health Strategy "changing minds, changing lives" was launched in December 2013, setting out Qatar's vision to provide the best possible mental health service, with primary deliverables of reducing stigma, expanding access to care, developing skilled workforce, work on mental health legislation, improving research capabilities and data collection, and focusing on transforming into a community based service. The strategy aspired to achieve integration between mental and physical health, especially for older adults and child and adolescent cases. It also aimed at establishing primary mental health service provision at primary healthcare facilities. An Independent evaluation in 2015 showed significant progress, especially toward community services. However, it highlighted challenges like workforce shortage and limited mental health budget, which equalled 0.36% of total health spending in 2014 (Sharkey, 2017).

Subsequently, mental health became a core component of the National Health Strategy 2018–2022, with a focus on prevention, early intervention, and integrated mental health within PHCC. Mental health ranked fourth out of the seven priority areas, preceded by healthy children and adolescents, healthy women, and healthy and safe employees. A national target was set to achieve 40% of service delivery at PHCC, in addition to targeting advances in research and data collection, increased awareness, and reducing stigma.

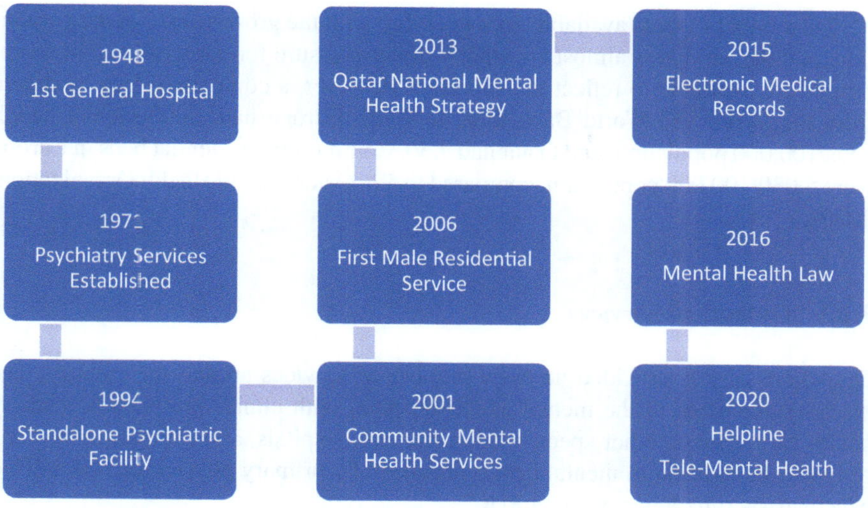

Fig. 2 Milestones of mental health services

3.1.1 Milestone of Mental Health Services

In the early years of service development, mental health was integrated with a general hospital facility. In the early 1990s, it moved to a standalone facility that was originally an obstetrics hospital. At the time, the facility hosted only 15 inpatients, reaching a maximum of 27 beds and 4 outpatient clinics (Fig. 2).

The service had grown steadily, expanding at various levels to meet the increasing demands. The number of mental health workers per 100,000 population increased from 15.00 in 2014 to 25.28 in 2020. The staffing increased to a total number of 63 psychiatrists, 515 mental health nurses, 46 psychologists, 14 social workers, and 78 other specialized mental health workers like occupational therapists, forming a total of 716, in addition to 47 mental health workers in child/adolescent mental health service in 2020 (World Health Organization, 2020).

3.1.2 Inpatient Services

The main psychiatric hospital moved to the south region of the country in 2024. It serves as the main hub for inpatient care and accommodates approximately 80 beds across several acute male and female units, and one long-term unit with a planned step-down unit. The original hospital became the center for forensic psychiatry and psychology clinics. A smaller inpatient unit is integrated with a general medical hospital in the mid-southern region with 15 beds. This unit provides crucial service for complex psychiatric cases with significant medical or surgical comorbidities. A perinatal subacute unit in a medical city accommodates around 15 beds.

The number of beds available does not align with the growing size of the population, and the service is almost constantly under pressure for admissions. No recent figures are available to reflect the shortage. However, a comparison can be drawn from the WHO and World Bank data. In 2020, Europe had 35.00 mental health beds/100,000 population, and Qatar had 2.30. Community residential beds in Europe were 53.30/100,000 population, compared to 5 in Qatar (World Health Organization, 2020).

3.1.3 Outpatient Services

Outpatient care is provided across a number of services around the country. The majority are based at the mental health hospital, with clinics provided at primary health care centers, other specialized or general hospitals, and in different regions of Qatar. In addition to mental health provision by primary physicians, specialized psychiatrists run clinics based at PHC.

The trend of outpatient activity has changed dramatically from 2018 to 2022 as the service expanded. The number of patients seen in clinics increased from 44,784 to 76,594. The number of no-show cases has reduced from 23 to 18%, reflecting better efficiency of the service and more willingness by the patients to be assessed and treated. The number of follow-ups has increased markedly from 39,986 to 66,562 (Khaled et al., 2024a, 2024b).

3.1.4 Community Health Services

Day care services started in 1998. Before that, a single nurse was responsible for conducting home visits and crisis intervention at an informal level. The service became an established entity in 2001, to include daycare, home visits, and crisis intervention (Mohammed et al., 2023). Residential care is provided in two villa compounds, for male and female patients separately. Currently, multidisciplinary care is provided for all. A compound in Doha was transformed into a multifunctional psychiatric facility that is the hub for adult and older adult outpatient services, child and adolescent mental health outpatient services, a home outreach program, and a long-term female residential unit. Another long-term care unit for male patients had to be accommodated within the acute general hospital.

3.1.5 Consultation Liaison Services

HMC provides 24-hour consultation liaison psychiatric services. In emergency situations, access to mental health services is through one of four emergency units integrated within the general hospitals, two in the capital, Doha, one in the north, and one in the south. Psychiatry consultations are also provided 24 hours for cases presenting in other disciplines such as medicine, surgery, the heart hospital, the women's wellness center, and others. Such services are provided through a multidisciplinary consultation liaison team during working hours, followed by an on-call system.

3.1.6 Helpline

Established in April 2020 as part of the country's response to the COVID-19 pandemic, this initiative provided accessible and confidential mental health support to the public during times of increased psychological stress. The helpline continues to provide an easily accessible support line for people in need of professional advice and care, free of charge. Currently, its scope is renewing medications, providing advice, redirecting patients toward consultation liaison services if needed, and scheduling appointments. The hours have expanded, but are not yet available round the clock. It is manned by mental health staff, including doctors, nurses, psychologists, and other allied health professionals who speak a variety of languages.

4 Challenges of Mental Health Care

4.1 Stigma

Stigma regarding mental health disorders has always been a major barrier to seeking help and acceptance of medical treatment in the region. This leads to major delays in presentation and deterioration of illness to the point of needing urgent intervention, mostly in inpatient settings. Discharges against medical advice (DAMA) are often requested by patients and/or their families. Stigma continues to affect the compliance with medications, leading to suboptimal follow-up even in outpatient settings and an increased sense of isolation and shame.

Several studies aimed at evaluating the level of stigma and factors associated with it across different target groups. Among healthcare professionals, stigma was found to be higher in nurses than in doctors and inversely associated with years of experience. Professionals with longer years of practice had lower stigma, as did those working within mental health services and long-term care, as opposed to working in other healthcare facilities. Stigma among families of people with mental illness was not high, reflecting the protective attitude families adopt in this culture. Families of higher education showed lower stigma levels. With regards to people with lived experience, their level of internalized stigma was lower than the international report, and again, inversely proportional to the level of education (Ghuloum et al., 2022; Kehyayan et al., 2021, 2024). Media portrayal of mental illness and misperceptions due to cultural beliefs contribute toward the problem. It is often experienced by proxy, resulting in people not disclosing their mental health challenges for fear of social consequences (Stirling et al., 2019).

Ongoing efforts are in place to reduce stigma by raising public awareness through campaigns. World Mental Health Day is recognized annually on October 10th with events organized by various health and educational institutions, discussing various aspects of mental health. The establishment of mental health clinics at primary healthcare and general hospitals is also a means of facilitating access to mental health care and reducing the associated stigma. However, more efforts are still needed.

4.2 The Impact of Religion on Mental Health Care

While spirituality is a major source of comfort and resilience, it could play a dual role in mental health care, a bidirectional effect. Traditional healing remains a viable option for many and is often the first option before seeking professional help. Misinterpretation of mental illnesses in a religious context could hinder presentation to the service and delay treatment. Illness may be attributed to "failing morality" or possession by a jinn. The belief in evil eye and sorcery or black magic is deeply engrained in the culture even among the higher educated population. The gaps in knowledge, met with misinformation provided by some traditional healers, contribute to delayed help-seeking behavior.

4.3 Demand Outpaces Forces

Despite ongoing efforts to expand the services, manpower remains a struggle due to the rapid expansion of society outpacing the available workforce. Qatar remains one of the leading countries in the region, with a rapid expansion in the infrastructure and numerous developmental projects, which require an influx of professional and skilled workforce, increasing population figures dramatically. Consequently, resources, especially for mental healthcare, remain stretched despite the continuous recruitment locally and internationally.

The strain on the inpatient services has also increased due to the limited beds in the face of growing needs. Hamad Medical Corporation (HMC) is the only provider of acute inpatient care for adults and older adults with mental illness, causing capacity constraints on the service.

Analysis of clinical services provided at the primary care levels in Qatar clearly suggested the need to strengthen and better adjust the services for mental health at the PHC levels. It was noted that it only makes up 0.1 percent of the total costs, and thus estimated that 430,720 people were unable to receive the needed services. In 2020, a comparison between mental health services in Qatar and the global situation was made. It was noted that it's below the average for high-income group countries. Facilities scored 0.04 in comparison to 0.05 globally, beds 2.30–10.80 globally, and number of admissions of 39.37–71.80 (Khaled et al., 2024a, 2024b).

4.4 Cost Pressure and Care Gaps

Qatar provides free healthcare to all citizens and subsidized health for non-national residents of the country. Despite that, due to concerns of stigma and unreasonable fear about confidentiality, private consultations are frequently sought. This is also to avoid delays in the public system. Private clinics, by nature, tend to be more readily accessible with shorter waiting times for appointments.

New changes have been applied to cost coverage, shifting away from a totally free healthcare to an insurance-based one. While expected and widely seen as rational, the shift introduces financial and logistical difficulties. The effect of this is already noted as financial barriers discourage scheduled help-seeking and increase emergency-only presentations. Mental health remains heavily subsidized by the government, and the extent of insurance coverage is yet to be considered.

4.5 Challenge of High Demand and Long Wait Time in Psychological Services

As the primary mental health care provider in the country, the mental health services of HMC face the biggest load. Efforts at minimizing the clinic waiting time are pressured by rising demands. This is more notable in psychology and therapy clinics, which have a long waiting time between appointments, affecting the continuity of therapy sessions and resulting in patients opting out. The quality of the outcome is disrupted. The gap in psychotherapeutic interventions contributes to a larger reliance on biological therapies.

4.6 Complexity of Mental Health Disorders and Co-morbid Physical Ill Health

Several factors explained earlier in this chapter contribute to the underreporting of symptoms and delays in presentation, leading to more complex disorders. Patients present with more acute and severe symptoms, are harder to treat, and at times have a worse prognosis. The interplay with organic etiology or comorbid presentations adds to the management challenge. The high prevalence of obesity, diabetes, and heart disease in the region can complicate or slow down the treatment process. The inequity in physical and mental healthcare is a known phenomenon worldwide. Mental health services in Qatar are therefore pushing for psychiatric emergencies to remain integrated with general hospitals and resist the occasional push for separation. The distance of inpatient units from general hospital services complicates the medical consultations when needed.

From the other perspective, the stigma associated with mental illness affects the diagnosis and treatment of comorbid anxiety or depressive disorders in those with chronic medical conditions.

5 Non-medical Management of Mental Disorders in Qatar

The healing of mental illness in Qatar is not limited to psychiatric interventions. The deep-rooted cultural and religious traditions play a major role in shaping the management. "Ruqya" is considered one of the most common non-medical healing approaches, where verses from the Quran (The holy book) are recited to individuals to provide spiritual relief, protection, and to counteract what many believe could be the effects of the evil eye or spirit possession. The government has taken steps to regulate the practice while recognizing the importance of faith in people's lives. For example, only registered traditional healers can practice the profession within the country. Extra steps were taken by employing healers, "Motawa," in hospital settings, with their role limited to Quranic Recitation and avoidance of any other traditional or spiritual rituals. The Ministry of Islamic Affairs provides recognized religious healers to safeguard those in need from exploitation.

This careful balance between faith and medicine has its advantages. For many patients, spiritual support can bring genuine comfort, offer hope, and help them feel more connected and understood within the healthcare system. It can also bridge the gap between patients and medical teams, especially when there's hesitation or fear around psychiatric care, in addition to the supervised efforts of Islamic centers to teach and guide the healers.

Challenges remain present, as if spiritual healing is seen as a replacement for medical treatment rather than complementing it, it can delay necessary care. There's also a risk that it reinforces the idea that mental illness is purely spiritual, which can increase stigma and lead families to overlook serious symptoms. Even with regulations, boundaries can be tested, especially if unregistered individuals try to get involved or if the healer's role expands beyond what's allowed. And when different belief systems are at play, it can sometimes create tension or confusion between families and medical staff. It is important for the practice to be grounded in clear rules and open communication to respect beliefs while making sure patients still receive the medical care they need.

6 Potential Ways Out

6.1 Augmented Research

Qatar is expanding in medical research in the region with the support of an increasing number of funding organizations offering a variety of funding programs that promote research collaborations and local capacity building. Mental health research output has steadily increased, though the majority is epidemiological in nature, with a rising interest in psychogenetic studies. Interventional and translation research is limited. The current resources support the progress of more integrated research, and opportunities are available for research training, especially targeting junior trainees.

6.2 Country-Wide Distribution of Mental Health Services

Involvement of the community mental health team has been a major contributor in facilitating earlier discharge from the acute inpatient settings and reduction of relapses. Moving toward catchment-area-based CMH services and subspecialized teams has provided further streamlining of the service and more focused care (Ahmed & Ghuloum, 2021). Despite the relatively small size of the country, resources are focused in the central capital, Doha, with difficulty in reaching the semi-rural areas. Allocating specialized clinics in primary health centers is of help. Private sector expansion to such areas would also be beneficial.

6.3 Health Insurance and Private Sector Involvement

Health coverage in Qatar was heavily subsidized by the government. An effort to introduce the insurance system was faced with challenges and subsequently put on hold. More recently, health insurance was reintroduced with a gradual build-up of its scope. Mental health coverage needs to be revisited and expanded, broadening mental health care to the private sector. This will encourage early help-seeking, support vulnerable populations, and improve public health impact. It's also important to note that the inclusion of mental health insurance validates mental illness and can contribute to reducing stigma. The overall costs will also reduce as early intervention is more cost-effective than crisis intervention.

6.4 Awareness Creation

Mental health awareness needs ongoing efforts with more persistent and collaborative, inter-agency activities. It needs to target different sectors of the population and different age groups, starting with prevention, through treatment, to rehabilitation and recovery. Mental health education in schools, workplace health programs, and community-based initiatives have all proven their benefits. Mental health First aid training and extensive allied health training are important to recognize and ensure holistic approaches in mental health care.

Narrower scale initiatives would include the provision of easy accessibility to mental health resources like brochures, websites, applications, and even a helpline. The use of different social media platforms to spread awareness is also an important step, as it provides a wide and instant reach. Engagement of influencers and celebrities can normalize mental health experiences, especially to the young. With the current level of stigma, engaging influencers in an open dialogue is quite a challenge.

6.5 Good Governance and Inter-Sectoral Collaboration

Leading progress and guiding innovation while managing an existing and expanding service is quite a challenge. A good governance structure is vital in the provision of good mental health services, recruiting the right expertise, enhancing the built environment, promoting staff wellbeing, training opportunities, and teamwork. This was recognized in the first Qatar Mental Health Strategy that invested in building the capacity of clinical and administrative leadership. A complete governance structure was created, moving mental health from a Psychiatry Department under a general hospital to an independent Mental Health Service with its own budget, resources, and staff allocation. Efficient resource allocation prevents gaps and ensures sustainability. Further efforts to support workforce development will help increase the efficiency of services provided. In the presence of good governance, equity and inclusion can be achieved. This will reduce disparities, enhance staff satisfaction and workforce retention, and reflect on the standard of patient care provided. Collaboration with the private sector, academic, and health institutes contributes to better mental health delivery.

6.6 Involvement of the Clients and Their Families in the Service Delivery Process

Promoting non-governmental organizations and patient advocacy groups and engaging service users in decision-making are all factors contributing to better, more equitable, and more accessible services. Clear communication with patients and their families will have positive outcomes on treatments, enhance adherence to treatment plans, and promote recovery, supporting continuity of care and empowering clients. Further involvement of the families and clients is needed in Qatar, by promoting more networks and establishing policy frameworks. Currently, only one NGO is available, and it has faced challenges threatening its functionality and existence. Efforts need to be in place to create education and support programs, use shared decision-making models, and tailor involvement according to client needs, providing truly individualized treatment plans. Continuous monitoring and evaluation of such services provides further data that can be used in establishing solid grounds for such associations.

6.7 Protection of Human Rights and Mental Health Law

Protecting the patients' rights, dignity, and autonomy is a priority that should be implemented with clear guidelines and policies. The human rights commission has played an important role in protecting patients' rights in the country. However, the Mental Health Act, which has been long on hold, needs to be implemented. This will ensure legal safeguards for hospitalization, including involuntary admissions, and protect patients and the healthcare providers. It requires renewed, extensive training of healthcare providers and other entities involved in the implementation of the law, e.g., the police force. Establishing the competent authority which provides oversight and monitoring is needed.

6.8 Human Resources Development

Training and continuous education ensure that professionals provide high-quality, evidence-based care. Qatar introduced the Psychiatry Residency Training Program in 1994. The program was under the Arab Board Medical Specialization Examinations, while more recently, the local Qatar Board Examination was introduced. The residency training is a 4-year program followed by 3 years of further training as a fellowship in subspecialties, including Addiction, neuromodulation, and advanced general adult, Geriatrics psychiatry, Child and adolescent, Perinatal mental health, Consultation liaison, and Learning disability training. This led to improved access to the right care and better coverage of the needed services. The program was among the first training programs in HMC to secure accreditation by the Accreditation Council of Graduate Medical Education, International (ACGMEI).

Further training of allied health care providers can enhance multidisciplinary collaboration. A clinical psychology training program was started recently. As nurses are recruited from across the globe with varying degrees of training and background in mental health nursing, an in-house training program is provided to standardize the care. Further training targeting allied health professionals with a focus on interdisciplinary care is needed.

Many Primary healthcare practitioners received training in recognizing mental illness, with a focus on screening for anxiety and depression, initiating treatment, and referring to tertiary services when needed. Such a program proved effective in introducing mental health delivery into primary care, and having periodic courses will strengthen the initiative.

7 Conclusion

Mental Health Services in Qatar witnessed steady and consistent progress in clinical services, education, training, and, to some extent, research. The sociodemographic structure of the population poses a challenge in providing the optimal care to the right person at the right time. Multifactorial stigma delays help-seeking and presents an obstacle to adhering to medication. Little data is available to understand the burden of mental illness on the health system and the individual. Writing this chapter provided an opportunity to reflect on all the achievements and progress made. However, we can not disregard the many challenges present. Recognizing these challenges, exploring them, and strengthening the arguments for improvement with research data will elevate the standard of care and improve the population's mental health.

References

Abou-Saleh, M. T., & Ibrahim, M. A. (2013). Mental health law in Qatar. *International Psychiatry, 10*(4), 88–90.

Ahmed, M. A. S., & Ghuloum, S. A. (2021). Qatar community mental health care: Achievements and challenges. *Consortium Psychiatricum, 2*(2), 76–80. https://doi.org/10.17816/CP78

Al Meezan. (n.d.). Qatar legal portal. https://www.almeezan.qa/

Bolorunduru, V. (2025). Four Qatari hospitals ranked among top-100 leading global hospitals. The Peninsula. Qatar/Health. https://thepeninsulaqatar.com/article/06/02/2025/four-qatari-hospitals-ranked-among-top-100-leading-global-hospitals

Ghuloum, S., Bener, A., Dafeeah, E., Al-Yazidi, T., Mustapha, A., & Zakareia, A. (2014). Lifetime prevalence of common mental disorders in Qatar using WHO Composite International Diagnostic Interview (WHO-CIDI). *International Journal of Clinical Psychiatry and Mental Health, 2*(1), 38–46. https://doi.org/10.12970/2310-8231.2014.02.01.4

Ghuloum, S., Mahfoud, Z. R., Al-Amin, H., Marji, T., & Kehyayan, V. (2022). Healthcare Professionals' attitudes toward patients with mental illness: A cross-sectional study in Qatar. *Frontiers in Psychiatry, 13*, Article 884947. https://doi.org/10.3389/fpsyt.2022.884947

Goodman, A. (2015). The development of the Qatar Healthcare System: A review of the literature. *International Journal of Clinical Medicine, 6*(3), 177–185. https://doi.org/10.4236/ijcm.2015.63023

Health and Medical Qatar. (n.d.). Hamad Hospital. https://www.healthandmedical.qa/clinic-single/hamad-hospital

IMO Qatar. (n.d.). *Qatar at a glance.* https://imo.gov.qa/state-of-qatar/qatar-at-a-glance

Kehyayan, V., Mahfoud, Z., Ghuloum, S., Marji, T., & Al-Amin, H. (2021). Internalized stigma in persons with mental illness in Qatar: A cross-sectional study. *Frontiers in Public Health, 9*, Article 685003. https://doi.org/10.3389/fpubh.2021.685003

Kehyayan, V., Omar, H., Ghuloum, S., Marji, T., Al-Amin, H., Abed Alah, M., & Mahfoud, Z. (2024). Internalized stigma and its correlates in families of persons with mental illness in Qatar: A cross-sectional study. *Current Psychology, 43*(39), 30937–30948. https://doi.org/10.1007/s12144-024-06686-y

Khaled, S. M., Al-Abdulla, M., Tulley, I., Al-Thani, S. M., & Woodruff, P. W. (2024a). Qatar's national mental health study—The World Mental Health Qatar (WMHQ). *International Journal of Methods in Psychiatric Research, 33*(S1), Article e2008. https://doi.org/10.1002/mpr.2008

Khaled, S. M., Alhussaini, N. W. Z., Alabdulla, M., Sampson, N. A., Kessler, R. C., Woodruff, P. W., & Al-Thani, S. M. (2024b). Lifetime prevalence, risk, and treatment of mood and anxiety disorders in Qatar's national mental health study. *International Journal of Methods in Psychiatric Research, 33*(S1), Article e2011. https://doi.org/10.1002/mpr.2011

Mitha, K. (2020). Approaches from the Islamic Golden Age. *Transcultural Psychiatry, 57*(5), 693–705. https://doi.org/10.1177/1363461520962603

Mohammed, M., Makki, I., & Ghuloum, S. (2023). Psychiatry in Qatar. *Bjpsych International.* https://doi.org/10.1192/bji.2023.23

Mohit, A. (2001). Mental health and psychiatry in the Middle East: Historical development. *Eastern Mediterranean Health Journal, 7*(3), 336–347. https://doi.org/10.26719/2001.7.3.336

Ouanes, S., Abou Hashem, L., Makki, I., Khan, F., Mahgoub, O., Wafer, A., Dulaimy, O., Amro, R., & Ghuloum, S. (2024). Mortality in Qatari individuals with mental illness: A retrospective cohort study. *Annals of General Psychiatry, 23*(1), 14. https://doi.org/10.1186/s12991-024-00499-w

Sharkey, T. (2017). Mental health strategy and impact evaluation in Qatar. *Bjpsych International, 14*(1), 18–21. https://doi.org/10.1192/S2056474000001628

Stirling, B., Hickey, J., Omar, H., & Kehyayan, V. (2019). Stigma towards mental disorders in Qatar: A qualitative study. *Qscience Connect, 2019*, 1–9. https://doi.org/10.5339/connect.2019.2

United Nations Statistics Division. (n.d.). *Demographic Yearbook*. https://unstats.un.org/unsd/demographic-social/products/dyb/

Wadoo, O., Al-Thani, S. H. A. Q. F., Latoo, J., & Alabdulla, M. (2023). Policy and legislation for the treatment of mental health and substance use disorders in Qatar. *Asian Journal of Psychiatry, 79*, Article 103368. https://doi.org/10.1016/j.ajp.2022.103368

World Health Organization. (2018). *Global Health Observatory data repository*. https://data.who.int/countries/634

World Health Organization. (2020). *Mental health atlas: Qatar country profile*. https://www.who.int/publications/m/item/mental-health-atlas-qat-2020-country-profile

World Health Organization. (2024). *Qatar: WHO statistical profile*. World Health Organization. https://www.who.int/data/gho/data/countries/country-details/GHO/qatar

World Health Organization, & United Nations Development Programme. (2021). *The cost of health services delivered at primary care facilities in Qatar. Doha, Qatar: WHO & UNDP*. https://uniatf.who.int/docs/librariesprovider22/default-document-library/qatar-phc-costing-report.pdf

Chapter 12
Mental Healthcare in Saudi Arabia

Mohammed A. Alarabi and Fahad D. Alosaimi

Abstract Mental healthcare is receiving growing attention in Saudi Arabia. Recent evidence points to a rising prevalence of mental disorders, particularly among younger Saudis. The majority of Saudis do not seek treatment for their mental health conditions, and when they do, many opt for non-medical traditional and faith healing. Existing mental health services are provided at primary care and specialized levels, and their delivery has been enhanced by advances in digital health. However, specialized mental healthcare services remain concentrated in urban areas, which are, in turn, underserved by primary care centers. This situation is complicated by a substantial shortage of healthcare providers required to deliver adequate mental healthcare. Although public opinion on mental illness and its treatment has improved in recent decades, many Saudis continue to face barriers to accessing care due to limited service availability. These challenges can be addressed by national efforts to enhance mental health literacy, strengthen inpatient, community, and primary care services, expand the implementation of the Mental Health Care Law, create more training opportunities for mental healthcare providers and improve their quality, and support culturally adapted interventions tailored to patients in Saudi Arabia.

Keywords Mental health · Saudi Arabia · History · Services · Psychiatry

---

The original version of this chapter was previously published without open access. A correction to this chapter is available at
https://doi.org/10.1007/978-981-95-0461-9_17

M. A. Alarabi (✉) · F. D. Alosaimi
Department of Psychiatry, College of Medicine, King Saud University, Riyadh, Saudi Arabia
e-mail: malarabi@ksu.edu.sa

F. D. Alosaimi
e-mail: falosaimi@ksu.edu.sa

S. Al-Huseini and S. M. Y. Arafat (eds.), *Mental Health Care in the Middle East*, South Asian Perspectives in Mental Health and Psychology ,
https://doi.org/10.1007/978-981-95-0461-9_12

1 Introduction

Mental healthcare in the Kingdom of Saudi Arabia is a rapidly developing area with expanding resources and unmet needs. The Kingdom has a population of over 32 million, with 38.8% of them being female. A large proportion of the Kingdom's inhabitants are non-Saudi expatriates, who constitute 13.4 million and are predominantly (76.5%) male (General Authority for Statistics, 2022). Saudi Arabia is home to the two holiest cities in Islam, Mecca and Medina, and is a Muslim-majority country. The Kingdom has a growing economy, with a GDP growth rate of 2.8% in the third quarter of 2024 compared to the same period of the previous year (General Authority for Statistics, 2024). It is categorized as a high-income country according to the World Bank and is one of the G20 forum countries, the leading venue for international economic and financial cooperation. National efforts to advance Saudi Arabia's economy and services have included healthcare as a primary focus. The Healthcare Transformation Plan is one of the eight themes of the National Transformation Program (NTP). It has been an integral part of the Kingdom of Saudi Arabia's broader "Vision 2030" strategy for economic development and national growth (Chowdhury et al., 2021). The NTP aims to transform the healthcare system in the Kingdom through technology and innovation to address challenges in healthcare delivery, including mental healthcare.

In this chapter, we first review the history of modern Saudi Arabia, then contextualize how mental healthcare services evolved within a country marked by rapid social and structural transformation. We then examine the epidemiology of mental disorders in the Kingdom, followed by a focused look at the current state of mental health services. This is followed by a review of the major challenges facing mental healthcare in Saudi Arabia today and a discussion of potential solutions to these challenges.

2 Historical Overview

Saudi Arabia comprises five historical regions of Arabia: Nejd, Eastern Arabia, Hejaz (including Mecca and Medina), Southern Arabia (including Asir), and Northern Arabia. These regions were unified during the reign of the first king of Saudi Arabia, King Abdulaziz (1875–1953). The current Kingdom marks the third establishment of the Saudi dynasty in Arabia, following the First Saudi State (1727–1818) and the Second Saudi State (1824–1891). The Saudi states emerged from Nejd in central Arabia and took Diriyah as the capital for the first state, and the adjacent city of Riyadh (which is Arabic for "meadows") for the second state and third, current state. The current Kingdom of Saudi Arabia was established in 1932 and consists of 13 administrative regions. The regions and the location of each administrative emirate, or *imarah*, are displayed in Fig. 1.

Note: All 13 administrative regions are labelled, and the location of each *Imarah* is marked (map is modified and used with permission from simplemaps.com).

Fig. 1 Regions of Saudi Arabia. *Note* All 13 administrative regions are labeled, and the location of each *Imarah* is marked (map is modified and used with permission from simplemaps.com)

Since the unification in 1932, these geographically dispersed regions of Arabia have been unified by a single identity despite the rich diversity in culture, tradition, and even language, as people from each region speak different dialects of Arabic. This unity is also reflected in the way Saudi Arabian society has experienced accelerated development and progress over the past century. As a country composed largely of arid deserts, the early economy was dependent on limited agricultural output and revenue from the Hajj, the annual Islamic pilgrimage to Mecca. However, the discovery of oil in the late 1930s marked a substantial shift in the country's economy, nurturing the development of the once-scattered Saudi people and laying the foundation for future growth. The transformations that followed in the latter half of the twentieth century and into the twenty-first have encompassed agriculture, water desalination, industrial production, literacy, education and training, and especially healthcare.

From a country that relied mainly on traditional medicine, Saudi Arabia has witnessed development in all domains of healthcare in the past century. The healthcare system evolved from small public health departments to a nationwide system of hospitals, specialized centers, and large medical cities (Walston et al., 2008). The majority of primary, secondary, and tertiary medical care services are regulated by the Ministry of Health (MOH), established in 1950. Still, a large proportion of healthcare is provided through other governmental agencies, such as military hospitals, National Guard hospitals, and university hospitals. In addition, there is a growing private healthcare sector, which provides care at the primary, secondary, and tertiary levels. For this reason, healthcare in Saudi Arabia can be characterized as a two-tier system. All healthcare services in the Kingdom continue to evolve under the NTP's Healthcare Transformation Plan. Current efforts include reorganizing healthcare services into clusters across the Kingdom, which form an "integrated ecosystem" encompassing all healthcare facilities within a designated catchment area, including central and general hospitals, as well as specialized centers. These health clusters are responsible for the health and wellness of the population within their respective areas and provide clinical care as well as prevention and health awareness. The World Health Organization (WHO) projects that more than one million individuals will be enjoying better health in Saudi Arabia in 2025 compared to 2018 (World Health Organization, 2025).

Formal mental health services in Saudi Arabia can be traced back to the establishment of the first mental health hospital, colloquially referred to as Shehar Hospital due to its location, in the city of Taif in 1952 with 250 beds. The second mental health hospital was opened in Medina in 1960, with a 36-bed capacity (Koenig et al., 2013). This was a period when North America was undergoing rapid deinstitutionalization, while modern Saudi Arabia was witnessing its first encounters with psychiatric hospitalizations. In the decades that followed, mental healthcare was delivered through these mental health hospitals, as well as general hospitals with psychiatric units and smaller short-stay mental facilities. For most of the history of mental healthcare in Saudi Arabia, psychiatric admissions were not regulated by national law and instead relied on individual hospital policy, the physician's judgment, and family consent. A significant step forward came with the issuance by royal decree of the Mental Health Care Law on July 17, 2014 (Almadani et al., 2023). Although implementation of the law has been uneven across the Kingdom, its provisions formally apply nationwide. In a subsequent section, we will review the law, its articles, and providers' perceptions.

The available reports from the latter half of the twentieth century indicate that men attended psychiatric services more than women, which reflected cultural practices around healthcare access in Saudi Arabia, but also the known higher severity of mental disorders in men. Mental healthcare was also characterized in that period by predominantly non-Saudi healthcare providers, including psychiatrists and mental health nursing staff (Al-Subaie, 1989). The shortage of mental health providers who are Saudi or informed of the cultural norms in Saudi Arabia is still a problem, which we will review in a subsequent section. A bigger problem has been the unavailability of specialized mental health providers for most of the history of the country. It was estimated that, up to the 1980s, no more than one psychiatrist was practicing for every 2 million individuals living in Saudi Arabia (Koenig et al., 2013).

Education and training in mental health were minimal in the Kingdom. Other than a few lectures on depression and organic brain syndromes, or a week-long clinical clerkship with a psychiatrist in one of the two existing mental hospitals at the time, exposure to psychotherapy or psychopharmacology was infrequent in Saudi medical schools for most of the second half of the twentieth century (Koenig et al., 2014). Besides a small psychiatric residency training program at King Saud University in Riyadh, specialty training in psychiatry was virtually nonexistent in the Kingdom. A second mental health training program existed at the Shahar Mental Health Hospital in Taif, which offered a diploma in psychological medicine. According to Dubovsky, this diploma did not fulfill residency requirements for certification (Dubovsky, 1983). A major turning point was the establishment of the Saudi Board in Psychiatry in 1997–1998, which was obtained following a four-year postgraduate residency training program. Initially, this residency offered training positions in Riyadh only. Over the past two decades, however, the residency program has expanded to other cities across the Kingdom, supplying the healthcare workforce with specialized psychiatrists (Koenig et al., 2013).

The history of mental healthcare in Saudi Arabia is also characterized by a shift from traditional healing practices, which were commonly considered the norm by Saudi individuals as late as the latter half of the twentieth century (Dubovsky, 1983). This shift is still ongoing, and the impact of continued traditional and alternative healing practices on mental healthcare delivery will be explored in another section.

As we conclude our historical overview, we should look at Saudi Arabia's rapid population growth and increase in life expectancy. Life expectancy was estimated to be 77.91 years in 2022, which is more than 30 years higher than the estimate in 1960. The latest estimate is 5 years higher than the global life expectancy and almost 7 years more than the regional average (World Health Organization, 2020a). Affluence and improvements in water and food availability likely played a role, but advancements in healthcare services were probably just as essential to this rise in life expectancy and the rapid population growth. Focusing on the past 30 years, the population of Saudi Arabia doubled between the years 1992 and 2022. The national census reported a population of 16,948,388 in September 1992, which rose to 32,175,224 in May 2022 (General Authority for Statistics, 2022). The population growth has been most prominent in urban areas, such as the capital city of Riyadh, where the population increased from 3,834,986 in 1992 to 8,591,748 in 2022. If we look at percentage growth instead, the General Authority for Statistics reported a national population growth of 4.5% between 2021 and 2022, with the highest percentage of growth reported as 5.1% in the central region, which includes Riyadh. Lastly, the national census reported an average age of 29 years, with most Saudis being under the age of 35 (General Authority for Statistics, 2022). The relevance of population growth and young population statistics to mental healthcare will be most apparent when we review the epidemiology of mental disorders in the Kingdom.

3 Epidemiology of Mental Disorders in Saudi Arabia

Recent estimates of the prevalence of mental disorders in Saudi Arabia have come from multiple sources. We begin our overview with estimates from the WHO, which compares prevalence data in Saudi Arabia to other countries within the WHO Regional Office for the Eastern Mediterranean (EMRO). It is worth noting, however, that these estimates are not based on data from healthcare agencies within Saudi Arabia and therefore may not represent the true burden of mental disorders or suicide in the country. In its 2020 Mental Health ATLAS, the WHO estimated that the age-standardized suicide mortality rate in Saudi Arabia was 5.43 per 100,000 in 2019 (World Health Organization, 2020b). For comparison, the average rate in other EMRO countries is lower at 3.6 per 100,000, while the global estimate is higher at 9.2 per 100,000 (World Health Organization WHO, 2021). The highest suicide rates in the Kingdom were estimated among males aged 85 and older (17.3 per 100,000) and those aged 35–44 years (13.7). Females had lower estimated suicide rates in all age groups compared to males, but the highest rate among females was in the 35–44 age group. The WHO has also published estimates of mental disorders in the Eastern Mediterranean Region in the Global Burden of Disease 2016 (GBD 2016) report, as well as in North Africa and the Middle East in the GBD, 2019 report. According to these estimates, depressive disorders contribute the highest percentage of disability-adjusted life years (DALYs) due to mental disorders in the region (42%), followed by anxiety disorders (21%), and schizophrenia, bipolar disorders, and idiopathic developmental intellectual disability (each at 8%) (Vos et al., 2017; GBD 2019 Mental Disorders Collaborators, 2022).

Unfortunately, these estimates did not rely on nationally representative samples from Saudi Arabia and, as mentioned previously, may mischaracterize the burden of mental disorders in the country. This limitation was recently addressed by the largest national survey examining the prevalence of mental disorders in the Kingdom. The Saudi National Mental Health Survey (SNMHS) was conducted as part of the WHO World Mental Health (WMH) Survey Initiative (Al-Subaie et al., 2020). It was based on a nationally representative sample of households, targeting Saudi citizens aged 15–65 years living in 11 of the 13 administrative regions (Jazan and Najran were excluded due to their proximity to the active military conflict in Yemen at the time of data collection). The sampling procedure selected 4302 representative households whose inhabitants were interviewed face-to-face by trained interviewers using the WHO Composite International Diagnostic Interview (CIDI) Version 3.0. The number of Saudis who completed the survey was 4004 (Mneimneh et al., 2020).

The survey estimated that 20.2% of Saudis met the criteria for any mental disorder in the previous 12 months. The most common CIDI disorders, grouped into broad categories, were anxiety disorders at 12.3% (including panic disorder, agoraphobia without panic, social phobia, generalized anxiety disorder, post-traumatic stress disorder, obsessive–compulsive disorder, and separation anxiety disorder). These were followed by mood disorders at 6.8% (including major depressive disorder and bipolar disorder), disruptive behavior disorders at 5.4% (attention-deficit/

hyperactivity disorder, conduct disorder, oppositional-defiant disorder, and intermittent explosive disorder), eating disorders at 3.2% (anorexia nervosa, bulimia nervosa, binge-eating disorder), and finally substance use disorders at 1.9% (including alcohol and drug abuse and dependence). Most individuals with 12-month mental disorders were classified as having either a serious disorder (7.9% of the surveyed sample, representing 39.0% of those with 12-month disorders) or a moderate disorder (6.8% of the surveyed sample, 33.7% of those with 12-month disorders), according to the WMH severity classification (Altwaijri et al., 2020a).

Looking at lifetime prevalence, the survey found that the lifetime prevalence of any mental disorder was estimated at 34.2%. Anxiety disorders had the highest lifetime prevalence at 23.2%. There was no significant difference between males and females in the overall lifetime prevalence of at least one mental disorder. However, females were more likely to meet the criteria for two lifetime disorders. Moreover, females had a higher lifetime prevalence than males of certain anxiety disorders, such as agoraphobia (3.2% vs. 1.4%), social phobia (7.0% vs. 4.3%), and generalized anxiety disorder (2.9% vs. 0.9%). Similar to other countries, female Saudis also had a higher lifetime prevalence of major depressive disorder (8.9% vs. 3.1%). The highest odds ratios for lifetime mental disorders were observed among the youngest Saudis, particularly those aged 15–24 years. Odds ratios were slightly higher in the 25–34 age group for some disorders, such as PTSD, separation anxiety disorder, binge-eating disorder, conduct disorder, and drug dependence.

Nevertheless, both young age groups (15–24 and 25–34) had significantly higher odds for mental disorders than older adults. Similarly, Saudis aged 35–49 had elevated odds ratios for lifetime mental disorders compared to older age groups, though to a lesser extent. The only exception was drug dependence, which was similarly prevalent in the 25–34 and 35–49 age groups. These findings suggest an increasing prevalence of mental disorders among younger individuals in Saudi Arabia. Alternatively, they may reflect underreporting of mental disorders among older Saudis (Altwaijri et al., 2020b).

A notable finding from the survey was the low proportion of Saudis who have sought treatment for their mental health concerns. Only 13.7% of Saudis received treatment for their mental disorder in any given year. And although disorders judged to be of serious severity were more likely to be treated, the survey found that adequate treatment was not associated with disorder severity (Al-Habeeb et al., 2020). At least one in ten Saudis sought treatment for their mental health concerns from a non-medical traditional or faith healer (AlTwaijri et al., 2019).

The estimates of the national survey indicate that mental disorders are common in Saudi Arabia as compared to other countries in which similar surveys were conducted. This was especially the case for anxiety disorders, and particularly separation anxiety disorder (lifetime prevalence of 11.9% in Saudi Arabia). In addition, the authors of the survey report note that these figures might have underestimated the true prevalence of mental disorders due to suspected underreporting by individuals and exclusion of those not living in households (Altwaijri et al., 2020c). The survey did not include diagnoses of psychotic disorders, which contribute a significant proportion of disability associated with mental disorders. It has been estimated, however, that the age-standardized prevalence of schizophrenia in Saudi Arabia is similar to other Middle Eastern and North African countries at around 250 per 100,000, with men having a higher prevalence than women (Safiri et al., 2024). Furthermore, since the national survey was conducted in the community, it did not provide estimates regarding inpatients and hospital-treated individuals in the Kingdom.

A national study of inpatients and outpatients in six hospitals across five different regions of Saudi Arabia, including 1205 patients, reported that the most common psychiatric diagnoses among inpatients were schizophrenia (55.8%), bipolar disorder (23.3%), and major depressive disorder (7.2%), whereas the most common diagnoses among outpatients were major depressive disorder (29.3%), schizophrenia (28.9%), generalized anxiety disorder (15.6%), and bipolar disorder (11.5%) (Alosaimi et al., 2017b). The study also reported sex differences, finding that males were significantly more likely to be diagnosed with primary psychotic disorders. In contrast, females were more likely to be diagnosed with bipolar or depressive disorders. Most patients (71.5%) were jobless, and around a third had a monthly family income of less than 3000 Saudi Riyals (Alosaimi et al 2017b). This mental health and social burden was further compounded by significant cardiometabolic morbidity. Although the sample consisted mostly of young adults (average age 38.1 ± 13.0), 29.3% were overweight, 37.9% were obese, and 9.3% were diagnosed with diabetes mellitus, with the latter being more common among inpatients. Cardiometabolic health is a major concern for Saudis with mental health conditions. The prevalence of metabolic syndrome is estimated to be more than 40% among psychiatric inpatients and outpatients (Alosaimi et al., 2017a). This significantly increases the risk of future cardiometabolic multimorbidity and mortality in a population that is young and struggling with increasing rates of mental disorders.

The reviewed estimates in this section highlight the growing prevalence and associated burden of mental disorders in Saudi Arabia. Notably, the most recent evidence points to a significantly higher prevalence of these disorders among younger Saudis, a finding of particular concern given the youthful demographic structure of the Kingdom. In the next section, we will review the mental healthcare services currently available in Saudi Arabia before covering the challenges that the mental healthcare system continues to face.

4 Mental Healthcare in Saudi Arabia

This section will review the current status of mental health services in the Kingdom and recent advances in digital health, hospital-based care, medication-based care, psychosocial interventions, and legal developments. Overall, mental health expenditures account for approximately 4% of the total health budget in Saudi Arabia, with around 22% of that budget allocated to mental health hospitals (Qureshi et al., 2013).

4.1 Primary Care for Mental Health

Primary care in Saudi Arabia serves as the foundational level of the healthcare system and is ideally the first point of contact between individuals and medical services. Despite this, healthcare utilization in the Kingdom continues to show a high reliance rate on secondary and tertiary care services and specialized private clinics.

Primary care centers were first established in 1989, and each Saudi family was registered with a center in their area of residence and received all their primary care needs from that center. Primary care centers are overseen by the MOH and provide essential services focusing on prevention, early diagnosis, and the management of chronic illnesses. By strengthening primary care services, the Ministry aims to reduce hospital overcrowding, improve access to healthcare, and enhance population health outcomes. In line with Vision 2030 and the NTP, extensive efforts have been directed toward expanding the capacity and reach of primary care centers, including integration of services through digital health solutions (Al-Kahtani et al., 2022).

Mental disorders are commonly encountered in primary care centers around the Kingdom, and they are more commonly seen in females, younger individuals in the 25–35 and 36–45 age groups, and those with obesity, diabetes mellitus, and stroke (Alangari et al., 2024). We see again the burden of mental disorders in the young and the associated cardiometabolic health burden in Saudi Arabia. A study at a single primary care center in Riyadh estimated that 28.5% of patients attending the center had a mental disorder (Alghadeer et al., 2018).

The delivery of mental healthcare at the primary care level depends on both the availability of primary healthcare centers and the ease of access to them. The distribution of these centers varies by region, from 20 primary care centers per 100,000 individuals in the smallest province of Al-Bahah to as few as 2.1 per 100,000 in the port city of Jeddah on the Red Sea. In Riyadh, there are around 7.5 primary care centers per 100,000 people. These numbers raise concerns over access to mental healthcare for the majority of the urban population in the Kingdom. A similar concern is that the recent population growth has led to a decline in the average number of primary care centers, from 8.0 centers per 100,000 individuals in 2017 to 6.6 in 2022 (Kattan, 2024).

Another barrier to providing mental healthcare to Saudis at the primary care level, besides the availability of centers, is the availability of a trained workforce. It has been estimated that short-term mental health training was provided only to 60% of primary care physicians and 65% of primary care nurses in the early 2010s (Qureshi et al., 2013). Given the high prevalence of mental disorders and the likelihood of encountering mental health conditions for all healthcare providers, it is evident that more training is needed. Recently, efforts have been made to implement a mental health training program for primary care physicians to enable them to assess and treat common mental disorders. One study suggested that trained primary care physicians following multi-step assessments were comparable to structured interviews by psychiatrists and more accurate than screening tools for the identification of depression and anxiety in the primary care setting (Alkhathami, 2022). An MOH initiative, called the Mental Healthcare Program, is being implemented to encourage early screening and assessment of mental disorders, particularly depression and anxiety, by family and primary care physicians and the use of pharmacotherapy using selective serotonin reuptake inhibitors (SSRIs) (Al-Khathami et al., 2025). It remains to be seen whether these initiatives will achieve the intended goal of providing high-quality care for mental disorders at the primary care level, rather than lead to overprescription of SSRIs (Arroll et al., 2023). A potential solution to improve mental healthcare in primary care centers using a collaborative care model will be discussed when reviewing policy solutions for mental healthcare in Saudi Arabia.

4.2 Hospital-Based Mental Care

The Kingdom has an estimated 12 psychiatric beds per 100,000 population. Around 90% of beds are found in mental health hospitals, with only a small proportion found in general hospitals. As previously noted, more than a fifth of the mental health expenditure is directed toward mental health hospitals (Qureshi et al., 2013). According to the MOH, dedicated mental health hospitals and complexes are distributed across the various regions of Saudi Arabia. Major cities such as Riyadh, Dammam, Jeddah, and Medina are served by Eradah Complexes, which provide comprehensive mental health and addiction services. *Eradah* (Which is Arabic for "will") is the name adopted by the Ministry when these facilities were rebranded in 2019 after being known for decades as *Al-Amal* Hospitals (*Amal* is Arabic for "hope"). The decision to rename was widely debated (Sabq News, 2019). "Will" is not necessarily preferable to "Hope" when addressing the burden and disability associated with mental health conditions, nor is renaming a solution to stigma in what is arguably a case of euphemism treadmill (Edward Schumacher-Matos, 2012). Table 1 shows the city and region for MOH mental health hospitals.

Among patients treated for mental disorders in Saudi Arabia, 40% receive care in mental health hospitals, 50% in outpatient clinics, and 10% in other clinical settings. Males continue to constitute a slightly larger proportion of inpatients, with females representing 46% of those treated in mental health hospitals and 50% of those treated in outpatient clinics. Patients diagnosed with substance use disorders account for 9% of inpatients and 20% of outpatients (Qureshi et al., 2013). The average length of stay is approximately 45 days in mental health hospitals, with continued efforts to reduce hospital-based durations of care. An obstacle to reducing the length of stay is the large number of hospital beds occupied by patients with severe chronic mental disorders who lack family support and options for supportive community housing. In community residential facilities, the length of stay ranges from 30 to 60 days. Psychiatric beds in general hospitals report shorter stays, typically ranging from 25 to 35 days per admission (AbuMadini & Rahim, 2002; Al-Sughayir, 2016).

Table 1 Location of Ministry of Health (MOH) Mental Health Hospitals across Saudi Arabia

Administrative Region	City	Hospital
Riyadh	Riyadh	Eradah Mental Health Complex
	Al-Kharj	Eradah Mental Health Complex
Makkah	Taif	Eradah Mental Health Complex
	Jeddah	Eradah Mental Health Complex
Eastern Region	Dammam	Eradah Mental Health Complex
	Hafr Albatin	Mental Health Hospital
	Al-Ahsa	Mental Health Hospital
Madinah	Medina	Eradah Mental Health Complex
Al-Qassim	Buraydah	Eradah Mental Health Complex
Tabuk	Tabuk	Eradah Mental Health Complex
Asir	Abha	Mental Health Hospital
	Bisha	Mental Health Hospital
Al-Jouf	Al-Jouf	Eradah Mental Health Complex
	Al-Qurayyat	Mental Health Hospital
Ha'il	Ha'il	Eradah Mental Health Complex
Northern Borders	Arar	Eradah Mental Health Complex
Al-Bahah	Baljurashi	Eradah Mental Health Complex
Jazan	Jazan	Eradah Mental Health Complex
Najran	Najran	Eradah Mental Health Complex

Source Ministry of Health (www.moh.gov.sa)

Unfortunately, only 1% of all general hospitals in the Kingdom provide specialized inpatient psychiatric services (Qureshi et al., 2013). This is regrettable, given that general hospitals offer better access to medical and surgical services compared to mental health hospitals and can ensure multidisciplinary care for patients who have medical comorbidities, who constitute a large proportion of inpatients (Alosaimi et al., 2017b). In 2018, the MOH reported an initiative to establish inpatient psychiatric wards in all general and specialized hospitals across the Kingdom with a bed capacity of more than 100 beds. The initiative was in response to a royal decree mandating that every general hospital with more than 100 beds should allocate an inpatient ward equivalent to approximately 5–10% of its total bed capacity, as a first phase, to psychiatric inpatient services. The aim of integrating mental health services into general and specialized hospitals was to facilitate access to these services and tackle widespread stigma. Although this initiative was situated within the NTP's Health Transformation Plan, it has seen little implementation since its announcement almost 7 years ago (Saudi Press Agency, 2018).

We now turn to hospital-based providers of mental healthcare. The number of providers in hospital settings remains low and variable. The estimated average number of providers per hospital bed is 0.39 nurses, 0.21 psychosocial staff, and 0.09

psychiatrists. These figures tend to be higher in urban areas and general hospitals, and lower in standalone mental health hospitals.

Besides mental health and addiction inpatient and outpatient services, mental health hospitals occasionally provide community-based services. These are, however, limited in their scope. There is a general deficiency in community-based services across the country for individuals with severe mental disorders who might benefit from home visits or supervised community treatments. Moreover, community residential facilities mainly function as halfway houses and continue to focus on medical care, rather than psychosocial efforts to reintegrate individuals back into the community (Qureshi et al., 2013).

So far, we have focused our review on governmental facilities. However, private mental healthcare services are available across the country as part of the Kingdom's two-tier system. The private mental health sector is largely outpatient clinic-based and mainly serves individuals with non-serious mental disorders. Most private mental health services are either stand-alone consultation centers or part of medical polyclinics. Some private general hospitals have psychiatric clinics, and an even smaller minority offer inpatient psychiatric services. Recent efforts under the NTP have encouraged investment in private inpatient general mental health and addiction services.

4.3 Medication-Based Care

Psychotropic medications are provided free of charge for patients receiving care in governmental or public hospitals and medical centers in Saudi Arabia. All psychotropic medications are regulated by the Saudi Food and Drug Authority (SFDA), which oversees a range of services including drug registration, regulation of controlled drug prescriptions, a pharmacovigilance system for reporting adverse drug effects, clinical trial registration, and drug tracking and tracing. Patterns of psychotropic prescriptions in the Kingdom indicate that antidepressants are the most commonly prescribed psychotropics at the primary care level. The prescription of selective serotonin reuptake inhibitors (SSRIs) by primary care physicians accounts for the majority of pharmacotherapy for mental disorders conducted at the primary care centers (Alsabhan et al., 2024). If instead we look at psychotropics prescribed to patients receiving specialized psychiatric care, the most commonly prescribed medications were antipsychotics, followed by antidepressants, then mood stabilizers, and finally anxiolytics and sedatives (Alosaimi et al., 2016a).

Nonadherence to pharmacological treatment of mental disorders does not seem to differ in Saudi Arabia from reported estimates in other countries and is estimated at around one-fifth to one-half of all patients (Al Jumah et al., 2014; Ali et al., 2023; Shahin & Daly, 1999; Surrati et al., 2020). The reported reasons for nonadherence were also similar, with drug adverse effects and polypharmacy being associated with higher rates of nonadherence.

4.4 Psychosocial Care

Psychosocial interventions in Saudi Arabia are provided by trained psychiatrists, psychologists, and social workers. Given the limited number of well-trained psychosocial care providers in the Kingdom, it is not surprising that these interventions are not commonly available. For many patients who are provided care, medication-based treatment is the only accessible form of treatment. This is regrettable given that a recent survey found that many Saudis find psychotherapy a preferable option when seeking mental healthcare (Senitan et al., 2024). The study also highlighted the importance of integrating spiritual and religious values and beliefs into therapeutic interventions to better adapt these interventions to the Saudi population.

Of the available psychotherapeutic interventions, the most commonly provided is cognitive behavioral therapy (CBT) (Alanazi et al., 2023). Furthermore, the availability of telehealth options has improved access to psychotherapy for many individuals in the Kingdom, with providers reporting positive attitudes toward virtual psychotherapy (AlHadi et al., 2021).

4.5 Digital Health and Telepsychiatry

As an integral part of the NTP, digital health has been a focus of the health transformation plan in Saudi Arabia since its proposal in 2015. The MOH has prioritized telemedicine as a core component of its national strategies, facilitating remote diagnosis, consultation, and medical assessment. The Kingdom's preparedness was put to the test during the COVID-19 pandemic, when virtual assessments and remote management became commonplace. The Ministry operates the National Health Information Center, which enables the automatic exchange of health data across healthcare sectors and oversees the Saudi Telehealth Network, connecting specialized facilities with primary care centers and hospitals in remote areas. As previously reviewed, the Ministry has also introduced digital platforms and applications. These digital applications include Sehhaty (Arabic for "My Health") for all individuals living in the Kingdom and Anat (Arabic for "Patience") for healthcare providers. These applications can be used to access digital health information, schedule medical appointments, prescribe medications, issue sick leaves, and ensure linkage of providers to their registration with the Saudi Commission for Health Specialties, which licenses healthcare providers in the Kingdom. Additionally, the 937 Call Center operates 24/7 to address public health inquiries, and ongoing surveys assess user satisfaction with telemedicine services (Ministry of Health, 2022).

In addition to MOH digital services, telepsychiatry has become a common practice in Saudi Arabia, with numerous online platforms and smart device applications dedicated to the delivery of mental healthcare. Some of these platforms connect users with therapists, while others also provide access to prescribers. Care is typically provided through text or video calls, and many of these platforms are private services that require out-of-pocket payment from the user. These telepsychiatry services constitute an increasing proportion of the mental health services provided in the country in recent years (Alanazi et al., 2023). And although the overall attitude of care providers toward telepsychiatry is positive, their level of knowledge regarding these services remains inadequate (Alghamdi et al., 2022).

It is unclear whether the service provided through online telepsychiatry platforms adheres to the ethical and professional standards required for the proper delivery of mental healthcare. The platforms are usually used for assessment and management, including psychotherapy and pharmacotherapy. But even though there is evidence for using telepsychiatry to provide some forms of therapy, such as CBT, the evidence for psychiatric assessment and management is severely limited (Brunt & Gale-Grant, 2023). Indeed, in the context of a comprehensive assessment involving a clinical examination and in-office measurements, it is evident that telepsychiatry platforms cannot replace the standard of care provided by in-person services. These issues can be overcome by telemedicine solutions that link one healthcare provider with a specialist when specialized providers are physically unavailable. However, this is not the service provided by current telepsychiatry platforms. There is a need, therefore, for regulatory efforts by policymakers in addition to practice guidelines for practitioners of telepsychiatry (Alqahtani et al., 2021). Current efforts by the MOH and the National Center for Mental Health Promotion aim to standardize telepsychiatry care across the various platforms and ensure adherence to the standard of care.

4.6 Saudi Mental Health Care Law

The Saudi Mental Health Care Law currently governs the mental healthcare system in Saudi Arabia. The law was issued by royal decree on July 17, 2014, and its implementation has been an ongoing effort across the Kingdom. Further regulations were issued in 2016 and later amended by the MOH in 2021. The Saudi Mental Health Care Law comprises 30 articles and establishes the legal and procedural framework for the care and protection of individuals with mental disorders in Saudi Arabia. Article 1 defines a mental disorder as "a disturbance in an individual's thought, mood, awareness, memory or other intellectual faculties, in whole or in part." The articles also establish the supervisory structure for the implementation of the law (Articles 3 to 8), outline the rights of psychiatric patients (Article 9), provide regulations for involuntary admissions including their duration (Articles 10 to 14), establish the responsibilities of psychiatric facilities (Articles 16 and 17), detail protocols for special treatments such as electroconvulsive therapy or special circumstances such as patient escape (Articles 18 to 24), and define violations of the law and specify the penalties (Articles 25 to 27).

Despite its potential to improve patient care in Saudi Arabia, the law continues to face challenges in implementation and provider awareness. A study on mental healthcare providers revealed that almost a third (28.7%) were unaware of the law's existence as of early 2023. Providers working in facilities where the law had been implemented were found to have more favorable attitudes toward the Mental Health Care Law (Almadani et al., 2023). There remains an urgent need to expand the Law's implementation across all mental healthcare facilities in Saudi Arabia and to ensure that all providers are trained to interpret and apply its articles in daily practice.

5 Challenges to Mental Healthcare in Saudi Arabia

We have already touched upon some of the challenges facing mental healthcare in Saudi Arabia. In this section, however, we provide an in-depth discussion of major issues such as workforce shortages, difficulties with access to care, the continued reliance on non-medical traditional and faith healing practices, persistent stigma and limited mental health literacy, concerns around cost, and poor mental healthcare practices.

5.1 Workforce Shortage

In terms of workforce availability, mental healthcare providers constitute an estimated 22 per 100,000 individuals in the country. Mental health nurses form the majority of this workforce (13 per 100,000), whereas psychiatrists remain few (2 per 100,000) (Qureshi et al., 2013). We have already reviewed the low number of providers per hospital bed. Despite increasing efforts to train healthcare providers in mental healthcare, it is unlikely that the current numbers will meet the needs. A decade-old estimate reported that recent graduates in mental health specialties remain few, with 1.8 nurses, 0.4 psychiatrists, 0.19 psychologists, and 0.95 social workers per 100,000 individuals (Qureshi et al., 2013).

How do these numbers compare to the actual need for mental healthcare providers in the country? A recent estimate reported that Saudi Arabia requires 49.2 healthcare providers per 100,000 individuals to meet the needs associated with mental disorders (Lee et al., 2024). The report estimates a workforce shortage of approximately 10,402 providers. It was further estimated that mental health nurses and psychosocial care providers account for 98.9% of the shortage. Overall, they report that current mental healthcare needs require an estimated additional 100 psychiatrists, 5700 nurses, and 4500 psychosocial care providers.

There are a number of reasons why these numbers are probably underestimates of the true shortage. Many mental healthcare providers have not received training in mental health, but have filled the position due to understaffing. For example, many "psychiatrist" positions are filled by service residents, that is, general practitioners who work in mental health hospitals under the supervision of a certified psychiatrist. The same is true for the majority of already working mental health nurses who have not received mental health training. Another reason is that a significant proportion of the healthcare providers are non-Saudi temporary workers, some of whom cannot even speak the language of their target population.

5.2 *Lack of Cultural Adaptation*

For many decades in Saudi Arabia, mental healthcare was provided by non-Saudis who did not have the cultural background of their target population and, at times, did not even speak Arabic (Al-Subaie, 1989). This deficit in culturally informed providers has been the main target of efforts to train Saudis as mental healthcare providers. As we reviewed, however, the shortage in mental healthcare providers is a major issue facing service delivery in the Kingdom (Lee et al., 2024). Since more than half of all healthcare providers in the country are non-Saudi, it is unclear how this issue can be tackled in the short term without extensive training of non-Saudi providers on the language and traditions of their Saudi patients.

Issues with cultural adaptation of care also include assessment tools, diagnostic categories, and interventions. Many diagnostic and assessment tools are developed in Western European and North American countries, and their appropriate use in the Saudi population requires careful translation and cultural adaptation. This is similarly the case for psychosocial interventions, which require appropriate translation and adaptation to serve the target population (Gearing et al., 2013).

Population-specific variables may be additionally relevant to pharmacotherapy, where most of the evidence for dosing, efficacy, and tolerability is derived from studies conducted outside the Middle East or North Africa. Recent efforts to conduct psychopharmacological research in Saudi Arabia aim to address this gap and are part of a broader global effort to consider race and ethnicity in psychopharmacological research (Olagunju et al., 2025). For example, a naturalistic study on patients treated with clozapine in Saudi Arabia revealed that the relationship between clozapine dose and serum level resembled that reported in Asian samples more than in European samples (Hassab Errasoul & Alarabi, 2022). More efforts are needed to ensure that available mental health interventions, whether pharmacological or psychosocial, are appropriate for the Saudi population.

5.3 *Difficult Access to Care*

We have already reviewed the disparities in regional availability of primary healthcare centers and how that can impact access to mental healthcare for many individuals around the Kingdom (Kattan, 2024). The limited integration of primary healthcare centers and specialized mental health services is another issue that is often highlighted in studies examining access to mental healthcare in Saudi Arabia. Fortunately, the recent implementation of electronic referral systems has enabled better integration of governmental services across the Kingdom.

In a recent nationwide study, an analysis of 10,033 electronic psychiatric referrals showed how digital health solutions may have enhanced access to care but also revealed a significant need for specialized mental healthcare in various regions (Alharbi et al., 2025). The study found that two-thirds of the referrals were due to the unavailability of psychiatric beds, while "unavailable subspecialty" was the primary reason for referrals across all regions. Notably, the highest rate of electronic psychiatric referrals came from the Northern Border and Al-Baha regions. On the other hand, the fewest referrals came from Medina, Riyadh, and the Eastern Region, where many specialized mental healthcare services are already available. These results point to the unmet needs for mental healthcare across the Kingdom and emphasize the urgency of establishing additional specialized services in the northern and southern regions.

5.4 Non-medical Traditional and Faith Healing

Historically, non-medical traditional and faith healing practices were not considered "alternative" but the norm for mental health conditions in Saudi Arabia (Dubovsky, 2006). Traditional medicine and faith healing continue to be widely practiced, especially among non-urban residents. In this regard, Saudi Arabia is similar to other countries in the region in which faith healing plays a central role in mental health (Al Shelali et al., 2024). Traditional and faith healing practices are often based on beliefs around the causes of mental complaints, including supernatural causes such as Jinn possession, witchcraft, or the evil eye, or unproven natural causes such as cranial hernias (Al-Habeeb, 2003). We will first review some of these practices and beliefs, then discuss their impact on mental healthcare in Saudi Arabia.

Traditional practices for mental health include cautery of the head, which is believed to treat different ailments and especially those of a mental nature. More extreme, but thankfully rare, measures include beatings as the healers believe psychotic patients do not feel pain when possessed. Such practices can cause severe injury in a population that is already vulnerable to harm (Alhamad, 2003). Some traditional healers rely on herbal concoctions and recipes to treat a variety of mental health complaints. Some apply the mixture directly to the head, believing that the ingredients can heal by direct effect on the patient's scalp. Ingestible herbal treatments are also commonly used and rarely supervised, raising concerns over potential toxic effects or drug interactions (Alghadir et al., 2022). Religious and faith healing often involves recitations from the Holy Quran, which is believed to have healing power as the literal word of God. It may also include washing with or drinking blessed water upon which the healer recited Qur'an (Al-Subaie, 1989). Although some of these healing practices draw on Islamic traditions, there are many issues with common faith healing practices in Saudi Arabia. Firstly, attributing mental health concerns exclusively to spiritual or supernatural causes is not attested in Islamic sources.

Secondly, faith healing through Quranic recitation is not a substitute for medicinal therapies, as those have been used and encouraged in prophetic traditions. Moreover, some faith healers conduct their practice without supervision or regulation, putting vulnerable individuals at risk of harm or exploitation (Alosaimi, 2021).

As we saw in the results of the National Mental Health Survey, traditional non-medical and faith healers are commonly sought by Saudis. At least 1 in 10 individuals reported seeking this modality of treatment for mental health concerns, often as a first line of help before turning to modern medicine (AlTwaijri et al., 2019). A study conducted on shopping mall visitors in Riyadh found that Saudis seeking faith healers had lower educational levels and income. They were also more likely to report a history of medical and psychiatric illness, particularly psychotic and bipolar disorders (Alosaimi et al., 2015). Another Saudi study utilizing a short structured diagnostic interview found high rates of mental disorders among 321 visitors of faith healing settings in Riyadh (Alosaimi et al., 2014). Among the visitors assessed, depressive disorders were the most common (34.9%), followed by anxiety disorders (18.7%). Psychotic and bipolar disorders were identified in 6.9% and 5.0% of the sample, respectively. Around 12.3% attributed their condition to the evil eye, 5.5% to black magic, and 16.5% to social and financial stress, while nearly half of the participants endorsed multiple explanations. Notably, none of the participants attributed their illness to biological causes. In terms of the treatment practices used, the most common was Quranic recitation and the use of blessed water. Alarmingly, nearly 5% of participants reported having been subjected to physical interventions such as beating, choking, or electric shocks as part of their treatment.

Besides potential harms of the physical or herbal "treatments" and the cost incurred by individuals seeking them, a major concern is that non-medical treatments can delay proper care. Indeed, in a study on the duration of untreated psychosis in Riyadh, the researchers found an average duration of almost one and a half years and found that this delay was associated with help-seeking from traditional healers (Al Fayez et al., 2017). In turn, these extended periods without appropriate care are associated with poorer prognosis.

Non-medical traditional beliefs and healing practices form a significant part of the cultural framework that shapes help-seeking behavior for mental health in Saudi Arabia (Al-Subaie, 1989; Dubovsky, 1983; Koenig et al., 2013). These beliefs have experienced a gradual shift in the past few decades, evident from improved awareness of the possible causes of mental health symptoms in recent surveys when compared to older studies in Saudi Arabia (Senitan et al., 2024; Wahass & Kent, 1997). Nevertheless, many Saudis continue to attribute signs and symptoms of mental disorders to supernatural causes, such as possession by Jinn or witchcraft, or even to weak faith (Almadani et al., 2025; Mohamed et al., 2024). Such beliefs shape people's awareness of mental health and can potentiate stigma against mental disorders.

5.5 *Stigma and Mental Health Literacy*

A 2024 systematic review examining barriers to seeking mental healthcare in Saudi Arabia found that stigma and poor mental health literacy were among the top barriers (Alhumaidan et al., 2024). Despite efforts to improve mental health awareness in the Kingdom, a lack of awareness continues to threaten access to needed care for many Saudis. A recent national study, including 4533 participants from all 13 regions of Saudi Arabia, reported that although Saudis were generally optimistic about the outcomes of mental disorders, they still held high rates of negative stereotypes about mental health conditions (BinDhim et al., 2024b).

However, public awareness of mental health conditions and their causes has been changing over the past few decades, leading to a lessening of the impact of stigma. A study on individuals with mood disorders found lower scores on the Inventory of Stigmatizing Experiences in Saudi Arabia compared to Canada and South Korea (Alateeq et al., 2018). In a study on Riyadh residents seeking psychotropic medications from retail pharmacies without prescriptions, the reasons given for avoiding visits to psychiatrists included the belief that their symptoms were not serious enough to warrant seeing a physician (42.4%), as well as the high cost of psychiatric clinics (28.5%), lack of trust in psychiatrists (22.5%), and lack of time (22.5%) (Alosaimi et al., 2016b). These findings highlight the importance of other barriers preventing access to mental healthcare services aside from stigma or poor mental health literacy. Indeed, a recent study using a validated mental health literacy scale administered to individuals across all 13 administrative regions of Saudi Arabia reported high mental health literacy scores (Bindhim et al., 2024a). For these reasons, some mental health experts in the country believe that the main barriers to mental healthcare for most individuals are no longer stigma or poor mental health literacy, but rather the unavailability and cost of mental health services.

5.6 *Cost of Mental Healthcare*

Although mental healthcare is provided free of charge at governmental and public facilities, cost is still a barrier for many individuals seeking treatment in Saudi Arabia. This is because governmental clinics are often overcrowded and, as previously reviewed, the workforce is not enough to serve the growing number of individuals needing care (Qureshi et al., 2013). In addition, some individuals may not be eligible for care in specialized mental healthcare facilities. For example, care provided in specialized psychiatric clinics in military or university hospitals cannot be easily accessed by individuals who lack eligibility for care under those governmental agencies.

Many Saudis find themselves seeking private mental health clinics for ease of access and the freedom to choose their provider. If care is provided outside of governmental facilities, drug treatment is also not free of charge, and patients have to pay for their medications out of pocket. The price of mental healthcare varies by clinic, and not all facilities accept insurance. In addition, the original basic medical insurance plan does not cover mental health services as comprehensively as it does other medical services. Although this problem has improved to some extent, it still creates a barrier against the private psychiatric sector investing in comprehensive primary, secondary, and tertiary care services for people with severe mental disorders.

On average, the service fee for a private psychiatric consultation ranges from 100 to 500 Saudi Riyals. Medications are similarly expensive, and generic formulations may not always be available to allow easier access. In the previously cited study, looking at reasons for seeking psychotropic medications without a prescription from retail pharmacies in Riyadh, around one-third of the sample reported that the high cost of seeking psychiatric care pushed them to obtain medications without prescriptions (Alosaimi et al. 2016b). The practice of psychotropic medication dispensing without prescriptions has since been restricted, as the MOH has been enforcing stricter laws against dispensing medications without valid prescriptions. Nevertheless, cost remains an issue and is compounded by poor mental healthcare practices.

5.7 *Gaps in Mental Healthcare Practices*

Poor healthcare practices constitute a challenge to good mental healthcare delivery in the Kingdom. One major challenge is the limited implementation of the Mental Health Care Law which, as previously reviewed, is essential for protecting patients' rights and clearly defines procedures for involuntary admission and treatment in Saudi Arabia (Almadani et al., 2023). The unavailability of therapists in many centers prompts physicians to offer pharmacological treatment in situations where psychosocial interventions should be the first-line approach. For individuals with severe mental disorders, the unavailability of community-based services shifts care to hospitals and perpetuates a revolving door phenomenon for many.

The lack of community care solutions is increasingly becoming a major issue as Saudi society continues its shift toward urbanization and nuclear family living as opposed to the traditional extended family structure. With these societal changes, homelessness and limited family involvement are now challenges facing a mental healthcare system that did not have to deal with them in the past. In turn, these challenges influence prescribing patterns, leading prescribers to use unproven pharmacological interventions to keep patients out of the hospital.

In addition, these prescribing patterns likely contribute to both the cardiometabolic burden and the high rates of nonadherence among patients with mental disorders. This is especially evident in cases of unwarranted polypharmacy. Many patients are prescribed antipsychotics for conditions where these agents are not the preferred treatment. On the other hand, medications with strong evidence of efficacy, such as clozapine for treatment-resistant schizophrenia and lithium as the gold standard for bipolar I disorder, remain underused. These prescribing trends likely contribute to the increased morbidity associated with mental disorders in the Kingdom.

6 Potential Solutions to Improve Mental Healthcare in Saudi Arabia

This final section explores potential solutions to the previously discussed challenges facing mental healthcare in Saudi Arabia. Before exploring these solutions in depth, we will provide a summary of expert opinions on potential solutions. In October of 2016, a workshop titled "Challenges Facing Mental Healthcare in Saudi Arabia" was held in Riyadh by the Human Rights Commission. The workshop gathered specialists in psychiatry, psychology, and sociology from governmental and private hospitals and centers in Riyadh, alongside members of the Human Rights Commission, and was chaired by Dr. Bandar bin Mohammed Al-Aiban, President of the Human Rights Commission. The mental healthcare institutions represented in the workshop included King Khalid University Hospital/King Saud University, Eradah Mental Health Complex in Riyadh, Prince Sultan Military Medical City, and private sector representatives. Moreover, participants included members of the Shura Council and members of the Human Rights Commission. The workshop concluded with the drafting of a set of recommendations to be submitted to the Royal Court, in accordance with the Commission's mandate (Alosaimi, 2021).

The recommendations included: (1) Establishing psychiatric units in general hospitals (which, as we have reviewed, was followed by a yet-to-be implemented initiative by the MOH in 2018 to allocate 5–10% of all large general hospital beds for psychiatric inpatient services); (2) Establishing mental health services within primary healthcare centers in neighborhoods; (3) Strengthening and supporting Eradah Complexes across the Kingdom; (4) Establishing day centers, halfway houses, and long-term residential care homes; (5) Enforcing regulations on the private mental health sector; (6) Accelerating the implementation of the Mental Health Care Law; (7) Encouraging universities and the Saudi Commission for Health Specialties to expand and implement clinical training programs in mental health; (8) Encouraging partnerships with the private sector; (9) Incorporating mental health education into curricula at the middle school, high school, and university levels; and finally (10) Establishing a national institute or authority for mental health, a recommendation which was followed by the establishment of the National Center for Mental Health Promotion by a decision from the Council of Ministers in 2019.

These recommendations offer a glimpse into the breadth of solutions available for mental healthcare in the Kingdom. In the following sections, we will look at some strategies, such as enhancing mental health literacy, strengthening policy and regulatory frameworks, expanding training opportunities for mental health professionals, and supporting culturally informed research to guide service development and delivery.

6.1 Mental Health Literacy

One of the recent positive developments has been the establishment of the National Center for Mental Health Promotion (NCMH) in 2019 to develop national and regional programs for mental health promotion. The center has been active in raising awareness of mental health disorders and fighting stigma. The center is also responsible for monitoring mental health claims, myths, and malpractices in the media and social media. The efforts of the national center have been cited as a possible contributing factor to recent findings of high mental health literacy scores across Saudi Arabia (Bindhim et al., 2024a). In addition to these efforts to raise awareness, several active consumer organizations exist in the Kingdom, representing people with lived experience of mental disorders and advocating for improved mental healthcare across Saudi Arabia (Qureshi et al., 2013). More efforts toward raising awareness of mental health and combating misconceptions about mental disorders will likely result in improved literacy and a lessening of the effect of stigma on access to care (Alhumaidan et al., 2024).

6.2 Mental Health Policies

In a policy document issued by the National Center for Mental Health Promotion in 2023, the center outlines policies and strategies to improve mental healthcare in the Kingdom (National Center for Mental Health Promotion [NCMH], 2023). One of the primary goals is to shift from institution-based to community-based mental healthcare. Another is the integration of mental health services in primary care settings and ensuring equitable distribution of mental health services across all regions. We have already seen that these are areas of particular concern when it comes to current service availability. Lastly, the center recommends the development of telehealth solutions, which, as we have covered, have led to improved access but still require appropriate regulation.

The document addresses the workforce shortage and recommends increasing the number and capacity of mental health providers and enhancing training and certification programs. One proposed solution is implementing incentives to attract graduates to pursue careers in mental healthcare. Raising awareness and combating stigma is also one of the center's primary goals. The center calls for increased efforts to implement the Mental Health Care Law to protect the rights of individuals with mental disorders and to establish mechanisms for complaints and redress.

As we have reviewed, a common theme in recent mental health policies in the Kingdom has been shifting the focus to primary care settings. In addition to recent attempts to train primary care physicians on the assessment and treatment of common mental disorders, more efforts are needed to achieve this goal as a part of the NTP. The Collaborative Care Model (CCM) is a promising solution, which has been shown to be a cost-effective strategy to improve patient outcomes (Vanderlip et al., 2016).

The model consists of a multidisciplinary group of professionals working within the primary care setting, led by a primary care physician; The team includes a behavioral health care manager, a consulting psychiatrist, and other mental health providers. Together, they provide population-focused care to a defined group of patients with regular review of treatment outcomes. Despite the expected difficulties in implementation, there is evidence to support the usefulness of this model of care to provide high-quality mental healthcare in the primary care setting (Holmes & Chang, 2022).

6.3 Mental Healthcare Training

The main problem facing the expansion of mental health training in the Kingdom is the unavailability of specialized mental healthcare services in many regions. This shortage of services, coupled with the limited number of specialists, restricts the options available for potential trainees, which in turn leads to a limited number of graduates in mental health programs for physicians, nurses, and psychologists. The solution, therefore, starts with the establishment and strengthening of specialized mental health services across the Kingdom.

Although incentivizing training in mental healthcare is likely to result in increased numbers of healthcare workers in this field, policymakers need to prioritize expanding the number of training positions. As reviewed previously, there is a significant need for psychosocial care providers, and addressing this shortage should be a priority for future policy decisions (Lee et al., 2024).

Additional training for already practicing physicians on the detection and management of mental disorders is needed. Equally important is training for registered specialists in appropriate prescribing practices to prevent polypharmacy and the overuse of antipsychotics. Moreover, training providers on recognizing and preventing medication errors can help improve outcomes for psychiatric patients (Alenzi et al., 2024). Physicians should be equipped to educate patients about psychotropic medications, including their indications and potential side effects (Alhur et al., 2024). Lastly, as the number of training programs in mental health expands, particularly with the increasing number of centers contributing to training for the Saudi Board in Psychiatry, efforts should be made to develop more subspecialty fellowship training in psychiatry, particularly for populations with unmet needs such as children, geriatrics, individuals with comorbid medical illnesses, and those with severe mental illness (Koenig et al., 2013).

6.4 Research in Mental Health

Advancing mental healthcare in Saudi Arabia also relies on conducting high-quality research within the Kingdom. As we have reviewed, recent studies on prevalence and morbidity have contributed to a better understanding of the unmet needs in mental health. Research must be culturally sensitive and consider the distinguishing features of Saudi society, including potential ethnic and regional differences (Lyons et al., 2025). Mental health research remains underfunded and is largely limited to a few centers in major cities. If we are to tackle the challenges facing mental healthcare delivery in Saudi Arabia, funding agencies and governmental policymakers must prioritize mental health research at the national level.

7 Conclusions

Saudi Arabia has experienced rapid social transformation and population growth over the past several decades. These demographic changes have produced a young population at increased risk of mental disorders and their associated disease burdens. Many challenges currently face mental healthcare services in the Kingdom, ranging from substantial workforce shortages to difficulties in accessing specialized care in many parts of the country. Perhaps the most prominent challenge is the limited number of specialized services, which has led to limited opportunities for specialized training, and in turn, restricted the number of well-trained specialists in mental healthcare in the Kingdom. The use of non-medical traditional healing remains common, and misconceptions about mental health, though lessened, persist as barriers to seeking help. Despite these challenges, recent advances in healthcare systems and policies, particularly through the efforts under the NTP's Healthcare Transformation Plan, have helped pave the way for improved mental healthcare delivery. For the mental healthcare system to overcome its challenges in the coming years, implementing existing policies and laws must be prioritized, including the Mental Health Care Law and national decisions to expand inpatient services, community services, and primary care services for mental health. However, the greatest step forward will probably be achieved by training more healthcare providers to serve the growing Saudi population adequately.

References

AbuMadini, M. S., & Rahim, S. I. (2002). Psychiatric admission in a general hospital. Patients profile and patterns of service utilization over a decade. *Saudi Medical Journal, 23*(1), 44–50.

Al Fayez, H., Lappin, J., Murray, R., & Boydell, J. (2017). Duration of untreated psychosis and pathway to care in Riyadh, Saudi Arabia. *Early Intervention in Psychiatry, 11*, 47–56. https://doi.org/10.1111/eip.12214

Al Jumah, K., Hassali, M. A., Al Qhatani, D., & El Tahir, K. (2014). Factors associated with adherence to medication among depressed patients from Saudi Arabia: A cross-sectional study. *Neuropsychiatric Disease and Treatment, 10*, 2031. https://doi.org/10.2147/NDT.S71697

Al Shelali, M., Alibrahim, H., Alomar, N., et al. (2024). The good, the bad, and the ugly of faith healers and psychiatric illnesses: A systematic review of the literature in the Arab world. *Journal of Religion and Health, 63*, 857–876. https://doi.org/10.1007/S10943-023-01898-1

Alanazi, T. N. M., McKenna, L., & Buck, M. (2023). The nature and availability of mental health services in Arab Gulf countries: A scoping review. *Saudi Journal of Health Systems Research, 3*, 10–34. https://doi.org/10.1159/000531699

Alangari, A. S., Fatani, F., Binhowaimel, N., et al. (2024). Factors associated with mental illness in a primary healthcare setting in the Kingdom of Saudi Arabia: A case-control study. *Healthcare, 12*, 1298. https://doi.org/10.3390/HEALTHCARE12131298

Alateeq, D., Aldaoud, A., Alhadi, A., et al. (2018). The experience and impact of stigma in Saudi people with a mood disorder. *Annals of General Psychiatry, 17*, 51. https://doi.org/10.1186/S12991-018-0221-3

Alenzi, K. A., Alsheikh, M. Y., Alsuhaibani, D. S., et al. (2024). Medication errors in psychiatric hospitals: A nationwide real-world evidence study in Saudi Arabia. *Pharmaceuticals, 17*, 1514. https://doi.org/10.3390/PH17111514

Alghadeer, S. M., Alhossan, A. M., Al-Arifi, M. N., et al. (2018). Prevalence of mental disorders among patients attending primary health care centers in the capital of Saudi Arabia. *Neurosciences, 23*, 238. https://doi.org/10.17712/NSJ.2018.3.20180058

Alghadir, A. H., Iqbal, A., & Iqbal, Z. A. (2022). Attitude, beliefs, and use of herbal remedies by patients in the Riyadh Region of Saudi Arabia. *Healthcare, 10*, 907. https://doi.org/10.3390/HEALTHCARE10050907

Alghamdi, S. A., Alshahrani, O. M., Alharbi, A. K., et al. (2022). Telepsychiatry: Knowledge, effectiveness, and willingness; assessments of psychiatrists in Saudi Arabia. *Neurosciences Journal, 27*, 79–86. https://doi.org/10.17712/NSJ.2022.2.20210125

Al-Habeeb, A., Altwaijri, Y. A., Al-Subaie, A. S., et al. (2020). Twelve-month treatment of mental disorders in the Saudi National Mental Health Survey. *International Journal of Methods in Psychiatric Research, 29*, Article e1832. https://doi.org/10.1002/MPR.1832

Al-Habeeb, T. (2003). A pilot study of faith healers' views on evil eye, Jinn possession, and magic in the Kingdom of Saudi Arabia. *Journal of Family and Community Medicine, 10*, 31. https://doi.org/10.4103/2230-8229.97830

AlHadi, A. N., Alammari, K. A., Alsiwat, L. J., et al. (2021). Perception of Mental health care professionals in Saudi Arabia on computerized cognitive behavioral therapy: Observational cross-sectional study. *JMIR Formative Research, 5*, Article e26294. https://doi.org/10.2196/26294

Alhamad, A. M. (2003). Physical injuries caused by traditional healers: A report of two psychiatric cases. *Annals of Saudi Medicine, 23*, 289–290. https://doi.org/10.5144/0256-4947.2003.289

Alharbi, A. A., Aljerian, N. A., Binhotan, M. S., et al. (2025). Digital surveillance of mental health care services in Saudi Arabia: Cross-sectional study of national e-Referral system data. *JMIR Public Health and Surveillance, 11*, Article e64257. https://doi.org/10.2196/64257

Alhumaidan, N. I., Alotaibi, T. A., Aloufi, K. S., et al. (2024). Barriers to seeking mental health help in Saudi Arabia: A systematic review. *Cureus, 16*, Article e60363. https://doi.org/10.7759/CUREUS.60363

Alhur, A., Alhur, A. A., Alrkad, E., et al. (2024). Assessing the awareness of psychotropic medications among the saudi population: Benefits, risks, and Prevalence. *Cureus, 16*, Article e66818. https://doi.org/10.7759/CUREUS.66818

Ali, M. M., Taha, M. M., Ahmed, A. E., et al. (2023). Psychotropic medication adherence and its associated factors among schizophrenia patients: Exploring the consistency of adherence scales. *Cureus, 15*, Article e46118. https://doi.org/10.7759/CUREUS.46118

Al-Kahtani, N., Alruwaie, S., Al-Zahrani, B. M., et al. (2022). Digital health transformation in Saudi Arabia: A cross-sectional analysis using Healthcare Information and Management Systems Society' digital health indicators. *Digital Health, 8*, 20552076221117744. https://doi.org/10.1177/20552076221117742

Alkhathami, A. D. (2022). An innovative 5-Step Patient Interview approach for integrating mental healthcare into primary care centre services: A validation study. *Gen Psychiatry, 35*, Article 100693. https://doi.org/10.1136/GPSYCH-2021-100693

Al-Khathami, A. D., Alharbi, L. S., Alomari, S. A., et al. (2025). Integrating mental healthcare into primary healthcare services: Saudi Arabia progress and achievements (1995–2022). *Current Research in Psychiatry, 5*(1), 42–49. https://doi.org/10.46439/PSYCHIATRY.5.035

Almadani, A. H., Alhadi, A. N., Aldawood, B. D., et al. (2025). Bipolar disorders in Saudi Arabia: What do we know so far? *Saudi Journal of Medicine & Medical Sciences, 13*, 1–6. https://doi.org/10.4103/SJMMS.SJMMS_306_24

Almadani, A. H., Altheyab, E. S., Alkheraiji, M. A., et al. (2023). Perceptions and attitudes of mental health professionals toward the Mental Health Care Law in Saudi Arabia. *Healthcare, 11*, 2784. https://doi.org/10.3390/HEALTHCARE11202784

Alosaimi, F. (2021). *Concepts and articles about mental health in Saudi Arabia*. The National Center for Mental Health Promotion.

Alosaimi, F. D., Abalhassan, M., Alhaddad, B., et al. (2017a). Prevalence of metabolic syndrome and its components among patients with various psychiatric diagnoses and treatments: A cross-sectional study. *General Hospital Psychiatry, 45*, 62–69. https://doi.org/10.1016/J.GENHOSPPSYCH.2016.12.007

Alosaimi, F. D., Alzain, N., Asiri, S., et al. (2017b). Patterns of psychiatric diagnoses in inpatient and outpatient psychiatric settings in Saudi Arabia. *Archives of Clinical Psychiatry (São Paulo), 44*, 77–83. https://doi.org/10.1590/0101-60830000000124

Alosaimi, F. D., Alhabbad, A., Abalhassan, M. F., et al. (2016a). Patterns of psychotropic medication use in inpatient and outpatient psychiatric settings in Saudi Arabia. *Neuropsychiatric Disease Treatment, 12*, 897–907. https://doi.org/10.2147/NDT.S100405

Alosaimi, F. D., Alruwais, F. S., Alanazi, F. A., et al. (2016b). Patients reasons for obtaining psychotropic medications without a prescription at retail pharmacies in Central Saudi Arabia. *Neurosciences, 21*, 338. https://doi.org/10.17712/NSJ.2016.4.20160245

Alosaimi, F. D., Alshehri, Y., Alfraih, I., et al. (2015). Psychosocial correlates of using faith healing services in Riyadh, Saudi Arabia: A comparative cross-sectional study. *International Journal of Mental Health Systems, 9*, 1–6. https://doi.org/10.1186/1752-4458-9-8

Alosaimi, F. D., Alshehri, Y., Alfraih, I., et al. (2014). The prevalence of psychiatric disorders among visitors to faith healers in Saudi Arabia. *Pakistan Journal of Medical Sciences, 30*, 1077. https://doi.org/10.12669/PJMS.305.5434

Alqahtani, M. M. J., Alkhamees, H. A., Alkhalaf, A. M., et al. (2021). Toward establishing telepsychology guideline. Turning the challenges of COVID-19 into opportunity. *Ethics, Medicine and Public Health, 16*, Article 100612. https://doi.org/10.1016/j.jemep.2020.100612

Alsabhan, J., Alanazi, A., Alhajaji, R., et al. (2024). Common mental health disorders and their current prescription patterns in Saudi Arabia's primary healthcare settings. *Cureus, 16*, 65562. https://doi.org/10.7759/CUREUS.65562

Al-Subaie, A. (1989). Psychiatry in Saudi Arabia: Cultural perspectives. *Transcultural Psychiatry, 26*, 245–262. https://doi.org/10.1177/136346158902600401

Al-Subaie, A. S., Al-Habeeb, A. H., & Altwaijri, Y. A. (2020). Overview of the Saudi National Mental Health Survey. *International Journal of Methods in Psychiatric Research, 29*, Article e1835. https://doi.org/10.1002/MPR.1835

Al-Sughayir, M. A. (2016). Effect of accreditation on length of stay in psychiatric inpatients: Pre-post accreditation medical record comparison. *International Journal of Mental Health Systems, 10*, 55. https://doi.org/10.1186/S13033-016-0090-6

AlTwaijri, Y., Al-Subaie, A., & Al-Habeeb, A. (2019). Saudi National Mental Health Survey Technical Report. In *Riyadh: King Salman Center for Disability Research*. Retrieved April 11, 2025, from https://faculty.ksu.edu.sa/sites/default/files/saudi_national_mental_health_survey_-_technical_report.pdf.

Altwaijri, Y. A., Al-Habeeb, A., Al-Subaie, A. S., et al. (2020a). Twelve-month prevalence and severity of mental disorders in the Saudi National Mental Health Survey. *International Journal of Methods in Psychiatric Research, 29*(3), Article e1831. https://doi.org/10.1002/MPR.1831

Altwaijri, Y. A., Al-Subaie, A., Al-Habeeb, A., et al. (2020b). Lifetime prevalence and age-of-onset distributions of mental disorders in the Saudi National Mental Health Survey. *International Journal of Methods in Psychiatric Research (In Press)*. https://doi.org/10.1002/mpr.1836

Altwaijri, Y. A., Al-Subaie, A. S., Al-Habeeb, A., et al. (2020c). Lifetime prevalence and age-of-onset distributions of mental disorders in the Saudi National Mental Health Survey. *International Journal of Methods in Psychiatric Research, 29*, Article e1836. https://doi.org/10.1002/MPR.1836

Arroll, B., Roskvist, R., Moir, F., et al. (2023). Antidepressants in primary care: Limited value at the first visit. *World Psychiatry, 22*, 340. https://doi.org/10.1002/WPS.21057

Bindhim, N. F., Althumiri, N. A., Ad-Dab'bagh, Y., et al. (2024a). Exploring mental health literacy and its associated factors: A National Cross-Sectional Study in Saudi Arabia, 2023. *Risk Management and Healthcare Policy, 17*, 355. https://doi.org/10.2147/RMHP.S442425

BinDhim, N. F., Althumiri, N. A., Al-Luhaidan, S. M., et al. (2024b). Assessing attitudes toward mental health illnesses in Saudi Arabia: A national cross-sectional study. *International Journal of Social Psychiatry*. https://doi.org/10.1177/00207640241263247

Brunt, T. J., & Gale-Grant, O. (2023). Telepsychiatry: What clinicians need to know about digital mental healthcare. *Bjpsych Advances, 29*, 230. https://doi.org/10.1192/BJA.2022.42

Chowdhury, S., Mok, D., & Leenen, L. (2021). Transformation of health care and the new model of care in Saudi Arabia: Kingdom's Vision 2030. *Journal of Medicine and Life, 14*, 347–354. https://doi.org/10.25122/JML-2021-0070

CityPopulation. (2025). *Saudi Arabia: Regions & Major Cities—Population Statistics, Maps, Charts, Weather and Web Information*. Retrieved April 4, 2025, from https://www.citypopulation.de/en/saudiarabia/cities/.

Dubovsky, S. L. (1983). Psychiatry in Saudi Arabia. *American Journal of Psychiatry, 140*, 1455–1459. https://doi.org/10.1176/AJP.140.11.1455

Dubovsky, S. L. (2006). Psychiatry in Saudi Arabia. *International Journal of Psychiatry, 140*, 1455–1459. https://doi.org/10.1176/AJP.140.11.1455

Edward Schumacher-Matos. (2012). *The Treadmill of Stigma, Language and Mental Illnesses*. Retrieved April 4, 2025, from https://www.npr.org/sections/publiceditor/2012/03/01/147727385/.

GBD 2019 Mental Disorders Collaborators. (2022). Global, regional, and national burden of 12 mental disorders in 204 countries and territories, 1990–2019: A systematic analysis for the Global Burden of Disease Study 2019. *Lancet Psychiatry, 9*, 137. https://doi.org/10.1016/S2215-0366(21)00395-3

Gearing, R. E., Schwalbe, C. S., Mackenzie, M. J., et al. (2013). Adaptation and translation of mental health interventions in Middle Eastern Arab countries: A systematic review of barriers to and strategies for effective treatment implementation. *International Journal of Social Psychiatry, 59*, 671–681. https://doi.org/10.1177/0020764012452349

General Authority for Statistics. (2022). *Nationality Statistics*. Retrieved April 4, 2025, from https://www.stats.gov.sa/en/w/%D8%A7%D9%84%D8%AC%D9%86%D8%B3%D9%8A%D8%A9-2?category=127396&tab=436327.

General Authority for Statistics. (2024). *Saudi economy grows by 2.8% during Q3 of 2024*. Retrieved April 4, 2025, from https://www.stats.gov.sa/.

Hassab Errasoul, A., & Alarabi, M. A. (2022). Factors predicting serum clozapine levels in Middle Eastern patients: An observational study. *BMC Psychiatry, 22*, 1–8. https://doi.org/10.1186/S12888-022-03910-6/TABLES/4

Holmes, A., & Chang, Y. P. (2022). Effect of mental health collaborative care models on primary care provider outcomes: An integrative review. *Family Practice, 39*, 964–970. https://doi.org/10.1093/FAMPRA/CMAC026

Kattan, W. (2024). The state of primary healthcare centers in Saudi Arabia: A regional analysis for 2022. *PLoS ONE, 19*, Article e0301918. https://doi.org/10.1371/JOURNAL.PONE.0301918

Koenig, H., Al Zaben, F., Sehlo, M., et al. (2013). Current state of psychiatry in Saudi Arabia. *The International Journal of Psychiatry in Medicine, 46*, 223–242. https://doi.org/10.2190/PM.46.3.A

Koenig, H. G., Al Zaben, F., Sehlo, M. G., et al. (2014). Mental Health Care in Saudi Arabia: Past, present and future. *Open Journal of Psychiatry, 4*, 113. https://doi.org/10.4236/ojpsych.2014.42016

Lee, E., Bruckner, T. A., Alluhidan, M., et al. (2024). Workforce estimate to treat mental disorders in the Kingdom of Saudi Arabia. *Human Resources for Health, 22*, 51. https://doi.org/10.1186/S12960-024-00929-6

Lyons, P., Edwardes, A., Bladon, L., & Abel, K. M. (2025). Culturally sensitive mental health research: A scoping review. *BMC Psychiatry, 25*, 190. https://doi.org/10.1186/S12888-025-06575-Z

Ministry of Health. (2022). *Telemedicine*. Retrieved April 4, 2025, from https://www.moh.gov.sa/en/Ministry/Information-and-services/Pages/Telemedicine.aspx.

Mneimneh, Z. N., Heeringa, S. G., Lin, Y. C., et al. (2020). The Saudi National Mental Health Survey: Sample design and weight development. *International Journal of Methods in Psychiatric Research, 29*, Article e1829. https://doi.org/10.1002/MPR.1829

Mohamed, A. A., Alomair, S. M., Alnijadi, A. A., et al. (2024). Barriers to mental illness treatment in Saudi Arabia: A population-based cross-sectional study. *Cureus, 16*, Article e53797. https://doi.org/10.7759/CUREUS.53797

National Center for Mental Health Promotion (NCMH). (2023). *National Mental Health Policies in the Kingdom of Saudi Arabia*. Retrieved April 4, 2025, from https://ncmh.org.sa/

Olagunju, A. T., Wang, J., Edet, B., et al. (2025). Racial and ethnic considerations for the clinical practice of psychopharmacology and research methodology: A narrative review of the growing body of literature. *Journal of Psychiatric Practice, 31*, 56–64. https://doi.org/10.1097/PRA.0000000000000845

Qureshi, N. A., Al-Habeeb, A. A., & Koenig, H. G. (2013). Mental health system in Saudi Arabia: An overview. *Neuropsychiatric Disease and Treatment, 9*, 1121. https://doi.org/10.2147/NDT.S48782

sabq News. (2019). *Where is the stigma in "Al-Amal"? Controversy over renaming psychiatric complexes to "Eradah": Experts assert the new designation implies disability and does not serve those seeking treatment*. Retrieved April 30, 2025, from https://sabq.org/saudia/msfdvl.

Safiri, S., Noori, M., Nejadghaderi, S. A., et al. (2024). The burden of schizophrenia in the Middle East and North Africa region, 1990–2019. *Scientific Reports, 14*, 1–13. https://doi.org/10.1038/s41598-024-59905-8

Saudi Press Agency. (2018). *Preparing Inpatient Wards for Psychiatric Patients in General and Specialized Hospitals*. Retrieved April 4, 2025, from https://www.spa.gov.sa/1845302.

Senitan, M., Alhabeeb, A. A., Althumairi, N. A., et al. (2024). Perceptions of mental disorder causes, treatments, and prevention among the general population in Saudi Arabia. *Front Psychiatry, 15*, 1404957. https://doi.org/10.3389/FPSYT.2024.1404957

Shahin, S. H., & Daly, E. B. (1999). Knowledge, attitudes and beliefs about psychotropic medication among Saudi hospitalized psychiatric patients. *International Journal of Nursing Studies, 36*, 51–55. https://doi.org/10.1016/S0020-7489(98)00057-1

Surrati, A., Harbi, N., Surrati, H., et al. (2020). Medication non-adherence factors and difficulties among psychiatric patients in Madinah. *Majmaah Journal of Health Sciences, 8*, 47. https://doi.org/10.5455/mjhs.2020.03.007

Vanderlip, E. R., Rundell. J., Avery, M., et al. (2016). *Dissemination of integrated care within adult primary care settings: The collaborative care model*. Retrieved April 30, 2025, from https://www.psychiatry.org/File%20Library/Psychiatrists/Practice/Professional-Topics/Integrated-Care/APA-APM-Dissemination-Integrated-Care-Report.pdf.

Vos, T., Abajobir, A. A., Abbafati, C., et al. (2017). Global, regional, and national incidence, prevalence, and years lived with disability for 328 diseases and injuries for 195 countries, 1990–2016: A systematic analysis for the Global Burden of Disease Study 2016. *The Lancet, 390*, 1211–1259. https://doi.org/10.1016/S0140-6736(17)32154-2

Wahass, S., & Kent, G. (1997). A comparison of public attitudes in Britain and Saudi Arabia towards auditory hallucinations. *International Journal of Social and Psychiatry, 43*, 175–183. https://doi.org/10.1177/002076409704300303

Walston, S. L., Al-Harbi, Y., & Al-Omar, B. (2008). The changing face of healthcare in Saudi Arabia. *Annals of Saudi Medicine, 28*, 243. https://doi.org/10.5144/0256-4947.2008.243

World Health Organization. (2025). *Saudi Arabia*. Retrieved April 4, 2025, from https://data.who.int/countries/682.

World Health Organization. (2020a). Life expectancy at birth (years). In *World Health Organization*. Retrieved April 30, 2025, from https://www.who.int/data/gho/data/indicators/indicator-details/GHO/life-expectancy-at-birth-(years).

World Health Organization. (2020b). *Mental Health Atlas 2020 Country Profile: Saudi Arabia*. Retrieved April 14, 2025, from https://www.who.int/publications/m/item/mental-health-atlas-sau-2020-country-profile.

World Health Organization WHO. (2021). The Global Health Observatory: Suicide rates. In *Mortality and global health estimates: Suicide rates*. Retrieved April 4, 2025, from https://www.who.int/data/gho/data/themes/topics/indicator-groups/indicator-group-details/GHO/gho-ghe-mortality-suicide-rate-estimates.

Chapter 13
Mental Health Care in Syria

Laetitia Gerbaka, Feten Fekih-Romdhane, Souheil Hallit, and Sahar Obeid

Abstract Syria is a Middle Eastern country that has recently suffered from several political and economic crises. This has resulted in a high prevalence of mental struggles and disorders among the Syrian population, the most frequent being stress, anxiety, depression, and Post-Traumatic Stress Disorder, with almost 85% of Syrians suffering from the latter. However, the preparedness of the country to meet these needs for mental health care is limited. This chapter begins with the presentation of Syria, noting the evolution of its mental health services, and also tackles the epidemiology of mental illness in this country. Afterward, the chapter discusses the current state of the mental health care sector in Syria, highlighting challenges that it is facing, and then presenting ways out of the limited access to and scarce resources in mental health care in Syria. Challenges included poor research and funding, lack of education about mental health and thus high stigma about the topic, restricted access to mental health services, fleeing of professionals post-war, over-the-counter psychotropic sales, gaps

L. Gerbaka · S. Obeid (✉)
Department of Psychology and Education, School of Arts and Sciences, Lebanese American University, Jbeil, Lebanon

L. Gerbaka
e-mail: Laetitia.gerbaka@lau.edu

F. Fekih-Romdhane
The Tunisian Center of Early Intervention in Psychosis, Department of Psychiatry "Ibn Omrane", Razi Hospital, Manouba, Tunisia

Faculty of Medicine of Tunis, Tunis El Manar University, Tunis, Tunisia

F. Fekih-Romdhane
e-mail: feten.fekih@gmail.com

S. Hallit
School of Medicine and Medical Sciences, Holy Spirit University of Kaslik, P.O. Box 446, Jounieh, Lebanon
e-mail: souheilhallit@usek.edu.lb

Department of Psychology, College of Humanities, Effat University, Jeddah, Saudi Arabia

Applied Science Research Center, Applied Science Private University, Amman, Jordan

S. Al-Huseini and S. M. Y. Arafat (eds.), *Mental Health Care in the Middle East*, South Asian Perspectives in Mental Health and Psychology ,
https://doi.org/10.1007/978-981-95-0461-9_13

in the distribution of treatment to the population, and disruption of basic services. Later, ways to manage and improve this state and these services are explained.

Keywords Syria · Mental health · Mental health services · Psychiatric services · Challenges in mental health care · Improvement of mental health care

1 Introduction

1.1 Country Profile

Located on the Mediterranean Sea, Syria represents one of the largest Middle Eastern countries, with a total area of 187,437 km^2, surrounded by Lebanon, Turkey, Iraq, Jordan, and Israel/Occupied Palestine (Adra & Duchonova, 2024; CIA, 2025; El Arnaout et al., 2019). The country is internationally known for its natural resources, such as petroleum, asphalt, marble, rock salt, and more, as well as its wide renewable water resources and major rivers, thus making it an attractive hub in the Middle East (Al-Ansari et al., 2019; Al-Bashaireh & Lazzarini, 2016; Aldahik et al., 2017; Ali & Sadek, 2013; CIA, 2025; Jassim & AL-Badri, 2019; Kattan, 2015). With a relatively large population of more than 23 million coming from different religions such as Muslim, Christian, or Druze, or ethnic groups, and who speak various languages, be it Arabic, English, French, Armenian, and Kurdish, Syria and its people undeniably have a rich cultural background and history (Adamczyk & Jomma, 2021; Bolton, 2020; CIA, 2025; Lakitsch, 2018). Yet, before becoming an independent country in 1946, it went through Ottoman colonization, French mandates, and several conflicts with different countries, until it became the Syrian Arab Republic of today, with Damascus as its capital (CIA, 2025; Khoury, 2014; Pierret, 2016, 2018; Reilly, 2020). It has been governed by the Al-Assad family since then, with the reign having been transferred from Hafiz Al-Assad to his son Bachar in 2000, who governed the country during its last civil war, which broke out in 2011 (CIA, 2025; Droz-Vincent, 2016; Mowafi & Leaning, 2018). However, the government established by Al-Assad was overturned at the end of 2024 by the Syrian Islamist movement, as tensions arose and opinions divided, leading to a period of instability in the country that remains unresolved (CIA, 2025; European Council on Refugees and Exiles, 2024). Millions have thus fled the country since both events (Hudson, 2018; Ilcan, 2018; Yazgan et al., 2015; Zisser, 2019), yet exact records about the country's economic, financial, social, or psychological situations remain undocumented. Nonetheless, before this event and since the civil war, the country had been going through debilitating inflation, unemployment, and poverty, with more than 80% of the population below the poverty line and damage to electrical and telecommunication infrastructure, which often left the population without these services (Badran, 2021; Buckner & Saba, 2010; CIA, 2025; Hamati, 2020; Muzzall et al., 2021; Nasan & Szpytko, 2020; Omar et al., 2020; Turkmani & Mehchy, 2020). Moreover, even the country's medical and health services often do not satisfy the needs of the population: for example, the physician density is around 1.3 physicians per 1000 inhabitants (Abbara et al., 2021; CIA, 2025; Taleb et al., 2015). Therefore, a wide array of services in the country needs to be tackled and improved, one of them surely being the mental health sector.

1.2 Evolution of Psychiatric Services in Syria

1.2.1 Pre-Syrian Arab Republic

Prior to the establishment of the Syrian Arab Republic that we know today, i.e., before the year 1946, the mental health sector of the country—similarly to all others—was ruled and controlled by the colonizers, whether it was under the Ottoman colonization or the French mandate (Neep, 2012; Ouahes, 2018; Reilly, 2020; Roussos, 2021). During this period, mental health was majorly stigmatized and its care and provision were significantly neglected, leaving a major part of the population untreated and struggling (Tsacoyianis, 2014). However, these services were not completely erased from the Syrian grounds, as some distinguished individuals acted upon that need for mental health services. Among them was Mr. Theophilus Waldmeier, who, in 1896, began providing mental health services for patients with mental disorders in the country (Assalman et al., 2008; Katchadourian, 1980; Launchbury, 2021). While his work impacted many, the national services were still lacking, as governmental institutions were still not providing funding for the psychiatric sector. Indeed, in 1922, Syria only had a single psychiatric hospital, proving that the resources for mental health services were severely scarce, leaving many patients' needs in this aspect unmet (Rafeq, 2015; Tsacoyianis, 2021). This hospital was visited by a professional, who described its services as not only very primitive, but even barbaric and abusive, observing chained patients among other things (Assalman et al., 2008).

1.2.2 After the Establishment of the Syrian Arab Republic

It was only after the independence gained by Syria and the establishment of the Syrian Arab Republic that mental health started being better acknowledged by the government and its services, whose Ministry of Health issued legislation in 1981 targeting the subject, from which the current mental health and psychiatric services of today are derived (Assalman et al., 2008; Gharaibeh & Amarica, 2008; Okasha et al., 2012). In 1996, the Syrian Psychiatric Association was created, to which most practitioners now adhere and organizes medical education and training for future members and professionals (Assalman et al., 2008; Hedar, 2017). In 2001, the Ministry of Health created a Psychiatric Directorate to tackle the issue surrounding mental health and the country's psychiatric services (Assalman et al., 2008; Gharaibeh & Amarica, 2008). Under this directorate, a decision was taken that after the professional referral of a patient, a committee of three psychiatrists must decide whether or not this patient needs or can be admitted to a psychiatric ward, decision which will be revised by the same committee a week after this admission who will also set the treatment plan (Assalman et al., 2008).

1.2.3 Public Psychiatric Services in Syria

Moreover, under this independent regime, two public psychiatric hospitals were established, Ibn Sina Hospital in Damascus, which has 800 beds, 600 for men and 200 for women, and Ibn Khaldoun Hospital in Aleppo, with 400 beds, 250 for male patients and 150 for female ones: both hospitals focused on psychiatric treatment and mental health services (Abou-Saleh & Mobayed, 2013; Assalman et al., 2008). An addiction center was also built in Damascus, Ibn Rushd Hospital, with a 30-person capacity (Abou-Saleh & Mobayed, 2013; Assalman et al., 2008; Hedar, 2017). Outpatient clinics have also been made available since the country's independence, which are distributed across the country's main cities and are run by professional psychiatrists under the national Ministry of Health (Assalman et al., 2008; Hedar, 2017; Shoib et al., 2022). Another public psychiatric ward is present at the Damascus University Hospital, and its main purpose is to train future psychologists and psychiatrists (Assalman et al., 2008; Sayed-Hassan et al., 2012). However, it is important to note that a severe shortage of psychiatrists in the country has been recorded, highlighting the importance of adapting the curriculum taken by these students for both the improvement of the services provided and the empowerment and encouragement of these students to go into this field (Albaba & Sahloul, 2023; Latifeh & Dashash, 2016; Latifeh et al., 2021).

1.2.4 Private Psychiatric Services in Syria

As for the private psychiatric sector, one private hospital is found in Damascus and services for both long-term and acute mental disorders are available, including specialized services for children suffering from autism (Assalman et al., 2008; Tsacoyianis, 2014). Many psychiatrists also run their private clinics across the country, the most being located in Damascus (Abou-Saleh & Mobayed, 2013; Assalman et al., 2008; Hamza & Hicks, 2021; Hedar, 2017). It is important to note that until 2008, adult psychiatry was a significantly bigger focus of the field, highly neglecting the child and adolescent aspects, as very few psychiatrists specialize in this subfield (Assalman et al., 2008; Clausen et al., 2020). In addition to that, even considering adult psychiatry, before the civil war, there were only 70 trained psychiatrists in Syria for the 22 million inhabitants, showing the extreme shortage of professionals and the significant lack of psychiatric resources in the country (Abbara et al., 2016; Hedar, 2017; Latifeh et al., 2021). The number declined to only twenty-seven in 2020 (WHO, 2020).

1.2.5 Post-civil War in 2011

Considering that the psychiatric services in Syria were already limited prior to the civil war that started in 2011, it is undeniable that these services were weakened even more as a result of the conflict, which caused massive destruction across the country, including to those sectors as attacks were made on the psychiatric facilities (Abbara et al., 2023; Albaba & Sahloul, 2023; Hamza & Hicks, 2021; Kakaje et al., 2021; Latifeh et al., 2021; Shoib et al., 2022). However, international help was provided, such as healthcare by expatriates or telepsychiatry by Arabic-speaking professionals through the Syrian American Medical Society (SAMS) and by the Syrian Expatriates Medical Association (Abbara et al., 2016; Hamza & Hicks, 2021; Nassan et al., 2015). Nonetheless, even with the implementation of these Mental Healthcare and Psychosocial Support services, psychiatric problems were on the rise and the help was limited, considering that the sociocultural factors constituted an obstacle and barrier as well (Hamza & Hicks, 2021). Moreover, it is crucial to note that many of the country's psychiatrists and professionals fled the country during the war, aggravating the amplitude of the preexisting shortage problem (Kallström et al., 2021; Latifeh et al., 2021; Shoib et al., 2022).

1.2.6 Mental Health Act

Finally, a Mental Health Act for Syria has been in progress for several years but has not yet been implemented (Assalman et al., 2008): its application could have a major positive impact on the improvement of the psychiatric and mental health services of the country, increasing the involvement of the government in the sector and thus potentially facilitating the access of the public to these crucial services.

2 Epidemiology and Burden of Mental Illness in Syria

The various crises and hardships that the Syrian population has been through over the past decades have clearly taken a toll on the mental health of the inhabitants, leading to the decline of the latter on average, creating a real burden of mental disorders in the country (Albaba & Sahloul, 2023; Hendrickx et al., 2020). Indeed, while the research and statistics are not wide, psychological distress has been noted for several years in Syria: for example, even in 2006, mental illnesses were recorded to be contributing to the causes of mortality among the inhabitants, also noting that more than 55% of Syrians were already suffering from psychiatric distress—without mental disorder diagnoses categorization (Abou-Saleh & Hughes, 2015; Assalman et al., 2008). Through the years, more data has proven that the rate of mental illness among the Syrian population has become a serious problem, with several disorders on the rise, especially after the civil war of 2011, the most severe and prevalent being post-traumatic stress disorder (PTSD), with levels ranging from

16 to 84%—a concerning rate—stress, anxiety, and depression (Abbara et al., 2016; Albaba & Sahloul, 2023; Ghumman et al., 2016; Hassan, 2019; Hendrickx et al., 2020; Kakaje et al., 2021; Latifeh et al., 2021; Nassan et al., 2015). Furthermore, the general prevalence of mental disorders among the Syrian population also constitutes a worrying number, as only 11% of the whole population tests negative for any mental disorder, with almost 45% of it exhibiting symptoms of severe mental disorders (Albaba & Sahloul, 2023). Additionally, the crisis also caused an augmentation in suicidal ideation and suicidal attempts, also inducing an escalation in the number of psychiatric hospitalizations among Syrians (Lama et al., 2016). It is important to note that suicide attempts are considered a crime in Syria (Adra & Duchonova, 2024; Almidani et al., 2024; Hamza & Hicks, 2021; Rayes et al., 2022). These serious numbers, related to the very low number of psychiatrists available in the country, especially post-crisis, show that most of these psychiatric cases are not followed up by professionals or even treated in the first place, with around 90% of severe cases not receiving the support and help they need (Hedar, 2017). Indeed, suicidality in Syria has become an increasingly severe problem, with suicidal ideation and behaviors noted among many individuals (Adra & Duchonova, 2024; Almidani et al., 2024; Lama et al., 2016; Swed et al., 2022). The main recorded factors behind suicidality in the country, besides the civil war (Lama et al., 2016; Selmo et al., 2021), range from sex and age—young females—to interpersonal and familial characteristics such as forced early marriages, domestic violence, or conflicts with partners, to socioeconomic factors like poverty or illiteracy, and even to personality traits and emotions like impulsivity, hopelessness, helplessness and trauma (Adra & Duchonova, 2024; Almidani et al., 2024; Swed et al., 2022). This once again raises the concern of the lack of involvement or implication of the Syrian government in the mental health of its population, calling for an improvement in the system of this sector (Swed et al., 2022).

In addition to that, as previously stated, most if not all of Syrian psychiatrists on ground are specialized in adult psychiatry, thus depriving the whole population of children and adolescents of psychiatric and mental health care, considering this group does suffer from many intellectual and developmental problems, as well as severe trauma, with most children having witnessed or even experienced atrocities (Hamza & Hicks, 2021; Hassan et al., 2016; Hedar, 2017; Kakaje et al., 2021). For example, Hamza and Hicks (2021) note that 60% of school-aged Syrian children suffer from at least one psychological disorder, the most frequent being PTSD, this trauma showing in various ways such as bedwetting, inactivity, or even the loss of their will to live. Separately, it is also crucial to note that, unfortunately, even setting the crises aside, Syrian women are prone to have suffered from physical and sexual abuse in terms of domestic abuse, child exploitation, and more, leaving them at severe risk for mental distress and trauma (Hamza & Hicks, 2021; Hedar, 2017).

Furthermore, substance abuse is another problem that the Syrian population struggles with, be it alcohol or other substances such as cannabis, opioids, or heroin (Abazid et al., 2020, 2023). Indeed, post-Syrian war, these rates of substance abuse among Syrians increased, which could be a result of trauma, of a need for an escape, or even to relieve pain in the case of opioid abuse (Abazid, 2022; Abazid et al., 2023).

Other factors that could come into play in the onset of drug abuse among Syrians are also academic failure, negative peer influence, and poor family situations (Abazid, 2022; Abazid et al., 2020, 2023; Alhyas et al., 2015; Eteish, 2024; Rasmussen et al., 2022). Additionally, this problem is widened by the combination of substances that are declared to be used by Syrians, as reports show that drug use is often paired with cigarette smoking (almost 80%) and/or drinking alcohol (57.3%) (Abazid et al., 2023). This problem is also aggravated by the idea that many Syrian drug users have that this practice does not necessarily lead to addiction, which was reported by more than half of the participants in the study conducted by Abazid et al. (2023). Considering once again that there is only one addiction rehabilitation center in Syria, only allowing for a 30-person capacity, the resources available for these struggling individuals are insufficient and need to be improved by the government to tailor to the needs of the population (Abou-Saleh & Mobayed, 2013; Assalman et al., 2008; Hedar, 2017). It is also important to note that substance abuse in Syria also includes the misuse, abuse, or unprescribed use of medications, be it psychotropics or others, which is also common in the country, thus needing higher control and attention from the government (Alaryan et al., 2021; Aljerf, 2017; Al Mais, 2023; Alsheikh et al., 2021; Bastaki et al., 2021; Chiappini & Schifano, 2020; Chiappini et al., 2020; Deeb et al., 2022; Jobnah et al., 2024; Latifeh et al., 2021; Rachidi et al., 2023; Schifano et al., 2021; Ward et al., 2013; Ylä-Rautio et al., 2020).

3 Mental Health Services in Syria

3.1 Conventional Services

While the stigma and taboo around mental health and specifically psychotherapy is still widely present in the Arab world including in Syria (Bär et al., 2021; Hamza & Hicks, 2021; Merhej, 2019; Özaslan et al., 2024; Shoib et al., 2022; Swed et al., 2022; Zolezzi et al., 2018), individuals' awareness of the importance of mental health has been increasing, especially after the struggles that the population has been through, bringing about the impending need to treat its repercussions, which is proven by their acceptance of provided help (Abou-Saleh & Hughes, 2015; Bou-Orm et al., 2023; Hassan et al., 2016; Hendrickx et al., 2020). However, these feelings of shame around psychotherapy still majorly affect the population's openness to the topic, resulting in a severe lack of data and research around the prevalence, availability, and access to psychotherapy in Syrian grounds. This could be related to the considerable ease of psychotropic treatment as opposed to psychotherapy, or to the similarity of psychiatry with physical health medication, relatively relieving the taboo and stigma around it. The internalization of this taboo and stigma around mental health and psychotherapy in the Arab world is also proven by the fact that psychological support and therapy are much more widely studied on Syrian refugees rather than Syrian inhabitants, as the former may become more open and accepting of the idea when surrounded by a culture that is educated about and comfortable with therapy (Ashfaq et al., 2020; Böge et al., 2022; Karnouk et al., 2019; Nakeyar & Frewen, 2016; Öztürk et al., 2024; Schlechter et al., 2023; Selmo et al., 2021; Sijbrandij et al., 2017; Yılmaz et al., 2024).

However, while psychiatric services are more widespread in Syria, they are still significantly scarce, as previously stated. Indeed, there are only two public psychiatric hospitals in Syria: Ibn Sina in Damascus with a 600-patient capacity, and Ibn Khaldoun in Aleppo, which can welcome 400 patients (Abou-Saleh & Mobayed, 2013; Assalman et al., 2008), along with an addiction center with 30 beds and a psychiatric ward in Damascus University Hospital (Abou-Saleh & Mobayed, 2013; Assalman et al., 2008; Hedar, 2017; Sayed-Hassan et al., 2012). The total number of mental health hospitals in Syria is thus three, a severely low number for such a large country (WHO, 2020). While the exact number of psychiatric hospitalizations in Syria is unknown, an approximate number of 1400 was set for 2020 (WHO, 2020), and it is certain that the need for it is much higher than the available beds and resources in the country, leaving a significant part of the population untreated (Abou-Saleh & Mobayed, 2013; Lama et al., 2016; Mowafi et al., 2016; Shoib et al., 2022). Furthermore, reports for the number of professionals working in the country were published by the World Health Organization in 2020 (WHO, 2020), that revealed that only 27 psychiatrists were working in the country, with 197 mental health nurses, 2955 psychologists, 2053 social workers, and 1127 other mental health providers, with a total of 7259 mental health professional on Syrian grounds (WHO, 2020). It is important to understand the scarcity of these resources as compared to the country's size and population, as the total number of mental health professionals results in around 43 providers for 100,000 Syrians (WHO, 2020).

Nonetheless, Syrian Non-Governmental Organizations (NGOs) have been offering their services to alleviate the burden of mental health and mental disorders among the Syrian population, providing the services of their professionals to support those in need on the grounds, for example, in specialized centers, teaching their patients to manage their symptoms or struggles and helping them improve their resilience (Almoshmosh et al., 2016).

In addition to that, the Syrian Association for Mental Health (SAMH) is also a nonprofit organization that works on the implementation of psychiatric and psychosocial programs and interventions in the country, to facilitate the inhabitants' access to psychotropic medications, to provide support to individuals who suffer from mental disorders or who have been through hardships such as sexual abuse, as well as to organize workshops to train future professionals in the country (Abou-Saleh & Hughes, 2015).

However, the disregard and lack of importance given to mental health by the Syrian government is still clear and overwhelming, which is highlighted by the fact that the governmental budget for mental health only consists of 2% of the total national health budget, proving once again that mental health does not represent a priority for the Syrian regime (Hendrickx et al., 2020; Okasha et al., 2012; Sijbrandij et al., 2017; Taha, 2022). It is also important to consider again that the services provided by this slim budget were severely affected by the 2011 civil war, as many of the mental health facilities were attacked and destroyed (Bou-Orm et al., 2023; Hedar, 2017; Kakaje et al., 2021; Latifeh et al., 2021).

3.2 Humanitarian Mental Health Services Post-civil War

Moreover, important humanitarian care was provided post-civil war, such as the aforementioned Mental Healthcare and Psychosocial Support (MHPSS) program implemented on the grounds, along with many other similar ones (Abou-Saleh & Hughes, 2015; Bou-Orm et al., 2023; Hassan et al., 2016; Hendrickx et al., 2020). These services allowed the targeted population to understand and manage their emotions better, such as anger, nervousness, or anxiety, and to know more about their symptoms should they have been suffering from any type of mental disorder, going from anxiety disorder, to depression, PTSD, and even suicidality (Hendrickx et al., 2020). These interventions included different types of therapy that ranged from Cognitive Behavioral Therapy (CBT), art therapy, Eye Movement Desensitization Reprocessing (EMDR), Psychological First Aid (PFA), and more, allowing for them to be varied, personalized and tailored to the cases (Hassan et al., 2016; Hendrickx et al., 2020).

Additionally, the World Health Organization (WHO) intervened to implement a specialized program for mental health in Syria, named the WHO Mental Health Gap Action Programme, which aimed at training medical doctors in Syrian hospitals and centers to understand and manage the ten most common mental disorders, i.e., PTSD, depression, suicidality, addiction, psychosis, developmental disorders such as autism, behavioral disorders in childhood, epilepsy and neurodevelopmental disorders such as Alzheimer's (Hedar, 2017). The WHO also applied a training program for psychologists in Syria, to train them to practice Cognitive Behavioral Therapy, family therapy, and Psychological First Aid (Hedar, 2017). The organization is also developing a school program aimed at emphasizing the role of teachers in supporting students' mental health. The program will introduce teachers to common mental health disorders, equipping them with the knowledge to recognize and respond to these issues effectively within the classroom and broader school environment (Hedar, 2017).

3.3 New Developments: Tele-Psychiatry

As previously mentioned, telepsychiatry, the virtual consultation of a psychiatrist through videoconferencing from a remote location (Alhur & Alhur, 2022; Chan et al., 2015; El Hayek et al., 2020; Farrell et al., 2022; García-Lizana & Muñoz-Mayorga, 2010; Hilty et al., 2002; Nassan et al., 2015), has been spreading since the COVID-19 pandemic and is being increasingly applied and adapted in Syria, (Jefee-Bahloul et al., 2016a, 2016b; Nassan et al., 2015; Parkes et al., 2022). For example, telepsychiatry has made its way to the WHO interventions implemented in the country (Nassan et al., 2015). Indeed, with the scarcity of psychiatric resources in the country and with the severely low number of psychiatry professionals on the grounds (Albaba & Sahloul, 2023; Assalman et al., 2008; Latifeh & Dashash, 2016; Latifeh et al., 2021), telepsychiatry provides an interesting solution to facilitate access of the Syrian population to psychiatric services without geographical barriers and transportation obstacles (Chan et al., 2015; Hassan & Sharif, 2019; Hubley et al., 2016; Kim et al., 2024; Penaskovic et al., 2022). Therefore, this practice offers a cost-effective solution, while being as efficient and accurate as face-to-face psychiatry, also ensuring patient satisfaction (Abbasy, 2020; Chan et al., 2015; Gajarawala & Pelowski, 2021; García-Lizana & Muñoz-Mayorga, 2010; Nassan et al., 2015; Waugh et al., 2015). However, this approach does present certain disadvantages and limitations. Many Syrians in need of psychiatric support lack the necessary equipment or internet access to attend videoconference sessions. Additionally, frequent electricity shortages and internet disruptions in Syria further hinder the effectiveness of this method (Al Halabi et al., 2021; El Hayek et al., 2020; Hassan & Sharif, 2019; Hendrickx et al, 2020; Jefee-Bahloul & Zayour, 2017; Omar et al., 2020; West, 2016). In addition to that, telepsychiatry seems to be more accessible and offered for Syrian refugees, as many studies and interventions have been implemented on this population—rather than on the Syrian inhabitants—ranging from telepsychiatry to CBT "e-mental health" interventions (Ashfaq et al., 2020; Hamza & Hicks, 2021; Hassan, 2019; Hassan & Sharif, 2019; Jefee-Bahloul & Zayour, 2017; Moustafa, 2015; Sijbrandij et al., 2017). It is also important to note that in this situation, cultural differences could constitute an obstacle if the psychiatrist is not Syrian or Arab, and language barriers could also be problematic, as the patient would need an interpreter, which is difficult and could also interfere with and jeopardize the therapeutic relationship (Ashfaq et al., 2020; Disney et al., 2021; El-Refaay et al., 2024; Hassan & Sharif, 2019; Jefee-Bahloul et al., 2014; Kerbage et al., 2020; Liem et al., 2021; Moustafa, 2015; Nassan et al., 2015).

4 Challenges of Mental Health Care

4.1 Poor Funding and Research

While some NGOs in Syria are putting in efforts, budget, and funding into improving the state of the mental healthcare system in the country, the Syrian government itself does not play a big role in the change and amelioration of this sector (Alhaffar & Janos, 2021; Almoshmosh et al., 2016; Jamal et al., 2020). Indeed, as previously stated, only a small fraction of the total national health budget is directed towards mental health, proving once again that this aspect of health is not prioritized and is significantly disregarded (Almoshmosh et al., 2016; Hendrickx et al., 2020; Okasha et al., 2012; Sijbrandij et al., 2017; Taha, 2022). Furthermore, much of the mental healthcare work in Syria is provided by international humanitarian services, such as the MHPSS programs implemented by the WHO and other organizations (Abou-Saleh & Hughes, 2015; Bou-Orm et al., 2023; Cratsley et al., 2021; Hassan et al., 2016; Hedar, 2017; Hendrickx et al., 2020). Even the World Federation for Mental Health (WFMH) has made a call to action in regards to the complex and urgent state of Syrian inhabitants' mental health, highlighting simultaneously the imperative need for mental healthcare in the country and the lack of involvement from the state (Abou-Saleh & Mobayed, 2013). Additionally, most of the research about mental health in Syria is done by internationals or Syrian expatriates, also showing the lack of funding from and research by the Syrian government (Cratsley et al., 2021; Hamza & Hicks, 2021; Hendrickx et al., 2020; Jefee-Bahloul & Khoshnood, 2014). In fact, only 1% of global peer-reviewed research in mental health is produced in the Arab World (Maalouf et al., 2019). Therefore, this leads to much wider literature about Syrian refugees' mental health instead of Syrian inhabitants' (Abou-Saleh & Hughes, 2015; Ashfaq et al., 2020; Hamza & Hicks, 2021; Hassan, 2019; Hassan & Sharif, 2019; Jefee-Bahloul & Zayour, 2017; Moustafa, 2015; Renner et al., 2020; Sijbrandij et al., 2017; Sirin & Rodgers-Sirin, 2015; Smeekes et al., 2017), even though studies have underlined the latter's greater psychological distress than that of refugees (Kakaje et al., 2021).

4.2 *Poor Mental Health Literacy and High Stigma*

In Syria, similarly to the rest of the Middle East and the Arab World, stigma around mental health, psychiatry, psychotherapy, and more is still omnipresent and very frequent (Bär et al., 2021; Merhej, 2019; Swed et al., 2022; Zolezzi et al., 2018). Indeed, Syrians still perceive receiving mental health care and psychological or psychiatric support as shameful, taboo, or even niche, thus making them reluctant to seek this help initially, thus prolonging their suffering (Assalman et al., 2008; Ashfaq et al., 2020; Yalim & Kim, 2018). In fact, in their article tackling the subject of mental health professionals specifically, Hamid et al. (2020) merge both data and personal experiences to explain the extent of this stigmatization in Syria, as it results in a reticence from the patient, but also a negative effect on the therapeutic relationship as well should it eventually take place.

Additionally, other stigma and taboos that are present in the Syrian society play a role in Syrian's perspectives and views of mental health care, such as the social perception of women in Syria and the internalization of gender roles and behaviors (Hendrickx et al., 2020). For example, Hendrickx et al. (2020) explain that in some cases the gender of the mental health professional plays a role, as some husbands refuse for their wife to consult a male psychiatrist, thus not allowing them to participate in the Eye Movement Desensitization and Reprocessing (EMDR) pilot conducted by the authors.

4.3 Restricted Access to Mental Health Services

The Syrian Arab Republic also suffers, as previously mentioned, from a restricted access to mental health services which is due to the scarcity of available resources, be it psychiatric hospitals or wards, psychotherapy clinics, mental health programs implementation, child and adolescent psychology services, and more, adding to that the destruction of mental health care facilities after the civil war (Abbara et al., 2016; Abou-Saleh & Mobayed, 2013; Albaba & Sahloul, 2023; Assalman et al., 2008; Clausen et al., 2020; Hamza & Hicks, 2021; Hedar, 2017; Kakaje et al., 2021; Latifeh et al., 2021; Shoib et al., 2022). Therefore, the inhabitants requiring psychiatric admission would have to be among the very few who do get admitted, considering the restricted number of beds in the wards, would have to find a psychiatrist or psychologist aboard considering the shortage of professionals and do telepsychiatry, which has many disadvantages, and more thus facing several challenges to access a service that should be easily available to all citizens (Abou-Saleh & Mobayed, 2013; Cratsley et al., 2021; Hassan, 2019; Hendrickx et al., 2020; Jamal et al., 2020; Shoib et al., 2022).

4.4 Fleeing of Professionals

Furthermore, the 2011 civil war, which caused widespread destruction and deep psychological trauma while severely damaging all sectors of the country, led many to flee, including numerous mental health professionals, particularly psychiatrists (Jamal et al., 2020; Kallström et al., 2021; Latifeh et al., 2021; Shoib et al., 2022). Therefore, the country that was already suffering from a shortage of mental health professionals was left with even fewer medical staff to service the inhabitants and to provide the required psychiatric and psychological services, thus reinforcing the already-existing gap between the number of professionals to the Syrian population (Abbara et al., 2016; Dewachi et al., 2014; Hamza & Hicks, 2021; Hedar, 2017; Latifeh et al., 2021).

4.5 Over-The-Counter Prescriptions and Misuse of Prescribed Medication

Moreover, the prescription of psychotropic medications over-the-counter has also become a common practice in Syria, as many people self-diagnose with several mental disorders and even prescribe themselves medication for them (Alaryan et al., 2021; Aljerf, 2017; Al Mais, 2023; Alsheikh et al., 2021; Bastaki et al., 2021; Deeb et al., 2022; Jobnah et al., 2024; Latifeh et al., 2021; Rachidi et al., 2023; Ward et al., 2013). This represents a severe problem for several reasons, a few of them being the high likelihood of misdiagnosis, the danger in not taking the right medication or the right dosage for a certain disorder, potentially leading to misuse or abuse, the lack of governmental control over the sales of unprescribed medication, and more (Alaryan et al., 2021; Chiappini & Schifano, 2020; Chiappini et al., 2020; Schifano et al., 2021; Ylä-Rautio et al., 2020). Therefore, the lack of involvement from the government also shows through this unregulated practice, which puts the population severely at risk and highlights once again the poor management of mental health care in Syria.

4.6 *Gaps in the Distribution of Treatment*

In terms of mental health care, the Syrian population also suffers from the problem of gaps in the distribution of treatment, notably psychiatric ones (Bou-Orm et al., 2023; Fuhr et al., 2020; Hamza & Hicks, 2021). In fact, as a considerable percentage of this treatment comes from the private sector, be it from private psychiatric hospitals or outpatient clinics, the services are not accessible to anyone (Abou-Saleh & Mobayed, 2013; Assalman et al., 2008; Hamza & Hicks, 2021; Hedar, 2017; Tsacoyianis, 2014). Indeed, Bou-Orm et al. (2023) prove in their study that more than 75% of the population who need mental health services do not have access to them, as 80% of the Syrian population is below the poverty line (Abu-Ismail et al., 2016; Bolton, 2020; CIA, 2025). This is related to the impactful differences in the social classes in Syria, which result in a wide inequality in purchasing power and economic stability among the different classes (Abu-Ismail et al., 2016; Azmeh, 2014; Goulden, 2011; Ismaiel, 2023; Rahimah, 2016). Thus, although psychiatric treatment and mental health services are already limited in Syria, access is further hindered by disparities in distribution, often determined by an individual's economic stability, purchasing power, and social class, highlighting the deeply rooted nature of this issue.

4.7 *Disruption in the Delivery of Basic Services*

In addition to that, the delivery of basic services in Syria, such as electricity, fuel, water or internet is also disrupted and limited, thus affecting all sectors of the country including the mental health care one (Al Halabi et al., 2021; Bou-Orm et al., 2023; El Hayek et al., 2020; Hassan & Sharif, 2019; Hendrickx et al, 2020; Jamal et al., 2020; Jefee-Bahloul & Zayour, 2017; Najy, 2022; Omar et al., 2020; West, 2016). Indeed, maintaining functioning systems is thus complicated for the different mental health facilities, such as the psychiatric hospitals—whether they are public or private. For example, Jamal et al. (2020) quote an employee of the mental health care system: "We don't have electricity at the moment […] Sometimes, we're using the flashlight of our mobiles to see." This thus shows the struggles of the workers in the mental health sector—and others—in Syria, who are attempting to provide the best service for their patients but are failing to do so because of a shortage of supplies of basic needs. This also present a problem for individuals who are using telepsychiatry, as internet connection, electricity and other essential components for videoconferencing are not always available or accessible, creating another barrier in the access to mental health care in Syria (Al Halabi et al., 2021; El Hayek et al., 2020; Hassan & Sharif, 2019; Hendrickx et al, 2020; Jefee-Bahloul & Zayour, 2017; Omar et al., 2020; West, 2016). Therefore, research suggests that interventions need to be implemented on a bigger scale, allowing for integrated policies and programs (Bou-Orm et al., 2023).

5 Non-medical Management of Mental Disorders in Syria

Considering that stigma around mental health in the Arab world and Syria is still widely spread (Bär et al., 2021; Hamza & Hicks, 2021; Merhej, 2019; Özaslan et al., 2024; Shoib et al., 2022; Swed et al., 2022; Zolezzi et al., 2018), the non-medical management of mental disorders in the country is still prominent. To start with, a practice named Traditional Arabic Medicine (TAM) in the Middle East represents the use of herbal therapies and plant treatments to heal different illnesses, including mental disorders (Alachkar et al., 2011; Khatib et al., 2021a, 2021b; Khoury et al., 2024; Sakr, 2017). This is widespread in Syria since 28% of patients who struggle with mental health and suffer from mental disorders first go to a traditional healer before consulting a mental health professional (Ghuloum et al., 2024). Therefore, while the efficiency and accuracy of these practices shall not be discussed, it is undeniable that mental health is still considered taboo in Syria and the Middle East, resulting in the resort to practices different than mental health care to treat the often misunderstood mental disorders.

Furthermore, Syria being a very religious country (Cardinal, 2009; Kelidar, 1974; Khatib, 2016; Lakitsch, 2018; Valter, 2014), religion, spirituality, and faith play a significant role in their relationship with and views on mental health. In fact, many Syrians rely on faith, God—or Allah, as per the Qur'an, both being relevant in Syria (Boshoff, 2024; Musick & Leitner, 2002; Pinto, 2011; Sayuti, 1999) and their religious beliefs to give them hope and strength to push through their mental struggles, seeking for help and healing through religious coping (Behere et al., 2013; Hamza & Hicks, 2021; Neftçi & Çetrez, 2017; Oxhandler et al., 2021; Schnabel & Schieman, 2022; Sen et al., 2022; Ukpo et al., 2024). Additionally, religious healers also often bring important comfort, consolation, as well as motivation and hope to struggling religious individuals, providing them with extra support outside of mental health care contexts, including in Syria (Ariani, 2021; Aseery, 2024; Dein, 2020; Drew et al., 2022; Higgins, 2014; Klass, 2018; Murharyana et al., 2024; Park et al., 2013; Quosh et al., 2013; Schmidt et al., 2020; Zarzycka et al., 2019). Some Muslim individuals in the Arab region have also found reciting the Quran to be a meaningful source of strength and motivation in coping with mental health challenges (Khoury et al., 2024). However, religion may sometimes interfere with the views and perspectives that individuals, namely Middle Easterns, including Syrians, have on mental health, reinforcing the stigma around the topic (Ghuloum et al., 2024). An example of this could be when God is seen as a source of reward and punishment, which can impact the way an individual thinks about mental health topics, like their outlook on suicidality (Hajiyousouf & Bulut, 2021; Ghuloum et al., 2024). Therefore, medical management of mental health struggles and disorders is not the only option available in Syria; however, while it is still limited and scarce, it is important to work on improving mental health services in the country to tend to the difficulties Syrians deal with on this level.

6 Potential Ways Out

6.1 Increased Mental Health Research and Funding

Mental health care and services are severely underfunded by the Syrian government, considering that only 2% of the governmental health budget goes to the mental health sector (Hendrickx et al., 2020; Okasha et al., 2012; Sijbrandij et al., 2017; Taha, 2022). Therefore, a way to tackle this issue and to improve mental health resources in the country would be to augment this funding and to encourage research about mental health in Syria, thus providing increased governmental help for a population who highly needs it, with almost half of the population suffering from various mental health struggles (Albaba & Sahloul, 2023). As previously mentioned, after the several crises it has been through, the Syrian population is in severe need for mental health interventions, be it to manage their stress and anxiety after major traumatic events such as the 2011 civil war, as well as to learn to cope and reduce their symptoms of PTSD, which has been noted to be very common since the events (Abbara et al., 2016; Albaba & Sahloul, 2023; Ghumman et al., 2016; Hassan, 2019; Hendrickx et al., 2020; Kakaje et al., 2021; Latifeh et al., 2021; Nassan et al., 2015). Therefore, government funding is required to alleviate these symptoms among the population.

6.2 Education and Encouragement of Mental Health Professionals

Furthermore, as the government gets more involved in the improvement of mental health care and services in Syria, more professionals should be encouraged to get into the field and trained to practice this to support inhabitants on the grounds. This also stems from the severe shortage of both psychiatrists and psychologists in the country—with less than 100 trained professionals until a few years ago, which results from immigration, poor education, an underdeveloped curriculum, a lack of awareness about the importance of mental health among the population, and more (Abbara et al., 2016; Dewachi et al., 2014; Hamza & Hicks, 2021; Hedar,

2017; Latifeh et al., 2021). Therefore, psychiatry and psychology curricula should be updated and tailored to the population's needs in a way that encourages students to participate and commit to helping other citizens in the country (Latifeh et al., 2021). Training and supervision should also be provided and extended to allow these future professionals to learn and adapt to the needs of the people.

6.3 Awareness About Mental Health Literacy and the Reduction of Stigma

As mental health stigma still constitutes an overwhelming problem in Syria and among the population, who often still sees mental health struggles as negligible or irrelevant, and who views mental health care as secondary or even shameful, raising awareness about the topic and reducing this stigma would be beneficial (Bär et al., 2021; Merhej, 2019; Swed et al., 2022; Zolezzi et al., 2018). Indeed, this could result in more individuals expressing their need for mental health care and seeking these services (Assalman et al., 2008; Ashfaq et al., 2020; Yalim & Kim, 2018), which would significantly relieve the mental health burden in the country. This can be done in several ways:

6.3.1 Social Media Campaigns

With the growing influence of social media globally and in the Middle East, namely, Syria (Feldkamp., 2021; O'Callaghan et al., 2014; Miconi, 2020; Radcliffe & Abuhmaid, 2020; Radcliffe & Abuhmaid, 2021; Rosman et al., 2014), raising awareness about mental health on social media could provide the computer-literate Syrian population easy access to information about mental health and its importance, as well as reachability of services should private psychiatrists or psychologists utilize their social media platforms to promote their services. Indeed, "mental health influencers" are becoming more and more popular, sharing crucial information on their social media while setting crucial boundaries—for this not to be confused with therapy and their practical, in-clinic services—a concept that could thus be interestingly applied in Syria to spread awareness (Florell, 2023; Pretorius et al., 2022; Triplett et al., 2022; White & Hanley, 2023, 2025).

Educational mental health content could also be created in several forms, be it through videos on social media—sharing expert information or interviewing professionals—through pictures and graphics that explain certain concepts, or even through podcasts that tackle various mental health topics, as these have become popular (Carrotte et al., 2023).

6.3.2 Educational Workshops

Moreover, to de-stigmatize mental health and to raise awareness about the importance of mental health care and services, educational workshops could be organized by the Syrian government or by mental health NGOs, as the latter are already carrying out campaigns and services in the country (Almoshmosh et al., 2016). These could be given on a nation-wide level, targeting several age groups and tailoring the workshops accordingly: for example, this could be given in school classrooms targeting bullying or body image, for parents about parent–child relationships, in retirement homes about struggles at this stage of life, and of course on a wider scale about the repercussions of national crises, the management of their aftermath and the potential struggles or disorders post-war.

6.3.3 Mental Health Apps

To further improve the accessibility of mental health content for the Syrian population, mental health apps could be made available, which could provide various services that could be beneficial to different individuals. Indeed, mental health apps could provide awareness and educational content, contact information of mental health practitioners, tips and exercises developed by professionals to handle different kinds of small-scale struggles, such as stress or anxiety, as well as trackers for mood, motivation, or even symptoms. These apps could then allow users to get more familiar with what mental health entails and how it affects them in several ways, providing them with immediate, short-term services or tips in times of need, and helping them discover more about their mental health patterns.

6.4 Control of Psychotropic Medication Prescription and Sales

As previously stated, the sales of over-the-counter psychotropic medications in Syria have become a serious problem, with self-diagnosis, self-prescription, as well as misuse and abuse of psychotropics now constitute a severe issue in the country (Alaryan et al., 2021; Aljerf, 2017; Al Mais, 2023; Alsheikh et al., 2021; Bastaki et al., 2021; Deeb et al., 2022; Jobnah et al., 2024; Latifeh et al., 2021; Rachidi et al., 2023; Ward et al., 2013). Thus, it is crucial for the Syrian government to establish rules and regulations for this aspect of psychopharmacology and psychiatry, to control for these dangerous consequences. Indeed, the purchase and use of psychotropics should happen through a regulated and controlled process that starts with professional diagnosis, moving on to psychiatric prescription and then legal purchase of the medication in a pharmacy. This is thus where the role of the Syrian government and its Ministry of Health lies: to regain control over these practices and ensure that their processes are legal, to provide the healthiest and safest care for all Syrian patients.

6.5 Equitable Distribution of Treatment

Considering that almost 80% of the Syrian population lives below the poverty line and does not have constant or stable access to mental health care (Badran, 2021; Buckner & Saba, 2010; CIA, 2025; Hamati, 2020; Muzzall et al., 2021; Nasan & Szpytko, 2020; Omar et al., 2020; Turkmani & Mehchy, 2020), it is important that governmental interventions aim to improve public mental health services and ensure their accessibility to the entire population. Additionally, as the public mental health sector remains limited and its resource severely scarce, with only two public mental health hospitals and around 1200 psychiatric ward beds in total (Abou-Saleh & Mobayed, 2013; Assalman et al., 2008) and only a few clinics and professionals, the Syrian population with limited financial capacity remains almost deprived from access to mental health care. Therefore, this is why even distribution of treatment and accessibility to mental health care and services need to be established in the country, allowing for the blossoming of the public mental health sector in Syria and growing the number of trained professionals available on the ground.

6.6 Availability of Basic Services

While the focus on the growth of the mental health care sector in Syria is undeniably important, this cannot be done without improving the availability of basic services, such as electricity, water, fuel and internet, which are, to this day, limited in Syria (Al Halabi et al., 2021; Bou-Orm et al., 2023; El Hayek et al., 2020; Hassan & Sharif, 2019; Hendrickx et al, 2020; Jamal et al., 2020; Jefee-Bahloul & Zayour, 2017; Najy, 2022; Omar et al., 2020; West, 2016). Indeed, without access to these, all sectors of the country, including those related to mental health, will remain restricted and partly functional, as they represent the basis of any given service. Therefore, the Syrian government and NGOs should work on making these basic services available in hospitals, clinics, universities and training centers, if not in the whole country, to allow for the expansion and growth of different sectors, in this case the mental health one, to provide the nation and the population with the mental health care that they require and deserve.

6.7 Dedicated Programs for Non-mental Health Workers

Having already tackled the training of professionals and the improvement of the educational programs in mental health in Syria, it is important to mention that educating individuals who do not work in the mental health sector but whose jobs entail frequent contact with others is important. Indeed, in the case of teachers, nurses, doctors, and more, knowledge and experience about mental health are often disregarded, even though they are crucial to know how to handle certain delicate cases (Carr et al., 2018; Ekornes et al., 2012; Kigozi-Male et al., 2023; Kutcher et al., 2016; McInnes et al., 2022; Minty et al., 2021; Skärsäter et al., 2018; Wijeratne et al., 2021; Yamaguchi et al., 2020). Such a program is already being developed in the context of schools (Hedar, 2017), which shows improvement but leaves room for more progress to be made. Therefore, more programs dedicated to these professions and populations should be implemented to teach and train these individuals about mental health, mental disorders, how to handle certain cases in their practice, and about the process and ethics of referrals.

6.8 Disaster Preparedness

With the unstable political situation in Syria, for example, in light of the recent events of 2024 (CIA, 2025; European Council on Refugees and Exiles, 2024), the country needs to have a mental health intervention program in case of crisis. Therefore, the Syrian government, with external humanitarian help (Abou-Saleh & Hughes, 2015; Bou-Orm et al., 2023; Cratsley et al., 2021; Hassan et al., 2016; Hedar, 2017; Hendrickx et al., 2020), should work on developing emergency services and programs to allow for fast and direct intervention in terms of mental health, should a crisis arise, and for prevention, steps to take to protect one's mental health in such a situation. This could entail educational programs about crises, as previously mentioned, but also the formation of a specialized team(s) trained and prepared to intervene for short-term interventions directly post-crisis.

6.9 Decriminalization of Suicide Attempts

Finally, as suicidal attempts are, to this day, considered a crime in Syria (Adra & Duchonova, 2024; Almidani et al., 2024; Hamza & Hicks, 2021; Rayes et al., 2022), stigma, shame, and taboo around mental health remain deeply entrenched in the population's beliefs and values, shaping their views and perspectives on the topic. Thus, the decriminalization of suicidal attempts would not only relieve the survivor, their family, and their surroundings of the pressure and heavy negative feelings like guilt, shame, or humiliation (Kealy et al., 2021; Lin et al., 2022; Ollivier et al.,

2022; Sadath et al., 2024; Westerlund et al., 2020), but would also alleviate the stigma around mental struggles and suicidality, potentially helping the families and the population as a whole understand this topic better, and improve their empathy, support, and compassion toward the victims (Abrams et al., 2022; Fitzgerald, 2021; Keller et al., 2021; Morgan, 2021).

7 Conclusion

Having suffered from several disabling crises, Syria remains a Middle Eastern country with several underdeveloped sectors, one of them being the mental health care sector. Indeed, while some effort is being extended by the government, NGOs, and international help to improve this area of healthcare, the resources and services on the grounds are still scarce and severely lacking. However, the need for mental health care in Syria is high and severe, as many individuals are suffering from stress, anxiety, depression, and most frequently PTSD after the recent civil war. Unfortunately, the mental health services available on the grounds do not meet these needs. Research and funding by the government are very minimal, the education around mental health is rare which reinforces the stigma and taboo around the topic, the presented services are scarce and thus do not fit the needs of the population, also considering that after the 2011 war, many professionals fled the country, noting that their number was initially low.

Furthermore, psychotropic medications are often sold over the counter. Even the available mental health services are unequally distributed over the country and the population, and access to them is restricted due to the frequent unavailability of basic services like electricity or water. To tackle this and improve the state of the mental health sector in Syria, several steps can be taken, such as raising the funding of the government to this sector, educating the population about mental health to destigmatize it, increasing mental health literacy in different ways, controlling the sale of psychotropic medications, making mental health care evenly available to Syrians, increasing the availability of basic services, training non-mental health workers to deal with certain cases, creating disaster emergency plans, and decriminalizing suicide attempts in the country. Therefore, there is still a long way to go for Syria to be fully meeting the needs of its population on the mental health level, but some effort is already being extended by different parties, which will hopefully develop to take the different steps to improve mental health care in the country.

References

Abazid, H. (2022). Drug abuse in the Middle East: A focus on Syria. In *Handbook of substance misuse and addictions: From biology to public health* (pp. 2629–2648). Springer International Publishing.

Abazid, H., Abou-Isba, S., Abu Farha, R., & Al-Jomaa, E. E. (2020). Drug abuse in Syria: Pattern of use, causes and perception as perceived by Syrian addicts. *Journal of Pharmaceutical Health Services Research, 11*(2), 183–188. https://doi.org/10.1111/jphs.12345

Abazid, H., Abu-Farha, R., Alsayed, A. R., Barakat, M., & Al-Qudah, R. (2023). A comprehensive overview of substance abuse amongst Syrian individuals in an addiction rehabilitation center. *Heliyon, 9*(4). https://doi.org/10.1016/j.heliyon.2023.e14731

Abbara, A., Coutts, A., Fouad, F. M., Ismail, S. A., & Orcutt, M. (2016). Mental health among displaced Syrians: Findings from the Suria public health network. *Journal of the Royal Society of Medicine, 109*(3). https://doi.org/10.1177/0141076816629765

Abbara, A., Marzouk, M., & Mkhallalati, H. (2021). Health system fragmentation and the Syrian conflict. In *Everybody's war: The politics of aid in the Syria crisis* (pp. 33–57). The Oxford University Press.

Abbara, A., Rayes, D., Tappis, H., Hamze, M., Wais, R., Alahmad, H., Almhawish, N., Rubenstein, L., & Haar, R. (2023). "Actually, the psychological wounds are more difficult than physical injuries:" a qualitative analysis of the impacts of attacks on health on the personal and professional lives of health workers in the Syrian conflict. *Conflict and Health, 17*(1), 48.

Abbasy, S. (2020). Importance and advantages of telepsychiatry in mental health during COVID 19 pandemic. *Psychology and Psychotherapy Research Study, 4*(2), 10-31031. https://doi.org/10.31031/pprs.2020.04.000585

Abou-Saleh, M., & Mobayed, M. (2013). Mental health in Syria. *International Psychiatry, 10*(3), 58–60. Https://doi.org/10.1192/S1749367600003854

Abou-Saleh, M. T., & Hughes, P. (2015). Mental health of Syrian refugees: Looking backwards and forwards. *The Lancet Psychiatry, 2*(10), 870–871. https://doi.org/10.1016/S2215-0366(15)00419-8

Abrams, M. P., Salzman, J., Espina Rey, A., & Daly, K. (2022). Impact of providing peer support on medical students' empathy, self-efficacy, and mental health stigma. *International Journal of Environmental Research and Public Health, 19*(9), 5135. https://doi.org/10.3390/ijerph19095135

Abu-Ismail, K., Abdel-Gadir, A., & El-Laithy, H. (2016). Poverty and inequality in Syria. *Arab Development Challenges Report, UNDP.* https://www.academia.edu/download/88603900/BG_15_Poverty_20and_20Inequality_20in_20Syria_FeB.pdf

Adamczyk, A. S., & Jomma, F. (2021). Religious minorities in the ideology and politics of Syria. *International Journal on Minority and Group Rights, 29*(2), 298–315. https://doi.org/10.1163/15718115-bja10057

Adra, A., & Duchonova, K. (2024). Suicidal behaviour in the Syrian Arab Republic. In *Suicidal behavior in Muslim Majority Countries: Epidemiology, risk factors, and Prevention* (pp. 287–301). Springer Nature Singapore. https://doi.org/10.1007/s12520-015-0239-2

Alachkar, A., Jaddouh, A., Elsheikh, M. S., Bilia, A. R., & Vincieri, F. F. (2011). Traditional medicine in Syria: Folk medicine in Aleppo governorate. *Natural Product Communications, 6*(1), 1934578X1100600119. https://doi.org/10.1177/1934578X1100600119

Al-Ansari, N., Jawad, S., Adamo, N., & Sissakian, V. (2019). Water quality and its environmental implications within Tigris and Euphrates rivers. *Journal of Earth Sciences and Geotechnical Engineering, 9*(4), 57–108. https://orcid.org/0000-0002-6790-2653

Alaryan, T., Hasan, T. A., Eshelli, M., & Alzeer, S. (2021). The misuse of prescribed drugs during the Syrian crisis: A cross-sectional study. *International Journal of Mental Health and Addiction, 19*, 714–723. https://doi.org/10.1007/s11469-019-00180-4

Albaba, D., & Sahloul, M. Z. (2023). A plea for psychiatric and humanitarian support in northwest Syria. *The Lancet, 402*(10409), 1236–1237. https://doi.org/10.1016/S0140-6736(23)01626-4

Al-Bashaireh, K., & Lazzarini, L. (2016). Marbles, granites and basalt used in the cruciform basilica of Abila (Decapolis, Jordan): Archaeometric characterization and provenance. *Archaeological and Anthropological Sciences, 8*, 545–554. https://doi.org/10.1007/s12520-015-0239-2

Aldahik, A., Schulz, H. M., Horsfield, B., Wilkes, H., Dominik, W., & Nederlof, P. (2017). Crude oil families in the Euphrates Graben (Syria). *Marine and Petroleum Geology, 86*, 325–342. https://doi.org/10.1016/j.marpetgeo.2017.05.030

Alhaffar, M. B. A., & Janos, S. (2021). Public health consequences after ten years of the Syrian crisis: A literature review. *Globalization and Health, 17*(1), 111. https://doi.org/10.1186/s12992-021-00762-9

Al Halabi, I., Das, S., Warkozek, G., & Misra, B. (2021, April). Status of energy in Syria-Study on how to meet the energy shortage by means of renewable resources. In *2021 12th International Renewable Engineering Conference (IREC)* (pp. 1–6). IEEE.

Alhur, A., & Alhur, A. A. (2022). The acceptance of digital health: What about telepsychology and telepsychiatry? *Jurnal Sistem Informasi, 18*(2), 18–35. https://www.researchgate.net/profile/Anas-Alhur/publication/364631149_The_Acceptance_of_Digital_Health_What_about_Telepsychology_and_Telepsychiatry/links/635680e86e0d367d91c094a6/The-Acceptance-of-Digital-Health-What-about-Telepsychology-and-Telepsychiatry.pdf?_sg%5B0%5D=started_experiment_milestone&origin=journalDetail&_rtd=e30%3D

Alhyas, L., Al Ozaibi, N., Elarabi, H., El-Kashef, A., Wanigaratne, S., Almarzouqi, A., Alhosani, A., & Al Ghaferi, H. (2015). Adolescents' perception of substance use and factors influencing its use: A qualitative study in Abu Dhabi. *JRSM Open, 6*(2), 2054270414567167. https://doi.org/10.1177/2054270414567167

Ali, B., & Sadek, M. (2013). Experimental analysis of the influence of crumb rubber addition on the short-term aging of Syrian asphalt. *Arabian Journal of Geosciences, 6*, 85–90. https://doi.org/10.1007/s12517-011-0342-3

Aljerf, L. (2017). Syrian medical legislation impacts stories on pharmacy in the millennium. *Chronicles of Pharmaceutical Science, 1*(5), 307–311. https://www.researchgate.net/profile/Loai-Aljerf/publication/320689183_Syrian_Medical_Legislation_Impacts_Stories_on_Pharmacy_in_the_Millennium/links/59f48df60f7e9b553ebbe195/Syrian-Medical-Legislation-Impacts-Stories-on-Pharmacy-in-the-Millennium.pdf

Al Mais, S. (2023). Clinical and pharmacological analysis of antidepressant use from the group of selective serotonin reuptake inhibitors. *Electronic Archive of the National Pharmaceutical University.* https://dspace.nuph.edu.ua/handle/123456789/31289

Almidani, S., Hilal, M. A., Alghadban, M., Abou Helal, O., Alkourdi, M., Kannan, J., Ekzayez, A., Patel, P., & El Achi, N. (2024). Demographics and risk factors for suicide in Syria: A retrospective media content analysis of online news sources. *Cambridge Prisms: Global Mental Health, 11*, e50. https://doi.org/10.1017/gmh.2024.47

Almoshmosh, N., Mobayed, M., & Aljendi, M. (2016). Mental health and psychosocial needs of Syrian refugees and the role of Syrian non-governmental organisations. *Bjpsych. International, 13*(4), 81–83. https://doi.org/10.1192/S2056474000001380

Alsheikh, M. Y., Alshahrani, A. M., Almutairi, R. D., Althobaiti, H. A., Fathelrahman, A. I., Seoane-Vazquez, E., & Alasmari, M. M. (2021). Analysis of gabapentinoids abuse-reports in the middle east and North Africa region utilizing the food and drug administration adverse event reporting system. *PTB Reports, 7*(1), 5–8. https://doi.org/10.5530/PTB.2021.7.2

Ariani, D. W. (2021). The role of religiosity and spirituality in motivating and improving students' performance in Indonesia. *Journal of Education, Society and Behavioural Science, 34*(8), 52–63. https://www.academia.edu/download/69635877/56947.pdf

Aseery, A. (2024). Enhancing learners' motivation and engagement in religious education classes at elementary levels. *British Journal of Religious Education, 46*(1), 43–58.

Ashfaq, A., Esmaili, S., Najjar, M., Batool, F., Mukatash, T., Al-Ani, H. A., & Koga, P. M. (2020). Utilization of mobile mental health services among Syrian refugees and other vulnerable Arab populations—A systematic review. *International Journal of Environmental Research and Public Health, 17*(4), 1295. https://doi.org/10.3390/ijerph17041295

Assalman, I., Alkhalil, M., & Curtice, M. (2008). Mental health in the Syrian Arab Republic. *International Psychiatry: Bulletin of the Board of International Affairs of the Royal College of Psychiatrists, 5*(3), 64–66. https://pubmed.ncbi.nlm.nih.gov/31507948/

Azmeh, S. (2014). The uprising of the marginalised: A socio-economic perspective of the Syrian uprising. *LSE Research Online*. http://eprints.lse.ac.uk/id/eprint/60243

Badran, Y. (2021). Syria: A fragmented media system. *Arab Media Systems, 3*(2). https://library.oapen.org/bitstream/handle/20.500.12657/47363/1/9781800640610.pdf#page=65

Bär, J., Pabst, A., Röhr, S., Luppa, M., Renner, A., Nagl, M., Dams, J., Grochtdreis, T., Kersting, A., König, H. H., & Riedel-Heller, S. G. (2021). Mental health self-stigma of Syrian refugees with posttraumatic stress symptoms: Investigating sociodemographic and psychopathological correlates. *Frontiers in Psychiatry, 12,* 642618. https://doi.org/10.3389/fpsyt.2021.642618

Bastaki, K., El Anbari, M., Ghuloum, S., & Jithesh, P. V. (2021). Prescription pattern and off-label use of antipsychotics in a middle eastern population. *Frontiers in Pharmacology, 12,* Article 753845. https://doi.org/10.3389/fphar.2021.753845

Behere, P. B., Das, A., Yadav, R., & Behere, A. P. (2013). Religion and mental health. *Indian Journal of Psychiatry, 55*(Suppl 2), S187–S194. https://doi.org/10.4103/0019-5545.105526

Böge, K., Hahn, E., Strasser, J., Schweininger, S., Bajbouj, M., & Karnouk, C. (2022). Psychotherapy in the Kurdistan region of Iraq (KRI): Preferences and expectations of the Kurdish host community, internally displaced-and Syrian refugee community. *International Journal of Social Psychiatry, 68*(2), 346–353. https://doi.org/10.1177/0020764021995219

Bolton, L. (2020). The economic situation for individuals and communities in Syria. *The Institute of Development Studies and Partner Organizations.* https://hdl.handle.net/20.500.12413/15126

Bou-Orm, I. R., Moussallem, M., Karam, J., deLara, M., Varma, V., Diaconu, K., Apaydin, M. C. B., Van den Bergh, R., Ager, A., & Witter, S. (2023). Provision of mental health and psychosocial support services to health workers and community members in conflict-affected Northwest Syria: A mixed-methods study. *Conflict and Health, 17(*1), 46. https://doi.org/10.1186/s13031-023-00547-4

Boshoff, R. P. (2024). A comparative study of the knowability of the Christian God and Allah: Strategic implications for Muslim evangelism. https://www.academia.edu/download/120971319/Rudolph_Boshoff_Master_Thesis_.pdf

Buckner, E. S., & Saba, K. (2010). Syria's next generation: Youth un/employment, education, and exclusion. *Education, Business and Society: Contemporary Middle Eastern Issues, 3*(2), 86–98. https://doi.org/10.1108/17537981011047934

Cardinal, M. C. (2009). Religious education in Syria: Unity and difference. *British Journal of Religious Education, 31*(2), 91–101. https://doi.org/10.1080/01416200802661100

Carr, W., Wei, Y, Kutcher, S., & Heffernan, A. (2018). Preparing for the classroom: Mental health knowledge improvement, stigma reduction and enhanced help-seeking efficacy in Canadian preservice teachers. *Canadian Journal of School Psychology, 33*(4), 314–326. https://doi.org/10.1177/0829573516688596

Carrotte, E. R., Blanchard, M., Groot, C., Hopgood, F., & Phillips, L. (2023). Podcasts, mental health, and stigma: Exploring motivations, behaviors, and attitudes among listeners. *Communication Studies, 74*(3), 200–216. https://doi.org/10.1080/10510974.2023.2196433

Chan, S., Parish, M., & Yellowlees, P. (2015). Telepsychiatry today. *Current Psychiatry Reports, 17*, 1–9. https://doi.org/10.1007/s11920-015-0630-9

Chiappini, S., & Schifano, F. (2020). What about "pharming"? Issues regarding the misuse of prescription and over-the-counter drugs. *Brain Sciences, 10*(10), 736. https://doi.org/10.3390/brainsci10100736

Chiappini, S., Guirguis, A., Corkery, J., & Schifano, F. (2020). Misuse of prescription and over-the-counter drugs to obtain illicit highs: How pharmacists can prevent abuse. *The Pharmaceutical Journal.* https://uhra.herts.ac.uk/bitstream/handle/2299/27008/Opioid_and_OTC_medicine_abuse.pdf?sequence=1

CIA. (2025). Explore all countries – Syria. *The World Factbook.* https://www.cia.gov/the-world-factbook/countries/syria/

Clausen, C. E., Bazaid, K., Azeem, M. W., Abdelrahim, F., Elgawad, A. A. A., Alamiri, B., AlAnsari, M., Alhamxzawi, A., Al Mai, A. M., Motwakil Bakhiet, A., Bashtawi, M., Çuhadaroglu, F., Hedar, M., Holdar, M., Jabr, S., Jafri, A. S., Jumaian, A., Moussa, S., Osman, A. H., …

Skokayskas, N. (2020). Child and adolescent psychiatry training and services in the Middle East region: A current status assessment. *European Child & Adolescent Psychiatry, 29*, 51–61. https://doi.org/10.1007/s00787-019-01360-2
Cratsley, K., Brooks, M. A., & Mackey, T. K. (2021). Refugee mental health, global health policy, and the Syrian crisis. *Frontiers in Public Health, 9*, Article 676000. https://doi.org/10.3389/fpubh.2021.676000
Deeb, G., Diaz, E., Haavik, S., Lupattelli, A. (2022). Medication use among immigrants from syria living in Western Norway: A Cross-Sectional Study. Pharmacoepidemiology, 1(2), 76–88. Deeb, G., Diaz, E., Haavik, S., & Lupattelli, A, 2022 Deeb, G., Diaz, E., Haavik, S., & Lupattelli, A. (2022). Medication use among immigrants from Syria living in Western Norway: A cross-sectional study. *Pharmacoepidemiology*, 1(2), 76–88. https://doi.org/10.3390/pharma1020008
Dein, S. (2020). Religious healing and mental health. *Mental Health, Religion & Culture, 23*(8), 657–665. https://doi.org/10.1080/13674676.2020.1834220
Dewachi, O., Skelton, M., Nguyen, V. K., Fouad, F. M., Sitta, G. A., Maasri, Z., & Giacaman, R. (2014). Changing therapeutic geographies of the Iraqi and Syrian wars. *The Lancet, 383*(9915), 449–457. https://doi.org/10.1016/S0140-6736(13)62299-0
Disney, L., Mowbray, O., & Evans, D. (2021). Telemental health use and refugee mental health providers following COVID-19 pandemic. *Clinical Social Work Journal, 49*(4), 463–470. https://doi.org/10.1007/s10615-021-00808-w
Drew, D., Banks, J., & Joseph, R. (2022). Religion and spirituality in clinical practice: An exploration of comfort and discomfort among practitioners. *Journal of Religion & Spirituality in Social Work: Social Thought, 41*(1), 104–120. https://doi.org/10.1080/15426432.2021.1994099
Droz-Vincent, 2016 Droz-Vincent, P. (2016). The Syrian military and the 2011 uprising. *Armies and Insurgencies in the Arab Spring,* 168–183. https://doi.org/10.9783/9780812293241-009
Ekornes, S., Hauge, T. E., & Lund, I. (2012). Teachers as mental health promoters: A study of teachers' understanding of the concept of mental health. *International Journal of Mental Health Promotion, 14*(5), 289–310. https://doi.org/10.1080/14623730.2013.798534
El Arnaout, N., Rutherford, S., Zreik, T., Nabulsi, D., Yassin, N., & Saleh, S. (2019). Assessment of the health needs of Syrian refugees in Lebanon and Syria's neighboring countries. *Conflict and Health, 13*, 1–14. https://doi.org/10.1186/s13031-019-0211-3
El Hayek, S., Nofal, M., Abdelrahman, D., Adra, A., Al Harthi, M., Al Shamli, S., AlNuaimi, N., Bensid, L., Cheaito, M. A., Emberish, A. M., Larnaout, A., & Bizri, M. (2020). Telepsychiatry in the Arab world: A viewpoint before and during COVID-19. *Neuropsychiatric Disease and Treatment,* 2805–2815. https://doi.org/10.2147/NDT.S277224
El-Refaay, S. M. M., Toivanen-Atilla, K., & Crego, N. (2024). Efficacy of technology-based mental health interventions in minimizing mental health symptoms among in immigrants, asylum seekers or refugees; systematic review. *Archives of Psychiatric Nursing, 51*, 38–47. https://doi.org/10.1016/j.apnu.2024.04.002
Eteish, H. A., & ALetesh, A. N. (2024). Prevalence of stimulants among students of the Syrian Private University and its relationship with academic achievement and psychological state. https://www.researchsquare.com/article/rs-4876823/latest.pdf
European Council on Refugees and Exiles. (2024). Syria: European reactions to the overthrow of the Assad regime. *European Council on Refugees and Exiles.* https://ecre.org/syria-european-reactions-to-the-overthrow-of-the-assad-regime/
Farrell, A., George, N., Amado, S., & Wozniak, J. (2022). A systematic review of the literature on telepsychiatry for bipolar disorder. *Brain and Behavior, 12*(10), Article e2743. https://doi.org/10.1002/brb3.2743
Feldkamp, J. (2021). The rise of TikTok: The evolution of a social media platform during COVID-19. In C. Hovestadt, J. Recker, J. Richter & K. Werder (Eds.), *Digital responses to Covid-19. SpringerBriefs in information systems*. Springer. https://doi.org/10.1007/978-3-030-66611-8_6
Fitzgerald, M. R. (2021). Examining suicide education materials to positively impact stigma and helping behavior, moderated by dispositional empathy (Master's thesis,

Northern Arizona University). https://www.proquest.com/openview/adbcce6609d2ec8884474880afe9d46b/1?cbl=18750&diss=y&pq-origsite=gscholar
Florell, D. (2023). Considerations before becoming a mental health influencer. *Communique, 51*(7), 36–37. https://link.gale.com/apps/doc/A749633350/HRCA?u=anon~280ad612&sid=googleScholar&xid=3ecc7991
Fuhr, D. C., Acarturk, C., McGrath, M., Ilkkursun, Z., Sondorp, E., Sijbrandij, M., Ventevogel, P., Cuijpers, P., McKee, M., & Roberts, B. (2020). Treatment gap and mental health service use among Syrian refugees in Sultanbeyli, Istanbul: A cross-sectional survey. *Epidemiology and Psychiatric Sciences, 29*, e70. https://doi.org/10.1017/S2045796019000660
Gajarawala, S. N., & Pelkowski, J. N. (2021). Telehealth benefits and barriers. *The Journal for Nurse Practitioners, 17*(2), 218–221. https://doi.org/10.1016/j.nurpra.2020.09.013
García-Lizana, F., & Muñoz-Mayorga, I. (2010). What about telepsychiatry? A systematic review. *The Primary Care Companion for CNS Disorders, 12*(2), 26919. https://doi.org/10.4088/PCC.09m00831whi
Gharaibeh, N., & Amarica, J. (2008). Psychiatry and Arab laws. *Arab Journal of Psychology, 20.* http://arabpsynet.com/Archives/OP/TopicJ20NumanGharaibeh2.pdf
Ghuloum, S., Al-Thani, H., Al-Amin, H. (2024). Religion and mental health: An Eastern Mediterranean region perspective. *Frontiers in Psychology, 15.* https://doi.org/10.3389/fpsyg.2024.1441560
Ghumman, U., McCord, C. E., & Chang, J. E. (2016). Posttraumatic stress disorder in Syrian refugees: A review. *Canadian Psychology/Psychologie Canadienne, 57*(4), 246. https://doi.org/10.1037/cap0000069
Goulden, R. (2011). Housing, inequality, and economic change in Syria. *British Journal of Middle Eastern Studies, 38*(2), 187–202. https://doi.org/10.1080/13530194.2011.581817
Hajiyousouf, I. I., & Bulut, S. (2021). Mental health, religion and suicide. *Open Journal of Medical Psychology, 11*(1), 12–27. https://doi.org/10.4236/ojmp.2022.111005
Hamati, S. (2020). A consequence of a tragedy: Nowcasting poverty rate in Syria. *Journal of Poverty and Social Justice, 28*(3), 299–336. https://doi.org/10.1332/175982720X15977681182347
Hamza, M. K., & Hicks, M. H. R. (2021). Implementation of mental health services in conflict and post-conflict zones: Lessons from Syria. *Avicenna Journal of Medicine, 11*(01), 8–14. https://doi.org/10.4103/ajm.ajm_141_20
Hassan, A. (2019). The Syrian mental health crisis: Present findings and future directions. *Harvard Public Health Review, 21*, 1.5. https://www.jstor.org/stable/48515225
Hassan, A., & Sharif, K. (2019). Efficacy of telepsychiatry in refugee populations: A systematic review of the evidence. *Cureus, 11*(1). https://www.cureus.com/articles/17340-efficacy-of-telepsychiatry-in-refugee-populations-a-systematic-review-of-the-evidence.pdf
Hassan, G., Ventevogel, P., Jefee-Bahloul, H., Barkil-Oteo, A., & Kirmayer, L. J. (2016). Mental health and psychosocial wellbeing of Syrians affected by armed conflict. *Epidemiology and Psychiatric Sciences, 25*(2), 129–141. https://doi.org/10.1017/S2045796016000044
Hedar, M. (2017). Mental health during the Syrian crisis: How Syrians are dealing with the psychological effects. *International Review of the Red Cross, 99*(906), 927–935. https://doi.org/10.1017/S1816383119000080
Hendrickx, M., Woodward, A., Fuhr, D. C., Sondorp, E., & Roberts, B. (2020). The burden of mental disorders and access to mental health and psychosocial support services in Syria and among Syrian refugees in neighboring countries: A systematic review. *Journal of Public Health, 42*(3), e299–e310. https://doi.org/10.1093/pubmed/fdz097
Higgins, P. (2014). "It'sa consolation": The role of Christian religion for people with dementia who are living in care homes. *Journal of Religion, Spirituality & Aging, 26*(4), 320–339. https://doi.org/10.1080/15528030.2014.880773
Hilty, D. M., Luo, J. S., Morache, C., Marcelo, D. A., & Nesbitt, T. S. (2002). Telepsychiatry: An overview for psychiatrists. *CNS Drugs, 16*, 527–548. https://doi.org/10.2165/00023210-200216080-00003

Hubley, S., Lynch, S. B., Schneck, C., Thomas, M., & Shore, J. (2016). Review of key telepsychiatry outcomes. *World Journal of Psychiatry, 6*(2), 269. https://doi.org/10.5498/wjp.v6.i2.269

Hudson, L. (2018). Syrian refugees in Europe: Migration dynamics and political challenges. *New England Journal of Public Policy, 30*(2), 9. https://scholarworks.umb.edu/nejpp/vol30/iss2/9

Ilcan, S. (2018). Fleeing Syria–border crossing and struggles for migrant justice. In *Mobilities, mobility justice and social justice* (pp. 54–66). Routledge.

Ismaiel, L. A. (2023). Testing the validity of purchasing power parity for Syria: Evidence from non-linear unit root tests. *Syrian Journal for Science and Innovation, 1*(2). https://journal.hcsr.gov.sy/archives/474

Jamal, Z., Alameddine, M., Diaconu, K., Lough, G., Witter, S., Ager, A., & Fouad, F. M. (2020). Health system resilience in the face of crisis: Analysing the challenges, strategies and capacities for UNRWA in Syria. *Health Policy and Planning, 35*(1), 26–35. https://doi.org/10.1093/heapol/czz129

Jassim, R. Z., & Al-Badri, A. S. (2019). Mineral resources and occurrences of sodium chloride in Iraq: An overview. *Iraqi Bulletin of Geology and Mining,* (8), 263–287. https://www.iasj.net/iasj/download/a91d668327c7fc98

Jefee-Bahloul, H., & Khoshnood, K. (2014). Mental health research in the Syrian humanitarian crisis. *Frontiers in Public Health, 2,* 44. https://doi.org/10.3389/fpubh.2014.00044

Jefee-Bahloul, H., Moustafa, M. K., Shebl, F. M., & Barkil-Oteo, A. (2014). Pilot assessment and survey of Syrian refugees' psychological stress and openness to referral for telepsychiatry (PASSPORT Study). *Telemedicine and e-Health, 20*(10), 977–979. https://doi.org/10.1089/tmj.2013.0373

Jefee-Bahloul, H., Barkil-Oteo, A., Shukair, N., Alraas, W., & Mahasneh, W. (2016a). Using a store-and-forward system to provide global telemental health supervision and training: A case from Syria. *Academic Psychiatry, 40*(4), 707–709. https://doi.org/10.1007/s40596-015-0423-9

Jefee-Bahloul, H., Duchen, D., & Barkil-Oteo, A. (2016b). Attitudes towards implementation of store-and-forward Telemental health in humanitarian settings: Survey of Syrian healthcare providers. *Telemedicine and e-Health, 22*(1), 31–35. https://doi.org/10.1089/tmj.2015.0021

Jefee-Bahloul, H., & Zayour, Z. (2017). Telemental health in the Middle East. In A. Barkil-Oteo & E. F. Augusterfer (Eds.), *Telemental health in resource-limited global settings* (pp. 67–68). Oxford University Press.

Jobnah, S., Latifeh, Y., Al Kabani, D., & Youssef, L. A. (2024). Ketamine and chronic treatment-resistant depression: Real-world practice and after relapse. *BMC Psychiatry, 24*(1), 745.

Kallström, A., Al-Abdulla, O., Parkki, J., Häkkinen, M., Juusola, H., & Kauhanen, J. (2021). I had to leave. I had to leave my clinic, my city, leave everything behind in Syria. Qualitative research of Syrian healthcare workers migrating from the war-torn country. *BMJ Open, 11*(11), e049941. https://doi.org/10.1136/bmjopen-2021-049941

Karnouk, C., Böge, K., Hahn, E., Strasser, J., Schweininger, S., & Bajbouj, M. (2019). Psychotherapy in Jordan: An investigation of the host and Syrian refugee community's perspectives. *Frontiers in Psychiatry, 10,* 556. https://doi.org/10.3389/fpsyt.2019.00556

Katchadourian, H. (1980). The historical background of psychiatry in Lebanon. *Bulletin of the History of Medicine, 54*(4), 544–553. http://www.jstor.org/stable/44441291

Kattan, Z. (2015). Chemical and isotopic characteristics of the Euphrates River water, Syria: Factors controlling its geochemistry. *Environmental Earth Sciences, 73,* 4763–4778. https://doi.org/10.1007/s12665-014-3762-z

Kakaje, A., Al Zohbi, R., Hosam Aldeen, O., Makki, L., Alyousbashi, A., Alhaffar, M. B. A. (2021). Mental disorder and PTSD in Syria during wartime: A nationwide crisis. *BMC Psychiatry, 21*(1). https://doi.org/10.1186/s12888-020-03002-3

Kealy, D., Treeby, M. S., & Rice, S. M. (2021). Shame, guilt, and suicidal thoughts: The interaction matters. *British Journal of Clinical Psychology, 60*(3), 414–423. https://doi.org/10.1111/bjc.12291

Kelidar, A. R. (1974). Religion and state in Syria. *Asian Affairs, 5*(1), 16–22. https://doi.org/10.1080/03068377408729692

Keller, S., McNeill, V., & Tran, T. (2021). The perceived stigma reduction expressed by young adults in response to suicide prevention videos. *International Journal of Environmental Research and Public Health, 18*(12), 6180. https://doi.org/10.3390/ijerph18126180

Kerbage, H., Marranconi, F., Chamoun, Y., Brunet, A., Richa, S., & Zaman, S. (2020). Mental health services for Syrian refugees in Lebanon: Perceptions and experiences of professionals and refugees. *Qualitative Health Research, 30*(6), 849–864. https://doi.org/10.1177/1049732319895241

Khatib, L. (2016). More religious yet still secular?-The shifting relationship between the secular and the religious in Syria. *Syria Studies, 8*(1), 40–65. https://ojs.st-andrews.ac.uk/index.php/syria/article/view/1316/1004

Khatib, C., Nattouf, A., & Hasan Agha, M. I. (2021a). Traditional medicines and their common uses in central region of Syria: Hama and Homs–an ethnomedicinal survey. *Pharmaceutical Biology, 59*(1), 776–786. https://doi.org/10.1080/13880209.2021.1936078

Khatib, C., Nattouf, A., & Agha, M. I. H. (2021b). *Traditional Medicines Used as Adjuvant Therapy for COVID-19 Symptoms in Syria: An Ethno-medicine Survey*. https://doi.org/10.21203/rs.3.rs-337854/v1

Khoury, P. S. (2014). *Syria and the French mandate: the politics of Arab nationalism, 1920–1945.*

Khoury, B., Rafeh, M., & Dargham, Z. B. (2024). Traditional healing for physical and mental problems in the Arab region: Past and current practices. *Bjpsych International, 21*(2), 44–46. 10.1192/bji.2024.3.

Kigozi-Male, N. G., Heunis, J. C., & Engelbrecht, M. C. (2023). Primary health care nurses' mental health knowledge and attitudes towards patients and mental health care in a South African metropolitan municipality. *BMC Nursing, 22*(1), 25. https://doi.org/10.1186/s12912-023-01188-x

Kim, J., Kelley, J., Choi, S., & Weir, P. (2024). Impact of transportation barriers on telehealth use during the COVID-19 pandemic. *INQUIRY: The Journal of Health Care Organization, Provision, and Financing, 61,* 00469580241266345. https://doi.org/10.1177/00469580241266345

Klass, D. (2018). The nature of religious consolation for the bereaved. Unpublished draft. https://www.academia.edu/download/30299255/The_Nature_of_Religious_Consolation_.pdf

Kutcher, S., Wei, Y., Gilberds, H., Ubuguyu, O., Njau, T., Brown, A., Sabuni, N., Magimba, A., & Perkins, K. (2016). A school mental health literacy curriculum resource training approach: Effects on Tanzanian teachers' mental health knowledge, stigma and help-seeking efficacy. *International Journal of Mental Health Systems, 10,* 1–9. https://doi.org/10.1186/s13033-016-0082-6

Lama, S., François, K., Marwan, Z., & Sami, R. (2016). Impact of the Syrian crisis on the hospitalization of Syrians in a psychiatric setting. *Community Mental Health Journal, 52,* 84–93. https://doi.org/10.1007/s10597-015-9891-3

Lakitsch, M. (2018). Islam in the Syrian war: Spotting the various dimensions of religion in conflict. *Religions, 9*(8), 236. https://doi.org/10.3390/rel9080236

Latifeh, Y., Hanafi, I., Alhoulaiby, S., & Alahdab, F. (2021). Crisis-based psychiatry curriculum update: A cross-sectional study and an expert reflection from Syria. *Asian Journal of Psychiatry, 61,* Article 102681. https://doi.org/10.1016/j.ajp.2021.102681

Latifeh, Y., & Dashash, M. (2016). A critical analysis and a suggested reform of psychiatric curricula in medical faculties during Syrian crisis. *American Journal of Health Research, 4*(6–1), 12–18. https://doi.org/10.11648/j.ajhr.s.2016040601.13

Launchbury, C. (2021). Aṣfūriyyeh: A history of madness, modernity, and war in the Middle East. *Contemporary Levant, 6*(2), 191–194. https://doi.org/10.1080/20581831.2021.1961457

Liem, A., Natari, R. B., Jimmy, & Hall, B. J. (2021). Digital health applications in mental health care for immigrants and refugees: A rapid review. *Telemedicine and e-Health, 27*(1), 3–16. https://doi.org/10.1089/tmj.2020.0012

Lin, Y. C., Wee, J. Y., Marks, R. B., O'Connell, K. L., Hassler, M. E., & Law, K. C. (2022). Shame-proneness and suicidal ideation: The roles of depressive and anger rumination. *Journal of Affective Disorders Reports, 7*, Article 100303. https://doi.org/10.1016/j.jadr.2021.100303

Maalouf, F. T., Alamiri, B., Atweh, S., Becker, A. E., Cheour, M., Darwish, H., Ghandour, L. A., Ghuloum, S., Hamze, M., Karam, E., Khoury, B., & Akl, E. A. (2019). Mental health research in the Arab region: Challenges and call for action. *The Lancet Psychiatry, 6*(11), 961–966. https://doi.org/10.1016/S2215-0366(19)30124-5

McInnes, S., Halcomb, E., Ashley, C., Kean, A., Moxham, L., & Patterson, C. (2022). An integrative review of primary health care nurses' mental health knowledge gaps and learning needs. *Collegian, 29*(4), 540–548. https://doi.org/10.1016/j.colegn.2021.12.005

Merhej, R. (2019). Stigma on mental illness in the Arab world: Beyond the socio-cultural barriers. *International Journal of Human Rights in Healthcare, 12*(4), 285–298. https://doi.org/10.1108/IJHRH-03-2019-0025

Miconi, A. (2020). News from the Levant: A qualitative research on the role of social media in Syrian diaspora. *Social Media+ Society, 6*(1), 2056305119900337. https://doi.org/10.1177/2056305119900337

Minty, Y., Moosa, M. Y., & Jeenah, F. Y. (2021). Mental illness attitudes and knowledge in non-specialist medical doctors working in state and private sectors. *South African Journal of Psychiatry, 27*(1), 1592. https://doi.org/10.4102/sajpsychiatry.v27i0.1592

Moustafa, M. (2015). *Telepsychiatry and mental health care for Syrian refugees in Turkey.* Yale University.

Morgan, E. (2021). Mental illness and suicide: combating stigma with compassion. *VOICES of USU, 125.*

Mowafi, H., & Leaning, J. (2018). Documenting deaths in the Syrian war. *The Lancet Global Health, 6*(1), e14–e15. https://doi.org/10.1016/S2214-109X(17)30457-6

Mowafi, H., Hariri, M., Alnahhas, H., Ludwig, E., Allodami, T., Mahameed, B., Koly, J. K., Aldbis, A., Saqqur, M., Zhang, B., & Al-Kassem, A. (2016). Results of a nationwide capacity survey of hospitals providing trauma care in war-affected Syria. *JAMA Surgery, 151*(9), 815–822. https://doi.org/10.1001/jamasurg.2016.1297

Murharyana, M., Al Ayyubi, I. I., Rohmatulloh, R., & Ikromi, S. N. (2024). The effects of Islamic religious education learning on students' motivation. *At-Tadzkir: Islamic Education Journal, 3*(1), 1–14. https://doi.org/10.59373/attadzkir.v3i1.44

Musick, E., & Leitner, M. (2002). *Allah and god–Different.*

Muzzall, E., Perlman, B., Rubenstein, L. S., & Haar, R. J. (2021). Overview of attacks against civilian infrastructure during the Syrian civil war, 2012–2018. *BMJ Global Health, 6*(10), Article e006384. https://doi.org/10.1136/bmjgh-2021-006384

Najy, Y. (2022). Water scarcity and development a case study of the Euphrates water shortages and their implications on northern Syria. *Lund University Libraries.* https://lup.lub.lu.se/student-papers/search/publication/9101928

Nakeyar, C., & Frewen, P. A. (2016). Evidence-based care for Iraqi, Kurdish, and Syrian asylum seekers and refugees of the Syrian civil war: A systematic review. Canadian *Psychology/Psychologie Canadienne, 57*(4), 233. https://psycnet.apa.org/doi/https://doi.org/10.1037/cap0000067

Nasan, A. W., & Szpytko, J. (2020). The concept of risk analysis of actions taken in the reconstruction of technical infrastructure in the areas after the disaster on the example of Syria. *Journal of KONBiN, 50*,. https://doi.org/10.2478/jok-2020-0001

Nassan, M., Frye, M. A., Adi, A., & Alarcón (2015). Telepsychiatry for post-traumatic stress disorder: A call for action in the Syrian conflict. *The Lancet Psychiatry, 2*(10). https://doi.org/10.1016/S2215-0366(15)00380-6

Neep, D. (2012). *Occupying Syria under the French mandate: Insurgency, space and state formation* (Vol. 38). Cambridge University Press.

Neftçi, N. B., & Çetrez, Ö. A. (2017). Resilience and mental health risks among Syrian refugees in Europe: a cultural perspective. *Acta Psychopathol, 3*(05), 1–4. https://www.hhri.org/wp-content/uploads/2022/02/Resilience-and-mental-health-2469-6676.100137.pdf

O'Callaghan, D., Prucha, N., Greene, D., Conway, M., Carthy, J., & Cunningham, P. (2014, August). Online social media in the Syria conflict: Encompassing the extremes and the in-betweens. In *2014 IEEE/ACM International Conference on Advances in Social Networks Analysis and Mining (ASONAM 2014)* (pp. 409–416). IEEE.

Okasha, A., Karam, E., & Okasha, T. (2012). Mental health services in the Arab world. *World Psychiatry, 11*(1), 52–54. https://doi.org/10.1016/j.wpsyc.2012.01.008

Ollivier, F., Soubelet, A., Duhem, S., & Thümmler, S. (2022). Shame and guilt in the suicidality related to traumatic events: A systematic literature review. *Frontiers in Psychiatry, 13*, Article 951632. https://doi.org/10.3389/fpsyt.2022.951632

Omar, F. A., Mahmoud, I., Hussian, A., Mohr, L., Abdullah, H. O., & Farzat, A. (2020). The effect of the Syrian crisis on electricity supply and the household life in North-West Syria: A university-based study. *Education and Conflict Review, 3,* 77–86. https://discovery.ucl.ac.uk/id/eprint/10109122

Ouahes, I. (2018). *Syria and Lebanon under the French mandate: Cultural imperialism and the workings of empire.* Bloomsbury Publishing.

Oxhandler, H. K., Pargament, K. I., Pearce, M. J., Vieten, C., & Moffatt, K. M. (2021). The relevance of religion and spirituality to mental health: A national survey of current clients' views. *Social Work, 66*(3), 254–264. https://doi.org/10.1093/sw/swab025

Özaslan, A., Yildirim, M., Guney, E., İlhan, M. N., & Vostanis, P. (2024). Mental health problems and help-seeking behaviours of Syrian refugee adolescents: Mediating role of self-stigma. *Psychological Medicine, 54*(4), 732–741. https://doi.org/10.1017/S0033291723002416

Öztürk, G., Timarcioğlu, K., Dikeç, G., Karali, E., Nacaroğlu, H., Çakir, H., & Harmanci Seren, A. K. (2024). Syrian refugees' experiences while receiving mental health services and psychiatric nursing care: A qualitative study. *Journal of Advanced Nursing, 80*(4), 1511–1522. https://doi.org/10.1111/jan.15894

Park, C. L., Edmondson, D., & Hale-Smith, A. (2013). *Why religion? Meaning as motivation.* In K. I. Pargament, J. J. Exline, & J. W. Jones (Eds.), *APA handbook of psychology, religion, and spirituality (Volume 1): Context, theory, and research* (pp. 157–171). American Psychological Association. https://doi.org/10.1037/14045-008

Parkes, P., Pillay, T. D., Bdaiwi, Y., Simpson, R., Almoshmosh, N., Murad, L., & Abbara, A. (2022). Telemedicine interventions in six conflict-affected countries in the WHO Eastern Mediterranean region: A systematic review. *Conflict and Health, 16*(1), 64. https://doi.org/10.1186/s13031-022-00493-7

Penaskovic, K. M., Zeng, X., Burgin, S., & Sowa, N. A. (2022). Telehealth: Reducing patients' greenhouse gas emissions at one academic psychiatry department. *Academic Psychiatry, 46*(5), 569–573. https://doi.org/10.1007/s40596-022-01698-x

Pierret, T. (2016). Syrian Arab Republic. In *The government and politics of Middle East and North Africa.*

Pierret, T. (2018). Syrian Arab Republic. In *The government and politics of the Middle East and North Africa* (pp. 47–78). Routledge.

Pinto, P. G. (2011). 'Oh Syria, god protects you': Islam as cultural idiom under Bashar al-Asad. *Middle East Critique, 20*(2), 189–205. https://doi.org/10.1080/19436149.2011.572414

Pretorius, C., McCashin, D., & Coyle, D. (2022). Mental health professionals as influencers on TikTok and Instagram: What role do they play in mental health literacy and help-seeking? *Internet Interventions, 30*, Article 100591. https://doi.org/10.1016/j.invent.2022.100591

Quosh, C., Eloul, L., & Ajlani, R. (2013). Mental health of refugees and displaced persons in Syria and surrounding countries: a systematic review. *Intervention Journal of Mental Health and Psychosocial Support in Conflict Affected Areas, 11*(3), 276–294. https://journals.lww.com/invn/abstract/2013/11030/mental_health_of_refugees_and_displaced_persons_in.6.aspx

Rachidi, M., Hatem, G., Hatem, M., Zein, S., Rachidi, S., & Awada, S. (2023). Impact of the COVID-19 pandemic on the consumption patterns of psychotropic drugs and predictors of limited access to medication. *The Journal of Medicine Access, 7*, 27550834231163704. https://doi.org/10.1177/27550834231163706

Radcliffe, D., & Abuhmaid, H. (2020). *Social media in the Middle East: 2019 in review.* University of Orgeon.

Radcliffe, D., & Abuhmaid, H. (2021). *How the Middle East used social media in 2020.* University of Orgeon.

Rafeq, A. K. (2015). Traditional and institutional medicine in Ottoman Damascus. *Turkish Historical Review, 6*(1), 76–102. https://doi.org/10.1163/18775462-00601007

Rahimah, B. E. (2016). The class oriented rationale: Uncovering the sources of the Syrian civil war. *Muslim World, 106*(1). https://www.academia.edu/download/55137866/The_Class_Oriented_Rationale-Badr_Eddin_Rahimah.pdf

Rasmussen, B., Sheehan, P., Symons, J., Maharaj, N., Welsh, A., & Kumnick, M. (2022). Syria education and development investment case: Economic, social and psychological costs and risks resulting from not investing in education systems in Syria: Report to UNICEF Syria. https://vuir.vu.edu.au/44933/1/2022_Ramussen_et_al_Syria_Education_%26_Development_Investment_Case.pdf

Rayes, D., Almoshmosh, N., El-Khani, A., Alkhalil, M., Basha, S., Fouad, F., Hilal, M. A., & Abbara, A. (2022). The epidemics of substance misuse and suicide in Syria: Casualties of protracted conflict and political instability. *Research Square,* Preprint. https://doi.org/10.21203/rs.3.rs-2070143/v1

Reilly, J. A. (2020). Ottomans in Syria: "Turkish Colonialism", or something else? *Comparativ: Leipziger Beiträge zur Universalgeschichte und Vergleichenden Gesellschaftsforschung, 30.* https://doi.org/10.26014/j.comp.2020.03-04.05

Renner, A., Hoffmann, R., Nagl, M., Roehr, S., Jung, F., Grochtdreis, T., König, H. H., Riedel-Heller, S., & Kersting, A. (2020). Syrian refugees in Germany: Perspectives on mental health and coping strategies. *Journal of Psychosomatic Research, 129,* 109906. https://doi.org/10.1016/j.jpsychores.2019.109906

Rosman, Y., Eisenkraft, A., Milk, N., Shiyovich, A., Ophir, N., Shrot, S., Kreiss, Y., & Kassirer, M. (2014). Lessons learned from the Syrian sarin attack: Evaluation of a clinical syndrome through social media. *Annals of Internal Medicine, 160*(9), 644–648. https://doi.org/10.7326/M13-2799

Roussos, S. (2021). The collapse of the Ottoman Empire and survival strategies of Christian communities in Greater Syria. *Contemporary Levant, 6*(1), 51–64. https://doi.org/10.1080/20581831.2021.1881719

Sadath, A., Kavalidou, K., McMahon, E., Malone, K., & McLoughlin, A. (2024). Associations between humiliation, shame, self-harm and suicidality among adolescents and young adults: A systematic review. *PLoS ONE, 19*(2), Article e0292691. https://doi.org/10.1371/journal.pone.0292691

Sakr, R. (2017). Traditional medicine in Syria: Knowledge, beliefs & experiences. In E. Falk (Ed.), *Traditional medicine, sharing experiences from the field* (pp. 72–78). ICHCAP.

Sayed-Hassan, R. M., Bashour, H. N., & Koudsi, A. Y. (2012). Patient attitudes towards medical students at Damascus University teaching hospitals. *BMC Medical Education, 12*, 1–8. https://doi.org/10.1186/1472-6920-12-13

Sayuti, N. (1999). *The concept of Allah as the highest god in pre-Islamic Arabia* (Doctoral dissertation, MA. Thesis, McGill University). https://central.bac-lac.gc.ca/.item?id=MQ64191&op=pdf&app=Library&oclc_number=1006818543

Schifano, F., Chiappini, S., Miuli, A., Mosca, A., Santovito, M. C., Corkery, J. M., Guirguis, A., Pettorruso, M., Di Giannantonio, M., & Martinotti, G. (2021). Focus on over-the-counter drugs' misuse: A systematic review on antihistamines, cough medicines, and decongestants. *Frontiers in Psychiatry, 12,* 657397. https://doi.org/10.3389/fpsyt.2021.657397

Schlechter, P., Hellmann, J. H., Kamp, S., Echterhoff, G., Wanninger, K., Wagner, U., & Knausenberger, J. (2023). Improving attitudes toward psychotherapy in residents and Syrian refugees in Germany: An interview vignette intervention study. *Journal of Cross-Cultural Psychology, 54*(4), 490–509. https://doi.org/10.1177/00220221231171060

Schmidt, C., Eickmeyer, J., Henningsen, M., Weber, A., Pleimann, A., & Koehler, S. (2020). Medical students' personal experiences, religion, and spirituality explain their (dis) comfort with a patient's religious needs. *Canadian Medical Education Journal, 11*(4), e29. https://doi.org/10.36834/cmej.69217

Schnabel, L., & Schieman, S. (2022). Religion protected mental health but constrained crisis response during crucial early days of the COVID-19 pandemic. *Journal for the Scientific Study of Religion, 61*(2), 530–543. https://doi.org/10.1111/jssr.12720

Selmo, P., Knaevelsrud, C., Mohamad, N., & Rehm, J. (2021). Prevalence and predictors of psychopathology in the war-afflicted Syrian population. *Transcultural Psychiatry, 58*(2), 226–238. https://doi.org/10.1177/1363461520937931

Sen, H. E., Colucci, L., & Browne, D. T. (2022). Keeping the faith: Religion, positive coping, and mental health of caregivers during COVID-19. *Frontiers in Psychology, 12*, Article 805019. https://doi.org/10.3389/fpsyg.2021.805019

Shoib, S., Swed, S., Alibrahim, H., Ezzdean, W., Almoshantaf, M. B., & Chandradasa, M. (2022). Syria's fragile mental health services in the midst of conflict and violence: Call for action. *Medicine, Conflict and Survival, 38*(4), 280–284. https://doi.org/10.1080/13623699.2022.2116552

Sijbrandij, M., Acarturk, C., Bird, M., Bryant, R. A., Burchert, S., Carswell, K., de Jong, J., Dinesen, C., Dawson, K. S., El Chammay, R., van Ittersum, L., Jordans, M., Knaevelsrud, C., McDaid, D., Miller, K., Morina, N., Park, A. L., Roberts, B., van Son, Y., Sondorp, E., … Cuijpers, P. (2017). Strengthening mental health care systems for Syrian refugees in Europe and the Middle East: Integrating scalable psychological interventions in eight countries. *European journal of psychotraumatology, 8*(sup2), 1388102. https://doi.org/10.1080/20008198.2017.1388102

Sirin, S. R., & Rogers-Sirin, L. (2015). *The educational and mental health needs of Syrian refugee children* (p. 13). Migration Policy Institute.

Skärsäter, I., Keogh, B., Doyle, L., Ellilä, H., Jormfeldt, H., Lahti, M., Higgins, A., Meade, O., Sitvast, J., Stickley, T., & Kilkku, N. (2018). Advancing the knowledge, skills and attitudes of mental health nurses working with families and caregivers: A critical review of the literature. *Nurse Education in Practice, 32*, 138–146. https://doi.org/10.1016/j.nepr.2018.07.002

Smeekes, A., Verkuyten, M., Çelebi, E., Acartürk, C., & Onkun, S. (2017). Social identity continuity and mental health among Syrian refugees in Turkey. *Social Psychiatry and Psychiatric Epidemiology, 52*, 1317–1324. https://doi.org/10.1007/s00127-017-1424-7

Swed, S., Sohib, S., Fathy Hassan, N. A. I., Almoshantaf, M. B., Alkadi, S. M. S., AbdelQadir, Y. H., Ibrahim, N., Khair, L. T., Bakkour, A., Muwaili, A. H. H., Muwaili, D. H. H., & Elkalagi, N. K. H. (2022). Stigmatizing attitudes towards depression among university students in Syria. *Plos One, 17*(9), e0273483. https://doi.org/10.1371/journal.pone.0273483

Taha, S. M. (2022). Literature review of the factors influencing access to mental health treatment services among adults in conflict-affected areas in the eastern mediterranean region. *Royal Tropical Institute, KIT.* https://bibalex.org/baifa/Attachment/Documents/MJKszYRpSE_20230509155121676.pdf

Taleb, Z. B., Bahelah, R., Fouad, F. M., Coutts, A., Wilcox, M., & Maziak, W. (2015). Syria: Health in a country undergoing tragic transition. *International Journal of Public Health, 60*, 63–72. https://doi.org/10.1007/s00038-014-0586-2

Triplett, N. T., Kingzette, A., Slivinski, L., & Niu, T. (2022). Ethics for mental health influencers: MFTs as public social media personalities. *Contemporary Family Therapy, 44*(2), 125–135. https://doi.org/10.1007/s10591-021-09632-3

Tsacoyianis, B. A. (2014). *Making healthy minds and bodies in Syria and Lebanon, 1899–1961.* Washington University in St.

Tsacoyianis, B. A. (2021). *Disturbing spirits: Mental illness, trauma, and treatment in modern Syria and Lebanon.* University of Notre Dame Press.

Turkmani, R., & Mehchy, Z. (2020). New Consumer Price Index estimates for Syria reveal further economic deterioration and alarming levels of humanitarian need. *Conflict Research Programme*. https://eprints.lse.ac.uk/103280/1/Turkmani_new_consumer_price_index_estimates_published.pdf

Ukpo, S. D., Imohiosen, C. E., Owot, J. A., & Ajuluchukwu, P. (2024). The impact of religious and spiritual counseling on mental health outcomes in geriatric care. *International Journal of Multidisciplinary Research and Growth Evaluation, 5*(6), 1538–1547. https://www.allmultidisciplinaryjournal.com/uploads/archives/20250222154230_MGE-2025-1-417.1.pdf

Valter, S. (2014). The Syrian war: Religious & political representations. *Syria Studies*. http://ojs.st-andrews.ac.uk/index.php/syria/article/view/1043

Ward, K. D., Asfar, T., Al Ali, R., Rastam, S., Weg, M. W. V., Eissenberg, T., & Maziak, W. (2013). Randomized trial of the effectiveness of combined behavioral/pharmacological smoking cessation treatment in Syrian primary care clinics. *Addiction, 108*(2), 394–403. https://doi.org/10.1111/j.1360-0443.2012.04048.x

Waugh, M., Voyles, D., & Thomas, M. R. (2015). Telepsychiatry: Benefits and costs in a changing health-care environment. *International Review of Psychiatry, 27*(6), 558–568. https://doi.org/10.3109/09540261.2015.1091291

West, D. M. (2016). Internet shutdowns cost countries $2.4 billion last year. In *Center for technological innovation at brookings, Washington, DC*.

Westerlund, M., Hökby, S., & Hadlaczky, G. (2020). Suicidal thoughts and behaviors among Swedish suicide-bereaved women: Increased risk associated with the loss of a child, feelings of guilt and shame, and perceived avoidance from family members. *Frontiers in Psychology, 11*, 1113. https://doi.org/10.3389/fpsyg.2020.01113

White, E., & Hanley, T. (2023). Therapist+ social media= mental health influencer? Considering the research focusing upon key ethical issues around the use of social media by therapists. *Counselling and Psychotherapy Research, 23*(1), 1–5. https://doi.org/10.1002/capr.12577

White, E., & Hanley, T. (2025). "What I share is not the same as therapy": Psychologist experiences of Instagram use as a mental health influencer. *Psychology and Psychotherapy: Theory, Research and Practice*. https://doi.org/10.1111/papt.12585

Wijeratne, C., Johnco, C., Draper, B., & Earl, J. (2021). Doctors' reporting of mental health stigma and barriers to help-seeking. *Occupational Medicine, 71*(8), 366–374. https://doi.org/10.1093/occmed/kqab119

World Health Organization (2020). Syrian Arab Republic. In *Mental health ATLAS 2020*. https://cdn.who.int/media/docs/default-source/mental-health/mental-health-atlas-2020-country-profiles/syr.pdf?sfvrsn=34510af_8&download=true

Yazgan, P., Utku, D. E., & Sirkeci, I. (2015). Syrian crisis and migration. *Migration Letters, 12*(3), 181. https://www.ceeol.com/search/article-detail?id=477035

Yalim, A. C., & Kim, I. (2018). Mental health and psychosocial needs of Syrian refugees: A literature review and future directions. *Advances in Social Work, 18*(3), 833–852. https://doi.org/10.18060/21633

Yamaguchi, S., Foo, J. C., Nishida, A., Ogawa, S., Togo, F., & Sasaki, T. (2020). Mental health literacy programs for school teachers: A systematic review and narrative synthesis. *Early Intervention in Psychiatry, 14*(1), 14–25. https://doi.org/10.1111/eip.12793

Yılmaz, T., & Karakuş, C. (2024). Psychotherapeutic interventions used in psychological treatment studies with Syrian refugees: A systematic review. *Trauma, Violence, & Abuse*, 15248380241306029. https://doi.org/10.1177/15248380241306029

Ylä-Rautio, H., Siissalo, S., & Leikola, S. (2020). Drug-related problems and pharmacy interventions in non-prescription medication, with a focus on high-risk over-the-counter medications. *International Journal of Clinical Pharmacy, 42*(2), 786–795. https://doi.org/10.1007/s11096-020-00984-8

Zarzycka, B., Śliwak, J., Krok, D., & Ciszek, P. (2019). Religious comfort and anxiety in women with cancer: The mediating role of hope and moderating role of religious struggle. *Psycho-Oncology, 28*(9), 1829–1835. https://doi.org/10.1002/pon.5155

Zisser, E. (2019). The Syrian refugees—Left to their fate. *British Journal of Middle Eastern Studies 46*(2), 293–309. https://doi.org/10.1080/13530194.2019.1569306

Zolezzi, M., Alamri, M., Shaar, S., & Rainkie, D. (2018). Stigma associated with mental illness and its treatment in the Arab culture: A systematic review. *International Journal of Social Psychiatry, 64*(6), 597–609. https://doi.org/10.1177/0020764018789200

Chapter 14
Mental Health Care in the United Arab Emirates

Waleed Ahmed, Faisal A. Nawaz, Leena Amiri, and Syed Fahad Javaid

Abstract The United Arab Emirates (UAE) is a constitutional federation consisting of seven emirates and is an evolving nation in terms of healthcare. The demographic landscape of the UAE presents a rich tapestry of cultures, religious customs, and evolving mental health perspectives. Rapid urbanisation, economic growth, and stresses on a diverse expatriate workforce present significant challenges. Reports estimate that about 15% of the Gulf Cooperation Council population suffers from a mental disorder annually, indicating the widespread nature of mental health issues. This chapter examines the UAE's progress in addressing mental health issues, provides historical perspectives, and aims to identify challenges in integrating equitable, culturally sensitive, and community-based mental health services for the region. It will also discuss policies and interventions as opportunities for improving mental health support strategies. As the country continues developing its health system, the UAE is well-positioned to emerge as a regional leader in mental health reform.

Keyword United Arab Emirates · Middle East · Mental health · Psychiatry · Culture · Emirati · Expatriates

W. Ahmed (✉)
Maudsley Health, Abu Dhabi, United Arab Emirates
e-mail: waleed.ahmed@maudsleyhealth.com

F. A. Nawaz
Al Amal Psychiatric Hospital, Emirates Health Services, Dubai, United Arab Emirates
e-mail: Faisal.Nawaz@ehs.gov.ae

L. Amiri · S. F. Javaid
Department of Psychiatry, College of Medicine and Health Sciences, United Arab Emirates University, Al Ain, United Arab Emirates
e-mail: lina.amiri@uaeu.ac.ae

S. F. Javaid
e-mail: sjavaid@uaeu.ac.ae

S. Al-Huseini and S. M. Y. Arafat (eds.), *Mental Health Care in the Middle East*, South Asian Perspectives in Mental Health and Psychology ,
https://doi.org/10.1007/978-981-95-0461-9_14

1 Country Profile

The United Arab Emirates (UAE) is a federation on the Arabian Peninsula's east coast, consisting of seven emirates: Abu Dhabi, Dubai, Fujairah, Sharjah, Ajman, Umm Al-Quwain, and Ras Al Khaimah. Established on 2 December 1971, it is a relatively new country with Abu Dhabi City as its capital, and operates as a constitutional federation. The UAE covers approximately 71,023.6 square kilometres, including islands in the Arabian Gulf and 27,624.9 square kilometres of territorial waters (The Official Portal of the UAE Government-Factsheet, 2025). Arabic is the official language, and Islam is the official religion (The Official Portal of the UAE Government-Factsheet, 2025).

The UAE is a "Very High Human Development" country, with a GDP of AED 1,486.3 billion (404.73 billion US dollars) in 2019 (United Arab Emirates Ministry of Economy, 2020; United Nations Development Programme, 2022). Its population, including nationals and expatriates, was 9,282,410 in 2020, with over 200 nationalities (The Official Portal of the UAE Government, 2025a, 2025b, 2025c; United Arab Emirates Ministry of Cabinet Affairs, 2025). Expatriates outnumber UAE nationals, with Indians being the largest group, followed by Pakistanis and Bangladeshis (United Arab Emirates Ministry of Cabinet Affairs, 2025). Life expectancy is 78.7 years (United Nations Development Programme, 2022). The literacy rate for those aged 15 and above is 98% (The Official Portal of the UAE Government, 2025a, 2025b, 2025c; United Nations Educational, Scientific and Cultural Organization, 2022).

The demographic landscape of the UAE presents a rich tapestry of cultures, religious customs, and evolving mental health perspectives. This chapter examines the UAE's progress in addressing mental health issues, provides historical perspectives, and aims to identify challenges. It will also discuss policies and interventions as opportunities for improving mental health support strategies.

2 Historical Context of Mental Health in the UAE

Traditional Middle Eastern culture struggles with accepting mental illness, often seeing it as something to hide (Arab Center Washington DC, 2025). Before Islam, the Arabian Peninsula attributed mental disturbances to supernatural causes, confusing mental illness with spiritual malaise and blaming demons for ailments of the mind and body (Dein & Illaiee, 2013; Yusuf & Javaid, 2025). With the advent of Islam in the seventh century, the understanding of mental illness shifted, blending compassion with existing beliefs. Mental disturbances were sometimes attributed to jinn or the evil eye, but cruel treatment was discouraged. "Insanity" was viewed as a condition beyond control, possibly a spiritual trial; thus, the afflicted deserved care over abuse (Okasha, 1999).

Broader cultural attitudes in Middle Eastern society towards mental illness were complex and nuanced. On the one hand, there was certainly stigma—the term *majnun* (madman) carried a social stigma (Dols, 2011). On the other hand, Islamic teachings fostered a degree of empathy for those who lost their reason. Cultural narratives provided a positive, or at least ambivalent, perspective on mental disturbance (Seyed-Gohrab, 2003). Middle Eastern Islamic culture balanced stigma with sympathy, often recognising the humanity in those deemed insane (Dols, 2011).

The prevalent culture in the UAE and the Middle East recognises that spiritual health benefits patient recovery. Treatments may include Quranic recitation, supplication, or visits from religious scholars for encouragement and prayer. This is not contradictory; the belief is that God created cures for diseases and provided knowledge to discover them—using both prayer and medicine is considered ideal (Ciftci, 2012; Haque & Kindi, 2015). The UAE's journey with mental illness—ranging from ancient supernaturalism, through the enlightened care of the Islamic Golden Age, disrupted by colonial imposition, to the present search for culturally authentic modern psychiatry—illustrates a region that continually negotiates the intersection of tradition and science. Historical perceptions of mental illness continue to resonate in contemporary attitudes and approaches (Malik, 2023).

3 Epidemiology of Mental Disorders in the UAE

Mental disorders are a significant public health concern in the UAE. A regional report estimates that about 15% of the Gulf Cooperation Council (GCC) population suffers from a mental disorder annually, indicating the widespread nature of mental health issues, despite varying national statistics (PricewaterhouseCoopers, 2022). Neuropsychiatric conditions account for roughly 20% of the UAE's disease burden, with depression and anxiety constituting about three-quarters of this burden (The Economist Impact, 2021). Although epidemiological data on specific disorders are limited, studies suggest that depression and anxiety are among the most prevalent mental health conditions in the UAE (Mahmoud & Saravanan, 2020).

In Dubai, a 2019 community survey found a depressive disorder prevalence of 2.3% among adults (Abdullatif et al., 2021), lower than the global 6% estimate (Bromet et al., 2011), suggesting underdiagnosis in the UAE. Conversely, a smaller study in Sharjah reported significantly higher rates: 31.5% of participants experienced depression, and 56.4% experienced anxiety, likely due to differences in sampling (Mahmoud & Saravanan, 2020). Schizophrenia and bipolar disorder occur less frequently; psychotic disorders have a point prevalence of about 0.5% and bipolar disorders approximately 0.7%, consistent with global trends (Zuberi et al., 2021). Overall, evidence suggests that common mental disorders, especially depression and anxiety, significantly affect the UAE's population, comparable to other Middle Eastern countries.

3.1 Suicide Epidemiology in the UAE

Suicide is a sensitive issue in the UAE due to legal, religious, and cultural factors. WHO estimates show that the UAE's age-standardised suicide rate was 1.7 per 100,000 in 2021, compared to a global rate of around 9 per 100,000 (World Health Organisation, 2025). The Abu Dhabi Department of Health Statistics reports that suicide caused 18 deaths in 2022, the second leading cause of injury-related deaths after road traffic accidents (Department of Health Abu Dhabi, 2025). A study of suicides in Dubai from 2003 to 2009 found a suicide rate of approximately 5.8 per 100,000 (Dervic et al., 2012). This study highlighted a disparity: the suicide rate was 6.3 per 100,000 for expatriates compared to only 0.9 for Emirati citizens (Dervic et al., 2012). These findings reveal that while the national average is low, specific subgroups, particularly migrant workers, face significantly higher suicide risks.

Over the past decade, reported suicide cases have gradually increased, particularly among expatriate labourers and foreign workers. However, comprehensive nationwide data on suicide in the UAE remains elusive (PROGRESS.guide, 2025). These figures often underestimate the true incidence of suicide, influenced by underreporting. Legal considerations historically played a role—until recently, attempting suicide was criminalised under UAE law. In late 2020, the UAE government reformed laws to decriminalise suicide attempts (Tabrez, 2020). Religious and cultural norms discourage suicide since, in Islam, it is viewed as a grave sin. Consequently, religion may explain the relatively low suicide rates in the UAE (Dervic et al., 2012). Families who lose a member to suicide often hesitate in reporting the cause of death, preferring it be classified as an "accident" or "undetermined" to avoid social disgrace or religious censure (Pritchard et al., 2020).

3.2 Substance Misuse Epidemiology in the UAE

The data pertaining to substance use in the UAE remains elusive. This is likely secondary to the deep-rooted religious and cultural beliefs about the use of illicit substances (Fouché et al., 2023). The UAE has a zero-tolerance policy for the use and possession of illicit substances and has a strictly regulated system governing the prescription of medications with a potential for misuse (The Official Portal of the UAE Government, 2024a, 2024b, 2024c). In terms of the commonly misused substances, a study conducted by the National Rehabilitation Centre in Abu Dhabi identified alcohol, followed by heroin, as the most common substances used among the participants (Alblooshi et al., 2016). Another study indicated that over 80% of adults with opioid use disorder in the UAE engaged in poly-substance use (Grauer, 2022). Substance misuse in the UAE is often comorbid with mental health disorders, notably mood disorders and anxiety, with female sex, young age, and chronic life difficulties being significant predictors of psychiatric morbidity (Abou-Saleh et al., 2001). There is a dearth of studies looking into the scale of illicit substance use, specifically in the Emirati population. A 2020 study on opioid use disorder in Emirati patients identified specific haplotypes associated with opioid use, suggesting a potential genetic predisposition (Alblooshi et al., 2020).

The UAE government has been proactive in attempts to bring a positive change in the face of the increasing substance use problem. In 2021, the new laws reflected a change in focus from prosecution to rehabilitation, providing a second chance for first-time offenders and averting prison sentences (The Official Portal of the UAE Government, 2024a, 2024b, 2024c).

4 Key Mental Health Risk Factors in the UAE Population

The mental health landscape in the UAE is influenced by various risk and protective factors. Rapid urbanisation, economic growth, and stresses on a diverse expatriate workforce present significant challenges. Conversely, cultural strengths—such as faith-driven resilience, strong family support, and emerging social networks—promote psychological well-being. Research highlights vulnerable groups like young people in transitions, expatriates under financial or social stress, and those with chronic medical conditions (Dervic et al., 2012; Koveshnikov & Lehtonen, 2024; Parkinson et al., 2023). The UAE's youthful demographic, with nearly 35% under 25 years old, is crucial for mental health epidemiology, as this age group faces higher risks of anxiety, depression, and substance use (The Economist Impact, 2021). Here, we explore UAE-specific factors affecting the UAE population's mental health.

4.1 Urbanisation and Lifestyle Changes

The UAE has rapidly urbanised over the past few decades, significantly altering its societal structure (Chowdhury, 2016). This fast lifestyle creates unique mental health pressures; social isolation in dense cities occurs despite crowds, as individuals may be distant from family and community support. The rising cost of urban living adds financial stress as housing, education, and other expenses increase. Additionally, shifts from close-knit tribal communities to nuclear families can weaken support networks (Helbich et al., 2020). Studies have linked urban living to higher mental disorder risks, such as anxiety and depression (American Psychiatric Association, 2021; Mechelli, 2019). In recent decades, the population has shifted from a traditional Bedouin heritage to a modern society, creating intergenerational clashes of values and identity struggles (Andrade et al., 2022). Recent research among UAE university students found worrisome levels of mental distress, with around one-third of students reporting moderate to severe anxiety (Faris et al., 2024). The shift to a fast-paced urban life has introduced stressors (crowding, noise, and competition) while diminishing some protective community bonds, thereby increasing mental health risks.

4.2 Rapid Economic Development and Work Stress

The UAE's rapid economic growth has brought prosperity, high stress, and intense competition. Ambitious development visions drive excellence but can lead to burnout and poor work-life balance. The stress of maintaining a standard of living in a fast-paced society further affects mental well-being. Thus, while the UAE benefits economically, its rapid development introduces psychosocial challenges, elevating mental health risks.

4.3 Expatriate Population's Unique Stressors

The UAE's population composition offers advantages and challenges (Haak-Saheem & Brewster, 2017). Expatriates have spurred the country's growth, enhancing business, education, and healthcare sectors. However, this diversity poses challenges; adapting to foreign culture can induce stress (Geros et al., 2020). Many expatriates live far from home, leading to social support deficits and isolation. This isolation, along with communication barriers, can cause loneliness and despair. In a study of Indian migrant workers during the pandemic, 77% reported profound feelings of loneliness (Khan et al., 2023). Migrant workers in lower income jobs are particularly vulnerable to workplace stress (Sönmez et al., 2011). In summary, despite the economic attractions, many expatriates—especially in low-wage sectors—face serious stressors, including adaptation strain, which increases their susceptibility to mental illness.

5 Mental Health Protective Factors in the UAE Population

5.1 Religious and Spiritual Influences

High religiosity is linked to lower depression levels, with faith communities providing spiritual solace and social support (Ghuloum et al., 2024). In UAE society, Islamic beliefs promote psychological resilience through coping mechanisms like prayer, faith in God's plan, and community charity. Mosques and religious gatherings act as community hubs, reducing isolation and contributing to the link between high religiosity and lower depression levels (Ghuloum et al., 2024). Overall, Islam's influence in the UAE serves as a protective factor, promoting routines, hope, charity, and collective support to enhance mental well-being.

5.2 *Family and Cultural Communal Support*

Emirati culture prioritises family, often involving extended families living together or maintaining close contact. These bonds provide individuals facing stress or sadness with immediate support from relatives who offer emotional comfort, advice, and practical help (Aspire, 2020; Thomas et al., 2017). Cultural norms encourage seeking help from family, community elders, or traditional healers during emotional need (Andrade et al., 2022). While this may delay formal treatment, it shows trust in informal support systems.

5.3 *Government Initiatives and Community Support Systems*

UAE authorities and communities increasingly recognise mental health as a priority, introducing appropriate support systems. The government has launched public awareness campaigns to reduce stigma and encourage help-seeking (Andrade et al., 2022). Volunteer support groups, including the "We Are Your Family" hotline established by the Ministry of Community Development, made over 12,000 calls to elderly citizens to combat loneliness and provide psychological assistance during the COVID-19 pandemic (The Economist Impact, 2021). The UAE government's commitment to happiness ensures mental health is integrated into public policy and community design (The Official Portal of the UAE Government-National Programme for Happiness and Wellbeing, 2025). Although progress is needed to reach marginalised groups and address deep-rooted stigmas, this multi-sectoral support network—spanning government policies, healthcare services, and community efforts—creates a protective framework to mitigate risks and support positive mental health.

6 Current Mental Health Services in the UAE

6.1 *Institutional Framework*

Mental health development has gained prominence in recent years. The UAE has embarked on significant initiatives to integrate mental health into its broader health agenda, enhance service provision, and tackle stigma. Despite these advancements, the UAE, like many countries, faces the dual challenge of scaling up services while ensuring culturally sensitive, accessible, and integrated care across its diverse emirates (Vigo et al., 2019).

In the UAE, mental health services are primarily managed under the Ministry of Health and Prevention (MoHAP), which oversees national health policies and initiatives (Ministry of Health & Prevention, 2025a, 2025b). The Emirates Health Services (EHS), established in 2022, consolidates mental health services previously offered by various entities, including MoHAP and local health authorities (Emirates Health Services, 2025). Furthermore, the Sakina initiative, part of the Abu Dhabi Health Services Company (SEHA), focusses explicitly on mental health, providing a centralised approach to psychiatric and psychological care across Abu Dhabi (Abu Dhabi Media Office, 2024). This comprehensive framework ensures that mental health services are integrated, accessible, and effective throughout the UAE. Governance of mental health in the UAE involves federal bodies like MoHAP and local emirate authorities such as the Dubai Health Authority (DHA), Abu Dhabi's Department of Health (DOH), and Emirates Health Services (EHS) (The Department of Health Abu Dhabi, 2025; Dubai Health Authority, 2025; Emirates Health Services, 2025). Each entity formulates policies suited to local population needs, coordinating with specialised psychiatric hospitals and clinics (The Official Portal of the UAE Government-Health regulatory authorities, 2024).

The Abu Dhabi Public Health Centre (ADPHC) is a government entity in the Emirate of Abu Dhabi, United Arab Emirates, focussed on promoting public health and wellness (The Abu Dhabi Public Health Centre, 2023). ADPHC develops and implements comprehensive mental health policies and strategies. Key initiatives include raising awareness through educational campaigns, collaborating with local healthcare providers and organisations, and supporting community-based mental health programmes that offer counselling and crisis intervention services. The landmark National Policy for the Promotion of Mental Health marked a turning point (United Arab Emirates Legislation, 2017). This policy aims to create a comprehensive, integrated mental health system, promote mental health awareness, reduce stigma, and ensure human rights protections for individuals with mental illnesses (Ministry of Health & Prevention, 2025a, 2025b).

The UAE's new Mental Health Law [Federal Law No. (10) of 2023 On Mental Health], effective from 30 May 2024, marks a major change in mental health care regulations. It supersedes the earlier legislation from 1981 and seeks to strengthen the protections and rights of individuals with mental health conditions while promoting their dignity (United Arab Emirates Legislation, 2023). Figure 1 outlines the evolutionary progression of mental health legislation in the UAE.

6.2 *Structure of Mental Health Services*

The UAE has significantly advanced its mental health services, reflecting substantial investments from both governmental and private sectors. While government-run institutions previously dominated the system, recent expansions have notably included private sector facilities, thereby enhancing inpatient psychiatric care capabilities and specialised service availability. However, challenges such as stigma, insufficient awareness, and cultural influences still persist, affecting the efficacy of these services (Alrumaithi & Moonesar, 2022; World Health Organization, 2020). Mental health services in the UAE are organised into primary, secondary, and tertiary care levels. Primary care primarily involves general practitioners who perform initial assessments

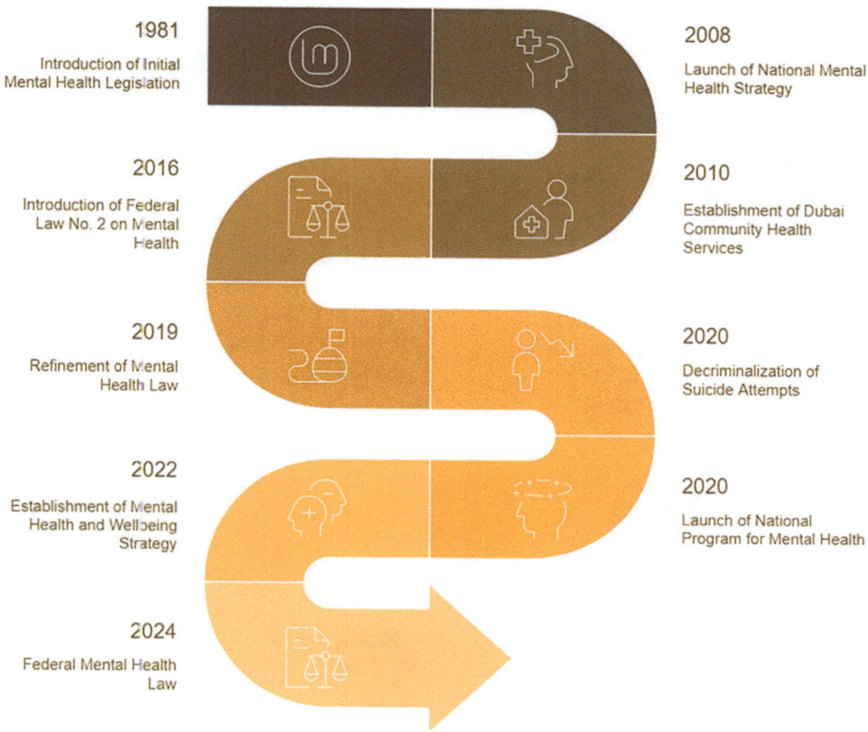

Fig. 1 Evolution of mental health legislation in the UAE

and referrals in primary healthcare centres (El-Rufaie & Absood, 1993). Secondary care includes specialised outpatient and community-based services (World Health Organization, 2020).

Tertiary services comprise specialised psychiatric hospitals providing extensive inpatient and outpatient care, including emergency and advanced psychiatric interventions. Major institutions include Al Amal Psychiatric Hospital, Behavioural Science Pavilion at Sheikh Khalifa Medical City, and Al Jalila Children's Speciality Hospital (The Official Portal of the UAE Government-Health regulatory authorities, 2024; World Health Organisation, 2020). Figure 2 highlights key milestones for mental health services in the UAE.

The private sector plays an increasingly vital role, particularly in outpatient psychiatry, psychology, and counselling services throughout major urban centres. These services cater to Emirati nationals and the expatriate community, offering accessible yet often high-cost care. The private sector is also active in digital mental health innovations, corporate wellness programs, and school-based mental health services (Department of Education and Knowledge (ADEK), 2024). Private sector growth has recently enhanced service capacity, significantly expanding inpatient and

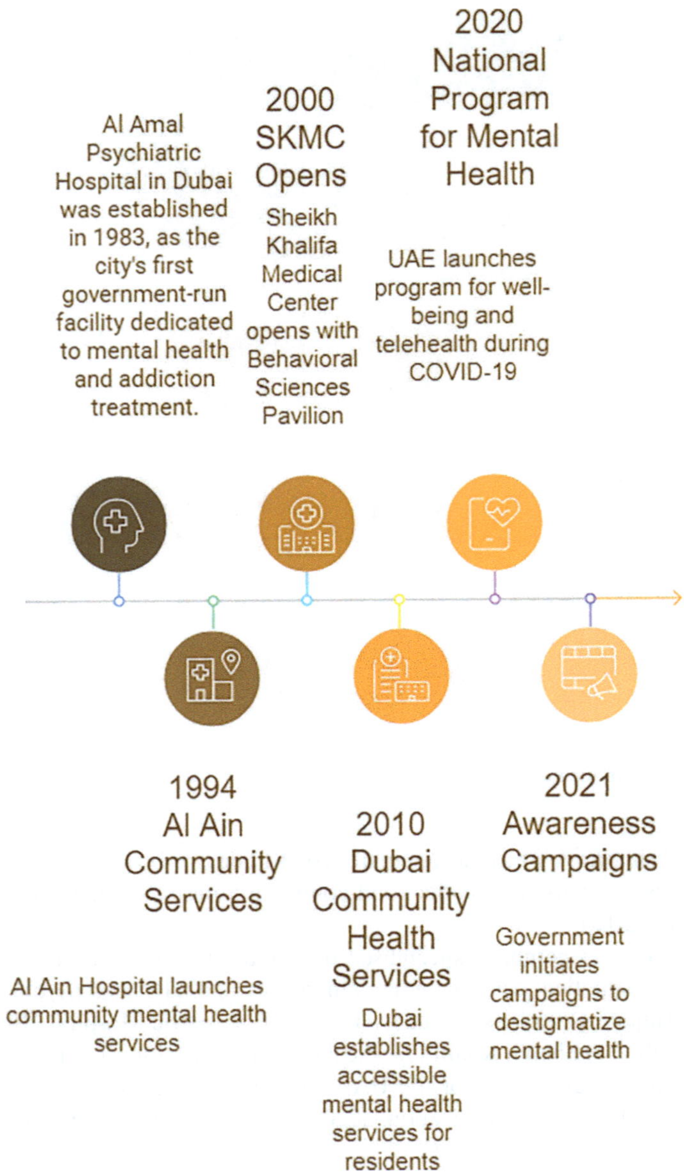

Fig. 2 Key milestones for mental health services and initiatives in the UAE

specialised psychiatric services (The Official Portal of the UAE Government-Health regulatory authorities, 2024; World Health Organisation, 2020).

Public sector services in the UAE encompass a range of mental health facilities, including outpatient clinics and specialised hospitals, aimed at providing comprehensive care to the population. As the UAE develops its mental health framework, the government prioritises integrating mental health services into primary care settings, ensuring better access for all citizens and residents. Sakina is a mental health division owned by the SEHA, serving as the centralised umbrella for all mental health services within Abu Dhabi's public healthcare system (Abu Dhabi Media Office, 2024).

7 Challenges in Mental Health Care in the UAE

The UAE's mental health care faces significant challenges with cultural dynamics, workforce, and accessibility. These issues require solutions grounded in international evidence but tailored to the local context. This section discusses prevalent challenges in detail.

7.1 Low Mental Health Literacy and Stigma

Mental health literacy—understanding mental illnesses and treatments—remains low in the UAE, with societal stigma as a major hurdle (Elyamani et al., 2021; Nair et al., 2022). Culturally, there are deeply rooted taboos around mental illness (Arab Center Washington DC, 2025; Sayed, 2015), leading to self-blame and shame. Low mental health literacy prevents many from recognising common disorders and knowing effective treatments. Even some primary healthcare providers have limited training in mental health, leading to missed diagnoses (Arab Center Washington DC, 2025). The impact of low literacy and stigma is seen in help-seeking patterns, with a preference for addressing issues privately or through family (Elshamy et al., 2023).

7.2 Funding and Research Limitations

Accurate data on mental illness prevalence in the UAE is historically challenging due to disparate sources. Available data includes hospital records, smaller academic studies, and estimates from international health agencies (Javaid et al., 2023; Marzouqi et al., 2022; Razzak et al., 2019), each with limitations. Hospital statistics mainly reflect acute cases, underestimating common disorders like mild depression or anxiety often managed in primary care. Although representative population-based studies for mental disorder screening exist (Abdullatif et al., 2021; Mubarak & Esaadouni, 2021), most data come from smaller studies focusing on specific subpopulations (Alameri et al., 2024; Hanach et al., 2023; Marzouqi et al., 2022), limiting their generalisability. Many studies use screening questionnaires instead of clinical diagnostic interviews, potentially inflating prevalence figures by including transient or mild symptoms (Mahmoud & Saravanan, 2020; Zuberi et al., 2021).

Improving epidemiological surveillance of mental health through enhanced health record reporting is vital for developing informed mental health policies in the UAE.

Globally, there is growing recognition that mental health needs adequate funding and research. High-income countries are urged to allocate at least 10% of health budgets to mental health (The Economist Impact, 2021). In the UAE, mental health services receive a smaller share of healthcare funding than physical health services, with primary care mental health programs accounting for less than 0.3% of total costs (Elmusharaf et al., 2023). The scarcity of funding relates to a lack of strong local research. The Arab region, which comprises over 5% of the world's population, contributes only about 1% of global mental health research output (Zeinoun et al., 2020). Adopting international best practices in the UAE would require increased funding for mental health research and the establishment of surveillance systems for mental illnesses (The Economist Impact, 2021).

7.3 *Inadequate and Inequitable Manpower*

An adequate mental health workforce is essential for quality care. High-income nations average about 64 mental health workers per 100,000 population, including 9–16 psychiatrists (PricewaterhouseCoopers, 2022). The UAE faces a notable shortage of mental health professionals, with uneven distribution. Despite improvements in mental health services, the ratio remains at 4.2 psychiatrists and 2.8 psychologists per 100,000 population (Eapen & El-Rufaie, 2008; World Health Organisation, 2020).

This limited workforce is concentrated in urban centres. Additionally, the mental health workforce heavily relies on expatriate professionals, as many psychiatrists, psychologists, and psychiatric nurses in the UAE are foreign-trained (Elmusharaf et al., 2023). This reliance poses challenges such as high turnover, exposure to global trends, and cultural and language barriers (Eapen & El-Rufaie, 2008). Without strengthening manpower, the UAE risks falling behind global best practices for accessible mental health care. International solutions like local training investments, rewarding practice in underserved areas, and integrating care into general health services could help bridge the gap (Elmusharaf et al., 2023).

7.4 *Access and Affordability of Mental Health Services*

The UAE has a stratified access landscape, with Emiratis enjoying better coverage and public options. In contrast, expatriates face financial and logistical barriers. The cost of mental health care is high relative to income: psychiatric consultations range from \$82 to \$163, and psychotherapy sessions can go up to \$272 (Gokulan, 2019). Migrant labourers and the unemployed face compounded challenges due to inadequate insurance and lower salaries. Historically, many health insurance plans excluded mental health coverage, with psychological disorders not considered insurable conditions until recently (Gargash Insurance, 2024). Although Abu Dhabi and Dubai now require employers to provide health insurance, coverage levels vary widely by job and tier. This economic barrier leads many to delay or avoid seeking help, acting as a significant obstacle to accessing care (Elshamy et al., 2023).

Language and cultural barriers impact access; expatriates from diverse backgrounds face challenges finding providers who speak their language or understand their culture. In 2019, an estimated 680,000 people in the UAE did not receive necessary mental health services (Elmusharaf et al., 2023), many of whom were expatriates slipping through the system. Additionally, access differs between urban and rural areas; residents in remote regions like desert communities or smaller northern emirates struggle as well. Urgent inclusive policies, strong insurance parity, and innovations like telehealth are needed to make mental health care accessible and affordable in the UAE.

7.5 Help-Seeking Patterns and Non-judicious Prescribing

Globally, mental health care has shifted towards a balanced approach combining medication, psychotherapy, and social support. In the Arab context, mental illness is often viewed medically, with the expectation of a "cure" through medication (Sayed, 2015). The stigma surrounding mental health, alongside cultural and religious beliefs, hampers effective help-seeking behaviour (Al-Darmaki, 2003; Niederkrotenthaler et al., 2014). Psychotherapy may be seen as trivial, and seeking psychological help can be viewed as a weakness (Sayed, 2015). Consequently, patients uncomfortable with therapy often request medication, which feels more private and immediate. Busy physicians may prefer prescribing drugs rather than convincing reluctant patients to consider therapy, leading to an over-reliance on pharmacotherapy, raising polypharmacy concerns. While specific UAE data are limited, studies in Gulf countries indicate high psychotropic polypharmacy rates, suggesting a regional trend (Aljawadi et al., 2022; Barakat et al., 2024; Elbakary et al., 2024).

Updating clinical guidelines and enhancing public understanding of therapy could reduce unnecessary polypharmacy and improve long-term outcomes.

7.6 Non-medical Management of Mental Disorders

The blend of traditional and modern practices is common globally, allowing healers to leverage community trust while ensuring patients receive medical care for serious issues (Green & Colucci, 2020). The first cultural instinct for psychological problems in the UAE is to consult traditional healers or religious figures. These healers use methods like Quranic recitation (ruqyah), prayers, blessings, or holy water, believing they can expel jinn or negative forces linked to the illness (Al-Shannaq & Aldalaykeh,

2023; Ciftci, 2012; Sayed, 2015). This form of spiritual healing is deeply rooted in the country's traditions (Eapen & Ghubash, 2004) and remains popular due to its social acceptability.

Herbal remedies and alternative medicine complement religious healing. Many individuals use Ayurveda, homoeopathy, or herbal medicine for stress, insomnia, or mood issues (Eapen & El-Rufaie, 2008; Eapen & Ghubash, 2004). Some prefer them as they are viewed as "natural" and culturally significant. Positive aspects of these non-medical practices include their cultural resonance and holistic approach, often addressing spiritual or social dimensions overlooked by formal healthcare. However, there are risks: relying solely on traditional and alternative methods can delay effective medical treatment. Severe conditions like schizophrenia or bipolar disorder may go untreated with only non-medical remedies. Unscrupulous healers might exploit patients by blaming them for a lack of "faith" if they do not improve.

Additionally, unregulated herbal concoctions can have unknown side effects. Many individuals combine approaches, taking prescribed medication and seeing religious healers for blessings, embodying "cognitive tolerance", holding both traditional and biomedical beliefs (Sayed, 2015). The UAE's mental health strategy should include culturally sanctioned healers as allies, mirroring global movements towards a more pluralistic mental healthcare approach that respects cultural backgrounds (Eapen & El-Rufaie, 2008; Sayed, 2015).

8 Technology and Innovations in Mental Health

The UAE has taken significant strides in cultivating a pro-technology culture within its health system. This also translates to several mental health initiatives that leverage digital mental health services for the population. Aligned with the National Strategy for Wellbeing 2031 (The Official Portal of the UAE Government, 2024a, 2024b, 2024c), the following domains are noteworthy examples.

8.1 Mobile Applications

Most government health services in the UAE are digitally transformed through secure, unified mobile applications for communication, appointment booking, laboratory results, and educational resources. This trend further extends to mental health services, which allow for continuity of care beyond the clinic (Sahatna Now, Your Gateway for Health in Abu Dhabi, 2025).

8.2 *Virtual Reality*

EHS launched the Virtual Reality Mental Health Lab to treat phobias and anxiety in an immersive environment. This enforced the role of cutting-edge technologies in spearheading novel treatment strategies on a broader community level for the country (Saseendran, 2024).

8.3 *Telemedicine and Remote Support*

Mental Health consultations provided via mobile applications have been a cornerstone for raising awareness and accessibility to care, particularly during the pandemic (Emirates News Agency-WAM, 2021). The deployment of the metaverse clinic is another example of optimising the patient experience through telemedicine, where patients can participate in consultations through a 3-dimensional space with the clinician (Emirates Health Services, 2022).

8.4 *AI-Enhanced Mental Health Support*

Artificial intelligence (AI)-based innovations hold a strong position in the UAE's governance system. This was solidified by appointing the world's first Minister of AI for the UAE in 2017. This further paved the way for proactive efforts in mental health development in the form of AI-assisted mental health applications that focus on user well-being and stress management (Saseendran, 2025).

9 Conclusions

The United Arab Emirates (UAE) has made considerable investments in healthcare, including mental health services, by leveraging its robust economic capacity. The country is advancing mental health care by integrating services, combating stigma, expanding insurance, and updating policies. As the country continues evolving its health system, integrating equitable, culturally sensitive, and community-based mental health services will ensure holistic care for all residents. With strategic focus and sustained leadership, the UAE is well-positioned to emerge as a regional mental health system reform leader.

References

Abdullatif, M., Farooq, S., Altheeb, A., Rishmawi, F., Jaradat, H., & AlAbady, K. (2021). Prevalence of depressive disorders and associated factors among adult population of Dubai 2019. *Dubai Medical Journal, 4*(4), 291–300. https://doi.org/10.1159/000518811

Abou-Saleh, M. T., Ghubash, R., & Daradkeh, T. K. (2001). A1 Ain community psychiatric survey. I. Prevalence and socio-demographic correlates. *Social Psychiatry and Psychiatric Epidemiology, 36*(1), 20–28. https://doi.org/10.1007/S001270050286

Abu Dhabi Media Office. (2024). Pure Health launches comprehensive mental health services platform Sakina. Abu Dhabi Media Office. https://www.mediaoffice.abudhabi/en/health/purehealth-launches-comprehensive-mental-health-services-platform-sakina/

Alameri, F., Yaslam, M., Alraeesi, N., Alshereif, S., Darwish, E., & Heena, H. (2024). Prevalence of anxiety disorders among visitors at a military primary health center in UAE. *Journal of Family Medicine and Primary Care, 13*(11), 4824. https://doi.org/10.4103/jfmpc.jfmpc_1658_23

Alblooshi, H., Hulse, G. K., El Kashef, A., Al Hashmi, H., Shawky, M., Al Ghaferi, H., Al Safar, H., & Tay, G. K. (2016). The pattern of substance use disorder in the United Arab Emirates in 2015: Results of a National Rehabilitation Centre cohort study. *Substance Abuse Treatment, Prevention, and Policy, 11*(1), 19. https://doi.org/10.1186/s13011-016-0062-5

Alblooshi, H., Al Safar, H., El Kashef, A., Al Ghaferi, H., Shawky, M., Hulse, G. K., Hulse, G. K., & Tay, G. K. (2020). Stratified analyses of genome wide association study data reveal haplotypes for a candidate gene on chromosome 2 (KIAA1211L) is associated with opioid use in patients of Arabian descent. *BMC Psychiatry, 20*(1), 1–9. https://doi.org/10.1186/S12888-019-2425-8

Al-Darmaki, F. R. (2003). Attitudes towards seeking professional psychological help: What really counts for United Arab Emirates University students? *Social Behavior and Personality, 31*(5), 497–508. https://doi.org/10.2224/sbp.2003.31.5.497

Aljawadi, M. H., Khoja, A. T., Alaboud, N. M., AlEnazi, M. E., Al-Shammari, S. A., Khoja, T. A., AlMuqbil, M. S., Alsheikh, A. M., & Alwhaibi, M. (2022). Prevalence of polypharmacy and factors associated with it among Saudi older adults – results from the Saudi National Survey for Elderly Health (SNSEH). *Saudi Pharmaceutical Journal: SPJ, 30*(3), 230–236. https://doi.org/10.1016/j.jsps.2022.01.003

Alrumaithi, F., & Moonesar, I. A. (2022). Psychological wellbeing: Toward an innovative provision of mental health and wellbeing in the United Arab Emirates. *Journal of Advanced Research in Social Sciences.* https://doi.org/10.33422/jarss.v6i1.788

Al-Shannaq, Y., & Aldalaykeh, M. (2023). Suicide literacy, suicide stigma, and psychological help seeking attitudes among Arab youth. *Current Psychology, 42*(8), 6532–6544. https://doi.org/10.1007/s12144-021-02007-9

American Psychiatric Association. (2021). *City living and mental wellbeing.* https://www.psychiatry.org:443/news-room/apa-blogs/city-living-and-mental-well-being

Andrade, G., Bedewy, D., Elamin, A. B. A., Abdelmonem, K. Y. A., Teir, H. J., & Alqaderi, N. (2022). Attitudes towards mental health problems in a sample of United Arab Emirates' residents. *Middle East Current Psychiatry, Ain Shams University, 29*(1), 88. https://doi.org/10.1186/s43045-022-00255-4

Arab Center Washington DC. (2025). *Increasing awareness of mental health needs in Arab populations.* Arab Center Washington DC. https://arabcenterdc.org/resource/increasing-awareness-of-mental-health-needs-in-arab-populations/

Aspire. (2020, March 26). How strong family ties wards off depression. *Aspire counseling services.* https://aspirecounselingservice.com/how-strong-family-ties-wards-off-depression/

Barakat, M., Nassar, R., Gharaibeh, L., Thiab, S., & Nashwan, A. J. (2024). Current landscape and future directions of deprescribing and polypharmacy practices in Jordan. *Medical Principles and Practice, 33*(6), 505–518. https://doi.org/10.1159/000541009

Bromet, E., Andrade, L. H., Hwang, I., Sampson, N. A., Alonso, J., de Girolamo, G., de Graaf, R., Demyttenaere, K., Hu, C., Iwata, N., Karam, A. N., Kaur, J., Kostyuchenko, S., Lépine, J.-P., Levinson, D., Matschinger, H., Mora, M. E. M., Browne, M. O., Posada-Villa, J., & Kessler, R.

C. (2011). Cross-national epidemiology of DSM-IV major depressive episode. *BMC Medicine, 9*, 90. https://doi.org/10.1186/1741-7015-9-90

Chowdhury, N. (2016). Integration between mental healthcare providers and traditional spiritual healers: Contextualising Islam in the twenty-first century. *Journal of Religion and Health, 55*(5), 1665–1671. https://doi.org/10.1007/s10943-016-0234-7

Ciftci, A. J. (2012). Mental health stigma in the Muslim community. *Journal of Muslim Mental Health, 7*(1). https://doi.org/10.3998/jmmh.10381607.0007.102

Dein, S., & Illaiee, A. S. (2013). Jinn and mental health: Looking at jinn possession in modern psychiatric practice. *The Psychiatrist, 37*(9), 290–293. https://doi.org/10.1192/pb.bp.113.042721

Department of Education and Knowledge (ADEK). (2024). ADEK school in-school specialist services policy. https://www.adek.gov.ae/-/media/Project/TAMM/ADEK/Policies/School-Policies/Teaching-and-Learning/ADEK_S_In-School-Specialist-Services-Policy_EN.pdf

Department of Health Abu Dhabi. (2025). *Open data dashboards*. https://www.doh.gov.ae/en/resources/opendata

Dervic, K., Amiri, L., Niederkrotenthaler, T., Yousef, S., Salem, M. O., Voracek, M., & Sonneck, G. (2012). Suicide rates in the national and expatriate population in Dubai, United Arab Emirates. *The International Journal of Social Psychiatry, 58*(6), 652–656. https://doi.org/10.1177/0020764011430038

Dols, M. W. (2011). *Majnūn: The madman in medieval Islamic society* (D. E. Immisch, Ed.; Reprinted). Clarendon Press.

Download Sahatna now, your gateway for health in Abu Dhabi. (2025). *Sahatna*. https://sahatna-app.doh.gov.ae/en/

Dubai Health Authority. (2025). *About us*. https://www.dha.gov.ae/en/AboutUs

Eapen, V., & El-Rufaie, O. (2008). United Arab Emirates (UAE). *International Psychiatry, 5*(2), 38–40.

Eapen, V., & Ghubash, R. (2004). Help-seeking for mental health problems of children: Preferences and attitudes in the United Arab Emirates. *Psychological Reports, 94*(2), 663–667. https://doi.org/10.2466/pr0.94.2.663-667

Elbakary, N., Abdallah, O., Ouanes, S., Hasanoglu, A., Abedlfattah-Arafa, E., Al-Shaikhly, M., Alqam, S., Alshakhs, S., Hijawi, Z., Al-Abdulla, M., Al-Khuzaei, N., & Hamad, S. (2024). Prevalence of polypharmacy and factors impacting psychotropic prescribing patterns in women of childbearing potential at inpatient mental health services in Qatar. *Neuropsychopharmacology Reports, 44*(4), 688–697. https://doi.org/10.1002/npr2.12467

Elmusharaf K., Poix S., Jung J. S., Al Farsi, Y., et al (2023). The cost of health services delivered at primary care facilities in the United Arab Emirates. UNDP, WHO, UNIATF, GHC. https://www.undp.org/sites/g/files/zskgke326/files/2024-02/uae_phc_costing_report.pdf#:~:text=Mental%20health%20services%20at%20the,in%20the%20UAE%20in%202019

El-Rufaie, O. E., & Absood, G. H. (1993). Minor psychiatric morbidity in primary health care: Prevalence, nature, and severity. *International Journal of Social Psychiatry, 39*(3), 159–166. https://doi.org/10.1177/002076409303900302

Elshamy, F., Hamadeh, A., Billings, J., & Alyafei, A. (2023). Mental illness and help-seeking behaviours among Middle Eastern cultures: A systematic review and meta-synthesis of qualitative data. *PLoS ONE, 18*(10), Article e0293525. https://doi.org/10.1371/journal.pone.0293525

Elyamani, R., Naja, S., Al-Dahshan, A., Hamoud, H., Bougmiza, M. I., & Alkubaisi, N. (2021). Mental health literacy in Arab states of the Gulf Cooperation Council: A systematic review. *PLoS ONE, 16*(1), Article e0245156. https://doi.org/10.1371/journal.pone.0245156

Emirates Health Services. (2022). *Emirates health services launches transformative project that deploys metaverse technology in healthcare delivery*. https://www.ehs.gov.ae/en/media-center/news/ehs-launches-transformative-project-that-deploys-metaverse-tech

Emirates Health Services. (2025). *About us*. Emirates Health Services. https://www.ehs.gov.ae/en/about-us

Emirates News Agency-WAM. (2021). *SEHA provides telemedicine services to mental health patients in Western Region*. https://www.wam.ae/en/article/hszrdpv8-seha-provides-telemedicine-services-mental-health

Faris, M., Macky, M. M., Badran, A. H., Saif, M., Yasser, M., Ibrahim, E., & Hussein, A. (2024). The prevalence of anxiety among university students in the United Arab Emirates following the COVID-19 lockdown. *Cureus, 16*(3), Article e56259. https://doi.org/10.7759/cureus.56259

Fouché, A., Albrithen, A., AlNuaimi, M., Al Riyami, K., Aruldoss, V., Cooper, K., Marta, R., & Tedam, P. (2023). Alcohol and substance dependence in the United Arab Emirates: A scoping review protocol. *British Medical Journal Open, 13*(5), Article e071208. https://doi.org/10.1136/bmjopen-2022-071208

Gargash Insurance. (2024). *Mental health coverage in insurance: A guide for UAE residents*. https://www.gargashinsurance.com/blogs/health-insurance/mental-health-coverage-in-insurance-a-guide-for-uae-residents/

Geros, H., Sizer, H., Mifsud, N., Reynolds, S., Kim, D. J., Eaton, S., McGorry, P., Nelson, B., & O'Donoghue, B. (2020). Migrant status and identification as ultra-high risk for psychosis and transitioning to a psychotic disorder. *Acta Psychiatrica Scandinavica, 141*(1), 52–59. https://doi.org/10.1111/acps.13099

Ghuloum, S., Al-Thani, H. A. Q. F., & Al-Amin, H. (2024). Religion and mental health: An Eastern Mediterranean region perspective. *Frontiers in Psychology, 15*, 1441560. https://doi.org/10.3389/fpsyg.2024.1441560

Gokulan, D. (2019). *The cost of keeping the mind healthy in UAE*. Khaleej Times. https://www.khaleejtimes.com/uae/the-cost-of-keeping-the-mind-healthy-in-uae

Grauer, A. D. (2022). Polysubstance use in adults with opioid use disorder receiving buprenorphine maintenance. *Journal of Addiction Medicine, 17*(1), 74–78. https://doi.org/10.1097/adm.0000000000001039

Green, B., & Colucci, E. (2020). Traditional healers' and biomedical practitioners' perceptions of collaborative mental healthcare in low- and middle-income countries: A systematic review. *Transcultural Psychiatry, 57*(1), 94–107. https://doi.org/10.1177/1363461519894396

Hanach, N., Radwan, H., Fakhry, R., Dennis, C.-L., Issa, W. B., Faris, M. E., Obaid, R. S., Al Marzooqi, S., Tabet, C., & De Vries, N. (2023). Prevalence and risk factors of postpartum depression among women living in the United Arab Emirates. *Social Psychiatry and Psychiatric Epidemiology*, *58*(3), 395–407. https://doi.org/10.1007/s00127-022-02372-1

Haak-Saheem, W., & Brewster, C. (2017). 'Hidden' expatriates: International mobility in the United Arab Emirates as a challenge to current understanding of expatriation. *Human Resource Management Journal, 27*(3), 423–439. https://doi.org/10.1111/1748-8583.12147

Haque, A., & Kindi, B. A. A. (2015). Mental health system development in the UAE. In *Mental Health and Psychological Practice in the United Arab Emirates* (pp. 23–34). Palgrave Macmillan. https://doi.org/10.1057/9781137558237

Helbich, M., Hagenauer, J., & Roberts, H. (2020). Relative importance of perceived physical and social neighborhood characteristics for depression: A machine learning approach. *Social Psychiatry and Psychiatric Epidemiology, 55*(5), 599–610. https://doi.org/10.1007/s00127-019-01808-5

Javaid, S. F., Hashim, I. J., Hashim, M. J., Stip, E., Samad, M. A., & Ahbabi, A. A. (2023). Epidemiology of anxiety disorders: Global burden and sociodemographic associations. *Middle East Current Psychiatry*, *30*(1). https://doi.org/10.1186/s43045-023-00315-3

Khan, M. I., Khan, M. A., Sherfudeen, N., Illiyan, A., & Ali, M. A. (2023). Mental health status of Indian migrant workers in the United Arab Emirates during the COVID-19 pandemic. *Healthcare, 11*(11), 1554. https://doi.org/10.3390/healthcare11111554

Koveshnikov, A., & Lehtonen, M. J. (2024). Stuck in a moment you can't get out of: The psychological effects of expatriates' coping with a crisis situation. *Journal of Global Mobility: The Home of Expatriate Management Research, 12*(4), 648–668. https://doi.org/10.1108/JGM-11-2023-0082

Mahmoud, I., & Saravanan, C. (2020). Prevalence of mental disorders and the use of mental health services among the adult population in United Arab Emirates. *Asian Journal of Epidemiology, 13*, 12–19. https://doi.org/10.3923/aje.2020.12.19

Malik, S. (2023). Reviving the legacy: Addressing Muslim mental health. *Academic Psychiatry, 47*(6), 620–621. https://doi.org/10.1007/s40596-023-01847-w

Mechelli, A. (2019). Cities increase your risk of depression, anxiety and psychosis – but bring mental health benefits too. The Conversation. http://theconversation.com/cities-increase-your-risk-of-depression-anxiety-and-psychosis-but-bring-mental-health-benefits-too-128911

Marzouqi, A. M. A., Otim, M. E., Alblooshi, A., Marzooqi, S. A., Talal, M., & Wassim, F. (2022). State of emotional health disorders of undergraduate students in the United Arab Emirates: A cross-sectional survey. *Psychology Research and Behavior Management, 15*, 1423–1433. https://doi.org/10.2147/PRBM.S365012

Ministry of Health and Prevention. (2025). *About the ministry*. https://mohap.gov.ae/en/about-us/about-the-ministryhttps://www.mohap.gov.ae

Ministry of Health and Prevention. (2025). The national policy for mental health promotion in the United Arab Emirates. https://uaephl.mohap.gov.ae/en/health-policies-and-legislations-advocacy/health-policies?itemId=fb25ead4-fed5-47f4-944b-1dfaebc9e16b

Mubarak, F., & Esaadouni, N. (2021). Prevalence of anxiety and depression in Abu Dhabi residents in the year 2019 (a pilot study). *Egyptian Journal of Psychiatry, 42*(1). https://doi.org/10.4103/ejpsy.ejpsy_30_20

Nair, S. C., Sreedharan, J., Satish, K. P., & Ibrahim, H. (2022). Health literacy in a high income Arab country: A nationwide cross-sectional survey study. *PLoS ONE, 17*(10), Article e0275579. https://doi.org/10.1371/journal.pone.0275579

Niederkrotenthaler, T., Reidenberg, D. J., Till, B., & Gould, M. S. (2014). Increasing help-seeking and referrals for individuals at risk for suicide by decreasing stigma: The role of mass media. *American Journal of Preventive Medicine, 47*(3 Suppl 2), S235-243. https://doi.org/10.1016/j.amepre.2014.06.010

Okasha, A. (1999). Mental health in the Middle East: An Egyptian perspective. *Clinical Psychology Review, 19*(8), 917–933. https://doi.org/10.1016/s0272-7358(99)00003-3

Parkinson, A., Mullan, B., Bebbington, K., Davis, E., Treadgold, C., & Finlay-Jones, A. (2023). Wellbeing and distress in young people with chronic conditions: How do positive psychology variables relate to mental health outcomes? *Health Psychology and Behavioral Medicine, 11*(1), 2274539. https://doi.org/10.1080/21642850.2023.2274539

PricewaterhouseCoopers. (2022). *The socioeconomic impact of untreated mental illness* https://www.pwc.com/m1/en/publications/documents/socio-economic-impact-untreated-mental-illness.pdf#:~:text=Foreword%20Within%20the%20GCC%2C%20approximately,build%20upon%20our%20previous%20report

Pritchard, C., Iqbal, W., & Dray, R. (2020). Undetermined and accidental mortality rates as possible sources of underreported suicides: Population-based study comparing Islamic countries and traditionally religious Western countries. *Bjpsych Open, 6*(4), Article e56. https://doi.org/10.1192/bjo.2020.38

PROGRESS.guide. (2025). *United Arab Emirates*. https://progress.guide/atlas/asia/united-arab-emirates/

Razzak, H. A., Harbi, A., & Ahli, S. (2019). Depression: Prevalence and associated risk factors in the United Arab Emirates. *Oman Medical Journal, 34*(4), 274–282. https://doi.org/10.5001/omj.2019.56

Saseendran, S. (2024). Arab health 2024: UAE launches 'immersive' virtual reality mental health lab to treat phobias, anxiety. *Gulf News* https://gulfnews.com/uae/health/arab-health-2024-uae-launches-immersive-virtual-reality-mental-health-lab-to-treat-phobias-anxiety-1.100742953

Saseendran, S. (2025). New mental health self-help app in Dubai will use AI to benefit users. *Gulf News*. https://gulfnews.com/uae/how-new-mental-health-self-help-app-in-dubai-will-use-ai-to-benefit-users-1.500027286

Sayed, M. A. (2015). Mental health services in the United Arab Emirates: Challenges and opportunities. *International Journal of Emergency Mental Health and Human Resilience, 17*(3), 3. https://doi.org/10.4172/1522-4821.1000263

Seyed-Gohrab, A. A. (2003). *Laylī and Majnūn: Love, madness and mystic longing in Niẓāmī's epic Romance*. BRILL. https://doi.org/10.1163/9789004492431

Sönmez, S., Apostolopoulos, Y., Tran, D., & Rentrope, S. (2011). Human rights and health disparities for migrant workers in the UAE. *Health and Human Rights, 13*(2), E17-35.

Tabrez, H. (2020). *UAE: Rules involving attempt and death by suicide*. Gulf News. https://gulfnews.com/living-in-uae/ask-us/uae-rules-involving-attempt-and-death-by-suicide-1.1605111089142

The Abu Dhabi Public Health Center. (2023). *About ADPHC*. https://www.adphc.gov.ae/AboutUs/AboutADPHC

The Department of Health Abu Dhabi. (2025). *About DoH*. https://www.doh.gov.ae/en/about

The Economist Impact. (2021). *Together for mental health: Towards a sustainable and scalable model of mental health care in the United Arab Emirates*. https://impact.economist.com/perspectives/sites/default/files/ei198_uae_mental_health_report_dv5.pdf

The Official Portal of the UAE Government. (2024a). *Drugs and controlled medicines*. https://u.ae/en/information-and-services/health-and-fitness/drugs-and-controlled-medicines

The Official Portal of the UAE Government. (2024b). *Health regulatory authorities*. https://u.ae/en/information-and-services/health-and-fitness/health-authorities

The Official Portal of the UAE Government. (2024c). *National strategy for well-being 2031*. https://u.ae/en/about-the-uae/strategies-initiatives-and-awards/strategies-plans-and-visions/social-affairs/national-strategy-for-wellbeing-2031

The Official Portal of the UAE Government. (2025a). *Factsheet*. https://u.ae/en/about-the-uae/fact-sheet

The Official Portal of the UAE Government. (2025b). *Mental health*. https://u.ae/en/information-and-services/health-and-fitness/mental-health

The Official Portal of the UAE Government. (2025c). *National programme for happiness and wellbeing*. https://u.ae/en/information-and-services/social-affairs/happiness/national-programme-for-happiness-and-wellbeing

Thomas, P. A., Liu, H., & Umberson, D. (2017). Family relationships and wellbeing. *Innovation in Aging, 1*(3), igx025. https://doi.org/10.1093/geroni/igx025

United Arab Emirates Legislations. (2017). *United Arab Emirates legislations*. https://www.uaelegislation.gov.ae/en/policy/details/the-national-policy-for-the-promotion-of-mentalhealth#:~:text=The%20UAE%20government%20issued%20the,to%20the%20highest%20global%20standards

United Arab Emirates Legislations. (2023). *United Arab Emirates legislations*. https://uaelegislation.gov.ae/en/legislations/2166

United Arab Emirates Ministry of Cabinet Affairs. (2025). *Statistics by subject*. https://fcsc.gov.ae/en-us/Pages/Statistics/Statistics-by-Subject.aspx#/%3Fsubject=Demography%20and%20Social&folder=Demography%20and%20Social/Population/Population

United Arab Emirates Ministry of Economy. (2020). *The annual economic report 2020*. https://www.moec.gov.ae/documents/20121/302471/English+Version+_MOE_Annual+Report.pdf/e89802b5-b321-126f-ccae-62c2103cac5b?t=1629712516757

United Nations Development Programme. (2022). *Human development report 2021–22*. https://hdr.undp.org/content/human-development-report-2021-22

United Nations Educational, Scientific and Cultural Organization. (2022). *United Arab Emirates*. https://uis.unesco.org/en/country/ae?theme=education-and-literacy

Vigo, D. V., Kestel, D., Pendakur, K., Thornicroft, G., & Atun, R. (2019). Disease burden and government spending on mental, neurological, and substance use disorders, and self-harm: Cross-sectional, ecological study of health system response in the Americas. *The Lancet. Public Health, 4*(2), e89–e96. https://doi.org/10.1016/S2468-2667(18)30203-2

World Health Organization. (2020). *Mental Health Atlas 2020*. https://cdn.who.int/media/docs/default-source/mental-health/mental-health-atlas-2020-country-profiles/are.pdf?sfvrsn=aa6c3081_6&download=true

World Health Organization. (2025). *Age-standardised suicide rates (per 100 000 population)*. https://www.who.int/data/gho/data/indicators/indicator-details/GHO/age-standardized-suicide-rates-(per-100-000-population)

Yusuf, R., & Javaid, S. F. (2025). Misconceptions about disabilities. In G. Bennett & E. Goodall (Eds.), *The Palgrave encyclopedia of disability* (pp. 1–6). Springer Nature Switzerland. https://doi.org/10.1007/978-3-031-40858-8_488-1

Zeinoun, P., Akl, E. A., Maalouf, F. T., & Meho, L. I. (2020). The Arab Region's contribution to global mental health research (2009–2018): A bibliometric analysis. *Frontiers in Psychiatry, 11*, 182. https://doi.org/10.3389/fpsyt.2020.00182

Zuberi, A., Waqas, A., Naveed, S., Hossain, M. M., Rahman, A., Saeed, K., & Fuhr, D. C. (2021). Prevalence of mental disorders in the WHO eastern Mediterranean region: A systematic review and meta-analysis. *Frontiers in Psychiatry, 12*. https://doi.org/10.3389/fpsyt.2021.665019

Chapter 15
Mental Health in Yemen

Mohammed Hussein Aljalei and Asma'a Munasar Alsubari

Abstract Yemen is undergoing a severe mental health crisis, exacerbated by prolonged armed conflict, economic instability, and a fragile healthcare infrastructure. The civil war has significantly disrupted health service delivery, leaving over half of the population without access to essential care, with mental health services among the most affected. This chapter examines the key barriers to mental health care in Yemen and explores potential strategies to enhance service accessibility. It provides an overview of the historical development of mental health services, assesses the current burden of mental disorders, and analyzes the growing demand resulting from widespread violence, forced displacement, and social fragmentation. Critical challenges include a severe shortage of trained mental health professionals, inadequate healthcare facilities, limited financial resources, and persistent cultural stigma surrounding mental illness. To address these challenges, the chapter proposes a multifaceted approach that includes increased investment in mental health, equitable distribution of human resources, integration of mental health into primary care, public education campaigns, and collaboration between traditional and biomedical practitioners to expand access and reduce stigma.

Keywords Yemen · Mental health care · Conflict and health · Access to care · Health system challenges · Cultural stigma · Mental health integration · Humanitarian response

M. H. Aljalei (✉)
National Center of Mental Health, Amman, Jordan
e-mail: mohammedaljalei0@gmail.com

A. M. Alsubari
Sana'a University, Sana, Yemen

S. Al-Huseini and S. Arafat (eds.), *Mental Health Care in the Middle East*, South Asian Perspectives in Mental Health and Psychology ,
https://doi.org/10.1007/978-981-95-0461-9_15

1 Introduction

1.1 Country Profile

Yemen is a nation situated in the southwestern region of the Arabian Peninsula, possessing an estimated population of approximately 40 million individuals and encompassing a total area of 555,000 km^2 (Health at a Glance, 2024). The country shares its boundaries with Saudi Arabia to the north and Oman to the east. At the same time, it is bordered by the Red Sea to the west and the Arabian Sea to the south (Fig. 1). Administrative divisions: The national administrative framework consists of twenty-three governorates, which are further divided into 333 districts, 2,210 sub-districts, and 38,284 villages, as reported by CSO statistics in 2019 (National Mental Health Strategy in Yemen 2022–2023, 2022). Historically, Yemen was home to ancient civilizations, including the Sabaean and Himyarite kingdoms, and subsequently became an important center for Islamic culture and trade. The nation was bifurcated into North and South Yemen until their unification on May 22, 1990. Nevertheless, since 2015, Yemen has been engulfed in a devastating civil conflict that has precipitated one of the most severe humanitarian crises worldwide. Despite its rich cultural legacy and advantageous geographical location, Yemen continues to be one of the poorest countries in the region, grappling with profound economic difficulties (El Bcheraoui et al., 2018). The ongoing strife,

Fig. 1 Map of Yemen

political turmoil, and external interventions have substantially obstructed developmental initiatives. Yemen is predominantly a Muslim nation, with over 99% of the population practicing Islam (World Population Review, 2023). The conflict has intensified problems such as food insecurity, inflation, and lack of access to vital services. Due to its historical connections and geographical proximity, Yemen has fostered cultural and trade relations with both Arab and African states. In recent years, migration trends have indicated that a considerable number of Yemeni citizens are seeking medical treatment and improved economic prospects in neighboring Gulf nations, notwithstanding the persistent challenges of mobility arising from the conflict and political instability (Qasem Saleh & Makki, 2008).

1.2 Evolution of Psychiatric Services in Yemen

The history of mental health care in Yemen is deeply intertwined with its cultural, religious, and socio-political evolution. From ancient healing traditions to modern psychiatric practices, Yemen's approach to mental health has been shaped by spiritual beliefs, colonial influences, and contemporary challenges. This historical trajectory can be divided into key periods: the pre-Islamic era, the Islamic Golden Age, the Ottoman and British colonial periods, post-independence developments, and contemporary challenges.

1.2.1 Pre-Islamic Period: Indigenous Healing and Spiritual Beliefs

Before the advent of Islam, mental health care in Yemen was primarily managed through traditional and community-based methods. The region's ancient civilizations, such as the Sabaeans and Himyarites, had rudimentary medical systems influenced by neighboring cultures like Mesopotamia and Persia. Mental illness was often perceived through a supernatural lens, attributed to possession by spirits "Jinn" or divine punishment. Healing practices included rituals, incantations, and herbal remedies, administered by priests and shamans. The strong emphasis on communal support ensured that individuals with mental health issues were cared for within their families and tribes rather than isolated from society. These practices, though rudimentary by modern standards, reflected an early attempt to address mental health within the framework of available knowledge and cultural beliefs (Elshamy et al., 2023).

1.2.2 Islamic Golden Age: Emergence of Medical Understanding

With the advent of Islam in the seventh century, Yemen became part of a vast Muslim empire that prioritized learning and scientific inquiry. During the Islamic Golden Age (eighth to thirteenth centuries), significant advancements in medicine occurred. Islam emphasized compassion and care for those suffering from mental illness, viewing it as a condition requiring treatment rather than punishment (Zafaran, 2023). Prominent Islamic scholars such as Al-Razi (Rhazes) and Ibn Sina (Avicenna) made significant contributions to the understanding of mental health (Pajević, 2021). These pioneers distinguished between physical and psychological ailments and advocated for human treatment of mental illness. Their works, which emphasized compassion and care, influenced medical thought across the Islamic world.

In Yemen, this intellectual flourishing led to the integration of psychiatric principles into local healthcare practices. While dedicated mental health facilities were rare, hospitals (bimaristans) established in other parts of the Islamic world may have inspired similar initiatives in Yemen. Mental health care during this period continued to rely heavily on religious and communal support networks, with mosques, shrines, and family structures providing solace and care for those suffering from mental illness.

1.2.3 Ottoman and British Colonial Periods: Institutional Beginnings

During the Ottoman rule (sixteenth–nineteenth centuries), Yemen remained largely dependent on traditional healing methods, as the empire focused more on military and administrative concerns rather than social services like mental health care. Mental illness was still addressed within religious and communal frameworks, with little evidence of formal psychiatric institutions. Some community members believe that mental health needs indicate the presence of a jinn inside them, prompting them to go to sheikhs to be cured of this (Mental Health Assessment IMC, 2019).

British colonial influence in southern Yemen, particularly in Aden (1839–1967), brought the first structured mental health facilities. The British established a mental asylum in Aden's Crater District during the late nineteenth century, initially for European officials and later for the local population. The asylum functioned as an isolation center rather than a therapeutic environment, reflecting prevailing attitudes toward mental illness as a source of shame or danger. Despite its limitations, this marked the institutionalization of mental health care in Yemen, albeit one rooted in containment rather than compassion.

1.2.4 Post-independence Developments: Struggles and Progress

Following the historic independence of North Yemen in 1962 and the liberation of South Yemen from British colonial rule in 1967, a significant milestone was reached with the unification of both states in 1990 (Elshamy et al., 2023). In Northern Yemen, al-Salaam Sanatorium was founded in Hudaydah in 1976 as a rudimentary facility for individuals with mental illnesses, which was devoid of adequate treatment resources. The initiation of mental health services occurred in 1978 with the arrival of a Bulgarian psychiatrist at the Republican Hospital in Sana'a, followed by a European physician who managed severe cases at the Military Hospital (A Neglected Crisis, 2017). A World Health Organization (WHO) study conducted in 1980 highlighted the presence of numerous mentally ill patients wandering in public spaces. In response, the WHO facilitated the establishment of psychiatric departments in three hospitals and provided training for local physicians. In 1981, Dr. Ahmed Makki emerged as the first specialized psychiatrist in Yemen. Thawra Hospital, alongside the contributions from Dr. Abdullah Al Kathiri in Aden. By 1986, Northern Yemen had a total of three psychiatrists. In Southern Yemen, mental health services became integrated into primary healthcare during the early 1980s through WHO initiatives, which were centered on training healthcare providers in various domains. Between 1986 and 1990, obsolete patient cells at the sanatorium in Aden were phased out. Following the unification of North and South Yemen in 1990, a consolidated Ministry of Health was established. Subsequently, the High Council for Mental Health was formed, comprising various ministries tasked with overseeing mental health programs, which included the creation of a national mental health strategy in 2004, supported by the WHO. This strategy aimed to enhance mental health awareness, increase access to care, and incorporate mental health services into primary healthcare, garnering support from multiple stakeholders. Nonetheless, sustained efforts were hindered by insufficient financial and human resources. A suggested Mental Health Act in 2004 failed to pass, as did a later draft bill in 2007. Yemeni physicians encountered difficulties in obtaining funding for clinics, and there was a lack of advocacy for mental health reforms (Alhariri et al., 2021). The societal stigma surrounding mental health issues persisted, deterring many from seeking assistance. This stigma may have also contributed to the low enrollment rates in psychiatry training programs.

1.2.5 Contemporary Challenges: War, Crisis, and Mental Health

The ongoing conflict in Yemen, which began in 2015, has severely undermined the country's already fragile healthcare infrastructure, with devastating consequences for mental health services. Prolonged violence, economic collapse, and the displacement of millions have created a humanitarian crisis marked by widespread trauma and psychological distress across the population.

By early 2015, the WHO reported that Yemen's health system had effectively collapsed, leaving over 14.8 million people, more than half the population, without access to basic healthcare services (Health System in Yemen, 2015). According to data from the Health Resources Availability Mapping System (HeRAMS), only 45% of the 3,507 health facilities surveyed across 16 governorates were fully functional, 38% were partially functional, and 17% were completely non-functional. Additionally, 274 facilities had sustained conflict-related damage, including 69 that were destroyed (HeRAMS Yemen, 2023).

Mental health services have suffered disproportionately within this broader collapse. The same HeRAMS survey indicated that only 21% of facilities provided services for non-communicable diseases and mental health conditions. The shortage of psychiatric professionals remains critical; WHO estimated that only 40 psychiatric specialists were present in the entire country in 2016, mostly concentrated in the capital, Sana'a. This number later declined to 36, according to the Ministry of Health. The mass emigration of healthcare workers and the severe shortage of psychotropic medications and clinical infrastructure have further exacerbated the crisis.

The mental health burden among Yemenis has escalated dramatically, particularly among vulnerable groups such as children, adolescents, and displaced populations. Mass displacement, both internal and cross-border, has led to widespread loss of homes, livelihoods, and family members, contributing to intense psychological stress (Jubari & Saifaldeen, 2014). Displaced individuals often face significant barriers to accessing care, including a lack of transportation, financial hardship, and limited availability of services within camps and host communities.

Children have been deeply affected. Many have witnessed extreme violence, experienced family separations, or endured prolonged periods of hunger. These exposures significantly increase their risk for post-traumatic stress disorder (PTSD), anxiety, and depression. Although data on child mental health in Yemen remain limited, a 2016 study involving 902 schoolchildren in Sana'a found that 79% exhibited symptoms of PTSD, 70% reported sleep disturbances, and 63% expressed uncertainty about their future.

Considering the increasing demands in this area, the WHO and several international non-governmental organizations (NGOs) have initiated programs such as the Mental Health Gap Action Programme (mhGAP). This program seeks to equip primary and community healthcare providers with the necessary skills to implement fundamental mental health interventions. Nevertheless, these initiatives remain constrained in terms of scope and funding, as humanitarian assistance continues to focus on urgent survival necessities, including food, shelter, and emergency medical services, rather than on mental health support (Keynejad et al., 2021).

In rural and underserved areas, where formal mental health services are nearly absent, communities often rely on traditional healing practices, family support, and informal coping mechanisms. While these culturally rooted approaches provide some psychological relief, they are not substitutes for structured psychiatric care. Recent initiatives have aimed to integrate mental health services into primary healthcare settings, but progress remains slow due to ongoing insecurity, logistical challenges, and economic constraints (Al-Krenawi, 2005).

1.2.6 Major Advocacy Group in Yemen

The Yemeni Psychiatric and Neurological Association (YPNA) was established in 1989, followed by the formation of the Yemeni Mental Health Association

(YMHA) in 1998. Many of these associations are relatively recent in their inception and encounter many challenges; however, they remain committed to advocating for and providing essential services. These organizations play a vital role in combating various forms of violence, including physical, mental, and sexual abuse aimed at women and children. They actively organize events to observe International Mental Health Day, which includes conferences, workshops, and seminars. Their initiatives also encompass publishing endeavors, and broadcasting activities via radio and television. Ultimately, these associations also advocate for the establishment of a formal code of ethics and the implementation of a Mental Health Act, often contending with significant personal and financial obstacles in the pursuit of these objectives.

1.2.7 Mental Health Legislation in Yemen

Yemen currently lacks a comprehensive Mental Health Act, and mental health services operate under general healthcare laws with no specific legal framework dedicated to psychiatric care. Efforts have been made to integrate mental health into national health policies, but challenges remain due to ongoing conflict, economic instability, and limited mental health infrastructure.

2 Epidemiology and Burden of Mental Illness

Over the past several decades, Yemen's healthcare system has suffered due to prolonged conflict, economic instability, and underinvestment in mental health services. The focus on communicable diseases has led to a rising double burden of diseases, with non-communicable diseases (NCDs), including mental disorders, now accounting for over 50% of Yemen's disease burden. Mental illness has emerged as a critical public health issue (Nawsherwan et al., 2025).

However, studies on the prevalence of mental illnesses in Yemen are scarce. Limited data indicates high prevalence, especially among those affected by war and displacement. Although a nationwide survey has not taken place, regional studies reveal troubling trends. For example, in 2018, over 25% of internally displaced persons (IDPs) exhibited symptoms of PTSD, while more than 30% of conflict-affected populations reported depression and anxiety (WHO 2019).

The prevalence of psychiatric disorders is notably higher among women (25.4%) than men (18.9%), and it also affects elderly individuals more significantly. A 2019 study by EPOS Consulting found PTSD was the most common mental health condition, impacting 45% of the surveyed population. Other disorders included depression (27%), anxiety (25%), schizophrenia (18%), and phobias (4%), (Abou Khalil & Owino Ouko, 2024).

Mental health services are more accessible in urban areas, while rural populations often depend on traditional healing. Suicide is rising, but is not recognized as a public health concern, with social stigma and limited services causing underreporting. Suicide rates fluctuate, with higher risks among young individuals, particularly women, housewives, and students. According to the WHO, in 2000, the suicide rate was about 6.1 per 100,000 people, varying over the years, with the lowest rate below 5.6 in 2013–2014. By 2019, the rate had slightly increased to 5.8 per 100,000, reflecting a 4.9% reduction compared to 2000. Underreporting and cultural stigma contribute to discrepancies in these statistics, and the leading methods of suicide include hanging and poisoning, alongside factors like economic hardship and psychiatric disorders (AL-Ahdal & Farahat, 2022). There is an urgent need for a comprehensive national mental health strategy in Yemen, emphasizing funding, psychiatric training, and integration of mental health services into primary healthcare to effectively tackle this crisis (Health at a Glance, 2024).

3 Mental Health Services in Yemen

3.1 Conventional Services

Mental illnesses are among the top health priorities in Yemen due to the significant burden imposed by prolonged conflict, displacement, and socioeconomic challenges. Yemen's health system is pluralistic, involving government services, private organizations, (NGOs), and donor agencies. Mental health care is delivered through formal and informal systems, with formal services including outpatient clinics, inpatient units, residential facilities, and psychiatric hospitals. However, most service users attend outpatient services, while fewer utilize inpatient or residential care. The government health system operates at three levels: primary care (community clinics and rural health centers), secondary care (district hospitals), and tertiary care (specialized hospitals). Psychiatrists are absent at the primary and secondary levels, with posts allocated only at tertiary care facilities. Alongside Western medicine, alternative medicine practitioners operate within the government system (Islam et al., 2021).

The private sector plays a dominant role, particularly in urban areas, offering both Western and traditional medicine through diagnostic centers, private clinics, and pharmacies. However, the private sector is poorly regulated, and unqualified practitioners dominate in rural regions, where traditional healers and religious leaders often serve as the primary source of psychosocial support for mental health issues. Despite the expansion of private mental health services. Yemen still lacks essential community mental health programs, crisis response units, and specialized outreach initiatives. NGOs and donor agencies play a crucial role in filling this gap, focusing on marginalized populations, internally displaced people (IDPs), and refugees, providing essential mental health and psychosocial support (MHPSS) services. Organizations such as the WHO, Médecins Sans Frontières (MSF), and local NGOs offer vital mental health interventions, including psychosocial counseling, crisis intervention, and community-based mental health programs. However, these initiatives are limited in scope, underfunded, and heavily reliant on external aid, making them unsustainable in the long term (WHO, 2019).

Barriers to accessing mental health care remain significant, including low mental health literacy, cultural stigma, chaotic help-seeking behavior influenced by supernatural beliefs, and weak referral systems. Individuals often consult informal providers such as family members, friends, or traditional healers before seeking formal care. In urban areas, patients typically visit specialized hospitals or private practitioners, while in rural areas, they rely on village doctors, pharmacies, or traditional healers. Unnecessary investigations, improper referrals, and financial exploitation are common in the private sector, further complicating access to care. Mental health care in Yemen is also hindered by a severe shortage of mental health professionals, a lack of mental health services in primary and secondary healthcare, geographical disparities in access, economic barriers, and the impact of conflict and displacement. The ongoing war has led to widespread trauma, increasing the prevalence of mental health disorders such as (PTSD), depression, and anxiety (Nawsherwan et al., 2025).

Addressing Yemen's mental health crisis requires urgent reforms, including increased funding, workforce development, and the integration of mental health services into primary care to ensure equitable access for all. A national mental health policy focusing on sustainable, community-based mental health care and crisis intervention services is urgently needed to improve the mental well-being of Yemen's population.

3.2 *The Role of the Private Sector*

The private sector has increasingly emerged as a critical component in the delivery of psychiatric care in Yemen, largely compensating for the severe deficiencies in public mental health services. This shift was initiated in the early 1990s with the establishment of the first private psychiatric clinic in Sana'a by Dr. Ahmed Al-Mansoori. Initially limited to outpatient consultations, the clinic eventually expanded to include medication management and comprehensive psychiatric services. Since then, the private mental health landscape has grown, though it remains under-resourced relative to the country's mental health burden.

Yemen, with a population exceeding 39 million, remains critically underserved in terms of mental health infrastructure. Currently, only four psychiatric hospitals across major governorates offer approximately 850 beds for adult patients. Public sector services are supplemented by seven outpatient psychiatric clinics within general hospitals. However, the country also hosts 45 private clinics, and three residential centers providing mental health care (Alhariri et al., 2021). Despite these developments, many services remain limited in scope and accessibility, particularly in rural regions. A closer examination of the private sector reveals substantial disparities in service delivery and capacity. Among private institutions involved in mental health care: 65% provide psychological support, and 69% offer broader mental health services.

In contrast, only 13% report adequate equipment, and just 20% maintain reliable access to psychiatric medications, highlighting critical supply gaps. Medication availability overall was reported at 56%, suggesting that pharmacological treatment is inconsistently provided. In terms of human resources, mental health professionals constitute only 48–64% of staff in relevant private facilities, reflecting a limited and variable level of specialization. Infrastructure within the private sector remains sparse:

Only three private hospitals provide mental health services, offering 173 beds. Eleven private mental health centers contribute an additional 53 beds (National Mental Health Strategy in Yemen 2022–2023, 2022). There are also 16 private psychiatric clinics operating independently (Fig. 2).

In the public–private intersection, just two mental health clinics are in public hospitals. This fragmented structure underscores the private sector's inability to fully compensate for systemic shortcomings. The country continues to face a severe shortage of qualified professionals, with fewer than 60 psychiatrists and 130 trained therapists nationwide. While this marks an improvement from the 44 psychiatrists reported in 2010, the ratio remains drastically insufficient. Compounding these issues, services are predominantly concentrated in urban centers, leaving rural populations with minimal or no access to care. Moreover,

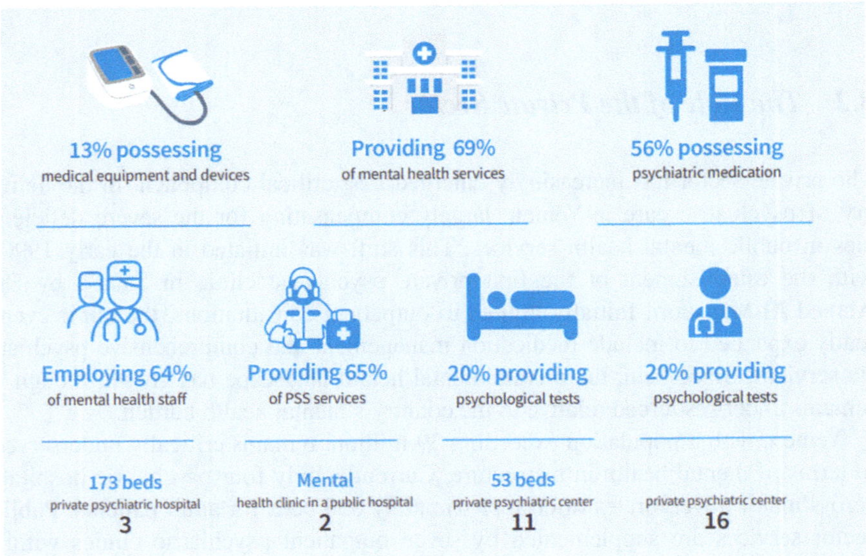

Fig. 2 Private mental health facilities in assessed governorates. Adapted from National Mental Health Strategy in Yemen 2022–2026 (National Mental Health Strategy in Yemen 2022–2023, 2022)

Yemen continues to lack critical mental health infrastructure such as community-based programs, crisis response services, and specialized outreach initiatives. Despite growth in the private sector, these structural and geographic limitations hinder the overall effectiveness and equity of mental health care in the country.

3.3 New Developments-Telepsychiatry

With the increasing availability of the internet, smartphones, and electronic devices, telemedicine has initiated a transformative phase in healthcare services within Yemen (Ishak et al., 2021). In recent years, significant advancements have been made in mental health care, propelled by the adoption of telepsychiatry, especially in a country where the accessibility of mental health services is often obstructed by persistent conflict, economic challenges, and a deficiency of mental health professionals (UNFPA, 2021).

Telepsychiatry in Yemen has gained momentum as an effective means of connecting mental health providers with patients, specifically targeting rural and underserved populations. Numerous mental health practitioners now utilize platforms such as WhatsApp, Zoom, Google Meet, Skype, and Messenger for patient communication, consultations, and the provision of psychotherapy or counselling. This method has proven especially beneficial during crises, such as the COVID-19 pandemic, when in-person consultations became challenging or infeasible (Ishak et al., 2021).

In Yemen, the delivery of telepsychiatry services frequently occurs through collaborations between local psychiatrists and international organizations. For example, Yemenis living abroad can access mental health consultations via telepsychiatry by coordinating with their relatives in Yemen. Family members consult local psychiatrists to describe the patient's condition and facilitate video calls between the psychiatrist and the patient. Following the consultation, prescriptions are issued, and medications are dispatched to the patient overseas. Notwithstanding its potential, tele-psychiatry in Yemen confronts considerable challenges, including inadequate internet infrastructure, electricity shortages, and the absence of regulatory frameworks to govern these services.

Nevertheless, initiatives led by local NGOs and international organizations have begun to mitigate these obstacles by providing training, resources, and support to mental health professionals (HeRAMS Yemen, 2023). At present, telepsychiatry in Yemen largely remains unregulated, with many services functioning through private practices or humanitarian entities. Although there is no formal government-led telepsychiatry initiative, the increasing demand for mental health services has spurred conversations regarding the integration of telepsychiatry into the national healthcare system. As tele-psychiatry continues to advance in Yemen, it holds the potential to enhance access to mental health care, alleviate stigma, and deliver vital support to individuals in distress. With further investments and regulatory frameworks, tele-psychiatry could evolve into a fundamental component of mental health services in Yemen, offering hope to numerous individuals in need.

4 Challenges in Mental Health Care in Yemen

Mental health care in Yemen faces severe challenges due to the ongoing conflict, economic instability, and weak healthcare infrastructure (Dureab et al., 2021). These challenges not only hinder access to mental health services but also perpetuate a cycle of neglect and suffering for millions of Yemenis. Below is an integrated discussion of the key issues affecting mental health care in Yemen (El Bcheraoui et al., 2018).

4.1 Limited Infrastructure and Funding

Yemen's mental health infrastructure is severely underdeveloped, with minimal funding allocated compared to other health priorities, such as infectious diseases and emergency care (Aya Hassanein, 2023). The lack of investment has resulted in:

Inadequate Facilities: There are only a few psychiatric hospitals in major urban centers like Sana'a and Aden. General hospitals rarely have dedicated mental health units, leaving patients with no choice but to seek care in overcrowded and ill-equipped facilities (National Mental Health Strategy in Yemen 2022–2023, 2022).

Outdated Equipment and Medication Shortages: Many health facilities operate with outdated diagnostic tools and treatment equipment. Essential psychiatric medications, such as antidepressants, antipsychotics, and mood stabilizers, are frequently unavailable due to supply chain disruptions caused by the conflict and economic sanctions (UNHCR, 2023).

Dependence on NGOs: With limited government funding, many mental health initiatives rely on international NGOs and humanitarian organizations. However, these efforts are often fragmented and unsustainable, leaving gaps in service delivery.

Conflict Damage: The war has destroyed or damaged numerous healthcare facilities, further reducing the availability of mental health services. Even when facilities remain operational, they are often understaffed and unable to meet the growing demand.

4.2 Shortage of Mental Health Professionals

The severe shortage of trained mental health professionals is one of the most significant barriers to accessing care in Yemen. Key issues include:

Severe Workforce Deficit: In Yemen, there are only 0.21 psychiatrists for every 700,000 people and 0.17 psychologists for each 100,000 individuals. This starkly contrasts with the higher ratios found in more developed countries, such as the United States, which boasts 12.4 psychiatrists and 29.03 psychologists per 100,000 individuals, and Norway, which has 29.68 psychiatrists and 54.28

psychologists for the same population. Additionally, there is a significant lack of reliable and comprehensive data regarding mental health services in Yemen, which hinders the possibility of making targeted investments in this crucial sector (Achieving Health for All in Yemen, 2023).

Urban Concentration: Most mental health professionals are concentrated in major cities, leaving rural populations without access to specialized care. This geographic disparity exacerbates inequalities in mental health service delivery.

Brain Drain: Many skilled healthcare workers, including psychiatrists, have fled the country due to insecurity, poor working conditions, and lack of opportunities. Those who remain often face burnout from overwhelming caseloads and inadequate resources (Médecins Sans Frontières, 2023).

Lack of Training Opportunities: Continuous professional development and advanced training programs are rare in Yemen. Mental health professionals often lack exposure to modern treatment modalities and evidence-based practices, limiting their ability to provide high-quality care (Zaid et al., 2024).

4.3 Stigma and Cultural Barriers

Stigma surrounding mental health remains deeply entrenched in Yemeni society, creating significant barriers to seeking help. Key aspects of this challenge include:

Misunderstanding of Mental Illness: Mental health disorders are frequently misunderstood and attributed to supernatural causes, spiritual possession, or moral failings. This perception discourages individuals from seeking professional help and reinforces harmful stereotypes.

Social Ostracism: People with severe mental illnesses are often ostracized by their families and communities. They may be subjected to neglect, abuse, or confinement, worsening their condition and violating their human rights (Human Rights Watch, 2021).

Gender-Specific Stigma: Women face additional stigma when seeking mental health care. Conditions such as postpartum depression or anxiety are often dismissed as weakness or inadequacy, preventing women from accessing timely treatment.

Religious Misinterpretations: Some religious leaders perpetuate misconceptions about mental illness, framing it as a test of faith or punishment rather than a medical issue. This can discourage individuals from seeking scientifically validated treatments (Elshamy et al., 2023).

4.4 Lack of Mental Health Awareness and Education

Public awareness of mental health remains alarmingly low in Yemen, contributing to misconceptions and reluctance to seek treatment. Key factors include:

Limited Public Discourse: Mental health is rarely discussed openly, leading to ignorance and fear surrounding mental illness.

Absence of School-Based Programs: Schools do not incorporate mental health education into their curricula, leaving children and adolescents uninformed about emotional well-being and coping mechanisms.

Workplace Neglect: Employers fail to address mental health concerns, offering no support systems or resources for employees experiencing stress, burnout, or other psychological issues.

4.5 Additional Challenges Specific to Yemen

Security Risks for Healthcare Workers: Mental health professionals face significant risks while providing care in conflict zones, including threats of violence and targeted attacks on healthcare facilities (Elnakib et al., 2021).

Telepsychiatry Limitations: While telepsychiatry offers potential solutions, its implementation is hindered by unreliable internet connectivity, power shortages, and low digital literacy among patients and providers (Alhammadi et al., 2024).

Cultural Resistance to Modern Treatments: Traditional healing practices, such as spiritual rituals or herbal remedies, are widely preferred over modern psychiatric interventions, delaying proper diagnosis and treatment.

Interplay Between Physical and Mental Health: Many Yemenis suffer from chronic physical illnesses, malnutrition, and disabilities caused by the conflict. These conditions often coexist with mental health disorders, requiring integrated care that is largely unavailable in Yemen's fragmented healthcare system (WHO, 2021).

5 Non-medical Approaches to the Management of Mental Health Disorders in Yemen

In Yemen, a considerable number of individuals experiencing mental health conditions seek care outside the established medical system due to inadequate access to psychiatric services. Traditional and faith-based practitioners, including Sheikhs, Imams, Ruqyah specialists, and herbal medicine practitioners, predominantly influence mental health care. They provide treatment grounded in religious rituals, Qur'anic verses, and conventional remedies. A study from the Ministry of Public Health and Population found that 30% of both adults and children with mental health disorders first approached traditional healers or alternative medicine practitioners, such as herbalists or spiritual advisors (Ministry of Public Health, 2021).

Such findings indicate that approximately one in four to one in two individuals in Yemen depend on non-medical caregivers during their initial engagement with mental health challenges, a tendency that commonly extends to later care-seeking efforts. The preference for non-medical interventions is shaped by prevalent cultural beliefs that link mental illness to supernatural phenomena, such as jinn possession, harm from black magic, or the evil eye. Lower educational levels and limited awareness of mental health were identified as major contributors to these beliefs. While these traditional practices may offer temporary psychological solace, they also have the potential to delay necessary medical intervention, exacerbate psychiatric symptoms, or result in direct harm. Consequently, fostering collaboration between mental health professionals and traditional healers is essential for enhancing mental health awareness and accessibility in Yemen (Cheffi Ahlem, 2021).

6 Strategies for Enhancing Mental Health Services in Yemen

6.1 Increased Research and Financial Support

A primary obstacle confronting mental health services in Yemen is the insufficient funding and resources allocated to mental health care (Dureab et al., 2021). To ameliorate this issue, it is crucial to enhance financial support for comprehensive mental health epidemiological research within Yemen. This can be accomplished by creating specialized mental health research funding agencies or by incorporating mental health research into the mandates of existing national and international research funding bodies. Additional financial resources are also needed to facilitate training and capacity building for researchers, clinicians, and other mental health practitioners, including the provision of scholarships and fellowships (Karam et al., 2023).

6.2 Nationwide Distribution of Mental Health Professionals

The allocation of mental health professionals in Yemen is characterized by inequity and centralization, with no designated positions for psychiatrists at primary and secondary care levels. There is an urgent need to ensure equitable distribution and effective use of available resources. Mental health services ought to be accessible through the current healthcare system. Strategic measures must be implemented to secure psychiatrists at the secondary level within government health services, and specialized training should be initiated to ensure that at least one individual knowledgeable in mental health is present at every primary health-care facility (Mental Health Assessment IMC, 2019). These measures aim to augment the number of mental health professionals and enhance the accessibility and availability of mental health services throughout Yemen. Resources should be distributed fairly to ensure service availability to individuals across all geographical, socioeconomic, racial, ethnic, and gender demographics (National Strategy, 2011). Mental health professionals should be encouraged to adopt a community care philosophy while receiving adequate compensation for their roles and being inspired by a commitment to community welfare.

6.3 *Establishment of Health Insurance*

Currently, Yemen lacks a national health insurance system that specifically covers mental health services. It is vital for the Yemen National Mental Health Strategic Plan to prioritize advocacy for the inclusion of mental health coverage in both government and private health insurance schemes. This should encompass coverage for evidence-based treatments for mental health disorders, including both medical and non-medical interventions. Financial mechanisms such as Direct Project Aid, Reimbursable Project Aid, and government funding will support this initiative. Moreover, certain private health insurance providers may offer mental health coverage within their policies. To enhance mental health insurance availability throughout the country, it is essential to educate the public about mental health insurance and develop specific insurance plans that encompass a wide array of mental health services, including psychotherapy, medication, and hospitalization. The government can also incentivize insurance providers through tax breaks, subsidies, or other financial benefits to promote the establishment of mental health insurance options.

6.4 *Promoting Mental Health Literacy*

Creating awareness about mental health literacy among the general population, health professionals, policymakers, and community leaders is a vital strategy for improving mental health knowledge (Okasa et al., 2012). Sustained digital media campaigns focusing on mental health can significantly influence public awareness, promote help-seeking behaviors, and diminish stigma. Enhancing awareness, particularly among the youth, may lead to increased utilization of modern digital health technologies for accessing mental health services and alleviating stigma associated with mental health issues in Yemen.

6.4.1 Social Media Initiatives

Leverage popular social media platforms such as Facebook, Instagram, Twitter, and TikTok to generate and disseminate content that highlights mental health issues, fosters mental health literacy, encourages discourse, and contributes to stigma reduction.

6.4.2 Educational Workshops

Conduct workshops in educational institutions and workplaces to inform individuals about various aspects of mental health, its significance, and strategies for recognizing and addressing mental health challenges.

6.4.3 Endorsements by Influencers

Collaborate with prominent figures or influencers to champion mental health literacy and assist in dismantling the stigma surrounding mental health challenges.

6.4.4 Public Service Announcements (PSAs)

Engage with local radio and television stations to broadcast public service announcements focusing on mental health literacy and the critical nature of seeking help when necessary.

6.4.5 Community Engagement Events

Organize community gatherings, such as mental health awareness walks, concerts, and art exhibitions, to unite individuals and disseminate information regarding mental health literacy.

6.4.6 Development of Mental Health Applications

Create accessible mental health applications that furnish users with resources, advice, and self-assessment tools to enhance mental health literacy and motivate help-seeking behavior.

6.4.7 Print Media Contributions

Generate articles, infographics, and opinion pieces for publication in newspapers and magazines to inform readers about mental health concerns and promote mental health literacy.

6.4.8 Collaboration with Mental Health Organizations

Establish robust alliances with esteemed mental health organizations to enable the exchange of valuable resources, specialized expertise, and profound insights. This cooperative initiative is intended to substantially improve mental health literacy on a wider scale, ultimately serving the interests of communities and individuals who require support the most.

6.5 Specialized Initiatives for Non-medical Care Providers

A substantial segment of mental health services in Yemen is catered to by non-medical care providers, such as traditional healers, religious figures, and community health workers. To synchronize traditional methods with contemporary psychiatric services, specialized initiatives should be established to educate these providers in mental health understanding, stigma alleviation, and referral processes. These programs can utilize existing cultural paradigms to encourage help-seeking behaviors while gradually incorporating evidence-based methodologies. The Yemeni government, alongside international partners, could create social and behavior change communication (SBCC) campaigns, encompassing television advertisements, radio programs, and community workshops. These campaigns ought to aim at diminishing stigma, enhancing mental health awareness, and training non-medical providers in recognizing and managing fundamental mental health issues. Such initiatives would resonate with global frameworks like the WHO's mhGAP, which has been effectively applied in various low-resource contexts (Cheffi et al., 2021).

6.6 Effective Referral Mechanisms

The Yemen National Mental Health Strategic Plan should prioritize the incorporation of psychiatric services at all tiers of the national healthcare framework. This approach seeks to bolster the current healthcare delivery system by augmenting providers' capabilities to recognize and address mental health issues. The establishment of referral protocols and pathways is crucial to ensure patients receive the appropriate level of care within the healthcare system. By decentralizing mental health services across divisions, districts, and subdistricts in both urban and rural settings, accessibility to mental health care can be assured for all citizens nationwide (Demographic Survey, 2015). The WHO's mhGAP might serve as a blueprint for scaling mental, neurological, and substance use disorder services in Yemen.

6.7 Principles of Good Governance

The successful provision of mental health services depends on the principles of good governance, which necessitate robust leadership and accountability structures to guarantee that services adhere to international standards and approved practices (Karam et al., 2023). Oversight of mental health services should be entrusted to the Directorate General of Health Services, including the management of both primary and secondary care in district hospitals and health centers. Clinical audits, supervision aimed at mitigating polypharmacy, and maintaining transparency, equity, and a non-discriminatory allocation of government resources can cultivate a culture of good governance within Yemen's mental health domain.

6.8 Accessibility of Psychotropic Medications

Ensuring a consistent availability of essential psychotropic medications such as antipsychotics, anti-anxiety medications, antidepressants, mood stabilizers, and antiepileptic drugs is imperative. These medications should be accessible from tertiary facilities down to the community level, bolstering mental health services and primary healthcare teams. Revising the essential medicine list to include new generations can assist in tackling accessibility challenges and ensuring that community mental health services maintain a reliable supply of necessary medications.

6.9 Engagement of Clients and Families in Service Provision

Involving clients and their families in the design and provision of mental health services is pivotal for creating models of care that center on patients. There is a scarcity of engagement from consumer associations and family groups within Yemen's mental health framework. To rectify this, initiatives should include: the establishment of Consumer Groups that advocate for the concerns of individuals experiencing mental health issues and their families; policy formulation that integrates client and family viewpoints in mental health policies, plans, and programs; and providing financial and logistical backing to sustain these efforts. Collaborative initiatives among mental health services and advocacy organizations can enhance mutual comprehension and improve the quality of care.

6.10 Collaborative Efforts Across Sectors

To strengthen mental health services in Yemen, it is vital to foster multisectoral collaboration among government bodies, NGOs, and international agencies. Partnerships across sectors can enhance funding opportunities, facilitate training programs, and improve service delivery outcomes. For instance, integrating mental health education into school curricula and promoting workplace mental well-being through awareness campaigns and support initiatives are examples of how such collaborations can nurture a supportive mental health environment and aid in reducing stigma (Wiedermann et al., 2023).

6.11 Preparedness for Disasters

The ongoing conflict and frequent natural disasters in Yemen necessitate a mental health strategy that is focused on disaster management. A biopsychosocial approach should inform the development of trauma-informed services that address both immediate and long-term mental health effects. Essential components should include establishing specialized trauma services featuring crisis intervention teams to provide immediate psychological assistance during emergencies; community resilience programs designed to equip affected populations with effective coping strategies; and the incorporation of disaster preparedness into national mental health policies and initiatives. This strategy is in alignment with recommendations for countries vulnerable to disasters, ensuring proactive measures are taken to address mental health needs during crises (Berring et al., 2024).

6.12 Development of Human Resources

Investing in human resources is essential for alleviating the shortage of mental health professionals in Yemen. Suggested approaches encompass the establishment of both short-term and long-term training initiatives for psychiatrists, psychologists, psychiatric nurses, and social workers on a national scale. It is imperative that undergraduate medical education includes comprehensive exposure to psychiatric disorders, and that the promotion of ongoing professional development is prioritized. Enhancements to the curriculum are necessary to guarantee adequate coverage of mental health subjects in undergraduate training. Facilitating continued education opportunities to enhance the skills of current healthcare practitioners will foster a sustainable workforce that can effectively meet the nation's mental health needs.

6.13 Administrative Enhancements

To enhance the governance of mental health, it is essential to establish a specialized mental health division within the Ministry of Health. This division would coordinate mental health initiatives, oversee budgetary allocations, and evaluate progress. By segmenting the country into designated service areas with assigned budgets, effective resource management and equitable provision of services will be ensured (National Mental Health Strategy in Yemen 2022–2023, 2022).

6.14 Regular Clinical Audits

The execution of systematic clinical audits is crucial to address the widespread concerns related to polypharmacy in the context of psychotropic medications. Integrating clinical psychopharmacologists within inpatient services can serve as a gatekeeping mechanism to promote the prudent utilization of these medications (Javelot et al., 2021).

6.15 Adaptive Approaches to Addressing Suicide Attempts

A recent 2024 study of 423 Yemeni youth aged 15–24 revealed alarming trends in suicide-related behaviors. It found that 65% had suicidal thoughts in the past three months, 48% made plans for suicide, and 61.4% attempted it at least once during that time. Additionally, 39.7% reported a lifetime history of suicide attempts (Abou Khalil & Owino Ouko, 2024). These findings highlight significant psychological impacts from ongoing conflict, displacement, and inadequate mental health services, pointing to a national crisis requiring urgent suicide prevention measures and community support systems. Implementing flexible strategies to manage suicide attempts is essential for evaluating the situation, improving care access, and crafting a national preventive strategy. The criminalization of suicide attempts obstructs critical mental health support for those in need. By adopting these approaches, Yemen can work toward better mental health services for all.

7 Conclusion

The mental health crisis in Yemen constitutes a significant humanitarian concern that necessitates immediate and coordinated intervention at the local, national, and international levels. Prolonged periods of conflict, economic deterioration, and systemic neglect have severely hindered the country's ability to respond to the increasing psychological needs of its populace. With a mere handful of psychiatrists catering to millions, an overstretched healthcare system, and deeply rooted cultural obstacles, it is imperative for Yemen to implement a comprehensive strategy to reform its mental health services. Essential strategies should encompass the enhancement of research funding, the decentralization of mental health care delivery, the bolstering of workforce capacity through specialized training initiatives, and the incorporation of mental health education within academic institutions and workplaces. Moreover, the utilization of technological advancements, such as tele-psychiatry, the establishment of effective referral systems, and the assurance of a consistent supply of psychotropic medications represent critical advancements. Engaging non-medical caregivers, including traditional healers and religious figures, can effectively address service delivery gaps while gradually altering societal perceptions surrounding mental illness. To alleviate the long-term consequences of trauma and displacement, Yemen must also emphasize disaster preparedness and resilience-building initiatives within its mental health strategy. Ultimately, resolving this crisis necessitates a sustained collaborative effort from all relevant stakeholders' government entities, non-governmental organizations, international allies, and local communities, to establish a sustainable and inclusive mental health system capable of accommodating the diverse requirements of Yemen's population.

References

A NEGLECTED CRISIS. (2017). https://sanaacenter.org/publications/analysis/51

Abou Khalil, I., & Owino Ouko, V. (2024). The analysis on the rise of mental health challenges among the youths in Yemen. *International Journal of Innovative Science and Research Technology (IJISRT)*, 1102–1156. https://doi.org/10.38124/ijisrt/IJISRT24SEP574

Achieving health for all in Yemen. (2023). www.emro.who.int/yemen

AL- Ahdal, T., & Farahat, R. A. (2022). The urgency of suicide prevention in Yemen: Challenges and recommendations—Correspondence. *International Journal of Surgery,* 106. https://doi.org/10.1016/j.ijsu.2022.106924

Alhammadi, O. A. S., Mohamed, H. I., Musa, S. S., Ahmed, M. M., Lemma, M. A., Joselyne, U., Roméo, B., Abdullahi, Y., Othman, Z. K., Hamid, M. R., Kasimieh, O., Lucero-Prisno III, D. E., Labyad, S., & Okesanya, O. J. (2024). Advancing digital health in Yemen: challenges, opportunities, and way forward. *Exploration of Digital Health Technologies, 2*(6), 369–386. https://doi.org/10.37349/edht.2024.00035

Alhariri, W., Mcnally, A., & Knuckey, S. (2021). The right to mental health in Yemen: A distressed and ignored foundation for peace. Health and Human Rights, *23*(1):43–53.

Al-Krenawi, A. (2005). Mental health practice in Arab countries. *Current Opinion in Psychiatry, 18*(5), 560–564. https://doi.org/10.1097/01.yco.0000179498.46182.8b

Annual Results Report 2023 Yemen. www.unhcr.org

Berring, L. L., Holm, T., Hansen, J. P., Delcomyn, C. L., Søndergaard, R., & Hvidhjelm, J. (2024). Implementing trauma-informed care—settings, definitions, interventions, measures, and implementation across settings: A scoping review. *Healthcare (Switzerland), 12*(9). https://doi.org/10.3390/healthcare12090908

Cheffi, A. (2021). Mental health and psychosocial support in primary health care (MHPSS PHC). *Yemen Red Crescent Society*. MHPSS-PHC-2022

Cheffi, A., Sejberg, Z., Logman, A., Harrison, S., & Steen Kryger, L. *Mental health and psychosocial support in primary health care* https://mhpsshub.org/wp-content/uploads/2022/04/MHPSS_PHC_English_19_04_2022.pdf

Dureab, F., Hussain, T., Sheikh, R., Al-Dheeb, N., Al-Awlaqi, S., & Jahn, A. (2021). Forms of health system fragmentation during conflict: The case of Yemen. *Frontiers in Public Health, 9*. https://doi.org/10.3389/fpubh.2021.659980

El Bcheraoui, C., Jumaan, A. O., Collison, M. L., Daoud, F., & Mokdad, A. H. (2018). Health in Yemen: Losing ground in war time. *Globalization and Health, 14*(1), 42. https://doi.org/10.1186/s12992-018-0354-9

Elnakib, S., Elaraby, S., Othman, F., BaSaleem, H., Abdulghani AlShawafi, N. A., Saleh Al-Gawfi, I. A., Shafique, F., Al-Kubati, E., Rafique, N., & Tappis, H. (2021). Providing care under extreme adversity: The impact of the Yemen conflict on the personal and professional lives of health workers. *Social Science and Medicine, 272*. https://doi.org/10.1016/j.socscimed.2021.113751

Elshamy, F., Hamadeh, A., Billings, J., & Alyafei, A. (2023). Mental illness and help-seeking behaviours among Middle Eastern cultures: A systematic review and meta-synthesis of qualitative data. *PLoS ONE, 18*(10). https://doi.org/10.1371/journal.pone.0293525

Hassanein, A. (2023). *Promoting Mental Treatment in the Arab world*. Liberty University – Master of Fine Arts Thesis. Liberty-MFA-2023-AyaH

Health at a glance. https://srhdpeuwpubsa.blob.core.windows.net/whdh/DATADOT/COUNTRY/PDF/887_Yemen.pdf

Health system in Yemen close to collapse. (2015). *Bulletin of the World Health Organization, 93*(10), 670–671. https://doi.org/10.2471/blt.15.021015

Human Rights Watch. (2021). *Social Ostracism*. https://www.hrw.org/world-report/2021/country-chapters/yemen

Ishak, A. A., Alhadi, A. M., & Al-Shamahy, H. A. (2021). Local experience of telemedicine: Examples of cases in Yemen. *Universal Journal of Pharmaceutical Research, 6*(1). https://doi.org/10.22270/ujpr.v6i1.537

Islam, Z., Rocha, I. C. N., Mohanan, P., Jain, S., Goyal, S., dos Santos Costa, A. C., Ahmad, S., Mehedi Hasan, M., & Essar, M. Y. (2021). Mental health impacts of humanitarian crisis on healthcare workers in Yemen. *Medicine, Conflict and Survival, 37*(2), 112–117. https://doi.org/10.1080/13623699.2021.1950519

Javelot, H., Dizet, S., Straczek, C., Langrée, B., Michel, B., Haffen, E., Bertschy, G., et al. (2021). *Enhancing the role played by clinical pharmacists in psychiatric settings to better integrate clinical psychopharmacology into the decision-making process. 76*(2), 149–156. https://doi.org/10.1016/j.therap.2020.12.011ï

Jubari, B., & Saifaldeen, A. (2014). *Estimated prevalence of mental disorders among war-affected population in Yemen during the period*. http://fcdf-ye.org/Uploads/637799113203088990.pdf

Karam, E. G., Okasha, A., Trojanovic, N., Al Barathie, J., Saab, D., Hakim, N., & Abbas, N. (2023). Research in mental health in the Arab speaking world 1920 to 2018. *Middle East Current Psychiatry, 30*(1). https://doi.org/10.1186/s43045-023-00382-6

Keynejad, R., Spagnolo, J., & Thornicroft, G. (2021). WHO mental health gap action programme (mhGAP) intervention guide: Updated systematic review on evidence and impact. *Evidence-Based Mental Health, 24*(3), 124–130. https://doi.org/10.1136/ebmental-2021-300254

Lea Zeinoun Understanding mental health in the Arab region. https://www.annd.org/uploads/publications/Understanding_mental_health_in_the_Arab_region_-_Lea_Zeinoun_-_En.pdf

Médecins Sans Frontières. (2023). *Yemen: The rise of severe mental health conditions in the country*. https://msfsouthasia.org/yemen-the-rise-of-severe-mental-health-conditions-in-the-country/

Mental Health Assessment, IMC. (2019). *Mental Health and Psychosocial Support Assessment*. https://cdn1.internationalmedicalcorps.org/wp-content/uploads/2017/07/IMC-Yemen-2019-MHPSS-Assessment.pdf

Mental Health and Psychosocial Support Programmes in Yemen. https://yemen.unfpa.org/sites/default/files/pub-pdf/mental_health_newsletter_jan_-_march_2021_-_update_-_final.pdf

National Mental Health Strategy in Yemen 2022–2023. (2022). *World Health Organization, Regional Office for the Eastern Mediterranean (WHO-EMRO)*. NMHS-Yemen-2022

Pajević, A., Pajević, I., Jakovljević, M., Hasanović, M., Kravić, N., & Žigić, N. (2021). Ibn Sina (Avicenna) as a Psychiatrist: A View from Today's Perspective. *Psychiatria Danubina, 33*(Suppl 4):1218–1226.

Qasem Saleh, M. A. B., & Makki, A. M. (2008). Mental health in Yemen: Obstacles and challenges. *International Psychiatry, 5*(4), 90–92.

Okasha, A., Karam, E., & Okasha, T. (2012). Mental health services in the Arab world. *World Psychiatry, 11*(1), 52–54. https://doi.org/10.1016/j.wpsyc.2012.01.008

Ministry of Public Health and Population. (2021). https://www.emro.who.int/images/stories/yemen/National_Mental_Health_Strateg__in_Yemen2022_2023_Eng.pdf

National Mental strategy. (2011). https://sfd.sfd-yemen.org/uploads/issues/health%20english-20121015-132757.pdf

Nawsherwan, Mubarik, S., Naeem, S., Mubarak, R., Yu, C., Yan, W., & Sang, M. (2025). Health dynamics in war-torn Yemen: Insights from 32 years of epidemiological data (1990–2021). *Population Health Metrics, 23*(1). https://doi.org/10.1186/s12963-025-00363-3

Operational status of the health system HeRAMS Yemen. (2023). http://www.wipo.int/amc/en/mediation/rules

Promoting Mental Treatment in the Arab World. https://digitalcommons.liberty.edu/masters/1002

Psychological health in Yemen. https://doi.org/10.1007/s12144-022-03617-7

Sana'. (2015). *Yemen National Health and Demographic Survey 2013 Ministry of Public Health and Population and Central Statistical Organization World Bank*. www.papfam.org

The devastating impact of war on the mental health of Yemen's children. https://resourcecentre.savethechildren.net/pdf/five_years_of_fear_and_loss_4th_pp.pdf/

WHO. (2021). *Yemen health system report*. https://cdn.who.int/media/docs/default-source/emergency-preparedness/jmo_who_ghea-2022_yemen.pdf

WHO. (2019). *Psychological impact of conflict in Yemen*. https://www.emro.who.int/yemen/news/millions-of-people-in-yemen-face-the-trauma-and-socioeconomic-pressures-of-9-years-of-conflict-with-limited-services.html

Wiedermann, C. J., Barbieri, V., Plagg, B., Marino, P., Piccoliori, G., & Engl, A. (2023). Fortifying the foundations: A comprehensive approach to enhancing mental health support in educational policies amidst crises. *Healthcare (Switzerland), 11*(10). https://doi.org/10.3390/healthcare11101423

World Population Review. (2023). (n.d.). *History of Yemen | How Old is Yemen?. World Population Review*. Retrieved April 20, 2025, from https://worldpopulationreview.com/countries/yemen/history

Yemen_HNO_2022 - Final Version (1). https://reliefweb.int/report/yemen/yemen-humanitarian-needs-overview-2022-april-2022

Yemen Population. (2025). *World Population Review*. https://worldpopulationreview.com/countries/yemen

Zafaran, M. (2023). The role of stigma in the barriers to mental health treatment in the arab culture. *Capstone Showcase, 100*. https://scholarworks.arcadia.edu/showcase/2023/pa/100

Zaid, S. M., Fadel, A. M., Taresh, S. M., Mohammed, L. A., & Fitriana, N. (2024). Psychologists' perspective of mental health in Yemen during the civil war and COVID-19: A qualitative inquiry. *Current Psychology, 43*(16), 14774–14785. https://doi.org/10.1007/s12144-022-03617-7

https://www.emro.who.int/yemen/news/millions-of-people-in-yemen-face-the-trauma-and-socio-economic-pressures-of-9-years-of-conflict-with-limited-services.html

Chapter 16
Mental Health Care in the Middle East: Bridging Gaps and Building Futures

Salim Al-Huseini and S. M. Yasir Arafat

Abstract This chapter examines the evolving landscape of mental health care in the Middle East, highlighting systemic disparities in service delivery, workforce distribution, and infrastructure across fourteen countries, including Bahrain, Egypt, Iran, Iraq, Jordan, Kuwait, Lebanon, Oman, Palestine, Qatar, Saudi Arabia, Syria, the United Arab Emirates, and Yemen. Drawing on data from the World Health Organisation Mental Health Atlas, it identifies persistent structural challenges while showcasing country-specific innovations in digital health, decentralised care, and culturally adapted interventions. The chapter draws attention to the predominance of cross-sectional studies and advocates for increased investment in implementation science and regional collaboration. It emphasises the region's unique strengths, faith integration, family-centred care, and collectivist resilience, which contribute to the global mental health discourse. It concludes with a forward-looking agenda, advocating for community-oriented, system-strengthening reforms that are culturally grounded and contextually appropriate, positioning the Middle East as a site of ongoing challenges and a source of scalable solutions for the region.

Keywords Middle East · Mental health care · Mental health services · Challenges of mental health care · Community mental health

1 Introduction

The Middle East is marked by profound historical, cultural, and religious continuities, yet it exhibits considerable political, economic, and infrastructural diversity. While countries across the region share commonalities in language, religion, and familial cultural norms, their health systems, particularly in the realm of mental

S. Al-Huseini (✉)
Department of Psychiatry, AL Masarra Hospital, Ministry of Health, Muscat, Sultanate of Oman
e-mail: salimalhuseini@gmail.com

S. M. Y. Arafat
Department of Psychiatry, Bangladesh Specialised Hospital, Dhaka, Bangladesh

S. Al-Huseini and S. M. Y. Arafat (eds.), *Mental Health Care in the Middle East*, South Asian Perspectives in Mental Health and Psychology ,
https://doi.org/10.1007/978-981-95-0461-9_16

health, are shaped by divergent trajectories of governance, the impact of historical and ongoing conflicts, disparities in resource allocation, and varying levels of institutional development (Gearing et al., 2013; Okasha et al., 2012). The region possesses a longstanding tradition of mental health care, tracing back to the Arab-Islamic Golden Age, during which progressive attitudes towards mental illness were reflected in the humane and holistic treatments provided in *bimaristans* (Maziak, 2006). Contemporary health systems within the region exhibit pronounced variability in accessibility, capacity, and quality. Wealthier states like Qatar (Mohammed et al., 2025) and the UAE (Ahmed et al., 2025) have invested heavily in modern infrastructure, integrating mental health into primary-care platforms and digital service delivery (Dent et al., 2017; Skuse, 2021).

In contrast, low- and middle-income countries (LMICs) like Egypt (Hassan & Elnoby, 2025), Jordan (Qutishat & Al-Hadidi, 2025), Iraq (Younis, 2025), and Palestine (Khatib et al., 2025) experience ongoing financing challenges, workforce shortages, and restricted institutional development (Okasha & Karam, 1998; WHO EMRO, 2021). Countries affected by war, including Syria (Gerbaka et al., 2025), Yemen (Aljalei & Alsubari, 2025), and Palestine (Khatib et al., 2025), and disasters in Lebanon (Arafat et al., 2020), frequently depend on underfunded public sectors or international non-governmental organisations (NGOs) for emergency psychological assistance, resulting in fragmented or ineffective routine care (Hassan et al., 2016). These system-level disparities intersect with powerful social determinants, prolonged armed conflict, mass displacement, rapid urbanisation, economic instability, and a predominantly young population to amplify rates of trauma, anxiety, and mood disorders (Karam et al., 2008). Enduring stigma, cultural misconceptions, and limited mental health literacy further impede early help-seeking, equitable access, and the prioritisation of mental health in national agendas (Gearing et al., 2015). Despite these common challenges, the region's robust familial networks and shared values can cultivate resilience and informal support. Nevertheless, worries regarding honour, reputation, and social visibility frequently hinder the disclosure of mental illness and postpone treatment (al-Krenawi & Graham, 2000). This intricate relationship highlights the necessity for culturally informed and contextually relevant reforms that close institutional gaps, bolster workforce capacity, and utilise existing social capital to improve mental health outcomes throughout the Middle East.

This chapter will show that, although the region faces common challenges such as underfunding, stigma, and fragmented service delivery, it also presents examples of innovation, resilience, and reform. The following sections will explore national mental health infrastructures, country-specific strengths, patterns of research productivity, and potential paths forward. By employing a comparative approach based on World Health Organisation (WHO) data and regional scholarship, this chapter seeks to synthesise the diversity and potential of mental health care systems in the Middle East, providing insights into future directions for equity-driven, culturally aligned, and system-strengthening reforms.

2 Mental Health Systems Across the Region

2.1 Service Delivery Models

The Middle East is undergoing a vital transformation in its mental health service delivery models. While the region is largely marked by a strong public sector presence and centralised, institution-based systems, there is a growing acknowledgement of the need for more integrated, decentralised, and innovative solutions. Strategies such as integrating mental health into primary and community health care, leveraging digital technologies, and fostering public–private partnerships are emerging as effective ways to bridge service gaps and improve accessibility (Musa, 2024). This section will explore these important developments, highlighting the current situation and future possibilities for integration and innovation in mental health care delivery throughout the Middle East.

2.1.1 Public Sector Dominance and Limited Private Sector Involvement

Traditionally, mental health systems in the Middle East have been overseen by government ministries, which have primarily financed, regulated, and provided services since modern health authorities were formed. Public funds have generally been directed towards significant, standalone psychiatric hospitals in major urban areas, reinforcing an institutional model isolated mainly from primary care and general hospital services (Saraceno et al., 2007; WHO EMRO, 2013). Despite the growing demand for mental health services, the private sector has found it challenging to address the gaps created by underfunded public systems. Both public and private insurance plans frequently exclude or heavily restrict coverage for outpatient psychotherapy and long-term medication treatments, leading to significant out-of-pocket costs for individuals and deterring many from seeking private care. Potential private providers encounter a complicated set of fragmented licensing, accreditation, and contracting requirements that complicate the process of opening and expanding clinics (WHO EMRO, 2021).

2.1.2 Integration of Mental Health into Primary and Community Health Care

The WHO has long advocated integrating mental health into primary health care (PHC), viewing it as essential for building effective and equitable health systems. The 2023 *World Health emphasis*ed that embedding mental health services within PHC enhances access, supports early identification, and ensures continuity of care (WHO EMRO, 2023) This recommendation holds particular relevance in the Middle

East, where demographic shifts, displacement, conflict, and socio-economic pressures have increased the burden of mental illness and underscored the need for community-based, sustainable models of care.

Integrating mental health into PHC requires equipping frontline providers, general practitioners, nurses, and community health workers to detect and manage common conditions such as depression, anxiety, and substance use disorders (Hijazi et al., 2011; Siddiqui et al., 2022). While progress across the region has been uneven, several reform-driven states have demonstrated promising models. Qatar's National Mental Health Strategy (2013–2018) shifted care from specialist tertiary centres to integrated PHC, enabling multidisciplinary teams to provide mental health support and expanding access significantly (Mohammed et al., 2025; Wadoo et al., 2021). In the United Arab Emirates, the Mental Wealth Framework (2024) builds on earlier well-being initiatives to integrate mental health across social policy, expand telepsychiatry, and develop community-based services (National Programme for Happiness and Wellbeing, 2024). Oman has taken initial steps to integrate mental health into PHC, training providers in polyclinics to deliver basic psychological support (AL-Huseini & Al Maqbali, 2025; Ministry of Health, 2023). Similarly, Bahrain has invested in PHC workforce development, reducing stigma and improving early intervention through targeted training programmes (Ebrahim et al., 2025). Lebanon's response illustrates the importance of cultural and gender-sensitive outreach (Nsouli et al., 2025). Psychoeducation and engagement strategies, particularly among women, have improved treatment adherence despite ongoing political and economic instability. These efforts align with the 2024–2030 National Mental Health Strategy, which emphasises rights-based and community-oriented care (El-Khoury et al., 2020; National Mental Health Strategy for Lebanon (2024–2030), 2024). Integration into PHC is critical in rebuilding trust and infrastructure in fragile and post-conflict settings. Iraq's 2014–2020 National Mental Health Strategy, supported by WHO, focussed on decentralisation and cross-sector collaboration to bring mental health services into general health centres (Sadik et al., 2011). In Palestine, WHO-assisted initiatives have adapted services to local cultural norms and expanded access through partnerships that extend care into refugee camps and rural communities (Marie et al., 2017, 2018). Despite these advances, challenges persist. In Egypt, mental health care remains largely hospital-based, mainly with psychiatry viewed as a highly specialised discipline. This perception continues to hinder integration into PHC (Loza, 2010). Regional integration requires more than mhGAP-informed training for mental health professionals.

2.1.3 Telepsychiatry and Digital Mental-Health Service Delivery in the Middle East

The mental health systems in the Middle East are experiencing a major transformation, with digitalisation playing a pivotal role in this change. Telepsychiatry, which involves delivering psychiatric services through digital platforms for evaluation, therapy, and follow-up, has shifted from being a supplementary service to a fundamental component of mental health strategies throughout the region. This shift was significantly hastened by the COVID-19 pandemic, highlighting the weaknesses of hospital-focussed care and pushing governments to implement more scalable, decentralised care models (Alnakhi et al., 2023; Taylor et al., 2020). Acknowledging this transition, the WHO has highlighted telemedicine as a crucial tool for ensuring service continuity, enhancing governance, and broadening mental health access, especially during crises (WHO, 2022).

The Gulf Cooperation Council (GCC) countries that have integrated telepsychiatry into their national health reforms are at the forefront of this digital transformation. In Saudi Arabia, the swift development of platforms like the 24/7 Call Centre and the Seha mobile app facilitated real-time psychiatric consultations and video-based therapy. These digital solutions were well-received by users and significantly contributed to integrating mental health services into primary care, enhancing overall accessibility and continuity (Al-Khathami et al., 2025). Similarly, the United Arab Emirates has progressed its digital mental health infrastructure through the National Programme for Happiness and Wellbeing. This initiative established the groundwork for the 2024 Mental Wealth Framework, which introduced AI-assisted self-help applications, school-based e-mental health interventions, and free telecounselling services, particularly benefiting working-age adults seeking confidential support (Digital, 2024). Qatar's shift from a single-hospital model to a community-based framework has also been supported by digital innovation. Through Hamad Medical Corporation, numerous psychiatric services were successfully transitioned to remote formats. A three-year evaluation of this transition showed a 50% reduction in missed appointments and improved continuity of care, especially for adult and geriatric populations (Wadoo et al., 2024). Bahrain has similarly integrated mental health tools into its national digital platforms, BeAware and Sehati, offering features such as e-prescriptions, culturally sensitive assessments, and remote consultations, all supported by strong regulatory oversight (MOH, 2025). In Oman, telephone-based psychiatric follow-up within the Al Shifa electronic health record system has improved service delivery; however, infrastructural challenges, including broadband access and clinician training, continue to impede complete optimisation (Hasani et al., 2020).

In contrast, Kuwait takes a more cautious approach to adoption. While clinicians have shown strong support for telepsychiatry, issues related to reimbursement models and regulatory clarity have delayed widespread implementation. In response, the Ministry of Health has begun co-designing a centralised mental health portal in collaboration with service users—a promising step towards systemic digital integration (Abdelghany et al., 2024).

Numerous LMICs have shown innovative adaptability outside the Gulf region despite limited resources. In Lebanon, around 73% of mental health professionals now utilise remote methods, facilitated by partnerships between the Ministry of Public Health and NGOs. These collaborations have made it possible to offer audio-based therapy in areas lacking sufficient internet infrastructure (Mohtar et al., 2025). Similarly, Iran has embraced telepsychiatry to continue providing services during clinic shutdowns. Although regulatory and insurance issues persist, trials of encrypted group therapy have proven both clinically effective and cost-efficient (Haghnia et al., 2019). In conflict-affected areas, telepsychiatry has become essential. Yemen's National Mental Health Strategy (2022–2026) emphasises low-bandwidth digital tools, such as SMS helplines and remote supervision systems for primary care providers, reportedly reaching over 100,000 users despite infrastructure collapse (Alhammadi et al., 2024). The Syrian TeleMental Health (STMH) programme similarly demonstrates how international cooperation, especially through diaspora psychiatrist networks, can aid skill development and supervision in crisis areas. This initiative underscores the importance of early partnerships with NGOs, sustainable funding, and the mobilisation of adaptable volunteer workforces (Almoshmosh et al., 2020).

With its well-established mental health infrastructure, Egypt uses digital tools to improve care access. A national survey found nearly universal support for e-mental health tools among psychiatrists, particularly for reaching underserved groups (Kamel et al., 2020). In Jordan, mobile technologies have similarly expanded mental health service access. A 2024 survey indicated that citizens and refugees were open to using mHealth platforms, leading to WHO-supported efforts to create chatbots and e-learning modules for adolescents and young adults (Ben-Zeev et al., 2024). Meanwhile, in the occupied Palestinian territories, movement restrictions have greatly limited traditional care delivery. To address this, organisations like WHO and Médecins Sans Frontières have set up encrypted telepsychiatry platforms that enable remote case discussions and secure video consultations for complex psychiatric cases (Aqtam, 2025). These advancements reflect a regional trend towards digitally enabled, context-sensitive mental health systems. While high-income countries lead in infrastructure and institutional integration, low-resource and conflict-affected areas are innovating under pressure, utilising mobile technologies and international partnerships. Looking ahead, the focus should be on harmonising governance frameworks, increasing digital literacy among providers and patients, and ensuring equitable access to telepsychiatry services that are culturally appropriate and scalable.

Telepsychiatry has increasingly facilitated access to mental health services across the Middle East, benefiting urban populations and underserved rural or conflict-affected regions (Jefee-Bahloul, 2014). Providing individuals with access to private care from their homes has helped diminish mental health stigma, a major obstacle to care in numerous areas of the region. Moreover, implementing virtual triage, remote follow-ups, and hybrid care models has proven effective in enhancing efficiency and resource management by optimising scarce specialist time (Al-Samarraie et al., 2020). Yet, challenges in implementation continue. These challenges include inconsistent internet access, varying levels of digital literacy, the absence of unified legal and ethical frameworks, and ongoing data security and confidentiality issues (Alaboudi et al., 2016; Alotaibi & Federico, 2017; Ataç et al., 2013). Looking forward, hybrid models that integrate asynchronous tools- like psychoeducational modules, chatbot-guided interventions, and digital self-help platforms- with synchronous video consultations provide a scalable and personalised approach to mental health care. Innovations in technology, such as artificial intelligence for triage and algorithm-driven care personalisation, could further improve service responsiveness and efficiency (Matlin et al., 2025). However, the effectiveness of these advancements relies on continuous investment, well-designed context-specific services, and the establishment of inclusive digital infrastructure to avoid exacerbating existing health disparities.

3 Availability of Mental Health Workforce Across the Middle East

Human resource capacity and infrastructure for mental health care in the Middle East expose stark disparities between high-income Gulf states and conflict-affected or lower-income countries (Alarabi & Alosaimi, 2025; Aljalei & Alsubari, 2025; AlNouri et al., 2025; Ebrahim et al., 2025; Gerbaka et al., 2025; Khatib et al., 2025; Nsouli et al., 2025; Younis, 2025). According to the WHO Mental Health Atlas (2022), psychiatrist-to-population ratios vary by more than 20-fold, with the United Arab Emirates reporting 4.24 psychiatrists per 100,000 population, followed by Saudi Arabia (3.4), Qatar (2.2), and Kuwait (2.35). In contrast, countries such as Iraq (0.57), Syria (0.16), and Yemen (0.2) remain critically underserved (WHO, 2022) (Fig. 1).

The allocation of psychiatric beds in the Middle East shows significant imbalances. Wealthy Gulf nations like Bahrain boast a relatively high density of 14.6 beds per 100,000 people, whereas Qatar has only 2.3 beds per 100,000 (World Health Organisation, 2021). In contrast, countries affected by conflict and those with lower incomes, such as Yemen, Syria, and Palestine, typically have fewer than 2 beds per 100,000, often with services limited to capital cities or hindered by infrastructure issues (WHO, 2022). These gaps underscore the pressing requirement for

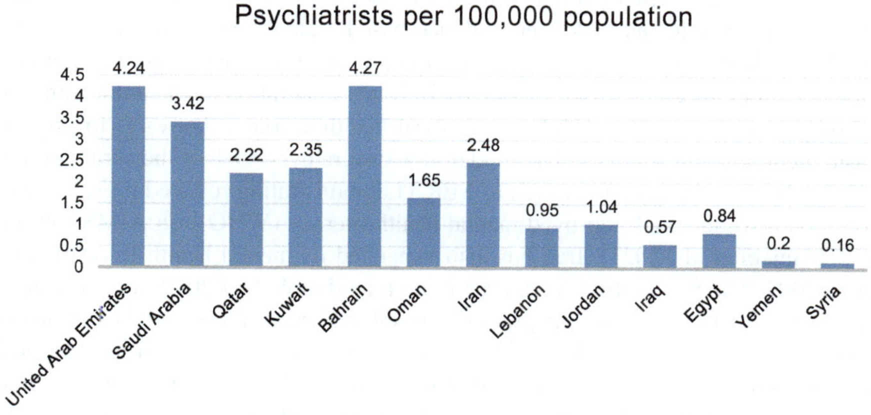

Fig. 1 Psychiatrists per 100,000 population in the Middle East 2022) (*Source* WHO Atlas)

increased investment in training, decentralised service delivery, and fair infrastructure development to facilitate mental health reform across the region.

4 Country-Specific Strengths and Innovations in the Mental Health System

Mental health systems across the Middle East face shared structural challenges, including workforce shortages, centralised hospital-based models, and widespread stigma. Yet, amid these constraints, several countries have demonstrated a capacity for adaptation and reform. A notable regional shift from institutional care towards decentralised, community-based, and culturally attuned approaches occurs.

Mental health is increasingly being integrated into national development agendas in the Gulf region. Saudi Arabia's Vision 2030 explicitly recognises mental health as essential to sustainable healthcare reform (Vision 2030, 2024). Similarly, the UAE's National Strategy for Wellbeing 2031 prioritises mental wellness, with significant investments such as Dubai's AED 105 million mental health initiative and Abu Dhabi's mental wellbeing programme (National Strategy for Wellbeing 2031, 2024). Qatar has advanced a community-oriented mental health model, enhancing service accessibility (Ministry of Public Health, 2018). Oman has expanded outpatient psychiatric units nationwide, addressing urban–rural disparities (WHO-Oman AIMS Report, 2006). Bahrain offers a comprehensive service anchored by its main psychiatric hospital, with supplementary outpatient and day-treatment facilities enhancing coverage (Al-Haddad & Al-Offi, 2009). Kuwait has adopted a decentralised model by embedding mental health clinics within primary healthcare centres, supported by tertiary care at the Kuwait Hospital for Psychological Medicine, which delivers regionally distributed specialist services (Bale, 2000; UNICEF Middle East, 2023).

Egypt has significantly improved service accessibility by training over 1200 primary care physicians to deliver evidence-based mental healthcare, supported by the 2009 Mental Health Law, which instituted protections and promoted community care (Jenkins et al., 2010; Loza, 2010). Iran's integration of mental health into primary care dates to the 1980s, using rural health workers (behvarz) to provide basic mental health services. The model now covers over 85% of the rural population, with recent programmes such as SERAJ demonstrating reduced prevalence of common disorders and improved mental health literacy (WHO-Iran AIMS Report, 2007; Hajebi et al., 2021). Iraq has also expanded its mental health infrastructure since 2003. The psychiatrist workforce more than doubled by 2010, inpatient units increased, and primary-care integration via mhGAP training improved early detection and treatment of disorders. Collaborative efforts with WHO and international partners have facilitated multidisciplinary training and the development of child mental health centres (Al-Uzri et al., 2012; Sadik & Al-Jadiry, 2006; Sadik et al., 2011). Despite conflict, Syria has sustained mental health service delivery through over 540 integrated primary health centres and targeted training of non-specialists and psychologists (WHO, 2013). International programmes such as STRENGTHS have supported Syrian refugees with scalable interventions like PM+, while NGOs have introduced telepsychiatry and mobile services to maintain care in insecure settings (Sijbrandij et al., 2017). Lebanon's National Mental Health Programme (2015–2030) has guided reforms focussed on decentralising services and integrating mental health into primary care. Civil society and NGOs have played a critical role in expanding coverage and promoting awareness amidst ongoing political and economic turmoil (Karam et al., 2016). Similarly, in Palestine, despite resource constraints and political instability, the mental health system benefits from a network of community-based organisations and international collaborations delivering Mental Health and Psychosocial Support (MHPSS) interventions (Aqtam, 2025). The government has prioritised decentralisation in Jordan to extend services to rural areas, allowing community-level customisation and more responsive care delivery. This model not only simplifies access and empowers local actors, resulting in improved outcomes and stronger community engagement (Abdalla, 2023).

These examples illustrate a region in transition, developing diverse, innovative, and contextually grounded approaches to mental health care. The trend towards integrated, community-based systems underscores the Middle East's evolving role in contributing to scalable and globally relevant mental health solutions.

5 Mental Health Research in the Middle East

Mental health research across the Middle East has grown substantially over the past two decades. However, its contributions to the global evidence base remain modest relative to population needs, geopolitical importance, and the region's burden of mental disorders. This section explores key developments in regional research productivity, methodological trends, research funding, and structural barriers, while highlighting future priorities for strengthening the mental health knowledge ecosystem across the Middle East.

5.1 Regional Contributions to the Global Evidence

Over the past 15 years, mental health research in the Middle East has grown rapidly, albeit from a historically low baseline. A bibliometric review covering 2009–2018 found that research activity remained concentrated in a few countries and institutions. Egypt (1419), Saudi Arabia (991), and Lebanon (502) were the top contributors, followed by the UAE (319) (Zeinoun et al., 2020). A broader analysis spanning 1920–2018 showed that Egypt, Saudi Arabia, and Lebanon accounted for 42% of the region's cumulative mental health research output, highlighting persistent disparities in national research capacity (Karam et al., 2023). Despite these disparities, regional research's overall quality and global participation have improved. By 2018, nearly

80% of publications were in non-local journals; international collaboration in authorship grew from 29% to 50%; and publications in leading quartile journals increased from 14% to 20% (Maalouf et al., 2019).

The GCC region has produced a smaller yet growing research. A 2016 scoping review found 55 studies on mental illness and user experiences in GCC countries (Hickey et al., 2016). Still, regional collaboration is restricted, with only a few multi-site or cross-border studies. Research on conflict-impacted areas like Yemen and Syria is limited, even though these populations face a significant burden of mental illness. Studies that culturally contextualise indigenous risk factors, explanatory models, and help-seeking behaviours are also lacking. Additionally, evaluations of the feasibility and effectiveness of locally adapted service delivery models are insufficient (Zeinoun et al., 2020).

Given the region's distinct epidemiological and structural challenges, including pervasive stigma, trauma exposure, and fragmented services, it is crucial to prioritise implementation science and interventions tailored to the local context. Important future research areas comprise scalable programmes to reduce stigma, digital mental health solutions, culturally adapted psychotherapies, and task-shifting methods appropriate for low-resource and humanitarian settings.

5.2 Challenges to Advancing Mental Health Research in the Middle East

Although research productivity in the region has significantly improved, major structural challenges impede the development of a sustainable and effective mental health research ecosystem in the Middle East. These challenges include inadequate institutional infrastructure, limited funding, and difficulties of publication, which result in the fragmentation and underuse of mental health scholarship in this field.

5.2.1 Health Research Infrastructure and Training

The mental health research infrastructure in much of the Middle East is still underdeveloped. As of 2023, there are only three WHO Collaborating Centres for Mental Health in the region: Iran and the UAE. This situation reveals a significant lack of institutional research capacity (WHO EMRO, 2023). Additionally, national academic and clinical systems frequently lack the structural support for ongoing research activities. Building a strong community of independent mental health researchers necessitates a long-term commitment to capacity-building efforts, such as funded fellowships, organised mentorship programmes, and designated academic time. In the absence of this support, research output is restricted, leaving intricate, policy-relevant issues unresolved due to a lack of interdisciplinary and enduring engagement inquiry (Altalib et al., 2019). Despite these challenges, institutions in the Middle

East and South Asia still generate high-quality research. Meeting these emerging demands necessitates strong institutional partnerships and the proactive engagement of committed scholars to promote enduring and mutually advantageous collaboration (Radwan, 1987).

5.2.2 Research Funding

Research on mental health in the Middle East continues to face significant funding challenges, hindering the development of evidence-based policies and services. Regional science and technology agencies frequently overlook mental health in their strategic priorities, resulting in a lack of specific institutional grants in this field. When funding is accessible, it typically falls short of addressing the needs for extensive, long-term research, such as clinical trials, longitudinal cohorts, or implementation studies. This lack of investment is particularly concerning when compared to the high incidence of mental illness in the region, which obstructs the formulation of effective policies and services (Regan et al., 2015).

6 Conclusion

The Middle East is pivotal in developing its mental health care system. It contends with a dual challenge: the persistent issues of insufficient resources, stigma, and political turmoil, alongside an increasing awareness of mental health as both a public health concern and a human rights issue (Okasha & Karam, 1998). This situation offers a unique chance to rethink mental health care in contextually relevant and globally aware ways. Realising this potential requires strategic investment in system strengthening, including scaling the mental health workforce, integrating services into primary care, and expanding access to community-based models. It also demands enhancing research capacity to generate locally relevant data that can drive policy and innovation. Embracing digital tools and tele-mental health platforms offers a promising path towards bridging geographical and resource-related gaps, particularly for youth and rural populations. Crucially, regional collaboration across academic, policy, and clinical domains can enable the sharing of expertise, the pooling of resources, and the creation of unified responses to shared challenges such as displacement, trauma, and service inequity (Musa, 2024; Sobhani et al., 2024). The future of mental health in the Middle East lies in bridging tradition with evidence-based care, aligning local needs with global mental health frameworks, and advancing national progress through regional solidarity. Cultural heritage and communal values, far from being barriers, can serve as powerful assets in designing care pathways that are holistic, inclusive, and resonant with the populations they serve (Mirzai et al., 2024).

As we conclude this book, we offer a final call to action to cultivate political will, enhance regional leadership, and implement culturally sensitive reforms prioritising mental health in public health agendas. The journey ahead is intricate; yet, with dedication, teamwork, and empathy, significant change is not only feasible but attainable.

References

Abdalla, D. (2023). A multi-factorial analysis of the sustainability of non-governmental organizations' psychosocial support programs in Jordan. *Independent study project (ISP) collection.* https://digitalcollections.sit.edu/isp_collection/3747

Abdelghany, I. K., AlMatar, R., Al-Haqan, A., Abdullah, I., & Waheedi, S. (2024). Exploring healthcare providers' perspectives on virtual care delivery: Insights into telemedicine services. *BMC Health Services Research, 24*(1), 1. https://doi.org/10.1186/s12913-023-10244-w

Ahmed, W., Nawaz, F. A., Amiri, L., & Javaid, S. F. (2025). Mental health care in the United Arab Emirates. In S. AL-Huseini & S. M. Y. Arafat (Eds.), *Mental health care in the Middle East.* Springer.

Alaboudi, A., Atkins, A., Sharp, B., Balkhair, A., Alzahrani, M., & Sunbul, T. (2016). Barriers and challenges in adopting Saudi telemedicine network: The perceptions of decision makers of healthcare facilities in Saudi Arabia. *Journal of Infection and Public Health, 9*(6), 725–733. https://doi.org/10.1016/j.jiph.2016.09.001

Alarabi, M. A., & Alosaimi, F. D. (2025). Mental healthcare in Saudi Arabia. In S. Al-Huseini & S. M. Y. Arafat (Eds.), *Mental health care in the Middle East*. Springer. https://doi.org/10.1007/978-981-95-0461-9_14

Al-Haddad, M. K., & Al-Offi, A. (2009). Psychiatric services in Bahrain: Past, present and future. *International Psychiatry, 6*(1), 14–16.

Alhammadi, O. A. S., Mohamed, H. I., Musa, S. S., Ahmed, M. M., Lemma, M. A., Joselyne, U., Roméo, B., Abdullahi, Y., Othman, Z. K., Hamid, M. R., Kasimieh, O., Iii, D. E. L.-P., Labyad, S., & Okesanya, O. J. (2024). Advancing digital health in Yemen: Challenges, opportunities, and way forward. *Exploration of Digital Health Technologies, 2*(6), Article 6. https://doi.org/10.37349/edht.2024.00035

Al-Huseini, S., & Al Maqbali, M. (2025). Mental health care in Oman: Current landscape, challenges, and future directions. In S. Al-Huseini & S. M. Y. Arafat (Eds.), *Mental health care in the Middle East*. Springer. https://doi.org/10.1007/978-981-95-0461-9_9

Aljalei, M. H., & Alsubari, A. M. (2025). Mental health in Yemen. In S. Al-Huseini & S. M. Y. Arafat (Eds.), *Mental health care in the Middle East*. Springer.https://doi.org/10.1007/978-981-95-0461-9_15

Al-Khathami, A. D., Alharbi, L. S., Alomari, S. A., Alqahtani, A. A., & Alfadhli, D. S. (2025). Integrating mental healthcare into primary healthcare services: Saudi Arabia progress and achievements (1995–2022). *Current Research in Psychiatry, 5*(1), 1. https://doi.org/10.46439/Psychiatry.5.035

al-Krenawi, A., & Graham, J. R. (2000). Culturally sensitive social work practice with Arab clients in mental health settings. *Health & Social Work, 25*(1), 9–22. https://doi.org/10.1093/hsw/25.1.9

Almoshmosh, N., Jefee-Bahloul, H., Abdallah, W., & Barkil-Oteo, A. (2020). Use of store-and-forward tele-mental health for displaced Syrians. *Intervention Journal of Mental Health and Psychosocial Support in Conflict Affected Areas, 18*(1), 66. https://doi.org/10.4103/INTV.INTV_53_19

Alnakhi, W. K., Mamdouh, H., Hussain, H. Y., Mudawi, M. S., Ibrahim, G. M., Al Balushi, A. J., Al Zarooni, N., Elnaeem, A., & Natafgi, N. (2023). Doctor for every Citizen: Telehealth visits at Dubai health authority during COVID-19 pandemic in Dubai, United Arab Emirates. *Healthcare, 11*(3), Article 3. https://doi.org/10.3390/healthcare11030294

AlNouri, N., AlSayegh, A., & AlIbrahim A. (2025). Mental health care in Kuwait. In S. Al-Huseini & S. M. Y. Arafat (Eds.), *Mental health care in the Middle East*. Springer.https://doi.org/10.1007/978-981-95-0461-9_7

Alotaibi, Y. K., & Federico, F. (2017). The impact of health information technology on patient safety. *Saudi Medical Journal*, *38*(12), 1173–1180. https://doi.org/10.15537/smj.2017.12.20631

Al-Samarraie, H., Ghazal, S., Alzahrani, A. I., & Moody, L. (2020). Telemedicine in Middle Eastern countries: Progress, barriers, and policy recommendations. *International Journal of Medical Informatics, 141*, Article 104232. https://doi.org/10.1016/j.ijmedinf.2020.104232

Altalib, H. H., Elzamzamy, K., Fattah, M., Ali, S. S., & Awaad, R. (2019). Mapping global Muslim mental health research: Analysis of trends in the English literature from 2000 to 2015. *Global Mental Health, 6*, Article e6. https://doi.org/10.1017/gmh.2019.3

Al-Uzri, M., Abed, R., & Abbas, M. (2012). Rebuilding mental health services in Iraq. *International Psychiatry. 9*(3), 58–60. https://doi.org/10.1192/S1749367600003209

Aqtam, I. (2025). A narrative review of mental health and psychosocial impact of the war in Gaza. *Eastern Mediterranean Health Journal*, *31*(2), 89–96. https://doi.org/10.26719/2025.31.2.89

Arafat, S. M. Y., Shoib, S., Kar, S. K., & El Hayek, S. (2020). Psychiatry in Lebanon. *The Lancet. Psychiatry, 7*(11), 932. https://doi.org/10.1016/S2215-0366(20)30415-6

Ataç, A., Kurt, E., & Yurdakul, S. E. (2013). An overview to ethical problems in telemedicine technology. *Procedia—Social and Behavioral Sciences, 103*, 116–121. https://doi.org/10.1016/j.sbspro.2013.10.315

Bale, R. (2000). A project to develop quality improvements in the Kuwait mental health service. *Psychiatric Bulletin, 24*(3), 111–112. https://doi.org/10.1192/pb.24.3.111

Ben-Zeev, D., Beaulieu, A., Guler, J., Larsen, A., & Bawaneh, A. (2024). Readiness for mHealth interventions in Jordan: Refugee camp and urban community survey. *Internet Interventions, 36*, Article 100746. https://doi.org/10.1016/j.invent.2024.100746

Dent, E., Toki, D., Dupuis, N., Marquis, J., Suyeshkumar, T., & Benlamri, M. (2017). Healthcare systems within the Middle East. *University of Western Ontario Medical Journal*, *86*(2), Article 2. https://doi.org/10.5206/uwomj.v86i2.2009

Digital, T. (2024). *Dubai Health Authority launches Mental Wealth Framework with a budget of AED105 million to advance Dubai Social Agenda 33*. Government of Dubai Media Office. https://mediaoffice.ae/en/news/2024/july/22-07/dubai-health-authority-launches-mental-wealth-framework-with-a-budget-of-aed105-million

Ebrahim, A. H., Jahrami, H., & Hamadeh, R., (2025). Bahrain's mental health sector: Pillars of excellence and strategic directions. In S. Al-Huseini & S. M. Y. Arafat (Eds.), *Mental health care in the Middle East*. Springer.https://doi.org/10.1007/978-981-95-0461-9_2

El-Khoury, J., Haidar, R., & Charara, R. (2020). Community mental healthcare in Lebanon. *Consortium Psychiatricum, 1*(1), 71–77. https://doi.org/10.17650/2712-7672-2020-1-1-71-77

Gearing, R. E., MacKenzie, M. J., Ibrahim, R. W., Brewer, K. B., Batayneh, J. S., & Schwalbe, C. S. J. (2015). Stigma and mental health treatment of adolescents with depression in Jordan. *Community Mental Health Journal, 51*(1), 111–117. https://doi.org/10.1007/s10597-014-9756-1

Gearing, R. E., Schwalbe, C. S., MacKenzie, M. J., Brewer, K. B., Ibrahim, R. W., Olimat, H. S., Al-Makhamreh, S. S., Mian, I., & Al-Krenawi, A. (2013). Adaptation and translation of mental health interventions in Middle Eastern Arab countries: A systematic review of barriers to and strategies for effective treatment implementation. *International Journal of Social Psychiatry, 59*(7), 671–681. https://doi.org/10.1177/0020764012452349

Gerbaka, L., Fekih-Romdhane, F., Hallit, S., & Obeid, S. (2025). Mental health care in Syria. In S. Al-Huseini & S. M. Y. Arafat (Eds.), *Mental health care in the Middle East*. Springer. https://doi.org/10.1007/978-981-95-0461-9_13

Haghnia, Y., Samad-Soltani, T., Yousefi, M., Sadr, H., & Rezaei-Hachesu, P. (2019). Telepsychiatry-based care for the treatment follow-up of Iranian war veterans with post-traumatic stress disorder: A randomized controlled trial. *Iranian Journal of Medical Sciences*, *44*(4), 291–298. https://doi.org/10.30476/ijms.2019.44944

Hajebi, A., Sharifi, V., Asgardoon, M. H., & Damari, B. (2021). The effectiveness of the pilot implementation of Iran's comprehensive mental and social health services (the SERAJ program): A controlled community trial. *Iranian Journal of Psychiatry, 16*(2), 168–176. https://doi.org/10.18502/ijps.v16i2.5818

Hasani, S. A., Ghafri, T. A., Al Lawati, H., Mohammed, J., Al Mukhainai, A., Al Ajmi, F., & Anwar, H. (2020). The use of telephone consultation in primary health care during COVID-19 pandemic, Oman: Perceptions from physicians. *Journal of Primary Care & Community Health, 11*, 2150132720976480. https://doi.org/10.1177/2150132720976480

Hassan, G., Ventevogel, P., Jefee-Bahloul, H., Barkil-Oteo, A., & Kirmayer, L. J. (2016). Mental health and psychosocial wellbeing of Syrians affected by armed conflict. *Epidemiology and Psychiatric Sciences, 25*(2), 129–141. https://doi.org/10.1017/S2045796016000044

Hassan, W., & Elnoby, S. (2025). Mental health care in Egypt. In S. Al-Huseini & S. M. Y. Arafat (Eds.), *Mental health care in the Middle East*. Springer. https://doi.org/10.1007/978-981-95-0461-9_3

Hickey, J. E., Pryjmachuk, S., & Waterman, H. (2016). Mental illness research in the Gulf Cooperation Council: A scoping review. *Health Research Policy and Systems, 14*(1), 59. https://doi.org/10.1186/s12961-016-0123-2

Hijazi, Z., Weissbecker, I., & Chammay, R. (2011). The integration of mental health into primary health care in Lebanon. *Intervention: International Journal of Mental Health, Psychosocial Work & Counselling in Areas of Armed Conflict, 9*(3), 265–278.

Jefee-Bahloul, H. (2014). Telemental health in the Middle East: Overcoming the barriers. *Frontiers in Public Health, 2*, 86. https://doi.org/10.3389/fpubh.2014.00086

Jenkins, R., Heshmat, A., Loza, N., Siekkonen, I., & Sorour, E. (2010). Mental health policy and development in Egypt—Integrating mental health into health sector reforms 2001–9. *International Journal of Mental Health Systems, 4*, 17. https://doi.org/10.1186/1752-4458-4-17

Kamel, M. M., Westenberg, J. N., Choi, F., Tabi, K., Badawy, A., Ramy, H., Elsawi, H., & Krausz, M. (2020). Electronic mental health as an option for Egyptian psychiatry: Cross-sectional study. *JMIR Mental Health, 7*(8), Article e19591. https://doi.org/10.2196/19591

Karam, E., El Chammay, R., Richa, S., Naja, W., Fayyad, J., & Ammar, W. (2016). Lebanon: Mental health system reform and the Syrian crisis. *BJPsych International, 13*(4), 87–89. https://doi.org/10.1192/s2056474000001409

Karam, E. G., Mneimneh, Z. N., Dimassi, H., Fayyad, J. A., Karam, A. N., Nasser, S. C., Chatterji, S., & Kessler, R. C. (2008). Lifetime prevalence of mental disorders in Lebanon: First onset, treatment, and exposure to war. *PLoS Medicine, 5*(4), Article e61. https://doi.org/10.1371/journal.pmed.0050061

Karam, E. G., Okasha, A., Trojanovic, N., Al Barathie, J., Saab, D., Hakim, N., & Abbas, N. (2023). Research in mental health in the Arab speaking world 1920 to 2018. *Middle East Current Psychiatry, 30*(1), 109. https://doi.org/10.1186/s43045-023-00382-6

Khatib, S., Alwawi, A., & Elissa, K. (2025). Mental health care in Palestine. In S. Al-Huseini & S. M. Y. Arafat (Eds.), *Mental health care in the Middle East*. Springer. https://doi.org/10.1007/978-981-95-0461-9_10

Loza, N. (2010). Integrating Egyptian mental health services into primary care: The policy maker's perspective. *International Psychiatry, 7*(1), 5–6.

Maalouf, F. T., Alamiri, B., Atweh, S., Becker, A. E., Cheour, M., Darwish, H., Ghandour, L. A., Ghuloum, S., Hamze, M., Karam, E., Khoury, B., Khoury, S. J., Mokdad, A., Meho, L. I., Okasha, T., Reed, G. M., Sbaity, E., Zeinoun, P., & Akl, E. A. (2019). Mental health research in the Arab region: Challenges and call for action. *The Lancet. Psychiatry, 6*(11), 961–966. https://doi.org/10.1016/S2215-0366(19)30124-5

Marie, M., Hannigan, B., & Jones, A. (2017). Resilience of nurses who work in community mental health workplaces in Palestine. *International Journal of Mental Health Nursing, 26*(4), 344–354. https://doi.org/10.1111/inm.12229

Marie, M., Hannigan, B., & Jones, A. (2018). Social ecology of resilience and Sumud of Palestinians. *Health, 22*(1), 20–35. https://doi.org/10.1177/1363459316677624

Matlin, S. A., Hanefeld, J., Corte-Real, A., da Cunha, P. R., de Gruchy, T., Manji, K. N., Netto, G., Nunes, T., Şanlıer, İ., Takian, A., Zaman, M. H., & Saso, L. (2025). Digital solutions for migrant and refugee health: A framework for analysis and action. *The Lancet Regional Health—Europe, 50*, 101190. https://doi.org/10.1016/j.lanepe.2024.101190

Maziak, W. (2006). Health in the Middle East. *BMJ, 333*(7573), 815–816. https://doi.org/10.1136/bmj.39006.478796.80

Ministry of Health. (2023). *Annual health report 2023.* https://moh.gov.om/en/statistics/annual-health-reports/annual-health-report-2023/?utm_source=chatgpt.com

Ministry of Public Health. (2018). *National mental health program—Home.* https://sehanafsia.moph.gov.qa/?csrt=7283037707818062786

Mirzai, F., Nasiri, Z., Naeim, M., Imannezhad, S., & Javedani, M. (2024). Advancing mental health in the Middle East: A paradigm shift. *Asian Journal of Psychiatry, 101*, Article 104220. https://doi.org/10.1016/j.ajp.2024.104220

MOH, B. (2025). *Telemedicine service—Ministry of Health.* https://www.moh.gov.bh/Services/TelemedicineService?lang=en

Mohammed, M., Mohammed, S., & Ghuloum, S. (2025). Mental healthcare in Qatar: Services, developments, and challenges. In S. Al-Huseini & S. M. Y. Arafat (Eds.), *Mental health care in the Middle East*. Springer. https://doi.org/10.1007/978-981-95-0461-9_11

Mohtar, L., Badr, N., Asmar, M. K., Bou-Orm, I., Maalouf, F. T., & Haddad, P. E. (2025). Adoption of tele health technology in mental and psychiatric services in Lebanon: A quantitative study. *Discover Mental Health, 5*(1), 40. https://doi.org/10.1007/s44192-025-00169-7

Musa, M. (2024). Mental health in the Middle East: Historical perspectives, current challenges, and future implications. *Saudi Journal of Humanities and Social Sciences, 9*(05), 138–148. https://doi.org/10.36348/sjhss.2024.v09i05.001

National Mental Health Strategy for Lebanon (2024—2030).pdf. (2024). Retrieved May 22, 2025, from https://www.moph.gov.lb/userfiles/files/National%20Mental%20Health%20Strategy%20For%20Lebanon%20%282024%20-%202030%29.pdf?utm_source=chatgpt.com

National Programme for Happiness and Wellbeing | The Official Portal of the UAE Government. (2024). Retrieved May 19, 2025, from https://u.ae/en/information-and-services/social-affairs/happiness/national-programme-for-happiness-and-wellbeing

National Strategy for Wellbeing 2031. (2024). *National strategy for wellbeing 2031 | The official portal of the UAE Government*. https://u.ae/en/about-the-uae/strategies-initiatives-and-awards/strategies-plans-and-visions/social-affairs/national-strategy-for-wellbeing-2031

Nsouli, A., Zeineldine, C., & Maalouf, F. (2025). Mental health care in Lebanon—History, challenges, and current status. In S. Al-Huseini & S. M. Y. Arafat (Eds.), *Mental health care in the Middle East*. Springer. https://doi.org/10.1007/978-981-95-0461-9_8

Okasha, A., & Karam, E. (1998). Mental health services and research in the Arab world. *Acta Psychiatrica Scandinavica, 98*(5), 406–413. https://doi.org/10.1111/j.1600-0447.1998.tb10106.x

Okasha, A., Karam, E., & Okasha, T. (2012). Mental health services in the Arab world. *World Psychiatry, 11*(1), 52–54. https://doi.org/10.1016/j.wpsyc.2012.01.008

Qutishat, M., Al-Hadidi, M. (2025). Mental health services in Jordan. In S. Al-Huseini & S. M. Y., Arafat (Eds.), *Mental health care in the Middle East*. Springer. https://doi.org/10.1007/978-981-95-0461-9_6

Radwan, A. (1987). Research and teaching in the Middle East. *The ANNALS of the American Academy of Political and Social Science, 491*, 126–133. https://doi.org/10.1177/0002716287491001012

Regan, M., Gater, R., Rahman, A., & Patel, V. (2015). Mental health research: Developing priorities and promoting its utilization to inform policies and services. *Eastern Mediterranean Health Journal, 12*(7), 517–521. https://doi.org/10.26719/2015.21.7.517

Sadik, S., Abdulrahman, S., Bradley, M., & Jenkins, R. (2011). Integrating mental health into primary health care in Iraq. *Mental Health in Family Medicine, 8*(1), 39–49.

Sadik, S., & Al-Jadiry, A.-M. (2006). Mental health services in Iraq: Past, present and future. *International Psychiatry, 3*(4), 11–13.

Saraceno, B., van Ommeren, M., Batniji, R., Cohen, A., Gureje, O., Mahoney, J., Sridhar, D., & Underhill, C. (2007). Barriers to improvement of mental health services in low-income and middle-income countries. *Lancet (London, England), 370*(9593), 1164–1174. https://doi.org/10.1016/S0140-6736(07)61263-X

Siddiqui, J. A., Qureshi, S. F., & Alotaibi, H. M. (2022). Perceived awareness of clozapine associated with socio-demographic status, clinical, and side effect profile among patients from Mental Health Hospital, Taif, Saudi Arabia. *Indian Journal of Mental Health, 9*(4). https://doi.org/10.30877/IJMH.9.4.2022.363-370

Sijbrandij, M., Acarturk, C., Bird, M., Bryant, R. A., Burchert, S., Carswell, K., de Jong, J., Dinesen, C., Dawson, K. S., El Chammay, R., van Ittersum, L., Jordans, M., Knaevelsrud, C., McDaid, D., Miller, K., Morina, N., Park, A.-L., Roberts, B., van Son, Y., … Cuijpers, P. (2017). Strengthening mental health care systems for Syrian refugees in Europe and the Middle East: Integrating scalable psychological interventions in eight countries. *European Journal of Psychotraumatology,8*(sup2), 1388102. https://doi.org/10.1080/20008198.2017.1388102

Skuse, D. (2021). Conflict and community: Mental health in the Arab world. *Bjpsych International, 18*(1), 1–1. https://doi.org/10.1192/bji.2020.59

Sobhani, M., Saeidi, P., Naeim, M., Kavand, R., Shojaei, B., Imannezhad, S., & Dehghani, D. (2024). Improving mental health infrastructure across the Middle East. *Asian Journal of Psychiatry, 93*, Article 103908. https://doi.org/10.1016/j.ajp.2023.103908

Taylor, C. B., Ruzek, J. I., Fitzsimmons-Craft, E. E., Sadeh-Sharvit, S., Topooco, N., Weissman, R. S., Eisenberg, D., Mohr, D., Graham, A., Jacobi, C., & Oldenburg, B. (2020). Using digital technology to reduce the prevalence of mental health disorders in populations: Time for a new approach. *Journal of Medical Internet Research, 22*(7), Article e17493. https://doi.org/10.2196/17493

UNICEF Middle East. (2023). *Integration of mental health and psychosocial support in primary health care.*

Vision 2030. (2024). *Health sector transformation program.* https://www.vision2030.gov.sa/en/explore/programs/health-sector-transformation-program

Wadoo, O., Ahmed, M. A. S., Reagu, S., Al Abdulla, S. A., & Al Abdulla, M. A. Y. A. (2021). Primary care mental health services in Qatar. *Bjpsych International, 18*(1), 15–18. https://doi.org/10.1192/bji.2020.45

Wadoo, O., Khan, F., Latoo, J., Saeed Khan, Y., Chandra, P., Iqbal, Y., Amro, R., Reagu, S., & Alabdulla, M. (2024). Telepsychiatry implementation in Qatar: A three-year analysis of no-show rates and its impact on mental health service delivery. *Qatar Medical Journal, 2024*(4), 50. https://doi.org/10.5339/qmj.2024.50

WHO. (2013). *mhGAP training creates more support for vulnerable people in Syria.* https://www.who.int/news-room/feature-stories/detail/mhgap-syria

WHO. (2021). *Mental health atlas 2020* (1st ed.). World Health Organization.

WHO. (2022). *Consolidated telemedicine implementation guide.* https://www.who.int/publications/i/item/9789240059184

WHO EMRO, (2013). *The work of WHO in the Eastern Mediterranean Region: Annual report of the Regional Director 2012* (No. EM/RC60/2). https://iris.who.int/handle/10665/124619

WHO EMRO. (2021). Understanding the private health sector in the Eastern Mediterranean Region. Retrieved May 13, 2025, from https://www.emro.who.int/images/stories/health-topics/uhc/understanding_phs_in_emr.pdf

WHO EMRO. (2023). Integrating mental health in primary health care. https://applications.emro.who.int/docs/9789292740924-eng.pdf

Who_aims_oman_report.pdf. (2006). Retrieved April 27, 2025, from https://cdn.who.int/media/docs/default-source/mental-health/who-aims-country-reports/who_aims_oman_report.pdf?sfvrsn=6830b334_3&utm_source=chatgpt.com

Who_aims_report_iran.pdf. (2007). Retrieved May 24, 2025, from https://cdn.who.int/media/docs/default-source/mental-health/who-aims-country-reports/who_aims_report_iran.pdf?sfvrsn=754baf8d_3&utm_source=chatgpt.com
Younis, M. S. (2025). Mental health services in Iraq. In S. Al-Huseini & S. M. Y. Arafat (Eds.), *Mental health care in the Middle East*. Springer.https://doi.org/10.1007/978-981-95-0461-9_5
Zeinoun, P., Akl, E. A., Maalouf, F. T., & Meho, L. I. (2020). The Arab region's contribution to global mental health research (2009–2018): A bibliometric analysis. *Frontiers in Psychiatry, 11*. https://doi.org/10.3389/fpsyt.2020.00182

Correction to: Mental Healthcare in Saudi Arabia

Mohammed A. Alarabi and Fahad D. Alosaimi

Correction to:
Chapter 12 in: S. Al-Huseini and S. M. Y. Arafat (eds.), *Mental Health Care in the Middle East*, South Asian Perspectives in Mental Health and Psychology, https://doi.org/10.1007/978-981-95-0461-9_12

The chapter "Mental Healthcare in Saudi Arabia", written by Mohammed A. Alarabi and Fahad D. Alosaimi, was originally published without open access. Following the authors' decision to option for open access, the copyright of the chapter changed on 03 December 2025 to ©The Author(s) 2025 and the chapter is now distributed under the terms of the Creative Commons Attribution-NonCommercial-NoDerivatives 4.0 International License (http://creativecommons.org/licenses/by-nc-nd/4.0/), which permits use, sharing, adaptation, distribution and reproduction in any medium or format, as long as you give appropriate credit to the original author(s) and the source, provide a link to the Creative Commons licence and indicate if changes were made.

The images or other third party material in this chapter are included in the chapter's Creative Commons license, unless indicated otherwise in a credit line to the material. If material is not included in the chapter's Creative Commons license and your intended use is not permitted by statutory regulation or exceeds the permitted use, you will need to obtain permission directly from the copyright holder.

The updated version of this chapter can be found at https://doi.org/10.1007/978-981-95-0461-9_12

S. Al-Huseini and S. M. Y. Arafat (eds.), *Mental Health Care in the Middle East*, South Asian Perspectives in Mental Health and Psychology ,
https://doi.org/10.1007/978-981-95-0461-9_17

MIX
Papier aus verantwortungsvollen Quellen
Paper from responsible sources
FSC® C105338
FSC
www.fsc.org

If you have any concerns about our products,
you can contact us on
ProductSafety@springernature.com

In case Publisher is established outside the EU,
the EU authorized representative is:
Springer Nature Customer Service Center GmbH
Europaplatz 3, 69115 Heidelberg, Germany

Printed by Libri Plureos GmbH
in Hamburg, Germany